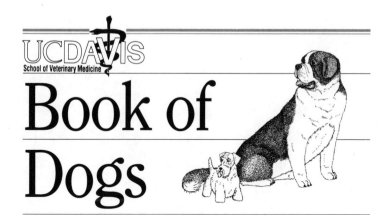

UC DAVIS
School of Veterinary Medicine

Book of
Dogs

Book of Dogs

UCDAVIS
School of Veterinary Medicine

The Complete Medical Reference Guide for Dogs and Puppies

By the Faculty and Staff,
School of Veterinary Medicine,
University of California, Davis

Edited by Mordecai Siegal

Consulting Editor, Jeffrey E. Barlough, D.V.M., Ph.D.

HarperCollins*Publishers*

To the Center for Companion Animal Health
at the University of California, Davis,
and all the men and women who work there.
This group of talented individuals has done much to
improve the health of companion animals everywhere.

FIRST EDITION

Pen-and-ink drawings of individual dog breeds and the American Kennel Club Breed Groups drawn for the *UC Davis Book of Dogs* by Cynthia Holmes.

All black and white photos by Mordecai Siegal, except where otherwise noted.

Anatomical illustrations, in addition to external and internal parasite illustrations, by Ernest W. Beck, anatomical artist, prepared from original illustrations by Fred J. Born, D.V.M., reprinted from *The Canine: A Veterinary Aid in Anatomical Transparencies with Supplemental Color Illustrations* (published by Solvay Animal Health, Inc.), with permission from Fred J. Born, D.V.M.

Illustrations appearing in chapter 11, "Normal Reproduction" (where noted), are from *Canine and Feline Endocrinology and Reproduction,* by Edward C. Feldman and Richard W. Nelson (W. B. Saunders, 1987), with permission.

Photos in chapter 42 and chapter 43 (where noted) are courtesy of Dr. Steve C. Haskins.

Sketch appearing in chapter 11, "Normal Reproduction," is from "Examination of the Genital System," by Shirley D. Johnston, published in *Veterinary Clinics of North America* 11: 543–559 (W. B. Saunders), with permission.

Illustration of the normal canine larynx appearing in chapter 43, "Procedures for Life-Threatening Emergencies," is reprinted with permission from J. Grandage and K. Richardson, in D. Slatter, ed., *Textbook of Small Animal Surgery,* (W. B. Saunders Co., 1985).

Table 3 and table 4 appearing in chapter 9, "Feeding Dogs," are from *Clinical Nutrition III* by Lon D. Lewis and Mark L. Morris, Jr. (Mark Morris Associates, Topeka, KS: 1987) with permission.

Library of Congress Cataloging-in-Publication Data

UC Davis book of dogs : the complete medical reference guide for dogs and puppies / by the Faculty and Staff,
   School of Veterinary Medicine, Ununersity of California at Davis ; edited by Mordecai Siegal, consulting editor,
   Jeffrey E. Barlough. -- 1st ed.
     p.   cm.
   Includes index.
   ISBN 0-06-270136-3 (alk. paper)
    1. Dogs--Diseases. 2. Dogs--Health. I. Siegal, Mordecai. II. Barlough, Jeffrey E. III. University of
California, Davis.
SF991. U325 1995
636.7'089--dc20
                                                 95-20198

03 02 01 00   ❖/RRD 10 9 8 7 6

Contents

Part VI: Infectious Diseases and Cancer

Part VII: Home Care

Contributors

Editor
Mordecai Siegal

Consulting Editor
Jeffrey E. Barlough, D.V.M., Ph.D.

Associate Editors
Victoria Blankenship Siegal
Donald G. Low, D.V.M., Ph.D.

Dog Breed and Group Illustrations
Cynthia Holmes

Photographs
Mordecai Siegal

This book represents the work of thirty-two authors. They are:

Janet Aldrich, D.V.M., is a staff veterinarian in the Emergency/Critical Care Service at the Veterinary Medical Teaching Hospital, University of California, Davis. She earned her D.V.M. at Michigan State University.

Cleta Sue Bailey, D.V.M., Ph.D., is a professor in the Department of Surgical and Radiological Sciences, School of Veterinary Medicine, University of California, Davis. She earned her D.V.M. at Oklahoma State University, and a Ph.D. in comparative pathology (neuroanatomy, neurophysiology) at the University of California, Davis. She is a Diplomate, American College of Veterinary Internal Medicine, Specialty of Neurology.

Jeffrey E. Barlough, D.V.M., Ph.D., is an NIH Postdoctoral Fellow in the Department of Medicine and Epidemiology, School of Veterinary Medicine, and Department of Medical Pathology, School of Medicine, University of California, Davis. He earned his D.V.M. at the University of California, Davis, and a Ph.D. in veterinary virology at Cornell University. He is a Diplomate, American College of Veterinary Microbiologists.

Vincent C. Biourge, D.M.V., Ph.D., is a Hill's Fellow in Small Animal Clinical Nutrition in the Department of Molecular Biosciences, School of

Veterinary Medicine, University of California, Davis. He received his D.M.V. at the University of Liège, Belgium, and a Ph.D. in nutrition at the University of California, Davis. He is a Diplomate, American College of Veterinary Nutrition.

Ann T. Bowling, Ph.D., is an adjunct professor in the Department of Population Health and Reproduction, School of Veterinary Medicine, University of California, Davis. She received her Ph.D. in genetics at the University of California, Davis.

Walter M. Boyce, D.V.M., Ph.D., is an associate professor in the Department of Pathology, Microbiology, and Immunology, School of Veterinary Medicine, University of California, Davis. He received his D.V.M. at Auburn University, and a Ph.D. in parasitology at Purdue University.

George H. Cardinet III, D.V.M., Ph.D., is professor emeritus in the Department of Anatomy, Physiology, and Cell Biology, School of Veterinary Medicine, University of California, Davis. He earned his D.V.M. and a Ph.D. in comparative pathology at the University of California, Davis.

Bruno B. Chomel, D.V.M., Ph.D., is an assistant professor in the Department of Population Health and Reproduction, School of Veterinary Medicine, University of California, Davis. He received his D.V.M. at the Lyon National Veterinary School, France, and a Ph.D. in microbiology at the University of Lyon.

Patricia A. Conrad, D.V.M., Ph.D., is an associate professor in the Department of Pathology, Microbiology, and Immunology, School of Veterinary Medicine, University of California, Davis. She earned her D.V.M. at Colorado State University, and a Ph.D. in protozoology and tropical animal health at the University of Edinburgh, Scotland.

Charles H. Courtney, D.V.M., Ph.D., is a professor in the Department of Infectious Diseases, College of Veterinary Medicine, University of Florida. He earned his D.V.M. at Auburn University, and a Ph.D. in veterinary parasitology at Ohio State University.

Larry D. Cowgill, D.V.M., Ph.D., is an associate professor in the Department of Medicine and Epidemiology, School of Veterinary Medicine, University of California, Davis. He received his D.V.M. at the University of California, Davis, and a Ph.D. in comparative medical sciences at the University of Pennsylvania. He is a Diplomate, American College of Veterinary Internal Medicine.

Autumn P. Davidson, D.V.M., is a veterinarian in the Outpatient Service at the Veterinary Medical Teaching Hospital, University of California, Davis, and a staff internist at the Encina Veterinary Clinic, Walnut Creek, California. She received her D.V.M. at the University of California, Davis. She is a Diplomate, American College of Veterinary Internal Medicine.

Edward C. Feldman, D.V.M., is a professor in the Department of Medicine and Epidemiology, School of Veterinary Medicine, University of California, Davis. He received his D.V.M. at the University of California, Davis. He is a Diplomate, American College of Veterinary Internal Medicine.

Clare R. Gregory, D.V.M., is an associate professor in the Department of Surgical and Radiological Sciences, School of Veterinary Medicine, University of California, Davis. He earned his D.V.M. at Cornell University. He is a Diplomate, American College of Veterinary Surgeons.

Benjamin L. Hart, D.V.M., Ph.D., is a professor in the Department of Anatomy, Physiology, and Cell Biology, School of Veterinary Medicine, University of California, Davis. He received his D.V.M. and a Ph.D. in neurobiology and behavior at the University of Minnesota. He is a Diplomate, American College of Veterinary Behaviorists.

Lynette A. Hart, Ph.D., is director of the Center for Animals in Society, School of Veterinary Medicine, University of California, Davis. She received her Ph.D. in zoology/animal behavior at Rutgers University.

Steve C. Haskins, D.V.M., M.S., is a professor in the Department of Surgical and Radiological Sciences, School of Veterinary Medicine, University of California, Davis. He earned his D.V.M. at Washington State University, and an M.S. in anesthesia at the University of Minnesota. He is a Diplomate, American College of Veterinary Emergency and Critical Care.

Peter J. Ihrke, V.M.D., is a professor in the Department of Medicine and Epidemiology, School of Veterinary Medicine, University of California, Davis, and an adjunct clinical associate professor in the Department of Dermatology, School of Medicine, Stanford University. He received his V.M.D. at the University of Pennsylvania. He is a Diplomate, American College of Veterinary Dermatology.

Claudia A. Kirk, D.V.M., is a Hill's Postdoctoral Fellow in Nutrition and a Ph.D. candidate in the Department of Molecular Biosciences, School of Veterinary Medicine, University of California, Davis. She received her D.V.M. at the University of California, Davis.

Mark D. Kittleson, D.V.M., Ph.D., is a professor in the Department of Medicine and Epidemiology, School of Veterinary Medicine, University of California, Davis. He received his D.V.M. at the University of Minnesota, and a Ph.D. in veterinary physiology and pharmacology at Ohio State University. He is a Diplomate, American College of Veterinary Internal Medicine, Specialty of Cardiology.

Robert L. Leighton, V.M.D., is professor emeritus in the Department of Surgical and Radiological Sciences, School of Veterinary Medicine, University of California, Davis. He received his V.M.D. from the University of Pennsylvania. He is a Diplomate, American College of Veterinary Surgeons.

Donald G. Low, D.V.M., Ph.D., is professor emeritus in the Department of Medicine and Epidemiology, and formerly associate dean for Public Programs and director of the Veterinary Medical Teaching Hospital, School of Veterinary Medicine, University of California, Davis. He earned his D.V.M. at Kansas State University,

and a Ph.D. in pharmacology at the University of Minnesota. He is a Diplomate, American College of Veterinary Internal Medicine.

Bruce R. Madewell, V.M.D., M.S., is a professor in the Department of Surgical and Radiological Sciences, School of Veterinary Medicine, University of California, Davis. He earned his V.M.D. at the University of Pennsylvania, and an M.S. in clinical sciences at Colorado State University. He is a Diplomate, American College of Veterinary Internal Medicine, Specialties of Internal Medicine and Oncology.

Richard W. Nelson, D.V.M., is an associate professor in the Department of Medicine and Epidemiology, School of Veterinary Medicine, University of California, Davis. He earned his D.V.M. at the University of Minnesota. He is a Diplomate, American College of Veterinary Internal Medicine.

Philip A. Padrid, D.V.M., is an assistant professor in the Department of Medicine, Section of Pulmonary and Critical Care Medicine, Pritzker School of Medicine, University of Chicago. He earned his D.V.M. at Cornell University.

Niels C. Pedersen, D.V.M., Ph.D., is a professor in the Department of Medicine and Epidemiology, and director of the Center for Companion Animal Health, School of Veterinary Medicine, University of California, Davis. He received his D.V.M. at the University of California, Davis, and a Ph.D. in experimental pathology and immunology at the Australian National University, Canberra, Australia.

Randall H. Scagliotti, D.V.M., M.S., is an associate clinical professor in the Department of Surgical and Radiological Sciences, University of California, Davis, and a staff ophthalmologist at the Sacramento Animal Medical Group, Carmichael, California. He earned his D.V.M. and an M.S. in comparative pathology at the University of California, Davis. He is a Diplomate, American College of Veterinary Ophthalmologists.

Mordecai Siegal is an author and journalist and has written 17 published books concerning domestic dogs and cats, including their behavior, nutritional needs, medical care, training, breed descriptions and human/animal bonding. His articles and monthly columns on pets have appeared regularly in national magazines, and he frequently appears on the broadcast media. He is the editor and a contributing author of *The Cornell Book of Cats*. He is the president of the Dog Writers Association of America.

Donald R. Strombeck, D.V.M., Ph.D. is professor emeritus in the Department of Medicine and Epidemiology, School of Veterinary Medicine, University of California, Davis. He received his D.V.M. from the University of Illinois at Urbana/Champaign, and a Ph.D. in physiology/gastroenterology from the University of Illinois at Chicago. He is an Honorary Diplomate, American College of Veterinary Internal Medicine.

Linda L. Werner, D.V.M., Ph.D., is a lecturer and clinical pathologist in the Department of Pathology, Microbiology, and Immunology, School of Veterinary Medicine, University of California, Davis. She received her D.V.M. at Ohio State University, and a Ph.D. in comparative pathology at the University of California, Davis. She is a Diplomate, American College of Veterinary Internal Medicine.

Leigh West-Hyde, D.V.M., M.S., is an associate clinical professor in the Department of Surgical and Radiological Sciences, School of Veterinary Medicine, University of California, Davis. She received her D.V.M. and an M.S. in nutrition at the University of California, Davis. She is a Diplomate, American College of Veterinary Ophthalmologists.

James F. Wilson, D.V.M., J.D., is a visiting lecturer in the Department of Medicine and Epidemiology, School of Veterinary Medicine, University of California, Davis, and an adjunct assistant professor in the Department of Clinical Studies, School of Veterinary Medicine, University of Pennsylvania. He earned his D.V.M. at Iowa State University, and his J.D. at the University of California, Los Angeles.

Acknowledgments

The *UC Davis Book of Dogs* is a medical reference work for dog owners, veterinarians, breeders, handlers, judges, groomers, trainers and all those who love dogs and have a need to understand canine veterinary care. The creation of this book and its contribution to the literature of the dog required the efforts of many people. It has come into existence because of the hard work and dedication of those who gave so generously of their time and brilliance.

The most important expression of appreciation and gratitude is for the educators and scientists who wrote the chapters of this book, enthusiastically giving their valuable time, knowledge and talent to its pages. These gifted members of the faculty made this book a tangible reality. It is, and will continue to be, a tribute to the invaluable work they perform every day on the UC Davis campus.

It is a rare event when a university reaches out beyond the boundaries of its campus to the larger world surrounding it, making available a portion of its academic wealth as represented in this book. Without cooperation and enthusiasm from the higher levels of administration and authority no project has good prospects. However, the *UC Davis Book of Dogs* was blessed from the beginning. We wish to thank Frederick A. Murphy, dean of the School of Veterinary Medicine, for his support, encouragement and gracious good will.

Many thanks are also extended to Kelly J. Nimtz, assistant dean for development, for his good offices and generous help with this project.

A special acknowledgment must be extended to Donald G. Low, emeritus professor of Veterinary Medicine and former director of the Veterinary Medical Teaching Hospital. During his tenure as associate dean for Public Programs (and afterwards, as well) his supreme efforts and cheerful optimism enabled this project to start and conclude successfully. One cannot overestimate how important to this project are the respect and affection held for him by members of the faculty.

Bill Balaban, the gentle advocate, is a kind, humane dog lover, who is greatly appreciated for his enthusiasm and generous support of the veterinary programs on the UC Davis campus. It was Mr. Balaban who opened the doors for the editor to walk through with the idea of this book. In no small way, he is responsible for its fulfillment. We say thank you with unreserved gratitude for his interest and devotion to the creation of this book. He is irreplaceable and his friendship is highly valued.

There is no way to sufficiently praise or thank Dr. Jeffrey E. Barlough, consulting editor and contributing author, for his unflinching efforts and prodigious work on this book. His editorial skills, writing talent and superior knowledge of veterinary medicine are evident on every page. Although his life is dedicated to science and education, there lurks behind his persona the sensibility of a writer. This book has been the beneficiary of his combined qualities. We are grateful for his important work on this manuscript.

The contributions to this book by Victoria Blankenship Siegal, associate editor, were extremely important. She has earned the recognition and esteem of her colleagues for the endless hours of editorial labor spent, scouring the stacks of manuscript pages handed to her each week. These are the results of her energetic editorial scrutiny and they are a shining reflection of her intelligence, keen judgment and good taste. Her dedication and superior skills have made a significant difference to the quality of this book. Hers was a major contribution.

We would also like to express our appreciation for the fine pen-and-ink drawings of an extremely gifted artist, Cynthia Holmes. Her illustrations of the many dog breeds and groups of dog breeds are sure to be a treat for those readers turning from page to page. Each stroke of her pen is certain to touch their hearts and minds.

While respecting her wish for anonymity, we nevertheless would like to openly thank the top professional dog person whose comments and corrections helped Cynthia Holmes create her breed portrayals as accurately and as close to accepted breed standards as possible.

Many thanks are also extended to Dr. Fred J. Born of the Town & Country Veterinary Clinics in Fond Du Lac, Wisconsin for his generous permission to reprint illustrations of the canine anatomy which appear in *The Canine: A Veterinary Aid in Anatomical Transparencies with Supplemental Color Illustrations* (Solvay Animal Health, Inc.).

Thank you, Mark Morris, Jr., for permission to use nutritional tables from your book, *Clinical Nutrition III* (1987) and for your telephone consultations, given on the run. He is a most generous person in a very generous industry. He always comes through.

A special note of gratitude is extended to James E. Dearinger, vice president, Obedience Events, American Kennel Club, for reviewing the nonmedical chapters and offering his constructive comments on them. Thanks also to Roberta L. Campbell, Administrator–Performance Events, American Kennel Club.

Fred Miller is the president of the United Kennel Club in Kalamazoo, Michigan, which is the largest working dog registry in the world and the second largest all-breed registry. Mr. Miller deserves a special mention of appreciation for the generous time and assistance given to the editor.

Sincere appreciation to Diane Vasey, editor in chief, American Kennel Gazette for her kind help, particularly when she was associate editor of the very beautiful magazine, *The Pointing Dog Journal.*

Many thanks to Connie Jankowski, editor of *DOGS USA Magazine.* Her sharp editorial comments on the nonmedical material in this book were perceptive, subtle and impressively expert. We gratefully appreciate her enthusiasm and encouragement.

Our thanks must also go to Linda Bentley and Eleanor Onoda for the administrative duties they performed so well. Their dedicated service contributed so much toward keeping the entire project moving forward.

Acknowledgment for help, assistance, advice and service beyond the call of duty go to Mel Berger, vice president and literary agent at the William Morris Agency; Phil Liebowitz, Esq. of the William Morris legal department; Ellen Sawyer of the Tree House Animal Foundation, Inc. of Chicago; and to Matthew Margolis, author and dog trainer.

Foreword

Frederick A. Murphy, D.V.M., Ph.D.

DEAN, SCHOOL OF VETERINARY MEDICINE
UNIVERSITY OF CALIFORNIA, DAVIS

From its beginning, the School of Veterinary Medicine at the University of California, Davis has had as its primary mission the care and treatment of all animals. The faculty and staff of the School of Veterinary Medicine have kept this mission before them every day as they have gone about educating generations of veterinary students, carrying out innovative research, and providing outstanding clinical services. The School was established in 1946 and accepted its first entering class in 1948. From that time the School has graduated 3,405 veterinarians who have dedicated their lives to maintaining and improving animal health. This book, dealing with the health and well-being of dogs, represents a special tribute to "man's best friend." It also represents a tribute to their caring owners who strive to be educated and responsive regarding their dog's health. Owners today, more than ever before, seek knowledge about health disorders and preventative steps to improve the overall quality of life and care for their pets.

The School's programs can best be described in terms of disciplines and technologies. Whereas in earlier years the classic disciplines of veterinary medicine such as anatomy, physiology, and pathology described a unidimensional perspective, today all of the disciplines of biomedicine—such as molecular biology, cell biology, developmental biology, etc.—have been added to the classical base. All of these disciplines and their technologies are brought to bear as we educate our students and solve the problems that society has assigned to us (i.e. companion animal health, including an increasing exotic pet population, public health, and the control of infectious and toxic diseases). This multidimensional approach has served the School well, but more importantly, it has greatly improved the capability of veterinarians to help animals of all species in all the different stages of life.

Many of our faculty focus on canine health and are working to advance our knowledge of canine diseases, nutrition and reproduction, all with the goal of assuring that dogs have a high quality of life that extends from birth into old age. Over the years, the School's faculty have developed vaccines, identified the causes of diseases, developed novel medical treatments, developed new surgical techniques, and promoted more advanced diagnostic tests. They have also shared this knowledge and technology with colleagues in private veterinary practice. An excellent relationship has been built between faculty members at the University of California, Davis and your veterinarian through consultation on referred cases, specialized treatment for difficult cases, continuing education offerings, and our annual seminar for practitioners on new, cutting-edge technologies and advances in clinical treatment of dogs and cats. This relationship helps everyone, not the least your dog.

Throughout the past decade an explosion of knowledge has substantially improved the understanding and application of medical principles that has greatly improved the general health of dogs. This has been particularly evident in the rise of clinical specialties (i.e. specialized surgery, ophthalmology, dermatology, infectious diseases, dentistry, pediatrics and geriatrics, genetics, etc.). This is just the beginning. People who care about dogs can expect much more in the future—medical science is undergoing a grand revolution which will pay off in better and better prevention, care and treatment approaches in the near future.

The school has proudly developed the reference book, the *UC Davis Book of Dogs*, with the goal of providing basic, everyday information to dog owners who want a more complete understanding of their pet's health. Many faculty members have participated in the writing of this book—their hard work is evident in the quality of the chapters. This book would never have come to be without the hard work of Dr. Donald G. Low, who organized and coordinated the project. I wish to thank all of Dr. Low's colleagues for a job well done. We hope that this book will provide dog owners with helpful information and will promote improved animal health. The *UC Davis Book of Dogs* is one more way in which the School of Veterinary Medicine is striving to be of service to society.

Preface

Donald G. Low, D.V.M., Ph.D.

EMERITUS PROFESSOR OF VETERINARY MEDICINE
SCHOOL OF VETERINARY MEDICINE
UNIVERSITY OF CALIFORNIA, DAVIS

Where does one get reliable, current information about the health of dogs? Obviously, members of the dog-loving public would prefer a source of information in which they can have confidence. We believe that the *UC Davis Book of Dogs* will go a long way in fulfilling that need. It is written by 32 authors, 29 of whom are veterinarians, all associated with the world-renowned School of Veterinary Medicine at the University of California, Davis. They are teachers, clinicians, specialists and researchers, all of whom are committed to finding answers to the most urgent health-related problems facing dogs today, problems that cause pain, suffering and premature death of animals that are loved and respected by their owners. I believe it would be difficult to find a better source of up-to-date health-related information than is provided here by these dedicated experts. This book is not intended to be a shortcut to becoming a veterinarian. Rather, it is a source of reliable information about canine diseases that may be of concern to you. This book is meant to serve as a handy, comprehensive reference, a book you can turn to in a time of need. This book is meant to allow you to understand better what your veterinarian tells you about your dog's health.

A major effort has been made to assemble the many knowledgeable veterinarians that came together for the production of this book. An enormous amount of research into the many questions all of us have about how to diagnose, prevent, manage and treat the specific diseases of dogs has gone into each of the following chapters. Behind each chapter is the lifelong experience and insight of the writer.

There is a long trail leading to the creation of this book. The first step along the trail was taken in 1973 when Dean William R. Pritchard established the School of Veterinary Medicine's Companion Animal Research Laboratory (CARL). The mission of the CARL was to advance our knowledge of health and disease in companion animals. Initially, progress was slow because of a lack of funding and space. Funding for companion animal research has always been difficult to obtain because most of the funding agencies that support other aspects of veterinary medical research do not support companion animal research.

In 1984 the Companion Animal Memorial Fund was established. Sponsoring veterinary hospitals contribute monetary donations to the fund in memory of fine pets who have died or who have been euthanatized to avoid continued suffering. The School of Veterinary Medicine then notifies the owner of the deceased animal of the gift. Owners frequently comment about how much this single act of kindness does to help them through the grief they experience as a result of losing their pet, who is often also their best friend. The number of sponsoring veterinary hospitals has steadily increased over the years. Pet owners, approving of the concept of the Memorial Fund, have likewise consistently increased their monetary support both through direct donations and through bequests. All money donated is used to support projects benefiting companion animals.

Clients of the Veterinary Medical Teaching Hospital have also become strong supporters of the Companion Animal Research Laboratory as they became aware of the major contributions that faculty were making to the health of companion animals.

In 1992, Dean Frederick A. Murphy recognized the broader mission to be fulfilled by the Companion Animal Research Laboratory and initiated planning for the UC Davis Center for Companion Animal Health. Dr. Niels C. Pedersen was appointed as the center's first director. Dr. Pedersen has an international reputation in companion animal research, specifically in the area of viral diseases. The Center for Companion Animal Health was dedicated on February 26, 1994 with an open house attended by more than 200 people who care about companion animals and their health. The Center is off to a grand start, initiating educational, clinical and research activities that are impressive, indeed. Currently 33 faculty members of the School of Veterinary Medicine have affiliations with the Center for Companion Animal Health. They represent a broad array of expertise in virtually every specialty that exists in veterinary medicine today.

It is Dr. Pedersen's dream to make the Center for Companion Animal Health the premier companion animal educational, research and public service facility in the world. He has made a good start toward attaining that goal. The Center has modern, up-to-date facilities and equipment. It is located adjacent to the School of Veterinary Medicine's Veterinary Medical Teaching Hospital. This location will permit the students to use the expertise and resources of the Center for Companion Animal Health at the teaching hospital to solve problems associated with hospital patients. At the same time it will keep the faculty associated with the Center for Companion Animal Health in close contact with the current problems faced by our pets.

Another of Dr. Pedersen's goals is to utilize the facilities of the Center for Companion Animal Health to help educate the next generation of teachers and researchers in companion animal medicine. This will be done by providing incentives for young veterinarians to come to the Center for training in research methodology. These veterinarians will come as postdoctoral fellows, as faculty members on sabbatic leave from other veterinary schools and as residents from the Veterinary Medical Teaching Hospital. The Center hopes to provide funding for these young clinician/scientists to help them get started in their scholarly careers. In addition, the Center will provide laboratory space, technical support, and equipment. Most important of all is the provision of mentorship, the advice and help senior faculty members will provide to incoming students. The creation of the Center for Companion Animal Health is the first step toward solving some of the most pressing medical problems of companion animals. However, success will be determined in large measure by the extent to which the animal-owning public is supportive of that Center.

To help contribute to that base of support for the Center for Companion Animal Health, the School of Veterinary Medicine has decided to assign royalties received from the sale of this book to the Center. For information on how to contribute, please contact the Development Office, School of Veterinary Medicine, University of California, Davis, Davis, CA 95616. Comments and suggestions are always welcome. This is an ongoing project, and therefore your comments will not only show your support for the Center but also will make the next edition even better.

Introduction

by Mordecai Siegal, Editor

A dog is a wet nose sliding across your face, a pair of eyes lit up at the sight of you, and a warm heart beating quickly with pleasure simply because of your presence. You are the extension of its very existence, the cause and the reason for its happiness. If nature hadn't created dogs, some clever, needful person would have, because dogs make it possible to survive some of the harsher aspects of life. They accomplish this with their unequivocal acceptance and devotion to their loved ones and with their tails swinging in merriment. Most dogs love most people. They are nature's reward to humankind for making the best of its realities, like a mother's kiss or a father's hug after a bruising fall. Always the consummate companion, a dog is both leader and follower, student and teacher, devoted friend and dedicated squire seeing us through the tangled weeds and tall grass of life's journey. A dog is the ultimate creature comfort.

Dogs come in many different sizes, shapes and types and may have any one or a combination of skills, personalities and temperaments. They may be shy or aggressive, stubborn or nervous, hyperactive or placid, aloof or outgoing. In some instances it is difficult to imagine how one breed could possibly belong to the same species as another. Still, dogs have more similarities than differences. What they share is a canine view of the world and the way they are destined to live in it. Most dogs can adjust to anything or anybody. They are practical, accepting, faithful to a purpose and childlike, in the best sense of that word, in the dispensation of their love and affection. Too often we only consider what dogs mean to us, and, of course, they mean a great deal. Why else would there be so many of them sharing our lives? To better know dogs, however, requires understanding what we mean to them.

When a dog moves into your home and bonds with you, it is accomplished with contact cement. The bonding factors are nutrition, shelter, warmth, comfort and your loving expressions of happiness with the new arrival's presence. In fact, a new dog almost immediately becomes a member of your family, which is the human equivalent of a wolf or dog pack. The pack structure is nature's canine household, complete with a head of the house and a subordinate group of leaders, followers, and territorial boundaries set aside for the activities of survival and procreation. Dogs are not only aesthetically pleasing, they are also skilled workers and enjoyable companions. However, in order to enjoy the benefits of these marvelous animals you must satisfy their needs and requirements, as they satisfy yours. Unlike most animals, dogs live in a human environment and therefore look to us for the requirements of survival which include food, friendship and affection, in addition to leadership, and medical attention.

When living with us, dogs must be shown love and appreciation, fed properly, kept clean, maintained in hygienic surroundings, protected from their own misbehavior and that of others, and given preventive and curative medical attention as it is needed. Like all living creatures, they are vulnerable to illness and injury. If a dog is struck by a car or cuts its paw it will experience pain and perhaps irreparable damage to the body unless medical treatment is provided. The canine body is a warm-blooded mammalian organism and as such is subject to invasion by viruses, bacteria and fungi which range from irritating to painful to life-threatening. Although the body's immune system defeats hundreds, perhaps thousands, of such invaders on an hourly basis it occasionally loses a battle and falls prey to disease which can only be defeated, if at all, by a highly trained professional. That is when we must reach out to the dog's doctor, the veterinarian. The science of veterinary medicine alleviates the suffering of animals to a very great degree and promotes longer, healthier lives.

Suffering is greatly reduced and life is extended because of the sophisticated training of veterinarians, highly skilled professionals who are essential to dogs and their families. The veterinarian is as much a part of our lives as the family doctor. Like general practitioners, they too must have a working knowledge of all aspects of the body and be prepared to treat as wide a range of disorders as heart disease, broken bones, cancer and skin allergies. Unlike general practitioners, they must also be prepared to diagnose and treat the medical problems of many different species, only one of which is the dog. Veterinary medicine is among the most remarkable professions in the world and those who teach it and those who go into private practice have the respect and undying gratitude of dog lovers everywhere.

How young men and women become veterinarians is not a mystery. First and foremost, they must possess intellectual gifts. They must express a thirst for highly technical and complex knowledge, demonstrate their willingness to perform hard, often grimy work, and choose to sacrifice many of the pleasures available to other young people during the time of their education and training. Through an unyielding schooling process consuming all of their time and a great deal of money, they systematically learn the medical sciences and healing arts that are taught at veterinary colleges. After three or four years of undergraduate school and four years of veterinary school, they become doctors of veterinary medicine. It is a considerable accomplishment. Many veterinarians then become board-certified specialists by completing a minimum of three years additional training, entering and concluding a residency program in their field of study and by passing examinations in their specialty. That is even a greater accomplishment.

The School of Veterinary Medicine of the University of California, Davis and its splendid faculty have educated and trained many of the world's finest veterinarians. Most dogs and their human families have benefited enormously from these highly trained doctors and would be quite lost without them. Thanks to this great institution, and others like it, medical riches are available to pet owners. Nevertheless, devoted dog people also require a source of veterinary information at their fingertips that enables them to act quickly, properly, and in the best interests of their canine family members when they become sick or injured. The *UC Davis Book of Dogs* offers a highly sophisticated source of medical information that is difficult to find outside the campus of veterinary colleges. This is a medical reference book written for dog owners, breeders, exhibitors, judges, groomers, kennel operators, and everyone involved in the world of dogs, including veterinarians themselves. This unique sourcebook was written by those who teach veterinary students.

The *UC Davis Book of Dogs* makes available medical information pertaining to dogs that is concise, understandable, but not shallow or over-simplified. It represents a major body of sophisticated information for those with a need or desire to understand the medical disorders of dogs and how they are dealt with by veterinarians. This reference book cannot enable any dog owner to diagnose an illness or treat a sick dog. It cannot, nor should it, attempt to replace professional veterinary care. Its purpose is to impart to conscientious dog owners, and those involved with dogs on a professional basis, medical information about the diseases and disorders that threaten the canine body and its various systems. Within the pages of this book is an important portion of collected knowledge from one of America's major learning institutions of veterinary medicine.

The purpose of the book is to clarify to the dog owner what his or her veterinarian is trying to explain within the time limits imposed by a waiting room filled with clients and patients, from dogs to cats to birds and snakes. When a veterinarian has only a few minutes to explain a complicated disorder or disease to a dog owner who may be distraught or choked with emotion, it is difficult for that person to come away from the experience with a full understanding of the veterinarian's discussion. The *UC Davis Book of Dogs* hopes to fill the gap and provide the dog owner and the veterinarian with the communication needed to explain and clarify the dog's illness. It is hoped that this book will function as an aid to both veterinarian and dog owner, serving both as a consulting reference tool.

When a dog owner fully understands what the veterinarian is trying to explain, the dog's chances for improvement are greatly enhanced. It is in the spirit of creating a partnership between dog owners and veterinarians that this book is added to the existing body of dog literature. All those responsible for this book, especially the contributing authors, who are on the faculty at the School of Veterinary Medicine at the University of California at Davis, believe that dogs in good health are an important source of pleasure and happiness to those fortunate to have a canine family member. Your dog's good health is the principal theme that moves throughout this volume.

On a personal note, this author and editor was singularly impressed with the quality of work, and those performing it, on the Davis campus, which benefits dogs everywhere. I particularly admire the various components of the Davis School of Veterinary Medicine which include:

Veterinary Medical Teaching Hospital
Veterinary Medicine Teaching and Research
    Center
Center for Companion Animal Health
The Center for Animals in Society
Pet Loss Support Hotline

The quality of these aspects of the University of California, Davis, School of Veterinary Medicine is reflected in these pages.

PART I

Getting a Dog

MOONSHINE: All that I have to say, is to tell you that the lantern is the moon; I, the man in the moon; this thornbush, my thornbush; and this dog, my dog.

—WILLIAM SHAKESPEARE
A Midsummer Night's Dream
Act V, Scene I

CHAPTER 1

Sources and Selection

by Mordecai Siegal

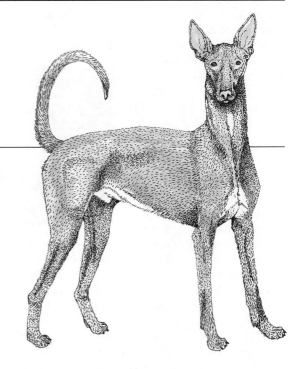

Some 4.8 billion years ago, the earth's crust solidified. Oxygen began to flow freely and circumnavigate the surface of our planet for the first time. The rays of the sun penetrated through the cloudy atmosphere. Biospheric chemistry combined to create air, water, light, heat, electricity and many ecosystems that stirred the earth. Life began. Its first form was probably blue-green algae. Across the geologic time divisions of 3 billion years came the biological genesis of bacteria, multicellular life, marine invertebrates, fish, fungi, plants, forests, amphibians, swamps, reptiles, volcanoes, dinosaurs, birds, insects, flowers, mammals, whales, apes and man.

Many scientists believe that the earliest mammal from which the domestic dog originated roamed the earth between 65 and 40 million years ago. This prehistoric creature is from an extinct genus of carnivores known as the *Miacis* that probably lived in the forests of North America, Eurasia and Asia. They are thought to have had low skulls, long slender bodies, long tails and short legs. They survived by preying on smaller animals. From this weasel-like mammal

sprang seals, raccoons, bear, cats, hyenas and the entire organization of canids that include the fox, jackal, wolf and dog.

The life we live today is inextricably bound to the chain of events that started with the creation of the earth itself and which has brought us to the next moment of experience. These are useful and interesting considerations as we sit enjoying the comfort and safety of the human family, which most certainly includes living happily with a dog.

A Guide to Dog Sources

It's easy to get a dog. Puppies are everywhere; some of them are even free. Acquiring a dog over the back fence may be easy but it is not the only way to get one nor is it the best possible source. The new dog in your life will become a member of your family and will be with you for approximately 15 years. Selecting a dog for long life and good health is greatly influenced by where you obtain the animal. Acquiring a healthy dog with a good temperament and emotional stability should not depend on luck alone.

There is a great variety of attractive dog breeds from which to choose, and if you are thinking about getting a dog you should consider them. The American Kennel Club recognizes 137 purebred dog breeds for registration and the United Kennel Club accepts 167 (most are the same breeds registered by AKC).

Therefore, it is not necessary to impulsively accept the first puppy that becomes available. There are so many ways to get a dog that it is foolish to rush the process and settle for one that is not necessarily appealing or one that is unsuitable for your life situation. When looking at the puppy in front of you, try to envision it as the dog it will grow into. The ability to choose, and choose intelligently, makes a great difference between developing an enjoyable relationship and one that ends in disappointment and failure. The first step in making the best possible choice is to become familiar with all the places one can find dogs. Where to look for a new dog should be determined by what kind of dog is desired, how much money one is willing to spend, and—most important of all—the reason for wanting a dog. The best reasons for getting a dog are to enjoy it as a companion animal, to compete in dog shows, obedience or field trials, or to breed it as part of a carefully planned line of purebred dogs. It is safe to assume that the vast majority of dogs are acquired by those who simply want a pet. Bear in mind that kennels, pet shops, shelters and pounds are only as good as the people or the administrative bodies regulating them. They may be excellent, adequate, inadequate or even worse. Only an informed, knowledgeable shopper can tell the difference and make the correct choice.

KENNELS

Purebred dog kennels are the most important source for acquiring a puppy that is most likely to possess the physical and behavioral qualities expected of its breed. A fact that may surprise first-time dog buyers is that some puppies purchased from a kennel are more expensive than those obtained from other sources. The higher prices are often due to the scarcity of the breed, but may also exist because of the time and expense involved in creating a fine line of dogs that meet the breed standards set forth by the American Kennel Club or the United Kennel Club. Producing beautiful, healthy, happy puppies is a time-consuming activity that demands skill, knowledge, and the expenditure of a considerable amount of money from the breeder. Breeding or showing purebred dogs is most often done for the love of it. Only a few ever realize a profit from this activity. However, some kennels are better than others.

The name of a kennel is simply a prefix to a dog's official name and is used by breeders in the registering and showing of dogs. It is recorded with the American Kennel Club (AKC) or the United Kennel Club (UKC) for a fee and, if approved, the kennel is granted the right to use the name exclusively for a specified period of time. In reality, however, a registered kennel name does not indicate or even imply an endorsement of that kennel by a registering organization or that it meets any standards for kennel operations. A kennel is merely a facility where one or more persons breed purebred dogs. Its quality must be evaluated personally. A proper kennel is operated by breeders who are devoted to hygiene, knowledgeable dog care, canine health, sound dog behavior and tempera-

ment, in addition to the genetic quality of their dogs based on selective breeding. Effective immunization regimens must be maintained. Veterinary medical attention is a vital aspect of kennel operations.

A kennel is not merely a name written on a pedigree. It is a place where dogs are bred, born and housed and is best evaluated by the quality of the dogs it produces. Most kennels are established inside or outside the homes of the breeders. It may be an elaborate building set apart on a large stretch of property or simply be a few dog runs made of chain link fence set in a concrete slab that is attached to the side of the breeder's home. Some homespun kennels consist of enclosed spaces for dogs inside the house or apartment. A kennel inside the home is usually improvisational and only suitable for small dog breeds. However, what is most important about a kennel is the excellence of its care and its reputation for producing sound, healthy dogs of high quality, rather than its luxurious facilities.

Good sanitation is important for the health of the animals as well as for the aesthetics of the kennel. Fecal matter should be removed as quickly as possible and urine washed away. Kennel floors and concrete slabs as well as food and water bowls and most other surfaces should be swept and mopped frequently with a 1 part bleach to 32 parts water (1:32) solution, or 4 ounces per gallon of water, and then rinsed with clear water. This simple mixture disinfects against many viruses and disease-causing microbes. Although hygiene practices vary, you should not be confronted with an unpleasant odor when entering a kennel. Good sanitation, however, is not the only criterion for evaluation.

First-time dog buyers should know that most breeders use the terms *pet quality* or *show potential* puppies as categories of dogs that are for sale at their kennels. Litters of puppies are produced on a limited basis by those who breed them for noncommercial purposes.

Those who produce purebred dogs that meet breed standards are likely to be involved in dog shows because dog shows provide an opportunity for breeders to compare dogs and exchange knowledge. A kennel need not win first place ribbons to produce outstanding dogs, however. Dogs entered in shows are exposed to the scrutiny of breeders, exhibitors, show judges and other knowledgeable dog people. Breeders gain credibility and recognition when they consistently show dogs of good quality. Competing at dog shows is a form of show-and-tell for breeders. The quality of their dogs reflect the quality of their breeding programs and the management of their kennels. Dog shows require their entrants to be pedigreed dogs that are registered with the AKC or UKC, depending on who is sponsoring the show or competitive event. Such dogs must be in good health and come from acceptable breeding lines as demonstrated by their pedigrees. They must also be of sound temperament and measure up to the established *standard* for their breed if they are to compete in dog shows and bring prestige to their breeders, owners and handlers.

A dog with *show potential* is usually more expensive than any other. It could cost thousands of dollars depending on the breeder's or the dog's reputation. Show dogs are the result of years of effort by a breeder who is aiming to meet the standards of perfection set down for his or her particular breed. To produce such dogs requires a knowledge of genetics, the mechanics and psychology of mating dogs, whelping puppies, nutrition, behavior, socializing puppies, and many other aspects of dog health and behavior. Breeders who develop quality show dogs rarely sell them or their puppies to those with no intention of showing them. It is a matter of pride and purpose that well-intended breeders and dog show exhibitors want their show quality dogs to be *campaigned*, which means to compete in major dog shows along a national circuit. *Campaigners* hope to win a *Champion* title for their dogs by winning at dog shows and scoring points toward that end. Furthermore, these exceptional dogs have much to offer to the breed and should become part of a program that aims to better the breed.

Not every puppy in a litter, however, meets the demanding standards for its breed and therefore must not be shown. Dogs that will not be shown, which make up the majority of most puppy litters, are casually called *pet quality* puppies and will be sold as companion animals. Pet quality puppies are healthy, beautiful animals that do not meet every strict requirement of the breed standard. Sometimes the coat color is slightly off or one paw may turn out just a bit, or the muzzle may be too short or too long, and so on. Nevertheless, breeders are quite fussy about the homes in which they place their babies. They try to evaluate a prospective purchaser and determine if that person will be good to the dog and provide a proper home. Many require that the prospective owners agree to neuter the puppies they buy or accept a limited registration certificate, which means that the offspring of the dog cannot be AKC registered. When purchasing a dog from a reputable breeder, expect to be asked many questions and try to understand how concerned they are about the well-being of the puppies they have brought into the world. Some breeders are quite emotional about letting go and saying good-bye to their puppies. It is like sending a child off into the world, away from home.

When selecting a kennel from which to purchase a puppy it is sensible to ask if the kennel owner is also an exhibitor. This is a fair question. The point of developing a sound breeding program is to have your dogs compete in dog shows. Of course, not every breeder is involved with dog shows. Some have retired from that activity or are involved only to the extent of supplying show dogs to exhibitors. The pedigree of your puppy tells the story. A pedigree is an official record of your dog's family tree and is on

file with a dog-registering body such as the American Kennel Club or the United Kennel Club. A good line of dogs may have one or more dogs with a Champion title in it, or is traceable to good show dogs or possibly even to the foundation stock of the breed. Ask if after-purchase support or a health guarantee is offered. If the breeder does not have the AKC registration application or registration certificate available at the time you acquire the dog, the seller should give you a written bill of sale that includes the name of the breed, sex and color of the dog. It should also include the date of birth, the registered name and number of the dog's sire and dam, and the name of the breeder. These should be written into a sales agreement.

One of the advantages of purchasing a puppy from a kennel is the opportunity to see it interact with some or all of its littermates and one or more of its parents. How a puppy behaves is an important aspect of selection. Much can be learned about a puppy by observing its parents. It is quite likely that one or both will be available. (*See* "Behavior," on page 12.)

A kennel must house its animals in adequate spaces or dog runs that are large enough for comfortable movement and rest. Anything less is inhumane and unacceptable. Dogs that are housed in outdoor facilities must also have some form of indoor shelter where it is warm and dry in the winter and cool in the summer. Dogs that are housed indoors should have light, ventilation, places to rest and room to move. A well-fed dog is obvious. It is healthy and energetic. These are basic necessities for all dogs, including males at stud. A special space, separate from the main group of dogs, is required as a whelping area for pregnant bitches to give birth in and to nurse their newborn puppies. A kennel that does not offer these basic necessities may be creating dogs with potential behavior problems.

Finding a good kennel is not as difficult as it sounds. The best method for starting your search is to attend a dog show. There, one can find many exhibitors who operate kennels and are willing to answer questions after they have met their obligations in the show ring. Kennels can also be found directly through national breed clubs. Ask about them at the American Kennel Club or the United Kennel Club. Look for breeders in the classified ads of dog magazines, which are available on newsstands and by subscription. Kennels from all parts of the United States and Canada advertise in these magazines. Both the AKC and the UKC offer a breeder referral program that will put you in direct contact with a member of a local dog club in your own community.

Current dog publications offering interesting dog articles, dog show information and breeder ads for prospective puppy buyers are:

Bloodlines (UKC)
Canine Chronicle
Coonhound Bloodlines (UKC)
Dogs in Canada
Dogs in Canada Annual (see "Puppy Buyer's
    Guide")
Dog Fancy
Dog News
Dogs USA Annual (see "Puppy Buyer's
    Guide")
Dog World
Front and Finish
Hunting Retriever (UKC)
Off-Lead
Pure-Bred Dogs/American Kennel Gazette
    (AKC)

PET SHOPS

In the past, browsers and customers would stand outside a pet shop to watch a window full of puppies either sleep in one large canine coil or tumble all over themselves as they competed for human attention. This reflected a time when pet shops were *not* the subject of controversy and criticism. More recently pet shops have been severely censured for the living conditions they provided for their puppies and the poor quality of their animal sources. As a result, many pet shops have changed how they house and display their animals. They no longer dump dozens of small dogs in a front window in order

to attract potential buyers. They have gotten the message that this practice causes the young dogs to injure each other or pass along contagious illnesses such as worms, fleas or various skin ailments. Most pet shops now show puppies in clean, well-lit, spacious cages that are wall-mounted and attractive to look at. For better or worse, pet shops are still a significant source of dogs that are purchased as companion animals, despite all the bad publicity they have earned concerning the so-called *puppy mills* where many pet shop dogs come from.

Some pet shops obtain their puppies from local breeders or from various reasonable commercial sources rather than from "livestock wholesalers" who in turn get their dogs from puppy mills. Chances are good that dogs in shops of this kind spent the first weeks of their lives in satisfactory living conditions and were bred from healthy dogs.

For some pet owners, it is of no significance whether a puppy is purebred or not. They only involve themselves with the pleasures of owning a companion animal and are not concerned with the dog's genetic history or its registered pedigree even though it may have a bearing on the animal's health and behavior. Few who want a dog know that many pet shops obtain their dogs from puppy mills. A puppy mill is not simply a dog factory churning out large quantities of cute little dogs.

A puppy mill is one of hundreds of breeding operations that is most often housed on a farm and is owned by those who do it for the extra money it brings in. It most often consists of kennels crammed with dogs housed in inadequate cages stacked one on top of the other. The kennel dogs are there for one purpose, to breed puppies in large quantities. In puppy mills dogs are not selected or rejected for mating on the basis of good or bad health, inherited diseases, or because of good temperament or severe behavior problems. All male dogs and all female dogs are mated. The puppies resulting from these matings receive little or no human attention and are sold to wholesale distributors irrespective of their state of health or behavior. In some instances, they bear little resemblance to the breed they are supposed to represent.

Although some good dogs have been purchased from pet shops, there is no way for inexperienced buyers to know in advance about the dog they have purchased and, therefore, they may be getting an animal with a serious illness or behavior problem. A number of serious medical conditions, such as hip dysplasia, are inherited and not apparent until long after the dog has been taken home, where he has crept into the emotions of the unsuspecting dog owner. To be fair, this can happen with any dog from any source. However, dogs from puppy mills are riskier buys than dogs from noncommercial breeders.

Obtaining a puppy from a pet shop is less risky if the animal is in obvious good health, has no apparent behavior problems, is handled by loving humans on a daily basis and is maintained in a clean, pleasant environment. A pet shop is a practical, if not ideal, alternative.

When obtaining a puppy from a pet shop one should be concerned about the shop itself. It should be well lit, clean, cheerful, odor-free and obviously hygienic. No more than one or two dogs should be in a single, spacious enclosure unless it is of generous proportions. It is potentially unhealthy, unsanitary and behaviorally damaging to place large numbers of puppies together in window displays. One sick dog can quickly spread its illness to the others. This is especially important to prevent the spread of internal or external parasites. Such an arrangement can also encourage the formation of abnormally aggressive or shy behavior. Sales personnel and others handling the dogs should be gentle, affectionate, knowledgeable and careful. Handling a dog incorrectly can be dangerous for the animal and the humans.

Dogs purchased from pet shops may be purebred (with or without registration papers) or mixed breeds (which are unregisterable). A purebred puppy is eligible to be registered as an individual dog if both its parents were registered with the American Kennel Club or the United Kennel Club and the litter from which it was whelped was registered by its breeder. It is only fair to say that many satisfactory and unsatisfactory companion animals have been purchased from pet shops. The same can be said of kennels and shelters.

Some pet shops do not sell any animals, but rather serve as an unofficial shelter and clearinghouse to give away unwanted or stray puppies and kittens. This service has important humane connotations despite the fact that business considerations are involved. The astute shopkeeper of such businesses create dog-owning customers who then purchase all their supplies at his or her establishment. It is good business.

Pet shops are magnetic attractions for those who are entertained by the look or the antics of animals on display. They offer prospective pet owners the convenience of being close to home. Many pet shop purchases are made on impulse which, of course, can be a disastrous mistake whether a pet is acquired from a breeder, a shelter or a shop. Acquiring a puppy should be a choice based on careful consideration and planning and not by reacting to one's own emotional responses or need for instant gratification. Many pet shops are beautiful to walk through, and many displays are designed to attract the attention of children so that they will influence their parents to make an impulse purchase. It is far less disastrous to impulsively buy a goldfish than a puppy.

When acquiring a puppy it is advisable to know what you want before making a purchase (male, female, mixed breed, which breed—longhaired, shorthaired, coat color, etc.). It is also critical that you understand the needs of a dog and your willingness to satisfy them. Longhair dogs require grooming and combing on a regular basis. Some breeds cannot bear to be left alone and require more personal attention than others. Terriers are high-energy, active dogs that are quite demanding. It is important to educate yourself about dog breeds and dog care. Dogs require medical care, personal attention, sound nutrition, clean surroundings, baths, grooming, obedience training and housebreaking. Be certain you are willing and able to provide the needs of a dog for the next fifteen years. Sales people at pet shops know how irresistible a puppy is once it is placed in a customer's arms. Just say "no" if the puppy is not the kind you wanted or if you have any doubts or reservations. (*See* "A GUIDE FOR SELECTING A DOG" on page 10.) Education, investigation and determination are the necessary elements for choosing the right dog.

ANIMAL SHELTERS

Selecting a dog from a shelter is a most important animal source to use. In many cases you are saving a dog's life by rescuing it from **euthanasia.** Shelters give dog lovers a wide range of choices plus the opportunity to provide safety and comfort for a homeless animal. The possibility of obtaining a good dog or puppy from one of the thousands of animal adoption agencies found all across the country is excellent. There are simply not enough homes for the many dogs that are lost, abandoned or born unwanted.

In some cases, homeless animals in a shelter spend the remainder of their lives in grim, indoor dog runs waiting to be adopted or euthanized. Animal shelters often bring people and dogs together, fulfilling the needs of each. They are often the safest, most efficient, economical source for acquiring healthy, endearing puppies and dogs. Their good works reward humans with the pleasures and delights of dog ownership while affording the opportunity to do something kind for an animal in need.

Many full-service animal shelters are sufficiently staffed with skilled professionals and expert workers, including veterinarians, veterinary technicians, administrators, animal handlers, peace officers, humane education specialists, and so on. There are also many volunteer rescue organizations with caring workers that are unfunded, unchartered and, in some cases, unlicensed. Although it is impossible to assess the quality of their efforts in general terms, it can be said that their work is often effective.

Some shelters are time-honored philanthropic associations underwritten by well-managed investment portfolios, bequests and wealthy donors. They may also receive funding from local or state governments in exchange for animal control services. Others rely solely on the contributions made by adopters. Many shelters and humane societies are affiliated with or recognized by national organizations such as the Humane Society of the United States or the American Humane Society. They can be found in the Yellow Pages under "Animal Shelters" or "Humane Societies." The larger establishments, such as the SPCA of San Francisco; SPCA of Boston, Massachusetts; ASPCA (New York City); or the Hamilton County SPCA (Cincinnati) are full-service organizations offering adoptions, veterinary service, information and education, animal abuse investigations and in some cases animal control. They provide their respective areas with essential animal services and have become indispensable to their communities.

There are many types of animal shelter operations in major urban areas. For example, Chicago has a city agency, the Commission on Animal Care and Control, and several important private agencies such as the Anti-Cruelty Society or the Tree House Animal Foundation, Inc. Functioning in a unique fashion is the privately funded and independently operated Tree House Animal Foundation. Although its adoption facilities are mostly for cats, it has pioneered many new programs which have had a direct impact on the stray animal and pet ownership problems which exist today. Their humane programs for dogs as well as cats include emergency veterinary medical assistance, cruelty investigations, low-cost neuter/spay, no-cost neuter/spay, low-cost vaccination, pet behavior counseling, pet-facilitated therapy, a pet-care hotline, and a pet food pantry for needy pet owners, in addition to public service radio and television announcements which supplement their many informative publications. The Tree House Animal Foundation is an innovative model for the ideal private shelter.

An extremely active adoption agency and animal shelter is the North Shore Animal League and Hospital in Port Washington, New York. This busy shelter is responsible for placing thousands of dogs and cats in decent homes every year. Unlike most shelters it reaches out for adoptions way beyond its own community.

To understand a shelter's policies one must become familiar with local animal laws and conditions. A nongovernment animal shelter, operating under the legal restrictions placed upon it by legislation, is often prohibited from collecting stray animals off the streets. In some communities private shelters are prohibited from accepting lost or abandoned animals. That responsibility may be reserved by statute as the work of a government agency, such as a city dog pound, or a private animal agency licensed by a city, town or county. The ASPCA (American Society for the Prevention of Cruelty to Animals) in New York City was typical of this arrangement. In addition to its adoption programs, veterinary hospital, animal shelter, humane education efforts, and cruelty investigations, the ASPCA was formerly commissioned by the City of New York to carry out animal control policies that included dealing with injured, lost, stray and abandoned animals from the streets. No other animal agency or shelter in that city was allowed to do so. The ASPCA employed a team of uniformed animal control officers whose job was to investigate violations of the various animal laws of New York City. They were empowered to issue citations and summonses. Recently, the city government of New York assumed many of these responsibilities.

Other private shelters in New York City may only accept unwanted animals from their owners. Even with these restrictions, private agencies such as the Humane Society of New York and the Bide-a-Wee Home Association, and hundreds of other adoption agencies throughout the country, accept thousands of unwanted dogs and cats from their owners each year. The animals are given medical attention, neutered when possible, fed, housed and cared for until proper homes can be found.

Many who have adopted dogs from shelters have described the experience as pleasant, exciting, interesting and always filled with emotion. The thumping of a tail hitting the sides of a crisp, new travel carton can only be interpreted as the sound of pleasure and gratitude as you take home your new puppy from an animal shelter.

VETERINARIANS

An important source for acquiring dogs and puppies is veterinarians. Thousands of clinics, private practices and animal hospitals throughout the country help dogs find new homes. Veterinarians have traditionally served their communities and their clientele as go-between for those who must find homes for their dogs and puppies and those who are looking for a pet. Many animal hospital and veterinary office bulletin boards are full of notices about puppies and dogs in need of a family. It is an important source to consider when acquiring a new pet.

A Guide for Selecting a Dog

The correct approach for selecting a pet is *not* to consider which is the best dog, but which is the best dog for you, your home and your lifestyle. Do you want a dog that demands a great deal of your attention and affection, or one that is somewhat reserved, has a more subtle personality and doesn't need that much personal interaction? There are breeds that are very active and some that sleep most of the time. Which is a plus or a minus for you? Some dogs need to be groomed often, particularly the longhaired breeds such as Afghans, Yorkshire Terriers, Lhasa Apsos, and so on. Some breeds hardly need any grooming.

Whether to live with a male or female is of no importance if the dog is to be neutered or spayed. A whole male dog will roam if given the opportunity and will fight with other males for territorial rights or for higher rank.

Unspayed females experience estrus ("heat") at least twice a year. A female in estrus is little understood by the novice dog owner. The behavior of a female in estrus is meant to attract a male dog and involves sexually oriented body language. It can be puzzling or even frightening to those who do not understand what is going on. Inexperienced owners are mistakenly convinced their dog is ill. During estrus the female dog secretes an odorous fluid intended to attract male dogs for the purpose of mating. (*See* CHAPTER 11, "NORMAL REPRODUCTION," and CHAPTER 12, "MATING.")

If the purpose of living with a dog is companionship only, then have your veterinarian spay a female (**ovariohysterectomy**) between the 6th and 8th month and neuter a male (castrate) between the 6th and 8th month of age. This will prevent undesirable sexual behavior and unwanted pregnancies. Some veterinarians are endorsing neutering dogs as early as 8 weeks of age.

Selecting a dog is not difficult once you ask yourself what you want. It has little or nothing to do with purebred dogs as opposed to mixed-breed dogs. Whether to purchase a purebred or a mixed-breed dog has more to do with personal preference and economic considerations.

Choosing a dog should be based on its intended purpose, aesthetic preference, cost and the behavior and health of a specific dog. *See* CHAPTER 2, "THE BREEDS," to better understand the differences between the existing purebred dog breeds.

SELECTING A HEALTHY DOG

After settling the questions of why you want a dog, how it will fit into your living pattern, its source, cost, breed and gender, you are ready to learn how to select a dog that is in good health and adaptive to the human environment. These considerations require a simple set of observations on your part when looking at a litter of puppies or an individual dog. You should be aware that looking at puppies is an emotional experience that can easily cloud your judgment. Nevertheless, it is essential to be as objective as possible and try to uncover existing medical or behavioral problems *before* you make your selection. Although the pedigree of a purebred dog is useful, it cannot tell you about the current state of health of the puppy sitting before you or whether it has the right temperament to suit you. Unless you have a veterinarian and an expert dog trainer to advise you, the selection is entirely up to you. You will be on your own.

You do not have to be a veterinarian to determine if you are looking at basically healthy dogs. Look for a litter of puppies that appear to be in obvious good health. This is the best possible situation. If there is one puppy, either in the breeder's kennel or in the pet shop, that is sluggish, or showing any of the signs of bad health indicated below, do not pick any dog from that group. Here are some important guidelines that will help you.

Coat

When examining a puppy for good health the most obvious aspect to inspect is its hair coat (fur). It should be soft, bright and vigorous-looking without clumps, mats, or bald patches. A dull, unwholesome looking haircoat is not necessarily a sign of poor grooming. It can indicate that the puppy is not being fed properly or that for some reason it cannot utilize the nutrition it is getting. In short, it could mean that the dog is sick.

Skin

Beneath the coat the dog's skin should be smooth with no lesions, scaly areas, or sores. A puppy's skin should also be free of minuscule debris appearing as a salt and pepper-like mixture, which indicates flea eggs and flea excreta. Active fleas may or may not be visible. Bald or bare patches of skin can be signs of skin diseases such as ringworm or mange. An abnormal appearance of the coat or skin may indicate parasitic infestation, allergies, eczema, bacterial or fungal skin infections, or any number of numerous other skin diseases. Clean, smooth, unspotted skin with no redness or soreness indicates the absence of infection and other medical skin conditions.

Eyes

Healthy eyes are clear, clean and alert with no excessive watering or sensitivity to light; no white skin showing from the corners; no ulcers on the surface, which appear as small indentations; and no whitish scars from previous medical conditions. Be watchful for unnatural markings or inconsistent coloring in the corneas (the transparent covering of the eyeball).

Ears

A puppy's ears should be clean with no unpleasant odor. Excessive dirt or a dark, waxlike substance accompanied by a bad odor is an indication of ear mites, which are microscopic parasites. Dogs with mites usually shake their heads and rub their ears with their paws.

Some puppies are born deaf and do not indicate it unless tested. Slap your hands together behind the puppy's ears and watch for a natural response. If you have any doubt concerning a puppy's ability to hear, speak to the seller and get an agreement to return the dog if a veterinarian determines deafness. Do not be inhibited about matters such as these.

Nose

Examine the nose. It should be cool and slightly damp. A runny discharge could indicate the presence of infection. Sneezing, coughing and a runny nose are signs associated with upper respiratory infections and other infectious diseases.

Teeth

Check the puppy's teeth. Within 2 to 8 weeks of age a puppy's mouth erupts with 28 deciduous or baby teeth. They begin to loosen and are replaced with 42 permanent teeth when the puppy is between 4 and 7 months. The process is complete within the puppy's first year of life. A dog's teeth should be smooth, white and clean with no stains. The gum tissue around the teeth should be firm, pink and calm-looking with no intense red color or bleeding of any kind. In some dogs the gum tissue is pigmented with one or two dark patches or spots. This is normal and not an indication of poor health. Pale-to-grayish white colored gums are a possible sign of anemia, which could be caused by internal parasites or some other medical condition.

Parasites

A bulging stomach may indicate the presence of internal parasites (worms) or a digestion problem. A bump on or near the navel of a puppy can be an umbilical hernia and may require medical attention. Important signs of parasitic infestation or the sicknesses they cause can be found in the anus or vulva areas. Signs of worms or diarrhea are apparent. Look for secretions, irritated tissue and hair loss, which may indicate chronic diarrhea possibly caused by virus infection. Acute diarrhea is a serious medical problem in puppies and could indicate a life-threatening infection such as parvovirus or coronavirus.

Vaccinations

If you decide to choose a dog and take it home with you, ask for the dog's vaccination record. In some respects, the vaccination record is more important than its pedigree. Most puppies should receive their first vaccination between 6 to 8 weeks of age, and the second vaccination should be given when the puppy is 12 weeks old. When purchasing your new dog, ask for a written record of vaccines given, their dates and type. Save this record for your veterinarian and give it to him or her at your dog's first examination. (*See* APPENDIX B, "VACCINATIONS.")

No matter how healthy or normal a puppy appears, it is always possible for it to have a medical problem that is not apparent. New puppies should always be given a complete veterinary examination soon after they arrive in their new homes. The first examination could be the most important one of its life.

Behavior

Of all the aspects to consider when selecting a puppy, temperament, emotional stability and acceptable behavior are among the most important. A playful yet calm and stable disposition is the ideal to look for in a puppy. A reserved puppy is different than a shy one. Some breeds hold themselves aloof from strangers and take a wait-and-see attitude before making direct contact. But that is not the same as shyness, which may be a behavior deficiency. The shy dog is abnormally frightened of anything unfamiliar and tries to avoid humans, animals, or change of any kind. Shyness is expressed by escape behavior, cringing, cowering and, when all else fails, by defensive aggression. Puppies that are not curious, energetic, playful, or anxious to greet you may either be ill or have a behavior problem. Of course, puppies can also be tired when being viewed and may simply be in need of a nap.

Another temperament type to avoid is the overly aggressive dog. Young dogs and even puppies that growl from deep within their throats are warning you to stop what you are doing or else they are going to bite you. That is undesirable and unacceptable behavior and indicative of an aggressive dog who will be dangerous as an adult. If you are suspicious of overly aggressive behavior, try placing the dog on his back and holding him there for a minute or two. A dog with a potential behavior problem will growl, snarl, howl, bark, and even snap and bite to get back on his feet. Avoid such a dog.

Puppies that have been handled by humans on a regular basis early in life have been "socialized." This means they should be better at interacting with humans and highly trainable. If they have

been allowed to remain with their mother and littermates for a minimum of seven weeks they are likely to adjust easily to other dogs as well as humans (providing they have been socialized). The transference of genetic characteristics plays an important role in dog behavior, too. If available, observe the puppies' mother and father. Chances are that the puppies will have a similar temperament. If they are at ease with strangers, congenial, curious, outgoing and friendly it is likely that their puppies will be the same.

When observing a litter of puppies, kneel to floor level and observe which ones are curious about you, friendly toward you, and want you to touch them. Lift them into your arms, one at a time, to see if they are at ease with you. A normal puppy will either thrash about playfully or settle in and enjoy the contact. A normal puppy should follow you about when it is set down on the floor once again. Try playing with it. A friendly, outgoing puppy will respond to your efforts. It will roll on its back and flail its paws, place your finger in its mouth, or try to climb on you and lick your face. There is more to canine health than clear eyes and a glossy coat. A happy, self-assured puppy that delights in the company of humans is likely to enjoy good health and a long life.

CHAPTER 2

The Breeds

by Mordecai Siegal

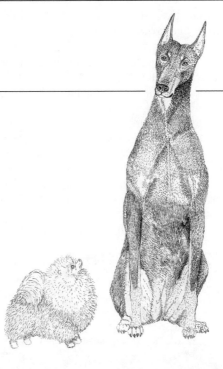

The first question that comes to mind for most people selecting a dog is, which breed do I want? For those with no set idea this is a difficult decision. There are so many dogs to choose from, more than 400 breeds in the world today. Deciding which one to live with can be a difficult choice. Dog selection is somewhat easier if you know something about the many breeds available and the groups into which they are divided.

The American Kennel Club, established in 1884, accepts 137 separate dog breeds for registration. They are classified into seven categories—Sporting Dogs, Hounds, Working Dogs, Terriers, Toys, Non-Sporting Dogs and Herding Dogs. Those breeds pending acceptance for registration are placed in the Miscellaneous Class, which currently contains six breeds. The AKC is the principal registry organization for purebred dogs in the United States. It establishes and administers rules and regulations for registering purebred dogs, dog shows, obedience and field trials, and many other related functions.

The United Kennel Club, established in 1898, is the second largest all-breed registry. It accepts 167 breeds for registration, which are categorized into eight groups—Guardian Dogs, Scenthounds, Sighthounds, Gun Dogs, Northern Breeds, Herding Dogs, Terriers and Companion Dogs.

There are many dog breeds native to foreign countries, many of which are not registrable by AKC, usually because of their scarcity in the United States. These international breeds offer more options for those seeking unusual dogs, but they are usually difficult to find outside their country of origin. In addition to all of the purebred dogs in the world, there is the option of choosing a mixed breed or mongrel.

Despite the incredible selection of breeds available it is a mistake to decide on one until you have asked yourself how a specific type of dog will fit in with the way you live. The size of your living space has a direct bearing on the success of your selection. Obviously, Saint Bernards are not a good choice for those living in cramped quarters, and toy dogs such as Chihuahuas may not be best for life on a ranch or farm.

It is also important to understand the characteristics of the breed that interests you because you may find they are incompatible with the way you live or with your likes and dislikes. For example, Bulldogs are rugged, endearing and interesting dogs, but they snore and wheeze in their sleep and frequently drool because of their unusual facial anatomy. They are also sloppy eaters. Some Bulldog owners carry a towel with them at all times to wipe their dog's jowls.

German Shepherd Dogs are extremely loyal and become emotionally attached to their owners and will protect them and their property to the death. However, they are all too often intolerant of other dogs and they also shed a great deal. Poodles are incredibly intelligent dogs, are bred in three sizes (toy, miniature and standard), can be fearless in the face of danger, and shed very little, but may annoy you with excessive barking or stubborn behavior. Shiba Inus are highly intelligent Japanese dogs that like to jump up on tables and in general behave somewhat like cats. Fox Terriers have charming, engaging personalities and attract quite a bit of attention wherever they go. Nevertheless, they are highly sensitive, excitable dogs that bark a lot and they can be scrappy.

As individuals, dogs differ from one another. The same is true from breed to breed and group to group. Although all dogs are appealing, it is important to learn as much as possible about the predictable breed characteristics of the dogs you are interested in before choosing which one you want. More important than breed selection, however, is determining the quality of the dog's breeding. The best dogs have no serious hereditary health problems, were vaccinated, were socialized as puppies by their breeder (handled gently on a daily basis), fed and housed properly, given attention and affection, and kept with their littermates and mother for at least 7 weeks.

Choosing a dog should be an intelligent decision based on the type of home you live in, how much time you can spend with the animal and whether you want an affectionate, outgoing pet or one that is reserved and somewhat aloof. Whether to get a male or female dog is another question to consider. (There are significant behavior differences between the two, especially among unaltered dogs.) Do you want a breed with a long coat or a short one? Do you mind if the breed you admire continually sheds hair on your carpet? Do you have small children? If so, it is best to get a sturdy dog that is somewhat large, and certainly one that is even-tempered so that he can tolerate and endure a child's play without becoming aggressive. A dog with a low tolerance for the exuberance of children may eventually bite them.

Is your home large enough for the breed you want? Is the dog going to live indoors or outdoors? Some breeds cannot tolerate an outdoor existence. Do you expect your dog to protect you? Acquiring a dog for protection is a large subject and one that requires the advice of experts. It is essential to consult a professional dog trainer about this before making a decision you may regret. Protection dogs are like loaded guns. They can be extremely dangerous to everyone, including their owners, if they are not professionally trained, handled properly and absolutely obedient. These are some of the issues to consider before looking for a dog. No one can answer these questions for you. Only you know how much time you can devote to grooming, exercise, play, training, or which canine personality you will enjoy the most. Each breed has its own characteristics, and it is up to the prospective dog owner to discover what they are, in addition to addressing the issues of their own needs and preferences.

A basic knowledge of dog breeds offers the best help to those deciding which dog to choose. There are many breed books available in bookstores, libraries, dog magazine advertisements and in pet supply catalogs. Another way to learn about specific dog breeds is by talking to exhibitors and breeders at dog shows, obedience trials and field trials. Most of them will generously answer your questions. Those who show dogs are usually breeders and are quite likely to be helpful, friendly and informative. They may even sell you one of their puppies if they think you will be a good dog owner. Professional dog trainers are another important source of breed information.

Most dog breeds possess one or more highly developed skills to perform specific tasks exceedingly well. These abilities were genetically promoted by resourceful breeders who selected dogs for mating that possessed a highly developed canine trait or characteristic that they wanted to emphasize. This, coupled with evolved physical and mental characteristics induced by environmental demands, created breeds that pull sleds, live in the snow, protect flocks of sheep, assist hunters, protect property, and so on.

Consider the West Highland White Terrier. Despite its white, fluffy, dainty appearance and its diminutive size, it was developed from several terrier breeds whose instincts were to vigorously pursue and flush out vermin from obscure ratholes. Most dog breeds were developed for their inclination to perform a specific task or because they could function well in some unusual circumstance, such as extreme weather. Few of these specialized dogs living as pets are given the opportunity to use their special skills in a meaningful way. Cocker Spaniels almost never hunt anymore and Collies rarely herd sheep. Nevertheless, it is extremely useful for pet owners to know about the specialized skills of their own dogs and allow them to express those inclinations in some constructive way. For example, a dog that is one of the retrieving breeds should be allowed to carry small packages or newspapers in its mouth and then be rewarded for it. It could avoid frustration or chewing problems in the home.

The one job that all pet dogs have in common is that of companion animal, which they accomplish with great success. Dogs have become an essential part of our day-to-day lives and can be found in the humblest and the most luxurious homes. Do you have any idea about the dog you want? The process of selecting a dog can be enhanced by the following information concerning AKC dog groups.

The American Kennel Club Groups

Presenting a complete description of the hundreds of existing dog breeds here would be impractical and inappropriate in view of the medical focus of this book and the limitations

of space. However, there is much to be learned by reading the concise descriptions of the seven AKC dog groups. If you are interested in a specific breed, look through the group description to which it is assigned. You will learn important information about a specific breed by taking into account what the dog was bred to do. In most cases, there are important similarities between the breeds within a group. Quite often they have the same abilities and special functions, which provide useful insights into a breed's potential behavioral traits.

GENERAL PRACTITIONERS AND SPECIALISTS

Dogs and wolves living in the wild require specific skills and behaviors that enable them to survive. These behaviors are instinctive and typical of most canine species. For example, dogs can see movement from great distances, which gives them obvious advantages. Their ability to locate a prey animal or an intruder by scent is exceptional. They live in a social structure known as a pack and hunt in groups enabling them to capture and eat animals larger than themselves. In the wild, all dogs can quickly dig holes in order to create a safe, warm place to sleep. They are proficient at guarding, fighting

and defending themselves. All dogs possess these and other traits with a general degree of skill.

In the course of domestication, breeders have cleverly selected and bred specific dogs for their accentuated size, type or ability. To illustrate: When wolves or wild dogs hunt, some members of the pack display a greater skill than others in separating the targeted animal from its herd. Over the centuries, those dogs with a greater ability to manipulate herd animals were selectively bred for that instinctive quality and then trained to emphasize that skill. Thus the herding breeds were created. Large, aggressive dogs that were born pack leaders, that were protective, that fought well, were selectively bred to emphasize those qualities and became the breeds used for guard and protection work.

Over the centuries many dog breeds came into existence because of the efforts of individuals who preferred that their dogs specialize in one of the canine skills to near perfection, rather than perform them all in a general way. For thousands of years humans have been selectively breeding dogs for their own practical purposes. As a result, domestic dogs now exist as specific breeds based on individual abilities such as guarding, herding, hauling, hunting, and so on. In some breeds physical characteristics were also emphasized to facilitate the utility of the dog. Some terrier breeds that chase their prey into holes, for example, have been selectively bred over the centuries for long bodies and short legs. Temperament has also been emphasized in some breeds. Individual dogs with a strong sense of territory have been bred for guard and protection work. In modern breeding programs dogs are also selected for a specific look or for their conformation as determined by a written standard for their breed.

The result of selective breeding has been the great diversity of size, type and temperament as seen in the hundreds of existing breeds. It is for this reason that the diminutive Yorkshire Terrier and the gigantic Irish Wolfhound both belong to the same species despite the incredible difference in size and behavior. The following introductions to the seven American Kennel Club Groups and the breeds within them will help you to understand some of the characteris-tics of the breeds that have been placed in them. This information may be useful when selecting the right breed of dog for you.

SPORTING DOGS
Brittany
Pointer
Pointer, German Shorthaired
Pointer, German Wirehaired
Retriever, Chesapeake Bay
Retriever, Curly-Coated
Retriever, Flat-Coated
Retriever, Golden
Retriever, Labrador
Setter, English
Setter, Gordon
Setter, Irish
Spaniel, American Water
Spaniel, Clumber
Spaniel, Cocker
Spaniel, English Cocker
Spaniel, English Springer
Spaniel, Field
Spaniel, Irish Water
Spaniel, Sussex
Spaniel, Welsh Springer
Vizsla
Weimaraner
Wirehaired Pointing Griffon

When the American Kennel Club began registering dogs in 1884, many of the breeds that now comprise the Sporting Group were the first to be listed. They have remained in that position of prominence ever since.

Dogs in the Sporting Group have been bred

for centuries to work side by side with humans, assisting in hunting upland birds and waterfowl. Almost all of the breeds in this group are subdivided as pointers, setters, retrievers or spaniels. They possess the highly refined ability to locate game birds by scenting them with a "high nose"—sniffing wind currents as they work in the fields. Their job is to catch the scent of game birds in hiding or on the move, locate the prey, indicate their presence to the hunter, flush them out if commanded, and then retrieve them once they are down. In England and several European countries these breeds are categorized in the Gun Dog Group. What distinguishes the breeds in one subdivision from another is their style of hunting when in the field.

Pointers

These breeds were developed in England in the mid-seventeenth century and did not begin as bird dogs. Their job was to find and then point to small game animals such as hares, which were then coursed or chased down by the faster Greyhounds. Later in that century they were employed to find and point to quail. Pointers are highly skilled dogs that find their quarry and hold their position with absolute stillness until the hunters take aim and flush the birds out of hiding.

The pointing breeds are aggressive in their work, move quickly, cover great distances, and are valued for their endurance. They are intelligent animals that are eager to dash onto the field and do their job locating upland birds such as pheasant and grouse and pointing to their whereabouts. Once a pointer has found its prey he must stay "on point," holding his position as though frozen to the spot, most often in the classic position with one forepaw held up and bent inward as his head and tail point the way like an arrow.

The pointing breeds in the Sporting Group are the Brittany, Pointer, German Shorthaired Pointer, German Wirehaired Pointer, Vizsla,

Weimaraner, and the Wirehaired Pointing Griffon. From 1934 to 1982 the Brittany was registered as the Brittany Spaniel. The AKC changed the name to Brittany. Its legs are longer than those of the typical spaniel and its manner of hunting is more setter-like. Brittanys are considered to be pointers.

The pointer breeds are lovable dogs that are affectionate and friendly, especially with their families. They are highly energetic with an irresistible need to run and move about vigorously. They are responsive to obedience training and make fine companion animals although they are not suited to city life, especially in apartments where they are too restricted. Because they are decision-making dogs in the field, they can be quite stubborn when not handled with authority. The pointer breeds must be obedience-trained as soon as possible if they are to live as companion animals inside the home. Like all sporting dog breeds, they were born to hunt.

Retrievers

Retrieving breeds do exactly what their name implies, which is to say they retrieve birds no matter where they have fallen. These highly skilled specialists will dive into icy waters without hesitation in the execution of their job, as well as plunge down hills covered with thorny thickets. They are particularly well suited for hunting wild ducks and geese, but are capable upland bird hunters as well. They are, however, considered waterfowl specialists.

Like other gun dog breeds, they too are capable of locating birds for the hunter and indicating where they are, but they excel at retrieving birds with a "soft mouth" (carrying them without causing damage), no matter where they have fallen. They are the expert swimmers of the dog world and do not hesitate to find and retrieve on command, no matter where they must go.

Of the five retriever breeds in the Sporting

Group, the Labrador Retriever and the Golden Retriever are considered by some to be the finest companion animals available and are the most suited to family life. They are always in the top 10 breeds for numbers of dogs registered by the AKC, which is attributed to their enormous popularity among dog lovers desiring a friendly, intelligent, even-tempered, family dog that loves children and just about anyone or anything. Many are used as guide dogs for the blind because of their fine temperament

and great trainability. They are, however, very energetic and require vigorous exercise and activity. All retrievers have an instinct to find something to retrieve and carry back to you in their mouths, and may develop chewing problems in the home if this need is not satisfied in a positive way. They are sensitive dogs and do not tolerate punishment well. They also have a tendency to dig holes. The Labrador Retriever and the Golden Retriever are the easiest of the retriever breeds to obedience-train

and are the most adaptive to family life.

Setters

These breeds are gun dogs and function by locating upland game birds, standing in point, and retrieving the birds once they are downed. In sixteenth- and seventeenth-century England, before guns were used for bird hunting, they were referred to as setting spaniels because they "set" the prey by keeping them pinned to the ground until nets could be cast over them. This partially accounts for the term "setter." At times their manner of pointing is to maintain a crouched position as they set or partially sit low to the ground.

Of the three setters registered by the AKC, the English Setter has the most sedate, relaxed temperament and is considered by some to be the easiest to live with. These are gentle dogs that are wonderful with children and elderly people.

Like all hunting breeds they are strong-willed and do not want to be left alone. They also tend to move slowly. English Setters of the Laverack strain are most often seen in AKC conformation shows and are appreciated for their pleasing appearance. Those of the Llewellin strain are considered the finest workers in the field, although they do not possess the look of the Laverack strain.

The Gordon Setter and the Irish Setter are high-energy dogs with a great need for exercise and activity. Like the English Setter, they too are gentle and friendly and love children, but are quite strong-willed and have difficulty adjusting to living in small city apartments. As hunting dogs they are easily distracted by anything that moves swiftly or suddenly, such as pigeons, squirrels or rabbits.

Spaniels

The spaniel breeds are among the oldest dog breeds in the world. They are thought to have originated in medieval Spain. The word "spaniel" means Spanish dog. There are nine spaniel breeds recognized by the American Kennel Club.

Spaniels are known as the flushing breeds for their propensity to flush birds from their hiding places once they have found them, so that hunters may take aim. Spaniels were important sporting dogs when hunting birds was accomplished with the use of nets and falcons. All of the spaniel breeds are capable of finding, flushing and retrieving both waterfowl and upland game birds.

Spaniels are smaller than other field dogs and consequently are used for their speed and ability to squeeze under places too tight for the larger gun dog breeds. All spaniels, even those walking along city streets, have a keen interest in the activities of birds and demonstrate an irresistible urge to chase them. Although the spaniel breeds have a great deal of energy as well as outgoing personalities, they are very obedient if they are socialized as puppies and trained when they are young. It is absolutely essential to acquire all spaniels, but especially Cocker Spaniels, from skilled, reputable breeders because of the bad results of overbreeding caused by commercialization. The English Springer Spaniel and the Welsh Springer Spaniel perform in the field in similar ways to the other spaniel breeds and are exceptional at flushing game birds from their hiding places.

Many dogs in the Sporting Group (no matter what the breed) are bred exclusively as field dogs. These are dogs expected to express their breed characteristics to the fullest. Dogs that live and work with hunters are highly energetic and intense in the performance of their hunting tasks, and (in some breeds) decide when to precipitate the moment of the hunter's action. To live with such dogs requires firm obedience and field training that is expert and without compromise. Many dogs in the Sporting Dog Group participate in American Kennel Club field trials and hunting tests, which are regulated events designed to test a dog's various hunting skills.

Many dogs in the Sporting Group are bred for the requirements of the show ring, which means the primary concern is for conformation and the overall look of the dog. Competition for championship points and winner's ribbons in dog shows involves physical appearance, sociability and a judgment of how the dog compares to the written standard for its breed. Rarely does a show dog of the Sporting Group work as a field dog or vice versa. It should be noted, however, that those dogs registered with the United Kennel Club are encouraged to be "the total dog," which involves both bench and field excellence. When acquiring a dog from the Sporting Group it is useful to know whether the puppy comes from field stock or show stock. Dogs that are purchased as pets from the Sporting Group are usually from show dog lines that for some reason did not quite match the breed standard. This has an important influence on the dogs' behavior in the home. Although all of the hunting instincts may be present, they will not be as intense or as pronounced as they are in superior field dogs. Of course, there are always exceptions to the rule.

HOUNDS
    Afghan Hound
    Basenji
    Basset Hound
    Beagle
    Black and Tan Coonhound
    Bloodhound
    Borzoi
    Dachshund
    Foxhound, American
    Foxhound, English
    Greyhound
    Harrier
    Ibizan Hound

Irish Wolfhound
Norwegian Elkhound
Otter Hound
Petit Basset Griffon Vendéen
Pharaoh Hound
Rhodesian Ridgeback
Saluki
Scottish Deerhound
Whippet

Breeds from the Hound Group are dogs whose hunting skills are not the same as those in the Sporting Group. Hounds do not hunt birds; they track and find larger game, from rabbits to humans. These are the great hunters and trackers of the dog world. The breeds in this group vary from one another in their look, size, behavior and hunting skills. The Greyhound couldn't be more different in every way from the American Foxhound, and the Saluki is worlds apart from the Bloodhound. They hardly appear to be members of the same species, much less the same dog group—but they are.

The hound breeds do not hunt in the same manner as those in the Sporting Group in that they do not keep their noses high in the air, scenting the air currents. In fact, they track their prey in one of two ways: by sniffing the ground or by sighting their prey visually from a great distance. The Hound Group is comprised of scenthounds and sighthounds.

The Scenthounds

These breeds differ in appearance and behavior from those hound breeds that hunt by sight. The scenthounds are, as a group, serious-looking dogs until they are set loose to track and find their quarry. Then they come alive with joy and pleasure. With their noses to the ground they can sniff their way for many miles until they find exactly what they are looking for. It is who they are and what they do.

Many of the scenthound breeds are short-legged and slower on the trail. They are stocky and powerfully built and they enjoy an active existence. Such breeds are the Beagle, Basset Hound, Dachshund and Petit Basset Griffon Vendéen. They work best in woodsy thickets.

They are capable of identifying one scent from thousands and pursuing it for great distances.

The most famous of the scenthounds is the Bloodhound, which is the legendary trail dog that searches for and usually finds escaped convicts, lost children and plane crash victims, as well as game for hunters. Bloodhounds are capable of catching a scent on the ground hours or even days after it has passed through. They are said to have the best nose in the dog world. Although they have an image of mercilessly chasing and attacking their prey, they are gentle, affectionate dogs who do no harm. Their job ends once they find who or what they were tracking. Unlike various other hunting dogs, they do not attack their prey. A Bloodhound on the trail makes his presence known by his musical voice as he barks and howls, calling out to the hunters with pleasure. Hunters refer to this as "singing" when "giving tongue" in "full cry."

The Beagle is the most popular and best-known of the scenthounds thanks to Snoopy, the famous dog in the Charles Schulz comic strip, "Peanuts." Possibly the most endearing scenthound breed for pet owners is the Dachshund, which is bred in three varieties (smooth, wirehaired and longhaired) and in two sizes (standard and miniature). These very clever dogs, beloved by all, are somewhat terrier-like, going after prey relentlessly, even into holes and tunnels in the ground. Although their natural prey was the German dachs, or badger, they are extremely interested in hunting mice and rats.

The following breeds are scenthounds: Basenji, Basset Hound, Beagle, Black and Tan Coonhound, Bloodhound, Dachshund, Foxhound (American), Foxhound (English), Harrier, Norwegian Elkhound, Otter Hound, Petit Basset Griffon Vendéen and Rhodesian Ridgeback. The United Kennel Club registers many of these same scenthound breeds and in addition they register the Bluetick Coonhound, Plott Hound, Redbone Coonhound, and Treeing Walker Coonhound (not illustrated).

The Sighthounds

Other breeds in the Hound Group are those whose hunting is accomplished with a highly

Group I: Sporting Dogs

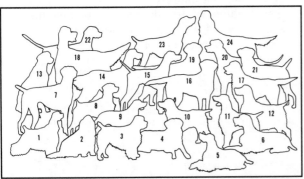

(1) Cocker Spaniel (2) Sussex Spaniel (3) Clumber Spaniel (4) Chesapeake Bay Retriever (5) English Cocker Spaniel (6) German Wirehaired Pointer (7) Weimaraner (8) Brittany (9) American Water Spaniel (10) Field Spaniel (11) Welsh Springer Spaniel (12) English Springer Spaniel (13) Curly-Coated Retriever (14) English Setter (15) Vizsla (16) Labrador Retriever (17) Flat-Coated Retriever (18) Gordon Setter (19) Golden Retriever (20) Irish Water Spaniel (21) Wirehaired Pointing Griffon (22) Pointer (23) German Shorthaired Pointer (24) Irish Setter

developed visual ability. These are known as sighthounds, or gazehounds or coursing hounds. The vision of these breeds is so acute that the slightest motion draws their attention, even from great distances. The reference to them as coursing hounds is based on their ability to outrun their prey once they sight it. Sighthounds are remarkably swift and command great physical endurance with their lithe, streamlined bodies. They hunt best in flat, open spaces where they are more capable of seeing their prey from a long way off. Once they locate their target they silently run it down at great speed.

The following breeds are sighthounds: Afghan Hound, Borzoi, Greyhound, Ibizan Hound, Irish Wolfhound, Pharaoh Hound, Saluki, Scottish Deerhound and Whippet.

What sighthound and scenthound breeds share in common is the supreme sense of performance when running free in the hunt. Scenthounds are good-natured dogs, fun-loving, somewhat docile, good-looking if not dainty (some drool). Beagles hunt in large packs; others, such as the Bloodhound, are likely to hunt in pairs. They are strong-willed dogs in their own laid-back but stubborn fashion. Most of these breeds require a firm hand in training. One must be authoritative but not harsh.

Sighthounds are different. They are much more sensitive and respond poorly to overly strong handling. They must be commanded firmly but delicately. These princely animals have a splendid bearing, especially when they run to the hunt. In times gone by, they hunted in groups of two and three. Many of the sighthound breeds, such as the Afghan Hound and the Borzoi, are absolutely elegant in their movement and appearance, especially when they run. The Irish Wolfhound, the tallest and most powerful of all breeds, is not as elegant in its movement (it canters when it runs), but is an extremely lovable and endearing dog, as is its slightly smaller cousin, the Scottish Deerhound. Sighthounds behave with reserve and aloofness and do not offer their attention to everyone. Finding a puppy with an easygoing tempera-

ment is the key to a happy relationship with any of these breeds.

Hounds bred for work in the field rather than the show ring have a hard time living indoors, especially in an apartment.

Working Dogs

Akita
Alaskan Malamute
Bernese Mountain Dog
Boxer
Bullmastiff
Doberman Pinscher
Giant Schnauzer
Great Dane
Great Pyrenees
Komondor
Kuvasz
Mastiff
Newfoundland
Portuguese Water Dog
Rottweiler
Saint Bernard
Samoyed
Siberian Husky
Standard Schnauzer

Although the breeds in the Working Group are loved and adored as companion animals, they were originally developed to perform a specific job in the human environment as canine specialists. Breeders have been selecting dogs with unique physical characteristics, specific temperaments, and special abilities for centuries and have shaped them into the breeds that we have come to love and employ. In all of recorded history, specific dog types have protected humans and their herd animals and hauled freight in wagons, carts and sleds. Dogs have been given military assignments since the beginning of human warfare. Breeds in the Working Group clearly demonstrate how humans have developed with exaggeration various aspects of canine behavior and physical characteristics.

The instincts to protect what belongs to them, to fight territorial intruders and to maintain pack integrity, in addition to being able to drag large animals that were brought down in the hunt, were the qualities that originally attracted the first dog breeders. With the exception of the various northern breeds such as the Samoyed and the Siberian Husky, Working Group breeds make good watchdogs and, in some cases, protection dogs. Breeds that willingly offer these abilities to the humans they live with have a territorial instinct, which is to say that they will defend their homes and their families as they would if they were living in a pack structure. Dogs that protect their human families do not tolerate the intrusion of those they do not know and will either chase them away or attack them.

For some people the intimacy and companionship that develops between them and their dogs is based on the dogs' instinct to guard and protect them. The working breeds are among the most social, the most loyal and the most misunderstood of all dog breeds. The aggressiveness that is part of the character of those breeds noted for it comes from a sense of connection with the humans that live on their territory. In human terms these are the qualities of loyalty and devotion. It is only when the aggressive dog's personality has been distorted that its behavior is unmanageable and therefore unacceptable.

Dogs that haul freight for humans in carts and sleds do so as the result of selective breeding based on the ability to bring home "the kill" and feed the pack. All dogs have this instinct, but not all of them are really good at it. Breeds that are heavier and stronger such as Alaskan Malamutes, Bernese Mountain Dogs and Newfoundlands can haul large, weighty loads. Smaller breeds such as Samoyeds and Siberian Huskies pull lighter loads, but do it with greater speed and agility. Dogs of the Working Group will guard their homes, protect their families, participate in war, rescue lost and endangered victims, pull heavy loads, guide blind citizens, and provide anyone who asks for it with love, devotion and companionship.

Breeds of this group that can be trained to protect you with various degrees of efficiency are the Akita, Alaskan Malamute, Bernese Mountain Dog, Boxer, Bullmastiff, Doberman Pinscher, Giant Schnauzer, Great Dane, Great Pyrenees, Komondor, Kuvasz, Mastiff, Portuguese Water Dog, Rottweiler, Saint Bernard and Standard Schnauzer. Breeds that will work for you by pulling sleds or carts or performing other physical tasks are the Alaskan Malamute, Bernese Mountain Dog, Newfoundland, Portuguese Water Dog, Samoyed and Siberian Husky. Rarely can a breed of the Working Group hunt as the breeds of the Sporting Group, Hound Group or Terrier Group do.

Newfoundlands and Portuguese Water Dogs are breeds that are exceptional swimmers and have traditionally worked with ocean fishermen on their boats. They were capable of swimming between boats, carrying messages or jumping into the water on rescue missions when necessary.

The northern or Spitz-type breeds began their lives as sled dogs (Siberian Husky, Samoyed, Alaskan Malamute) and have a strong instinct to live and work in snow and cold climates. The natural habitat of these breeds was frigid and necessitated that they dig holes in the

Group II: Hounds

(1) Longhaired Dachshund   (2) Wirehaired Dachshund   (3) Smooth Dachshund   (4) Beagle (5) Basset Hound   (6) Petit Basset Griffon Vendéen (7) Shorthaired Ibizan Hound   (8) Basenji (9) Wirehaired Ibizan Hound   (10) Whippet (11) English Foxhound   (12) Rhodesian Ridgeback (13) Harrier   (14) Norwegian Elkhound   (15) Afghan Hound   (16) Pharaoh Hound   (17) Black and Tan Coonhound   (18) American Foxhound   (19) Otter Hound   (20) Greyhound   (21) Borzoi   (22) Saluki (23) Scottish Deerhound   (24) Bloodhound   (25) Irish Wolfhound

snow in which to sleep. Consequently, they have the habit of digging holes no matter where they live, even if it is in a backyard or front lawn. Although it is quite unacceptable behavior in most human environments, it makes perfect sense to the dogs. But when dogs are living as pets this is an upsetting behavior problem and must be dealt with as such.

The behavior patterns of the working breeds that offer some form of protection are based on the natural imperative to protect territory and preserve the pack. If you understand this aspect of their behavior you will understand everything useful about them. In a sense, dogs that perform hard physical work do it for the same reason.

Terriers

Airedale Terrier
American Staffordshire Terrier
Australian Terrier
Bedlington Terrier
Border Terrier
Bull Terrier
Cairn Terrier
Dandie Dinmont Terrier
Irish Terrier
Kerry Blue Terrier
Lakeland Terrier
Manchester Terrier
Miniature Bull Terrier
Miniature Schnauzer
Norfolk Terrier
Norwich Terrier
Scottish Terrier
Sealyham Terrier
Skye Terrier
Smooth Fox Terrier
Soft Coated Wheaten Terrier
Staffordshire Bull Terrier
Welsh Terrier
West Highland White Terrier
Wire Fox Terrier

Although there are several behavioral similarities among all of the terrier breeds, there are important differences requiring their mention. Obviously, there are profound physical differences among the terrier breeds that pertain to size, body shape and coat type. Many of the terrier breeds are peevish and scrappy, but not all of them. However, all terriers are hunting dogs. With few exceptions, the terrier breeds were skillfully developed to perform important hunting tasks in agrarian societies. Through selective breeding these breeds were created because they were needed to control rodents and other pests that consume the contents of cultivated gardens and cash crops, in addition to harming the land and feeding off such farm animals as chickens and pigs. The Airedale, largest of the terrier breeds, was an effective hunter of fox, badger, weasels, otters and water rats, although other terrier breeds were also employed to hunt these animals. As societies moved from an agrarian to a more industrial-urban form of lifestyle, farming and gardening required less and less of the efficient hunting skills of the terriers.

The American Kennel Club lists 25 recognized terrier breeds in this group, most of which are now living as pets or show dogs. Their image as ratters or controllers of vermin has changed drastically. Such elegant breeds as the Sealyham Terrier with its glistening white coat can, with the slightest encouragement, go digging into a rat's hole as it snarls and snaps for the kill. As hard as that might be for the modern pet owner to imagine, nonetheless, that is exactly what it was created to do.

Even the name of their breed type, terrier, indicates why these dogs were created. The word terrier is from the Latin *terra* meaning "earth." Terrier breeds are persistent, headstrong and obstinate, which drives them to pursue their quarry across watery marshes and through thickets of brush and thorns, scurrying into tunnels and holes as the fox, rat or badger "goes to ground." For this purpose many of the terrier breeds have been developed with exaggerated short legs and long bodies.

Most terriers are small to medium-sized dogs. All but a few of the breeds were developed in England, Wales, Scotland and Ireland, and originate from various terrier-type dogs that were commonly found in the British Isles and employed opportunistically to hunt vermin, rabbits and other small game.

Up until the turn of the nineteenth century,

some terriers were thrust into the so-called blood sports such as pit fighting, where dogs fought each other to the death. Another of these purported "dog sports" was bull baiting, which gathered much attention until it became socially unacceptable and was permanently banned in the beginning of the twentieth century.

The terrier breeds originate from dogs that were developed as small-game hunters, ratters and fighting dogs. Dogs performing such tasks had to be stubborn, contentious and aggressive combatants. Time, and the efforts of concerned breeders, have changed, or at least attenuated, the aggressive qualities of the terrier breeds, especially those used in the blood sports. After many generations as companion animals their behavior has softened, making them highly desirable as pets. The terrier breeds are, for the most part, intelligent, clever, loyal, devoted and completely lovable dogs. They are among the most prized and admired house dogs.

Small to medium-sized terrier breeds are the Australian Terrier, Bedlington Terrier, Border Terrier, Cairn Terrier, Dandie Dinmont Terrier, Smooth and Wire Fox Terriers, Irish Terrier, Kerry Blue Terrier, Lakeland Terrier, Standard Manchester Terrier, Miniature Bull Terrier, Miniature Schnauzer, Norfolk Terrier, Norwich Terrier, Scottish Terrier, Sealyham Terrier, Skye Terrier, Soft Coated Wheaten Terrier, Staffordshire Bull Terrier, Welsh Terrier and West Highland White Terrier.

The larger terrier breeds (50 pounds or more) are the Airedale Terrier, American Staffordshire Terrier and the Bull Terrier. The American Pit Bull Terrier (not illustrated) is one of the most important terrier breeds, but is only registered by the United Kennel Club, not the American Kennel Club. It is a delightful, pure breed that is a highly trainable dog and wonderful to live with when bred properly, socialized, obedience-trained, and handled gently and respectfully.

Toys

Affenpinscher
Brussels Griffon
Chihuahua
Chinese Crested
English Toy Spaniel
Italian Greyhound
Japanese Chin
Maltese
Manchester Terrier
Miniature Pinscher
Papillon
Pekingese
Pomeranian
Poodle (Toy)
Pug
Shih Tzu
Silky Terrier
Yorkshire Terrier

The Toy Group is comprised of breeds that only appear to be similar because of their very small size. In fact, many of the breeds in the Toy Group are quite different from one another. The Pomeranian, for example, can be traced to Spitz-type or sled dogs; the Yorkshire Terrier comes from the larger terrier breeds. In both examples, some of their physical and behavioral characteristics are similar to those of their derivative breeds. A number of the toy breeds are obviously bred down from their standard-size counterparts such as the Toy Poodle, Italian Greyhound and Toy Manchester Terrier. The breed sources for some of the toy breeds are impossible to determine, however, because their lineage has been lost in antiquity. Such ancient breeds are the Chihuahua, Maltese, Japanese Chin and the Pekingese, among others. For these reasons it is more useful to consider what these breeds have in common rather than to examine their differences, of which there are many.

What all toy breeds have in common is that they are small and are the ultimate companion animals. In reality, these diminutive dogs should not be referred to as toys because that label creates the false impression that they are playthings. These vertically challenged breeds are mighty dogs in tiny bodies. Providing unqualified friendship and constant companionship is not idle play or shallow distraction. For many people the emotional fulfillment provided by these dogs is life-giving and life-saving. No companion animal is more capable of developing as close a relationship with its family as any one of

Group III: Working Dogs

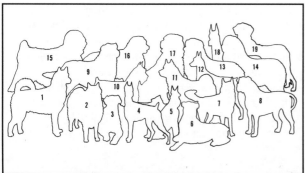

(1) Alaskan Malamute   (2) Samoyed   (3) Portuguese Water Dog   (4) Boxer   (5) Standard Schnauzer (6) Rottweiler   (7) Siberian Husky   (8) Bullmastiff (9) Bernese Mountain Dog   (10) Giant Schnauzer (11) Akita   (12) Doberman Pinscher   (13) Great Pyrenees   (14) Newfoundland   (15) Komondor (16) Kuvasz   (17) Saint Bernard   (18) Great Dane (19) Mastiff

Group IV: Terriers

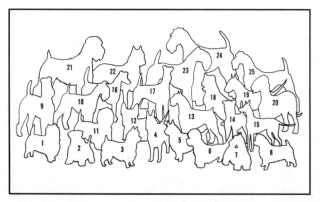

(1) Cairn Terrier   (2) Sealyham Terrier
(3) Australian Terrier   (4) Miniature Bull Terrier
(5) Norwich Terrier   (6) Dandie Dinmont Terrier
(7) Scottish Terrier   (8) Norfolk Terrier   (9) Wire
Fox Terrier   (10) Lakeland Terrier   (11) West
Highland White Terrier   (12) Skye Terrier
(13) Miniature Schnauzer   (14) Border Terrier
(15) Manchester Terrier   (16) Smooth Fox Terrier
(17) Welsh Terrier   (18) Staffordshire Bull Terrier
(19) Bull Terrier   (20) Bedlington Terrier   (21) Soft
Coated Wheaten Terrier   (22) American
Staffordshire Terrier   (23) Kerry Blue Terrier
(24) Airedale Terrier   (25) Irish Terrier

the toy breeds. Their size allows them to be carried about and taken anywhere, which provides the possibility of a much more intimate relationship. Consequently, toy dogs very often sense the emotional fluctuations of human behavior as they happen. The toy dogs seem to understand the subtle differences in the speech, body movement and behavior patterns of their human companions and as a result respond sensitively to happiness, sadness and changes in the day-to-day routines. Toy dogs are remarkable pets. Their ability to respond to human feelings also allows them to manipulate those who love them and get their own way in almost all matters. It is a quality that is usually associated with cats. Nevertheless, breeds in the Toy Group are not anything like cats. They behave exactly as the larger dogs, but on a smaller scale. With only a few exceptions, the toy breeds are very territorial and will incessantly bark at the slightest intrusion. In some instances they will even attack an intruder and try to drive him away.

There are few similar characteristics among the breeds of the Toy Group beyond their companionship capabilities. The American Kennel Club has placed these breeds in the same group, obviously, because of their size and because of their lap-dog image. The Toy Group, however, has within it

miniaturized versions of breeds that are found in all the other AKC groups. The miniaturization of a breed causes some personality and temperament changes, but it is safe to state that there are many behavioral responses that are similar between the standard and smaller versions of a breed. For example, Italian Greyhounds are as quiet, mild-mannered, hardy and eager for a good run as their cousins, the Greyhounds. Toy Poodles are as intelligent and as trainable and endearing as their counterparts, Standard and Miniature Poodles. English Toy Spaniels are similar to other spaniels in that they are friendly and gentle and somewhat reserved with strangers. The Toy Manchester Terrier is similar in temperament to the larger Standard Manchester Terrier. The toy version exhibits many of the terrier traits including high energy, scrappiness with other dogs and stubbornness, in addition to being as sensitive as any other toy breed. The Toy Manchester Terrier is also lively yet gentle, and totally lovable.

All of the breeds in the Toy Group are amiable, companion animals that readily serve as watchdogs because of their propensity to yap and bark at the slightest intrusion or noise. Breeds that have frequent grooming requirements are the Affenpinscher, English Toy Spaniel, Japanese Chin, Maltese, Papillon, Pekingese, Pomeranian, Toy Poodle, Shih Tzu, Silky Terrier and Yorkshire Terrier. All breeds in the Toy Group demand a great deal of attention and affection.

They consider themselves the babies of their families and never let you forget it.

NON-SPORTING DOGS

Bichon Frise
Boston Terrier
Bulldog
Chinese Shar-Pei
Chow Chow
Dalmatian
Finnish Spitz
French Bulldog
Keeshond
Lhasa Apso
Poodle, Miniature
Poodle, Standard
Schipperke
Shiba Inu
Tibetan Spaniel
Tibetan Terrier

Of all the AKC group designations this one is the least understood, especially by newcomers to the dog fancy. Non-Sporting Group breeds appear to have little or nothing in common with each other. There is an explanation for this that comes from Victorian England. The idea of the Non-Sporting Group springs from late-nineteenth-century English values concerning dogs. The Kennel Club, the primary dog-registering organization of England and the model for the American Kennel Club, registered approximately 40 dog breeds when it was formed in 1873. Soon afterwards, it began registering more breeds than it could manage without some form of division for the sake of administrative efficiency. Victorian values at the time dictated that sporting dogs were the breeds of choice for country gentlemen. Consequently, the breeds were split into two sections, those that participated in the hunt in any way and those that did not. Thus was born the Sporting Division and the Non-Sporting Division. The two divisions represented a clear reflection of the value placed on dogs at the time.

When the need eventually arose for further demarcation the Toy Group was created, which resulted in the removal of a number of breeds from the Non-Sporting Division. When the American Kennel Club was formed in 1884 it followed the English format in addition to forming the Working Group, which required removing more breeds from the Non-Sporting Group. As each of the seven AKC groups were created the appropriate breeds were removed from the Non-Sporting Group and reassigned. As a result the Non-Sporting Group has become a general category for breeds that meet all American Kennel Club requirements for registration and competition but do not logically fit into the other groups. Few, if any, of the Non-Sporting breeds appear to have any relationship to each other except as companion animals. Ironically, the Kennel Club of England abolished the Non-Sporting Group and replaced it with the Utility Group.

With no exceptions, the Non-Sporting Group breeds are excellent companion animals as well as winners in the show ring. Part of the reason these breeds cannot be classified within the other six groups is that many of them no longer perform their original function because it is either irrelevant or obsolete.

The Bulldog, for example, was originally developed in England as a breed for fighting, particularly in the ugly spectacle of bull baiting. Until it was outlawed in 1835 bulldog-type canines were matched against tethered bulls. They were encouraged to mutilate each other until one was either dead or totally incapacitated. This was but one of the blood sports. Since that terrible time the ferocity of the dog's temperament has been bred away and the modern Bulldog has become an even-tempered, good-natured pet. Because of its legendary tenacity, this breed has become a symbol of English pride, especially important during the darker days of World War II.

The origins and early functions of the breeds in the Non-Sporting Group are as interesting as they are varied. The Bichon Frise originated as

Group V: Toys

(1) Chinese Crested   (2) Japanese Chin
(3) Chihuahua—Smooth Coat   (4) Chihuahua—Long
Coat   (5) Pug   (6) Pekingese   (7) Miniature Pinscher
(8) Brussels Griffon   (9) Maltese   (10) Manchester
Terrier   (11) Papillon   (12) Shih Tzu
(13) Silky Terrier   (14) English Toy Spaniel
(15) Affenpinscher   (16) Italian Greyhound
(17) Pomeranian   (18) Yorkshire Terrier
(19) Poodle (Toy)

an early water spaniel. The Boston Terrier, one of the few American breeds, developed as a cross between the Bulldog and various terrier breeds from England. The Bulldog began as a professional dog fighter but developed into one of the most beloved of all house pets. The Chinese Shar-Pei is of obvious Mastiff origin and possesses a dominant personality that was originally exploited in staged dog fights. Their loose and wrinkled skin made it difficult for canine opponents to get a grip on them. The Chow Chow is of Spitz origins and originated in China for hunting, fighting and guard work. The Dalmatian is a versatile breed that was used as a draft dog, as

a hunter, a watchdog and even as a herding dog. These are high-spirited, playful dogs that are vigorous and active. The Finnish Spitz, the national dog of Finland, is a bird hunter, strong-willed and stubborn. The French Bulldog looks like a bulldog but is in fact an even-tempered toy breed that is gentle and playful. The Keeshond is an alert watchdog, territorial but good-natured. The Lhasa Apso originated in Tibet as a watchdog. It is an affectionate and vigorously playful dog. The Poodle (Standard and Miniature) is intelligent, highly energetic, and somewhat stubborn, although easily trained. Poodles were originally developed as retrieving water dogs. The Schipperke (pronounced skipper-key) is a working dog originally used in Belgium as a watchdog on water barges. It is an active, stubborn, yet easily trained dog. The Shiba Inu is a

Spitz-like breed from Japan that is small, active and somewhat catlike in its behavior. It has a dominant temperament and can be aggressive. The Tibetan Spaniel is not a spaniel but did originate in Tibet. The breed was developed as a watchdog and as a companion animal. It is shy with strangers but happy and outgoing at home. The Tibetan Terrier is not a terrier but did originate in Tibet. These small dogs were used (in Tibet only) as herding dogs and as watchdogs. They are excellent companion animals. They are playful, friendly and somewhat stubborn.

HERDING DOGS
Australian Cattle Dog
Australian Shepherd
Bearded Collie
Belgian Malinois
Belgian Sheepdog
Belgian Tervuren
Bouvier des Flandres
Briard
Collie, Rough
Collie, Smooth
German Shepherd Dog
Old English Sheepdog
Puli
Shetland Sheepdog
Welsh Corgi, Cardigan
Welsh Corgi, Pembroke

In 1983 the American Kennel Club divided its Working Group in two. A number of breeds were taken out of that group and placed in the newly formed Herding Group. This action was part of a continuing process of refinement for the purpose of administrative efficiency and the logical reclassification of breeds. The reasoning for this change was obvious. Many breeds placed in the working group could be identified as sheep or cattle dogs and there were enough of them to justify getting their own group designation, just as the terriers were eventually reclassified out of the Sporting Division and given their own group.

Sheep and cattle dogs were placed in the Working Group originally because many of them were extremely versatile and were called upon for guard work, for pulling carts (and sleds), and, where possible, to help hunters. Shepherds and cattle drovers not only expected their dogs to herd sheep or cattle, they called on them to protect the flocks and herds from bears, wolves and other predators, including humans. In some situations, where the flocks were kept in remote places, the dogs were left alone with their sheep for weeks at a time with a hidden reserve of food to live on.

The Herding Group currently consists of 15 breeds. What they share is an adaptive temperament that enables them to be trained by humans for almost any task asked of them. The ability and the willingness to drive livestock from one place to another as well as protect it has been a traditional function for these dogs which, over the centuries, have been prized by shepherds, farmers and ranchers.

Herding behavior in dogs is better understood once it is seen in the context of the hunting techniques of canines living in a natural state. Shepherding or herding grows from two aspects of wolf behavior. Wolves (and wild dogs) hunt in groups in order to bring down animals much larger than themselves. An important technique in accomplishing this involves deliberately chasing the prey, usually part of a herd, in a specific direction while other members of the pack separate the old, sick or very young from the main group. Once isolated, the targeted animal is brought down and eaten by the canine hunters. Sheep and cattle dogs bring to bear these instinctive behaviors, which are classified as herding techniques, as they are trained by shepherds, drovers or farmers to move, control and protect their livestock.

The other aspect of wolf behavior found in herding dogs is the instinct to safeguard their fallen prey from the mouths of scavengers or to guard their den from encroachers who are not part of their pack. These hunting and guarding instincts carry over to the behavior of domestic herding dogs that work with sheep and cattle and also to those who live as pets and companion animals.

In days long since gone, older herding dogs taught their skills and techniques to younger herding dogs. This is no longer the case. Valuable herding dogs that are put to work in the pastures are the result of selective breeding and highly refined training. Such dogs are obedience-trained at an early age. The ability to come when called (the recall) and to drop instantly when given the signal are of great importance. Herding dogs must also learn the advanced training of responding properly to voice commands, whistles and motions or the movements of the shepherd's crook from a great distance. The dogs must learn to control sheep and cattle by intimidating them with a piercing stare from their strong, dominant eyes. When such a dog stares directly into your eyes it is an intense challenge and can be an unnerving experience. In an effort to preserve the classic skills and techniques of canine herding the American Kennel Club maintains a herding program, which is divided into Testing and Trial sections. Both divisions award titles for demonstrations of inherent herding abilities and proficiency in herding situations.

The herding dog breeds are notable for their stamina, speed and agility. Most of them are adaptive to all sorts of people and to all sorts of living conditions that are imposed on them, including various climates and weather extremes. These breeds come in large, medium and small sizes and are all dominant, highly trainable dogs. They are animals with fine sight and scent, good hearing and great intelligence.

Group VI: Non-Sporting Dogs

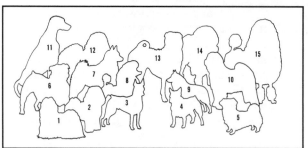

(1) Lhasa Apso   (2) Bichon Frise   (3) Boston Terrier
(4) French Bulldog   (5) Tibetan Spaniel   (6) Bulldog
(7) Finnish Spitz   (8) Miniature Poodle
(9) Schipperke (10) Tibetan Terrier (11) Dalmatian
(12) Keeshond   (13) Chinese Shar-Pei   (14) Chow
Chow (15) Standard Poodle

Group VII: Herding Dogs

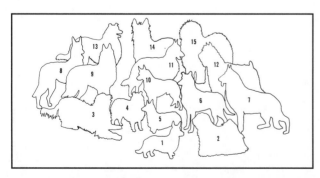

(1) Cardigan Welsh Corgi   (2) Puli
(3) Bearded Collie   (4) Shetland Sheepdog
(5) Pembroke Welsh Corgi   (6) Smooth Collie
(7) German Shepherd Dog   (8) Belgian Malinois
(9) Belgian Sheepdog   (10) Australian Cattle Dog
(11) Belgian Tervuren   (12) Bouvier des Flandres
(13) Rough Collie   (14) Briard   (15) Old English
Sheepdog

Protecting their families and homes is instinctive for these dogs. However, they must be obedience-trained at an early age and handled firmly and with a dominant manner. Herding breeds have a strong desire to please, but some are more stubborn than others because of their decision-making behavior. Most dogs in this group are protective by nature and consequently are reserved with strangers. To avoid overly aggressive dogs in such large breeds as the German Shepherd Dog, Old English Sheepdog, or Bouvier des Flandres, they should be bred from carefully selected, even-tempered dogs, socialized as very young puppies, and vigorously obedience-trained.

Dogs of the herding breeds are very sensitive animals and must never be hit or verbally abused. Eventually, they will defend themselves if necessary and that could be dangerous. If they are confined in small living quarters they tend to behave destructively and are capable of chewing up personal property when left alone too long. All of the herding breeds can live happy, normal lives in the city as well as in the country if they are obedience-trained and exercised adequately.

PART II

Living with Your Dog

I class myself with Rin Tin Tin. At the end of
the Depression, people were perhaps looking
for something to cheer them up. They fell in
love with a dog, and with a little girl. . .

— SHIRLEY TEMPLE
on her success as a child star,
New York Post, Sept. 13, 1956

CHAPTER 3

The Human-Animal Bond: Attachment to Dogs

by Lynette A. Hart

Why is it that dogs seem to be such perfect companions for so many people? Throughout the ages, dogs have been taken for granted as partners living side by side with people. Human culture in fact seems to have coevolved with the presence of dogs, perhaps over a span of a hundred thousand years. Hundreds of dog breeds were created to fulfill specific human needs such as hunting, herding and guarding.

Stemming from their wolf ancestry, dogs naturally enjoy living in a "pack," even one populated by human beings, and this predisposes them to a compatible relationship among us. Dogs tirelessly seek out social contact with their human companions, initiating interactions and affection. They understand the rules of a social hierarchy and thus are easily trainable and obedient. They have the mental capacity and the motivation to adapt flexibly to a wide range of requirements imposed by human companionship. And they come in so many varieties—all sizes, shapes, temperaments and activity levels. This provides prospective owners with a wide selection when choosing a compatible breed, one

that can fulfill the owners' specific expectations; that is, that the dog exercise with them, guard the house, serve as a lapdog, or be easy to train.

The Dog As Active Companion

Despite the wide diversity of dog breeds, there is concrete evidence of the general compatibility of dogs and people. In one study 57 dog owners rated their own dogs versus a hypothetical "ideal dog" on 22 behavioral traits. The owners consistently assigned high ratings to their dogs on five traits that they also rated as very important in an ideal dog. The dogs excelled in the following traits that were considered of crucial importance by their owners:

- expressiveness
- enjoyment of walks
- loyalty and affection
- welcoming behavior
- attentiveness

These five traits typify how a dog can facilitate social interactions by always being available to its owner for social activities. The dog participates in countless daily interchanges with its owner, tirelessly performing such behaviors as whining, begging, making noises, obeying and just being with the owner—all behaviors in which cats would rarely engage. The dog even serves as a conversational companion. Transcribed conversations that occurred while people were walking their dogs have revealed that all walkers spoke frequently to their dogs during walks. With frequent use of the dog's name and numerous commands, these conversations strongly resembled the "motherese" language that mothers use with small children.

Conceivably a dog's level of enthusiasm could become excessive in a busy household. It appears that dogs may adjust their interactions with people depending on the living situation, turning up the level of interaction in a quiet home and scaling it down in a busier household. In-home observations of adult family members and dogs while children were not present showed that in childless families the people and the dog interacted more frequently and with greater complexity, and that the dog spent a greater amount of time being close to someone. Dogs in childless families interacted in five or more bouts per hour per person, as compared to one or two bouts in families with children. This suggests that a dog living with a solitary and perhaps lonely person may actually increase its interaction rate and become a more involved companion than if it were living with several people.

The Dog As Facilitator of Human Companionship

Dogs excel at recruiting human companionship. Even small animals such as turtles or rabbits attract passerby and become a focus for conversation. Dogs go beyond this by greeting, soliciting attention and play, and actively seeking human responsiveness. People walking their dogs almost invariably are provided opportunities for friendly social interchanges with passersby, in contrast to people not walking with dogs.

The socializing effect extends to adults and children with disabilities, persons who are often subjected to social rejection. Evidence suggests that the animal enhances how the person is perceived so that the person is viewed as being more attractive. Because of this, and because of the great attractiveness of dogs, adults and children using wheelchairs and accompanied by service dogs receive friendly approaches from strangers that apparently would not occur in the absence of the dog. The service dog acts as a social adjunct that assists in normalizing the responses of able-bodied people to those in wheelchairs. Especially for a child, creating a more normal social context is critical to healthy social development.

The Dog As Something to Nurture

In the past families more easily functioned as tiny communities than they do today. More individuals lived in larger family groups with more children, and relatives were not spread over such vast distances. Family members shared the responsibilities of child care and farm animal care. Today, few young children reside near their aunts, uncles, cousins and grandparents,

who now often lack any creatures for which to care. And the children themselves, usually growing up in smaller families, gain little or no experience in caring for younger children.

A dog can fill the need for something to love and for which to care. With close parental guidance, a dog can serve as an introduction to nurturing for a small child. Only and youngest children apparently are drawn to an opportunity to experience nurturing with their pets, and spend more time with the animal than do children who have younger siblings.

For older people a dog is something to love that loves them back. The rituals of each day, from waking up to going to sleep, often are built around daily activities with the dog. Feeding the dog and walking with it provide an essential framework for a daily schedule. Dog owners need not face coming home to an empty house because they know that the dog is waiting for them and needs attention.

The Dog As Motivation to Exercise

Awareness is growing of the value of consistent exercise in enhancing mood and promoting lifelong health. For example, even modest amounts of exercise exert a protective effect against hip fracture, a debilitating injury for elderly people from which many never recover. A dog offers support and motivation to take daily walks. After non–dog owners in one study adopted a dog, they increased their routine walking severalfold. The ability of a dog to motivate someone to take outdoor walks every day is arguably one of the most significant benefits of dog ownership.

The Dog As Social Support and a Well-being System

A dog can enrich anyone's life. For someone who is experiencing particular stress, a dog can serve as a buffer and provide essential support. By serving as a companion, eliciting other human support, requiring nurturing, and motivating to exercise, a dog can keep a person moving ahead even during difficult times. In a study

of elderly persons whose spouses had recently died and who had no close confidants, those with a pet were less likely to describe themselves as seriously depressed. Among bereaved elderly pet owners with few or no friends, those who were closely attached to their animals fared better than did the unattached pet owners in self-reports concerning depression.

One study of elderly people and their medical visits found that dog ownership was particularly effective in protecting against the effects of life stresses. For most people, increasing amounts of stress resulted in a greater number of medical visits. However, dog owners did not show this pattern. Dog owners reported spending extensive time talking to their dogs, playing with them outdoors, and walking with them. Perhaps these regular and pleasurable activities played a role in the dog owners' decreased need for medical attention.

Since the early 1980s, some studies have suggested that companion animals may exert a beneficial role in cardiovascular health. In a recent Australian report, companion animal owners were found to have lower **systolic blood pressure** (blood pressure during heart muscle contraction) and **plasma triglycerides** (a measure of circulating fatty acids) than did nonowners. Further evidence of healthful effects of dog ownership was found in an English study, where improved general health and fewer minor health problems occurred for at least ten months after dog adoption.

Coping with the Death of a Companion Dog

For many people a companion dog's importance ranks near that for the human members of the family. In fact, more than a third of dog owners surveyed in one study pictured themselves as being closer to their dog than to any other family member! When a dog is so important to someone, the loss of that animal inevitably will have a profound effect. The person whose dog has died must suddenly stop routine activities. No longer is the dog the first and last creature seen each waking day. No longer can the dog be walked and fed, or share countless interchanges with its owner throughout the day.

Awareness has grown over the past few years that bereavement is to be expected following the death of a companion animal. Support groups for grieving pet owners now are available in many communities, and a pet-loss support hotline has been established that accepts telephone calls Monday through Friday evenings, 6:30 to 9:30 P.M. Pacific time, at (916) 752-4200.

CHAPTER 4

Puppies and Pediatrics

by Autumn P. Davidson

The acquisition of a new puppy is a momentous occasion, whether it is the first dog owned by an individual or family, or one of many. A new puppy represents the start of a new relationship. A puppy offers unconditional friendship for life, complete with affection, loyalty, entertainment and companionship. The dog owner needs only to provide responsible husbandry (feeding, housing, exercise and grooming), supervision (including adequate training and play), and health care. Few situations in life offer such a rewarding return on an investment. Most dog owners agree that the only major disadvantage in establishing a relationship with a puppy is the shorter life span of that beloved canine friend.

The bond that develops between a dog and its owner is unique, its character molded primarily during the animal's first year. A large body of knowledge exists concerning relationships between dogs and human beings. Bookstores and libraries abound with books on puppy selection, raising and training, and communities often have many dog trainers available. This chapter provides important, basic guidelines that are applicable to a puppy's first year of life.

A Puppy's Roots

The decision to acquire a dog is one that should be made with great care. As the responsible human being in the relationship, the dog owner should have a lifestyle appropriate for having a dog (time and energy for the dog), a home amenable for keeping a dog (with either an enclosed yard or plenty of time available for leash walks), and adequate financial resources (ongoing expenses for food, veterinary care, licensing and equipment). Once the decision to obtain a pet has been made, the type (mixed-breed vs. purebred), gender and source must be decided upon. A mixed-breed puppy will have a unique physical appearance and personality, and may have "hybrid vigor" (fewer health problems due to greater genetic diversity), when compared to a purebred puppy. Today's daunting pet overpopulation problem can also be addressed by acquiring a mixed-breed puppy.

A purebred puppy will have more predictable

physical characteristics and personality owing to preceding generations of selective breeding. (*See* CHAPTER 6, "CANINE BEHAVIOR.") Genetic variability overall is minimized. Responsible breeders are aware of potential heritable problems in their particular breeds and will take steps to avoid them, will educate their clients about them, and will follow their puppies throughout their lives.

Many wonderful breeds of dogs are available, each unique in many ways. Deciding between a mixed-breed and a purebred, or between purebreds, will depend on what an individual is looking for in a dog. Prospective owners should take plenty of time to consider the different breeds and mixes, their physical characteristics (haircoat type, body size, exercise and food requirements) and personalities (tractable vs. strong-willed, vocal vs. quiet, energetic vs. sedentary, timid vs. aggressive, etc.), and select accordingly.

The person selecting a pup should find someone knowledgeable to converse with concerning the characteristics of a selected breed or individual dog. Mixbred puppies are best acquired either from private parties who are aware of the qualities of one or (preferably) both parents, or from animal shelters and welfare groups whose staff have had sufficient time to observe a puppy's personality. Purebred puppies are best acquired from breeders in good standing with the American Kennel Club (AKC), who have been involved with their breed for a number of years and who are knowledgeable concerning the breed's qualities and problems. One should be able to obtain references from a breeder, including clients, veterinarians or trainers; to visit dogs at their home; and to examine certificates of genetic screening, as from the Orthopedic Foundation for Animals, the Canine Eye Registry Foundation, and the Institute for Genetic Disease Control. Purebred puppies should generally not be acquired through newspaper advertisements, because quality breeders place their puppies by word of mouth and rarely need to advertise. One should also avoid so-called "backyard" breeders; that is, those who haphazardly mate two purebred dogs for financial gain or simply for fun and who lack knowledge of the breed's potential problems.

Deciding between a male or a female puppy depends again on personal preference. Both sexes make excellent pets when raised correctly. Both make good watchdogs, athletes and children's companions. Male and female dogs do have some differences with regard to health problems, but these are insignificant to their overall life expectancy. All pet puppies—male or female—should be neutered, leaving breeding to the professionals.

Although raising a dog from puppyhood is extremely rewarding, obtaining a new adult dog can offer several advantages. Some of the work and time necessary for raising a puppy can be avoided by adopting an adult dog from an animal shelter, purebred rescue group, or animal welfare organization. Adopting an adult dog also contributes positively to the pet overpopulation problem. Although puppy raising is avoided, dogs acquired as adults often need basic training too (including housebreaking), so their first year in the new home is of great importance just as it is for pups.

A Puppy's Health

Within 48 hours of bringing a new puppy home, a trip to the veterinarian for a physical examination is in order. This initial visit is a most important one, providing the veterinarian with an opportunity to evaluate the puppy's health and personality and to outline preventive health measures. Any physical defects, behavioral problems or illnesses need to be uncovered immediately, enabling the owner to make an informed decision about whether to keep the puppy. The history of the puppy's origin and its attitude, appetite and activity level in its new home should be summarized for the veterinarian. The puppy's diet, medications or supplements given, water consumption and nature of eliminations should be examined. Any vaccinations or medications given previously by the breeder or shelter should also be noted for the record. Guidelines or instructions received from the breeder should be reviewed critically. The pet owner should not hesitate to ask the veterinarian about proper husbandry and training for his or her new puppy.

On the first visit a complete physical examination will be performed, which should include measurement of body temperature and vital signs (pulse and breathing rate), and evaluation of the skin, eyes, ears, mouth, bones, muscles, nerves, heart, lungs, abdominal organs, genitals and lymph nodes. The puppy should be weighed, and a fresh sample of its stool, usually brought in by the owner, should be evaluated for the presence of internal parasites, such as roundworms. Further blood or urine tests may be applicable depending on the history and results of the physical examination.

The new puppy owner should receive instruction in the proper techniques of oral hygiene (brushing of the teeth), ear care, nail trimming and grooming to be performed at home. Methods of flea control and heartworm prevention, when applicable, should be outlined. The administration of a deworming medication will be based upon the veterinarian's judgment and the results of the stool evaluation. The puppy's temperament should be evaluated and home exercises in proper socialization reviewed. Finally, the initial series of immunizations against viral and bacterial diseases ("puppy shots") should be initiated (*see* CHAPTER 34, "VIRAL DISEASES"; CHAPTER 35, "BACTERIAL DISEASES"; and APPENDIX B, "VACCINATIONS").

Immunization techniques have improved the life expectancy of puppies dramatically in the last two decades. Proper administration of vaccines at optimal time intervals, in conjunction with prudent husbandry, will minimize the chances that a puppy will contract an infectious disease. Although vaccines can be obtained from feed stores and given by pet owners themselves, their administration by a licensed veterinarian or veterinary technician at an animal hospital is optimal for several reasons:

1. vaccines must be handled and administered properly to maintain potency;
2. the veterinarian has invested considerable time and expertise in obtaining the best and most efficacious products from the many brands on the market based on current, validated research;
3. the most up-to-date knowledge concerning the administration of multiple vaccines in a series is also made available to veterinarians, again through validated research;
4. the veterinarian will discuss with the pet owner the pros and cons of various immunization protocols, and make the owner comfortable with the program selected for his or her puppy;
5. some geographic variation exists with regard to vaccine recommendations, e.g., vaccination against Lyme borreliosis;
6. allergic (**anaphylactic**) reactions, although rare, can occur a short time after receiving a vaccine (these sudden, life-threatening events are best handled immediately in a veterinary hospital).

In general, the expense of the pup's receiving immunizations at a veterinary hospital is minimal when compared to the lifelong health care of the dog. (*See* APPENDIX B, "VACCINATIONS.")

Appropriate measures to reduce exposure to infectious disease agents must accompany proper vaccination schedules. Puppies acquire passive immunity (antibodies) to many infectious diseases from the bitch's first milk, or **colostrum.** Colostral antibodies provide important, temporary protection against infectious diseases early in a puppy's life. This type of immunity gradually diminishes over the first 20 weeks. The presence of these antibodies can interfere with the mechanism by which vaccinations stimulate the puppy's own more permanent immunity, however (*see* CHAPTER 33, "THE IMMUNE SYSTEM AND DISORDERS"). Unfortunately, certain infectious diseases can sometimes overwhelm this maternally derived immunity, resulting in illness in a properly vaccinated puppy. Isolation of young puppies from dogs with infectious diseases is therefore of the utmost importance. Puppies should not be taken to public areas such as parks or public sidewalks where other dogs have wandered, and they should be carried when taken into the veterinary clinic. Boarding and grooming facilities should be avoided until puppies have completed their full course of immunizations. Early efforts at socialization and training should take place at home or in a clean environment frequented only by other healthy, vaccinated dogs. Similarly, traffic through the home should be limited, because some viral diseases may be readily transmitted on the soles of shoes. Young puppies should not be allowed in kennels housing dogs that have traveled from shows or trials, or where unquarantined dogs may be introduced.

Regardless of owners' and veterinarians' precautions, however, puppies do have a knack for getting sick. The puppy owner needs to know which signs of illness warrant a simple call to the veterinarian for discussion, and which require an emergency visit. Events necessitating *an immediate trip* to the clinic include:

- serious trauma
- exposure to extreme temperatures, either hot or cold
- contact with toxins or caustic substances
- altered states of consciousness
- severe pain
- hemorrhage
- difficulty breathing
- collapse

A quick call to the veterinarian's office, forewarning arrival, is always appreciated. Common problems worthy of consultation on a *nonemergency basis* include:

- persistent vomiting or diarrhea
- lack of appetite
- any change in urinary habits
- constipation
- excessive sneezing
- eye or ear pain
- malodorous skin, ears or mouth
- abnormal discharge from the eyes, ears, mouth, genitals or anus
- coughing
- abnormal swellings
- lameness

Generally, veterinarians would rather have an unnecessary telephone consultation than an excessively polite client with a seriously ill pup. *When in doubt, call!*

Dog owners should be familiar with the normal appearance of their pet's gums, be able to take a rectal temperature, and be able to report on the puppy's appetite, thirst and eliminations when calling the veterinarian. After consultation, the veterinarian may request a visit or may suggest an interim plan of home management.

Common sense and good husbandry can prevent many puppy health problems. One should avoid allowing the puppy freedom in areas not carefully "puppy-proofed." Chewed electric cords, ingestion of toxic or caustic substances from the house, garden or garage, garbage raids, and contact with unfriendly or overly exuberant dogs, children or cats can often be avoided. Certainly puppies (and most adult dogs) have no concept of the danger of automobile traffic. Puppies also exhibit exceedingly poor judgment, often jumping off heights or falling into pools. Puppies should be treated as toddlers; that is, they should be monitored closely and confined in a safe spot when not supervised.

A spacious crate or exercise pen can serve as an ideal "playpen" for a young pup. Playthings that are generally safe and acceptable are those that are meant to be chewed upon, that are non-toxic, and that are not readily dismantled or ingested. Best avoided are toys with easily removed bells or squeakers, small objects that could be swallowed or inhaled, and items that resemble the owner's own valuables (shoes, socks, leather goods). Most veterinarians advise against giving puppies real bones, goat hooves, pig ears or rawhide pieces that can be swallowed because digestive upsets commonly follow ingestion of such objects.

Puppy Husbandry

Good husbandry will optimize one's chances of raising a pup to healthy, well-adjusted adulthood. New puppy owners should familiarize themselves with proper canine nutrition, housing, exercise and grooming. The field of canine nutrition has advanced significantly in recent years, and many types of high-quality commercial foods are now widely available. When selecting a dog food, one should choose a well-known national brand backed by years of research and experience. The veterinarian should be able to make several suggestions in this regard. The food should be nutritionally complete for all canine life stages. Kibble (dry dog food) is adequate in most situations, although canned food may be necessary for more discriminating canine palates. Puppies older than 5 to 6 weeks of age do not need to be fed milk. (*See* CHAPTER 8, "CANINE NUTRITIONAL REQUIREMENTS," and CHAPTER 9, "FEEDING DOGS.")

Establishment of good eating habits occurs during the puppy's first several months of life. Puppies do not require great variety in their diets if they have been properly trained at mealtime. Dogs are intelligent; if they learn as pups that refusing to eat kibble results in better-tasting items being offered, they will hold out for the latter.

Two general feeding styles prevail, meal feeding and free-choice feeding. *Meal feeding* involves the preparation and administration of small amounts of food, usually three times daily, for puppies less than 6 months of age, and ideally twice a day thereafter. Puppies should be placed in a quiet area (a crate is ideal) for 10 minutes of uninterrupted eating time. If the food has not been completely eaten during the allotted time, the remains should be removed and no further food offered until the next designated mealtime. Such a method of feeding promotes prompt eating habits.

Free-choice feeding involves leaving a calculated amount of dry dog food available throughout the day and on which the puppy can nibble intermittently. Although exceedingly convenient for owners, this style of feeding does not permit close scrutiny of the puppy's appetite, encourages prolonged feeding, and can contribute to overeating. Free-choice feeding also may not work well in a multiple-dog household or when traveling.

Puppies are frequently placed on growth formulations of dog food that provide increased energy and mineral levels. No further supplementation with vitamins and minerals is required or advised. Overnutrition and oversupplementation can contribute adversely to the development of orthopedic problems in growing dogs (*See* CHAPTER 26, "THE SKELETON AND DISORDERS"). The addition of any dietary supplements should be discussed with a veterinarian or, if necessary, a veterinary nutritionist. Myths abound concerning feed additives and supplements and their supposed value. The volume of food should be adjusted according to the pup's weight and activity. Dog-food labels frequently overestimate daily requirements. Puppies should be lean rather than chubby, with the ribs easily felt but with fat padding over the spine. Difficulty in maintaining a healthy body weight can necessitate switching from a growth formula to an adult formula of dog food at an earlier age. (*See* CHAPTER 8, "CANINE NUTRITIONAL REQUIREMENTS," and CHAPTER 9, "FEEDING DOGS.")

The correct type of housing for a dog depends on the breed and climate. All dogs require space to exercise and eliminate and a warm, dry, draft-free bed. Warm weather necessitates shaded, well-ventilated areas. Fresh water should always be available. Young puppies should not have access to an entire yard unsupervised, but should be confined to a puppy-proofed area when alone. Dogs are social animals; leaving a puppy alone for long stretches of time (over 4 hours) encourages destructive behavior born of boredom. (*see* CHAPTER 7, "MISBEHAVIOR.") Petsitters, neighbors and friends can provide important midday entertainment for a puppy during the work week.

Adequate and proper exercise is as important to dogs as it is to people. Puppies should not, however, be expected to exercise rigorously until they are fully grown. Exercise on turf, rather than on paved surfaces, is preferred. A short to moderate leash walk or a romp in the park are ideal. Road conditioning, such as accompanying a jogger or bicycle rider, is not advised for growing dogs owing to the potential for concussive damage to growing bones and joints.

Good grooming habits are also best established early in a puppy's life. Dogs need to be trained to cooperate during tooth brushing, ear cleaning, nail trimming and haircoat care. Dog owners also need to learn correct techniques to make grooming a pleasant experience. The initial problem with puppies is usually their inability to hold still for long periods of time. One should work in short time slots, rewarding the puppy for cooperating each time, and gradually increasing the demand. The veterinarian can assess the degree of cooperation encountered during normal physical examinations, determine if training is proceeding on schedule, and offer tips if necessary.

Special Events of the First Year

Several events during the puppy's first year warrant special attention. Although genetics dictate most aspects of a dog's disposition, experience plays a large role in personality development. Proper socialization cannot be overemphasized, particularly during the first 4 months of age. (*See* CHAPTER 6, "CANINE BEHAVIOR.") Puppies should be exposed to all situations that they will be expected to face with good graces as adults, such as children, people of all sizes, shapes and colors, other animals, veterinarians, noises, travel, confinement, physical contact and so on. Adequate socialization can be hampered by attempts to avoid exposure to infectious disease during the critical first 4 months of life, so owners may need to be creative.

Six-week-old puppies have a set of **deciduous** (baby) **teeth,** all of which will be replaced by permanent teeth through the process of *teething* (*see* CHAPTER 21, "CANINE DENTISTRY"). Chewing behavior is often attributed to teething. Adequate supervision and confinement, and materials for the relief of teething discomfort are important, to avoid the establishment of a destructive chewing habit. Puppies should not be allowed to chew on an owner's hands or clothing because such habits are hard to break once they become established.

The tendency to vocalize varies with the breed of dog and to some degree with the sex. Barking can develop into a vice, causing serious problems with neighbors. A puppy's first efforts at vocalization, especially when becoming protective of the home, may seem cute, but firm guidelines must be set to establish what is acceptable. "Mindless" barking should be discouraged. The best watchdogs will become quiet when commanded to.

Sexual maturity occurs in both male and female dogs between 6 months and 1 year of age. Ideally, neutering should be performed in bitches before the first heat cycle occurs, thereby diminishing the chances of later mammary cancer and unwanted pregnancies. Male dogs should be neutered around the same time. The longer a male dog remains intact (unneutered), the greater the tendency it will have to develop behaviors such as aggression, urine-marking and mounting, and wandering for bitches in season. The tendency to protect the home is not mediated by sex hormones; thus, neutering does not prevent a puppy from developing into a fine watchdog. (*See* CHAPTER 6, "CANINE BEHAVIOR.")

Although the trials and tribulations of raising a puppy may make the process seem overwhelming at times, the time invested is well-rewarded. Most dog owners can barely remember the time when their canine companions were still small enough to carry everywhere, and when their personalities were still developing. Enjoy your dog's first year. Make it a time of learning together to nurture one of life's most fulfilling relationships.

CHAPTER 5
Geriatrics

by Janet Aldrich

Geriatrics is the branch of medical science dealing with the diseases, disabilities, and care of aged patients. Geriatric dogs (or aged dogs) are those that have reached the age at which the diseases associated with aging are likely to begin. The exact age at which this occurs varies with individual dogs and with the various breeds. Small-breed dogs age more slowly and in general live longer than do the large and giant breeds. As an estimate one might say that small-breed dogs become aged at approximately 11 years, medium-sized dogs at 10 years, large-breed dogs at 9 years, and giant-breed dogs at 7 years.

The gradual deterioration of body processes associated with aging is expected by most owners, because they recognize that the same processes occur in their family and friends and in themselves. Some of the signs of aging include:

- decreased strength and flexibility
- decreased tolerance of cold and heat
- increased susceptibility to certain diseases
- gradual deterioration of organ functions

Despite widespread recognition of such signs, the specific mechanisms by which aging occurs remain incompletely understood. However, advances in the study of the life processes within cells continue to contribute to our knowledge of aging, increasing the likelihood that certain aspects of aging can be effectively managed.

Several theories exist on exactly why aging occurs. One theory holds that the genetic structure of every cell has a built-in "biological clock," which at a certain prescribed time "runs out" so that the substances necessary for cellular function and repair are no longer made. The result is cell degeneration and death. A second theory postulates that errors in cell replication (reproduction) that occur randomly throughout life become more frequent with advancing age, causing abnormal function and cell death. A third theory is that errors in cell replication are less frequent in long-lived species because such species simply have a better replication mechanism. Because fewer errors are made, fewer cells are produced that function abnormally.

Each of these theories probably accounts for part but not all of the aging process. Aging represents an extremely complex series of events and at our present level of knowledge cannot be simplified into one single, simple theory. No matter what the mechanism, however, we all recognize that aging is characterized by a gradual loss of organ function and an increased susceptibility to disease. Such knowledge is sufficient to convince us that aging dogs require greater protection from environmental stresses, greater attention to health problems, and earlier and more complete evaluation and treatment of abnormal body function.

The geriatric dog has special needs that usually develop slowly over time. These needs include a proper diet (especially weight control), a comfortable environment, adequate exercise appropriate for abilities, and regular health evaluation as well as prompt and thorough attention to any changes in the state of health.

Care

ROUTINE HEALTH EVALUATION

For the older dog the benefits of a complete physical examination every year include the early identification of problems such as obesity, dental disease, heart or lung dysfunction, and abdominal, skin or **subcutaneous** (beneath the skin) masses. If indicated, a general health screen with blood and urine analysis can aid in the early identification of treatable conditions. As an example, the management of kidney or heart disease is usually more successful when these problems are identified early. Masses may be benign or malignant. If malignant, early identification may allow removal and a possible cure.

DIET

One of the most common problems of geriatric dogs is obesity. Unfortunately, this problem is often underrated by owners who do not recognize the adverse health effects of the condition. Overfeeding and obesity result in decreased resistance to infectious diseases, possibly

because of adverse effects on the function of the immune system. Obese animals also do not live as long as do animals in lean body condition.

Stable weight is maintained by a balance between food intake and energy expenditure in metabolism and exercise. As dogs age the body's metabolic rate slows, and this together with orthopedic or other concomitant problems that reduce the amount of tolerable exercise can contribute to a slow, often unnoticed, weight gain. A gain of 10% of body weight is considered significant (note that this may be only a gain of 1 pound in a small dog normally weighing 10 pounds). If this weight gain continues each year from the 7th year on, the dog will weigh 14 pounds at 11 years of age, a weight gain to 40% above normal.

Weight control for dogs follows the same principles as for all other animals (and people). Food intake must be reduced, expenditure of energy must be increased, or both must occur in order for weight to be lost. The best prescription is a permanent change in eating and exercise habits rather than a "crash" diet. Because a dog's diet often is under the total control of the owner, the responsibility for reducing food intake rests with the owner and not the dog. Every morsel of food that drops into a dog's mouth must be counted as part of the dog's daily caloric intake.

Methods for decreasing food intake include:

- reducing the total amount of the dog's usual daily diet by 25%
- switching to a commercial diet specially formulated for overweight dogs
- substituting low-calorie snacks for the usual between-meal treats

It is important that the majority of the caloric intake each day comes from dog food and not from treats. In other words, the calories from treats should be reduced before the amount of the daily diet is decreased. This does not necessarily mean eliminating treats entirely. The feeding of treats or table scraps is often an important part of the social interaction between dog and owner. Substituting low-calorie snacks can preserve this social interaction while contributing to the goal of reduced caloric intake. The use of low-calorie dog foods can also be helpful if the amount fed is controlled.

Geriatric dogs may also have special dietary needs related to problems such as kidney or heart disease. High-fiber diets may be useful in the management of diabetes mellitus, while still other diets are designed for dogs with sensitivities to certain foods. Diets specially formulated for prescription by a veterinarian are available for these and other age-related problems. (*See* CHAPTER 9, "FEEDING DOGS.")

HOUSING

Geriatric dogs housed outdoors require increased protection from extremes of heat and cold. The damp, cold weather of certain climates can mean increased discomfort for dogs that do not have a warm, dry sleeping place. Likewise, excessive environmental heat can pose a serious problem to the geriatric dog that may not be able to regulate its body temperature as effectively as when it was young.

Geriatric dogs kept indoors usually have established favored sleeping places in the house. A soft, padded bed placed in one of these areas may be accepted by the geriatric dog experiencing joint pain and stiffness. Older dogs may have significant difficulty getting up and down the stairs for a variety of reasons ranging from orthopedic problems to neurologic disease. A change in the usual routine may need to be made if an aged dog cannot be assisted in negotiating the stairs.

EXERCISE

Older dogs should be encouraged to take reasonable amounts of regular exercise unless there is a specific reason not to do so. If there are any signs of difficulty in exercising, these should be brought to the attention of the veterinarian. Older dogs may have a slowly diminishing ability to exercise vigorously, but they should retain an active interest in their usual activities and exhibit a reasonable degree of tolerance for moderate exercise. A common mistake is to overemphasize the significance of aging and use it as an explanation for abrupt changes in behavior, such as a sudden disinterest in a dog's usual activities (which is much more likely to be a sign of disease than a sign of aging and should be carefully investigated).

Problems of Aging

BEHAVIOR CHANGES

Senility, as is seen occasionally in old people, may occur in dogs but it would be a mistake to attribute a behavior change to senility until other possible causes have been investigated. Such causes could include liver or kidney disease, in which toxins accumulate in the blood and alter brain function, or disease of the brain itself, which might be the result of inflammation, bleeding, a tumor, or a variety of other disorders. Behavior changes may also be due to disabilities such as impairment of hearing or vision, or chronic pain in the joints or back. Even healthy older dogs may exhibit certain behaviors that reflect their changing needs. They may prefer warmer sleeping places because their tolerance for cold has decreased, or softer resting places to relieve pressure on arthritic joints. Older dogs may not see or hear as well and thus may be less interactive with the family. They may experience pain with vigorous activity and therefore be less willing to play in the same way as they used to. Older dogs may also experience isolation from the family if they have health problems that make them less than acceptable companions. One common example is a problem with urination or defecation that causes an owner to isolate the dog in easily cleaned areas of the house, or to banish the longtime house dog to an outdoor existence. The dog is deprived of the companionship it has known all its life and may respond by attention-seeking or destructive behavior or, in some cases, by withdrawing from interaction with its human companions. (*See* Chapter 6, "Canine Behavior," and Chapter 7, "Misbehavior.")

Chronic Coughing

Chronic coughing in geriatric dogs can represent a worsening of a condition that has been present for many years but is becoming more noticeable. Conditions of this type include tracheal collapse, chronic bronchitis (inflammation of the **bronchi,** the larger air passages leading from the trachea and branching within the lungs), and heart failure.

Tracheal collapse is a syndrome often found in small- and toy-breed dogs. It is caused by a structural defect that renders the trachea softer than normal and easily collapsed by external pressures such as a collar, or by internal pressures such as a sudden intake of breath (as may occur when the dog becomes excited and is barking vigorously). With age the trachea becomes softer and even more collapsible. The condition is often made substantially worse by obesity. Management of tracheal collapse involves weight reduction if needed, switching from a collar to a harness to relieve pressure on the trachea, and avoiding behaviors that clearly induce coughing episodes.

Chronic bronchitis may be caused by exposure to irritating substances (especially cigarette/cigar smoke and other pollutants) or substances to which the dog is allergic (pollens, house dust). The lungs respond to such insults by increasing their production of secretions, which as a consequence partially obstruct airways and stimulate coughing. Chronic bronchitis is best controlled by removing the offending substance. Other treatments must be tailored to individual patient needs.

Heart failure can result in the accumulation of fluid in the lung (**pulmonary edema**) when the pumping action of the heart fails to provide adequate blood circulation. This is manifested by an increased respiratory rate, chronic cough-

ing and reduced tolerance to exercise. Effective management of the underlying cardiac disorder will usually lessen the severity of the cough, and sometimes eliminate it. (*See* Chapter 24, "The Circulatory System and Disorders"; Chapter 29, "The Respiratory System and Disorders"; and Chapter 33, "The Immune System and Disorders.")

Dental Disease

Excellent dental care for geriatric dogs is readily available from the veterinary profession. Because the cleaning of teeth requires general anesthesia, the geriatric patient with dental disease should be completely evaluated in terms of the major body systems (heart, lungs, kidney, liver, red and white blood cells) before anesthesia for dental work. The benefits of a healthy mouth almost always outweigh the risks of the anesthesia, since advances in anesthetic agents and anesthetic techniques have allowed veterinarians to anesthetize even aged dogs without excessive risk. (*See* Chapter 21, "Canine Dentistry.")

Impaired Hearing

Deafness, either partial or complete, is fairly common in old dogs. Chronic ear infections can cause deafness, but often deafness occurs with no previous history of ear infections. In such cases the deafness is thought to be caused by degeneration of the sound receptors in the ear. The hearing loss usually occurs gradually, and it may be difficult at first for an owner to determine whether the dog actually cannot hear or simply doesn't wish to respond.

An affected dog should be examined by a veterinarian to rule out the possibility of an ear infection or generalized neurologic disease. If the dog is otherwise healthy, the hearing loss can be managed simply by adjusting home management around the disability. One should always keep in mind that deaf or partially deaf dogs may be easily startled, and depending on an individual dog's temperament, it may be inclined to respond aggressively to surprises.

Ocular (Eye) Problems

Older dogs may develop age-related **cataracts,** in which the lens of eye becomes opaque and interferes with vision. As the cataract forms it causes lens protein to leak into the eye, initiating an immune reaction and subsequent inflammation. Surgery to remove cataracts is available from veterinary ophthalmologists, who will make a thorough evaluation of each individual case before providing a recommendation for therapy. Many dogs adapt well to gradual vision loss and are not particularly bothered by it, provided the environment is kept stable so that they can learn to avoid obstacles.

Older dogs also develop age-related changes in the structure of the lens known as **nuclear sclerosis.** This condition occurs in all aged dogs and causes a cloudiness of the lens, but does not significantly interfere with vision or produce an inflammation.

Glaucoma in older dogs is often due to displacement (**luxation**) of lens of the eye such that the outflow of fluid from the eye is obstructed. Glaucoma may also occur because of blockage of the outflow tract in the absence of a displaced lens. Fluid buildup within the eyeball results in a pressure increase that causes pain and eventually destroys the **retina** (the light-sensitive layer of cells at the back of the eye), causing blindness.

Tumors involving the eyelid occur in older dogs and may be malignant or benign. Either type of mass may contact the eyeball and cause irritation and possibly ulceration. Malignant masses are likely to spread to involve the eye itself or the tissues around the eye. Masses that are surgically removed should always be examined microscopically by a veterinary pathologist to determine if a malignancy is involved.

Paralysis of the nerves that close the eyelids can produce an inability to blink and therefore to distribute the film of tears over the eyeball. This type of partial paralysis is seen in the older dog and does not necessarily mean that other neurologic problems are present.

Decreased tear production can cause drying of the eye and the tissue around the eye, a condition known as **keratoconjunctivitis sicca (KCS),** or "dry eye." If left untreated drying of the eye can cause permanent damage. Fortunately, current treatments for KCS are much more effective than those used in the past and may resolve the problem. (*See* Chapter 19, "The Eye and Disorders.")

Heart Disease

The heart is a pump that is divided into four chambers. Inflow and outflow of blood are controlled by valves that open and close in order to direct blood through the heart. The blood receives oxygen as it passes through the **pulmonary** (pertaining to the lungs) vessels, and then is pumped out as the heart muscle contracts. The movements of the valves and the flowing blood create the normal heart sounds.

Heart valves may become so worn that they fail to close completely with each beat of the heart. This allows some blood to flow backward through the partially closed valves, creating an abnormal heart sound called a **heart murmur.** Many older dogs, particularly of small breeds, commonly develop heart murmurs as the result of worn heart valves. Heart murmurs do not necessarily mean heart failure; the reserve capacity of the heart is substantial, and even moderately leaky valves can be compensated for by increased pumping action. Thus the identification of a heart murmur in a dog does not mean that immediate treatment is required. What it does mean is that regular monitoring of the condition by a veterinarian should be instituted so that signs of heart failure can be detected if and when they do occur. (*See* Chapter 24, "The Circulatory System and Disorders.")

Lameness or Weakness

Lameness or weakness in the geriatric dog should not immediately be assumed to be due to **arthritis** (joint inflammation) because there are many causes of these two problems, certain of which are potentially reversible with proper diagnosis and treatment. Other causes include neurologic disease of the spinal cord or peripheral nerves or muscles, infection of vertebrae or joints, bone tumors, and a variety of metabolic diseases in which the necessary substances for muscle movement are lacking.

Many older dogs do, in fact, have arthritis and require special management. The diagnosis usually requires X-ray studies of the affected joint(s). Once a diagnosis of arthritis has been established, the veterinarian may prescribe anti-inflammatory and/or pain-relieving medication.

The pain reliever or arthritis that an owner may be taking for his/her own arthritis should never be substituted for that prescribed for the dog. One of the most common errors is to assume that the dog will have the same response to a medication as a person will. One must, in fact, exercise special caution when administering pain relievers and anti-inflammatory drugs to dogs. Severe adverse reactions can occur, including life-threatening bleeding into the stomach and kidney failure.

Pressure on the spinal cord can produce weakness and eventually paralysis. In many older dogs of the small breeds this condition is commonly caused by disc disease, wherein one or more **intervertebral disks** (cushioning structures positioned between the vertebrae of the spinal column) gradually lose their structure and eventually protrude into the spinal canal, putting pressure on the spinal cord. Most commonly the hind limbs are affected. Older dogs of the large breeds may suffer from pressure on the spinal cord in the neck caused by malformation of the ligaments surrounding the cord, malformation of **cervical** (neck) vertebrae, or protrusion of an intervertebral disk.

LOSS OF BALANCE

Another disease of older dogs is **idiopathic vestibular disease,** also known as **vestibular syndrome,** which is characterized by a sudden loss of balance, a head-tilt, abnormal eye movements in which the eyes continually move from side to side in an abrupt jerky fashion (**nystagmus**), and an inability to walk normally (sometimes an inability to walk at all). These signs are caused by malfunctioning of the **vestibular** (balance) mechanism, which involves parts of the inner ear and brain. Idiopathic vestibular disease does not have a known cause but does have a good prognosis, since most dogs recover spontaneously in a few weeks. Unfortunately, other more serious diseases such as tumors and infections can cause similar signs. For this reason, loss of balance should be carefully evaluated by a veterinarian in order to arrive at a correct diagnosis.

URINARY HABITS

Older female dogs often develop urinary **incontinence** (loss of voluntary control over urination). Characteristically a small puddle of urine will be found in the sleeping area, or urine will be seen to drip from the vulva with the dog apparently unaware of it. Involuntary urination should be evaluated by the veterinarian, particularly to determine whether a urinary tract infection is present. In many cases urinary incontinence may be easily treated with oral medication given once or twice daily. (*See* CHAPTER 27, "THE URINARY SYSTEM AND DISORDERS.")

INCREASED WATER CONSUMPTION AND URINE PRODUCTION

Older dogs of either sex may exhibit increased water consumption owing to a variety of causes, including diabetes mellitus, kidney disease, uterine infection, or other hormonal or metabolic diseases. Often, owners are unaware of this condition until the dog begins making increased demands to be let outside to urinate, or is found urinating in the house. A change in urinary habits should be carefully evaluated by a veterinarian. (*See* CHAPTER 14, "REPRODUCTIVE DISORDERS"; CHAPTER 27, "THE URINARY SYSTEM AND DISORDERS"; and CHAPTER 32, "THE ENDOCRINE SYSTEM AND METABOLIC DISORDERS.")

KIDNEY DISEASE

At any age the kidneys may be injured by infection, toxins, drugs trauma, shock or immunologic attack. The geriatric dog may also be subject to the effects of a gradual deterioration of kidney function known as chronic kidney disease. Management of kidney disease begins with knowledge that the disease is present and identification and elimination (if possible) of any underlying cause(s). The benefits of a controlled protein diet in the management of chronic kidney disease have been well established. Additional management may involve the use of drugs to control some of the abnormalities commonly found in kidney disease, such as anemia, acid-base imbalance, high serum phosphorus levels, and others. Although chronic kidney disease is often incurable, vigorous management can improve both the quality and length of life. (*See* CHAPTER 27, "THE URINARY SYSTEM AND DISORDERS.")

Prostate Disease

Gradual enlargement of the **prostate gland** (gland in male mammals that surrounds the neck of the bladder and is important in the production of **semen**) occurs in uncastrated male dogs. The prostate also becomes more susceptible to infection and structural abnormalities with advancing age. A bloody discharge from the tip of the penis, often following urination or mixed with voided urine, can be a sign of prostate disease. The prostate can become so enlarged that the dog may have difficulty passing stool, and the stool may be smaller in diameter than normal. An infected prostate gland may be painful and can cause a fever and, occasionally, a generalized infection of the body. Treatment of prostate infections with appropriate antibiotics is often successful. Depending on the individual case, neutering following elimination of the infection may be recommended. (*See* Chapter 14, "Reproductive Disorders" and Chapter 27, "The Urinary System and Disorders.")

Cancer

Cancer is a frightening diagnosis, and the fear of having such a diagnosis made can cause owners of older dogs to delay seeking care for their pets longer than they might have when the dogs were younger. While cancer can occur at any age it is more common in older dogs. However, every lump, bump or abnormality in an older dog is not necessarily cancer. Only a proper evaluation by a veterinarian can make the diagnosis. If the diagnosis is cancer it is important to know that great strides have been made in the treatment of veterinary cancer patients and that helpful treatment may be available to prolong life and preserve its quality. Even if the final decision is not to pursue therapy for the cancer, it is still useful to have made the diagnosis so that subsequent decisions about quality and length of life will be made based on knowledge of the likely course of the cancer and what clinical signs it is likely to cause. (*See* Chapter 38, "Cancer.")

Anesthesia

The prospect of anesthesia for the geriatric dog may be uncomfortable for owners, who believe that their dog's life will be placed at substantial risk by such a procedure. This fear can be beneficial if it leads an owner to seek a thorough preanesthetic evaluation and postanesthetic monitoring for the geriatric dog. The fear can be harmful, however, if the owner is led instead to refuse needed procedures just because the dog is old and not because of any specific contraindication to the anesthesia itself. A common example is the geriatric dog in need of dental work—a dog that would benefit greatly from improved oral health but does not receive the needed care simply because it is "too old." As the animal continues to grow older, the dental disease worsens and the adverse effects on overall health increase.

The concept of risk versus benefit is of primary importance in deciding on anesthesia for the older dog. The need for the contemplated procedure should be clearly established and the risks to the patient thoroughly identified. Only then can an informed decision be made. Risk factors for anesthesia include the status of the heart, lungs, blood, liver and kidneys, as these are the organs most affected by and having the most effect on anesthesia. While these organs may have been assumed to be functioning properly in the younger dog, it is not safe to make the same assumption in an older patient. Older dogs may have less reserve capacity in their organ systems, and this can make them more sensitive to the effects of preanesthetic and anesthetic drugs. Therefore a more extensive preanesthetic workup usually is in order for geriatric patients. In addition to a thorough physical examination, this workup usually includes analyses of blood and urine, which may reveal diseases of which the owner was unaware. The geriatric dog may have compensated for a gradual decrease in kidney function by increased water consumption, which the owner either does not recognize or does not perceive as a problem. The decrease in exercise tolerance associated with some forms of heart or lung disease may not be noticed at all if the dog and owner do not exercise regularly together.

Less-than-optimal functioning of any of these body systems does not necessarily mean that anesthesia cannot be performed, however. Great advances have been made in veterinary anesthesiology in recent years that have improved the ability to anesthetize safely animals having significant health problems. Identification of these problems prior to anesthesia allows for sufficient preparation and increases the likelihood that complications can be effectively managed. The geriatric patient requires closer monitoring and greater support during anesthesia and in the postanesthetic recovery period. Certain high-risk patients may appropriately be referred to veterinary hospitals in which special expertise and equipment are available. Anesthesia always carries some risk; the goal of thorough preanesthetic evaluation is to keep that risk as low as possible.

SURGERY

For patients of any age the benefits of surgery must be balanced against the risks. For the geriatric patient additional risk considerations include an expectation of decreased organ reserve capacity, which especially affects anesthetic risk and decreases speed of healing, which in turn affect recovery time and completeness of healing. Although age alone is not a contraindication to surgery it does mean that certain precautions are warranted. Many geriatric dogs benefit greatly from appropriate surgery. For example, an infected uterus (**pyometra**) in the geriatric bitch is a life-threatening condition that can be treated by prompt surgical removal of the uterus and ovaries. Intensive care is required in both the pre- and postsurgical periods as well as during surgery. The results of surgery are usually good, with the geriatric patient recovering fully from what would almost certainly have been a fatal illness.

Presurgical evaluation includes a complete review of the medical history of the patient and any current medications, as well as blood and urine analyses similar to those discussed above for preanesthetic evaluation. Chronic medical problems that may have been tolerated but not treated might require a more thorough evaluation before proceeding. For example, hair loss, increased water consumption and mildly decreased exercise tolerance may have all been thought unimportant or simply signs of aging. A thorough medical evaluation might reveal that these are instead signs of a hormonal dysfunction—in this case, **Cushing's syndrome**—that is treatable, and that if untreated can have an adverse effect on the healing of surgical wounds.

Many drugs that have been given with no apparent ill effect can pose a problem when surgery is anticipated. For example, aspirin, which is commonly given to geriatric dogs to treat arthritis, also reduces blood clotting, while corticosteroids given for flea allergy control can delay surgical wound healing.

(*See* CHAPTER 40, "SURGERY AND POSTOPERATIVE CARE.")

EUTHANASIA

Attitudes concerning euthanasia arise from a combination of an individual's life experiences and belief system. These attitudes are usually complex and often deeply held, and are certainly a private matter. If euthanasia is an option the decision is frequently based on the owner's evaluation of the quality of the dog's life. Evaluation of quality of life usually is based on beliefs about whether or not pain is present, and on observations of appetite, activity level and participation in usual activities. Although the decision is entirely the owner's responsibility, it may be helpful to discuss euthanasia with the veterinarian who is familiar with the dog and its medical problems. The veterinarian may be able to contribute a perspective on the likelihood of pain, the likely course of the disease, which signs may be alleviated by treatment, and what form significant clinical deterioration of the patient is most likely to take. It is well to discuss with the veterinarian all aspects of euthanasia, including what will happen before, during and after the procedure. Nothing can change the fact that the decision is a painful one, but planning and open discussion with all the people involved can make this difficult time easier to bear.

CHAPTER 6

Canine Behavior

by Benjamin L. Hart

To understand the behavior of any domestic species, it is important to know something about the ancestry of that species. This is particularly true for dogs. With dogs we also have a special advantage in that we can look at their existing wild relatives, whose progenitors formed the common ancestral stock, and so can examine the natural context of canine behavioral patterns.

The Ancestry of Dogs

The wolf, in particular the smallish Indian wolf (Canis lupus pallipes), was the most likely ancestor of the domestic dog. However, other **canids** (members of the family to which dogs belong), including coyotes, jackals and dingoes, will interbreed with dogs, so it is likely that the dog of today possesses genetic input from several ancestral lines. Most canine behaviorists use the wolf as the behavioral reference point for understanding the behavioral patterns of dogs.

The dog was the first animal species domesticated by early human beings. In North America, Europe and Asia, archaeological finds have revealed an association between wild canids and people beginning as long as 10,000 to 12,000 years ago. The most suggestive evidence for domestication of the dog lies in an excavated site in northern Israel that dates back approximately 12,000 years. In this excavation the skeleton of a puppy was found in close association with a human skeleton, the hand of the human lying across the chest of the puppy, clearly implying an affectionate (rather than a gastronomic) relationship.

It may be that there was no purposeful intent on the part of early human beings to domesticate wild canids. Rather, the scavenging habits of the wild progenitors of the dog may have

been responsible for maintained contact with human settlements. With breeding groups of wolves close by, and given the habits of people in caring for young animals, wolf pups may have been kept as pets. From there it would have been only a short step to establishing a more enduring relationship, perhaps as hunting companions, in which there would have been obvious advantages for both partners. The ancestors of dogs were territorial, making them good watch animals and excellent guards over a human family's territory. They were also highly social, which meant that wolves raised by people could have taken a subordinate role and allowed their human companions to dominate and control them, just as wolves may be subservient to other wolves in a pack.

The dog is the domestic species that has been the most profoundly altered through selective breeding over centuries of living with human beings. Differences in size and shape among the various breeds are so striking that if we did not know better, we would be tempted to consider some breeds as belonging to separate species. Over the centuries dogs have been bred for various anatomical or behavioral traits that suited certain utilitarian functions or simply a breeder's fancy. Some breeds were developed with behavioral tendencies particularly useful for hunting, with different breeds specializing in different methods of gathering prey, such as pointing to game birds, barking and chasing foxes, or retrieving waterfowl. Other breeds were developed for the quick learning of complex tasks, such as herding cattle or sheep while following the hand signals of the herdsman. Protection of an owner's property by barking or attacking was another desirable trait. In general, behavioral functions characterizing the individual breeds represent an enhancement or suppression of natural canine behavioral characteristics, rather than the emergence of new behavioral patterns from the ancestral stock.

Dog Breeds

In current societies the utilitarian aspects of dogs are becoming less relevant, but the behavioral characteristics related to breed identification are still of great importance to pet owners. As past selective breeding concentrated on enhancing behavioral characteristics for utilitarian purposes, intentional or unintentional alteration of other behavioral patterns that play a role in a dog's integration into the human family occurred. Thus dogs that were bred for barking and chasing foxes, such as the Beagle, are more predisposed to vocalize around the house (with not a fox in sight) than are other breeds. Dogs that were bred primarily for aggressive territorial protection seem to have become aggressive in a more general sense, some even acquiring a tendency to challenge an owner for dominance, particularly if the owner is not an assertive "pack leader."

How have behavioral scientists learned about the behavioral characteristics of different breeds? In one study researchers conducted extensive laboratory tests on several breeds of dogs (Basenjis, Beagles, Cocker Spaniels, Shetland Sheepdogs, Fox Terriers), using specific measures of emotional reactivity, trainability and problem-solving ability. They found clear differences among the breeds. For example, Fox Terriers, Beagles and Basenjis were judged significantly more reactive than Shetland Sheepdogs or Cocker Spaniels. Cocker Spaniels were the easiest to train, while Basenjis and Beagles were consistently the most difficult. Although some breeds excelled at particular problem-solving tasks, no breed consistently outscored the others on all problem-solving tasks. Based on this work and on other information we have, it is probably fair to say that there is no evidence for one breed's being more "intelligent" than any other.

Authorities on dogs are frequently asked, "What is the best breed of dog?" This question is actually not possible to answer because there is no "best" breed. Different breeds are better suited for different environments and lifestyles. For example, a breed of dog that would be ideal for a young man living alone and who is away at work every day might be different from one suited for a family with children, who would frequently play with the dog in a large backyard all day. The best breed for a single person in a crime-ridden neighborhood may not be the best breed for someone who lives where there is less crime and who is concerned about excessive barking. A person who is not very assertive will surely be disappointed with a breed characterized by a tendency to challenge the owner for dominance, whereas an assertive person with a fund of experience in raising dogs would not find such a breed unattractive.

Unfortunately, people often choose a dog because of its size, coat, or distinctive coloration, or because it is cute as a puppy. The primary reason for choosing a particular dog should be its behavior. Tendencies to challenge an owner for dominance, engage in excessive barking, seek affection, or be easily trained are certainly more important than a dog's color, size or shape. When choosing a dog a prospective owner should evaluate his or her own personality traits and lifestyle and a select a breed (and gender) that is most appropriate. This can be accomplished by consulting a number of sources, including books (for example, Benjamin L. Hart & Lynette A. Hart, *The Perfect Puppy: How to Choose Your Dog by Its Behavior,* W.H. Freeman & Co.), breeders, members of local dog clubs and obedience trainers, for insights into the behavior of the various breeds. While one can expect breeders to be partial to their own breeds, they are generally in the business for their love and enjoyment of dogs rather than for any monetary considerations, and their comments and advice will usually be honest and candid. There is also a great deal of variability among individual dogs within any particular breed, which must be taken into account as well when comparing the different breeds.

What about adopting mongrels, which are commonly available from local animal shelters? Mongrels are, by definition, the product of an intermingling of at least two purebreds, rarely intentionally; thus no generalizations can be applied equally to all mongrels. People often claim that mongrels are calmer and not as highly strung as purebreds, are better with children, less fragile, and so forth. However, if calmness is what the prospective owner is seeking, a purebred breed characterized by low excitability is usually a safer bet than a mongrel of unknown genetic background. The advantage of selecting a purebred puppy over a mixed breed is the ability to predict the characteristics of the dog as an adult. It is known, for example, that an Irish Setter puppy will differ from a Golden Retriever pup in certain predictable attributes of behavior, as well as in coat color, length and body build.

Having said this, however, millions of mongrels do become ideal family dogs. Delightful mixed-breed puppies are always available from neighborhood breeders and animal shelters, usually for no more than the cost of vaccinations (and in some places, the cost of spaying or neutering). When a mongrel is an obvious cross between two recognizable breeds, as is often the case, one can generally learn something about the dog's probable adult behavior by consulting the behavioral profiles of the component breeds. Certainly with mongrels it is important to inquire about the background of the puppy and the behavior of its sire and dam.

Behavioral Effects of Spaying and Neutering

Today dog owners are strongly encouraged (if not required) to have their male dogs neutered (castrated) and their female dogs spayed.

Questions naturally arise as to the influences these two procedures have on dogs' subsequent behavior.

In male dogs the following changes can be expected after neutering, whether the procedure is performed before or after the dog reaches puberty:

- less aggression toward other male dogs
- less inclination to seek dominance over the owner
- less urine-marking in the house
- less predisposition to mount other dogs or people
- less tendency to roam for extended periods of time

Evidence suggests the likelihood that neutering will alter these behavior patterns is approximately 50%; that is, a neutered male is about half as likely to engage in these objectionable behaviors as is an "intact" male. Whether male dogs are neutered before or after they reach puberty does not alter the influence of the neutering on these behaviors. It is apparent from clinical studies that neither the prior history of a dog's engaging in objectionable behavior, nor the dog's age when it is neutered, influences the probability of a behavior's being altered. Neutering is not expected to make a dog calmer, less destructive, less active, or better with children. There is also no evidence that neutering makes a dog fat or lazy. While neutering does result in eventual replacement of some muscle tissue by fat, neutered males exhibit no marked predisposition toward weight gain.

What are the changes one might expect in female dogs from the spay operation known as an **ovariohysterectomy,** in which both the uterus and ovaries are removed? Most owners usually have their female dogs spayed to prevent their coming into breeding condition. During **estrus** ("heat") female dogs usually vocalize more frequently, often act in a nervous manner and move about more. The urine and genital tract secretions of females approaching estrus or in estrus contain chemical attractants **(pheromones)** that are noticed by male dogs living in the vicinity. Although there are stories about male dogs being attracted to females in heat from miles away, the pheromones are probably not that potent, but instead are picked up by male dogs as they trek through a female's territory.

After a female dog has been spayed, whether before or after it has experienced a heat period, it almost never displays typical female sexual behavior again. There is no basis to the common notion that female dogs may develop differently if they are spayed prior to their first heat or before having a litter of puppies. Do spayed female dogs gain weight? Interestingly, there is some evidence to indicate that spayed bitches may experience a 5 to 10% gain in body weight as a result of the loss of hormonal secretions from the ovaries, even if food intake and exercise level are kept constant. This difference is not profound, however, and one can usually assume that the weight gain is mostly a function of the amount of food ingested rather than the amount of exercise received.

Social and Territorial Behavior

By nature dogs are highly social, a reflection of the fact that their wild ancestor, the wolf, lived in closely knit packs with a social structure built around a dominance hierarchy. From a dog's standpoint people become part of the pack structure; thus dogs interact with us utilizing the same behavioral patterns they would for canine members of their pack. Dogs love social interaction, and, as most people who have trained a dog know, they will learn skills and perform "parlor tricks" simply for the praise and affection received in return (a principle that only rarely applies to their feline counterparts).

One reason dogs were domesticated is that they protected their adopted homes as vigorously as they would a pack den. An assertive watchdog or guard dog can be a real asset in a crime-ridden neighborhood. However, in other environments such territoriality may become exuberant and present a serious problem to owners when friends come to call. (*See* Chapter 7, "Misbehavior.")

Reflecting their social nature, dogs will accept a subordinate role to people who assume an air of dominance or assertiveness towards them. The degree to which a dog accepts this role depends upon breed, gender, and individual differences. Females in general are more ready to accept dominance by human members of the pack than are males. Acting in a way that encourages a dog to take a subordinate role does not in the least diminish their affection for us; indeed, subordinate members of a pack appear to enjoy being around the dominant members.

Feeding Behavior

Dogs exhibit the behavioral characteristics of their ancestral pack hunters, which were able to bring down large prey sufficient to provide food for several days. Thus, we often refer to the dog's ancestral feeding behavior as "feast or famine." On occasion, dogs have been observed

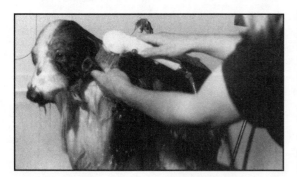

to consume the equivalent of one-tenth or even one-fifth of their body weight at one time. When social **carnivores** (meat-eaters) kill prey there is an inevitable competition for food; those animals that eat the most rapidly will receive the most food and succeed better over the long run. Thus, by nature dogs are not leisurely eaters. They have the capacity to overeat if their food is particularly palatable because they are able to consume a quantity of food sufficient to last for several days, even if they are fed every day. In other words, dogs cannot be trusted to reduce their dietary intake to that required simply to maintain optimal body weight.

An interesting aspect of canine feeding behavior is the tendency to bury food or bones, sometimes to the chagrin of the pet owner when the burying occurs in the vegetable garden. Even when caged, some dogs may attempt to cover a bone by using the papers strewn about the cage floor. The purpose of this behavior is food storage, or caching. It is another inheritance from dogs' wild ancestors, for many wild canids, including wolves and some species of fox, will bury small prey items for retrieval and eventual consumption during the lean months of the year.

Food Aversions

Dogs, like other animals, may develop an aversion to a food that has made them ill and created a digestive upset. This behavior has been well studied in the laboratory. It is known that the **postprandial** (occurring after a meal) sickness is connected to the taste or smell of the offending item. The function of such conditioned food aversions is to protect animals against future ingestion of a food that produces gastrointestinal illness.

Anorexia and Obesity

There are several conditions that can cause a dog to lose its appetite, a condition known as **anorexia.** Anorexia, for example, is a normal response to many illnesses and may be a clue that a dog is coming down with an infectious disease. Anorexia almost always accompanies a fever. Sometimes loss of appetite occurs when a dog loses its ability to smell, as may happen during an infection of the upper respiratory tract. Dogs may stop eating for emotional reasons as well, such as the death of a family member to which a dog was particularly attached. In such cases the dog usually will adapt to the new situation and regain its appetite, so long as people have not given it too much attention while it refused to eat, thus unintentionally "rewarding" it for the anorexia.

Obesity in dogs is a more frequent occurrence than anorexia. One common cause is that dogs often eat much more than their daily energy expenditure requires. As previously mentioned, the chief reason for such behavior is that dogs, like wolves, have a tendency to consume larger amounts of food at one time than they actually need. This inherited characteristic, related to the irregularity of prey availability in the wild, can lead to repeated overeating and subsequent obesity when appetizing food is provided on a daily basis.

Many people believe that an ideal diet for carnivores consists solely of meat. In reality, however, dogs "cannot live by meat alone." The diet of wild canids consists not only of the carcass of prey items, but also occasional vegetable matter. The skin, bones and intestinal tract contents of the prey also constitute a substantial portion of the diet. Thus, when one contemplates providing a dog with the same diet that its natural ancestors would have consumed, it will be necessary to include a variety of food constituents. Fortunately, almost all major commercial dog foods (which are a mixture of animal and plant products) contain the nutrients appropriate in both quality and quantity for dogs' daily maintenance. (*See* CHAPTER 8, "CANINE NUTRITIONAL REQUIREMENTS" and CHAPTER 9, "FEEDING DOGS.")

Eliminative Behavior

This is an area where much misunderstanding exists. When a dog is housebroken it is not being taught eliminative habits; rather, the owner is simply relying on the dog's natural eliminative instincts to keep its nest or den clean. Most dogs are naturally fastidious about keeping their home area clean, a reflection of the sanitary behavior of their wild ancestors. In wild canids the feces often contain the eggs of intestinal parasites, which hatch into infective immature forms called **larvae** and would be readily consumed by both pups and adults if the feces were deposited in and around the den (*See* CHAPTER 37, "INTERNAL PARASITES"). By eliminating in an area distant from the den, feces are deposited where the parasites are much less likely to be acquired by den members.

The ease with which dogs can be toilet-trained makes them favorite pets. A great many dogs are probably housebroken regardless of owners' attempts to assist in the process. When "accidents" occur we assume (often wrongly) that the dog knows it has been bad, and then sometimes proceed with punishment. But there is no way to explain to a dog that the reason it is being punished now is because it soiled the bedroom two hours ago. Certainly, rubbing the dog's nose in the soiled area or pointing out the mess several hours after the fact can only hinder, rather than help, the housebreaking process.

When housebreaking a dog one must realize that it is difficult for a puppy to perceive of the entire house as a den. Thus, if permitted immediately to range over the entire home, a puppy is likely to consider the living room and dining room as legitimate toilet areas. For this reason it is usually recommended that toilet training begin by restricting the puppy to one small room, or even part of a room, thereby making it easier for the pup to identify its present living space with the den of its ancestors. The pup should be taken outdoors frequently when the tendency to eliminate is high, especially after consuming a meal or waking from a nap. If the training procedures are followed faithfully, the puppy may not eliminate at all in the small training area, but will tend instead to hold its urine and feces until it has the opportunity to eliminate outside. Once the pup has proven that it can keep its small living space reliably clean, it is gradually allowed greater access to the house, always under the watchful eye of the owner.

If the pup cannot be taken outside frequently,

it is advisable to place it within an enclosure strewn with newspapers opposite the sleeping and feeding area. After it is routinely eliminating on newspapers the pup then can be allowed additional space within the house. By taking a series of small steps at roughly 2-week intervals, the pup may eventually be given access to all parts of the house.

Reproductive Behavior

It is important to understand the normal patterns of reproductive behavior in dogs, so that when they are bred and a litter of puppies is delivered one can differentiate the normal from the abnormal, and know when it is advisable to intervene.

Elements of reproductive behavior are seen even in puppies. Male pups often exhibit sexual mounting as a part of normal play behavior. In fact, this behavior appears necessary for the development of normal adult sexual responses. If raised in isolation from other dogs, puppies will not experience sexual play and, as a consequence, may have difficulty executing normal sexual behavior as adults.

Mating behavior generally begins with genital investigation of the female by the male, some attempts at play, and a few mounting attempts. When penetration (**intromission**) occurs it is usually by a type of trial-and-error pelvic thrusting. The male may mount and thrust several times before achieving intromission. With receptive responses the female aids intromission by a sideways curvature of the rear quarters, deviation of the tail, and vertical movement of the external genitalia. When the male first achieves intromission, the front legs are pulled backwards, the tail is deflected downwards, and alternate stepping of the hind limbs is initiated along with oscillation of the pelvis. The stepping of the hind limbs is sometimes so high that the male is thrown off balance. This intense reaction usually lasts for 15 to 30 seconds, and it is at this time that the sperm-dense fraction of the **semen** (the thick, milky-white secretion or ejaculate) is expelled from the penis. The penis swells enormously (engorges) within the female's genital tract, essentially locking the male and female together in what is commonly known as a "tie." During this time the female usually stands rigidly, but towards the end may start twisting and turning and may even throw off the male before he can dismount. The male usually turns and lifts one leg over the penis after dismounting, so that during the genital tie the animals end up in a tail-to-tail orientation. The tie usually lasts for 10 to 30 minutes, although it may range from 5 to as long as 60 minutes. There has been some speculation as to why the genital tie evolved in canids. Probably the best explanation is that the penis becomes so completely engorged that the sperm are propelled directly into the uterus of the female, thus promoting very rapid fertilization of the eggs. A tie of 30 minutes may be long enough to assure that a male's sperm are well on their way up the female genital tract, so that any other male that happens to breed with the female afterward will be much less likely to fertilize the eggs and produce offspring.

One additional aspect of the reproductive behavior of female dog requires some explanation. The ovaries of females reaching puberty secrete the sex hormone **estrogen** twice a year. Estrogen has a number of important influences, one of which is to increase overall activity. Thus, a female usually moves about more, vocalizes more frequently, and may seem "nervous" during estrus. Estrogen is also responsible for the secretion of pheromones for attracting males. Female dogs in heat may evoke mounting behavior from both male and female dogs. Also, when placed with a male dog, a female in heat may mount the male, especially if the male's sexual advances are relatively slow. Pet owners with two female dogs may observe one female mount the other female when in estrus. This behavior is relatively normal.

(*See* Chapter 11, "Normal Reproduction"; Chapter 12, "Mating"; and Chapter 13, "Pregnancy and Parturition.")

Maternal Behavior

Proper maternal behavior is so important to the survival of offspring that evolutionary forces have programmed it rather precisely. Thus, a bitch that has given birth but has had no previous opportunity to observe or engage in the care of newborns nevertheless is capable of performing a relatively complex sequence of maternal tasks, with almost perfect timing and precision, until the offspring are weaned. The emotional attachment between the mother and her young represents one of the strongest interindividual bonds in nature, and is so powerful that a canine mother is even willing to risk her life for her newborn pups that she hardly even knows.

Pregnant females often become overtly restless and nervous a few days prior to **parturition** (giving birth). They may follow their owners around and alternate often between standing and lying down. At the time of birth the pups are delivered while the female is recumbent (although she may frequently move and change position during the birthing process). As the pups move through the birth canal the mother may break the fetal membranes with her teeth. This tugging on the membranes may actually help pull the newborn through the birth canal. After the birth of a puppy, the female usually consumes the fetal membranes and licks the newborn vigorously, which initiates the pup's breathing efforts. The mother also will bite off the umbilical cord while eating the fetal membranes. Pulling and stretching of the umbilical cord seems to cause constriction of the umbilical blood vessels and thus results in very little bleeding. The mother will lick and groom the hindquarters of the pups, stimulating urination and expulsion of the first bowel movement, which is referred to as **meconium.** Between deliveries the mother continues to lick and groom the newborn pups as well as her own genital region, and will also clean the bedding. Usually, the total duration of the birthing process does not exceed 12 hours. (*See* CHAPTER 13, "PREGNANCY AND PARTURITION.")

Nursing is a focus of interaction between a mother and her puppies that begins as soon as the young begin to suckle. Finding a teat to suck is not as random a process as it might seem. The pup moves toward the warmth of the mother's body, crawling with paddlelike movements of the forelimbs and moving its head from side to side, until eventually it comes into contact with the mother's lower body wall and

mammary area. There is reason to believe that there are **olfactory** (pertaining to smell) cues coming from the teats that help guide the newborn and promote attachment to the nipple.

In the first three weeks of **lactation** (production of milk by the female) the mother initiates virtually all nursing sessions. After this time, when the young have become more mobile and their eyes and ears are functioning, nursing sessions may occur inside or outside the bed and for the most part are initiated by the pups. The mother then usually cooperates by lying down and exposing her teats, if she is not already recumbent. Later, as the time of weaning approaches, the mother will begin avoiding the pups' nursing attempts.

Among wolves the pack members, including the dam and sire, introduce pups to solid food by regurgitating or disgorging a freshly consumed meal. The wolf pups usually beg for such partially processed food by pulling and biting the lips of an adult that has just returned to the den. Such behavior occasionally occurs in domestic dogs, although it may not be recognized as a normal part of maternal behavior.

Social interactions between the pups and their mother, and among the pups themselves, prepare the young for later social behavioral patterns. Such interactions are crucial for shaping behaviors that will make the pups desirable as pets. The mother spends practically 24 hours a day interacting with her puppies. Deprivation of this interaction, such as can happen by very early weaning or orphanage, may predispose the pups to be excessively fearful and socially maladapted as adults. Although maternal behavior is programmed into the brain, this programming is not immutable. When people in their enthusiasm step in and help a bitch when some aspect of her maternal behavior is insufficient, they are allowing for the survival of offspring with potential defects in the neural programming for maternal behavior, which then perpetuates some of the abnormal mismothering seen in dogs.

While the basic social responses of dogs are innate, the early experience of a pup with its mother and littermates refines and develops these responses, which include the appropriate use of submissive gestures and the behavior of a subordinate. If puppies are exposed only to littermates and have little contact with human beings, they tend to develop strong attachments only to dogs and may never form close attachments with people. In fact, they may exhibit fear and escape responses when a human being approaches. Conversely, if a pup is removed from its littermates before 6 weeks of age and exposed only to people, it may become primarily attached to people and exhibit abnormal social responses towards other dogs. Normally, puppies are exposed to both dogs and human beings during their period of socialization. It is for this reason that it is recommended that a puppy be taken from the litter to its permanent home at about 7 to 8 weeks of age in order to allow for adequate socialization, first to its canine littermates and subsequently to its new human companions.

One aspect of canine maternal behavior not seen in any other domestic animal is the phenomenon of **pseudopregnancy,** a condition wherein the bitch exhibits signs of pregnancy following estrus. This condition can be confusing or frustrating to the owner of a dog that has been mated. Affected dogs may undergo mammary gland development and produce milk, and display maternal behavior identical to that of a female with a true pregnancy. Before this behavioral syndrome was understood, pseudopregnancy in dogs was considered an abnormality. We now know that in the wolf ancestors, pseudopregnancy in the barren female wolves of the pack most likely served a functional purpose, in that the pseudopregnant females could serve as nursemaids and thereby contribute to the survival of the offspring of the pack. Since female pack members are usually related to the females with pups, the helpers are in actuality contributing toward the survival of offspring with which they share some genes. (*See* Chapter 14, "Reproductive Disorders.")

Misbehavior

The primary enjoyment of having a dog comes from interacting with the dog and observing its behavior. When this behavior presents a problem and becomes a misbehavior, however, dogs are no longer quite as enjoyable. The following chapter presents an overview of the solutions to some of the more common misbehaviors of dogs.

CHAPTER 7
Misbehavior

by Benjamin L. Hart

Most behavior problems in dogs involve behavior that is normal from the animal's standpoint but objectionable to people. We require pets to live in our homes and adapt to our human culture and daily schedules. While domestication of the dog undoubtedly has increased the species' compliance and adaptability, human requirements sometimes exceed the tolerance of the pet.

Often, objectionable behavior may arise simply from a specific living situation. For example, a dog that barks excessively in a tiny apartment may not bark if housed on a small farm. A dog that aggressively attempts to assert its dominance over an owner may not be a problem for an owner who is a strong "pack leader." It would be inaccurate to refer to such behavioral problems as these as abnormal. Rather, the term "abnormal" should be reserved for behavioral problems that are actually maladaptive and serve no purpose, even for animals in the wild. In dogs, for example, unpredicatable and unprovoked aggression, flank-sucking and tail mutilation would be representative examples of

abnormal behavior. Behavioral changes that sometimes occur secondary to disease processes are also considered abnormal and can be important in diagnosing the underlying disease condition.

People sometimes attempt to handle behavioral problems in dogs by being overly **anthropomorphic;** that is, by infusing a human persona into their pets. A common example would be an owner's arriving home and finding some object that a dog has broken. There is a natural human tendency to believe that the dog is acting "guilty" about the ruined object when its behavior is merely submissive. Submission is the dog's innately determined way of preventing aggression or punishment on the part of a dominant individual (in this case, the owner). The dog, by reacting to the owner's behavior and anticipating punishment, acts in a submissive manner. The owner then interprets this behavior as evidence of guilt. *It is almost impossible to overemphasize, however, that canine behavioral problems cannot be approached in the same way as human behavioral problems.*

Aggressive Behavior

Aggression is the most frequent behavioral problem in dogs. However, aggression is not always an undesirable trait. Problems usually arise simply because aggressive behavior varies considerably from time to time and between dogs. We expect dogs to exhibit aggression when warding off an intruder, but not to threaten or attack our friends. They should not back down from a bully dog, but neither should they growl at other, nonthreatening animals. Moreover, a dog whose level of dominance assertiveness is just right for one owner may be deemed too assertive or aggressive for another person.

Aggression Toward People

Dominance-Related Aggression
The most common type of aggressive behavior in dogs is that seen when dogs growl or snap at owners, not out of fear or pain but simply because they want their own way. They may threaten or snap when attempts are made to put them outdoors or move them from the bed. A dog may even "dare" an owner by grabbing something like a shoe or glove and displaying it; when the owner attempts to take the object away the dog growls and threatens. This type of misbehavior, referred to as *dominance-related aggression,* is usually prevented by an owner's establishing his or her authority over the dog from puppyhood.

There are two rather different approaches to resolving this problem, one indirect and one direct. The *indirect approach* involves controlling the affection and food rewards that are customarily given to the dog throughout the day; that is, using affection and food treats as an inducement to obey. Initially, the dog is deprived of affection and treats for at least four hours, after which the owner calls the dog and issues a command such as "Sit" or "Lie down." When the dog responds it is favored with lots of affection for 30 seconds and possibly a food treat. This exercise is repeated frequently throughout the day. If repeated enough times the dog is able to obtain a day's worth of social contact and food

treats, or even its entire ration of food, on terms set by the owner and not the dog. *The dog is never rewarded unless it obeys.* In this way it is possible to control a dog and indirectly assume an assertive and dominant position, while the dog is consistently reminded of its subordinate role. For the duration of the training period one should avoid circumstances likely to evoke an aggressive response from the dog. The success of this approach depends on all members of the family adopting the technique and withholding affection except when commands are given and obeyed.

Once the procedure begins to have the desired effect, one can use a little more force by pushing the dog outdoors if it is reluctant or slow, or jerking the choke chain if the dog does not lie down readily upon command. Gradually, human members of the family can increase the degree of force with which they handle the dog until they are at a point where they can physically control the animal without fear of reprisal. In situations wherein just one member of a family has trouble with a dog, all members of the family should ignore the dog except for the person having the trouble. This person should then be the only one to command the dog and be its only source of affection and food rewards.

The *direct approach* in dealing with dominance-related aggression exploits the dog's natural tendency to assume a subordinate role once it learns that being dominant is not possible. It takes advantage of the fact that in a pack, dominant-subordinate relationships are established and maintained by force or the threat of force. Physical control is a type of nonverbal communication that dogs understand, for dogs clearly use force with each other. This procedure is most suitable for puppies just learning their place in the family, or where no one is in danger of being injured when attempting to control a dog. To apply the direct approach, one confronts the dog's aggression only with the degree of force or restraint necessary to subdue it. Restraint or shaking by the scruff of the neck is often appropriate for small dogs or puppies. A convenient technique for larger animals is to use a control halter or a choke chain. Meeting force with force should not be considered inhumane or inappropriate, provided one only uses the degree of force necessary to maintain control and establish dominance.

Aggression Toward a New Baby

Another type of aggression is that displayed toward a new addition to the family. A well-mannered dog may develop a nasty temperament as a result of the new arrival, and family members may become concerned that they cannot trust the dog not to bite or snap at the child. The problem often arises because people in the family lavish excessive affection on the dog, assuming that the animal needs assurance it has not lost favor with them. When the dog growls or in other ways exhibits a dislike for the strange human intruder, they may put the dog outside or in another room while the baby is present. The dog may subsequently be showered with attention and affection while the baby is asleep because the members of the family do not want the dog to feel unloved. Thus, affection is lavished when the baby is not around, but is terminated or the dog put outside when the baby is present. The dog naturally develops a dislike for the child *because it feels that if it were not for the baby it would be receiving the increased affection all day long.*

The solution to this problem is similar to the indirect approach to dominance-related aggression, in that affection and food treats are used to achieve the desired effect. All affection and attention should be withdrawn from the dog when the baby is not present. When the baby is in the room the dog should be given lots of attention and affection and highly favored food treats. The goal is for the dog to view the baby as a signal that it will receive praise, attention and food. The problem usually resolves itself rather quickly if one is conscientious in controlling affection.

Fear-induced Aggression

A third type of aggressive behavior is fear-induced and is often directed towards specific people or types of people, such as children, adult men, or people in uniform. A dog may have been mistreated by a man, for example, and subsequently developed a fear of all men.

To cope with this fear, the dog drives people away by growling when they approach. When the growling does not suffice the dog often responds by snapping. If for some reason snapping loses its effectiveness the dog may resort to biting. Thus, a dog may be trained or "shaped" to escalate its level of aggression to relieve its fear.

Direct punishment is not useful to resolve this problem. When one forces a dog to hold still while the fear-evoking individual approaches, the dog's emotional response will be even more intense the next time. The first step in treating the problem, as with any phobia or fear, is to institute a program that includes systematic presentation of the fear-inducing stimulus. This involves gradually exposing the dog to the fear-evoking person by presenting it with rewards to create a desirable emotional response.

The best way to use affection and attention for reward is to withdraw affection from the dog except during training sessions. Training sessions involving exposures to the fear-evoking person should be scheduled on a daily basis. The most common procedure is to have the dog sit in a room with the person placed about 20 feet away. Assuming the dog's behavior is somewhat neutral, it is then petted and given a food reward by an individual who the dog trusts. This procedure is repeated 10 times in a row, with good behavior rewarded on each presentation. At least one or two sessions of this type should be conducted per day. Over a period of days the fear-evoking individual is placed gradually closer and closer to the dog, so that eventually he or she can give the dog a food treat and become a source of affection. During the course of the training sessions every attempt should be made to prevent the dog from being exposed to the fear-inducing person outside of the training session.

Territorial Aggression

A fourth type of aggressive behavior is territorial aggression, which often is manifested by a dog's becoming wild and excited when the doorbell rings and people come in. A convenient way of dealing with this problem is to employ a restraint such as a control halter, with friends taking turns knocking on the door or ringing the doorbell and entering while a partner controls the dog from the inside. This should be repeated at 30-second intervals until the reaction subsides. The next step is to have a person who is a stranger to the dog come to the door repeatedly until no reaction is seen. The training sessions should be kept up for several days. What one is actually doing with this technique is desensitizing the dog's territorial defense behavior so that it becomes more controllable.

An alternative to desensitization is for people in the family to withdraw all attention and affection from the dog several hours before staged visits by friends. The visitors are instructed that when they arrive they should lavish affection on the dog, which soon learns to look forward to such visits. Later, visits by individuals less well-known to the dog can then be instituted. The aim is to induce the dog to generalize that anyone who comes to the house is going to be rewarding and enjoyable.

Aggression Toward Other Dogs

People often have two or three dogs in a single household, usually with no problem because the dogs have established a dominance hierarchy among themselves. Difficulties may arise, however, when this hierarchy is interfered with by owners. Often the dogs get along fine with each other while the owners are away, but fighting may break out once the owners have returned. The causes of such fighting are related to the subordinate dog's feeling protected when the owners are present and not yielding as it normally would to subtle signals from the dominant dog to move aside. The dominant dog usually will start a fight to reinforce its position. The owners then proceed to punish the dominant dog, thereby reinforcing the tendency for the subordinate to feel protected when they are around. As the dominant dog continues to retaliate against the subordinate dog the situation worsens. The fighting occurs essentially because the dominance relationship that keeps peace when the owners are away breaks down when they are present.

The solution to this problem is for the owners first to play down the greeting response. The dominant dog should then be treated as a favorite by petting it first, letting it outdoors (or indoors) first, and so on. When growling occurs, whether by the subordinate or dominant dog, the *subordinate* dog should be punished because it is usually the subordinate dog's not obeying the signals given out by the dominant dog that is at the root of the problem. Complications can arise when people in the family are more attached to the subordinate dog and somewhat reluctant to play favorites, or when two people living together are each attached to a different dog and cannot agree about treating one as the favorite. Assuming, however, that the human members of the household can agree to cooperate and show the dogs that the same rules that apply when they are away also apply when they are home, this type of aggression can often be quickly resolved.

Sometimes dogs fight even when the owners are away, because they may not have yet established a dominance hierarchy. This is most common when the dogs are closely matched in breed, size and gender, so that one dog does not easily attain dominance. People may be reluctant to encourage one dog to become dominant, or may suppress aggressive behavior when one dog is trying to assert dominance. The goal in resolving this problem, whether owners like it or not, is to help one of the dogs establish dominance. This requires making some determination as to which dog would more likely be dominant in a natural setting.

One can facilitate dominance of one dog by treating it as a favorite. If both dogs are intact males, one can also tip the balance by having the designated subordinate dog neutered. Neutering removes some of the incentives of a male dog to engage in fighting. A neutered dog also loses some of the **olfactory** (pertaining to smell) characteristics derived from male sex hormones, making it a less interesting target for the dominant dog to attack. In some cases it may be necessary to have both dogs neutered to reduce fighting tendencies. If the dogs cannot be left alone together in the same room, one can consider installing a physical barrier that allows the two dogs to see and smell each other without contact and so gradually become adapted to each other. Eventually the barrier can be removed.

Fear Reactions and Phobias

Most fear- or anxiety-related behavior in dogs stems from normal reactions to situations where, in the wild, such fear or anxiety would be adaptive and hence advantageous. Usually, fear and emotional reactions diminish through habituation and maturation, but when they do not they can become problems that require attention. The goal in solving such problems is to desensitize or **habituate** the reactions through structured training sessions, removing any reward the dog may possibly have gotten from emotional behavior that attracted human attention or comfort.

REACTIONS TO LOUD NOISES

Usually dogs become habituated to loud noises, fireworks, automobile backfires or thunderstorms during puppyhood and adolescence. If habituation does not occur, however, severe emotional reactions to such stimuli may be the result. Although such noises are in most cases physically harmless, the anxiety and aversive internal feelings that they engender in a susceptible dog often worsen the problem. Fear responses are often enhanced because people try to comfort a dog and give it extra attention at the time of the fear. Thus, one should stop all comforting or other reinforcements of the fear reaction. One should instead act indifferent to a dog when it exhibits fear. In resolving the situation it is important first to establish the identity of the fear-evoking stimulus. Then, once the fear-evoking stimulus has been identified, one can develop a stepwise gradient of noises, increasing from very soft to very loud, to conduct desensitization training sessions.

A workable way of grading the noise produced by firecrackers, for example, is to use multiple nested cardboard boxes or even blankets to muffle the sound. A starter pistol with blank .22 shells can be used to mimic the firecrackers. (Before starting the training session one needs to test the stimulus at full strength to make sure that it does, in fact, evoke fear.) The training sessions are scheduled for once or twice a day. Sessions involve first discharging the starter pistol fully muffled by the boxes or blankets. The muffled pistol should make such a soft sound that it hardly gains the dog's attention. After every shot the dog should be presented with a food reward, affection and praise. (Obviously, if the dog is quite hungry the training sessions will go better.) Every two days or so remove one layer of muffling, so that over the course of a couple of weeks the sound of the discharge becomes louder and louder. Under ideal circumstances, once the desensitization training has been completed the pistol can be discharged at full intensity with the dog exhibiting little emotional response.

The treatment of thunderstorm phobias follows along the same lines, except that it is usually necessary to use a recording of thunder (commercially available on "sound-effects" tapes or CD's) for playback at gradually increasing volume. In some cases this may be insufficient to evoke a full-blown fear reaction in the dog. To reproduce the complete stimulus really requires a dark room, strobe lights, and even the spray of water on windows, which unfortunately can complicate the desensitization process.

SEPARATION ANXIETY

Separation anxiety is a common problem in dogs, particularly when they are pets in households where everyone must work. It is natural for a dog to be upset when members of the pack abandon it, and its behavior in the wild would be quite adaptive. On the domestic scene this type of behavior is usually manifested by excessive vocalization and other signs of emotional disturbance, such as inappropriate urination and defecation or chewing on woodwork or furniture. Such behaviors usually occur within the first few minutes of an owner's departure from the house. When people lavish excessive attention on a dog before leaving (perhaps hoping that the dog can "store up" some of this affection for later use during the day), *they are simply enhancing in the dog's mind the contrast between the owner being home and being away,* and so are only making the problem worse.

Resolution of separation anxiety requires habituating the dog by using a planned series of absences, initially as brief as one or two minutes in length. Gradually, the absences are lengthened during training sessions over the succeeding several days. (In some cases it may be necessary to habituate a dog to predeparture cues if it becomes anxious before people actually leave.) One can conduct several trials each day. After a few short absences have been staged, one should reward the dog with a long-lasting food treat (such as a knucklebone) given at the time of the next departure. This will produce in the dog a pleasurable internal state that is incompatible with the anxiety state evoked by separation. Such a food treat will be welcomed if the dog has recently experienced only short-term owner absences and exhibited only very mild anxiety reactions. The owner should then schedule a series of absences of a few minutes each, giving the dog the bone when it is left alone and then taking it away (bagging and refrigerating it) when he or she returns. As the dog sees it, there is no bone unless the owner is gone. The object thus is to make the dog *want* the person to leave so that it can have the bone back.

Absences are scheduled so that they last for only 1 or 2 minutes initially, progressing to 3 or 4 minutes, then 10 or 15 minutes, up to 30, 45 and 60 minutes each. If the procedure is carefully implemented the dog will gradually become habituated to these separations. It is imperative that little or no attention be given to the dog prior to departure, and that greetings upon return be subdued. If it is necessary to leave the dog alone for a lengthy period of time before the training sessions have been completed, friends, relatives or a dog-sitter should be employed to keep the dog company during the owner's absence.

Submissive Urination

Submissive urination is another manifestation of anxiety that is widely misunderstood by dog owners. It is most often a problem in young dogs and in females, and usually occurs when the dog is greeted. This behavior in the wild is normal, and functions to defuse or preclude aggression on the part of dominant pack members. The urination innately blocks or inhibits aggression on the part of dominant dogs. Thus, when an owner physically punishes a dog for submissive urination, the problem only becomes more pronounced *because the dog must urinate even more in order to block the owner's aggression.*

Resolution of the problem can be easily achieved by habituating the dog to greetings. Greetings should be staged and performed repeatedly several times an hour until the dog no longer urinates whenever it is approached.

Once resolution has reached the half-way point (i.e., when the dog urinates only about half the time that it is approached), it is helpful to introduce a bridging stimulus, such as a duck call, which is sounded as soon as the dog urinates. Immediately after sounding the duck call the owner should leave the dog alone. After several such experiences the dog will learn to associate the duck call with the abrupt departure of the people the dog wants to be with. *In human terms, we want the dog to think that urinating is driving family members away, whereas not urinating will make them stay.* Use of the duck call as a bridging stimulus allows one to pinpoint within a fraction of a second the exact misbehavior that is causing the people to leave.

Problems with Elimination

House-soiling may reflect urine-marking, submissive urination, or separation anxiety. It can also be caused by a medical disorder, such as a urinary tract infection, intestinal inflammation, or arthritis, that may make moving to a toilet area painful. House-soiling may also occur following a long bout of uncontrollable diarrhea. To resolve a house-soiling problem it is necessary first to determine the underlying cause. If either submissive urination or separation anxiety is to blame, then treatment should follow the guidelines outlined above for those problems. Urine-marking in the house by male dogs frequently responds to neutering.

Aside from the above, an initial approach to house-soiling may be to determine if the dog has a den-sanitation instinct by restraining it in its bed and observing if the dog soils the bed when left alone for a reasonable period of time. If the dog soils its bed, one should search for physical causes to the problem and direct treatment accordingly. If there are indications that the sanitary instinct still exists, one should renew house-training. If the elimination occurs at night, the dog may be restrained by its bed overnight and taken out in the middle of the night to prevent accidents. One then gradually sets back the time of the night trips. If the elimination occurs during the day, the dog may be confined to a small area and taken out frequently. In establishing house-training or retraining, one should also keep in mind the three factors that evoke elimination—exercise, eating and drinking.

PART III

Nutrition

Our dog Fred
Et the bread.

Our dog Dash
Et the hash.

Our dog Pete
Et the meat.

Our dog Davy
Et the gravy.

Our dog Toffy
Et the coffee.

Our dog Jake
Et the cake.

Our dog Trip
Et the dip.

And—the worst,
From the first,—

Our dog Fido
Et the pie-dough

— JAMES WHITCOMB RILEY
"The Diners in the Kitchen"

CHAPTER 8

Canine Nutritional Requirements

**by Vincent C. Biourge
and Claudia A. Kirk**

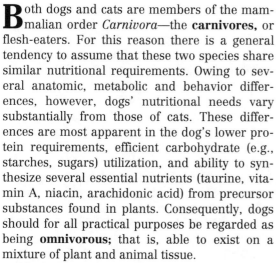

Both dogs and cats are members of the mammalian order *Carnivora*—the **carnivores,** or flesh-eaters. For this reason there is a general tendency to assume that these two species share similar nutritional requirements. Owing to several anatomic, metabolic and behavior differences, however, dogs' nutritional needs vary substantially from those of cats. These differences are most apparent in the dog's lower protein requirements, efficient carbohydrate (e.g., starches, sugars) utilization, and ability to synthesize several essential nutrients (taurine, vitamin A, niacin, arachidonic acid) from precursor substances found in plants. Consequently, dogs should for all practical purposes be regarded as being **omnivorous;** that is, able to exist on a mixture of plant and animal tissue.

Their stomach capacity allows most adult dogs to ingest their daily required intake of food in a single meal. Feeding several meals (two to four) throughout the day is recommended for dogs having higher energy requirements (puppies, pregnant and lactating bitches, and active working dogs), and for large-breed dogs with a predilection to **bloat** (distension of the stomach,

also called *gastric dilation-volvulus; see* CHAPTER 10, "DISEASES OF DIETARY ORIGIN" and CHAPTER 30, "THE DIGESTIVE SYSTEM AND DISORDERS"). Although less particular than cats in their choice of diet, dogs do have several innate food preferences, including preferences for:

- meat over nonmeat diets
- canned or semimoist food over dry food
- new foods over familiar foods
- sugar

Dogs exhibit tremendous differences among the various breeds in size (a Chihuahua weighing 2–6 pounds versus a Saint Bernard Dog weighing 150–180 pounds) and daily activity (a house pet versus a sledge dog). These differences translate into substantial variations in energy and nutrient requirements (*see* CHAPTER 9, "FEEDING DOGS"). The overall goals in fulfilling a dog's nutritional requirements are optimal health and a prolonged life span. These are difficult to measure, however, and this difficulty explains some of the challenges and controversies surrounding the general subject of nutrition.

Dog's normal nutritional needs include water, energy (obtained from carbohydrates, fats and proteins), **amino acids** (the nitrogen-containing building blocks of proteins), **glucose** (blood sugar) precursors (found in carbohydrate and protein), fatty acids (from fat), minerals and vitamins. Collectively these compounds are called nutrients. (Oxygen in the air is usually not regarded as a nutrient; however, it is essential for the body's utilization of nutrients.) Most common foods represent a complex mixture of these nutrients. Basic minimum nutritional requirements and nutrients allowances for dogs have been determined by the subcommittee on canine nutrition of the National Research Council (NRC), and the pet-food committee of the American Association of Feed Control Officers (AAFCO). These standards are used as guidelines by pet-food manufacturers when formulating canine diets.

Water

The body of an adult dog is composed of about 60% water; this value is even higher in puppies. Water is vital for cellular functioning and is an essential component of nutrition. Water deprivation leads to death much more rapidly than does starvation. Dogs obtain water not only from drinking, but also from food and from the breakdown of ingested fats, carbohydrates and proteins (**metabolic water**). Water is lost through urine, feces, lactation, respiration and panting. Excessive losses may occur during hot weather, severe exercise or disease (e.g., diarrhea, vomiting, kidney disease). Increased consumption of salt may also increase water requirements. The body's water content is remarkably constant, making **dehydration** (loss of body water) a potent inducer of thirst. Dogs should therefore have access to fresh, clean water at all times.

Energy

Dogs require energy for all cellular functions (e.g., muscle contraction, transport of substances across cell membranes, maintenance of cellular integrity, synthesis and breakdown of molecules, etc.). Dogs obtain this energy in the form of chemical energy derived from the processing of ingested food. The mechanism by which this is accomplished can be arbitrarily divided into four phases:

1. digestion, which occurs when large molecules (proteins, carbohydrates, fats) are broken down into smaller ones (amino acids, glucose, fatty acids) in the gastrointestinal tract;
2. absorption, wherein these smaller molecules are transported from the intestine to individual cells;
3. **oxidation,** the "burning" of glucose, amino acids, and fatty acids to produce **adenosine triphosphate (ATP),** the true form of energy used by cells (some cells, including brain cells, a portion of the kidneys, and red blood cells, can burn only glucose to produce ATP);
4. energy expenditure, representing the consumption of ATP by the cellular machinery for specific cell functions.

When excess energy (i.e., food) is ingested, the superfluous amino acids, glucose and fatty acids are stored as **glycogen** (animal starch, a complex carbohydrate) or fat for use at a later time. If excess energy intake becomes chronic, as by overfeeding, the expansion of the body's fat stores will lead to obesity (*see* Chapter 10, "Diseases of Dietary Origin").

The energy derived from foods can be quantified in units known as calories. A **calorie** (abbreviated *cal*) is defined as the amount of energy needed to raise the temperature of 1 gram of water 1 degree Celsius (centigrade). Because this amount of energy is very small, nutritionists prefer to use the term **kilocalorie** (abbreviated *kcal;* also referred to as a *Calorie,* with a capital "C"), which represents 1000 calories. The kilocalorie or Calorie is the one familiar to most readers. (In order to standardize the different systems of energy units in use around the world, energy may also be expressed in joules (*J*) or kilojoules (*kJ*), 1 kcal being equivalent to 4.184 kJ.)

No animal is able to utilize all the energy in its food. In dogs most of the energy that is not utilized is lost in feces and urine. The **gross** energy (GE) of a food is the amount of energy produced by its complete *combustion* (burning). The difference between GE and the energy that is lost in urine and feces is referred to as **metabolizable energy (ME).** ME represents the energy that is ultimately available to the dog for use. In veterinary texts and in pamphlets distributed by pet-food manufacturers, the energy content of diets and the energy requirements of dogs are usually expressed as ME.

The **maintenance energy requirement (MER)** is the amount of energy used by a moderately active adult dog in a *thermoneutral* environment, that is, at the optimal ambient temperature. It represents the energy expended in obtaining and using food in an amount sufficient to maintain body weight, but not to support growth, pregnancy or lactation. Owing to the extreme variations in size within the canine species, the total MER varies widely among the different breeds. The relationship between MER and body weight is expressed by an exponential curve (*see* FIGURE 1). The equation that best represents the curve is still a topic of controversy, but the one most commonly used is:

$$MER = 132 \times (\text{body weight})^{0.75}$$

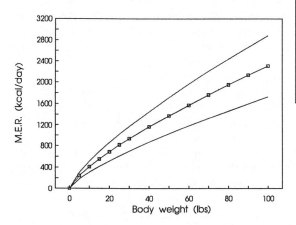

Figure 1. Maintenance energy requirements (MER) of adult dogs. The open square represents the curve calculated by the equation $MER = 132 \times (\text{body weight})^{0.75}$, where MER is expressed in kcal and body weight is in kg. The two other curves represent 75% and 125% of these requirements. Body weight in the figure is expressed in pounds for ease of reference.

where MER is expressed in kcal and body weight is expressed in kilograms (kg).

The line of open squares in figure 1 represents the curve predicted by the above equation. Because some dogs may need more or fewer calories than the amount derived from this curve (owing to the large variation in MER among dogs of similar size), curves representing 75% and 125% of the MER are shown as well. Table 1 illustrates the use of this equation to calculate the MER for a 10-pound dog. It is important to remember that the calculated MER only represents an *estimate* of energy need; energy intake should always be adjusted to maintain body weight. (The caloric requirements for other physiologic conditions—exercise, pregnancy, lactation, growth—are discussed in CHAPTER 9, "FEEDING DOGS.")

Table 1
Calculation of the maintenance energy requirement (MER) of a 10-lb dog using the equation
$$MER \text{ (kcal)} = 132 \times (\text{body weight in kg})^{0.75}$$

Step 1: Conversion of lb to kg (1 lb = 0.453 kg)
10 lb × 0.453 = 4.53 kg

Step 2: Determination of metabolic body weight $(kg^{0.75})$
$4.53^{0.75} = 3.11$

Step 3: Determination of MER
MER = 132 × 3.11 = 410 kcal of metabolizable energy (ME)

Proteins

Dietary proteins serve as a source of amino acids and nitrogen. Amino acids are used to synthesize hormones, enzymes, body secretions and various other body proteins. Nutritionists divide amino acids in two categories: **essential amino acids** (those that cannot be synthesized in sufficient quantities by the animal and must be provided in the diet) and **dispensable amino acids** (those that can be synthesized by the animal so long as a source of nitrogen [i.e., other amino acids] is present in the diet). The essential amino acids for dogs are arginine, histidine, isoleucine, leucine, lysine, methionine, pheny-lalanine, threonine, tryptophan and valine.

Proteins that provide optimal proportions of the essential amino acids, such as egg protein, are said to be of *high quality*. Proteins that are deficient in one or more essential amino acids (e.g., wheat protein is deficient in lysine) are said to be of *poor quality*. An amino acid present in insufficient quantity in a protein is said to be *limiting*. The quality of a protein can be improved by supplementing it with the limiting amino acid (i.e., by adding lysine to wheat protein) or by adding a protein that contains the limiting amino acid in excess.

Although an amino acid may be present in sufficient quantity in a protein, if the protein is difficult to digest the amino acid may be "trapped" in the protein and lost in the feces. The lower the *digestibility* (ease of digestion) of a protein, the more of that protein will be required to meet individual amino acid needs. As a general rule, proteins from animal sources are more digestible than are proteins from plant sources. For the synthesis of proteins, cells require the simultaneous presence of all the amino acids. Even if only one amino acid is lacking, protein synthesis will be halted and the amino acids that are present will instead be **catabolized** (broken down). A protein that results in such a waste of amino acids is said to have poor *biological value*.

Protein and amino acids are also used by dogs to manufacture glucose and energy. If the total energy (food) intake is limited, the use of amino acids as a source of energy will take precedence over protein synthesis. If excessive amounts of energy and protein are ingested, the superfluous amino acids will be used for making glucose, glycogen and fat, while the nitrogen the amino acids contained will be eliminated in the urine.

Protein deficiency in dogs results in decreased food intake, poor growth, weight loss, muscular wasting, depressed milk production, a rough and dull haircoat, depletion of blood proteins, and ultimately death. These signs are not specific, however, and may result from either severe caloric restriction or a deficiency of a single essential amino acid. Specific signs charac-

teristic of individual amino-acid deficiencies in the dog have not been adequately documented. Conversely, the role of excess dietary proteins in inducing certain disease states (e.g., kidney disease) in dogs remains controversial.

Carbohydrates

Sugars, starches and dietary fibers make up this class of nutrients. Sugars and starches are digested in the small intestine, and their products of digestion, such as glucose and fructose, are used primarily as energy sources. Dietary fibers typically constitute the cell walls of plants and for the most part remain undigested during their passage through the intestine.

SUGARS AND STARCHES

Sugars and starches are commonly referred as **digestible carbohydrates.** Their digestion and metabolism result in the formation of glucose, which is used for energy and for the synthesis of fat and dispensable amino acids. During lactation, glucose is necessary for the synthesis of **lactose** (milk sugar). Sugars and starches are not strictly required in the canine diet, however, because the amino acids in protein and the glycerol present in fat can be used to make glucose. Diets lacking digestible carbohydrates should contain enough protein to ensure normal protein and glucose synthesis. This is particularly true in pregnant and lactating bitches, which require carbohydrates to meet the large glucose needs of the growing fetus and to synthesize lactose for the milk. Because starches are a less expensive source of energy than either protein or fat, digestible carbohydrates constitute a substantial portion of most commercial dog foods. The addition of small amounts (5%) of digestible carbohydrates to an all protein and fat diet (i.e., a diet for sledge dogs) will minimize the diarrhea often associated with such a diet.

In the dog, the digestibility of cooked starches (gelified starches) is high, while raw starches are less well-utilized. Healthy dogs efficiently digest sucrose (table sugar), provided the amount ingested is not excessive or the introduction to the diet too suddenly. Lactose is not well-tolerated by weaned and adult dogs, particularly if large amounts are introduced suddenly. *Small* quantities of both of these sugars (5% of the diet) will be well-tolerated by most dogs. Sucrose and all sweet substances will enhance the palatability of foods for dogs.

DIETARY FIBERS

Dietary fibers (pectins, gums, hemicellulose, cellulose, lignin) are not considered essential for a dog's diet, although they may be beneficial in regulating the passage of food through the intestinal tract. In general, dietary fibers interfere with the absorption of some nutrients, modify the composition of the bacteria normally present in the large intestine, and increase the volume of the stool. Most of these effects have not been well-documented in dogs, however.

Dietary fibers have been classified as **soluble fibers** (as in fruits, oat bran, and psyllium [the chief component of many commercial stool softeners]) and **insoluble fibers** (cellulose, wheat bran). Soluble fibers attract water and form a gel, are highly fermentable (able to be digested by bacteria) in the large intestine, and have been shown in people to slow emptying of the stomach and to inhibit the absorption of cholesterol. Insoluble fibers are good bulk-forming agents and are poorly fermentable in the large intestine. Insoluble fibers are commonly added to commercial dog foods to dilute their caloric density, in order to reduce caloric intake without exacerbating hunger (*see* CHAPTER 9, "FEEDING DOGS").

Fat

Dietary fat represents a highly concentrated source of energy. Fat supplies 2.25 times as much energy as proteins and carbohydrates and provides the body with essential fatty acids. It also acts as a carrier of fat-soluble vitamins (vitamins A, D, E and K) and is an important factor in the acceptability of food by influencing its palatability and texture. In people fatty meals are more satisfying because they slow stomach emptying and prolong the feeling of **satiety** (appeasement of the appetite).

Dogs are able to digest and absorb high levels of dietary fat. Fat constitutes the most important energy source in diets for dogs having high energy requirements (e.g., puppies, lactating bitches and working dogs). A transition from a low- to a high-fat diet should be made gradually in order to allow the digestive tract time to adapt. Intake of a high-fat diet should be restricted in adult dogs at maintenance in order to avoid excessive energy intake and obesity.

Dietary fat consists of a mixture of **triglycerides** (compounds containing fatty acids linked to glycerol), **phospholipids** (fats containing phosphorus) and cholesterol. The differences between one fat and another are largely the result of their different fatty-acid compositions. Fatty acids are chains of carbon and hydrogen atoms in which the carbon atoms are linked by simple or double bonds. Saturated fatty acids have no double bonds, while unsaturated fatty acids have one (monounsaturated) or more (polyunsaturated) double bonds. Neither dietary fat nor cholesterol induces heart disease in healthy dogs.

ESSENTIAL FATTY ACIDS

The only demonstrable need for dietary fat is as a source of essential fatty acids and as a carrier of fat-soluble vitamins. **Essential fatty acids** (linoleic acid and arachidonic acid) are polyunsaturated fatty acids that have structural functions in the cell membranes and serve as precursors for **prostaglandins** (regulators of a number of important physiological processes involving allergic reactions, contraction of smooth muscle, dilation of blood vessels, blood clotting, and others) and **leukotrienes** (modulators of allergic and inflammatory reactions). Linoleic acid is very abundant in vegetable oil; dogs (but not cats) can convert linoleic to arachidonic acid. Arachidonic acid is found only in animal products.

A deficiency in essential fatty acids results in poor general condition and a coarse, dull, dry haircoat. The skin often is thickened and excessive flaking of dandruff is evident. Growth in puppies is inadequate, while adult dogs reproduce poorly. A deficiency in a commercial dog food may result from poor formulation or inadequate or lengthy storage.

Linoleic and arachidonic acids belong to the

n-6 (or *omega-6*) family of fatty acids, so-called because there is a double bound between the sixth and seventh carbons from the terminal end of these fatty acids. Fish oil (α-linoleic acid, eicosapentaenoic acid) belongs to the *n-3* family (double bond between third and fourth carbons). It is not known if dogs have a requirement for fatty acids of the n-3 family. In people, ingestion of n-3 fatty acids has been associated with clinical improvement in some skin and joint diseases. Whether dogs may be beneficially affected by n-3 fatty acids remains to be determined.

Minerals

Our knowledge of the minerals required in the canine diet is limited. Requirements for calcium, phosphorus, potassium, sodium, magnesium, iron, copper, zinc and iodine have been demonstrated. A requirement for chloride and selenium is also strongly suggested. Based on information available for other animal species, it is assumed that manganese, sulfur, cobalt, molybdenum, fluorine, chromium, silicon, tin, nickel and vanadium are also essential for dogs. Currently it is common practice to include all of these minerals in commercial canine diets.

Limited data are available to determine the mineral concentrations that should be used in the formulation of dog food. The recommendations that have been made are based on studies involving dogs, on estimates extrapolated from the requirements of other species, and on experience with diets that have resulted in acceptable performance. The determination of mineral requirements is further complicated by interactions between dietary minerals (e.g., calcium's interference with the absorption of zinc) and insufficient knowledge of the biological availability of minerals (e.g., zinc in the form of zinc oxide is very poorly absorbed). Finally, mineral requirements for pregnancy, lactation, maintenance and work, as well as differences among breeds, have not been well-defined.

Minerals are the major constituents of bones and teeth and help to maintain the body's acid-base, electrolyte and fluid balances. They act as intracellular signals and their release induces a cascade of chemical reactions. Minerals that are required in the diet in very minute amounts are referred to as **trace elements**. These include zinc, iron, copper, manganese, cobalt and iodine. Trace elements serve as essential components of enzymes, hormones, and various other compounds.

As a general rule, mineral supplementation of commercially available canine diets should be avoided. Available diets already fulfill all known requirements and any added minerals may interfere with the absorption of the minerals already present in the diet. Mineral supplementation may be required for some homemade diets, however (*see* CHAPTER 9, "FEEDING DOGS").

CALCIUM AND PHOSPHORUS

Calcium and phosphorus are the major minerals in bones and teeth. Calcium is also involved in blood clotting and in the transmission of nerve impulses. Phosphorus is essential for the activation or inhibition of many enzyme systems, the generation and transfer of energy, and for many other metabolic processes. A common mineral imbalance involving calcium and phosphorus is caused by the feeding of an all-meat diet, or a homemade diet that is not supplemented with a source of calcium such as bonemeal. As a consequence, the body removes calcium from the skeleton in order to maintain blood calcium levels, resulting in deformed and excessively fragile bones (*see* CHAPTER 10, "DISEASES OF DIETARY ORIGIN"). Calcium deficiencies may also result in **tetany** (seizure-like tremors). A deficiency in phosphorus has not been reported in dogs fed common foods or commercial dog food. Excessive intake of calcium during growth may result in skeletal abnormalities, while excessive dietary phosphorus has been shown to promote kidney damage in dogs having a reduced amount of functioning kidney tissue.

POTASSIUM

Potassium is found in high concentration in body cells and is required for fluid balance and proper nerve and muscle function. A deficiency results in muscular weakness, poor growth, an irregular heartbeat and kidney lesions. Animal tissue contains higher levels of potassium; therefore, higher animal tissue (protein) diets should contain sufficient amounts of potassium.

SODIUM AND CHLORIDE

Sodium and chloride are found in high concentration outside body cells; that is, in the extracellular fluids. They help to maintain body fluid and electrolyte balances. Common table salt (sodium chloride) is usually added to dog food to increase palatability, and it is most unlikely that a normal diet will be deficient in either of these two minerals. Signs of deficiency when it does occur include fatigue, poor growth, dehydration, hair loss and dry skin.

MAGNESIUM

Magnesium is found in bone and is important for proper heart, muscle and nerve functioning. It is also involved in enzymatic reactions responsible for the generation and transfer of energy within cells. Signs of deficiency include muscular weakness, and in severe cases convulsions, inappetence, poor growth, and deposition of calcium in the wall of the **aorta** (the great vessel arising from the left ventricle of the heart, which feeds blood through the arterial system into the body).

IRON

Iron is an essential component of **hemoglobin** (the red pigment in red blood cells that serves as the carrier of oxygen to the tissues) and many other molecules involved in the transport, utilization and storage of oxygen in the body. Iron deficiency is associated with **anemia** (decreased red blood cell count), which causes weakness and fatigue. Excessive quantities of iron result in inappetence and weight loss.

COPPER

Copper is a constituent of many enzymes. Among them is an enzyme responsible for hair and skin pigmentation and another important for bone formation. Copper is also involved in the absorption and transport of iron. A deficiency will result in anemia, loss of hair pigmentation, and bone abnormalities, while an excessive quantity of copper also induces anemia as well as liver damage. Breeds such as the

Bedlington Terrier and West Highland White Terrier have a defect in the handling of copper by the liver and should be fed diets containing only low or moderate amounts of this element.

MANGANESE

Little is known about specific requirements for manganese in the dog. In other species, manganese is important for reproduction and proper bone formation.

IODINE

The only recognized function of iodine is in the synthesis of thyroid hormones. Thyroid hormones regulate the overall rate of body metabolism and are important for the development of the brain. Iodine deficiency results in **goiter** (enlarged thyroid gland), hair loss, skeletal deformities, and apathy.

SELENIUM

The best-known function of selenium is as a constituent of **glutathione peroxidase,** an enzyme important for protecting cells against damage caused by by-products of normal metabolic processes. In that function selenium acts in conjunction with vitamin E. Deficiency of selenium and vitamin E results in muscular weakness, muscle and heart damage, inappetence and death. On a practical basis, dogs consuming commercial diets are very unlikely to become deficient in selenium because this mineral has a wide distribution in dog-food ingredients.

OTHER TRACE ELEMENTS

Cobalt, molybdenum, chromium, silicon, tin, nickel and vanadium are required in other animal species in very minute concentrations. Requirements have not been established for dogs. However, the quantities of these minerals in the natural ingredients used in commercial dog foods meet the known requirements of other mammalian species.

Vitamins

Vitamins are required in very small amounts because dogs cannot manufacture sufficient quantities to fulfill their daily needs. Vitamins are classified as either **fat-soluble vitamins** (vitamins A, D, E, K) or water-soluble vitamins (vitamins B, C). Several vitamins (principally A, E, C and thiamine [vitamin B_1]) are readily destroyed by light, heat, oxidation, moisture, fat rancidity or combination with certain minerals. Food processing, lengthy storage and poor storage conditions (humidity, heat) will substantially affect the vitamin content of a diet. Pet foods are formulated to compensate for the loss of vitamins during processing. Thus, vitamin supplements are unnecessary in healthy dogs consuming a commercial dog food before the indicated expiration date. Supplementation may be required with some homemade diets, however, and in certain disease states (kidney, liver and intestinal diseases) (*see* Chapter 9, "Feeding Dogs").

FAT-SOLUBLE VITAMINS

The absorption of fat-soluble vitamins is facilitated by the presence in the diet of moderate levels of fat and is inhibited by conditions that prevent normal fat absorption (e.g., pancreas, liver or intestinal malfunction). Fat-soluble vitamins are stored in the body. This explains why, when compared to water-soluble vitamins, deficiencies take a longer time to become evident and excesses result more rapidly in toxicity.

Vitamin A (Retinol)

Vitamin A is essential for normal vision, growth, reproduction, and the maturation of the surface lining cells of the skin and mucous membranes. A deficiency results in retarded growth, night blindness, inappetence, weight loss, increased susceptibility to infection, ocular infections, skin lesions, tumors and skull abnormalities. Excessive intake of vitamin A (e.g., 100 times the daily requirement) causes weight loss, lethargy, inappetence and bone abnormalities. If excessive vitamin A is given during pregnancy it can produce a cleft palate in puppies. Liver is an excellent source of vitamin A, so dogs fed liver as the main component of the diet can develop vitamin A toxicity.

Vitamin D

Vitamin D is involved in the metabolism of calcium and phosphorus for the formation of bones and the maintenance of blood calcium concentration. A deficiency in vitamin D results in bone deformities (**rickets**) in puppies. Vitamin D is the most toxic of all the vitamins; overdosing with as little as 10 times the daily requirement will raise blood calcium levels and deposit calcium in the blood vessels, kidney and heart. Irreversible kidney damage is a common consequence of vitamin D toxicity. It appears that dogs, unlike other mammals, may not be able to synthesize vitamin D as the result of exposure to sunlight, and thus require vitamin D in their diet.

Vitamin E (Alpha-tocopherol)

Vitamin E is an antioxidant, protecting fats in the diet and in the body from **oxidation** (rancidity). Vitamin E is important for maintaining the stability of cell membranes and in this function it is closely allied with selenium. Increasing polyunsaturated fatty acids (vegetable oils, fish oils) in the diet will increase vitamin E requirements. A deficiency in vitamin E results in degeneration of the **retina** (the light-sensitive layer of cells at the back of the eye), muscle degeneration and muscle weakness, inappetence, depression and death. Vitamin E is not generally thought of as being toxic, but some adverse effects on blood clotting have been observed in other animal species.

Vitamin K

Vitamin K regulates the formation of several factors involved in blood clotting. A dietary source of vitamin K is not necessary because sufficient amounts are produced by the bacterial population of the large intestine. Dietary supplementation with vitamin K may be indicated, however, in cases of chronic intestinal or liver disease, or during long-term (more than 4 weeks) antibiotic therapy. Vitamin K is potentially toxic (anemia, blood abnormalities) if taken in very large quantities.

WATER-SOLUBLE VITAMINS

Water-soluble vitamins are not stored (except for vitamin B_{12}) in the body; signs of deficiency thus can occur more rapidly than for the fat-soluble vitamins. Conversely, because these vitamins are excreted rapidly their potential for toxicity is low.

B Vitamins

The B vitamins—thiamine (B1), riboflavin (B2), niacin, pantothenic acid, pyridoxine (B6), folacin, choline, biotin and cyanocobalamin (B12)—are important constituents of many enzyme systems that regulate most cellular processes. Natural deficiencies of B vitamins often occur as multiple vitamin deficiencies. Clinical signs generally result in loss of appetite, impairment of gastrointestinal tract function, skin lesions, poor haircoat, nervous system impairment (weakness, paralysis, lethargy, hyperexcitability, confusion), and anemia. Brewer's yeast, wheat germ and animal products are good sources of B vitamins.

Folacin and biotin are not required in the diet of healthy dogs because both are synthesized by the bacteria of the large intestine. Supplementation may be indicated, however, in cases of chronic intestinal disease or long-term antibiotic therapy. Deficiencies in folacin, riboflavin, pantothenic acid and pyridoxine are unlikely to occur when dogs are fed commercial food and the usual table foods. The absorption of biotin is impaired by a constituent protein of raw egg whites called **avidin.** This effect can be avoided by thorough cooking of eggs. Vitamin B12 deficiency is a concern in dogs fed a completely vegetarian diet (*see* CHAPTER 9, "FEEDING DOGS") and those with intestinal disease or pancreatitis (inflammation of the pancreas).

Thiamine is very sensitive to heat, so that a deficiency may result during the commercial processing of food. In the pet-food industry it is common practice to supplement commercial diets with large quantities of thiamine before processing. Thiamine deficiency may also result from the simultaneous ingestion of a **thiaminase** (an enzyme that breaks down thiamine), such as the one present in raw fish. Thiaminases are, however, inactivated by heating (i.e., cooking). The primary clinical signs of thiamine deficiency in dogs are inappetence and muscular weakness.

Choline plays an important role in the transport of fat from the liver and in the stimulation of nerve cells. Methionine (an amino acid) can be used by the dog to manufacture choline. A choline deficiency (poor growth, excessive deposition of fat in the liver) is most unlikely in dogs fed a normal diet.

Vitamin C (Ascorbic Acid)

Unlike people, dogs are able to synthesize vitamin C from glucose and thus do not require a dietary source. Manufacture of vitamin C occurs primarily in the liver. Vitamin C plays an important role in the functioning of several enzymes. Careful studies have failed to find evidence of a beneficial effect of vitamin C in either alleviating or preventing infectious diseases, or in growth-associated skeletal disease in large-breed dogs. Vitamin C supplementation may, however, be of benefit in active, working dogs (sledge dogs) and in dogs with liver disease (reduced vitamin C formation in the damaged liver).

CHAPTER 9

Feeding Dogs

by Vincent C. Biourge
and Claudia A. Kirk

Dog owners are often concerned about what to feed their pets. Making a choice from the extensive roster of available brands and varieties can at times seem overwhelming. Pet foods are marketed very aggressively, thus it is not always a simple matter to differentiate between legitimate and invalid claims. Small-animal nutritionists are often consulted by concerned owners seeking advice on diet, dietary supplementation, disease prevention, and on other, more controversial issues such as the health risks associated with food additives. Unfortunately, there are few simple answers to these questions; however, by reviewing basic concepts and presenting some representative options, pet owners are usually able to make an educated choice on what to feed their dogs. (For a full understanding of the basic nutrition terms used in this and the following chapter, readers are urged to consult CHAPTER 8, "CANINE NUTRITIONAL REQUIREMENTS.")

A Balanced Diet

The primary factor that determines the amount of food a dog is going to eat is energy, that is,

calories. Consequently, commercial dog foods are formulated so that the amount of food needed to fulfill dogs' energy requirements will contain the required quantities of all the other nutrients as well. A diet that provides the correct balance of energy and nutrients is said to be *complete and balanced.* Because nutrient requirements vary depending on age, physiological status (e.g., pregnancy, lactation), activity level and disease state, diets are usually qualified as complete and balanced "for adult maintenance," "for all stages of life," "for growth," et cetera.

Determining whether a diet is nutritionally balanced can be a difficult undertaking. Despite significant progress in our understanding of the nutritional needs of dogs and the interactions between different nutrients, unknowns still remain. Consequently, no evaluation of a dog food can be considered complete until the food's adequacy has been assessed in a *feeding trial;* that is, by demonstrating that dogs do well when the food is consumed over a defined period of time.

Once a diet is complete and balanced on the basis of its energy content, one need only be concerned with meeting a dog's energy requirement, since the diet already fulfills the requirements for the other nutrients at that particular level of food intake. The energy requirement, like nutrient requirements, is a function of age, physiological status and level of exercise. The procedures used to estimate a dog's energy requirement and the energy content of a diet are described below.

Energy, although the most important factor, is not the only factor affecting the amount of food a dog will eat. If the **energy density** (amount of energy per pound of a diet) is too low, physical limitations, such as the size of the stomach, will prevent the dog from eating enough to fulfill its dietary needs. This may be an advantage when feeding an obese dog but will be detrimental for a dog with a high energy requirement, such as a lactating bitch. On the other hand, the more palatable the diet the more willing the dog will be to eat, and possibly overeat. A highly palatable diet thus may be advantageous for a lactating bitch but will clearly be inappropriate for an obese dog.

Types of Foods

Dog foods can be classified into several categories based on their source, ingredients, moisture content and other factors. In the United States most pet owners prefer the cost, convenience and nutritional balance provided by commercial pet foods. Yet many owners do prepare homemade diets for their pets, often due to medical necessity, but also for personal satisfaction or because of particular beliefs.

COMMERCIAL DOG FOODS
Commercial dog foods are those that are purchased prepackaged from grocery, pet, or feed stores, or from a veterinarian. Diets from specialty stores are often referred to as *premium brands*. Although premium-brand dog foods cost more than popular grocery-store brands, they do not guarantee superior nutrition. In general, premium brands use high-quality ingredients that are highly digestible, which accounts for part of their increased cost. Additional costs arise from the practice of using a "fixed formula"; that is, the recipe used by a premium-brand manufacturer remains exactly the same batch after batch. Some popular-brand manufacturers, while not altering the overall nutrient content of their diet, may shift the ratios of similar ingredients within a recipe (i.e., ground corn vs. ground wheat) owing to cost changes dictated by the commodities market. This practice allows popular brands to keep their overall costs lower than those of premium brands (which must compensate for potential cost fluctuations in their pricing structure). Some dogs are exquisitely sensitive to variations between batches and may develop a mild stomach upset when fed a new batch. In such cases choosing a fixed-formula brand is preferable. For the majority of dogs, however, minor variations in diet have relatively little impact.

Dry Foods
Dry-type dog foods contain approximately 10% moisture. These diets are made using a variety of cereal grains or meals, animal or poultry meats, meals and by-products, soybean meal, animal fats, fibers, vitamins, minerals and preservatives. Cereal grains are often the primary ingredient in dry foods. The wet mixture of ingredients is pressed through a patterned opening or *die* in the presence of steam (a process called *extrusion*) and then dried to the desired moisture content. The steam cooks the starches, making them highly digestible, and expands or "puffs" the food pellet into a desirable texture. After drying, the fat as well as other flavor enhancers are sprayed on the outside of the food. This increases the palatability as well as the energy content of the diet. Some manufacturers elect to add all the fat to the ingredients prior to extrusion; however, this

probably makes little difference in the overall digestibility or quality of the diet. The average dry dog food contains approximately 350 kcal per cup of food.

There are several advantages to feeding dry diets to dogs. First of all, dry diets cost considerably less than semimoist or canned foods. They are more convenient to feed, and do not spoil as quickly as canned diets do when left out for free-choice feeding. Dry-type diets may result in fewer dental problems as well. A drawback to some dry diets is their lower energy content. Dogs with high energy requirements, such as puppies and lactating bitches, may have difficulty eating enough of a dry food to meet their energy needs. Choosing a high-energy (i.e., high-fat) dry food can compensate for this disadvantage. Another drawback lies in the large quantity of food some dogs can bolt down at a single meal—a feeding pattern that can lead to life-threatening **bloat** (gastric torsion) in large-breed dogs (*see* Chapter 10, "Diseases of Dietary Origin"; Chapter 30, "The Digestive System and Disorders"; and Chapter 40, "Surgery and Postoperative Care"). Finally, some dogs (particularly of the small or toy breeds) find dry foods to be less palatable or more difficult to eat than either canned or semimoist diets.

Semimoist Foods

Semimoist foods contain approximately 25–30% moisture. They are often shaped to resemble human foods, like ground beef, in order to improve their visual appeal. To bind the water and prevent spoilage, high levels of sucrose (table sugar), sorbates and propylene glycol are used. The ingredients are similar to those of dry diets except for a reduction in cereal grains. Thus, semimoist diets tend to have a higher digestibility than dry-type foods. The average energy content is 275 kcal per 6-ounce package. The newer "soft-dry" products have less fresh meat than a semimoist diet and may also contain mold inhibitors and acids to prevent spoilage. Advantages of semimoist foods include improved digestibility, increased palatability, and feeding convenience. Semimoist diets cost more than dry foods, however, and because of their high sugar content may promote dental disease.

Canned Foods

Canned foods have a very high moisture content (in the United States the average moisture content is 74–78%). The composition of canned foods varies widely from primarily meat-based or gourmet-style diets to high-cereal grain products. Similarly, the digestibility of canned diets varies from extremely high to moderate. A clue to the actual meat content of a diet can be found on the label. Diets named for their meat source (e.g., beef) must contain at least 70% of the labeled meat protein. Diets called meat *dinners* or *platters* must contain a minimum of 10% of the labeled meat source, while meat *flavors* may contain none of the actual meat but have only a recognizable meat flavor. Dinners and flavored canned diets often use textured vegetable proteins to simulate chunks of meat, providing visual appeal for the pet owner. This may seem a bit deceptive; however, textured vegetable proteins are nutritious and do improve the texture of the diet. Canned diets labeled complete and balanced are designed to be fed alone and need no additional supplementation.

Canned diets are the most expensive dog foods to feed. However, they tend to be the most palatable owing to their high water, meat and fat content. The energy content of the average canned food is approximately 500 kcal per 14- to 15-ounce can. Canned diets are often used as well to enhance the flavor of dry-type foods, as the sole diet in toy breeds, and as a weaning food for puppies.

Treats and Biscuits

The popularity of commercial treats and biscuits has expanded considerably over the years. Feeding treats enhances the human-animal bond, provides a positive reward during training, and adds calories to the diet. Treats vary widely in their ingredients, nutrition and texture. In general they are higher in salt, fat and sometimes sugar than are "complete" dog foods. Because they are not intended to serve as the sole nutritive source, they are not required to meet any standardized nutrient requirements and may or may not be complete and balanced. This is of little concern if these foods are fed only in small quantities. Excessive feeding of treats (greater than 10% of a dog's daily intake), however, may negatively affect the nutritional quality of a diet. Treats and biscuits are not recommended for obese dogs or those on therapeutic diets.

HOMEMADE DIETS

Homemade diets are most often fed for medical reasons or when a therapeutic diet is available but the dog refuses to eat it. In other cases, pet owners simply choose to prepare homemade foods because they derive personal satisfaction from cooking for their pet or because of specific personal beliefs or concerns. Providing a complete and balanced homemade diet is possible, but entails a good deal of time, effort and money. Homemade diets are rarely less expensive than commercial products when properly supplemented. They do tend to be highly palatable, however. A typical homemade diet contains good-quality protein and carbohydrate sources supplemented with essential fatty acids, vitamins and minerals. (Owners should consult a veterinarian regarding proper supplementation.) The chief disadvantage of homemade diets, beyond the time and expense involved in their preparation, is the uncertainty regarding nutritional adequacy. Homemade diets of necessity have not been subjected to nutrient analyses or feeding trials and must therefore be used with a certain degree of caution. Having said this, it appears that most dogs do quite well on properly prepared homemade diets.

Vegetarian Diets

Owing to the increase in numbers of pet owners practicing a vegetarian lifestyle, feeding a vegetarian diet to dogs has become more common. Unlike cats, dogs can do quite well on a vegetarian diet, so long as adequate amounts of protein, amino acids and vitamin B_{12} are provided. Commercial brands are available, and in general are recommended over home-prepared diets simply because they must meet the standard nutritional guidelines established for dogs. With effort, however, a balanced homemade diet can be prepared so long as owners do not skip required supplements or are not overzealous with others.

Selecting a Dog Food

Selecting an appropriate dog food can cause great anxiety for some pet owners. Many owners are unclear on how to assess the quality of the various diets or how to use the nutritional information provided on pet-food labels. Pet-food manufacturers, large and small, must adhere to nutrition and labeling guidelines set forth by the American Association of Feed Control Officers (AAFCO). The individual state governments are responsible for enforcing approved regulations. These regulations provide a standard of nutrition and labeling so that consumers have some means of evaluating the product and its labeling claims.

QUALITY (NUTRITIONAL ADEQUACY)

The first step in evaluating a dog food is to read and understand the label. All pet-food labels must contain the product name, weight, manufacturer, the guaranteed analysis, a list of ingredients, a statement of nutritional purpose and adequacy, and the basis on which this latter claim is made. After determining the product is for dogs, the owner should determine if the product is complete and balanced and for which life stage the food is intended. This is found in the statement of nutritional adequacy and purpose and may read: "Complete and balanced nutrition for growth and maintenance of adult dogs." A diet so labeled would be intended to provide the sole nutrition for growing puppies and adult dogs, but *not* for pregnant or lactating bitches. How the manufacturer determined this nutritional claim should then be assessed. Claims based on "AAFCO feeding protocols" are considered superior to those based solely on a nutrient analysis stating that the diet "meets AAFCO nutrient profile recommendations." Feeding trials are more likely to detect nutrient imbalances or interactions that reduce the quality of a diet.

After determining that the correct product has been selected for a pet and appears to be nutritionally complete and balanced, an examination of the list of-ingredients will help determine the diet's quality. Ingredients in a product must be listed by order of weight on an "as is" basis. It is important to note that fresh meats (about 60% water) added "as is" at the top of an ingredient list may actually provide fewer nutrients than a meat meal (about 10% water) that is lower on the list. This is because fresh products, owing to their higher water content, are simply heavier than meal-form products. Generally speaking, meat, fish, and poultry meats and meals are good-quality ingredients and often are listed as one of the first few ingredients in a dog food. Meat or poultry bonemeal or by-products tend to be of lesser quality and are typically lower on an ingredient list. Cereal grains and soybean meal provide both energy and protein and are among the top ingredients in most foods. Cereal or plant middlings and hulls are of low nutrients value but may be added to increase fiber content. Vitamins, minerals and

---

Table 1
Dry-matter (DM) calculation for comparing diets

Step 1: Calculate the total percent dry matter (% DM) for the diet
total % DM = 100% - % moisture

Step 2: To estimate the carbohydrate content, subtract all listed nutrients from 100
% carbohydrate = 100 - (% moisture + % protein + % fat + % fiber + % ash)

Step 3: Calculate the % of each nutrient listed in the proximate analysis on a DM basis
% nutrient (DM) = (% nutrient ÷ total % DM) × 100

Example: Compare the nutrient content of a dry and canned diet using DM

Proximate Analysis

	Dry (as is)	*Canned* (as is)
Moisture	12%	78%
Crude protein	28%	8%
Crude fat	10%	4%
Crude fiber	5%	1%
Total	55%	91%
Total % DM:	100 – 12 = 88% DM	100 – 78 = 22% DM
% carbohydrate:	100 – 55 = 45%	100 – 91% = 9%

% Nutrient DM:

	Dry (dry matter)	*Canned* (dry matter)
Crude protein	28 ÷ 88 × 100 = 31.8%	8 ÷ 22 × 100 = 36.4%
Crude fat	10 ÷ 88 × 100 = 11.4%	4 ÷ 22 × 100 = 18.2%
Crude fiber	5 ÷ 88 × 100 = 5.7%	1 ÷ 22 × 100 = 4.5%
Carbohydrate	45 ÷ 88 × 100 = 51.1%	9 ÷ 22 × 100 = 40.1%

preservatives are added last because they are required in such small quantities.

When comparing diets for nutrient content, the **proximate analysis** is a useful measure. The proximate analysis includes the maximum moisture, maximum fiber, minimum crude protein, and minimum crude fat. The carbohydrate fraction is either listed as *nitrogen-free extract (NFE)* or can be determined by subtracting all the listed percentages from 100 (the remainder is predominately carbohydrate). A direct comparison between labels can be made if the moisture contents are the same. If not, these values must first be converted to *dry matter* for comparison (*see* TABLE 1). The dry matter in a diet is simply the percentage of available nutrients minus the water.

A diet comparison may also be made on a caloric (energy) basis. Diets higher in fat are generally higher in energy. Because dogs will consequently eat less of a high-energy diet, it must contain increased amounts of protein, vitamins and minerals, as compared to a lower-energy diet. The caloric content or **metabolic energy (ME)** of a diet can be included on the label at the manufacturer's discretion or can be roughly estimated from the proximate analysis by following the example in table 2.

FOOD STORAGE

Proper storage and handling of dog food helps assure that the maximal amount of nourishment will be obtained from the product. Commercial foods should be purchased and used promptly before their expiration date. Opened dry foods are generally good for 6 months if stored in a cool, dry place. Excessive heat and humidity destroys vitamins and fat and encourages mold growth. Unused portions of canned foods should be immediately refrigerated. Homemade diets can be made in large batches and frozen for later use. If immediately frozen, most diets can be stored for 2 or 3 months. Vitamin supplements should always be added after cooking. Warming refrigerated diets to room temperature or slightly above improves diet acceptance, but excessive heat should be avoided. If a microwave is used for heating, always stir the food well and check for hot spots.

Table 2
Estimation of the caloric content of dog foods

Step 1: Calculate the carbohydrate content (as is) as shown in table 1

Step 2: Calculate the caloric content using the values from the proximate analysis and the following factors for each nutrient
Crude protein $\times$ *3.5* = protein kcal per 100 grams
Crude Fat $\times$ *8.5* = fat kcal per 100 grams
Carbohydrate $\times$ *3.5* = carbohydrate kcal per 100 grams

Step 3: Added together the three values from Step 2 equal the total caloric content per 100 grams of diet

Step 4: Divide the total by 100 to determine kcal per gram of diet

Example:
% carbohydrate: 100 - 55 = 45%

Calculate caloric content of each nutrient:

	Dry (as is)	*Factor*	*Calories*
Crude Protein	28%	3.5	98.0
Crude Fat	10%	8.5	85.0
Carbohydrate	45%	3.5	157.5

Total kcal per 100 grams of dog food: 340.5
Total kcal per gram of dog food:
340.5 ÷ 100 = 3.4 kcal per gram

Guidelines for Feeding Dogs

The nutritional needs of dogs are affected by age (puppy, adult, senior), physiological status (pregnancy, lactation), level of activity, disease, and external factors such as ambient temperature or stress. The energy requirements of the adult dog at maintenance are often used as the standard, and the requirements for the other stages of life expressed as a multiple of the maintenance requirements (*see* TABLE 3). The variation in energy, protein and some mineral (calcium, phosphorous) requirements between maintenance and the other stages of life has been relatively well-established in dogs. Although age,

---

Table 3
Metabolic energy (ME) requirements of dogs

Maintenance energy requirements (MER)

Body weight *(lb)*	MER *(kcal)*	Factors to apply to MER to obtain daily energy requirements*
2	125	Adult maintenance = 1 × MER
4	205	Adult inactive = 0.8 × MER
6	280	Pregnancy: First 5 weeks = 1 × MER
8	345	—Last 4 weeks = 1.1–1.6 × MER
10	410	Lactation = 2 - 4 × MER
15	555	Growth: 0–50% adult body weight = 2–4 × MER
20	690	—50–80% adult body weight = 1.6 × MER
30	935	—80–100% adult body weight = 1.2 × MER
40	1160	Cold or hot = 1.25–2 × MER
50	1370	Work: Light = 1.1 × MER
75	1860	—Moderate = 1.4 × MER
100	2305	—Heavy = 2–4 × MER

(Source: Modified from Lewis, L.D., M.L. Morris & M.S. Hand, *Small Animal Clinical Nutrition III* (1987), Mark Morris Associates, Topeka, KS.)

*Multiply MER by the appropriate factor to obtain the approximate daily energy requirements for a given situation. These amounts represent a guideline only. For long-term feeding, adjust the amount fed to maintain optimal body weight.

---

physiological status, work levels, and disease probably also affect the requirements of the other minerals and vitamins, little information is available to make accurate recommendations.

ADULT MAINTENANCE REQUIREMENTS

The **maintenance energy requirement (MER),** or the amount of energy required by a moderately active adult dog in a thermoneutral environment (optimal ambient temperature), have been described in chapter 8, "Canine Nutritional Requirements" (*see* TABLE 1). It is important to remember that there is a great deal of variability among individual dogs with regard to energy requirements (up to 25% above or below MER). Therefore, the actual amount of food provided should be adjusted to body condition (*see* CHAPTER 10, "DISEASES OF DIETARY ORIGIN"). The recommended energy densities and concentrations of protein, fat, and fibers in diets for maintenance vary widely and are summarized in table 4. Diets formulated for puppies or lactating bitches will fulfill all the dietary needs of adult, nonpregnant, nonlactating dogs, but their higher energy density may cause excess energy intake and obesity in this latter category of animals. Such diets are also more expensive. Outdoor dogs require additional energy (and therefore food) to maintain body temperature when the ambient temperatures are low (below 45° F) or high (above 85° F) (*see* TABLE 3).

The best criteria for judging the adequacy of a feeding regimen in an adult dog are haircoat and skin condition and maintenance of optimal body weight (*see* CHAPTER 10, "DISEASES OF DIETARY ORIGIN"). If ideal body weight is exceeded when feeding standard maintenance diets, a nutritionally complete low-energy diet ("Lite diet") should be considered as an alternative. When the amount of feces produced is of concern (indoor dogs), diets with higher digestibility, such as premium or puppy diets, are recommended. Most adult dogs can fulfill their nutritional requirements eating one meal per day. In more active dogs or in large-breed dogs that are predisposed to bloat, two or three smaller meals per day are more appropriate.

PREGNANCY AND LACTATION

Ensuring the best possible start in life for puppies begins with proper nutrition of pregnant and lactating bitches. Two-thirds of the fetal growth of pups occurs during the final three weeks of **gestation** (pregnancy). Consequently, energy and nutrient requirements increase substantially above maintenance only after the fifth week of pregnancy. It is generally recommended that the bitch's energy intake be increased by 10–15% per week, beginning at week 5 or 6 of gestation, in order to provide 150–160% of MER by the time the pups are born (*see* TABLE 3). Although a maintenance diet would fulfill all the nutrient requirements during the first six weeks of gestation, it is a good idea to introduce the high-energy diet early so that the digestive tract has plenty of time to adapt to the change. Diets recommended for late gestation and lactation are more digestible and contain higher levels of protein and energy (i.e., more fat and less fiber)

(*see* TABLE 4). Bitches should be fed once or twice a day early in gestation, increasing to three to four times a day by late gestation.

Pregnant bitches must consume large amounts of nutrients to produce sufficient milk of adequate composition to support the growth of their puppies. At peak lactation (3 to 6 weeks after **whelping** [giving birth]) energy requirements can be as high as two to four times MER, depending on the size of the litter (*see* TABLE 3). Practically, this means that bitches should be allowed to eat as much as they want of a diet formulated for lactation and growth (*see* TABLE 4). To allow for adequate food intake, feedings should be divided into at least four meals. Mixing canned food and dry food may also enhance food intake.

Milk production requires calcium. In small breeds, seizures associated with depletion of blood calcium (**eclampsia,** or **puerperal tetany**) are not uncommon soon after whelping (*see* CHAPTER 14, "REPRODUCTIVE DISORDERS"). However, adding calcium to a complete and balanced diet during pregnancy will not prevent eclampsia; thus calcium supplements are not routinely recommended during gestation. If a diet devoid of carbohydrates is fed to bitches in gestation or

Table 4
Diet characteristics recommended for dog foods

	Minimum Metabolizable Energy Density* (kcal/100g)	Minimum Digestibility %	Nutrients in diet dry matter**		
			Protein %	Fat %	Fiber %
Maintenance	350***	75	15–34	8–30	5–10***
Growth/pregnancy/lactation	390	80	29–35	12–30	0–5
Old age	375***	80	14–21	10–15	5–10***
Work/stress	420	80	25–42	20–30	0–3

(Source: Modified from Lewis, L.D., M.L. Morris & M.S. Hand, *Small Animal Clinical Nutrition III,* (1987) Mark Morris Associates, Topeka, KS.)

*Minimum metabolizable energy of food per 100 grams (3 1/2 oz) of dry matter.

**Dry matter is what remains of the food after the water contained in that food has been evaporated.

***Obesity-prone dogs may be fed a diet lower in energy density and higher in fiber.

lactation, the amount of dietary protein should be high enough to allow for sufficient glucose (blood sugar) and lactose (milk sugar) production to meet the needs of the growing puppies (*see* Chapter 8, "Canine Nutritional Requirements").

Puppies and Growing Dogs

For the first several weeks of a puppy's life the bitch's milk is its sole source of nutrients. Within the first 1 or 2 days, the milk contains antibodies that provide some protection against infectious diseases (*See* Chapter 33, "The Immune System and Disorders"). Puppies should be encouraged to take small but increasingly larger amounts of solid food as early as 3 to 4 weeks after whelping (the same diet offered to the bitch can be used). Initially, water is added to form a liquid slurry and then reduced to increase the consistency. Puppies can be fully weaned onto a highly digestible, energy- and nutrient-dense diet (*see* Table 3) between 6 and 8 weeks of age. When a new puppy is acquired, it is important to avoid rapid dietary changes; instead, the old diet should *gradually* be replaced with the new one.

Energy (two to four times MER) and nutrient requirements are greatest between weaning and the time dogs reach 50% of their adult body weight (about 3 to 5 months of age for most breeds). Energy requirements then decrease to about 1.6 times MER until 80% of the adult body weight has been achieved. Finally, about 1.2 times MER is recommended until growing dogs reach adult body weight. Adult body weight can be determined by comparison to the parents' weight or to breed standards.

Daily energy intake should be divided into four daily meals just after weaning, with the frequency reduced to one or two daily meals by adulthood. Excessive energy and nutrient intake during growth promotes obesity and in larger breeds may impair skeletal development (*see* Chapter 10, "Diseases of Dietary Origin"). Free-choice feeding thus is not recommended for puppies; rather, food quantities should be adjusted to maintain a steady growth rate and proper body condition. Diets formulated for growth will fulfill all the requirements of adult dogs. A change to a maintenance diet should be considered if a dog has a tendency toward obe-

sity or in order to reduce feeding costs. Complete and balanced diets for growth should *not* be supplemented with minerals and vitamins. (*See* Chapter 8, "Canine Nutritional Requirements," and Chapter 10, "Diseases of Dietary Origin.")

Working Dogs

Working dogs are assigned many different tasks, from showing and guarding to pulling sledges in subfreezing conditions. For these reasons their energy requirements vary widely, from 1.1 to 4 times MER (*see* Table 3). Psychological stresses, as endured by sentry or show dogs, have been reported to increase energy requirements by as much as 40%. To allow working dogs to ingest such large amounts of energy, as well as overcome the appetite suppression common in stressed animals, highly palatable, highly digestible, high-energy (high fat, reduced carbohydrate, low fiber), high-protein balanced diets have been recommended (*see* Table 4). Very little is known about the vitamin and mineral requirements of hardworking dogs. Supplementation with iron, vitamin C, and vitamin E has been suggested, but the benefits of such a practice have not been demonstrated.

Hypoglycemia (abnormally low levels of blood glucose) can result in weakness, collapse and seizures. This is sometimes observed in hunting dogs at the beginning of the season ("hunting-dog hypoglycemia"), and is primarily the result of poor conditioning and poor nutrition. Hunting dogs should be fed stress/working diets for 1 to 3 weeks before conditioning, and conditioned for at least 3 weeks before hunting.

Geriatric Dogs

The average life span of dogs is largely a function of breed. Small and medium-sized dogs have a longer life expectancy than larger breeds (*see* Chapter 5, "Geriatrics"). Little is known about the dietary needs of older dogs. The recommendations are mostly based on studies in human beings. It is assumed that older dogs, like older people, tend to become overweight and have reduced kidney and heart function. For these reasons, diets formulated for older dogs generally contain fewer calories (less fat, more fiber), moderately restricted levels of high-quality protein (*see* CHAPTER 8, "CANINE NUTRITIONAL REQUIREMENTS"), moderately restricted phosphorus and sodium concentrations, and increased amounts of the B vitamins. The benefits of such dietary modifications for prolonging life span and reducing aging-related organ damage are highly controversial, however. Scientific studies to confirm or refute the validity of these modifications are not available. As a general rule, such diets are not recommended for older animals that are thin, because of the food's low energy density.

Feeding Management

OVERFEEDING

Overfeeding occurs when an owner feeds too much of a food or feeds a high-energy food to a dog with low-energy needs. Overfeeding is thus a common cause of obesity. (*See* CHAPTER 5, "GERIATRICS," and CHAPTER 10, "DISEASES OF DIETARY ORIGIN.")

INAPPETENT DOGS

Although it is uncommon, some dogs may refuse to eat a new diet, particularly if it is less palatable than the old diet. This problem may be avoided by introducing the new diet progressively. Sick and debilitated animals often lose their appetite and refuse to eat. They may be encouraged to eat with tender loving care, hand-feeding, and by increasing the palatability of the diet that is offered. Palatability can be improved by increasing the protein and/or fat content of the diet, warming the food, and increasing the water content either by directly adding water to make a slurry or by purchasing a product high in moisture, such as a canned food. If a dog refuses to eat for more than a few days, the veterinarian may recommend force-feeding. When and how to force-feed should be left to the discretion of a veterinarian. Usually, food is made into a paste and fed into the dog's mouth through a syringe.

CHANGING DIETS

Any change in a dog's diet should take place gradually over a 4- to 7-day period. The sudden introduction of a new food can cause abdominal discomfort, vomiting or diarrhea. A new diet can be introduced by replacing ¼ of the old diet with the new one on day 1; ½ on day 2; ¾ on day 3; and then feeding the new diet exclusively by day 4. If a dog is particularly food-sensitive, or if the new diet is considerably different from the old (i.e., a low-fat diet changed to a high-fat diet), these changes should take place more gradually. This method allows the intestinal enzymes and microorganisms time to adapt to the new diet. The practice of fasting dogs the day before a rapid diet switch does *not* promote intestinal adaptation to a new diet.

DISEASE MANAGEMENT

Some disease conditions (e.g., certain kidney, liver and intestinal disorders) can be managed through the use of specialized diets designed to reduce or correct altered metabolism or metabolic waste products. These specialized or *therapeutic diets* should be used under the direction of a veterinarian and must be tailored to an individual dog's needs. (Nutritional management of disease is discussed in the individual chapters dealing with the specific body systems.)

SUPPLEMENTS

Dogs fed commercial dog foods that are complete and balanced do not require any additional vitamin or mineral supplementation. Supplements, when given in excessive quantities, can inhibit the absorption and availability of other nutrients and produce toxicities (*see* CHAPTER 10, "DISEASES OF DIETARY ORIGIN"). Exceptions include dogs with specific medical disorders and, possibly, hard-working dogs such as sledge dogs. Dogs fed homemade diets should have a balanced supplement added to the diet or given to them directly. This type of supplementation should be tailored to the diet recipe.

Commercial diets have sufficient quantities of vitamins and minerals to maintain nutritional quality if moderately supplemented. However, supplementing commercial diets with treats or table foods should not exceed 10% of the daily intake. This rule of thumb applies as well to supplementation with other dietary components, such as fresh organ or muscle meat. Feeding uncooked, fresh meat is *not* recommended, for both nutritional and health reasons. Typical commercial dog foods more than meet dogs' daily requirements for protein. Added dietary protein does not promote increased muscle growth, but instead is used by the body as an expensive energy source or is stored as fat. In addition, raw meat sometimes contains parasites or harmful bacteria, which are readily destroyed by cooking.

A variety of other supplements are commonly given by well-intentioned owners. Foods and spices such as garlic, parsley, bee pollen and brewer's yeast rarely cause harm, but do little to improve the nutritional status of a dog. Such supplements often are spin-offs of current fads in human nutrition.

PRESERVATIVES AND FOOD ADDITIVES

Many owners are concerned about preservatives and other food additives in their dogs' diets. To date much of this concern has been unfounded. Nevertheless, several manufacturers have succumbed to public pressure and are marketing diets that contain "natural" preservatives and are free of additives. Preservatives are added primarily to dry and semimoist foods to prevent the destruction of vitamins and fats when exposed to oxygen (i.e., they act as *antioxidants*). Without preservatives, the nutritional quality of a food can be severely compromised during storage. The most common chemical preservatives are butylated hydroxytoluene (BHT) and ethoxyquin. Vitamins C and E and beta-carotene also have antioxidant functions and have been called "natural" preservatives. The benefits and drawbacks of preservatives remain areas of hot debate in both human and pet nutrition. Although well-controlled studies have failed to show any detrimental effects of chemical preservatives, concerned pet owners today have the option of feeding canned diets that tend to be preservative-free.

Food additives include dyes, color stabilizers, humectants (moistening agents), gums and gels. Their purpose is to enhance the aesthetic quality of a diet or to act as a preservative (in the case of humectants). They are generally considered safe, although some animals may exhibit dietary intolerance to such ingredients.

CHAPTER 10

Diseases of Dietary Origin

by Claudia A. Kirk
and Vincent C. Biourge

Our understanding of the impact of nutrition on health and disease in dogs has expanded considerably over the last decade. Diseases resulting from nutritional deficiencies are unusual now in dogs fed appropriate amounts of complete and balanced commercial pet foods (*see* CHAPTER 8, "CANINE NUTRITIONAL REQUIREMENTS" and CHAPTER 9, "FEEDING DOGS"). However, diseases of dietary origin still occur because dietary excesses and imbalances can be as detrimental as deficiencies. This chapter will discuss diseases resulting from imbalanced diets, incomplete homemade diets and improper feeding methods. It will also cover some of the more common disorders that are diet-related but not caused by diet alone.

Obesity

Recent information indicates that 25–44% of pet dogs in the United States are overweight, making obesity the most important nutritional disease of dogs. A dog is considered obese when its body weight exceeds 20% of the ideal for its age, sex and breed. Although obesity alone may not signif-

icantly shorten a dog's life span, it does increase the risk of developing certain diseases that can impair the quality of life. Obesity has been shown to increase the risk of diabetes mellitus, infections, cancer, and skin disease. It may also be associated with an increased incidence of **hypertension** (elevated blood pressure) and orthopedic, neurologic, cardiac, and reproductive disorders. Thus, maintaining a dog's optimal body weight will enhance its overall health and well-being.

CAUSES OF OBESITY

Simply stated, obesity is caused by excess energy intake (too many calories) or decreased energy output (too little exercise), or a combination of the two. The excess energy is stored in the body as fat. Obesity is sometimes found in neutered, female and older dogs due to the decreased physical activity observed among these dogs. Other dietary factors contributing to the high incidence of obesity include highly palatable (i.e., flavorful) commercial diets or table foods, which promote overconsumption of calories, and high-fat diets, which, bite-for-bite, are more calorie-packed than are low-fat diets.

A hormonal disturbance such as **hypothyroidism** (decreased thyroid gland activity) can promote obesity by reducing the body's basal metabolic rate, thereby decreasing energy needs. Although hypothyroidism is common in dogs, most obese dogs are not hypothyroid. (*See* Chapter 32, "The Endocrine System and Metabolic Disorders.")

Signs of Obesity

The onset of obesity may go unnoticed by owners, particularly when longhaired dogs are involved. Objective methods for determining an "ideal" body weight or measuring obesity in dogs are either unavailable, expensive or unproven. Thus, both owners and veterinarians must rely on a more subjective "look and feel" technique to determine the body condition of a dog.

A dog is considered to be at its ideal weight if the ribs can easily be palpated (felt) as the hands are swept over the chest. The chest, abdomen ("waist") and hips should form an "hourglass" shape when viewed from above. If pressure must be used to feel the ribs beneath a layer of **subcutaneous** (beneath the skin) fat and the "waist" is absent, the dog is likely obese. Other signs of obesity include:

- a broadened face, neck and shoulders
- accumulation of fat over the hips and at the base of the tail
- a shortened stride or "waddle"
- lethargy
- reduced exercise capacity
- respiratory noise or effort

It is important to remember that many of these signs may be caused by other conditions or diseases (e.g., pregnancy, heart disease, hormonal imbalances, etc.). Obese dogs thus should be evaluated by a veterinarian prior to initiation of a weight-reduction or exercise program, in order to rule out the possibility of an underlying physiological abnormality.

Weight Management

The best way to manage obesity is by preventing it. By providing plenty of exercise, feeding a moderate- to low-fat, moderately palatable diet, and not feeding table foods or scraps (which typically are high in fat and calories), many cases of obesity can be avoided. Because obesity is caused by the chronic consumption of more calories than are needed to meet daily requirements, one has only to decrease the caloric intake or increase the energy expenditure of a dog to achieve weight loss. While this is easy in principle, it is difficult in practice for most pet owners.

Increasing Energy Expenditure

Increasing energy expenditure is most easily accomplished by increasing a dog's level of exercise. A brisk daily walk is a good start. The exercise level should be gradually increased over time, since vigorous exercise may add excessive strain to bones, joints and ligaments, leading to injury.

Certain medications may increase energy expenditure. The adrenal gland hormone dihydroepiandrosterone (DHEA) has been evaluated in dogs, with some success reported. Unfortunately, a few dogs experienced side effects, and until further studies can prove safety and efficacy the use of this medication is not advised. Thyroid-hormone replacement therapy commonly increases energy expenditure and often results in weight loss. However, its use should be confined to dogs diagnosed as hypothyroid; general use may lead to thyroid gland suppression and cardiac abnormalities.

To lose 1 pound of fat, 3500 kilocalories beyond that required for body maintenance must be expended. This is roughly the equivalent of 7 cans (15 oz.) of canned dog food or ten cups of dry food. For most dogs, exercise combined with reduced caloric intake will be required for satisfactory weight loss.

Reducing Caloric Intake

Reduction of caloric intake can be accomplished by any of the following methods:

- feeding smaller quantities of the normal diet
- feeding a reduced-calorie diet (usually a low-fat, high-fiber reducing diet)
- feeding a diet with low palatability

Feeding smaller quantities of the normal diet often leads to begging or restlessness between meals. These behaviors can be reduced by feeding smaller meals more frequently or by using reducing diets. Reducing diets are advantageous in that the bulk of the food has not been reduced, giving owners and dogs the perception that a full meal has been fed. Further, the high-fiber content reduces the digestible energy of the diet, so that fewer calories are eaten as well as absorbed. Feeding low-palatability diets may help some dogs voluntarily reduce food intake. This method is probably less successful than close regulation of food intake.

"Starvation diets" (total food deprivation) have also been used for achieving rapid weight loss in dogs. Unlike cats, dogs do not appear to suffer any significant metabolic derangements from this approach. During starvation, the dog's metabolism becomes extremely efficient. When the dog is refed, however, this metabolic efficiency will increase the risk of becoming obese once again. Because of this, and also for humane reasons, a more moderate approach to weight loss is advisable. Food deprivation should be reserved for extreme cases when rapid weight loss is essential.

The overall goal is to reduce a dog's caloric intake to 60–70% of the requirement for its estimated ideal body weight. Table 1 illustrates how to calculate the caloric requirement for weight loss and the estimated rate of loss. If the rate of weight loss is significantly faster or slower than desired, caloric intake should be adjusted accordingly. Food acquired from other sources (neighbors, children, etc.) should be considered if weight loss remains sluggish. Food treats and table scraps add unwanted calories to the diet of obese dogs and should not be fed. To avoid temptation on the part of both dogs and owners, "dieting" dogs should not be allowed in the kitchen or dining area during food preparation or meals. If the pet owner cannot refrain from feeding treats to an obese pet, low-calorie alternatives such as rice cakes or small slices of raw carrots can be substituted for the usual snacks.

Diarrhea

Diarrhea is a common disorder in dogs. It may be caused by parasites, metabolic or infectious

---

Table 1
How to calculate the caloric requirement for weight loss and to estimate the rate of loss

To calculate the caloric requirement for weight loss:

Step 1: Convert the desired body weight to kilograms (kg):
1 lb = 0.453 kilograms
Example: 22 lbs × 0.453 = 10 kg

Step 2: Calculate the estimated caloric requirement at the desired weight:
Estimated caloric requirement in kilocalories (kcal) = 132 × (body weight in kg)$^{0.75}$
Example: $132 \times 10^{0.75} = 742$ kcal

Step 3: Determine the number of calories to feed for weight loss (60 or 70% of the value for step 2):
Multiply caloric requirement from step 2 × 0.60 (or 0.70) = kcal to feed per day
Example: 742 × 0.60 = 445 kcal per day

Step 4: Once the desired weight has been achieved, gradually increase the number of calories to the amount calculated in step 2.

To determine the estimated rate of weight loss:

Step 5: Determine daily caloric deficit:
Value from step 2 - value from step 3 = kcal deficit
Example: 742 kcal - 445 kcal = 297 kcal deficit

Step 6: Divide 3500 by the daily deficit to determine the number of days needed to lose 1 pound:
Example: 3500 ÷ 297 = 11.8 days required to lose 1 pound

---

diseases, toxicities, diet or feeding practices. Dogs with diarrhea should be examined by a veterinarian. If parasites, toxins and disease have been eliminated as causes of the diarrhea and the dog seems otherwise healthy, dietary factors are likely to be involved. A common dietary cause of diarrhea is "dietary indiscretion"; that is, when a dog eats scraps, spoiled food, or nonfood items from the garbage or environment, or consumes an unusually large quantity of its normal diet. Most cases resolve without treatment in 1–2 days. More severe cases may require bowel rest or temporary institution of a bland diet (*see* CHAPTER 30, "THE DIGESTIVE SYSTEM AND DISORDERS").

Sudden dietary changes or refeeding after prolonged inappetence may lead to diarrhea. Dietary changes should always be made gradually, so that the digestive enzymes may adapt and to avoid sudden shifts in the composition of the microbial population of the intestine. Changing the diet is best accomplished by adding increasing amounts of the new food to the old diet over 4 to 7 days (*see* CHAPTER 9, "FEEDING DOGS"). Feeding smaller meals more frequently allows the digestive enzymes and intestinal microorganisms to adjust to a new food more easily. When refeeding dogs that have been inappetent, small frequent meals as well as a bland diet may be necessary.

Dental Disease

Wild dogs often eat foods that are hard (bones) or fibrous. This provides a natural abrasive action for the gums and teeth, reducing plaque and calculus buildup and subsequent dental disease. Although feeding bones is not advocated, hard biscuits, chews, or diets that mimic this abrasive action can be beneficial for dental health. Canned and semimoist diets lack abrasive action and, depending on the sugar content, may promote dental disease. For further information on dental disease and its prevention, *see* CHAPTER 21, "CANINE DENTISTRY."

Skin Disease (Dermatoses)

Many nutritional deficiencies are known to cause skin and haircoat disorders in dogs. However, deficiencies in **essential fatty acids** (**EFA;** i.e., linoleic acid and arachidonic acid) and zinc are the only ones commonly recognized. Less common causes are protein, vitamin E, vitamin A, biotin and copper deficiencies. Nutritional deficiencies are difficult to diagnose because different deficiencies can cause similar clinical signs and specific diagnostic tests are not easily performed. The most common signs are a dull, dry, brittle coat and hair loss. The skin often becomes flaky, greasy and sometimes thickened in areas such as the nose and foot pads. Hair **depigmentation** (fading of the coat color) is seen with protein or copper deficiencies. As the normal architecture and protective function of the skin is compromised, bacterial infections become more common and intense **pruritus** (itching) may be evident.

EFA DEFICIENCY
EFA deficiency may be seen when feeding a diet that is of poor quality, has been inadequately stored, is severely fat-restricted, or lacks adequate fat stabilization with antioxidants such as vitamin E or ethoxyguin. Changing to a higher-quality or higher-fat diet will usually improve the condition within a few weeks.

ZINC DEFICIENCY
Zinc deficiency has been described in dogs fed poor-quality or generic diets or oversupplemented with minerals, and has also been reported as a specific problem in the Siberian Husky, Alaskan Malamute and Bull Terrier breeds. Excessive amounts of **phytates** (a form of inositol [a sugarlike compound] found in plants) in the diet and iron, copper or calcium supplementation will interfere with zinc absorption. This is an excellent example of how the balance of the different nutrients in a diet can be equally as important as meeting minimum requirements, and why supplements should not be given indiscriminately. When zinc deficiency is caused by a dietary deficiency or imbalance, a change in diet and short-term zinc supplementation will result in rapid improvement. Zinc deficiency associated with specific breeds is more likely a zinc-absorption defect and may require lifelong zinc supplementation under veterinary supervision.

VITAMIN A DEFICIENCY
Vitamin A deficiency (or excess) can cause an abnormal thickening of the skin. Some skin diseases in dogs and people have responded well to treatment with vitamin A–like substances. This response is most likely due to the druglike effect of these substances, and is not evidence of a dietary deficiency in vitamin A. Vitamin A can be highly toxic when oversupplemented (*see* below) and should be given to pets only on the advice of a veterinarian.

BIOTIN DEFICIENCY

Biotin deficiency has been produced by feeding large amounts of uncooked egg white, which contains a heat-sensitive inhibitor of biotin absorption called **avidin.** (This fact, as well as concerns over contamination of eggs by *Salmonella* bacteria, should prompt owners to cook all eggs fed to dogs.) Biotin deficiency is very uncommon in dogs fed properly stored, good-quality commercial pet foods. If a nutritional deficiency is suspected, the diet brand, its nutrient profile and list of supplements, and storage procedures should all be evaluated.

Skeletal Diseases

Certain skeletal disorders may be caused by nutritional deficiencies, excesses and imbalances. Nutritional deficiencies are rare when feeding commercial diets. Nutritional excesses and imbalances are common, however, particularly when diets are supplemented with large amounts of meat, vitamins and minerals. In adult dogs, skeletal diseases of nutritional origin usually respond well to dietary changes. In growing puppies, however, skeletal abnormalities can result in permanent impairment and may require both dietary management and surgical correction.

RICKETS AND OSTEOMALACIA

Rickets and **osteomalacia** are consequences of a vitamin D deficiency. Dogs appear unable to synthesize vitamin D through the action of sunlight and thus require vitamin D in the diet. Vitamin D deficiency in young dogs (rickets) results in joint enlargement, bone fractures, bowed legs, and abnormal jaw formation and tooth eruption. Deficiency in adult dogs (osteomalacia) is characterized by bone pain and tenderness, and fractures in severe cases. Vitamin D is widely distributed in most foods. However, deficiencies may occur in poorly formulated homemade or high-cereal grain diets.

NUTRITIONAL SECONDARY HYPERPARATHYROIDISM

Nutritional secondary hyperparathyroidism is the result of a calcium deficiency, a marked imbalance in the ratio of calcium to phosphorus in the diet, or a combination of both. The parathyroid glands will compensate for low or imbalanced blood calcium levels by increasing the release of parathyroid hormone, which draws calcium out of the bones. This results in bone thinning and clinical signs similar to vitamin D deficiency. In severe cases **tetany** (seizure-like tremors) may occur if the blood calcium level falls too low. Typically, nutritional secondary hyperthyroidism is seen in animals fed high- or all-meat diets or improperly formulated homemade diets. Treatment entails a change to a complete and balanced diet. Calcium supplements are rarely needed except with tetany, which constitutes a medical emergency.

DEVELOPMENTAL DISORDERS

Developmental disorders of the skeleton include **osteochondrosis dissecans** (OCD; bone degeneration in joints), hip dysplasia, osteochondritis (disturbed cartilage growth), cervical vertebral malformation, angular limb deformities, and retained cartilage cores. Such disorders are most often seen in large- and giant-breed dogs that undergo rapid growth. Nutritional, environmental and genetic factors all contribute to these problems. The nutritional factor is one of excess (overconsumption and oversupplementation), particularly during the first 6 months of life. There is no evidence that vitamin C deficiency is responsible for any of these disorders. (*See* CHAPTER 26, "THE SKELETON AND DISORDERS.")

Overconsumption occurs by overfeeding a regular diet or feeding a high-energy diet. These feeding practices promote such rapid growth that normal cartilage and bone development cannot keep pace. High-protein diets have been associated with developmental bone disorders because they provide increased energy intake and not because the protein level in the diet causes disease. Excess protein does not make more bone or muscle; it makes more energy. Overconsumption of food and rapid growth thus should be avoided in the large and gaint breeds. Food intake may need to be restricted or lower-energy diets provided to achieve a steady but moderate rate of growth. (*See* CHAPTER 9, "FEEDING DOGS.")

Oversupplementation occurs when mineral preparations or supplements are added to a complete and balanced diet. High dietary calcium has been shown to increase the occurrence of certain developmental skeletal disorders. Excess dietary calcium increases calcium absorption across the intestinal tract and into the blood. In response the thyroid gland releases **calcitonin,** a calcium-regulating hormone that acts to balance the activities of parathyroid hormone. The increase in calcitonin levels in young growing dogs stimulates rapid calcium uptake into the developing bone and cartilage, resulting in growth abnormalities. Most commercial dog foods contain surfeit amounts of calcium and phosphorus; mineral supplements thus are unnecessary. In general, growing dogs fed commercial dog rations and supplemented with calcium or mineral preparations will be oversupplemented. Owners concerned about the quality of their pet's diet should feed higher-quality diets instead of adding vitamin or mineral supplements indiscriminately.

A new area of research in this area has focused on the association of development skeletal disorders and the **dietary anion gap,** the balance of negatively and positively charged particles in the diet. The results to date have suggested an association, but remain too preliminary to allow any meaningful nutritional recommendation.

Vitamin Toxicities and Deficiencies

Vitamin toxicities typically occur when commercial rations are supplemented with additional vitamin preparations. Vitamin A and D toxicities are the most common because these vitamins are fat-soluble and are stored in the body. (*See* CHAPTER 8, "CANINE NUTRITIONAL REQUIREMENTS.") When given in excess the normal elimination pathways are overwhelmed and toxic effects result. Toxicities of water-soluble vitamins can occur, but are rare unless the vitamins are given in megadoses. Deficiencies are most often detected in dogs fed homemade diets that have been inadequately formulated or prepared.

VITAMIN A TOXICITY

Vitamin A toxicity can occur when very large amounts of liver, cod liver oil or vitamin A sup-

plements are added to the diet. It is most often seen in conjunction with vitamin D toxicity because many nutritional supplements contain both vitamins. Early clinical signs of vitamin A toxicity include inappetence, lethargy, weight loss, skin sensitivity, and bone and joint pain. In chronic toxicities bulging eyes, bone defects, skin thickening and degenerative changes in blood vessels may occur. During pregnancy, excessive vitamin A can cause deformations in the developing fetuses. Treatment of vitamin A toxicity consists of removing the source of vitamin A excess.

VITAMIN D TOXICITY

Vitamin D toxicity leads to increased dietary calcium uptake and increased levels of calcium in the blood. The excess calcium is deposited in various organs and soft tissues as the body's regulatory mechanisms attempt to lower blood calcium levels. Common areas of abnormal calcium deposition (calcification) include the kidneys, lungs and gastrointestinal tract. Extensive calcification can result in specific organ failure or formation of kidney stones. Early clinical signs are nonspecific and include inappetence, lethargy, weakness and sometimes diarrhea. Later signs are usually related to specific organ failure. Vitamin D toxicity is most often caused by excessive vitamin D supplementation. However, dogs ingesting rat bait containing cholecalciferol (a vitamin D precursor) have experienced sudden and severe vitamin D toxicosis. Treatment of vitamin D toxicity entails removing the excess source of vitamin D, lowering blood calcium levels by the use of various medications, and managing any evident organ dysfunction. The prognosis is guarded, however, once organ failure has occurred.

VITAMIN B12 DEFICIENCY

Vitamin B12 deficiency has been reported in dogs with severe intestinal and pancreatic disease. Strict vegetarian diets are deficient in vitamin B12 and have the potential to cause a deficiency. However, vitamin B12 deficiency resulting from the feeding of a vegetarian diet to dogs has not been reported to date. This may reflect a very low vitamin B12 requirement in the dog, or appropriate supplementation of vegetarian diets by owners aware of the potential for deficiency. A deficiency of vitamin B12 causes an **anemia** (low red blood cell count) that responds readily to vitamin B12 injections.

Diet-Related Diseases

Diet-related diseases are not nutritional diseases, but are diseases strongly influenced by the type of diet, dietary ingredients or particular feeding practices. Nutritional management often controls their occurrence or severity. These diseases are briefly mentioned here because of their common occurrence and the fact that veterinary nutritionists are frequently consulted regarding their management.

DIETARY INTOLERANCE AND FOOD ALLERGIES

Dietary intolerance and food allergies occur when the immune system becomes sensitized to various ingredients present in the diet. Most often the immune reactions are directed against a protein component of the diet. However, sensitivities to other food components (preservatives, dyes) have also been reported. Clinical signs usually involve the gastrointestinal tract or skin. (*See* CHAPTER 22, "THE SKIN AND DISORDERS"; CHAPTER 30, "THE DIGESTIVE SYSTEM AND DISORDERS"; and CHAPTER 33, "THE IMMUNE SYSTEM AND DISORDERS.") Typical gastrointestinal signs include vomiting, gas buildup, abdominal discomfort and diarrhea. Skin manifestations can include reddened, irritated skin and severe itching.

Diagnosis most often entails removal of the suspected offending food and subsequent monitoring of the patient for improvement. This is done by feeding novel diets that use a single protein and starch source. Such diets are often referred to as "**hypoallergenic**" diets. (This is really a misnomer, since it implies that other diets cause allergies. "Hypoallergenic" diets are simply limited-ingredient diets that use novel proteins.) Following an improvement in signs, the food suspected of causing the sensitivity is reintroduced to confirm its effect. Once the offending ingredients have been identified they are eliminated from the diet. This may require feeding the dog a specially formulated or home-made diet. (*See* CHAPTER 30, "THE DIGESTIVE SYSTEM AND DISORDERS.")

GASTRIC DILATATION-VOLVULUS

Gastric dilatation-volvulus (GDV), commonly known as **bloat** or gastric torsion, is a life-threatening condition most often seen in large- and giant-breed dogs. In this disease the stomach twists around until it cannot empty, trapping fluid and gas within it. The underlying causes are not completely understood; however, feeding practices may influence its occurrence. Episodes have been associated with heavy exercise following the consumption of a large meal. In general, dogs should not be allowed to consume mass quantities of food and/or water before or following exercise. In dogs predisposed to GDV, smaller meals should be fed three to four times a day, instead of the usual one or two large meals. If dry kibble is fed, soaking it with water prior to feeding may help reduce a dog's overall food intake and avoid consumption of large quantities of water after feeding. (*See* CHAPTER 30, "THE DIGESTIVE SYSTEM AND DISORDERS" and CHAPTER 40, "SURGERY AND POSTOPERATIVE CARE.")

PANCREATITIS

Inflammation of the pancreas appears to result from a variety of factors. Nutritional factors are thought to be important because pancreatitis is often seen in middle-aged or older, obese dogs following consumption of a fatty meal. Signs of pancreatitis include inappetence, lethargy, vomiting, diarrhea, abdominal pain and fever. Severe or untreated cases can lead to shock and death. Treatment of mild cases consists of avoiding stomach distention and pancreatic enzyme secretion by withholding food and water for 2–5 days, while supporting the dog with intravenous fluid therapy. When feeding is resumed, small, frequent amounts of a bland, low-fat diet should be offered. Once recovery is complete, the low-fat diet should be continued on a normal feeding schedule. More severe cases with particular complications will require correspondingly intensive treatment. Dietary management of pancreatitis should always be conducted under a veterinarian's supervision. (*See* CHAPTER 31, "THE LIVER, PANCREAS AND DISORDERS.")

CARNITINE CARDIOMYOPATHY

Carnitine cardiomyopathy has been reported in Boxers and some large-breed dogs. **Carnitine** is an amino acid that carries fatty acids into the cellular **mitochondria** (specialized structures within body cells that are responsible for producing energy) where they can be used to make energy (in the form of **adenosine triphosphate, or ATP**). When ATP levels are low the heart cannot effectively contract and relax, a situation leading to heart failure.

The dog is able to synthesize carnitine in the liver and a dietary requirement has not been demonstrated. Carnitine cardiomyopathy is therefore not a true nutritional deficiency, but instead appears to be an inherited metabolic defect. Affected dogs have low levels of carnitine in the blood and/or heart muscle, owing to their inability to absorb, manufacture or conserve carnitine. Carnitine supplementation may improve cardiac function in these cases, but will not affect cardiomyopathies arising from other causes. (*See* CHAPTER 24, "THE CIRCULATORY SYSTEM AND DISORDERS.")

PART IV

Reproduction

Then in late summer a new rival appeared—
to be accurate, three rivals. And they took
up all of Lady's time and thought and love.
Poor old Lad was made to feel terribly out in
the cold. The trio of rivals that had so suddenly claimed Lady's care were fuzzy and
roly-poly, and about the size of month-old
kittens. In brief, they were three thorough-
bred collie puppies.

—ALBERT PAYSON TERHUNE
Lad: A Dog

CHAPTER 11

Normal Reproduction

**by Edward C. Feldman
and Richard W. Nelson**

The Normal Female

The reproductive system of the bitch consists primarily of the **vulva** (the external genitalia), **clitoris, vagina, cervix** (lower portion of the uterus), **uterus,** the paired **uterine horns,** the paired uterine or **fallopian tubes** (also called **oviducts**), the paired **ovaries,** and two rows of **mammary glands** distributed along the chest and abdomen. (*See* CHAPTER 18, "ANATOMY.")

The ovaries are found in the lower abdominal cavity near the kidneys. They are held in place by a fold of tissue, the **mesovarium,** which provides them with blood vessels and nerves. Each ovary is a relatively small, lima-bean-shaped structure approximately 2 cm long and 1.5 cm wide. In most bitches the left ovary is heavier than the right ovary. The ovaries of a female puppy contain approximately 700,000 **ova** (eggs; singular: **ovum**).

The uterus is a *Y*-shaped, hollow, muscular organ that is the site for implantation of fertilized eggs. The body of the uterus forms the base of the *Y,* connecting through the cervix to the vagina. The paired uterine horns are long and narrow and form the arms of the *Y.* At the end of each arm the horn merges into its continuation, a uterine (fallopian) tube. The uterine tube has a funnel-like opening that is located near the corresponding ovary. The size and weight of the uterus both increase as the bitch matures and enters the *estrous cycle,* the recurrent, rhythmic cycle of sexual receptivity that is characteristic of most female mammals. During **estrus** ("heat"; from the Greek oistros, "vehement desire") the bitch *ovulates* (periodically releases eggs from the ovaries), secretes a watery, lubricating fluid into the lower genital tract, and becomes sexually receptive to the male. The eggs pass through the "funnel" and travel down into the uterine tube or oviduct, where fertilization with *sperm* from the male takes place. The fertilized eggs or **zygotes** move down the uterine horn and thence into the uterus, where they implant in the uterine wall. (*See* CHAPTER 12, "MATING," and CHAPTER 13, "PREGNANCY AND PARTURITION.")

The cervix is an oval-shaped mass whose opening connects the uterus with the more external vagina. The vagina is a long narrow tube that sits above the urinary bladder (membranous sac for the collection of urine) and below the **rectum** (lowermost portion of the large intestine). Below the bladder is the **pelvic symphysis,** the joint formed by the union of the two halves of the pubic bone of the pelvis. The vagina extends from the cervix to the **hymen** (membranous tissue that, in virgin bitches, partially or completely covers the external opening of the vagina). The main purpose of the vagina is to serve as the repository for the *penis* of the male during **coitus** (mating). The **vestibule** is the outer segment of the vagina into which the **urethra,** the connecting tube from the urinary bladder, empties. Beyond the vestibule and hymen the vagina merges with the vulva, which comprises the external genital structures of the female, including the external lips or folds (**labia**) and the clitoris. The clitoris is a small mound of **erectile tissue** (capable of erection; i.e., able to stiffen following engorgement with blood) that sits within the clitoral **fossa** (channel) and is considered to be the female analog of the male penis.

The Normal Male

The reproductive system of the male dog consists primarily of the *penis* (the organ of intercourse), the paired **testes** or **testicles** (in which the sperm are produced), the **scrotum** (dependent pouch of skin in which the testicles rest), the **prostate gland** (which surrounds the urethra where it joins the urinary bladder), and the **vas deferens** (testicular tubules that transport the male reproductive cells, or sperm, from the testes to the urethra, which tunnels through the penis). The **spermatic cord** is a combined structure extending from the groin area to the testes, through which run the vas deferens and a number of vessels and nerves. The testes are the site of production of **testosterone,** the major sex hormone of the male. Male dogs also have several pairs of nonfunctional mammary glands.

The **prepuce** is a protective fold of skin that encloses the penis in its non-erect state. The shaft of the penis terminates in a caplike structure, the **glans penis.** Within the penis—which, like the female clitoris, is composed of erectile tissue—is a strengthening bone, the **os penis,** or

baculum (such a structure is absent in human males). At one end of the os penis is a penile swelling known as the **bulbus glandis.** During an erection the bulbus glandis markedly enlarges, effectively "locking" the male inside the female during intercourse (*see* CHAPTER 12, "MATING"). The urethra, a long hollow tube, runs through the penis from its origin at the neck of the bladder and serves to transport urine to the exterior. It also acts as the conduit for **semen,** the thick, milky white fluid that is deposited in the female's vagina during an *ejaculation.* The semen is composed of several elements, including the sperm (which form and mature within the testes, and are transported to the urethra through the vas deferens) and secretions from the prostate gland.

The Ovarian Cycle

The cyclic sexual cycle of the bitch differs in certain aspects from that of other domesticated mammalian species. Most mammals, including dogs and human beings, are spontaneous ovulators; that is, at periodic intervals an *ovum* is produced from one of many developing *follicles* (precursor forms of the eggs) within one of the ovaries. (Each ovarian follicle, after shedding its ovum, matures rapidly into a hormone-producing **corpus luteum** [plural: **corpora lutea**] before eventually degenerating.) By contrast, cats are reflex ovulators; that is, eggs are produced from ovarian follicles only following stimulation by sexual intercourse. Bitches are also **seasonally monoestrous** or *seasonally monocyclic,* having only a single group of follicles mature during each heat or "season." Each season is separated by a prolonged period of sexual quiescence (*see* below). Cats, however, are seasonally polyestrous or seasonally polycyclic, the female experiencing several heat cycles per season.

Breed has a significant effect on the timing of a dog's first heat. Generally, bitches exhibit their first cycle several months after achieving adult height and body weight. There exists, however, considerable variability within a breed as well as among different breeds. Beagles, for example, usually exhibit their first **proestrus** (*see* below) between 7 and 10 months of age; even in a controlled laboratory environment, however, the first proestrus may occur as early as 6 months of age or as late as 13 months. Thus it is reasonable to expect some small breeds to enter their first heat between 6 and 10 months of age. While a large-breed bitch may also begin her first proestrus before 1 year of age, some normal, large-breed dogs may not begin to cycle until 18 to 24 months of age or even later. This natural variability, coupled with the occurrence of cycles referred to as silent heats, can confound a veterinarian's or owner's ability to predict the timing of a first season. (**Silent heat** is a period that goes unnoticed by the owner simply because there may be little vulvar swelling, bleeding, attraction of males, or behavior change. *See* CHAPTER 13, "PREGNANCY AND PARTURITION.")

The owner's experience, the hair length of the dog (vulvar bleeding is easier to see in a shorthaired dog), cleanliness of the dog (one that licks a great deal is more apt to hide bleeding), and presence of a male dog in the home are just a few of many variables that determine the ease with which an owner may notice estrus. Clinically, veterinarians tend not to begin evaluating a female dog for failure to experience an ovarian cycle until she is at least 2 years old. The ideal age for breeding is between 2 and 6 years of age. First breeding is recommended during the second or third estrus, *after* an owner has witnessed at least one complete, normal ovarian cycle.

It is commonly believed that dogs experience ovarian cycles twice yearly, once in the spring and again in the autumn. However, bitches actually experience ovarian cycles throughout the year, averaging one ovarian cycle every 7 months. Owner preferences may play a role here. Certainly, the bitch's **whelping** (giving birth to) pups in October provides a breeder with "goods to sell" for an upcoming Christmas season. Secondary peaks in whelping tend to occur later in the year (December) in dogs living in warmer climates, and earlier (July) in colder areas.

The "average" bitch enters the first stage of estrus (proestrus) approximately every 7 months. Thus, she will begin an ovarian cycle at least once in every month of the year during her life if she maintains this schedule (African breeds such as the Basenji cycle only once a year, however). The tendency to vary somewhat is quite acceptable. With this in mind, the typical **interestrus** interval (the period from the end of standing heat to the beginning of the next heat or proestrus) is 5 to 11 months in duration, with the normal interval as short as 3.5 months and the longest being 13 months. Intervals more frequent than every 4 months, however, are commonly associated with **infertility** (diminished ability to produce offspring), and those as infrequent as every 12 months or longer *may* be associated with **subfertility** (less than normally fertile) or infertility (the breed and individual variability can be striking). It appears that most dogs 2 to 6 years of age are relatively consistent in cycle length as well as in the duration of each phase.

As dogs advance beyond the optimum breeding ages of 6 to 8 years, various changes are likely to occur, including a progressive lengthening in the duration of the interestrus interval, reduction in litter size, increases in congenital birth defects, and problems at **parturition** (giving birth). Healthy bitches typically experience ovarian cycles throughout life.

PROESTRUS

Duration

The beginning of proestrus is usually defined as the time when vaginal bleeding is first seen, the end when the bitch allows a male dog to mount and breed. Other criteria have been utilized in describing the onset of proestrus, including enlargement of the vulva, attraction of males to the female, and changes in behavior toward males (*see* FIGURE 1). Additional criteria include changes in the appearance of the vaginal mucosa (surface of the vagina), as viewed with special equipment by the veterinarian, or changes in exfoliative cytology (microscopic appearance of shed cells) of vaginal epithelial cells (surface-cell layer), a procedure known commonly as *vaginal cytology* (*see* below). No single criterion for noting the onset of proestrus is as simple and reliable, however, as observing the first day of a bloody vaginal discharge. The length of time from the onset of proestrus to the time of first breeding is usually 6 to 11 days, with an average of 9 days. Variations in what is considered normal can be extreme in some cases (i.e., as brief as 2 or 3 days, or as prolonged as 25 days).

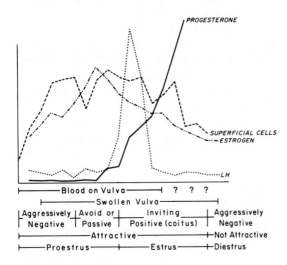

Figure 1. Diagrammatic illustration of the behavior changes, hormonal fluctuations and vaginal cytology of a bitch experiencing proestrus and estrus.

Clinical Signs

The female in early proestrus exhibits an increase in playful, teasing behavior but actively discourages any mounting attempt by a male. This may involve antisexual growling, moving away, baring of the teeth, and snapping. She also may keep her tail tight against the **perineum** (region between the thighs encompassing the anus and genitalia), between the rear legs and covering the vulva. This initial behavior pattern gradually changes as proestrus progresses. The female usually becomes more receptive as demonstrated by increasingly seeking out males, playing and teasing. The response of the bitch to male mounting attempts becomes more asexual and passive. In late proestrus the behavior of the bitch may be described as passive or confused; she may sit or stand passively when mounted, with or without intermittent displays of tail deviation.

Proestrus is typically, but not always, associated with varying quantities of bloody vaginal discharge. The blood comes from the rapidly changing uterine lining; the blood trickles through the slightly relaxed cervix and enters the vagina. The volume of uterine bleeding and the subsequent bloody vaginal discharge varies from bitch to bitch. Some dogs cease bleeding as proestrus proceeds into estrus. In these bitches, the bloody discharge fades and becomes yellow and transparent (straw-colored). However, changes in the color of the vaginal discharge are inconsistent, with some bitches showing bloody discharge throughout proestrus, estrus, and into diestrus, while others bleed little or only at the beginning of proestrus.

The vulva slowly enlarges throughout proestrus. Proestrus, early to late, is associated with a swollen and turgid vulva that impedes **intromission** (insertion of the penis) by a male. As proestrus proceeds into estrus the vulva softens dramatically, eliminating this obstacle.

Hormonal Changes and Ovarian Anatomy

The bitch in proestrus is under the influence of the female sex hormone **estrogen.** The estrogen is produced by the developing ovarian follicles— the same follicles that are responsible for the production of the ova, and the primary site for estrogen synthesis in the body (*see* FIGURE 1). Estrogen is responsible for the characteristic behavioral changes of proestrus—the vaginal discharge, attraction of males, and uterine preparation for pregnancy. The potent effects of estrogen are exemplified in the **ovariohysterectomized** (spayed) female, which can easily be brought into a classic proestrus state (though without vaginal bleeding) by the administration of estrogens.

Vaginal Anatomy

The vaginal lining in **anestrus** (between estrus periods) is only a few cell layers thick and relatively fragile. The rising estrogen concentrations of proestrus cause a rapid increase in the number of cell layers lining the vagina. Intromission of the penis into the estrogen-primed vagina is not harmful to the female, because this tougher, thickened wall is more capable of resisting damage. The thickening pushes the lining cells farther and farther away from their blood supply, resulting in cell death, a change easily recognizable by vaginal cytology (*see* FIGURE 2) or **endoscopy** (examination of the interior of the vagina through an inserted tube, or endoscope).

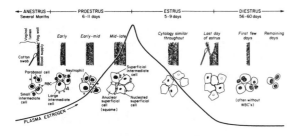

Figure 2. Illustration of the changes in vaginal wall thickness, vaginal cytology and relative plasma estrogen concentrations in an average bitch experiencing an ovarian cycle. Note that near the last day of estrus, one may encounter "rafts" of vaginal cells that are all sloughed at that time. *Lumen,* interior of the vagina; *nucleated,* having a nucleus; *anuclear,* lacking a nucleus; *parabasal cells,* small, rounded, nonsuperficial cells; *intermediate cells,* well-nucleated cells more superficial than parabasal cells; *superficial cells (squames),* large, irregularly shaped cells (with diminished or absent nuclei) that are about to be sloughed from the vaginal surface; *RBC,* red blood cells; *WBC,* white blood cells; *neutrophil,* type of white blood cell, having a lobulated nucleus.

ESTRUS

Hormonal Changes
The first day the female allows breeding (**standing heat**) is the beginning of estrus. This phase ends when she no longer accepts the male. The bitch will usually begin to exhibit signs of standing heat only when circulating estrogen concentrations, once elevated, begin to fall (*see* FIGURE 1). In concert with declining estrogen levels, later in proestrus and immediately preceding the onset of estrus, the ovaries produce significant amounts of the hormone *progesterone.* The combination of increasing serum progesterone levels and declining serum estrogen concentrations, in the final days of proestrus, stimulates

two major events. The first is the change in behavior of the bitch, in which an animal passively resistant to breeding is transformed into one that actively seeks breeding. The second and equally important event is the release of the following hormones from the **pituitary gland** at the base of the brain: **follicle-stimulating hormone (FSH)** and **luteinizing hormone (LH)**, which induce ovulation (*see* FIGURE 3).

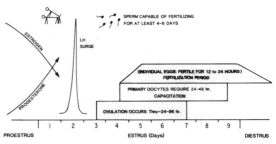

Figure 3. An illustration of the hormonal changes and sequence of events concerning the timing of ovulation and fertilization of ova in the average bitch. *Primary oocytes,* newly released eggs; *capacitation,* process of maturation by which eggs become capable of being fertilized by sperm.

Clinically, measuring plasma progesterone concentrations as the bitch progresses through proestrus and estrus can be extremely valuable. Several "in-hospital" test kits are now available to veterinarians for estimating progesterone concentrations. The more frequently the bitch is sampled, the more precise the veterinarian can be in determining the day that progesterone begins to increase in the blood. This can assist in the recommendation of breeding dates and in more precisely predicting whelping dates.

Ovary and Uterus
Ovulation occurs 24 to 72 hours following the release or "surge" of LH from the pituitary gland. The number of eggs released for future fertilization is somewhat dependent on the breed of the bitch. Smaller breeds, with their small litter size, ovulate fewer numbers of eggs (2 to 10) when compared to larger breeds, which may ovulate 5 to 20 ova. Follicles rupture

within a relatively short time of each other (12 to 96 hours). Even though eggs are not released at precisely the same time, they are in similar stages of development, ensuring that development of fetuses will progress together. This illustrates the exquisitely sensitive and synchronous balance that exists among falling estrogen concentrations, rising progesterone concentrations, the "LH surge," and ovulation.

The number of ova present in the ovaries of a newborn bitch has been estimated at 700,000. By puberty this number has been reduced to about 250,000 to 350,000, at 5 years of age 30,000 to 33,000, and at 10 years only a few hundred. Fertility appears to decline progressively once a bitch has reached 7 years of age or older. However, a corollary to the menopause of women is not typically seen in the bitch.

Duration

The duration of estrus is usually 5 to 9 days. As with proestrus, the exact length may vary dramatically among normal dogs, as brief as 1 to 2 days in some dogs and as prolonged as 18 to 20 days in others. Individual bitches are usually consistent from cycle to cycle when they are about 2 to 6 years of age. However, variability within and among breeds makes it difficult to predict the length of proestrus or estrus in any particular dog.

Clinical Signs

The behavioral alterations in the female entering standing heat are those of reflexive receptivity to mounting and attempts at copulation by the male. Estrus bitches may crouch and elevate their rear quarters toward the male. Any pressure placed on or near the lower back will cause the tail to be held off to one side, accompanied by an obvious tensing of the rear legs to support the weight of the mounting male. The bitch may attract males from long distances, owing to the production of potent odors called **pheromones.** At this stage the vulva has progressed through the turgid phase and becomes soft and flaccid, no longer the difficult barrier for a male to penetrate. The vaginal discharge is often a straw-colored or pink fluid; less commonly, it continues obviously bloody.

DIESTRUS

Hormonal Changes and Duration

Diestrus is defined as the phase of "progesterone dominance," beginning with the cessation of standing heat and continuing throughout the time during which progesterone is secreted by the corpora lutea (derived from follicles that have shed their eggs) in the ovaries. An alternative definition for the onset of diestrus would relate to the dramatic shift of cell types observed on vaginal cytology.

Progesterone concentrations in the plasma rise to levels > 1.0 ng/ml (ng/ml = nanograms [one billionth of a gram] per milliliter) at approximately the onset of estrus. The progesterone rise contributing to the onset of estrus is derived from cells within follicles on the ovaries. After ovulation, corpora lutea develop on the ovaries within the ruptured follicular cavities. These cells are capable of producing progesterone throughout pregnancy. The zenith in progesterone concentration is usually achieved 20 to 30 days post-ovulation, approximately 2 to 3 weeks after the beginning of diestrus. A transient plateau in progesterone concentration persists for an additional 1 to 2 weeks. The progesterone concentrations at that time are dramatically higher than basal concentrations, usually in the range of 15 to 60 ng/ml.

Statistically, pregnant bitches have higher progesterone concentrations than nonpregnant bitches, beginning several weeks after the onset of diestrus. Individual variation, however, precludes the usefulness of progesterone assays for pregnancy diagnosis. *This is extremely important.* All nonpregnant healthy bitches that have progressed through standing heat are "pseudopregnant" in the sense that they have functioning corpora lutea even if they are not pregnant. Therefore, the corpora lutea function throughout a normal gestational period regardless of the presence or absence of a fetus (or fetuses). In fact, the corpora lutea of nonpregnant bitches have a longer functioning life expectancy than do corpora lutea of pregnant bitches.

Once the plateau period in diestrus plasma progesterone concentrations has passed, there follows a prolonged decline in luteal function. The luteal phase ends abruptly in the pregnant bitch (approximately 65 days after fertilization) as part of the onset of whelping. However, the luteal phase wanes more slowly in the nonpregnant bitch, often lasting an additional 10 to 30 days.

Clinical Signs

Diestrus begins when a previously receptive bitch abruptly refuses to breed. She may also no longer attract males. The vulva returns to a normal or anestrus size and is no longer flaccid. There are in reality no readily recognizable clinical differences when comparing a spayed bitch, an anestrus bitch, and one that is nonpregnant and in diestrus. There is also no obvious method of distinguishing a pregnant bitch early in diestrus from one that is not pregnant.

Mammary Glands

The increasing progesterone concentrations of standing heat initiate glandular development in mammary tissue. These changes usually become obvious to the owner approximately midway through diestrus. The hormone **prolactin,** whose concentration in the blood rises during the final weeks of gestation, induces **lactation** (milk production) in preparation for the newborn.

ANESTRUS

Duration and Clinical Signs

Anestrus is the phase of the female reproductive cycle following diestrus, during which the uterus returns to an inactive state (i.e., it **involutes**). Anestrus begins with whelping and ends with proestrus. The beginning of anestrus is not readily discernible in a nonpregnant bitch; no obvious demarcation between diestrus and anestrus is *clinically* detectable. Thus, the reproductive tract during anestrus is preparing for the onset of another cycle, which begins with the upcoming proestrus. The period from the end of standing heat to the end of anestrus is interestrus.

As with the other phases of the ovarian cycle, anestrus varies in duration. This variability depends on breed, health, age, time of year, environment and many other factors. The typi-cal female begins proestrus every 7 months, with proestrus lasting 9 days, estrus 7 to 9 days, diestrus 58 days, and anestrus 4½ months. The duration of diestrus progesterone secretion is likely to be the major factor determining the interval between nonfertile (nonpregnant) ovarian cycles.

There are no readily obvious clinical differences when comparing an anestrus bitch with a spayed bitch. In fact, sometimes one cannot tell if a bitch has been spayed or not.

Vaginal Exfoliative Cytology

CLINICAL USEFULNESS OF VAGINAL CYTOLOGY

Management of Normal Breeding

Vaginal exfoliative cytology is one of the most commonly used diagnostic tools in clinical canine reproduction. In this context, vaginal cytology is most useful for helping an owner determine the proper time to breed a bitch. Observation of the behavior of a bitch with a stud is the most reliable method of learning when a bitch has entered standing heat (i.e., when the bitch is ready to breed, she will breed). However, many exceptions to this philosophy highlight the value of vaginal cytology.

Vaginal cytology is an excellent aid for distinguishing between proestrus, estrus and diestrus. A minimum of two or three smears, taken over a period of 4 to 7 days, should always be examined. Vaginal cytology, behavior of a bitch, and monitoring of serum progesterone concentrations are of real value in breeding management.

Knowing precisely the first day of a cycle, beginning with the first day of vulvar swelling or vaginal bleeding, is helpful, but should not be relied upon as the sole criterion for determining when a bitch should be bred. Remember: only the "average" dog enters standing heat on the 10th day after beginning proestrus! Three to 6 days may pass after the vaginal smear is suggestive of estrus before natural breeding commences, because of the overlap in vaginal cytologic appearance observed at the end of proestrus and throughout estrus. Once breeding begins it should be allowed to continue until the bitch refuses to breed. *This is the most important advice we provide to owners.* We recommend breeding dogs every 2nd, 3rd, or 4th day of estrus. More frequent intervals are suggested if it is the bitch's first breeding or if the bitch is known to have an abbreviated estrus. A less frequent breeding schedule is suggested if the bitch is known to have been in standing heat for 9 days or longer on previous heats.

Shipping or Receiving a Bitch

Bitches often are transported long distances for breeding. Cytology can be used to aid an owner in deciding when to ship a bitch. The duration of proestrus can be difficult to predict, and early shipping is recommended. When receiving a bitch, her behavior status can be checked immediately. If she is not standing for the stud, a vaginal smear and a serum progesterone should be assessed. Both parameters may be monitored in serial fashion; that is, by repeated testing over a defined period of time.

Unusual Cycles

Any bitch that appears to have normal reproductive cycles but that never stands for the stud may be hormonally normal and fertile. Some bitches fail to stand for a male because they are not exposed to him during *their* standing heat (i.e., standing heat is often unrecognized because it is not occurring between days 9 and 12 of the cycle). Vaginal cytology will help determine when a bitch will be likely to breed.

Predicting Whelping Dates

Vaginal cytology is a superb tool for predicting the approximate date of whelping. This is based on the knowledge that whelping occurs near day 57 of diestrus. Obtaining a series of vaginal smears from a bitch on a daily basis will readily allow recognition of the first day of diestrus. This method is more reliable than utilizing breeding dates.

Infertility Problems

Vaginal cytology is a crude reflection of plasma estrogen concentrations and, as such, can be considered a test of ovarian function. Infertility cases should be evaluated using vaginal cytology and serum progesterone concentrations (the serum samples for this latter test must be submitted by the consulting veterinarian to a testing laboratory) to determine if the problem is one of mismanagement (incorrect timing), inadequate estrogen (poor follicular development), or some less common disorder.

Techniques and Methodology for Making Vaginal Smears

The method used should meet several relatively simple criteria:

1. It should be simple to perform and inexpensive
2. It should be applicable to dogs regardless of their size or temperment
3. It must not be painful
4. It should be successful regardless of the presence or absence of a vaginal discharge
5. It should be able to be performed by owners after they have been given a brief lesson

Briefly, the lips of the vulva are gently separated with one hand. The other hand holds a sterile, 5- to 7-inch cotton-tipped applicator. The cotton-tipped end of this swab is passed into the vulva. The cotton tip initially is pressed gently against the top surface of the vagina, to avoid the clitoral fossa, and then advanced forward and upward toward the vertebral column, until it goes over the floor of the pelvis (*see* Figure 4). The applicator is rotated one complete revolution in each direction and then withdrawn. The entire procedure should only take seconds and is rarely painful. A bitch may appear uncomfortable if there is no vaginal discharge. Therefore, the cotton should be moistened with two or three drops of sterile saline to act as a lubricant if a discharge is not obvious.

Once the cotton swab has been withdrawn, the cotton tip is *rolled* gently from one end of a glass microscope slide to the other. There should be space on the slide for 3 separate linear impressions (*see* Figure 5). One must remember not to press firmly and not to rub or smear the cotton against the glass, because the result of either procedure will be a nondiagnostic slide. Usually, two slides are prepared using one or cedure for an owner or breeder. It must be pointed out, however, that vaginal exfoliative cytology will not answer some common questions. For example, vaginal cytology cannot identify the day of ovulation or fertilization; therefore, the "perfect" day for breeding cannot be determined from an evaluation of smears. Retrospectively, once the first day of diestrus is identified, ovulation can be assumed to have occurred approximately 6 to 7 days earlier. Vaginal cytology also cannot be used for pregnancy diagnosis. Lastly, vaginal cytology, while a valuable tool, is an imperfect substitute for observations of behavioral estrus. Observation of behavior along with a review of vaginal cytology is an optimum means for evaluating stages of the canine reproductive cycle.

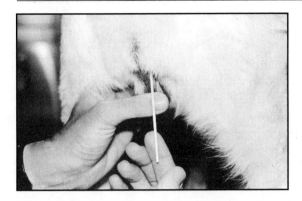
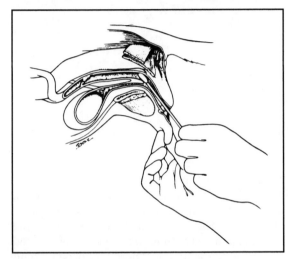

Figure 4. Obtaining a vaginal smear with a cotton-tipped swab. (Top) The swab is inserted into the vagina. (Bottom) A diagram illustrating the location of the cotton-tipped swab.

two cotton swabs. The slides should then be left to dry or dipped once or twice (fixed) in 95–100% methanol to prevent cellular deterioration or distortion. Finished slides can be stained immediately or stored and stained at a later date.

LIMITATIONS OF VAGINAL CYTOLOGY
Understanding the clinical applications of vaginal cytology will increase the value of the pro-

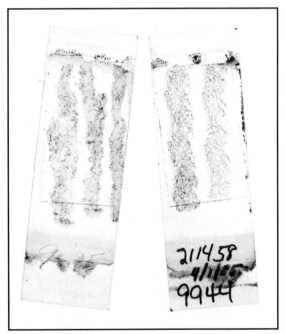

Figure 5. Two stained glass slides after the cotton swab has been correctly rolled across the surface to make two or three columns containing vaginal smear material.

CHAPTER 12
Mating

**by Edward C. Feldman
and Richard W. Nelson**

Natural Breeding

In discussions concerning breeding management of both the bitch and stud, a good deal of emphasis is placed on normal "instincts" or normal "behavior." There is little doubt, however, that humans have an influence on dogs and their behavior patterns. Understanding and assessing the interaction of owner influence and a variety of other environmental factors on dogs that do have strong instinctive behavior patterns can be difficult.

DEVELOPMENT OF SEXUAL BEHAVIOR
It appears that sexual behavior may be recognized in male puppies as young as 3 to 4 weeks of age. They are often observed to mount littermates of either sex and display pelvic thrusting actions. Female puppies only occasionally show mounting behavior, and if mounted they usually remain passive. This is considered normal play behavior.

Lack of socialization may markedly affect copulatory behavior. In one study, comparisons were made between male beagles raised in semi-isolation and those in a heterosexual group. The semi-isolation group, as adults, were not as successful in copulating as the other group of males. Dogs raised with exposure only to humans may respond incorrectly when placed in a breeding situation. There has been a trend in the past several decades to sell pups at quite a young age. With pups arriving in their new homes at 6 to 7 weeks of age, it is possible that they are being deprived of some "sex education" which they would have received had they remained with their littermates for a longer period of time. However, the importance of mounting behavior during play and of interaction with other dogs for the development of normal adult sexual behavior remains speculative.

COURTSHIP
Pre-mating behavior is initiated by the male, with responses to these actions by the female. Most males are aggressive in their behavior, forcing positive or negative responses from the bitch. Courtship behavior includes the male's sniffing at the bitch's nose, ear, neck, flank and vulvar area, while the bitch sniffs the male in

return. Licking of the vulvar area, chasing, wrestling and urinating induce actions of a similar nature by the female. If the female is in proestrus, further advances by the male, such as standing near her or placing his paw or head on her back, results in the bitch's sitting, crouching, growling, snapping or wheeling around.

CHANGES IN SEXUAL BEHAVIOR IN PROESTRUS AND ESTRUS

In response to increases in plasma estrogen concentrations, the bitch is frequently observed to be restless, nervous, have an increase or decrease in appetite, drink more, and/or urinate more frequently. The increase in urination may aid in dispersing odors present in the urine and vaginal secretions that attract male dogs.

The female changes from being outwardly hostile to the male to becoming passive and resistant, and finally actively receptive. Obviously, the key behavioral change during this series of events is the time that the female becomes overtly receptive to the male. As estrus progresses, the female may then become less interested in mating. (For a review of the canine reproductive cycle, *see* CHAPTER 11, "NORMAL REPRODUCTION.")

THE TIE

Courtship behavior, as previously described, usually precedes copulation. Courtship may be prolonged or may consist of the male's briefly licking the vulva prior to mounting. The bitch typically "presents" her hindquarters to the male, with her tail deviated to the side. Any attempt at mounting by the male causes the bitch to stand firmly in place. Mounting consists of the male clasping the flanks of the female with his forelegs. **Intromission** (insertion of the penis) appears to be achieved through tentative trial-and-error pelvic thrusting of the penis toward the vaginal opening. Intromission is accomplished without the male's having an erection, because the **os penis** (penile bone) provides rigidity. If the male had an erection prior to intromission, the enlarged **bulbus glandis** of the penis (portion of the penis that surrounds one end of the os penis and swells markedly during erection) would actually prevent intromission.

With normal breeding, intromission takes place, erection then begins, and stepping movements of the male's rear legs are seen. Engorgement of the bulbus glandis takes place simultaneously with the stepping movements. The pelvic thrusting becomes more aggressive and ejaculation of sperm-free prostatic fluid (discharge from the prostate gland) takes place during the initial 15 to 60 seconds of intromission.

Following pelvic thrusting, the male typically dismounts by placing both front legs to one side of the bitch and lifting one hind leg over her back to stand tail to tail with her. Swelling of the bulbus glandis makes withdrawal of the penis from the relatively small vaginal opening impossible. Thus, the male and female are locked, or tied together. This is described as an inside tie. If the male's erection precedes intromission, the relatively large bulbus glandis cannot enter the vagina, and the result is an outside tie.

Dogs that have achieved an inside tie remain locked together for 5 to 60 minutes. They may actually drag each other around during this time. During the first 1 to 5 minutes of a tie, the male is ejaculating sperm-rich semen. The ejaculate throughout the remainder of a tie consists of sperm-free prostatic fluid.

FACTORS AFFECTING SEXUAL BEHAVIOR

Environment

Male dogs are more territorial than females, and it has been suggested that when a female is dominant to an individual male, he is not likely to succeed in breeding. Dominance of a male may be quite pronounced in his territory. Therefore, females usually are brought to the male for breeding.

Humans may also influence canine behavior. Some dogs respond to the presence of the owner, while others do not. Some dogs will allow human assistance during breeding. Some males perform better if another male dog is in the area. Noise, lighting, flooring (traction), and a myriad of other environmental factors can also influence breeding.

Experience

Young and inexperienced adult male dogs may become overexcited when near bitches in heat.

They may attempt to mount the head, side or flank before orienting correctly. Inexperience can result in a failure to dismount the female, until she literally throws the male off her back. Maiden bitches in heat are reported to display longer play behavior prior to allowing copulation than do experienced females. Sexual behavior, therefore, is likely to reflect both innate and learned responses.

Mate Preference and Dominance

Studies have suggested that bitches show distinct preferences for particular males during mating by either accepting or actively rejecting one male. Preferences remain during several cycles and are unrelated to social affinity for males during **anestrus** (sexually inactive period between two heat cycles). The role of dominance is difficult to address, but the female rarely allows a submissive male to breed. This is the reason that the female is brought to the male, for he is more likely to be the dominant one in his own territory. Males, however, are rarely particular if the female is receptive. Therefore, the female is thought to determine the success of copulation when a pair of dogs is chosen for mating.

Artificial Insemination (AI)

COLLECTION OF SEMEN

Artificial insemination is a procedure wherein semen is taken from the male and inoculated into the vagina of the female, avoiding natural breeding.

Semen can be collected from most stud dogs in a clean, quiet room with a nonslippery floor. An artificial vagina and a clear plastic tube are used. A bitch often is not needed. However, for experienced males accustomed to natural breeding, a bitch in heat makes collecting semen from the male much easier. With the owner holding the stud to protect the collector from being bitten, the penis and bulbus glandis are gently massaged within the penile sheath. When the bulbus glandis begins to enlarge, the sheath is slipped posteriorly, and the penis with the bulbus glandis is exposed. Failure to extrude the penis and the bulbus glandis from the sheath usually results in an incomplete erection and failure to ejaculate, presumably due to pain.

Once the penis and bulbus glandis are extruded from the sheath, the collector firmly holds onto the base of the penis, above the bulbus glandis. The thumb and index finger are used, providing both massaging movements and downward pressure around the base of the bulbus glandis. During or immediately after achieving an erection, aggressive pelvic thrusting movements by the stud that accompany the onset of ejaculation may make it difficult to place the artificial vagina over the penis. However pelvic thrusting is typically short-lived (5 to 30 seconds) and the initial 5 to 30 seconds of ejaculate is usually free of sperm. There is no need to collect this sperm-free fluid and, therefore, there should be no alarm over the pelvic thrusting, ejaculate which is not collected, or failure quickly to situate the artificial vagina over the penis.

The sperm-rich second fraction of the ejaculate usually begins as the pelvic thrusting stops. At the same time, many males will "step over" the collector's arm, as if dismounting from the bitch. The collector should simply allow this movement by the male and bring the penis between the rear legs of the stud for continued collection. Semen is usually collected for a period of 2 to 5 minutes. The clear plastic tube should already have been connected to the rubber artificial vagina, which can be held under the collector's arm during the initial stimulation period to provide some warmth. Canine semen is relatively resistant to cold shock, alleviating the need for warm-water tanks or incubators for holding semen.

The use of a clear plastic collection tube will allow visualization of the semen. The semen is usually collected for approximately 3 to 4 minutes, keeping one hand over the plastic to avoid excessive light exposure. As long as the ejaculate is obviously whitish or creamy and cloudy (normal and sperm-rich), the ejaculate continues to be collected. Whenever the ejaculate becomes clear (sperm-free), one can discontinue collecting. If one is not certain when the male has ceased ejaculating the sperm-rich fraction, stop the collection after 4 minutes. Continued collection only dilutes the sperm with sperm-free prostatic fluid, resulting in cumbersome fluid volumes.

The most difficult task in AI is stimulating the male to ejaculate. Once this is accomplished, the balance of the procedure is quite simple. The bitch should be inseminated within 10 to 15 minutes of collecting the semen from the male. If the semen appears normal, we inseminate the bitch immediately after collecting the semen, saving several drops for post-insemination microscopic evaluation. If the ejaculate is abnormal in color or consistency, it is evaluated prior to insemination. During any delay, the semen is kept warm by holding the tube in one's hand, which also keeps the semen out of potentially harmful ultraviolet rays.

INSEMINATION PROCEDURE

During the insemination procedure the male is taken out of the room to avoid any distractions. Using sterile gloves, the inseminator draws the semen into a sterile, new, 12- or 20-ml syringe. Once the semen is in the syringe a new, clean urethral catheter is attached. The owner is usually given the job of holding the bitch's head, and also keeping the bitch's tail to one side. A gloved, non-lubricated index finger (except in very small dogs) is placed into the vagina, palm up. If a lubricant is used it must be non-spermicidal. The urethral catheter is then slid over the top of the finger and passed into the vagina until resistance is met. Because of the unique anatomy of the canine cervix, one is not able to pass the catheter through the cervix and into the uterus. The index finger aids in avoiding both the clitoral **fossa** (a blind pouch) and the **urethra** (outflow tract from the urinary bladder). The catheter usually will follow the curvature of the vagina.

The semen is flushed into the vagina and the catheter is removed. Then the owner can help— he or she can sit in a comfortable chair, place a drape over his or her lap, and hold the rear legs of the bitch up for at least 10 to 15 minutes. During this time the remaining semen is examined microscopically by the collector.

The entire insemination procedure is rarely a problem for the bitch. There should be no pain or discomfort associated with the procedure, which is rather simple and not at all time-consuming.

INDICATIONS FOR ARTIFICIAL INSEMINATION (AI)

There are many reasons for an owner to choose AI over natural breeding, but the most common is a perceived inability of the male and female to breed. This inability may be the result of the presence of a vaginal **stricture** (narrowing), which impedes intromission by the male and causes pain during breeding for the female. Additional reasons for failure to breed include orthopedic problems, such as back disease, rear leg problems, or muscle weakness. Artificial insemination may also be chosen because of a major size difference between the mates. Either the male or female may be inexperienced, or there may be a history of one dog's refusing to mate or allow mating by the other. If the male or female has a history of attacking the other, the owner may simply want to avoid another confrontation. Some bitches appear never to enter standing heat, refusing all breeding attempts by any male.

Less commonly, medical reasons account for the use of AI. Some owners wish to avoid any possible venereal contact between their dog and its mate. This seems uncalled for when working with *Brucella*-free animals (*see* CHAPTER 35, "BACTERIAL DISEASES"). Inseminating semen into the vagina still provides intimate contact between bitch and stud. Any agent that could be transmitted from stud to bitch during natural mating will not be avoided with AI. However, AI avoids transmission of any agent from bitch to stud.

SUCCESS RATES FOR ARTIFICIAL INSEMINATION

Artificial insemination may be associated with lower conception rates and smaller litter sizes than would be achieved with natural breeding. This is likely the result of several factors. During natural breeding semen is pressure-forced through the cervix into the uterus and oviducts, whereas in AI, the semen is placed outside the cervix. With natural breeding, uterine contractions aid in semen transport, an unlikely event in most AI situations. Also, in natural breeding the duration of the tie may contribute to improved conception rates.

CHAPTER 13

Pregnancy and Parturition

**by Edward C. Feldman
and Richard W. Nelson**

Breeding Management of the Bitch

The most common problem encountered by veterinarians working in the field of canine reproduction is the potentially infertile bitch or stud. Owners bring these dogs to their veterinarian with the major concern that the dogs are failing to produce puppies. The vast majority, however, are perfectly healthy, fertile animals whose apparent infertility problems are related to a misunderstanding of proper breeding management. Thus, it is advisable to review proper breeding protocols before embarking on an investigation of infertility.

Age at First Ovarian Cycle
It appears that the bitch reaches sexual maturity and experiences her first ovarian cycle within 1 to 6 months of attaining adult height and weight. Therefore, the average Miniature Poodle begins her first **proestrus** at a younger age than the average Great Dane (*see* CHAPTER 11, "NORMAL REPRODUCTION").

Silent Heat
A **silent heat** is simply an estrous cycle that proceeds unseen by an owner. Bitches experiencing a silent heat either exhibit little or no vaginal bleeding, keep themselves scrupulously clean, or maintain little contact with male dogs. Virtually all but the most experienced owners will fail to detect proestrus and estrus in such animals. Silent heats appear to be most common in the first and second heat cycles of a bitch's life.

Split Heat
A **split heat** occurs when a bitch with proestrus vaginal bleeding, vulvar swelling, and attraction of males proceeds into an apparent diestrus, only to begin proestrus again 2 to 10 weeks later. This sequence may be repeated several times. Each apparent proestrus fails to be followed by ovulation, allowing a new group of follicles to develop, reexposing the bitch to increases in circulating estrogen concentration and the signs of another proestrus. Once the follicles fully mature and ovulation does take place,

the cycle is fertile and the expected interestrus interval, consisting of diestrus and anestrus, will take place. Split heats are frequently seen as a female behavior problem; such dogs may need to be force-bred or artificially inseminated. Split heats may occur at any age, but are most commonly encountered in young bitches. Split heats are not associated with any major underlying health problem.

Inexperience and Ovulation Failure
It is not surprising that the young bitch, even one apparently in estrus, may not respond to a stud as would be expected. Together, the inexperienced bitch and stud, controlled by inexperienced owners, often fail to achieve a tie, with one of two healthy dogs usually taking the blame. (*See* CHAPTER 12, "MATING.")

THE GOAL IN BREEDING—WHEN SHOULD BREEDING BEGIN?
The simple goal in any breeding program is to deliver sufficient numbers of sperm to the uterus and oviducts of the female to achieve the optimal chance for fertilization of mature eggs. Employing reliable, clinically practical criteria for estimating the correct days to breed can be a quite valuable adjunct to any breeding program. These criteria include behavior observation, use of vaginal cytology, **vaginoscopy** (visual inspection of the vagina and cervix using a speculum, an instrument that facilitates access to a body passage), and serial serum progesterone concentrations (*see* CHAPTER 11, "NORMAL REPRODUCTION"). None of these four criteria is considered perfect in and of itself, but when all are used together they represent a superb means of insuring that a bitch will be inseminated at the proper time.

The Best Criterion: Behavior
Behavioral estrus (**standing heat**) is "the" factor in determining when breeding of the bitch should begin. In most bitches, estrus ("heat") behavior is synonymous with the phase of fertility. Therefore, observation of the bitch's response to a male, beginning 5 or 6 days after vaginal bleeding is detected and continuing every 2 or 3 days, is an inexpensive, straightforward and reliable means of determining when to begin and end the breeding phase of the ovarian cycle. Occasionally it is advisable to have both the male and the female leashed, with one handler for each in case of fighting. However, if possible, it is better to allow the male and female some freedom of movement. If the female stands for the male, breeding should begin regardless of the color of the vaginal discharge, the vaginal cytology, or the calculated day of the cycle.

The one factor whose variability cannot be overemphasized is the inability to predict the number of days a bitch will remain in estrus (will allow mating). The average duration is typically 7 to 9 days. We recommend breeding the bitch every 2 to 4 days, beginning with the first day of acceptance and continuing *throughout* the acceptance period. It is of paramount importance that the male *continue breeding the bitch until the day of first refusal.* Fertilization of eggs is most likely to occur in the final 4 or 5 days of standing heat, regardless of the length of the heat.

Other Criteria
Vaginal cytology, vaginal endoscopy and serum progesterone concentrations provide a good reflection of events occurring within the female prior to observation of breeding behavior (*see* CHAPTER 11, "NORMAL REPRODUCTION"). However, none of these tools is perfect and all require that owners and veterinarians not be influenced by preconceived notions.

Criteria That Are Not Reliable
It is never recommended to breed the bitch routinely on predetermined days, dating from the first observed day of proestrus. Thus, breeding bitches on days 9 and 11, or 10 and 13, is not as reliable or as likely to result in conception in all bitches as those criteria previously described as valuable. Rather, while such an approach may be sufficient for most average bitches, it is not for all normal dogs.

It is often suggested that the optimal time to begin breeding is when the vaginal discharge changes from bloody to a translucent yellow, straw color or clear. *This is a totally incorrect and misleading approach.* Some normal bitches may never have a bloody discharge, while others may bleed throughout standing heat. The color or consistency of the vaginal cytology should not determine breeding dates.

As the bitch progresses from proestrus into estrus, the swollen and enlarged vulva evolves from being tense and turgid to being soft and pliable. This change is not easily appreciated, however. Because most owners are not experienced in assessing this alteration, use of such a subjective criterion is not encouraged.

The male dog is typically willing to breed any bitch in standing heat. Experienced studs have been observed that will only breed the bitch on the "correct" day. However, it would appear that the bitch usually is the factor determining when and if breeding is to occur. When bringing the bitch and stud together, observation of the bitch's behavior is more informative than observation of the behavior of the male.

RECOMMENDATIONS FOR BREEDING PROGRAMS

Specific recommendations for canine breeding programs include the following:

1. Record the first day of vulvar swelling, bloody vaginal discharge, and when males become obviously interested in the bitch.

2. Begin "teasing" the bitch with a male dog on day 5 or 6 of proestrus, and repeat this procedure every 2 or 3 days to determine the first day of standing heat. In cases of previous infertility, begin on day 1 of proestrus.

3. Allow the bitch to be bred, beginning on her first day of acceptance of the male, and continue to breed every 2 to 4 days *throughout* the acceptance period.

4. Complete records should be kept on the dates of proestrus, breeding and vaginal smears. Notes should be made on the presence or absence of ties, the length of each tie, and the behavior of both the male and female. The success of the male in siring litters with other bitches should be recorded. Records should also be kept on whelping dates, litter size, health of puppies, duration of pregnancy, interval between births, etc. This should include the reason for destroying any puppies.

5. Vaccinations should be current for the breeding bitch before she enters proestrus. If not, the bitch should be vaccinated early in proestrus. Vaccinating any potentially pregnant or known pregnant bitch is *not* recommended (*see* APPENDIX B: VACCINATIONS).

PUPS OF DIFFERENT AGES *IN UTERO*

One reason some dog owners resist breeding a bitch and stud repeatedly once a day on a 2-to-4-day schedule is their fear of having fetuses develop that are distinctly different in age. However, eggs are probably being fertilized over a rather short time (1 to 4 days), and the age differences of codeveloping fetuses are not significant. Gross differences in size, weight and apparent maturity of newborn puppies are more likely to be related to the overall health of each pup, its placenta (fetal connection to the uterus), the genetic background of the individual fetus, and the health of that area of the uterus in which each puppy develops. It is important to remember that sperm from more than one male can account for disparity in size or color of puppies (i.e., one litter can have more than one father).

FERTILIZATION

The Egg

If one appraises an "average" bitch, there is a consistent sequence of events leading to pregnancy as she progresses through proestrus and into estrus. Twenty-four to 96 hours after the onset of breeding behavior—averaging about the 4th day of standing heat—ovulation begins. It takes 72 hours for approximately 75% of the follicles to rupture and 96 hours for greater than 90% of the follicles to rupture. The eggs released are primary oocytes that require 24 to 48 hours of maturation (capacitation) before fertilization can occur. Once mature, the fertile life of each egg may be only 12 to 24 hours. Fertilization, therefore, would on average take place on the 7th day of standing heat. When one realizes that most bitches are not precisely "average," it seems obvious that predicting the precise day of fertilization is impossible.

It appears that there is no single optimal day for a stud to breed the normal bitch. Nature has developed a system to ensure conception if a single breeding should occur within a wide period of days (see FIGURE 3 IN CHAPTER 11, "NORMAL REPRODUCTION"). The primary goal in breeding a bitch is to obtain at least one mating every 2 to 4 days during standing heat.

The Sperm

Sperm from a natural mating may reach the oviduct of the bitch within 25 seconds of ejaculation. More importantly, canine sperm have a relatively long survival period within the uterus, usually lasting for 4 to 6 days after a single breeding. Significant numbers may survive for as long as 11 days. The length of time that fertile eggs remain within the oviducts (several days), coupled with the longevity of sperm capable of fertilization following a single mating, suggests that a single breeding is quite likely to result in conception.

Pregnancy

GENERAL EXPECTATIONS

Litter Size

Generally speaking, the larger the breed of dog (not including fat), the larger the average litter size. Toy breeds usually have litters of 1 to 4 puppies, while larger breeds can average 8, 10, or even 12 pups per litter. Litter size also correlates with the sperm count of the male (a normal count is 2.5 to 8 hundred million sperm per ejaculate), the timing of breeding, the health of the bitch and the condition of her uterus, plus numerous other factors.

Sequence of Events

Fertilization and early fetal development begin within the oviducts. The embryos enter the uterus 6 to 10 days following the onset of ovulation. Attachment sites within the endometrium (uterine wall) are formed 17 to 18 days after ovulation. Implantation occurs at these sites 17 to 21 days after fertilization. It appears that fetuses become equally spaced throughout both uterine horns, regardless of the ovary of origin. By day 35, canine body characteristics become recognizable. By day 40 the eyelids are formed with fused lids, each digit has its claw, hair and color markings are visible, and the sex can be determined. The skeleton can be visualized on X rays after 42 to 45 days of pregnancy.

The Bitch

The bitch's body weight will usually increase a total of 20 to 50%, with an average of 36% during pregnancy. Between 30 and 40 days of gestation, the uterus may turn in on itself to some degree and create some discomfort for the bitch. Also during this time period, the bitch may start to experience a mild increase in serum white blood cell numbers as well as a mild anemia.

Gestation Length

Variation in the timing of ovulation, multiple breeding dates, and the inconsistent length of estrus make it difficult to know precisely the day of fertilization or the due date of a litter. The traditional 63 to 65 days from the time of first breeding is *not* a perfect formula. A range of potential due dates—56 to 72 days from the day of first breeding—would have a greater likelihood of proving correct.

A method for choosing the potential due date can be relatively simple and precise. This is valuable information when working with a bitch likely to require a caesarean section, or of interest to an owner who simply has a strong desire to know precise whelping dates. Vaginal exfoliative cytology smears, prepared by the owner or veterinarian, should be obtained daily throughout standing heat and for several days beyond the date of first refusal to breed (see CHAPTER 11, "NORMAL REPRODUCTION"). The whelping date is likely to be 56 to 58 days after the first day of diestrus, as determined by vaginal cytology. Further, after day 42 to 45 of gestation, X rays of the abdomen can be reviewed and the number of fetuses counted. The larger litters tend to have shorter gestation lengths (55 to 57 days), while bitches with only one or two puppies tend to have longer lengths of gestation (57 to 59 days).

PREGNANCY DIAGNOSIS

Palpation

Clinically, **palpation** (feeling with the hands) of the abdomen by a veterinarian is an easy, relatively inexpensive, and reliable means of recognizing pregnancy, if performed at the proper times. Between days 20 and 30 of gestation (or 20 to 30 days after first breeding), the uterine swelling at the individual placental sites is usually **palpable.** Palpation is always easier to describe than to perform in practice. Palpation of a lean and relaxed dog is not equivalent to palpating one that is overweight or nervous.

Radiographs (X rays)

Radiographic evaluation of the abdomen is an excellent tool for diagnosing pregnancy and

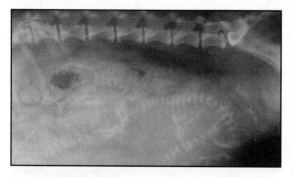

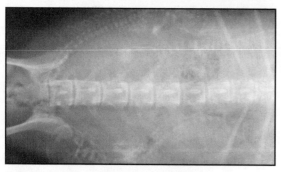

Figure 1. Lateral (top) and ventrodorsal (bottom) abdominal X rays of a pregnant dog on day 50 of diestrus. The easiest methods for estimating litter size are counting fetal skulls or vertebral columns.

probably the most reliable aid for determining the number of developing fetuses. In order to recognize a fetus radiographically, there must be fetal skeleton development (*see* FIGURES 1 and 2).

Fetal skeletal elements may be first detected 20 to 21 days prior to parturition, which represent 42 to 52 days after mating. Usually, radiographic evaluation is used not only for pregnancy diagnosis, but also for determination of fetal numbers and as a tool for predicting **dystocia** (difficult whelping) problems. Collapse of the skeletal elements may indicate fetal death.

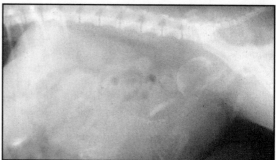

Figure 2. Lateral (top) and ventrodorsal (bottom) abdominal X rays of a bitch with a single fetus. Notice the skull (arrow) width versus the pelvis width in (bottom), suggesting that dystocia (difficult whelping) may occur. Ligament relaxation, however, is difficult to predict. This fetus was delivered normally without difficulty.

Diagnostic Ultrasound

The use of ultrasonic equipment in pregnancy diagnosis has been extremely rewarding. Ultrasonography has consistently recognized fetal forms within the uterus between days 16 and 20 of gestation (*see* FIGURE 3). Visualization of the functioning fetal heart can usually be accomplished by day 25 of gestation. The equipment for these procedures can be extremely expensive, but is becoming widely available nevertheless. Differentiation of pregnancy versus **pyometra** (severe uterine infection) and early recognition of pregnancy can be accomplished quickly and safely with ultrasound.

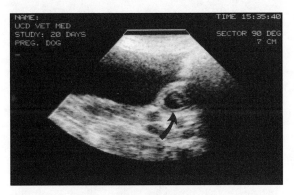

Figure 3. One fetal vesicle (arrow) on an ultrasound view of the abdomen, in a bitch on day 20 of gestation.

Blood and/or Urine Tests for Pregnancy Diagnosis

There have been no routine blood or urine assays available for the diagnosis of pregnancy in dogs. This is a reflection of the fact that serum hormone concentrations are not significantly different when comparing nonpregnant bitches after the breeding phase of their ovarian cycle with pregnant bitches. However, the hormone relaxin is detectable with special assays and its measurement is potentially a reliable indicator of pregnancy.

NUTRITION AND GENERAL CARE DURING PREGNANCY AND LACTATION

Nutrition

The diet for a breeding bitch or one that is in the first one-half to two-thirds of gestation should consist primarily or totally of good commercial "maintenance" dog food. The dog should be fed normal quantities of food during the 4 weeks following standing heat. Increases in the quantity of food offered, if desired by the bitch, should begin during the 5th and 6th weeks of gestation. The initial mild increase of 20–25% may progress to a total increase in food quantity of 50% by the 8th and 9th weeks of gestation and the 1st week post-whelping. The final period of gestation and the period of lactation should be nutritionally supported with a diet containing higher levels of protein, energy and minerals. Ideally, the label of the gestation/lactation diet should state that the food has passed the American Association of Feed Control Officers trials. The 2nd and 3rd weeks of lactation are often associated with the greatest stress to the bitch, and the caloric requirement may be twice that of anestrus. During the 4th week of lactation the food allotment should start being reduced.

It is wise to increase the number of meals offered to a bitch during the last few weeks of pregnancy. It is not unusual for dogs with large litters to have a limited stomach or abdominal capacity for food owing to physical compression by the fetuses. Offering small meals, separated from disruption by other dogs, is helpful. It is also advantageous to allow the lactating bitch plenty of time to eat. Be certain that the dogs are eating and that the puppies do not interfere with the meals. Some bitches lose significant amounts of weight while nursing a large litter because they have had no real opportunity to eat.

Note: Some owners have a strong desire to supplement a pregnant or lactating bitch's diet. Multipurpose veterinary B-complex vitamins may be beneficial and should not be harmful, but bonemeal and any other calcium supplement should not be given to a bitch at this time. Commercial dog foods contain adequate amounts of calcium and the correct calcium:phosphorus ratio (1.2 to 1.0). Excessive calcium supplementation to bitches in late gestation has been incriminated in predisposing the puppies to gastric dilatation-volvulus or bloat (*see* CHAPTER 30, "THE DIGESTIVE SYSTEM AND DISORDERS"); will interfere with the absorption of zinc, manganese and certain other essential minerals; and may predispose the bitch to dystocia. Calcium supplementation may actually increase the chance of **eclampsia** ("milk fever"; calcium deficiency in a lactating bitch). (*See* Chapter 14, "Reproductive Disorders.")

Mid-Gestation Examination

Many veterinarians recommend routine examination of bitches at days 35 to 45 of gestation. This provides an opportunity to have questions answered and to review diet, supplements, exercise, wormings and any other pertinent factors. Ideally, the breeding bitch should have been vaccinated prior to breeding. The bitch should be tested for heartworm and intestinal parasites prior to proestrus, but can be tested if pregnant. Heartworm **microfilaria** (minute prelarval stage of the heartworm parasite) can cross the placenta into the fetus. Hookworms and roundworms can be treated even if the bitch is pregnant. Veterinarians often recommend that abdominal X rays be taken after day 45 to confirm the pregnancy, count the fetuses and (subjectively) assess their health and viability.

Exercise

Walking a bitch daily throughout the period of pregnancy should be beneficial to the owner as well as the dog. Dogs accustomed to jogging may continue to do so for the initial 4 to 6 weeks of pregnancy. The owner must be careful not to overexert the pet, however.

Parturition (Birth)

CARE OF THE BITCH

Whelping Box

Providing the bitch with a special area for whelping and nursing her pups can prevent her from choosing an undesirable location. Many breeders build a whelping box to meet certain criteria (*see* Figure 4). The box should be large enough for the bitch to stretch out comfortably and have room for a litter of puppies. The sides should be high enough so that young puppies cannot jump out, but low enough so that the bitch can escape easily whenever she wants.

The whelping box should be made available

Figure 4. Whelping box for a Laborador retriever. Note the ledge, which prevents the bitch from accidentally crushing a pup between herself and the wall of the box.

to the bitch beginning 7 to 14 days prior to the whelping date, in order to allow her ample opportunity to become comfortable with the new environment. It should be placed in relatively familiar surroundings that also provide some degree of privacy. The wall of the box should have a ledge near the floor to prevent the reclining bitch from accidentally crushing a pup between herself and the wall (*see* Figure 4).

The whelping box or area should be bedded down with towels. Towels are preferred over newspapers because they are clean, provide nesting material, and can be washed and reused many times. Newspapers are not nearly as soft or warm, and newspaper print can discolor the puppies. The ideal temperature for the box floor should be approximately 75°F, and can be provided by ordinary light bulbs (hot water bottles are cumbersome). There should be some small towels available, as well as scissors, thread, tincture of iodine, and a rectal thermometer for monitoring the temperature of the bitch.

The Final 30 Hours

Eighteen to 30 hours before parturition begins, the plasma progesterone concentration declines below 2 ng/ml (*see* Chapter 11, "Normal Reproduction"). Ten to 14 hours after this critical hormone change, the rectal temperature of the bitch falls below 100°F, and often below 99°F.

The decline in temperature usually precedes labor by 10 to 24 hours.

STAGES OF LABOR

Stage I

This stage begins with the onset of uterine contractions and ends when the cervix is fully **dilated** (opened). Contractions of the uterine musculature are not usually visible externally. The duration of stage I labor in the bitch averages 6 to 12 hours, but may last as long as 24 hours. The bitch during this time may appear restless and nervous, and often refuses to eat. She may be seen to shiver, pant, vomit, chew, scratch at the floor, or pace. Most dogs seek seclusion and/or exhibit nesting behavior (digging or tearing material to create a nest) during or near the end of this phase. There is little for the owner to do aside from providing the bitch with some privacy and an area for whelping.

Stages II and III

Stage II begins with full dilation of the cervix and ends with complete expulsion of the fetus, while stage III begins after expulsion of the fetus and ends with expulsion of the placenta (fetal connection with the uterus). A bitch with more than one puppy will alternate between stage II and stage III. The length of these two stages is highly variable; bitches may deliver pups over a period of a few hours or as many as 24 to 36 hours. Contractions are usually visible. The bitch will be either on her side or in a squatting position. With passage of each pup, the membranes covering the fetus rupture or the bitch frees the pup by removing them.

The time between initiation of stage II labor and birth of the first puppy is variable. Commonly, this period is only 10 to 30 minutes. Active straining for more than 30 to 60 minutes may indicate a problem, and a veterinarian should be consulted. The time interval between the birth of subsequent pups is also variable. It is not unusual for a bitch to deliver several puppies, then rest for a period before beginning the delivery process again. In this situation, a lag of more than 4 to 6 hours is cause for concern. A disturbed, frightened or nervous bitch may stop whelping altogether.

Placentas will usually be passed within 5 to 15 minutes of the birth of each pup. Occasionally, one or two placentas may follow the birth of two puppies that had no placentas, (i.e., one puppy may be born from each uterine horn without placentas, but subsequent pups from either horn are typically preceded by the placenta associated with the previous birth). Approximately 40% of puppies are born in a **breech** (rear-end first) **presentation**. Breech presentation is not abnormal and does not predispose to dystocia in dogs.

The bitch may eat the placentas, although there is no known benefit to this, and the practice is not encouraged. Subsequent vomiting of the placental material is a common occurrence. The bitch should lick each newborn vigorously to remove all fetal membranes from the face and to promote the pups' breathing. If this does not occur within 1 to 3 minutes, the owner can carefully intervene. *Some bitches may not appreciate or understand the human desire to help and may react by attempting to bite.*

The residual fetal membranes should be removed by placing the puppy on a clean, soft towel and vigorously rubbing the pup with the other end of the towel. There is often a large amount of fluid within the membranes of each **neonate** (newborn); failure to use a new *dry* towel for each pup can result in the sensation that one is attempting to squeeze a wet and slippery bar of soap.

The bitch often will sever the umbilical cord with her teeth. If this is not done the owner can intervene, using thread to tie two knots in the cord, the first approximately 1 inch from the pup and the second an additional ¼ inch away (*see* FIGURE 5). Using clean scissors, a cut should then be made between the knots and the severed end dipped in a mild antiseptic, such as tincture of iodine or povidone-iodine (Betadine). The pups should then be left with their mother, except in unusual circumstances, and handled as little as possible. Some bitches will nurse early puppies while delivering subsequent pups, while others will not.

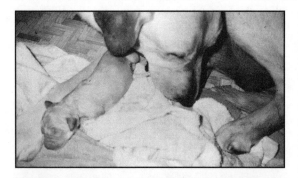

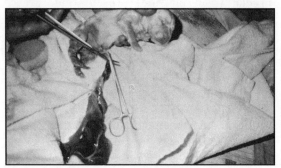

Figure 5. (Top) Yellow Labrador retriever severing the umbilical cord of one of her pups; (bottom) cutting the cord beyond a clamp, if the bitch fails to sever it.

Normal Uterine Involution

After whelping the uterus undergoes a period of repair called **involution.** During this time an odorless green, dark red or brown, or obviously bloody fluid called **lochia** will be discharged from the vulva. This is normal and may vary from a rather significant amount immediately following parturition to quite small amounts 4 to 8 weeks later. This discharge is often licked clean by the bitch. The bitch should ideally remain in good health during the period of uterine involution. The continued good health of the bitch is important; an ill animal with a vaginal discharge postpartum may have a uterine infection requiring veterinary care.

CHAPTER 14

Reproductive Disorders

**by Edward C. Feldman
and Richard W. Nelson**

Disorders of the Female Reproductive Tract

MISMATING

Unwanted pregnancies frequently occur in dogs. Veterinarians in turn are often requested to terminate pregnancies early in gestation, in order to avoid the difficulties encountered with a pregnant bitch or an unwanted litter of puppies. The problem of an unwanted breeding may arise because dog owners are not aware that their pet is "in heat," or because they underestimate the will of a stud or bitch that wants to encounter the opposite sex. Even the best educated and most conscientious owners, however, may still encounter an episode of *mismating.*

Treatment of Bitches Not Intended for Breeding Programs

Several treatment options are available. **Ovariohysterectomy** (spay) is the treatment of choice for the mismated bitch that is not intended for breeding. This procedure permanently eliminates chances of an unwanted pregnancy. It is safe, relatively inexpensive, and eliminates any chance of reproductive problems in the future. Spaying avoids contributing to the more than 6 million unwanted dogs and at least an equal number of unwanted cats that are killed each year in shelters and pounds.

Treatment of the Valuable Breeding Bitch

Estrogens (female sex hormones), administered at the correct dosage and time after an unwanted breeding, tighten the junction between the uterus and the oviducts, preventing migration of developing embryos into the uterus and thus ending pregnancy. However, estrogens are associated with several serious side effects, and the safest estrogen compounds are the least effective in preventing pregnancy. The most effective estrogens dramatically increase the chances for development of **pyometra** (severe uterine infection). Overdosage of estrogens may result in fatal destruction of the bone marrow. Estrogen administration to prevent pregnancy thus is not recommended.

The *recommended* method for managing a mismated, valuable breeding bitch is to examine her 30 days post-breeding with abdominal **ultrasonography** (**ultrasound,** a method for visualizing internal body structures using reflected sound waves). If the bitch is not pregnant, no therapy is required. If she is pregnant, treatment with injections of **prostaglandins,** which eliminate the production of the hormone **progesterone,** can be instituted. Without progesterone, pregnancy terminates in abortion. Use of prostaglandins is a safe and consistently successful means of pregnancy termination in dogs. Physical side effects (panting, increased salivation, vomiting, diarrhea) are transient in nature and not life-threatening. Of course, pregnancy should be confirmed prior to treatment with prostaglandins.

CLINICAL PSEUDOPREGNANCY (FALSE PREGNANCY; PSEUDOCYESIS)

After **estrus** (standing heat), normal bitches enter a phase of the reproductive cycle called **diestrus,** during which progesterone dominates (*see* CHAPTER 11, "NORMAL REPRODUCTION"). Laboratory assays have demonstrated no significant difference in progesterone levels between nonpregnant bitches in diestrus and pregnant bitches. All nonpregnant bitches in diestrus, therefore, can be considered pseudopregnant. However, this **physiologic** (normal) condition needs to be differentiated from *clinical pseudopregnancy,* a disease syndrome recognized by breeders and veterinarians.

The signs of clinical pseudopregnancy are those commonly seen in pregnancy. They may be so convincing that the bitch appears truly pregnant and about to whelp. Clinical signs usually begin 6 to 12 weeks after standing heat. They may be subtle in nature, reflecting simply a change in appetite, weight gain or some abdominal enlargement. Sometimes the signs are suggestive of impending whelping, and can include restlessness, decreased activity, nesting behavior, loss of appetite, vomiting, or mothering of inanimate objects. The signs may also be quite overt and confusing, involving lactation or abdominal contractions. Bitches have been examined for delayed parturition, uterine inertia, or **dystocia** (difficult whelping), and have subsequently been shown to be pseudopregnant!

Diagnosis and Interpretation

The diagnosis is made by confirming the typical signs in the absence of demonstrable pregnancy. Thus, no blood, urine or other tests are required, assuming that abdominal X rays or ultrasonography are negative for pregnancy. It is not usually possible to determine whether a bitch was once pregnant and subsequently aborted or resorbed a litter (*see* below), although this would be considered rare.

Clinical pseudopregnancy is an exaggeration of the normal state. A bitch that fails to ovulate, one with abnormal ovaries or an abnormal *pituitary gland,* would not be able to exhibit clinical pseudopregnancy (*see* CHAPTER 11, "NORMAL REPRODUCTION"). Clinical pseudopregnancy demonstrates that a bitch is normal, rather than being a source of concern with respect to future ovarian cycles.

Treatment

Therapy may not be recommended for mild clinical pseudopregnancy, primarily because it is usually self-limiting within 1 to 3 weeks. The most worrisome clinical problems of pseudopregnancy are nesting behavior and lactation. Nesting may result in destruction or staining of household furnishings. Lactation may be uncomfortable for the bitch and represents a potential infection problem. Whenever possible, no treatment should be instituted.

Persistent lactation, a response to continuing stimuli for milk letdown, sometimes requires therapeutic intervention. Most bitches stimulate themselves by licking, by mothering inanimate objects or by having an unrelated litter of puppies in close proximity. Other stimuli include warm or cold packing of the mammary glands or running water over the glands, efforts by owners to make their pets more comfortable. Placing an **Elizabethan collar** (a wide collar that restricts contact between the head and the body) around the neck of the bitch and removing any objects she may be mothering should hasten the resolution of pseudopregnancy. If these measures do not succeed, or if a more aggressive strategy is deemed necessary, we recommend that water be removed from the bitch for a 6- to 10-hour period, each night, for

3 to 7 consecutive nights. Water deprivation forces fluid conservation and so lactation should quickly cease. Alternatively, the bitch should be treated by a veterinarian.

Spontaneous Abortion or Resorption of Fetuses

Premature expulsion of dead or living fetuses during late gestation (abortion), or **resorption** (biochemical dissolution) of a fetus or fetuses, pose difficult diagnostic dilemmas for veterinarians. The incidence of abortion or resorption of canine fetuses is extremely difficult to estimate, because there is no reliable method for confirming pregnancy during the first 3 weeks of gestation, and because most bitches are never evaluated with abdominal ultrasonography or X rays. It is quite possible that many bitches thought to have aborted or resorbed a litter were never pregnant at all.

Causes

Even when aborted fetuses or placentas are evaluated by a pathologist, the exact cause for pregnancy failure may not be discovered. The causes of pregnancy failure can encompass congenital/hereditary defects, infections, drugs, toxins, trauma, uterine disease, hormonal abnormalities, severe malnutrition, and significant systemic illness. In general terms, these causes are usually divided into three broad categories: fetal defects, abnormal maternal environment, and infectious agents.

Diagnosis and Management

Abdominal ultrasonography is a highly sensitive and reliable means of diagnosing pregnancy (as early as 16 days of gestation) and detecting viable fetuses by recognition of their functioning hearts (as early as 24 days of gestation). Early confirmation of pregnancy gives a veterinarian the opportunity to recognize loss of a few fetuses or an entire litter. The bitch that has aborted a litter and is ill requires veterinary care, but one that remains clinically healthy is easier to manage. If the bitch has aborted only once, she should be checked for *Brucella* infection (*see* Chapter 35, "Bacterial Diseases"); if negative, she can be bred during the following heat period. If a bitch is *Brucella*-negative and has aborted several times, a different stud should be tried. If that fails, examination by a veterinary specialist is warranted. Every attempt should be made to obtain a fetus or several fetuses immediately after they are aborted for **necropsy** (postmortem examination) and culture for infectious agents.

Dystocia

Dystocia is defined as difficult birth or the inability to expel the fetus from the uterus through the birth canal. Dystocia is a fairly common occurrence in dogs; however, management of dystocia is not always a straightforward procedure.

Practical Considerations

The uterus. Dystocia may be caused by primary uterine inertia (uterine weakness or insufficient uterine force to propel the pup through the birth canal). This category of dystocia is most likely to respond to medical management.

The pelvis. Dystocia can also result if the birth canal is too small. This constriction may be the result of heredity, or may be an acquired defect such as a fracture. Such dystocias usually require surgical intervention.

The fetus. Occasionally the fetus is too large for the birth canal. The most common explanation is development of only one fetus, creating a single large pup. Another common problem is an abnormal fetal position. These problems usually require surgery.

The vagina. A bitch may be examined and found to have a puppy wedged in the vagina. This may be caused by fetal oversize or an undersized pelvis. The vagina itself may be too small, as would occur with a vaginal **stricture** (narrowing). A vaginal stricture or band of tissue can obstruct fetal passage, resulting in the need for surgery or extensive manipulation.

Breed Incidence

Brachycephalic breeds. Brachycephalic (flat-faced) breeds typically have a narrow or small pelvis. To complicate matters, brachycephalic breeds such as Bulldogs, Pugs, Boston Terriers, Sealyham Terriers, Scottish Terriers and others are also among the breeds having large heads and wide shoulders—additional impediments to normal birthing (secondary uterine inertia problems).

Miniature and small breeds. These dogs are, subjectively, more often nervous, apprehensive and prone to single-pup litters. The psychological state of the bitch can disrupt or interrupt parturition and result in primary uterine inertia. A single fetus may be quite large, resulting in fetal obstruction.

Large breeds. As a group, large-breed bitches have a low incidence of dystocia problems. Occasionally an extremely large litter of puppies is encountered. In such situations, uterine fatigue may be a potential problem.

Diagnosis

History. The diagnosis of dystocia is usually based on observation of one or more of the following:

Thirty to 60 minutes of strong abdominal contractions without successful expulsion of a pup

Greater than 4 to 6 hours since the birth of a pup

Failure to deliver pups 24 to 36 hours after the rectal temperature was noted to fall

Crying, and licking or biting at the vulvar area during whelping

Prolonged pregnancy, lasting beyond 70 to 72 days from the first breeding or beyond 60 days from the first day of diestrus

On average, puppies should be delivered every 45 to 60 minutes. Several pups may be born within a period of minutes, but bitches may "rest" periodically during whelping for several hours. These rests are not associated with abdominal contractions and usually do not persist beyond 4 to 6 hours. The general condition and health of the bitch are important information for the owner and veterinarian. The veteri-

narian must be informed of any medications the owner may already have administered or other treatments attempted.

In general, the size of the stud dog is not helpful in the diagnosis of dystocia. Use of large males, relative to the height and weight of the bitch, does not result in an increased incidence of dystocia. The bitch and uterus are the major determinants of fetal size *in utero*.

Radiographs and ultrasonography. The most valuable tests that a veterinarian can perform on a bitch suspected of having a dystocia problem are radiography (X rays) and ultrasonography of the abdomen. X rays can confirm or dismiss the presence of pregnancy, and are an excellent tool for locating and identifying malpositioned fetuses that cannot be delivered normally. Ultrasonography is a superb means of assessing fetal viability.

Treatment

Treatment of dystocia as determined by the veterinarian is based on a multitude of factors. It may consist of doing absolutely nothing, administering a mild sedative to the bitch, or administering drugs to stimulate uterine contractions. Surgical removal of puppies from the uterus (**caesarean section**) is a relatively safe and successful procedure. When other means of management fail, caesarean section is well warranted.

Planning. Certain breeds are highly prone to dystocia; thus it is wise to estimate whelping dates in order to avoid unnecessary surprises or emergencies. Such predictions are relatively reliable and easy to achieve, allowing for ready application to practical clinical situations (*see* CHAPTER 13, "PREGNANCY AND PARTURITION").

The owner of a bitch likely to require caesarean section should learn how to prepare smears for vaginal cytology (*see* CHAPTER 11, "NORMAL REPRODUCTION"). Smears should be obtained from the first day of standing heat until 7 days after the day of first refusal to breed. The entire series of slides should be evaluated by a veterinarian. The first day of diestrus should be identified. Approximately 45 to 50 days into diestrus, abdominal X rays can be taken and the number of fetuses counted. Small litters (only one or two puppies) should be assigned a due date on day 58 or 59 of diestrus. Large litters typically have a shorter gestation period and should have a due date of day 55 or 56 of diestrus. Average-sized litters should be delivered on day 57 of diestrus. Such predictions are not infallible, but they have proven to be quite accurate. Any bitch with a previous history of dystocia or from a breed prone to this problem should undergo this simple procedure.

Post-whelping Oxytocin Injection

Many veterinarians and breeders recommend administration of the hormone **oxytocin** at the end of parturition. This injection is thought to aid in expelling any retained placentas or fetuses, hasten uterine involution (*see* CHAPTER 13, "PREGNANCY AND PARTURITION"), and decrease postpartum hemorrhage. Others have claimed that the injection does little good and is completely unnecessary. Currently this is provided at UC Davis, but it is not strongly encouraged.

SUBINVOLUTION OF PLACENTAL SITES

Normal reconstruction of the uterine wall following parturition (**involution**) is typically associated with a bloody vaginal discharge. As judged by ultrasonography, involution requires approximately 15 weeks to be completed. The bloody vaginal discharge usually persists for 1 to 6 weeks. Some healthy bitches, however, may exhibit a bloody discharge (one without odor or that is off-color) lasting well beyond 6 weeks (**subinvolution**). These normal dogs typically have no fever or other worrisome clinical signs other than the vulvar discharge. The pups in their litters are also healthy. The bitches affected are usually less than 3 years of age and the syndrome follows their first or second litter.

ECLAMPSIA (PUERPERAL TETANY)

Eclampsia is an acute, life-threatening syndrome caused by decreased circulating calcium concentrations (**hypocalcemia**). It is seen most commonly in small- to medium-sized bitches during early lactation post-whelping or, rarely, in late pregnancy. The hypocalcemia is most likely due to calcium loss in lactated milk coupled with poor dietary calcium utilization. The stresses of nursing a litter can reduce the bitch's appetite, further lowering calcium intake without reducing calcium loss into the milk. Also, in an effort to prevent eclampsia, pregnant bitches are sometimes fed bone meal and calcium supplements, which may actually increase the chances for eclampsia's development.

Clinical Signs

Eclampsia is most common in small dogs and least common large dogs. The signs seen by the veterinarian are usually dependent on how quickly the owner recognizes a problem and seeks professional care. The initial signs of hypocalcemia may be subtle and vague, especially to the inexperienced owner. The behavior changes are similar to those seen prior to whelping (i.e., restlessness, nervousness, pacing, panting and whining). But, in addition, the bitch is likely to lose maternal responses to her pups and begin to exhibit some of the early signs of hypocalcemic tetany (including irritability, restlessness, increased salivation, stiffness of gait, unsteady gait, and pain on walking).

Within minutes to several hours of the first signs a bitch may progress into a much more severe, potentially fatal clinical state. **Tetany** can be exhibited as severe muscle spasms or an inability to stand. These signs are usually associated with fever and a rapid heart rate. If untreated, the bitch will experience **seizures** (fits). Noise or touch may initiate muscle spasms or seizure-like activity.

Diagnosis and Treatment

The diagnosis is based on typical signs (neurologic signs or nervousness) in a lactating bitch. In addition to the treatment and recommendations provided by a veterinarian, the owner can and should take additional measures to prevent recurrence of eclampsia. Older pups (> 3 weeks) can be permanently removed from the bitch and hand-raised. Younger puppies can also be hand-raised, reducing the likelihood of a relapse but requiring a large amount of work by the owner. It would be helpful to alternate nursing and bottle-feeding daily for 10 days (i.e., either hand-feed one-half of the litter every day or the entire litter every other day). These approaches will reduce milk production and thereby reduce the chances for a relapse of hypocalcemia. If a relapse should occur, all nursing by the pups should be permanently discontinued. The diet of any bitch that has had eclampsia should consist of a quality commercial dog food containing the correct canine calcium:phosphorus ratio of 1.2 to 1.0.

PYOMETRA

Pyometra is one of the most common, serious, and worrisome disorders in the bitch. It is a hormonally mediated disorder of diestrus, which means that the disease is invariably associated with the progesterone-dominated phase of the ovarian cycle (*see* CHAPTER 11, "NORMAL REPRODUCTION"). The disease results from overwhelming bacterial growth within the uterus. The infection causes a mild to severe, potentially life-threatening **septicemia** (presence of bacteria in the bloodstream, accompanied by related clinical signs of disease) and **toxemia** (presence of toxins in the blood, accompanied by clinical signs), which require aggressive therapy. The uterus may have undergone pathologic changes prior to development of the disease, which is assumed to be caused by an exaggerated response to progesterone stimulation. It is extremely rare for pyometra to occur in a bitch that is not under the influence of progesterone.

The Older Bitch

Bitches older than 7 to 8 years of age are increasingly prone to the development of pyometra. The syndrome is the result of repeated exposures to progesterone during normal diestrus phases. After years of cyclic ovarian activity, the predisposition for and incidence of pyometra increase. The risk of developing pyometra thus becomes exaggerated in an otherwise healthy older dog.

The Younger Bitch

A significant number of young bitches (6 months to 6 years of age) have been diagnosed with pyometra. It is unlikely that the same process seen in older dogs would account for their uterine disease. However, there is a strong correlation between the incidence of pyometra in young dogs and estrogen administration, given in an attempt to prevent pregnancy. Estrogen administration for accidental breedings is not recommended (*see* "MISMATING," above). If the misbred bitch is not valuable as a brood bitch, she should be spayed. If she is of value, an unwanted pregnancy or induced abortion is far preferable to the side effects of estrogen therapy.

History and Clinical Signs

Clinical signs will depend upon the patency of the cervix. An obvious sign seen in bitches with an open-cervix pyometra is a vaginal discharge which looks and smells like pus. The discharge is usually first noticed 4 to 8 weeks after standing heat. Pyometra has been diagnosed as early as the end of standing heat and as late as 12 to 14 weeks after standing heat. Other common signs include lethargy, depression, lack of appetite, increase in water intake and urine output, vomiting and diarrhea. The overall health of the affected dog is most dependent on how quickly the owner recognizes the problem and seeks veterinary assistance.

The bitch with closed-cervix pyometra is more often quite ill at the time of diagnosis due to the lack of an obvious and easily recognized vaginal discharge as is seen in open-cervix infection. Instead, owners notice an insidious onset of signs that usually include depression and inappetence. In conjunction with the vomiting and diarrhea associated with this syndrome, dogs with closed-cervix pyometra may become critically ill or even die.

Diagnosis and Complications

Pyometra can often be diagnosed rather easily. *A diagnosis of pyometra should be suspected in any ill bitch.* The diagnosis is confirmed when the appropriate clinical signs are present in conjunction with typical abnormalities on physical examination, laboratory studies, and X-ray or ultrasonographic evaluation. A definitive diagnosis becomes a challenge when the history is vague (especially regarding ovarian cycle activity) or when a vaginal discharge is not present (closed-cervix pyometra).

Surgical Treatment

Spaying is the preferred treatment for pyometra unless the owner strongly wishes to maintain the reproductive potential of the affected dog. Relatively healthy bitches are usually excellent surgical risks; severely ill animals should receive intensive care. In some dogs surgery should not be postponed for more than a few hours.

Medical Treatment

Medical therapy utilizing hormones and quinine produces inconsistent results and is not often successful. In addition, systemic antibiotics are usually ineffective as the sole therapy for canine pyometra. However, results using prostaglandins have been extremely encouraging, and these compounds now offer a reliable medical alternative for therapy. The medication causes contraction of the uterus, reduction in circulating progesterone concentrations, and (the least consistent effect) relaxation of the cervix. This therapy as used by an experienced veterinarian can be extremely effective.

INFERTILITY

Problems of infertility or apparent infertility occur commonly in the bitch. Veterinary advice will often be sought after a bitch fails to conceive, if she fails to exhibit "normal" breeding behavior, when her cycles appear to be unusual, or for a myriad of other disturbances. Further, a championship or other important title may be earned by the bitch, insuring demand for and value of her puppies before any attempt has been made at breeding. "Infertility," therefore, is a huge category comprising a long list of anatomic, physiologic and behavioral problems, as well as a number of apparent husbandry misunderstandings.

Before embarking on an investigation into the potential cause(s) of infertility in a bitch, the male should first be assessed. The normal male is continuously fertile (i.e., continuously producing sperm), while the female is usually fertile only 1 to 3 weeks per year.

Most bitches examined by us for an apparent infertility problem are healthy but are not being bred by normal males, or are not being allowed to breed when they are in estrus. Occasionally, however, the fault lies with the female: some bitches cycle too frequently, fail to cycle, suffer systemic illness, or have some predisposing congenital abnormality. Invariably, these bitches require veterinary care.

CONGENITAL ABNORMALITIES OF THE VAGINA AND VULVA

Five major types of abnormalities in embryonic development of the vagina have been reported in the dog, each resulting in a narrowing of the reproductive tract (vaginal stricture). These abnormalities include:

1. a band of fibrous tissue crossing and narrowing the **lumen** (interior) of the vagina;
2. a fibrous ring compressing the vaginal lumen;
3. vulvar **hypoplasia** (underdevelopment), which narrows the opening of the vulva;
4. incomplete fusion of two embryonic ducts, causing a "double" vagina;
5. hypoplasia of the vagina (as opposed to hypoplasia of the vulvar opening).

Clinical Signs

Bitches with any of the above defects are usually brought to veterinarians for one, two, or all three of the following concerns: vulvar discharge, chronic vulvar licking, or attracting male dogs. These three signs are the result of **vaginitis** (inflammation of the vagina), usually recurrent, and caused by the stricture. Inflammation of the vagina results in an increasing amount of vaginal secretions (discharge); irritation which causes the licking; and both of these problems together with secondary bacterial overgrowth cause odors that attract males.

Much less commonly, a bitch may be unwilling to breed, unable to breed, or appear to be in pain when the male attempts or succeeds in breeding. These latter concerns are least common because most female dogs owned in this country have had an ovariohysterectomy and have never been bred.

Treatment

Before making any treatment recommendation, the owner must understand the problem and must appreciate that no treatment except surgery will permanently resolve the clinical signs. Many owners elect not to treat their pets once they understand that the problem is self-limiting, almost never causes systemic illness, and that the signs, while likely to wax and wane throughout the dog's life, are not life-threatening and may not be as serious or dangerous as corrective surgery. If treatment is deemed necessary, less aggressive therapy should be recommended before surgery is considered.

Treatment is given usually because the bitch is extremely uncomfortable and appears to be in significant pain. In these dogs, the approach is to treat with a vaginal douche one to three times daily until the signs abate. This can be accomplished by filling a FleetR enema bottle with a commercially available antiseptic solution and flushing the vagina one to three times daily. The procedure should be continued until the bitch regains her normal appearance and attitude. Prior to treatment, all dogs with a vaginal discharge should be examined by a veterinarian.

VAGINITIS AND VAGINAL INFECTIONS

The difficulties and controversy associated with vaginitis are its causes, frequency of occurrence, and frequency of occult (not clinically apparent) disease. It would seem that primary, uncomplicated vaginitis is not common. Our experience indicates that, in most cases, infection is secondary to other problems, such as strictures, trauma or foreign bodies.

Is a positive vaginal culture meaningful?

Bacterial infections have been implicated as a cause of infertility in the bitch and as a source of disease for breeding males. However, approximately 95% of normal bitches carry bacteria in the vagina. Merely isolating bacteria from the vaginal tract does not constitute the basis for a diagnosis of disease. Conversely, some organisms, such as *Brucella canis,* may be difficult to isolate; thus, a negative culture does not ensure that a bitch is free of an infectious disease.

Some owners of stud dogs require a "negative" vaginal culture from the bitch to be used in breeding. However, most male dogs harbor microorganisms in the **prepuce** (fold of skin

enclosing the penis) and **urethra** (membranous tube carrying urine from the bladder to the exterior of the body) that are similar to those classified as "normal vaginal flora." It is unjustified to refuse to allow a stud dog to breed a particular bitch because bacteria have been isolated from her vagina. It is also unjustified to associate all positive vaginal cultures with infection, vaginitis or infertility. Furthermore, administration of antibiotics has not been demonstrated to alter the bacterial flora of the vagina.

Disorders of the Male Reproductive Tract

DISORDERS OF THE PENIS AND PREPUCE

Persistent Penile Frenulum

Persistent penile frenulum refers to the abnormal persistence of a thin band of connective tissue that extends from beneath the tip of the penis to either the prepuce or the underside of the penile shaft itself, producing a downward or lateral deviation of the tip of the **glans penis** (cap-shaped termination of the penile shaft). This abnormality usually is identified during the physical examination when a pup is presented to a veterinarian for its initial immunizations. Clinical signs of persistent penile frenulum may include:

- Streaming of urine onto the hind feet or in other unexpected directions during urination
- Subsequent **dermatitis** (skin inflammation) of the hind limbs caused by urine scald
- Inability to extrude the penis from the prepuce during penile engorgement (erection)
- Discomfort or pain during penile engorgement
- Repeated licking of the preputial area

Diagnosis of persistent penile frenulum is made by visual observation. The frenulum usually is avascular (lacking blood vessels) and can easily be removed surgically.

Phimosis

Phimosis refers to an abnormally small preputial opening, such that the penis is unable to be extruded properly. Phimosis may occur as a birth defect or be acquired as a complication of inflammation, **edema** (tissue swelling), cancer, or scar-tissue formation. Small preputial openings may interfere with urination and result in accumulation of urine within the preputial cavity. Constant urine dribbling, abnormal streaming of urine, persistent preputial swelling, and secondary bacterial infections may develop. More commonly, phimosis interferes with extrusion of the penis during mating. An inability to copulate will be quickly obvious to the observer. Treatment involves surgical enlargement of the preputial opening.

Paraphimosis

Paraphimosis is a condition wherein an engorged or swollen penis cannot be retracted back into the preputial sheath. Paraphimosis is most commonly associated with mating difficulties. Either the preputial hairs become entangled around the base of the glans penis, forming a restrictive band, or the extruded penis becomes trapped when the preputial opening adheres to the penis and is pulled down into the preputial cavity as the erection subsides.

Paraphimosis is an acute medical emergency. Failure or delay in treatment will increase the risk for development of obstruction of the **urethra** (the membranous tube that transports urine from the bladder to the exterior of the body) or **gangrene** (death and decay of tissue caused by obstruction of the blood supply) of the penis. Amputation of the penis may be necessary if paraphimosis has been present for longer than 24 hours and no therapy has been applied. Treatment is designed to reestablish normal blood flow through the penis by removing restrictive bands of tissue, hair or foreign objects, cleansing **necrotic** (dead) areas of the penis, and replacing the penis into the prepuce. Surgical enlargement of the preputial opening may be required in severe cases that do not respond to medical management.

Taking precautions before and after mating can aid in preventing paraphimosis. Hairs around the preputial opening should be clipped prior to breeding. After mating the penis and prepuce should be inspected frequently, to be sure that the penis retracts completely into the prepuce. The prepuce itself should ride easily over the penis and should not be turned in on itself.

Balanoposthitis

Balanoposthitis (inflammation of the glans penis and prepuce) should be suspected whenever pus is observed dripping from the preputial opening. In normal dogs there should be either no preputial discharge or an occasional small amount of yellow-white smegma (a thick glandular secretion accumulating beneath the prepuce). Balanoposthitis typically develops following a change in the ecology of the preputial cavity (e.g., a foreign body, trauma) that fosters overgrowth of the microorganisms normally present there. Mild balanoposthitis is a common clinical finding in dogs and usually causes no problems. Dogs with severe balanoposthitis, however, may exhibit acute swelling and inflammation of the prepuce, abundant preputial discharge, pain, and abscess formation.

Diagnosis is usually self-evident; however, a thorough examination of the penis and prepuce should be performed by a veterinarian to identify possible foreign bodies, lacerations, masses or abscesses. Treatment involves elimination of any predisposing factors, cleansing of the preputial cavity and penis with mild antiseptic solutions or a sterile salt solution, and infusion of antibiotic ointments into the preputial cavity over a 2- to 4-week period. Oral antibiotics may also be indicated. Recurrence of balanoposthitis is common despite therapy, especially when an underlying, predisposing factor cannot be identified.

Penile Trauma

Trauma to the penis typically results from automobile accidents, mating, aggressive confrontations with other dogs, or impalement on a fence during a jump. Bruises, lacerations, puncture wounds, **hematomas** (localized pockets of blood under the skin), fractures of the penile bone, and urethral obstruction may develop. Hemorrhage, swelling and pain are common findings. Dogs with penile trauma should be examined by a veterinarian, who can assess the extent of damage, the integrity of the urethra, and the status of the penile bone. Treatment is aimed at controlling hemorrhage, cleansing the wounds, **suturing** (stitching) any lacerations, and applying antibiotic creams to the penis until the damaged tissue has healed.

Tumors of the Penis and Prepuce

The most common tumor is the **transmissible venereal tumor,** which is transmitted from dog to dog by sexual contact. Other tumors that may occur include mast cell tumors, squamous cell carcinomas, fibromas, and **papillomas.** (*See* Chapter 22, "The Skin and Disorders.") With the exception of transmissible venereal tumors, penile tumors typically occur in older dogs. Clinical signs of a penile tumor can include swelling in the region of the prepuce, abnormal preputial discharge, excessive licking of the prepuce and penis, **hematuria** (blood in the urine), and straining to urinate. A definitive diagnosis requires microscopic examination of a biopsy sample. Therapy and prognosis are dependent on the tumor type. (*See* Chapter 38, "Cancer.")

Disorders of the Testes

Cryptorchidism

Cryptorchidism refers to failure of one or both **testes** (testicles) to descend into the **scrotum** (dependent pouch of skin containing the testicles) by 8 weeks of age. Retention of a testis within the abdomen is most common, although the testis may occasionally lodge in the **inguinal canal** (passage between the groin area and the scrotum) or alongside the penis. Although nongenetic factors may be involved, there is no doubt that genetic predisposition plays an important role in the development of cryptorchidism. The occurrence of cryptorchidism is higher overall in purebred dogs, in certain breeds, and within certain families of a breed. The mode of inheritance has been difficult to establish, however.

Diagnosis is usually made on routine physical examination, with the finding of only one or no scrotal testes. Because of the strong genetic implications, further breedings of an affected male and its parents are discouraged, and neutering is recommended. Surgical therapy to place the retained testis into the scrotum is considered an unethical practice.

Testicular Tumors

Tumors of the testes are common in dogs. The three most common tumors are *Sertoli cell tumors* (derived from cells within the testicular tubules that are important for nurture and development of sperm), *seminomas* (derived from sperm-producing cells), and *interstitial tumors* (derived from male sex hormone-producing cells). All three tumor types occur with approximately equal frequency in the canine population. The average age for development of testicular tumors is 10 years, with a range of 3 to 19 years. The age of onset is earlier when the involved testis is outside the scrotum, as in cases of cryptorchidism (*see* above). There is a much greater incidence of testicular cancer in cryptorchid testes than in normally descended testes.

Clinical signs are variable and can include enlargement of the involved testis, distention of the abdomen, infertility, *prostate gland* problems (e.g., blood dripping from the penis, bloody urine, difficulty urinating, constipation), and signs of **feminization** (development of female sex characteristics). Male feminization results from the production of **estrogen** (female sex hormone) by the tumor. Clinical signs include non-itchy, symmetrical hair loss, **hyperpigmentation** (localized, abnormal darkening of the skin), **gynecomastia** (overdevelopment of the male mammary glands), attraction of other male dogs, and standing in a female (squatting) posture to urinate.

Definitive diagnosis of a testicular tumor requires microscopic examination of a biopsy specimen or a surgically excised testis. Therapy involves surgical removal of the involved testis. Chemotherapy or radiation therapy may be indicated in dogs whose tumors have spread (**metastasized**) beyond the initial tumor site. (*See* Chapter 22, "The Skin and Disorders" and Chapter 38, "Cancer".)

Infectious Orchitis/Epididymitis

Inflammation of the testis (**orchitis**) and **epididymis** (epididymitis, inflammation of the coiled, elongated duct used for storage, maturation and movement of sperm) usually occurs together and typically is caused by bacteria. The bacteria gain access by direct trauma (e.g., puncture wounds), retrograde passage of infected urine or prostate gland secretions, or spread from a blood-borne infection. Bacteria commonly isolated include staphylococci, streptococci, *Escherichia coli, Proteus,* and *Brucella canis.* If the infection goes untreated, chronic inflammation and destruction of the sperm-producing capacity of the infected testis may result.

Clinical signs of acute disease include sudden pain, scrotal swelling, lethargy, inappetence and a reluctance to stand or walk. *Such dogs should be examined by a veterinarian immediately.* Because of the pain, affected dogs often resist physical examination. The primary clinical sign of chronic disease is infertility.

Diagnosis is based on the history, physical findings, isolation of the causative bacterium by culture of urine and semen, and appropriate blood tests for *Brucella canis.* (*See* "CANINE BRUCELLOSIS" IN CHAPTER 35, "BACTERIAL DISEASES".) Treatment involves the administration of appropriate antibiotics for a minimum of 3 weeks, supportive therapy (e.g., intravenous fluids), and possibly neutering (depending on the intended use of the dog). The prognosis for maintaining fertility in dogs following orchitis/epididymitis is guarded. If the sperm-producing cells remain intact and tubule obstruction does not occur, sperm production and fertility may be restored in several months. At the earliest, a dog should not be declared infertile based on semen evaluation until at least 3 months have elapsed following treatment.

Lymphocytic Orchitis
Lymphocytic orchitis is caused by failure of the host's immune system to recognize the testis as "self"; that is, it results from an autoimmune reaction. Eventual destruction of the testis generally follows. The immunologic attack may be triggered following testicular trauma, infection or inflammation, or may occur spontaneously in dogs with a genetic predisposition. The primary clinical sign is infertility and lack of sperm in the semen when both testes are involved. Because of the progressive nature of this condition, the prognosis for return of fertility is poor. Treatment is difficult and, because of the potential genetic implications, is probably not warranted.

Idiopathic Testicular Degeneration
This disease is characterized by loss of function of the sperm-producing cells, with variable involvement of the sex-hormone-producing cells. It is a progressive disorder of unknown cause that eventually results in testicular atrophy, sterility, and a variable loss of libido (sexual drive). Idiopathic testicular degeneration usually develops in dogs between 3 and 6 years of age. The primary clinical sign is infertility. Diagnosis requires identification of changes in the consistency and size of the testes, lack of sperm in a semen evaluation, and noninflammatory tubule degeneration as determined by microscopic examination of a biopsy specimen. There is no known treatment.

DISORDERS OF THE PROSTATE GLAND

Benign Prostatic Hyperplasia
Benign prostatic **hyperplasia** (BPH) refers to enlargement of the prostate gland caused by multiplication of the cells of the prostate gland. BPH is the most common disorder affecting the prostate gland in dogs. It is believed to result from excessive exposure of the prostate to **androgens** (male sex hormones, such as **testosterone**). Clinical signs usually are absent, although occasionally constipation, difficulty in defecating, and blood in the urine may be evident. Diagnosis is based on rectal examination of the prostate. Treatment is not required if there are no clinical manifestations. Neutering is the treatment of choice in dogs exhibiting clinical signs. The prostate gland will decrease in size within weeks of the neutering operation.

Bacterial Prostatitis
Bacterial infection of the prostate gland with resulting inflammation is common in dogs. The bacteria involved in general are similar to those causing urinary tract infection, and include

Escherichia coli, staphylococci, streptococci, *Klebsiella, Enterobacter,* and *Mycoplasma.* In cases having an acute onset, the clinical signs may include lethargy, inappetence, urethral or preputial discharge (blood, pus), and abdominal pain. The veterinarian usually can make a tentative diagnosis of bacterial prostatitis on the basis of the history and physical findings. A positive bacterial culture of urine, semen or prostatic fluid will confirm the diagnosis and aid in selecting an antibiotic for therapy. Bacterial prostatitis should be treated with the appropriate antibiotic for a minimum of 3 weeks.

Prostatic fluid should be recultured for bacteria while the patient is receiving antibiotics and after antibiotics have been withdrawn, in order to be certain that the infection has resolved. Failure to control the infection or recurrence of the infection after antibiotics have been withdrawn can lead to chronic bacterial prostatitis. Chronic prostatitis usually is not associated with signs of **systemic** (throughout the body) illness, but is a cause of recurrent urinary tract infections, chronic orchitis, and infertility or sterility in an otherwise healthy, intact male dog. Long-term antibiotic therapy is required for treatment of chronic prostatitis. Antibiotics should be administered for a minimum of 3 months, and potentially for the remainder of the dog's life, if the infection cannot be eliminated. (*See* "INFECTIONS OF THE PROSTATE GLAND" IN CHAPTER 27, URINARY SYSTEM AND DISORDERS).

INFERTILITY

Because most male dogs are neutered at a young age in this country, infertility in the male tends to be an uncommon problem. Development of infertility in a valuable stud dog can be disastrous, however, owing to difficulties in identifying the underlying cause and the limited number of viable therapeutic options available to restore fertility.

Diagnostic Approach

The usual diagnostic approach taken by the veterinarian is to classify the infertility into one of several broad categories, based on the presence or absence of libido and whether the dog has previously sired a litter. The most common sce-nario involves a proven stud dog that subsequently becomes infertile. Typically, the development of infertility is accompanied by a waning of sexual drive. Such dogs are considered to have acquired infertility. A dog that has never sired a litter despite numerous attempts is considered congenitally (from birth) infertile until proven otherwise. Acquired infertility would be a possibility in the latter case, however, if the problem happened to arise before the animal had been used for breeding purposes. Disorders of sexual development, anatomic defects, and functional defects of sperm production are among the possibilities that must be weighed in making a diagnosis.

The presence of normal sexual drive in an infertile dog would imply dysfunction of the testis, epididymis, or prostate gland but normal testosterone concentrations. Conversely, decreased libido in an infertile dog may result from destruction of the cells in the testes that produce testosterone. Other hormonal diseases (e.g., hypothyroidism), hormone-producing testicular tumors, drug therapy, and psychological problems resulting from trauma or pain during sexual arousal, represent other potential diagnoses that must be ruled out.

The diagnosis ultimately is based on information obtained from the history and on the physical examination. A complete reproductive history as well as relevant information concerning the dog's environment, breeding use, previous illnesses, medications and incidents of trauma must be gathered. Particular attention should be paid to the age of the dog, frequency of sexual use, breeding practices of the kennel, presence or absence of previous reproductive problems, and previous or current use of any hormones or medications. Several drugs and hormone preparations have been associated with infertility in dogs. As a general rule, any administered drug potentially can result in infertility. Genetic factors also may contribute to infertility and should be suspected if inbreeding, infertility in related dogs, or problems with other hormonal disorders are identified.

A *Brucella canis* test and semen evaluation are usually performed in all infertility cases. Abnormalities found on semen evaluation provide clues to the underlying cause and dictate the next steps in the diagnostic process. Several typical abnormalities have been identified on semen analysis.

Azoospermia. *Azoospermia* is a complete absence of sperm in the ejaculate. Azoospermia is usually an acquired disorder that develops secondary to dysfunction within the testes. Testicular disorders resulting in azoospermia include idiopathic testicular degeneration, lymphocytic orchitis, infection, trauma and cancer. Other potential causes include incomplete ejaculation, drugs, environmental insults, systemic disease, hormonal disorders (e.g., hypothyroidism), complete obstruction of the testicular ducts or tubules, retrograde ejaculation (i.e., passage of semen into the urinary bladder during ejaculation), and underlying genetic disorders.

Oligospermia. *Oligospermia* is a decrease in the total number of sperm per ejaculate. Most of the disease processes resulting in azoospermia also can cause oligospermia. Whether oligospermia or azoospermia develops may be dependent on the severity of the disease process, the extent of involvement of the reproductive tract (e.g., partial versus complete obstruction of the duct system), and the timing of semen evaluation in relationship to the disease course (e.g., early versus late). With time, oligospermia may eventually progress to azoospermia.

Teratozoospermia. *Teratozoospermia* is an increase in the number of abnormal sperm in the ejaculate. Anatomic defects of sperm are classified as either primary or secondary. Primary abnormalities are believed to represent defects in sperm development within the testes, while secondary abnormalities are nonspecific and may arise during transit through the duct system (i.e., within the epididymis), during handling of the semen or preparation of semen smears for evaluation, or following infection, trauma or fever. Anatomic defects may result from environmental insults, drugs, systemic illness, infectious or lymphocytic orchitis/epididymitis, prostatitis, or congenital defects in sperm development.

Asthenozoospermia. *Asthenozoospermia* is a decrease in **motility** (ability to move) of sperm in the ejaculate. Progressive forward motility is considered normal movement for sperm, and probably reflects viability and ability to fertilize an egg. In a normal canine ejaculate, greater than 70 percent of sperm should exhibit normal motility. The most common cause of asthenozoospermia, especially when the remainder of the semen evaluation is normal, is faulty semen collection technique or sample handling. Persistent problems with sperm motility may reflect a problem in the testes or epididymis. Many of the disorders producing anatomic abnormalities of sperm can also affect sperm motility.

Abnormal Seminal Fluid. Abnormal *seminal fluid* (fluid secretion component of the ejaculate) may be apparent at the time of semen collection or may become apparent during subsequent microscopic examination of the sample. Grossly visible changes usually involve alterations in color and opacity. Canine semen normally is white to opalescent in color, and opaque. Clear and colorless semen suggests azoospermia, which can be confirmed during the microscopic examination. A yellow discoloration suggests contamination of the semen with urine, while a red or brown tint is suggestive of hemorrhage. Hemorrhage does not necessarily imply an underlying disease process, however, and mild hemospermia (blood in the semen) may not interfere with fertility. With a severe inflammatory process involving the reproductive tract, the semen may exhibit a greenish tint, and clumps, clots or flakes may be visible in it. Such inflammation usually is the result of infectious prostatitis, infectious orchitis/epididymitis, or lymphocytic orchitis.

Additional diagnostic tests for infertility may be warranted depending on the results of the semen evaluation. Such tests can include diagnostic **ultrasound** (noninvasive technique for visualizing internal structures of the body by means of sound [echo] reflections) of the testes and prostate gland, culture of the semen, testicular aspiration smear or biopsy, and evaluation of testosterone levels in the blood.

Treatment

Specific therapy for infertility will be dependent on the nature of the underlying problem. Fifty-five to 70 days normally are required for sperm to develop and appear in the ejaculate. Thus, any therapy that is expected to increase the sperm count must be administered for at least 3 months before its efficacy can be critically weighed.

Abstinence from sexual activity is an important adjunct therapy for many infertility problems, and in some cases may be all that is required to resolve transient insults to the testes. Stress, sexual overuse, excessive heat (sperm are sensitive to elevated temperatures), and certain medications are all potentially reversible problems, given sufficient recovery time. Oligospermic and azoospermic dogs should always be reevaluated 3 to 6 months after the initial examination before declaring a problem with sperm production permanent.

CHAPTER 15

Birth Control

by Edward C. Feldman
and Richard W. Nelson

Prevention of Ovarian Cycles

The options available for the prevention of ovarian cycles in dogs are limited. For permanent sterility and complete prevention of cycling, **ovariohysterectomy** (removal of the ovaries, oviducts and uterus) is the most obvious and popular treatment. Reversible contraception by pharmacologic means (drugs) is occasionally requested to prevent or delay **estrus** (heat) without precluding future fertility. These drugs are usually used in hunting, field trial and show dogs because an ill-timed estrus could interfere with performance or participation.

SURGICAL STERILIZATION: OVARIOHYSTERECTOMY
(SPAY OPERATION)

Recommended Procedure
Ovariohysterectomy (OVH) is the recommended method of sterilization in the bitch. The surgery is performed commonly and has few drawbacks. It is a procedure with distinct advantages over **tubal ligation** (tying off the oviducts) or hysterectomy (removal of the uterus). Both of these latter procedures sterilize the bitch but do not

prevent ovarian cycles or the behavior alterations accompanying estrus. Furthermore, the ovaries are left intact and could become a site for cancer or infection. **Ovariectomy** (removal of the ovaries) would leave the uterus as a site for potential infection. Ovariectomy, as a component part of the OVH procedure, has the advantage of substantially reducing the risk of **mammary** (breast) cancer if the procedure is performed before the first ovarian cycle. (Breast cancer in dogs is often observed.)

Some owners may be concerned about depriving a bitch of the benefit derived from ovarian hormones. It is known however that the estrogen and progesterone concentrations of a dog in *anestrus* are similar to those in a spayed bitch (*see* CHAPTER 11, "NORMAL REPRODUCTION"). Therefore, there is no obvious medical reason to avoid or delay OVH.

Spay in Prepuberal Bitches
(Prior to the First Estrus)
The veterinary community and related concerns have debated the age at which bitches should undergo ovariohysterectomy. Common advice, suggesting that a bitch not be neutered until 6

months of age, is being questioned. Conclusions from one recent study were that skeletal, physical and behavioral development did not differ in puppies (of either sex) neutered at 7 *weeks* of age from those neutered at 7 months of age. The primary reason to neuter a bitch (or a male) earlier than 5 or 6 months of age is to decrease the number of unwanted puppies with which our society must deal. Millions of unwanted puppies and kittens are euthanized (put to sleep) yearly. The prepuberal neutering of puppies will not eliminate this problem, but it may reduce the numbers. Early neutering has not been demonstrated to be harmful in any way. The cost, emotionally and financially, for millions of euthanasia procedures every year *is* harmful. Unless serious damage can be shown to follow the neutering of 7- to 9-week-old puppies, the procedure should be applauded and supported by the public and the veterinary profession.

Post-OVH Obesity

Ovariohysterectomy has been implicated in the incidence of obesity in our pet population. Prospective studies have demonstrated that neutering tends to promote increased food intake and body weight gain, while another study has indicated that neutering does not influence these same factors! Some dogs may be predisposed to weight gain after OVH, which can be controlled with exercise and limited feeding; reducing food intake alone may not resolve the tendency toward obesity in some bitches.

LAPAROSCOPIC STERILIZATION

Laparoscopic sterilization can be performed in the bitch. The laparoscope is a special optical instrument that can be inserted into the abdomen without making a large incision. The uterine horns or the uterotubal junctions are located visually and can then be destroyed by electrocoagulation (electrocautery) or the use of plastic clips. Laparoscopic sterilization is quick and safe, can be performed on young bitches, and could be a practical method for mass sterilization. However, most veterinarians do not have the necessary equipment, and laparoscopically sterilized dogs still continue to cycle, breed and attract males.

STEROID HORMONE SUPPRESSION OF OVARIAN CYCLE ACTIVITY

A variety of natural and synthetic substances are known to inhibit ovarian cycle activity in the bitch. Typically there is a transient response that depends on the continued presence of the drug. When drug administration is discontinued and the effect of the drug dissipates, ovarian cycle activity *usually* resumes. Such drugs can have side effects. **Progestogens** (compounds with progesterone-like activity) can promote development of uterine disease with or without development of infection (**pyometra**) (*see* Chapter 14, "Reproductive Disorders") or mammary gland development with or without post-therapy lactation. **Androgens** (male sex hormones) can induce masculinization of behavior and appearance. Owners must be cognizant of the side effects of these powerful medications. Attention to dosage, timing of administration within ovarian cycles, and review of the bitch's complete medical history and physical examination are always warranted.

Megestrol Acetate

Megestrol acetate (synthetic progesterone) is available in the United States in 5 to 20 mg tablets under the trade name Ovaban. The daily oral dosage and treatment protocol depend on whether therapy begins during anestrus or proestrus. There are several major contraindications to the use of megestrol acetate, including the presence of disease in the reproductive organs, or mammary tumors or other growths. The drug should not be administered to bitches that are or could be pregnant because of potential masculinization of female fetuses, and because progestogens can delay **parturition** (whelping).

Megestrol acetate should not be used in dogs prior to or during their first ovarian cycle. If estrus occurs within 30 days of discontinuing therapy, mating should be prevented. The drug should not be administered for more than two consecutive treatment periods owing to the potential for uterine damage. Megestrol acetate should not be administered to dogs known or suspected to have diabetes mellitus because of the insulin antagonistic effects (*see* Chapter 32, "The Endocrine System and Metabolic Disorders").

Mibolerone

Mibolerone is useful for preventing estrus in adult female dogs not intended primarily for breeding purposes. The drug is an extremely potent, synthetic male hormone. It is available in liquid form under the trade name Cheque and can be added to the food. Mibolerone should not be used in pregnant bitches or bitches with **perianal adenoma,** perianal adenocarcinoma, or other androgen-dependent tumors. The drug is not recommended for use in dogs with a previous history of either liver or kidney disease, since it appears to be metabolized in the liver and excreted into the urine (by way of the kidneys) and feces. A few dogs have become jaundiced while receiving this drug, necessitating termination of treatment. Bitches treated for a prolonged period (longer than 8 months) should undergo periodic liver function testing. The medication is to be used with caution (or not at all) in bitches younger than 7 months of age, because of the potential for inducing premature inhibition of bone growth.

It should be mentioned that a few of the side effects of mibolerone therapy actually encourage some owners to employ this drug. Being a potent androgen, mibolerone appears to increase muscle strength, stamina and aggressiveness in the bitch, traits that may be considered positive side effects in field-trial bitches. Other androgenic effects include enlargement of the clitoris, mounting behavior and musky body odor. Approximately 10% of treated bitches develop a whitish, viscid vaginal discharge, and some have had small **vesicles** (blisters) appear on the vaginal surface.

Depot Injectable Progesterone

A single intramuscular injection of medroxyprogesterone acetate maintains effective circulating levels of this progestogen for several months. This drug was marketed as a canine contraceptive (Promone) until 1969. Although successful in delaying heat cycles, the drug was not considered safe because it induced uterine disease and pyometra in a large number of bitches. High doses also contributed to the development of breast cancer. *The drug is not recommended.*

Testosterone Injections

Intramuscular injections of testosterone propionate and the use of oral androgens (methyltestosterone) given weekly for as long as 5 years have been used to prevent ovarian activity in Greyhounds. Apparently it is believed by some that the drug also carries the benefit of enhanced racing performance. Why such drug usage is allowed is not clear, nor can it considered acceptable.

VAGINAL AND INTRAUTERINE DEVICES

Various devices designed to block **intromission** (insertion of the penis) by the male have been marketed. None has gained wide acceptance because of unacceptably high failure rates, lack of practicality, problems with fit, harm to the bitch and owner dissatisfaction. Intrauterine devices cannot be used owing to the difficulties associated with entry through the canine cervix.

IMMUNIZATION

An immunization procedure (contraceptive vaccine) designed to provide reversible contraception in the bitch has been developed. However, the procedure has not yet undergone large-scale clinical trials, and its importance to the future management of canine contraception remains to be determined.

Castration (Orchiectomy) and Vasectomy

Options available for fertility control in the male are exclusively surgical. Castration (orchiectomy) involves complete removal of the testes, rendering the dog permanently infertile and modifying or eliminating many typically male behavioral traits. These include roaming, urine-marking in the home, mounting of dogs or people, and dominance aggression directed at other male dogs. Owners often report that their dogs become more docile, affectionate and people-oriented following castration. Territorial aggression is a trait of both male and female dogs and so is unlikely to be altered by castration. **Vasectomy,** in which the testicular tubules (the **vas deferens**) are severed, is a less drastic but equally permanent method of fertility control. Vasectomized dogs retain normal libido and male-associated behaviors but are unable to sire a litter.

CHAPTER 16

Genetics

by Ann T. Bowling

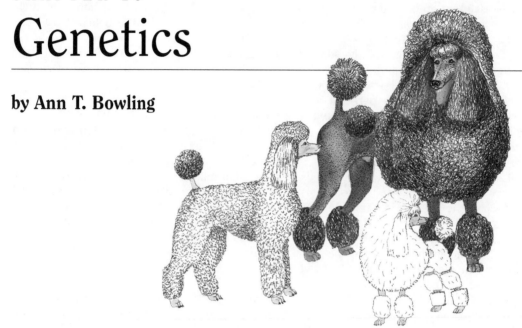

An understanding of the general principles of genetics can be important for the breeding of healthy, beautiful dogs. Many physical and behavioral attributes of dogs have an inherited basis, while others are due primarily to environmental influences. To make effective breeding decisions for or against selected traits, it is essential to determine whether an individual trait is inherited. Most responsible breeders are familiar with the basics of canine genetics, particularly with information pertaining to their chosen breeds. Interest in canine genetics is not limited to people with a breeding program, however. Many dog owners are fascinated to learn how a favorite pet comes to differ in color, size, shape or ability from the dog that lives next door. Using dogs as an example, this chapter discusses general principles of genetics to illustrate the physical basis of inheritance, which was first clearly defined by the Austrian monk and naturalist Gregor Mendel (1822–1884) in his studies of garden peas.

The Physical Basis of Inheritance

Genes, the individual units of inheritance, are composed of **DNA (deoxyribonucleic acid)** and

occur as components of the very large and complex DNA molecules known as **chromosomes,** which are found in the nucleus of every cell. Genes encode information that directs the manufacture of **proteins,** the molecules that control the developmental stages from egg and sperm through puppy to adult. Proteins also are needed to maintain all normal body functions. It is estimated that 50,000 to 100,000 genes, each coding for different proteins, are required to direct the incredibly complex processes of life.

The DNA of canine genes is packaged in 78 chromosomes within the cell nucleus. It is impossible to observe or photograph chromosomes without the aid of a microscope and special cellular dyes that stain the normally colorless genetic material. The 78 chromosomes can be cut out from a photographic print and arranged as a series of 39 pairs in a photographic print. The array of paired chromosomes prepared from such a print is known as a **karyotype.**

Although the different breeds generally can be distinguished from one another by visual comparison, dogs of all breeds have the same number, sizes and shapes of chromosomes within their cells because the genetic information of all dogs is nearly identical. The fact that crosses between breeds of dogs widely differing in appearance will produce fertile offspring is evidence of this basic similarity. The only distinguishing feature found in most canine karyotypes is the difference between males and females, which is manifested in a single pair of chromosomes (the X and Y) whose inheritance will be discussed below.

The genes arrayed along the chromosomes are so minute that they cannot be "seen" by any direct process, even microscopy. Classically speaking, genes are only recognized by their end effects (e.g., black hair versus blonde hair). The new era of biotechnology now is making it possible to delineate the precise molecular sequence of the DNA of many specific genes. Few canine genes, if any, have yet been sequenced, but it probably is only a matter of time before the basic information gleaned from genetic research on mice and human beings can be applied effectively to dogs as well.

Mendelian Genetics

THE BEHAVIOR OF CHROMOSOMES

An understanding of inheritance patterns can be obtained by a thorough knowledge of the behavior of chromosomes, even though chromosomal processes were not known to Mendel when he made his discoveries. Two division processes are characteristic of cells and their chromosomes. The first process, known as **mitosis,** occurs in all cells of the body. When a body cell divides, the cell's chromosomes precisely duplicate themselves. As the cell transforms from a single cell into two, each daughter cell receives an exact replica of the chromosomes of the original cell. The second division process, known as **meiosis,** is directly involved in the formation of **gametes** (the reproductive cells—the sperm and **ova,** or eggs) and occurs only in the reproductive organs. Gametes contain only 39 chromosomes, exactly half the number found in the other cells of the body. Each pair of chromosomes contributes only a single chromosome to a gamete. When sperm (containing 39 chromosomes) and egg (also containing 39 chromosomes) combine during fertilization, the chromosome number of the resulting fertilized cell or **zygote** is 78, thus reconstituting the normal chromosomal composition of canine body cells.

THE INHERITANCE OF SEX

A puppy's sex is determined by the genetic contribution of its sire alone. As mentioned earlier, a clear difference exists between the chromosomes of male and female dogs and can be visually observed in a karyotype. For one particular pair of chromosomes—the sex chromosomes—the pair members are distinctly different from each other in the male, whereas in the female the paired chromosomes are essentially identical. The two sex chromosomes of the male are designated X and Y. The two sex chromosomes of the female both resemble the X of the male and thus both are designated X. As indicated above, the members of every chromosome pair are split up as the gametes form during meiosis. All gametes of the female (ova) have only a single X chromosome, while male gametes (sperm) represent an equally divided mixture of X- and Y-bearing cells. An ovum fertilized by an X-bearing sperm will develop into a female puppy, while an ovum fertilized by a Y-bearing sperm will develop into a male puppy.

Geneticists often employ a simple diagrammatic tool called a **Punnett square** (shown below) to predict the expected outcome of individual matings. On the top of the diagram are listed the alternative traits (in this case, chromosomes symbolized X and Y) that can be contributed by one parent; at the left are listed the alternatives contributed by the other parent (in this case the female, who can only contribute an X chromosome). In the squares formed by the intersection of the columns and rows of the parental contributions are listed the possible combinations that can be produced in the offspring. For sex, only two outcomes are possible: XX (female) and XY (male).

	MALE CONTRIBUTION (sperm)	
	X	Y
X	XX Female	XY Male
X	XX Female	XY Male

FEMALE CONTRIBUTION (ovum)

From our understanding of the chromosomal basis of sex determination, it is clear why the YY alternative has never been found. The X chromosome contains genes for many essential functions, the absence of which would be incompatible with life. By contrast, few genes other than those for the determination of maleness are found on the Y chromosome.

Probably the most important genetics lesson to be learned from the study of sex determination is that the inheritance of traits follows the inheritance pattern of the chromosomes. Since chromosomes occur in pairs, only one of two trait alternatives may be transmitted from each parent to its offspring. Equal ratios of the trait alternatives (in this case, sex) are expected among the offspring. Thus, genetic differences among siblings may be determined solely by a difference in the contribution of one parent (for other traits, this will not always be the male parent).

DOMINANT AND RECESSIVE GENES

Occasionally, matings are observed in which an offspring is distinctly different from both parents. For example, a pair of black Labrador Retrievers may produce some yellow puppies as well as the anticipated black ones. The inheritance of coat color provides some wonderful examples for an understanding of basic concepts of genetics.

Many studies have verified that the yellow coat of Labradors is produced by the action of a gene whose alternative form produces black pigment in the hair. The alternative forms of a particular gene are known as **alleles.** In many species, if the DNA molecular sequences of different alleles of a gene are compared, they characteristically are found to differ in only a single **nucleotide** (an individual unit of DNA) out of the thousands of nucleotides of which the alleles are composed. The nucleotides of the DNA code for the production of specific sequences of **amino acids,** the building blocks of protein molecules. A change in a single amino acid (resulting, for example, from a single nucleotide change in the corresponding gene) may destroy the activity of a protein or cause it to produce an altered product.

In the coat-color example illustrated above, yellow coat factors were carried by the black-coated Labrador parents without being physically apparent. The yellow allele is said to be **recessive** to the black, and the black allele is said to be **dominant** to the yellow. A dominant allele is one that is expressed even when carried by only one member of a chromosome pair. In this example, the presence of just one dominant allele (coding for the production of a black hair coat) will drive the production of black hair pigment, resulting in a black coat, even if the yellow allele is present as the other member of the chromosome pair. Only when both members of a chromosome pair contain the recessive yellow allele, rather than the dominant black allele, will the coat color be yellow.

To provide a simplified notation, geneticists assign letters to genes and their different alleles. In the coat-color example, the responsible gene is called extension (the name is assigned due to its similarity to a previously designated gene of mice) and symbolized by the letter E. The dominant and recessive alleles are designated by a superscript notation. The dominant allele is assigned a capital letter, E^E, which can be simplified for discussion to E, while the recessive allele is referred to as E^e, or more simply, e. Three possible combinations of these alleles are thus possible for individual animals: EE, Ee, and ee.

Because the chromosomes bearing the genes occur in pairs, the coat color will be determined by the interaction of the pair of alleles of the E gene. The term **genotype** is used for the letter symbols describing a gene pair, while the term **phenotype** is used to describe the external attributes resulting from a gene's action. Thus the genotype of black dogs is either EE or Ee, while the genotype of yellow dogs is always ee. Conversely, the phenotype of EE and Ee dogs is black, while the phenotype of ee dogs is yellow. When both alleles in a pair are the same (here, EE or ee), the dog is said to be **homozygous** for that trait. When each of the two alleles is different (Ee), the dog is said to be **heterozygous.** Because the black allele E is dominant to the yellow allele e, for black dogs the genotype (either EE or Ee) is not always readily apparent from the phenotype (black). Thus, a yellow pup can be produced from the mating of black dogs if both of the parents are heterozygous for the color trait, as shown in the following Punnett square diagram.

HETEROZYGOUS MALE PARENT

		E	e
HETEROZY-GOUS FEMALE PARENT	E	EE Black	Ee Black
	e	Ee Black	ee Yellow

The diagram provides additional information about the pups in a potential litter resulting from the mating of these two dogs. The ratios expected for a cross between heterozygotes is 3:1 (in this case, 3 black pups:1 yellow pup), although the genotypic ratio underlying the colors is 1 homozygous black pup:2 heterozygous black pups:1 yellow pup. Among the black pups, the EE dogs can never have yellow puppies even if bred to a yellow mate, while Ee dogs in combination with either Ee or ee mates will produce both yellow and black puppies.

At this time the only way to determine which black dogs are EE and which are Ee is through a **test cross** to an ee (yellow) mate, since no direct laboratory test for the e allele is available. A test cross is a mating between a homozygous recessive (here, ee) and an animal with the phenotype of the dominant allele. Sometimes pedigrees or family studies can help determine genotypes that may not always be obvious from phenotypes. For example, a black Labrador with a yellow parent, and any black dog that produces a yellow pup, will necessarily be Ee. A useful characteristic of a recessive trait such as e is that it will always "breed true," that is, yellow bred to yellow will always produce yellow, since no E factor is present in the cross to contribute the ability to manufacture black hair pigment.

Occasionally it may be possible to differentiate homozygous and heterozygous genotypes by observation of the phenotype. This is known as *incomplete dominance*. Another coat-color trait can provide an example of this. In heterozygotes the *merle* gene M causes a distinctive, blotchy dilution effect of hair color and a variable white-patch pattern, which is considered highly desirable in many breeds, particularly Australian Shepherds. Homozygotes for the merle gene usually have a coat that is markedly white. Also associated with the homozygous condition, however, are undesirable defects of sight and hearing that may cause breeders to avoid mating two heterozygotes. On the other hand, a homozygote (white) can be expected to produce all merle-marked puppies when bred to a non-merle (i.e., a recessive) and thus can be a valuable producer for a breeder of Australian Shepherds or other breeds for which the merle pattern is considered desirable.

MULTIPLE ALLELES

For any given gene many variations (multiple alleles) potentially may exist, but seldom are more than two variants known. One explanation for the low numbers of recognized multiple allelic systems is that some changes (mutations) in gene sequence may lead to defective or inactive products, and thus be associated with embryonic or fetal death. Another potential explanation is that the phenotypic effects of the variants may be so minute that, barring direct sequencing of the molecular structure of the DNA, the differences will not be detectable. In any case, canine coat-color studies provide examples of multiple allelic systems that can show how multiple alleles contribute to the variety of color types produced.

The *spotting* gene S controls the production of white markings. Four possible alleles have been hypothesized for Cocker Spaniels. The dominant allele S produces a colored dog without white markings. The s^i recessive alternative produces a so-called Irish spotting pattern consisting of a white collar, chest, toes and tail tip. A third allele, s^p, recessive to both the previous alternatives, produces a variably piebald (having patchy pigmentation) spotting pattern. A fourth allele, s^w, recessive to all the others, produces an all-white dog. In a mating between a solid parent and one with Irish spotting (each parent being heterozygous for different spotting alleles), three patterns potentially could be produced in the offspring:

	SOLID PARENT	
	S	s^w
IRISH SPOTTING PARENT — s^i	Ss^i Solid	s^is^w Irish spotting
s^p	Ss^p Solid	s^ps^w Piebald

GENE INTERACTIONS

Because the genetic makeup of every dog is composed of thousands of genes, it is important to develop a working understanding of the results expected from the complex interaction of the products of more than a single gene. Using already familiar examples, one can predict the outcome of a mating when two traits are considered simultaneously, such as sex and black or yellow coat color (both parents being heterozygous for coat color).

FACTOR TYPES FOR SPERM

		XE	Xe	YE	Ye
FACTOR TYPES FOR OVA	XE	XX EE Black female	XX Ee Black female	XY EE Black male	XY Ee Black male
	Xe	XX Ee Black female	XX ee Yellow female	XY Ee Black male	XY ee Yellow male

The four different parental types of sperm can combine with the two different types of egg to generate eight potential genotypic classes of off-spring. Each class is equally likely to occur owing to the random processes that determine whether a sperm will be XE, Xe, YE, or Ye, and whether it will combine with an XE or an Xe ovum. Based on the dominance interaction between alleles of the E locus (E being dominant to e), these eight genotypic classes will appear as four phenotypes of pups (black males, black females, yellow males, and yellow females). Notice that a litter of eight puppies can be expected, *on average,* to include a single yellow female and a single yellow male. Due to chance, any particular litter of this type may have no yellow females or males, while others may have two or three of each. When data from many litters resulting from such a mating are combined over time and evaluated by statistical tests, however, the predicted ratio of genotypic classes in the Punnett square becomes quite evident, even though any given litter of eight pups

will only occasionally match the expected proportions exactly.

Sometimes the actions of alleles of one gene may obscure the actions of alleles of another gene. Dominance refers to the interaction of alleles of a single gene; the masking of one gene's activity by another gene is more properly called **epistasis,** rather than dominance. The gene that is masked by epistasis is said to be **hypostatic.** (Often this terminology is considered cumbersome and abandoned by lay geneticists, but misuse of the term dominance is also a fundamental source of confusion when determining the relationship between alleles of different genes.) We can consider an example with a mating between parents each heterozygous for genes at two chromosomal locations, or **loci** (singular: **locus**). In this case, we can use the familiar E gene in combination with the white spotting pattern gene S. In the presence of the dominant allele S, no white spotting is present, while an s^ws^w homozygote is all white, suppressing the expression of any E alleles. The following Punnett square representation provides an understanding of the interactions of the allelic combinations of these two genes.

FACTOR TYPES FOR SPERM

		SE	Se	s^wE	s^we
FACTOR TYPES FOR OVA	SE	SS EE Black	SS Ee Black	Ss^w EE Black	Ss^w Ee Black
	Se	SS Ee Black	SS ee Yellow	Ss^w Ee Black	ss^w ee Yellow
	s^wE	Ss^w EE Black	Ss^w Ee Black	s^ws^w EE White	s^ws^w EE White
	s^we	Ss^w Ee Black	Ss^w ee Yellow	s^ws^w Ee White	s^ws^w ee White

The complex interactions of genes may produce phenotypic ratios that at first glance seem unrelated to those expected by the simple random assortment of genes on chromosomes. In the above example, three colors of pups could be produced by black parents: black, white, and yellow, in expected proportions of 9:4:3. Even more complicated examples could be constructed, but the point to be made is that a basic understanding of the allelic actions of genes when considered in isolation from each other can aid in predicting the outcome of more complex interactions.

GENE LINKAGE

Each individual gene is located on one particular chromosome and at a specified place (locus) on that chromosome. Most genes chosen for study are by chance located on different chromosomes. Occasionally traits of interest are located on the same chromosome and tend to be inherited together more often than they are split apart, a phenomenon referred to as **gene linkage.** Linked genes can be separated from one another as part of the normal process of chromosomal recombination occurring during meiosis. The proportion of offspring in which linked traits occur in different combinations from those of the parents is related to the physical distance between the genes on the chromosome. One of the ways for an undesirable trait to become widespread in a breed is through close linkage with another trait that is highly prized. It is important to understand just how many offspring and how much careful testing may be required to produce a puppy possessing the valued gene without the linked defective trait, if the genes are closely situated on the same chromosome.

A special case of linkage is related to the genes on the X chromosome (the female sex chromosome), particularly several that produce factors necessary for normal blood clotting. Males, it will be recalled, have only one X chromosome per cell. Some may inherit from their mothers an X chromosome with a defective gene whose expression in females usually is masked by the normal gene on the other X chromosome. The inheritance of so-called **X-linked** disease-causing genes has a pattern of expression that follows the pattern of transmission of the sex chromosomes. Typically, males inherit the defective gene from mothers that are heterozygous (i.e., carriers) for the abnormal gene. Half the male offspring of a carrier mother on average will be affected, but none of the female offspring will be affected, although half will be carriers like the mother. Male offspring of affected fathers never receive the defective gene from the father. Female offspring of affected fathers are usually free of the disease but may transmit the problem to half of their male offspring. X-linked inheritance can be demonstrated with a Punnett square, where X* is used to symbolize the X chromosome with the disease-associated gene.

		FACTORS CONTRIBUTED BY SPERM	
		X	Y
FACTORS CONTRIBUTED BY OVUM	X*	XX* Carrier Female	X*Y Affected male
	X	XX Normal female	XY Normal male

X-linked genes are often called **sex-linked** genes, to contrast them with **autosomal** genes which are located on any of the other 38 pairs of chromosomes.

POLYGENIC (MULTIPLE-GENE) TRAITS

Most traits are influenced by more than a single gene, but for many we can only discern the action of a so-called major gene, which appears to produce the bulk of the genetic variation in the trait of interest. Particularly for traits that can be measured (quantitative traits), the phenotype can be produced by additive effects of several genes at different loci (and can also typically be influenced by environmental components as well). In traditional animal science, breeding programs concentrating on production traits (milk, meat, eggs) can be assisted by mathematical analyses of production records among related animals, in order to choose the best individuals for breeding stock. In dog breeding, where such production traits are not highly selected, polygenic inheritance is encountered primarily in association with detrimental traits, such as hip dysplasia. Progress in selecting against such a trait can be frustratingly slow when several genes affect the trait and cannot be readily identified. Moreover, quantitative traits may exhibit a "threshhold effect," so that breeders may not be aware of the accumulation of problem genes until a critical mass of additive alleles has been attained, producing a phenotypic abnormality. The ability of DNA biotechnology to identify marker genes holds promise for selecting desirable production traits and seemingly could be used to select against deleterious multiple-gene traits as well.

Determination of Inheritance Patterns

To apply genetics to a breeding program requires an understanding of how traits are inherited, in order to design a breeding and selection scheme directed toward a given goal. How can one determine whether a trait is inherited (or due to environmental effects such as diet or microorganisms), and if inherited, whether it is dominant, recessive, sex-linked, autosomal, multiple allelic, or polygenic? Several years of genetic research may be necessary to provide definitive answers. The components of such research may include:

- searching the scientific literature for similar conditions in dogs of other breeds or in other mammalian species
- collecting pedigrees of dogs expressing the trait to search for relationships
- collecting complete litter data to determine the pattern of transmission in a lineage
- designing test matings

Among the above projects, pedigree collection is ultimately the least informative, since purebred dogs are likely to be related to each other and to be produced from matings between stock that are at least distantly related. Test matings, on the other hand, are likely to provide a good deal of information. Characteristic inheritance patterns of different classes of genes can be recognized and matings designed to investigate trait transmission.

Characteristics of autosomal dominant genes include:

- transmission from an affected parent (except in the unlikely event the trait has just appeared as a new mutation)
- approximately 50% of offspring of both sexes will have the trait

Recessive traits will usually be seen initially in both males and females as a result of matings between normal parents, but when affected animals are mated together, the offspring (inheriting two recessive alleles) will all exhibit the trait. Generally, X-linked traits are obvious from their apparent association with males. Several examples exist in the scientific literature wherein an erroneous conclusion about the inheritance of a trait was reached before a thorough genetic study was completed, so it is important not to rush to conclusions before test matings have been performed.

Inbreeding, Linebreeding, Outcrossing

To produce dogs with desirable traits, most breeders work with purebred dogs of known pedigree. Studbook regulations prevent the use of animals outside the registry, effectively creating a closed genetic pool. The aim of this restriction is to encourage the breeding of stock of a consistent type, with excellence for a selected set of breed characteristics. Outcrossing between different breeds is seldom practiced as a selective dog-breeding technique, although many "good" dogs probably are produced as a result of its inadvertent application when dogs are left to their own devices!

Owners generally see no more than a five- or six-generation pedigree of their animals, owing perhaps to constraints as trivial as paper size for printing pedigrees, but also to the time necessary to research and compile the more distant generations (which seldom seem to be readily available in computer databases). If distant generations could be viewed as easily on paper as the more immediate ones, breeders might be surprised to learn how few founders their purebred animals trace. Of course, this will vary widely from breed to breed, but nonetheless purebred animals are by definition more inbred than are animals outside a closed studbook format.

Inbreeding is a breeding technique which pairs closely related animals, such as father-daughter, brother-sister, or cousins. However, the strict scientific definition of inbreeding counts all relationships that are duplicated on both sides of a pedigree, no matter how distant. Animal breeders by tradition consider distantly related crosses to be linebreeding rather than inbreeding, but the scientific basis of this concept is not obvious; linebreeding is in essence a moderate form of inbreeding.

The theoretical purpose of inbreeding (or linebreeding) is to produce stock of consistent excellence through creation of a homozygous type. Inbreeding increases the probability that any gene will be homozygous by descent. Of course, inbreeding favors homozygosity of genes of excellence as well as deleterious genes, so a thorough understanding of the process is vital for a sound breeding program. Among some animal stocks, inbreeding leads to reproductive problems (ultimately infertility) and reduced disease resistance. Breeders are continually warned of these possibilities, although documented examples in many animal species are difficult to find.

The premise of inbreeding (or linebreeding) is that homozygosity is desirable. It is well known that at times the optimal type is obtained in heterozygotes (for example, the merle pattern gene) rather than in homozygotes. Although heterozygosity does not produce a consistent breeding animal, it should not be considered an inappropriate breeding tool. In fact, so little is known about the genetics of desirable conformation traits that it probably is premature to say that inbreeding, as a general technique for structuring pedigrees, produces either consistently good or bad stock.

The best approach for responsible dog breeding includes an awareness of pedigree structure, but focuses on breeding for quality, while not ignoring real or potential problems of defective genes. It is irresponsible to assume that any animal is without deleterious genes; the task is to minimize the risk of producing a defective pup, while at the same time producing an example of true excellence for the particular breed of concern.

Additional Examples of Canine Genes

BASIC COLORS

In mammals, **melanin** is the most important pigment of coat color. Melanin occurs as granules of pigment in the hair, skin, and **iris** (the circular, pigmented tissue behind the cornea of the eye) in two basic forms: eumelanin (black or brown in color) and pheomelanin (red or yellow). Genes of coat color produce their effects by influencing the switch between eumelanin and pheomelanin production, or by altering the presence, shape, number or arrangement of pigment granules.

The basic coat colors of dogs are produced by the interactions of alleles at nine different gene loci (see TABLE 1). The genetics of coat color variants in dogs has been determined from canine family studies, while the biochemistry of pigment production is assumed to be similar to that for other mammalian species. A comprehensive understanding of the interactions of the many gene loci involved requires a review of the basic effects of each gene.

The major color-producing genes are agouti (A), brown (B), and, as has already been described, extension (E). Of these the simplest is B, which has only two alleles. The recessive allele b causes the production of brown pigment in place of the more commonly seen black. Weimaraners and Chesapeake Bay Retrievers are examples of breeds in which all animals have a pair of the recessive alleles (bb); that is, they are homozygous recessives. Breeds in which both B and b occur include Doberman Pinschers and Poodles.

Alleles at the E locus either extend (E) or diminish (e) the amount of eumelanin in the coat, with the opposite effect on the extent of pheomelanin. This gene is responsible for producing the difference between black-coated dogs and red- or yellow-coated dogs. Golden Retrievers are an example of a breed in which all animals are ee. Coat-color patterns known as brindle and black mask (e.g., in Great Danes) are attributed to alleles e^br and E^m, respectively, at the E locus.

The agouti gene also influences the distribution pattern of eumelanin. The dominant allele A causes eumelanin to be uniformly distributed in hairs over the entire body to produce a black coat. A series of recessive alleles is the major source of color variation. The red/yellow/black-tinged color known as sable (Collies, Great Danes) is produced by the variant symbolized a^y. The black banded hairs of Norwegian Elkhounds and some German Shepherd Dogs are produced by the variant symbolized a^g. The tan points pattern characteristic of Doberman Pinschers is due to the breed's being homozygous for the recessive allele a^t at the agouti locus.

Color dilution is produced by the recessive allele d at the D locus, which affects the clumping of pigment granules in hair. Examples of dd dogs are seen among some Doberman Pinschers and all Weimaraners. Another dilution effect is produced by a recessive variant of the C locus (c^{ch}), which is thought to be responsible for the golden color of ee Golden Retrievers, in contrast to the rich red of ee Irish Setters, which are homozygous for the dominant alleles at C.

A dominant gene for progressive graying (G) causes the hair of Bedlington Terriers to become white or nearly white with age, although pups may be born in a variety of black, brown and red colors.

The variants of the S (spotting) gene were discussed above in the section on multiple alleles. They are responsible for white markings in Basenjis and Collies, and the absence of such markings in Airedale Terriers and Rottweilers. In association with the variants that produce white markings, a separate dominant-acting gene T causes the production of discrete color spots (ticking) in the areas of white, such as is seen in all Dalmatian dogs and some English Springer Spaniels. In dogs without white markings, the presence or absence of T remains undefined, except perhaps through analysis of offspring from selected matings.

The final coat color variant to mention is the merle gene (M), which also has been previously described. An unusual feature of M, however, is the apparently high mutation rate of the dominant allele back to the normal, recessive condition. This phenomenon has been proposed to explain the production of occasional non-merle puppies from homozygous merle females. Instability of mutant genes has been observed infrequently in other organisms.

Blood Groups, Protein Polymorphisms, and DNA Markers

Although dogs do not have the same ABO and Rh blood groups as human beings, they do have their own systems of red blood cell antigens, which vary from individual to individual and from breed to breed. Determination of blood groups is important for selecting a compatible blood donor when a whole-blood transfusion is required.

Blood is composed of a complex mixture of proteins that can be sorted out by **electrophoresis** (separation of components of a mixture by their differing migration in an electric field) and visualized with protein-specific dyes or stains. The resultant banding patterns represent the protein products of genes. The genetic basis of band pattern variation for a specific protein can be studied using blood samples from members of family groups. Inheritance of variants is due to **codominant alleles,** wherein both members of an allelic pair are fully expressed.

The high degree of **polymorphism** (genetic variation) for blood group, protein, and DNA marker systems, combined with the codominant pattern of inheritance of variants, makes such markers useful for identification, parentage testing, and gene mapping. Genetic tests may exclude a parent because it fails to share a genetic factor with its alleged offspring. Alternatively, an offspring may be excluded because it possesses a factor not present in at least one of the parents. If no excluding systems can be detected, the parentage relationships are said to *qualify.* Any system of genetic markers can be employed in parentage tests, provided that a solid foundation of published research supports interpretation of the results, so that any legal challenge can be successfully met.

Establishment of a genetic map for the dog will require the identification of hundreds of genetic markers. When an extensive canine gene map is available, it may allow breeders to design matings that are more certain to meet specific production goals than is possible with the empirical techniques now available. Identification of markers closely linked to a disease for which no biochemical test is available could allow selection of mating pairs in order to avoid the breeding of inapparent carriers. In the future, special performance abilities, seldom the result of a single gene, could be more effectively selected using assayable linked marker genes, rather than by relying on the performance records of parental stock.

Breeders can use the following table for coat color alleles to create a Punnett square and predict the most probable coat colors in a known mating.

Table 1
Coat Color Alleles of Dog Breeds

Coat Color Loci

Breeds	A	B	C	D	E	G	M	S	T
Airedale Terrier	a^s a^t	B	C	D	E	g	m	S	?
Basenji	a^y a^s a^t	B	C	D	E	g	m	s^i	t
Basset Hound	a^y a^t	B	C c^{ch}	D	E	g	m	S s^p	T t
Bedlington Terrier	A a^t	B b	C c^{ch}	D d	E e	G	m	S	?
Chesapeake Bay Retriever	A	b	C c^{ch}	D	E	g	m	S	?
Cocker Spaniel	A a^y a^t	B b	C c^{ch}	D d	E e		m	S s^i s^p s^w	T t
Collie	a^y a^t	B	C	D d	E	g	M m	s^i s^w	t
Dachshund	a^y a^t	B b	C	D	E	g	M m	S	?
Dalmatian Dog	A a^t	B b	C	D	E e	g	m	s^w	T
Doberman Pinscher	a^t	B b	C	D d	E	g	m	S	?
German Shepherd Dog	a^y a^g a^s a^t	B b	C c^{ch}	D d	E^m E e	g	m	S	?
Golden Retriever	A	B	C c^{ch}	D	e	g	m	S	?
Great Dane	A a^y	B	C	D d	E^m E e^{br}	g	M m	S s^p s^w	t
Irish Setter	A	B	C	D	e	g	m	S	?
Kerry Blue Terrier	A	B	C	D	E	G g	m	S	?
Labrador Retriever	A	B b	C	D	E e	g	m	S	?
Newfoundland	A	B b	C	D	E	g	m	S s^p	T t
Norwegian Elkhound	a^g	B b	c^{ch}	D	E^m	g	m	S	?
Poodle	A a^t	B b	C c^{ch}	D d	E e	G g	m	S	?
Rottweiler	a^t	B	C	D	E	g	m	S	?
Samoyed	?	B	c^{ch}	D	e	g	m	s^w	t?
Springer Spaniel (English)	A a^t	B b	C	D	E e	g	m	s^p s^w	T t
Weimaraner	A	b	C c^{ch}	d	E	g	m	S	?

Legend

Uppercase = the dominant gene of that locus
lowercase = the recessive gene of that locus
superscript = variations of that characteristic

A = uniformly colored hair shaft
a^g = black banded hair shaft
a^s = black saddle
a^t = tan point of feet, nose and eyebrows
a^y = sable (hair shaft banded with red/yellow/black)
B = black
b = brown
C = red

c^{ch} = golden yellow
D = nondiluted color
d = diluted color
E = (extension) black
E^m = black mask
e = yellow
e^{br} = brindle
G = progressive graying
g = nonprogressive graying
M = merle

m = non-merle
S = solid colored coat
s^i = Irish spotting of white (collar, chest, toes and tail tip)
s^p = piebald (patchy white spotting)
s^w = white (all white)
T = ticking (color spots in white patches)
t = nonticking

CHAPTER 17

Congenital and Inherited Disorders

by Ann T. Bowling

A congenital abnormality is any defect of structure or function that is present at birth (birth defect). Congenital abnormalities may or may not be inherited. Many congenital problems have a direct effect on pup mortality. In one study, the mortality rate in groups of purebred puppies under 3 weeks of age was shown to be 15%. Either inheritance of an abnormal gene, or environmental influences interfering with the normal developmental process, could have played a role in the pups' deaths. Environmental factors to consider in such a situation include nutritional deficiencies or excesses, inhaled or ingested chemicals, drugs, infectious agents and toxins. Although inherited diseases may be classified as congenital, many do not become evident for several months or even years after birth. To prevent their recurrence in future litters, it is important to delineate the basis of the problem; unfortunately, many congenital abnormalities have no recognized, established cause.

This chapter will focus primarily (but not exclusively) on inherited defects. A variety of examples encompassing many different dog breeds will be presented. In addition, the quality of evidence needed to arrive at definitive conclusions regarding the genetic basis of defects will be reviewed. Abnormalities that are **familial** (i.e., those that run in family lines) and are thought to be of genetic origin, but for which definitive evidence is currently lacking, will also be discussed. Most of these defects are presumably the result of an interaction of the environment with several genes, each having a small, additive effect (i.e., a **polygenic** mode of inheritance). A discussion of carrier testing and selective breeding schemes will be presented at the conclusion as a guide for owners and breeders. (For definitions and explanations of the genetic terms that are used extensively in this chapter, readers are strongly urged to read chapter 16, "Genetics.")

Normal development of the canine fetus requires approximately 9 to 10 weeks, on average approximately 63 days, which is the normal gestation period. The fertilized ovum, or **zygote,** representing the union of the egg from the female and sperm from the male, proceeds by way of cell division through a series of developmental stages on its way to becoming a newborn pup. One of the earliest recognized stages in this process is the **blastocyst,** which develops by about 8 days post-fertilization. The blastocyst is essentially a hollow sphere of a few hundred embryonic cells, looking nothing at all like the eventual end product of the gestation process. Further development occurs in the uterus, where the embryo is implanted in the uterine wall and survives by receiving nourishment from the mother through a specialized tissue known as the **placenta,** which serves as the physical connection between mother and off-spring. As the pup continues to develop, it passes through several successive stages, including the **gastrula** and the neurula.

By about three weeks post-fertilization, the embryo is approximately 4 mm in diameter (about ⅛ inch). Within the next 8 days or so it quadruples in size. During the second half of gestation rapid development occurs, as the future pup grows larger and larger and the different organ systems within it take on recognizable shapes and begin to function.

During any of these stages of development, genetic or environmental influences may interfere with one or more of the normal developmental events and so produce a birth abnormality. (For additional information on the reproductive and birth processes in dogs, *see* CHAPTER 11, "NORMAL REPRODUCTION," and CHAPTER 13, "PREGNANCY AND PARTURITION.")

In general, genetic diseases can be broadly categorized as belonging to one of three groups:

1. chromosomal defects
2. single-gene defects
3. polygenic (multiple-gene) defects

Abnormalities in the first two categories are ultimately the easiest to document and understand, but are much rarer than abnormalities brought about by complex, polygenic effects.

Usually the first evidence of a problem is the birth of some pups in one litter, or in litters from repeated matings between the same set of parents, exhibiting similar defects of structure or function. (It is unlikely in the extreme that *every* pup in a given litter would be affected by the same genetic disease; such a situation would be presumptive evidence of a nongenetic, or environmental, problem). Another clue that an abnormality may have a genetic basis is an association with a particular breed. Breed association is more indicative of a genetic disease than is familial association because families, coexisting in the same environment, would be more likely to be exposed to any problem peculiar to that environment than would an entire breed, whose members are spread out over many families in many individual environments.

Disruption of normal development during the early stages is usually incompatible with life, resulting either in immediate death of the embryo or in failure of the embryo to implant in the uterine wall. Dominantly inherited defects often have extreme effects on the organism, and animals with such genes seldom survive to breeding age (although there are rare exceptions). The majority of identified genetic anomalies are inherited as recessive genes, meaning that the parents are heterozygotes (carriers) but are unlikely to be clinically affected. Recessive genes are "hidden" in heterozygotes by the dominant normal gene and may be more widespread within a breed than is generally acknowledged. Those mutations that survive are usually chance "hitchhikers" in highly successful breeding lines, otherwise the homozygous genotype producing the problem condition would be so rarely encountered as to be overlooked.

Pedigree studies of affected animals may provide tentative evidence for inheritance of some diseases. However, because most purebred animals tend to be related to varying degrees, pedigree relationships alone cannot be used to substantiate the inheritance of a defect. Clinical and other studies may relate the abnormality to an analogous, proven genetic disease in another species. Verification of inheritance of a trait in dogs usually requires data documenting the number of affected and unaffected pups produced from selected, informative matings. To determine whether a genetic basis exists for problems in which the affected dogs survive to reproductive age, it is possible to design matings (test crosses) between affected and normal animals. If the defect in question is produced by a lethal gene, however, matings can only be designed between animals that have sired or produced an affected pup (i.e., presumptive heterozygotes), and many more offspring will be needed than in a test cross of a nonlethal gene.

Chromosomal Defects

Most chromosomal abnormalities are eliminated before they can be observed or studied because they are associated with the loss or rearrangement of a large number of genes—a usually lethal event. Although rarely seen, the most common (viable) chromosome problems involve the sex chromosomes, X and Y. For certain problems of infertility, karyotyping may be an important diagnostic tool for identifying the basis of the problem. Unfortunately, karyotyping for domestic animals is only available at a few veterinary research hospitals, and relatively few veterinary clinicians are fully familiar with presenting signs that may be linked to abnormal chromosomes.

77, X Gonadal Dysgenesis

A rare few infertile bitches have been determined to be missing one of the pair of X chromosomes. The karyotype is analogous to that described for human female gonadal dysgenesis, also known as **Turner's syndrome.** Bitches exhibiting a small size compared to expectation for the breed, chronic, primary infertility, and failure to cycle through estrus regularly or at all are candidates for a diagnosis of chromosomal disease. The condition appears to occur sporadically, probably from failure of the sex chromosome pair to separate during meiosis, and no compelling evidence has been found to indicate an inherited tendency. Because affected bitches are infertile, the condition is essentially self-limiting.

79, XXY Testicular Hypoplasia and Aspermogenesis

An extra X chromosome in males is associated with infertility in several species, including human beings (**Klinefelter's syndrome**), cats and pigs. In one reported male dog, the initial clinical problem was a heart defect (ventricular septal defect, or VSD). As part of the thorough research workup the chromosome abnormality was uncovered, although it was not initially anticipated. Upon maturity, the dog was about half the normal weight anticipated for males of the breed (German Shorthaired Pointer), had small testicles and failed to produce sperm (**aspermogenesis**).

Single-gene Defects

Generally, single-gene defects are confined to one breed or to breeds with similar origins. Once the necessary research has been completed conclusively proving the single-gene origin of a defect, the breeder's work has just begun. If a laboratory test for carriers of the defective gene is available, breeders may choose to breed only from noncarriers or, alternatively, to select breeding stock in subsequent generations that are free of the problem gene. If no laboratory carrier test is available, avoidance of breeding with carriers will be an imperfectly lofty goal. While every effort may be made to avoid breeding from carriers, a large number of carriers will by chance remain undetected. Clearly, a laboratory carrier test is a highly desirable goal for the management of any single-gene defect.

Skeletal System Disorders

When comparing the different breeds, it is readily apparent that dogs exhibit great variation in shape and size. What is normal in some breeds may be considered abnormal in others. The examples described here will delineate within-breed skeletal defects having a single-gene origin.

Anemic Dwarfism

A syndrome of short-limbed (*achondrodysplastic*) dwarfism, resembling human **rickets** (vitamin D deficiency), has been identified in Alaskan Malamutes. Whereas rickets is caused by a nutritional deficiency, the syndrome in dogs is produced by an autosomal recessive gene and cannot be corrected by dietary supplementation. The supporting genetic evidence was obtained from an analysis of breeding data. Litters produced by matings between presumed heterozygotes produced 19 affected pups of both sexes out of a total of 71, closely approximating the

3:1 ratio anticipated for a breeding of two heterozygotes. Breedings between affected and carrier dogs (test crosses) produced 11 normal and 8 dwarf offspring, approximating the predicted 1:1 ratio. Breedings between affected animals produced only affected pups. Affected dogs exhibit signs of mild **hemolytic** anemia (loss of red blood cells characterized by direct red blood cell destruction), with red cells demonstrating physical abnormalities, so this disease can also be classified as a blood disorder.

Dwarfism with Retinal Dysplasia
The autosomal recessive form of dwarfism has also been documented in Labrador Retrievers. In this breed it is also associated with a variety of eye defects involving the **retina** (the light-sensitive layer of cells at the back of the eye). The most severe eye defects are seen in homozygotes. Less severe eye abnormalities are also observed in heterozygotes, although the dwarfism is not evident. (*See* CHAPTER 19, "THE EYE AND DISORDERS.")

Craniomandibular Osteopathy (CMO)
Formation of excessive dense bone in the jaw, first manifested as painful chewing at 3 to 4 months of age, is an autosomal recessive disorder of Scottish Terriers and West Highland White Terriers. The disease can be controlled by corticosteroid therapy. If any breedings are proposed from treated animals, it is important to remember that the offspring may perpetuate a genetic liability for the breed.

CENTRAL NERVOUS SYSTEM DISORDERS

Progressive Neuronal Abitrophy (PNA)
This brain disease in Kerry Blue Terriers is inherited as an autosomal recessive gene. It is characterized by **ataxia** (incoordination), lack of balance equilibrium, and head tremors, reflecting abnormalities within the *cerebellum* (the portion of the brain concerned with motor function, balance and the coordination of movement). Signs generally develop between 2 and 4 months of age. No laboratory carrier test is available. The disorder appears to be prevalent in many of the top Kerry Blue show lines and

can serve as an example of the ethical quandary faced by serious dog breeders. Culling the top stock will potentially affect the future type and quality of the breed. Breeding from a known carrier of mediocre type and quality cannot be condoned, but it may not be wise to exclude outstanding breed representatives from the breeding pool. This dilemma would not be nearly as devastating were a carrier test available. The same or a similar disease may also occur in Smooth Fox Terriers and Lapland Dogs.

GM₂ Gangliosidosis
This disease is inherited as an autosomal recessive disorder in German Shorthaired Pointers. The onset usually occurs at about 6 months of age. Pups exhibit increasing nervous behavior, clumsiness, partial blindness and deafness. Death usually occurs by 2 years of age. The cause of the disease is a defective enzyme that allows *lipids* (fats) to accumulate in the brain.

Globoid-cell Leukodystrophy
An inevitably lethal disorder of Cairn Terriers and West Highland White Terriers, **globoid-cell leukodystrophy** is inherited as a simple autosomal recessive defect. Signs of incoordination and hind-limb stiffness beginning at 4 months of age are associated with the gradual and symmetrical destruction of white matter in the brain and loss of **myelin** (a fatty substance forming the outer tunic or sheath around many nerve cells).

Neuronal Ceroid-lipofuscinosis
In this degenerative and lethal disease, signs of impaired vision and mental degeneration are noticeable by 12 to 15 months of age. The disease is caused by deposition of lipid granules in nerve cells, due to the reduced activity of an enzyme, *PPD-peroxidase*. It is inherited as an autosomal recessive in English Setters. Fortunately for breeders who encounter this disease, laboratory tests that identify **heterozygotes** (carriers) are now available.

OCULAR (EYE) DISORDERS
Progressive Retinal Atrophy, Peripheral Type (PRA) is documented as an autosomal recessive disease. It is known to occur in many breeds,

and few breeds are completely free of the defect. In Irish Setters the characteristic retinal changes may already be present by 8 weeks of age, but in other breeds the signs usually do not appear for up to 6 to 10 years. The disorder is characterized by defective night vision, which gradually progresses to involve normal daylight vision until the dog is completely blind in both eyes. Many owners do not notice the developing vision deficiency or are unaware of the hereditary nature of the disorder, so that affected dogs often are used for breeding. As breeders become more aware of the importance of eye examinations for their dogs and begin to select against defects, the incidence of PRA in the canine population should decrease. (*See* Chapter 19, "The Eye and Disorders.")

Skin Disorders

Ehlers-Danlos Syndrome
(Cutaneous Asthenia)

This disease of human beings, dogs, cats and mink is characterized by hyperextensibility and extreme fragility of the skin, probably due to a defect of **collagen** (a protein constituent of connective tissue). The skin is usually of normal thickness, but may be stretched well beyond what is possible in normal dogs. As a consequence, wounds occur easily and heal very slowly. The large, gaping wounds characteristic of Ehlers-Danlos syndrome have been compared descriptively to "fish mouths." Genetic studies in English Springer Spaniels suggest that the disease is inherited as an autosomal dominant, as it is in people and mink. (*See* Chapter 22, "The Skin and Disorders.")

Acrodermatitis

Puppies with this disease, inherited as a recessive gene in Bull Terriers, are undersized, have difficulty nursing, exhibit a progressively worsening **dermatitis** (inflammation of the skin), diminished mental capabilities, inflamed ears and diarrhea. Death usually occurs at about 7 months from respiratory infections.

Hairlessness (Congenital Hypotrichosis)

In this rare, inherited X-linked condition hair is missing from much of the body, but fine hairs occur on the head, feet and tail. Affected individuals have been reported in many breeds of dogs. Associated abnormalities of teeth and tear production have also been described. Hairlessness represents a breed trait for the Chinese Crested Dog, Mexican Hairless Dog, Abyssinian Dog, African Sand Dog, and Turkish Naked Dog, and thus is not considered a disease per se in such breeds.

Circulatory System Disorders

Neonatal Isoerythrolysis
(NI; Hemolytic Disease of the Newborn)

An otherwise healthy newborn pup may develop signs of lethargy, elevated pulse and respiration rates, and clinical evidence of an acute **hemolytic** (characterized by destruction of red blood cells) anemia within 2 to 5 days of birth. Antibodies to surface components of the pup's red blood cells are present in the **colostrum** ("first milk"), milk produced by the bitch during the first day or two after the birth of her puppies, and are the cause of the red blood cell destruction. Affected pups are usually from the second or later pregnancies of the bitch. Recovery may be spontaneous or the disease may progress to severe anemia and death. NI is a genetic disease only in that the red blood cell components involved in the immunologic reactions are inherited. The presence of strongly reactive antibodies to those components in the dam is the result of prior sensitization, either through blood transfusions, traumatic birthing, or immunization with vaccines contaminated with red blood cells. With this disease, dog owners need not assume that sires or dams of affected pups possess a transmissible liability that would ethically command their removal from the breeding pool.

Hemophilia A (Factor VIII Deficiency)

This recessive, X-linked disease represents the most common bleeding disorder of dogs and has been reported in most of the popular breeds. Signs of hemophilia include episodes of recurrent **subcutaneous hematoma** (localized pockets of blood under the skin), **hemarthrosis** (bleeding into joints), and internal hemorrhage with anemia, the latter commonly being the ultimate cause of death. Affected individuals lack a factor (factor VIII) essential to the blood-clotting process. Because of the severity of the disease, it is not likely that affected males will be used for breeding, but bitches and (on average) half of the sisters of affected males will perpetuate the disease if used as breeding stock.

Von Willebrand's Disease (VWD)

Like other bleeding diseases, VWD is characterized by hematomas, intermittent lameness (from bleeding into joints) and nosebleeds. As with hemophilia A, affected dogs are deficient in clotting factor VIII activity. Unlike hemophilia A, however, this disorder is not X-linked. Based on data from German Shepherd Dogs, VWD is caused by an autosomal dominant gene, perhaps lethal to homozygotes. The problem is not confined to German Shepherd Dogs, but has been reported also in Golden Retrievers, Doberman Pinschers, and Miniature Schnauzers, presumably with the same mode of inheritance.

Cyclic Neutropenia/Cyclic Hematopoiesis of Gray Collies

One type of gray coat color in Collies is associated with lowered resistance to infection, loss of appetite, lameness and fever. The signs are correlated with periodic declines in number of circulating blood **neutrophils,** white blood cells that are critical scavengers of invading bacteria and other disease agents, immune complexes and cell debris. Most affected puppies die within 6 months from overwhelming infections. Blood **platelet** (clotting cell) levels may also drop precipitously, resulting in bleeding episodes. Breeding data support the inheritance of this trait as an autosomal recessive.

Pyruvate Kinase Deficiency

A syndrome of hemolytic anemia in Basenjis is caused by a deficiency of an essential red blood cell enzyme, pyruvate kinase. The defect is inherited as an autosomal recessive. Breeding plans can be managed through use of laboratory tests that can identify heterozygotes, although some overlap exists in the ranges for enzyme

values between homozygous normal animals and heterozygote carriers.

Phosphofructokinase Deficiency

A syndrome of hemolytic anemia in English Springer Spaniels is characterized by the typical lethargy and weakness after exercise usually associated with anemias, but does not appear markedly to shorten life span. It is caused by another red blood cell enzyme deficiency and is inherited as an autosomal recessive. A laboratory test can be used to confirm the diagnosis and to distinguish carriers from normal animals.

UROGENITAL SYSTEM DISORDERS

XX Sex Reversal

Occasionally Cocker Spaniels of indeterminate sex **(intersexuality)** are reported, with characteristics of both sexes intermingling in the same individual. Some appear more closely to resemble (sterile) males, while others exhibit a mostly female phenotype, although their **gonads** (reproductive organs) are **ovotestes** (abnormal gonads containing both testicular and ovarian tissue). On chromosomal analysis the animals exhibit a female (XX) karyotype. Data suggest that an autosomal recessive gene, when homozygous, causes an XX animal to develop either partially or completely into a male.

METABOLIC AND ENDOCRINE DISORDERS

Pituitary Dwarfism

Somatomedins, also called **insulin-like growth factors,** are small proteins that exert a growth effect upon the body, promoting the proliferation of bone, cartilage, and soft tissues, and the enlargement of certain body organs. Low levels of somatomedin activity have been demonstrated in the rarely encountered disorder of pituitary dwarfism in German Shepherd Dogs. The dwarfism is inherited as an autosomal recessive trait.

Copper Toxicosis

Accumulation of high levels of copper in the liver, leading progressively to **hepatic cirrhosis** (liver disease characterized by replacement of functioning liver cells with scar tissue) and death, has been shown to be inherited as an autosomal recessive trait in Bedlington Terriers. Liver biopsy can diagnose the disease in young animals, but many owners are reluctant to have this invasive diagnostic procedure performed on their pet. A new, relatively noninvasive procedure using radioactively labeled copper offers promise for the diagnosis of affected animals. No carrier test is currently available. It has been suggested that the high prevalence of the disease in Bedlington Terriers is related to restriction of the gene pool resulting from aggressive efforts to decrease the incidence of an eye disorder, *retinal dysplasia* (*see* CHAPTER 19, "THE EYE AND DISORDERS").

Intestinal Cobalamin Malabsorption

Chronic inappetence and failure to thrive have been associated with an autosomal recessive disorder in Giant Schnauzer puppies. Failure to absorb **cobalamin** (a cobalt-containing component of vitamin B12) in the digestive tract is a potentially lethal defect, as this vital nutrient cannot be manufactured by the body, but must be ingested from outside sources.

Polygenic (Multiple-gene) Defects

Most traits are influenced by more than a single gene. This is particularly evident in dogs when considering the multifaceted aspects of conformation. Progress in selection against an undesirable trait can be frustratingly slow when several genes affect the trait and cannot be readily identified. Moreover, polygenic traits may exhibit a "threshhold effect," so that breeders may not be aware of the accumulation of problem genes in the selected breeding stock until a critical mass of additive alleles has been attained, producing a phenotypic abnormality.

CRYPTORCHIDISM

This sex-limited condition in which either one (**unilateral** cryptorchidism) or both (**bilateral** cryptorchidism) testicles fails to descend into the **scrotum** (dependent pouch of skin containing the testicles) is suspected to be hereditary, but data are inconclusive on the mode of inheritance. Bilateral cryptorchids usually are sterile, while unilateral cryptorchids are usually fertile. The problem may be caused by the action of several genes, each exerting a small influence with a resulting threshhold effect. This hypothesis proposes that affected males have a sufficient number of genes to manifest the problem, while unaffected relatives have nearly as many of the critical genes. Because expression of the trait is limited to males, female relatives never exhibit the problem regardless of the number of detrimental genes they carry.

Cryptorchidism is considered undesirable owing to the theoretical potential for male sterility within a breeding line (or an entire breed). Practical considerations for selecting against cryptorchid males for breeding include the following:

Retained testicles appear more likely than descended ones to develop tumors
Castration is a surgically more complex procedure in cryptorchids than in normal males

(*See* CHAPTER 14, "REPRODUCTIVE DISORDERS.")

COLLIE EYE ANOMALY

This vision problem occurs in the Collie and Shetland Sheepdog breeds. At one time as many as 80–90% of animals were affected, but with appropriate breeding selection the incidence appears to be declining. With this disease normal development of the back of the eye is disrupted. Lesions can be seen in the retina, blood vessels, and **optic disk** (that portion of the **optic nerve,** the neurologic connection between the eye and brain, visible at the surface of the retina) in puppies as young as 6 to 8 weeks old. The severity of the disorder varies greatly from dog to dog, and the disease does not progressively worsen with age. Although the published data have been said to support the inheritance of the problem as an autosomal recessive trait, critics point out that the data would also support a polygenic model. Additional data are needed to sort out the current confusion. There is no doubt, however, that the problem is inherited, and the difficulties in eradicating it lend support to the suggestion that the trait is not caused by a single recessive gene. (*See* CHAPTER 19, "THE EYE AND DISORDERS.")

HIP DYSPLASIA

This crippling defect is of special concern to dog owners because of its widespread incidence in many breeds. Hip dysplasia is the result of a complex set of inherited traits, including failure of the head of the **femur** (thigh bone) to fit into its socket in the **pelvis** (hip), and insufficient muscle mass in the hip area. An imperfect fit can cause slippage and eventual osteoarthritis (joint inflammation). Overfeeding causing rapid growth may be more likely to elicit the problem in a predisposed animal. Both sexes appear to be affected with equal frequency.

Generally, the larger breeds are at greater risk for developing hip dysplasia. The problem may be congenital, but can develop anytime up to 18 months of age. Eventually lameness, reluctance to exercise, and hip muscle wastage become obvious. It is generally accepted that the underlying defect is caused by a series of genes. The evidence consists of such data as:

  The severity of the problem fits a graded
    series from normal through mildly affected
    to severely affected
  Normal parents can produce affected off-
    spring
  The incidence of affected offspring increases
    with increasing severity of disease in the
    parents

Selection programs that have concentrated on reducing or eliminating breedings using severely or moderately affected animals have succeeded in reducing the percentage of affected puppies, but not in eradicating the defect. (*See* CHAPTER 26, "THE SKELETON AND DISORDERS.")

Carrier Testing

To avoid producing pups with an inherited defect resulting from the action of a dominantly inherited gene, it is sufficient to avoid breeding from an affected parent. To avoid producing affected pups resulting from the effects of recessive genes, matings between two carriers (heterozygotes) must be avoided. Matings involving a single carrier will not, of course, produce an affected puppy. Practically speaking, identification of carriers represents an extremely vexing problem. In the absence of a specific biochemical or DNA test for the defective gene, carriers can be recognized only by having sired or given birth to affected puppies. Many carriers will go undetected with such a screening method. Providing lists of known carriers serves to establish guilt by association, when in fact 50% of the offspring of carriers, on average, will not have inherited the defective gene and they (as well as the carriers) may be a source of valued genes at other loci.

The requirements of progeny testing to ascertain carrier status require a certain level of statistical assurance, based on a number of complex statistical analyses. For example, to determine whether a young male dog carries a specific recessive lethal gene requires breeding to bitches known to be carriers for the disease. If no affected pups are produced from a litter (or combined litters) of 12 puppies, then statistically the male is considered at the 97% level of certainty not to be a carrier for that gene. Progeny testing is slightly easier for recessive traits that are deleterious but not lethal. No affected puppies in a litter of at least 5 pups from an affected bitch strongly suggests, at the 97% level of statistical certainty, that the sire is not a carrier. Of course, birth of even one affected pup would immediately prove that the male being tested is a carrier for the trait of concern. If a greater degree of certainty were required, more matings would be necessary. With the increasing interest in gene sequencing in mammals, it is quite likely that within the decade DNA-based diagnostic tests could be available for certain inherited canine diseases, so that for these diseases at least such costly and time-consuming progeny tests would be unnecessary.

PART V

Canine Body Systems and Disorders

The dog is man's best friend.
He has a tail on one end.
Up in front he has teeth.
And four legs underneath.

— OGDEN NASH
An Introduction to Dogs

CHAPTER 18

Anatomy

by Jeffrey E. Barlough

Anatomy is the study of body structure, and supplies the basic framework for understanding **physiology,** the study of body function. Anatomical structure represents the sum total of the parts of the individual body systems—the skin, muscles, respiratory tract, digestive tract, urogenital tract, circulatory and immune systems, **endocrine** (hormonal) system, and nervous system. The many different components of these systems all interact with each other to varying extents, to produce the functional, living organism.

This chapter provides a broad overview of canine anatomy through a series of anatomical illustrations. The material presented here does not represent an exhaustive review of the subject; more detailed information on individual components of the body are available in the other relevant chapters.

The Muscles

MUSCLES OF THE HEAD AND NECK
The *scutularis* (39) helps draw the ears forward, while the *auricular* muscles (2) draw the ears up and back. The *malaris* (27) depresses the lower eyelid. The *levator nasolabialis* (24) serves to raise the upper lip and dilate the nostrils. The *masseter* (28) is one of the muscles of chewing, helping to close the jaw. The *buccinator* (4) forms part of the cheek, raises the lips, and aids in the movement of food within the mouth. The *occipitomandibularis* (29) is involved in general movement of the head and lower jaw. The *zygomaticus* (45) pulls the corners of the mouth upward. The *brachiocephalicus* (3), a large expanse of muscle reaching from the upper forelimbs to the head, acts to flex the neck and extend the shoulder. Part of this muscle also contains embedded within it the *clavicle,* or collarbone (9). The *omotransversarius* (30) helps to draw the forelimb forward.

DORSAL MUSCLES
The cape-like *trapezius* muscle (1) raises the head and shoulder. The *latissimus dorsi* (26) is fan-shaped and flexes the shoulder. The thick *lumbodorsal fascia* (25) extends across the lower back and serves as the anchor for a number of muscles.

MUSCLES OF THE THORAX, ABDOMEN AND TAIL

The *intercostal* muscles (22) connect the ribs to one another. The *posterior deep pectoral* (33) helps to flex the shoulder. The *external abdominal oblique* (13) is a large, superficial muscle that forms part of the abdominal wall. The *rectus abdominis* (36) borders the abdominal midline. The *caudalis* (7) and *sacrococcygeus* (37) are important for movements of the tail.

MUSCLES OF THE FORELIMB

The *brachiocephalicus* (3) and the *supraspinatus* (41) help in extending the shoulder, while the *deltoid* (10), divided into two parts, helps to flex the shoulder. The *infraspinatus* (23) serves to support the shoulder joint. The *brachialis* (5) is involved in flexing the elbow, while the *triceps brachii* (44) helps to extend it. The forepaw is controlled by a number of muscles, including the *extensor carpi radialis* (14), *flexor carpi radialis* (17), *extensor carpi ulnaris* (15), *flexor carpi ulnaris* (16), and the *pronator teres* (34). The digits (toes) of the forepaw are controlled by several *digital flexors* (11) and *digital extensors* (12).

MUSCLES OF THE HINDLIMB

The *sartorius* (38) is a straplike muscle that, together with the important *quadriceps femoris* (35), flexes the hip and extends the *stifle* (knee joint). The *gluteus medius* (18) and *gluteus superficialis* (19) are major muscles of the rump. The *caudofemoralis* (8) extends the hip and rotates the thigh inward. The *biceps femoris* (6) and *popliteus* (32) both flex the stifle. The *tensor fascia latae* (42) is a triangular muscle that flexes the hip. The *semitendinosus* (40) is the hindmost muscle of the thigh. The *gracilis* (20) helps to draw the thigh inward toward the body. The major calf muscle, the *gastrocnemius* (21), flexes the stifle and helps to extend the foot. The *peroneus* (31) and the *tibialis anterior (cranialis)* (43) aid in movement of the hindpaw.

The Skeleton

FORELIMB

The *scapula* (63) is known more commonly as the shoulder blade. The major portion of the forelimb consists of a middle bone, the *humerus* (51,114), and two lower bones, the *radius* (61,132) and *ulna* (66,140). The bones of the forepaw include the *carpals* (46,106), *metacarpals* (55,122), and *phalanges* (58,127).

HINDLIMB (PELVIC LIMB)

The pelvis is composed of three bones: the *ilium* (52), *ischium* (53), and *pubis* (60). The *obturator foramen* (124) is a large opening between the pubis and ischium for the passage of important vessels and nerves. The hindlimb consists of an upper bone, the *femur* (49,112), which is attached to the pelvis by a ball-and-socket joint; the *patella* (kneecap) (57,126); one or more *fabellae* (111); and two lower bones, the *tibia* (65,138) and the *fibula* (50,113). The bones of the hindpaw or foot include the *tarsals* (64,136), *metatarsals* (56,123), and *phalanges* (59,128)

TRUNK

Enclosing the thorax (chest cavity) are thirteen pairs of *ribs* (62) with their associated *costal cartilages* (47). The *lungs* (54) are the organs of breathing; their expansion and contraction are controlled by a powerful and important muscle, the *diaphragm* (48,72). The diaphragm serves as a physical separation between the thorax and the abdominal cavity. The *sternum* (135), or "breastbone," is composed of eight *sternebrae* and connects the ends of the ribs at the body midline.

SKULL, VERTEBRAE, RIBS

Bones of the canine skull (cranium) include the *maxilla,* or upper jaw (121); the *mandible,* or lower jaw (120); and the *zygomatic arch* (141). The *orbit* (125) is the bony socket within which sits the eye. The *external auditory meatus* (110) is the passageway leading to the eardrum and inner ear. (The *trachea* [139], which is not part of the skeletal system, is made of cartilage and serves to conduct air between the larynx and lungs.) The remainder of the axial skeleton is composed of seven *cervical vertebrae* (108), of which the first is called the *atlas* (104) and the second is called the *axis* (105); thirteen *thoracic vertebrae* (137); seven *lumbar vertebrae* (118); the *sacral vertebrae* (133); and a variable number of *caudal vertebrae* (107), these latter making up the tail. Through the vertebrae runs the *spinal cord,* the vital neurologic conduit that connects the brain, protected within the skull, with the sensory and motor nerves running through the body.

The Thoracic and Abdominal Organs (Viscera)

The *heart* (73), the pumping organ that circulates the blood, is covered by a thin external layer of tissue, the *pericardium* (80). The heart is composed of four chambers, two *atria* with appendages called *auricles* (70), and two *ventricles* (90). The *pulmonary artery* (83) sends blood from the heart to the lungs for oxygen uptake. The *cranial vena cava,* or *precava* (82), returns blood from the head and upper body to the heart, while the *caudal vena cava,* or *postcava* (81), returns blood from the abdomen and lower body. The *pulmonary veins* (84) return deoxygenated blood to the lungs. The *aortic arch* (69) is the vessel through which freshly oxygenated blood from the lungs and heart is pumped out into the body. This blood is passed to the head and upper body by the *brachiocephalic* (74), and *subclavian* (88) *arteries,* and to the lower body by the *aorta* (68), the continuation of the aortic arch.

The *liver* (77,95) is a large, chocolate-colored organ that, among its many other functions, filters blood from the digestive tract and stores energy. The *spleen* (87) is an "immunologic filter" of the blood, containing many important cells of the immune system. The *kidneys* (75) remove toxic waste products of metabolism from the blood, producing urine. The *small intestine* (86) and *large intestine,* or *colon* (76), form the largest portion of the digestive tract, wherein nutrients are absorbed and solid waste (feces) is generated. Fecal material accumulates in the colon and is excreted via the *rectum* (85) through the *anus* (67).

In the female, eggs (ova) are formed in *ovaries* (78,96), travel down the corresponding *oviduct* (79,97), and, if fertilized by spermatozoa from the male, will implant in the *uterus* (89,101), initiating a pregnancy.

The *trachea* (139) transports air between the larynx and lungs. The air passes through the large *bronchi* (71) before actually entering the smaller airways within lung tissue. The *pulmonary arteries and veins* (83,84), together with the coronary arteries, are the main blood conduits for the lungs. The muscular *esophagus* (93) carries food from the oral cavity to the *stomach* (99), where it can be acted upon by acid and digestive enzymes. Also involved in the process of digestion (in addition to the intestines) are the *liver* (77,95), *gallbladder* (94), and *pancreas* (98). The pancreas is the source of insulin, a hormone important in the absorption of nutrients. Insulin is lacking or deficient in many animals and humans with diabetes mellitus. Food exits the stomach into the *duodenum* (92), which is the upper portion of the small intestine.

Metabolic waste products in the blood are filtered out by the *kidneys* (75), resulting in the production of urine. The urine is transported through the ureters to the *urinary bladder* (100), and is discharged through the urethra. In the female, the urine is excreted by way of the *vestibule* (103). The *ovaries* (78,96), *oviducts* (79,97), *uterus* (89,101), along with the *cervix* (91), *vagina* (102), and the more external vulva, comprise the female reproductive tract. The male reproductive tract is located almost entirely outside the abdominal cavity.

CHAPTER 19

The Eye and Disorders

by Randall H. Scagliotti

The perception of an object by the sense of vision is a highly complicated physiological process. But what exactly *is* vision? An oversimplification, perhaps—but one that allows for a clearer definition and appreciation of vision's intricacies—involves dividing vision into several individual senses. The light sense is the perception or awareness of light and its intensity. What is known as "light" is in actuality radiation, covering a narrow band of the electromagnetic spectrum—wavelengths about 400 to 700 millionths of a millimeter (400 to 700 nanometers [nm]) in length. The spectacle of color as seen through the color sense is the differentiation between two or more wavelengths (colors) of light within this spectrum range. The longer wavelengths appear as reds and oranges, while the shorter wavelengths are visualized as greens and blues. Finally, the *form sense* makes possible discrimination of different parts of a visual image. To create and perceive the images called vision requires the detection and integration of the senses of light, color and form. This is accomplished through the eyes and their connections with the visual centers of the brain.

When disease affects the eye or brain, it may cause a disturbance in one or more of these vision categories, leading to vision impairment or blindness.

The Normal Canine Eye

The structure of the canine eye and vision centers of the brain evolved along the lines of the carnivorous hunter because of environmental pressures. Because dogs are members of the animal kingdom's **arrhythmic** activity group (i.e., animals remaining active at all times and under all conditions), canine eyes had to evolve to accommodate both day and night vision under extremes of all climatic conditions. Consequently, the entire anatomy of the eye is adapted to these activities. Dogs are predators, so their eyes are placed well forward in the head, promoting greater attention to detail and concentration. To appreciate this advantage, one need only reflect on the intense stare of the hunting wolf and contrast it to the searching, frightened gaze of an alarmed sheep. When an imaginary line is drawn through the central axis

THE LEFT EYE

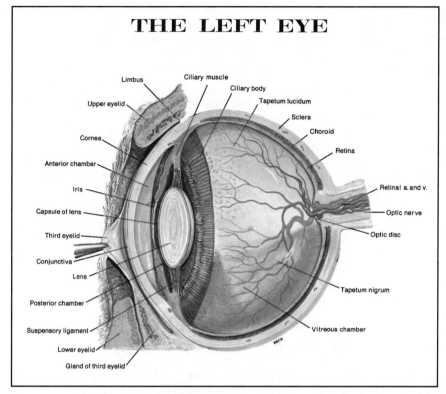

Limbus
Ciliary muscle
Ciliary body
Upper eyelid
Tapetum lucidum
Sclera
Choroid
Cornea
Retina
Anterior chamber
Retinal a. and v.
Iris
Optic nerve
Capsule of lens
Optic disc
Third eyelid
Conjunctiva
Lens
Tapetum nigrum
Posterior chamber
Suspensory ligament
Vitreous chamber
Lower eyelid
Gland of third eyelid

of each eye of a dog, and another is drawn down the long axis of the nose, an angle is created that varies, because of different breed head types, between 30° and 52° in each eye, with a resultant angle of 60° to 104° between the two eye axes. Compared to the larger angles of herbivores such as sheep, the eyes of a dog are placed relatively close together. This forward eye position affords the dog **binocular fixation** (both eyes looking at the same object simultaneously) and **stereopsis** (depth perception), both of which promote improved coordination and better judgment and accuracy when stalking and leaping. However, this does restrict the field of view when compared to the "wraparound" vision of herbivores such as cows and sheep. It also increases the size of the **blind spot,** the portion of the visual field, behind the line of sight, that cannot be seen without changing eye and head position.

ANATOMY OF THE CANINE EYE
The bones of the skull (including their covering, the **periosteum**) that house and protect the eye-

ball are referred to as the **bony orbit.** The **soft-tissue orbit** includes the nonbony structures (muscles, nerves, blood vessels) that lie within the bony orbit. A movable protective shield is provided for the eyeball by the upper and lower eyelids and the third eyelid, or **haw.** The mucous membrane lining the inner surface of the eyelids, both sides of the third eyelid, and the white surface of the eyeball is called the **conjunctiva.** The third eyelid, located in the inner angle of the eye (called the **medial canthus**), between the lower eyelid and the eyeball, is usually hidden or camouflaged from view. It is normally pink in color, with a thin, black-pigmented band at its leading edge. Sometimes dogs are born without pigmentation in this band; as a consequence, the third eyelid is more noticeable. This trait is undesirable to some breeders and is considered a breed blemish. If the eyeball is injured or inflamed, or there is disease elsewhere in the body (e.g., a gastrointestinal disorder), the third eyelid will partially cover the eye until the dog is healthy. The third eyelid and its internal support structure, composed of T-shaped **cartilage** (a specialized type of connective tissue), are designed to conform to the shape of the eyeball. The base of the cartilage is surrounded by a tear gland, or **lacrimal gland,** known as the gland of the third eyelid, that secretes up to 35% of the eye's tears. The remaining 65% is secreted by another lacrimal gland located in the outer portion of the upper eyelid.

The eyeball itself, also known as the **globe,** is composed of three basic layers or tunics. The outer layer is the **fibrous** (composed of thickened connective tissue) **tunic;** the middle layer is the highly **vascular** (supplied with blood vessels) and pigmented **uvea,** containing the **iris, ciliary body,** and **choroid;** and the innermost layer is the **nervous tunic,** or **retina.** The shape of the eyeball is imparted by the tough outer fibrous tunic, which consists of a central, circular, transparent window, the **cornea,** and a surrounding white portion called the **sclera.** The line of demarcation between the cornea and sclera is known as the **limbus.** The globe is divided into three chambers, which are filled with transparent material. The iris divides the front third of the eye into an **anterior chamber** and a **posterior chamber,** both of which contain liquid **(aqueous humor),** while the more deeply placed **lens** separates the posterior chamber from the inner **vitreous chamber,** which is filled with the gel-like **vitreous body** or, more simply, *vitreous.*

The transparent cornea is the primary structure responsible for bending the incoming light rays and focusing them onto the light-sensitive retina at the back of the eye. An injury to the cornea will not lead to bleeding because a healthy cornea has no blood vessels. When blood vessels are present, as seen in some corneal diseases, they impair vision. Corneal injury is very painful because the cornea is abundantly supplied with sensitive nerves. The inner surface of the cornea is bathed and nourished by the aqueous humor of the anterior chamber. The aqueous fluid exits the eyeball by passing through lattice-like layers of fine strands known as the **pectinate ligaments** and the **trabecular network,** which bridge the angle created by the cornea and the iris (the **iridocorneal filtration angle**). Some ocular disorders lead to a decreased ability of aqueous humor to exit the eye. This decreased outflow of aqueous humor causes an increase in pressure within the eye **(intraocular pressure)** known as **glaucoma,** which will result in blindness if left untreated.

The iris and ciliary body (a circular muscle located directly behind the iris) are referred to together as the **anterior uvea.** The iris determines the color of the eye, and controls the quantity of light entering the eye by adjusting the size of the opening in its center, the **pupil.** Partial but not total absence of iris pigmentation is referred to as **subalbinism,** or partial albinism, which results in a partly or entirely blue iris. The pink or red iris associated with a total absence of iris pigment in the middle and deepest layers of the iris (a true *albino*) has not been reported in dogs.

The lens is located behind the iris. It is a transparent refractive structure that finely focuses images onto the retina for clear and sharp vision. To fulfill this function the lens must not only be transparent, but must also occupy a stable position and be able to change its shape as required (i.e., undergo *accommodation*). The lens is held in a stable, secure position by numerous strands **(zonules,** or—more collectively—the **suspensory ligament**) that extend from the ciliary body to the equator of the lens. As the circular muscle of the ciliary body contracts, the zonules slacken, thereby allowing accommodation that results from the natural elasticity of the outer capsule that invests the lens.

The large vitreous chamber behind the lens is filled with a clear, gel-like material that serves to keep the posterior two-thirds of the eye properly shaped, while also applying pressure on the retina to hold it in place. The retina, along with the **optic nerve,** is actually an extension of brain tissue outside the skull. When the deep internal structures of the eye are viewed with a special instrument (an **ophthalmoscope**), one can observe an irregularly circular disk known as the **optic disk,** or *optic nerve head,* which represents the entry point of the optic nerve at the back of the eyeball. *It is startling to realize that, when one is observing the optic disk, one is actually viewing a portion of the brain.* The retina itself is a multilayered structure, but very thin and very transparent. It contains specialized light receptors **(photoreceptors)** known as **rods** and **cones,** which convert the incoming packets of light energy **(photons)** into nerve impulses that are relayed up the optic nerve to the vision centers of the brain. A specialized area near the optic disk, called the **area centralis,** possesses an abundance of cone photoreceptors and is largely responsible for the most precise and accurate vision.

In the upper portion of the interior of the eyeball, directly behind the retina, lies the highly reflective and colorful tapetum (also called **tapetum lucidum**). The tapetum is responsible for the colorful "eye shine" observed when light is reflected from its surface (e.g., by automobile headlights at night). The shape, size and color of the tapetum vary greatly in dogs. Sometimes this layer is absent or severely underdeveloped. In a puppy's first three months of life, the color of the tapetum progresses from an initial gray to violet, to blue, and finally to its permanent adult coloration, which may be blue, yellow, green or orange. Attempts have been made, without success, to relate tapetal coloration to a dog's coat color. The purpose of the tapetum is to enhance the dog's ability to see during low-light conditions by utilizing all available light; that is, light not absorbed during initial passage through the retina is reflected back onto the retina for a second chance at absorption and vision. The lower half of the **fundus** (back of the eye) lacks a tapetum lucidum; instead, there is a broad area of heavy pigmentation (the **tapetum nigrum**) that guards the sensitive retina from overhead glare during the daylight hours.

MOVEMENTS OF THE EYE

Ocular movement is the result of sophisticated, coordinated activity by the **extraocular** (outside the eyeball) muscles, or EOMs, and the **cranial nerves** (nerves coming from the brain) that stimulate them. By moving the eyes, the EOMs not only increase the field of view, but also allow the area of finest vision in the retina, the area centralis, to move as well and thus maintain optimal visual acuity. Ocular movements in dogs are of two principal types:

Voluntary movements that jump or change the line of sight or object of fixation of both eyes to a new location

Movements that keep images steady on both retinas during head movement by means of the balancing apparatus in the inner ear, i.e., by sending messages to "correct" the EOMs, which in turn "right" the eyeballs, regardless of the position of the head in space

Without eye movement, the visual world would "slip" on the retinas, with every movement of the head creating a dizzying blur for an image. To accomplish these highly intricate and coordinated movements, the EOMs can be divided functionally into four groups:

Three opposing pairs of muscles that rotate the eyeball around three axes: the vertical, horizontal, and anterior-posterior (forward-backward)

Four muscles that can retract the eyeball deeper into the orbit

COLOR VISION

Determining the presence and type of color vision in dogs has proved difficult and has required three different methods of study: *morphologic* (i.e., studying the forms and structure of the entire vision-producing anatomy), *physiologic* (chemical and electrical), and *behavioral*.

Dogs do see color, but it is based on a dichromatic (i.e., two primary colors) system covering wavelengths of light ranging from 429 nm to 555 nm, rather than the trichromatic (three primary colors) system present in primates, including human beings. The ability to extract the color from any field of view is a combined function of the retina and the vision areas of the brain.

Disorders of the Eye

DISORDERS OF THE EYELID

These disorders constitute a common clinical problem in dogs and may be manifested by a variety of clinical signs. Painful injury to the nerves supplying the eyelid margins will cause **blepharospasm** (squinting) and rubbing of the eyelids with the forepaw or by brushing along household objects such as a carpet or furniture. Any inflammatory disease affecting the well-vascularized eyelids will result in eyelid **hyperemia** (reddening caused by increased blood flow) and **edema** (swelling). **Epiphora** (an overflow of tears) may be present, especially if adjacent eye tissue (cornea, conjunctiva) is irritated as a result of the eyelid problem. A deformed or malpositioned eyelid can mechanically irritate the cornea or eyelid surfaces. Alternatively, eyelid bacteria or their by-products (e.g., certain toxins) can extend from the eyelid to injure the surrounding tissues.

Dermoids

Dermoids are a *congenital* (present at birth) problem wherein single or multiple abnormal patches of skin and hair are present on one or more eyelids, in either a pigmented or nonpigmented form. The hair shafts can extend out in many directions or form tufts of wild hair. Most frequently, the lateral (towards the side) halves of both lower eyelids are involved. Dermoids may extend onto the conjunctival surface and occasionally as far as the cornea. They badly distort the eyelids and interfere with proper evaluation of the eyelid margins. Occasionally, the eyelid margin is destroyed by the dermoid. If the abnormal hairs touch the cornea or conjunctiva, these surfaces will become irritated or ulcerated. Dermoids may occur as an inherited problem in the Saint Bernard, German Shepherd Dog, and Dalmatian breeds. Cure is provided by surgical removal of the dermoids, although topical antibiotic-corticosteroid ointments may provide some temporary relief.

Ankyloblepharon

The eyelids of newborn pups remain fused along the eyelid margins for about 10 to 15 days after birth, after which they open completely. **Ankyloblepharon** (failure of one or both eyelids to open) after this time can lead to bacterial infection, most commonly with staphylococci, beneath the closed or partially closed eyelids. The pus that forms in response to the infection accumulates under the eyelids, causing a bulging of the eyelid surface. Any delay in resolving this infection may lead to ulceration and scarring of the cornea, or even corneal perforation with subsequent loss of vision.

Home therapy includes the application of hot compresses and attempts to separate the eyelids gently with the fingertips. Veterinary assistance should be sought if the above measures fail, since surgery will then be necessary to preserve the eyelid margins and remove the pus. An appropriate antibiotic should be administered until all signs of infection disappear.

Macroblepharon/Macropalpebral Fissure

Normally, the eyelids cover and protect the eyeball such that only a small portion of the white sclera is visible. The abnormality known as **macroblepharon** (excessively long eyelids) can lead to **macropalpebral fissure** (an enlarged eyelid opening), which exposes large amounts of sclera around the cornea. This alteration not only reduces the amount of protection the eyelids provide for the eyeball, but also excessively exposes the eyeball to the environment and renders it more vulnerable to any number of damaging ocular conditions. Notably, **brachycephalic** (flat-faced) breeds have the highest incidence of ocular disease resulting from this problem, although certain other breeds (Saint Bernard, Bernese Mountain Dog, Basset Hound, Cocker Spaniel) may also be affected.

The disorder usually occurs in both eyes. Macroblepharon affecting only one eye is more likely to occur in the nonbrachycephalic breeds. Macroblepharon is first observed in puppyhood in the brachycephalic breeds, while in other breeds it may not be apparent until adulthood. Two other factors contributing to this condition, at least in the brachycephalic breeds, include a shallow bony orbit that forces the eyeball forward, and an inability to close the eyelids completely, resulting in a condition called **lagophthalmos.**

The ocular consequences of macroblepharon vary among individuals of a breed and among breeds. In its most benign form the complaint comes from the pet owner, rather than the pet. Owners typically report increased ocular redness, which is caused by excessive exposure of the conjunctival surfaces because of the enlarged eyelid opening. Alternatively, the large amount of visible sclera raises complaints about poor cosmetic appearance or elicits concern that the eyes are not normal. In its most dramatic and serious complication, the eyeball is extremely susceptible to **proptosis** (forward protrusion of the eye). The eyeball can roll forward out of the orbital socket, leaving the front half of the eyeball resting in front of the eyelid margins, while the upper and lower eyelids scroll inward on themselves behind the eye. This is most commonly seen in the brachycephalic breeds and usually follows a blunt blow or bite wound to the ocular area. *This is a medical emergency and requires immediate veterinary care.* If one has the presence of mind to grab the skin of the upper and lower eyelids and give a quick jerk forward toward the nose, the eyeball will snap back into place before excessive swelling and damage can occur. This maneuver can save the eyeball and vision. Only timely medical attention by a veterinarian is likely to preserve vision should the maneuver prove unsuccessful. Other (less dramatic and less serious) complications of macroblepharon include chronic ocular discharge (tears or mucus), **corneal melanosis** (black or brown pigmentation of the cornea), **keratitis** (inflammation of the cornea), and defective eyelid position or movement. These conditions may require medical therapy or surgery to alleviate discomfort or vision loss.

Entropion

Eyeball irritation or injury can result from this conformational defect of the eyelid wherein an "inrolling" of the eyelid margin occurs, such that the eyelid hairs rub against the smooth, sensitive cornea. This causes mechanical injury to the corneal surface cells and a disruption of the thin layer of tears that serves to feed and protect the cornea. Entropion may be present along part of all of one or more eyelids. In dogs, entropion displays a high incidence of inheritance in certain breeds and is thought to be influenced by the simultaneous action of several genes (e.g., a *polygenic* mode of inheritance). (*See* CHAPTER 16, "GENETICS.") These genes define the skin and other structures making up the eyelids, the amount and weight of skin covering the head and face, the orbital contents, and the conformation of the skull. Many breeds are predisposed to entropion, including Chow Chows, Chinese Shar-Peis, Saint Bernards, Basset Hounds, Bernese Mountain Dogs, Bloodhounds, Bulldogs and Chesapeake Bay Retrievers, among others. Surgical correction of the defect is usually indicated.

Ectropion

Unlike entropion, this eyelid conformational defect results in eversion (a turning outward) of the affected eyelid margin, causing irritation and injury owing to increased exposure of the conjunctival and corneal surfaces. The lower eyelid is usually involved. Although most ectropions are developmental in origin, some are acquired. When the extent of eversion leads to secondary conjunctival or corneal disease, surgical correction is required.

Abnormal Eyelashes and Facial Hair

The variation in skull types, eyelid conformation, and haircoat lengths and stiffness in the various breeds present many opportunities for either eyelashes or facial hair to contact and damage the sensitive cornea and conjunctiva. Eyelashes growing from an abnormal location along the lid margin and causing ocular irritation are referred to as distichia, and the condition is called **distichiasis.** It is commonly seen in Cocker Spaniels, Golden Retrievers and Weimaraners, and may be inherited. **Trichiasis** is a condition wherein facial hair or eyelashes arising from normal sites are misdirected and contact the cornea or conjunctiva. Those hairs arising from the prominent nasal folds of breeds such as Pekingese, English Bulldogs, and Pugs, frequently contact the cornea and produce excessive tearing with corneal inflammation. Sometimes **ectopic** (displaced) eyelashes may emerge from the conjunctival surface itself. They are usually short and stubby, and are most commonly situated beneath the upper eyelid, in the outer to middle third near the eyelid margin. These aberrant lashes cause extreme pain and profound squinting and tearing. Eventually a corneal ulcer may develop in the upper and outer quadrant of the cornea, just inside the limbus. The discomfort and ulceration will not resolve until the abnormal lashes are removed. Therapy for all of these eyelash or facial hair disorders consists of removal of the offending lashes or hairs by surgical excision or by **cryosurgery** (a procedure by which local application of intense cold [freezing] is used to destroy unwanted tissue).

Blepharitis

Inflammatory disease of the eyelids is known as **blepharitis.** The origins are many and varied, and include bacterial, fungal, parasitic, allergic, traumatic and **neoplastic** (cancerous) causes. Staphylococci and streptococci are the most common bacterial infections encountered and require appropriate antibiotic therapy, either topically (local administration) or **systemically** (i.e., by the oral route or by injection). Sometimes an allergic component exists, particularly with staphylococci, which necessitates the addition of a corticosteroid to the therapeutic regimen. A common complication of chronic staphylococcal infections of the eyelid glands is the development of **hordeolums** (sties) and **chalazions** (chronic inflammatory lesions) along the lid margins. Sties appear as well-demarcated, reddened bumps and may be effectively treated with hot compresses and topical antibiotics. Chalazions are more chronic in nature and can be confused with eyelid tumors. They appear as irregularly firm, pigmented masses along the lid margins. Surgical excision is required in most cases. Styes and chalazions can lead to secondary corneal problems if they are not adequately controlled.

Reddened, itchy eyelids that appear to be losing hair may be infected with parasitic mites, either *Demodex* or *Sarcoptes*. Mite infestations can involve other areas of the body as well. The diagnosis can be made by examination of scrapings from eyelid skin or other affected areas. Treatment involves an appropriate **miticide** (a medication that kills mites) applied to all affected areas of the skin, including the eyelids. It is wise to use a protective lubricating ointment in the eyes if the miticide is applied to the eyelids. (*See* CHAPTER 23, "EXTERNAL PARASITES.")

Eyelid Tumors

Eyelid tumors in dogs usually are benign. Those that are malignant are very slow to spread and tend to invade local, rather than distant, tissues. The most common tumors are adenomas, adenocarcinomas, benign and malignant melanomas, and papillomas (warts). They are best treated by surgical excision or cryotherapy. (*See* CHAPTER 38, "CANCER.")

DISORDERS OF THE CONJUNCTIVA

The most common conjunctival disorder in dogs and one that elicits much owner concern is con-

junctivitis (conjunctival inflammation, or "pinkeye"), which may appear quite innocuous at the outset and not sight-threatening. Determining the cause of a conjunctivitis can sometimes be difficult, because the inflammation may be the result of disease within the conjunctiva itself (*primary conjunctivitis*) or a manifestation of disease elsewhere in the eye or body (*secondary conjunctivitis*). When conjunctivitis is secondary, it is often the earliest and most visible sign of **systemic** (body-wide) illness or ocular diseases such as blepharitis, keratitis, glaucoma or **iridocyclitis** (inflammation of the iris and ciliary body). The diagnosis of primary conjunctivitis is made by ruling out systemic and other ocular diseases as the cause. Inflamed conjunctival surfaces exhibit red ("pink") eyes, watery or **mucoid** (mucus-containing) discharge, increased frequency of blinking and/or slight squinting, and protruded third eyelid. One or both eyes may be involved. Primary conjunctivitis can be caused by bacterial, viral, fungal or parasitic agents, as well as by allergic reactions or contact with irritating substances. Treatment will be dictated by identification of the underlying cause.

Infectious (Bacterial or Fungal) Conjunctivitis

The conjunctival surfaces have their own indigenous population of bacteria and fungi, just like the skin, which serves to keep these surfaces healthy. The normal bacterial and fungal population of the canine eye changes throughout life and also varies depending on the breed, local environment, geographic location, and season of the year. The predominant microorganisms include the bacterium *Staphylococcus aureus* and several fungi, primarily *Candida* and *Curvularia. Acute bacterial conjunctivitis* is a common ocular disorder of dogs most frequently caused by *Staphylococcus aureus,* and results from compromised host-defense mechanisms which allow exuberant overgrowth of the indigenous population. Bacterial conjunctivitis may also be associated with eye injury, misdirected eyelashes, **keratoconjunctivitis sicca (KCS,** "dry eye"), chronic skin diseases such as **seborrhea** (a disease characterized by excessive scaling, crusting and greasiness) and **pyoderma** (any skin disease characterized by pus formation), and chronic outer-ear disease. (*See* CHAPTER 22, "THE SKIN AND DISORDERS.") These and any other associated problems should always be treated when therapy for the conjunctivitis is initiated. Treatment with appropriate antibiotics or antifungal agents following bacterial or fungal culture of the conjunctiva usually resolves the conjunctivitis.

Viral Conjunctivitis
Canine distemper virus (CDV) infection and canine adenovirus type 1 (CAV-1, the cause of infectious canine hepatitis) infection are the two most serious viral infections associated with conjunctivitis in dogs. Both of these viruses may also cause upper respiratory tract disease. CDV causes acute and chronic conjunctivitis and dry eye. In the earliest phases of distemper, intracellular viral *inclusion particles* can be seen in cells scraped from the affected conjunctival surface and properly stained. Later, antibody detection techniques may assist in making a diagnosis. Treatment for viral conjunctivitis is nonspecific and supportive in nature; that is, it is directed at eliminating secondary bacterial invaders, dry eye, and other ocular signs until the virus infection has run its course. A proper and timely vaccination program as advised by a veterinarian will almost always prevent disease caused by CDV and CAV-1. (*See* CHAPTER 34, "VIRAL DISEASES," and APPENDIX B, "VACCINATIONS.")

Parasitic Conjunctivitis
The conjunctival sac (the space between the eyelids and the eyeball) of dogs in the western United States may contain a worm parasite, *Thelazia californiensis,* which can cause a conjunctivitis known as **thelaziasis.** Removal of the worm with *forceps* (a medical instrument for grasping tissues) as it wriggles over the surface of the cornea or conjunctiva, or flushing the eye with antiparasitic medication, is effective in ridding the eye of this parasite.

DISORDERS OF THE THIRD EYELID
A great deal of concern often is expressed when the third eyelid is **prolapsed** (drawn across the eye) and visible, rather than hidden in its usual

location. A prolapsed third eyelid with an enlarged tear gland protruding from behind its leading edge, but seeming to present no discomfort to the affected dog, accounts for the great majority of third-eyelid disorders. The third eyelid only becomes visible by passive movement, because there is no neuromuscular system in the third eyelid to direct its voluntary or involuntary, active movement across the surface of the cornea. Any change in eyeball size (especially a decrease) or shape will result in passive protrusion of the third eyelid. If the eyeball remains normal in size, but ocular irritation or injury causes it actively to be retracted more deeply into its socket by the strong pull of the ocular musculature, the third eyelid will passively prolapse, even to the extreme of shrouding the entire eyeball. When this occurs, concerned owners often describe the condition by remarking that the eyeball has "rolled back into the head," even though this is physically impossible! Prolapse of the third eyelid also occurs when the eyeball passively alters its position in the orbit (most frequently moving deeper) as the result of a change in size, position or shape of the soft-tissue structures of the orbit. For example, temporary or permanent reduction in orbital soft-tissue mass occurs during:

• **dehydration** (excessive loss of body water) and muscle wasting from serious systemic illness
• severe dental disease with tooth **abscesses** (pus-filled lesions) that extend into the orbit
• severe head-muscle **atrophy** (shrinkage or wasting)

A change in the shape or size of the bony orbit caused by tumors, fractures or infection will also lead to prolapse of the third eyelid by a similar mechanism.

Protrusion of the Gland of the Third Eyelid
The tear gland that normally occupies the base of the third eyelid sometimes undergoes enlargement and protrudes beyond the leading edge of a prolapsed third eyelid, appearing as a round, red mass ("cherry eye"). The cause of

this condition remains speculative. It can occur in one or both eyes and in any breed, although breeds such as Beagles, Bloodhounds, Boxers, Bulldogs, American Cocker Spaniels, Lhasa Apsos, Neapolitan Mastiffs and Chinese Shar-Peis are at particular risk. Treatment involves returning the tear gland to its normal position in order to preserve its tear-producing capability, removing the potential for corneal or conjunctival irritation from prolonged exposure, and returning the eye to a normal appearance. Repositioning of the gland using the fingers and/or treatment with topical anti-inflammatory medication occasionally restores the gland to normalcy; more commonly, however, one of several surgical techniques is needed to achieve a resolution of the problem.

Tumors of the Third Eyelid

These are not common, but when present are usually benign. **Excisional biopsy** (surgical removal of the entire mass and submission of the tissue for microscopic examination) is an appropriate means of both diagnosis and treatment. If the tumor is malignant (adenocarcinoma, basal cell carcinoma, or squamous cell carcinoma), the entire third eyelid should be removed. Except for extensive traumatic injury, this is the only recognized indication for surgical removal of the third eyelid. (*See* CHAPTER 38, "CANCER.")

Eversion of the Cartilage of the Third Eyelid

In this condition, a scroll-like curling of the cartilage that provides internal support for the third eyelid develops, resulting usually in an eversion of the margin or leading edge of the third eyelid. The condition may occur in one or both eyes and may produce mild ocular irritation, decreased third-eyelid function, and a poor cosmetic appearance. It may be inherited, and is commonly observed in the following breeds: Doberman Pinscher, German Shepherd Dog, German Shorthaired Pointer, Great Dane, Irish Wolfhound, Neapolitan Mastiff, Newfoundland and Weimaraner. Treatment for the disorder is the surgical removal of the folded portion of the cartilage.

DISORDERS OF THE CORNEA

The cornea acts as an impermeable mechanical barrier between the eye and the environment. Because it is transparent and smooth, the cornea also serves as the main **refractive** (light-bending) surface for focusing the visual image on the retina. Preservation of the cornea's surface smoothness and transparency is enhanced by adequate tear production and proper eyelid movement. Any condition that alters the transparency of the cornea will lead to diminished vision. Conditions that disturb tear production or proper distribution of the tears can secondarily decrease corneal transparency. Corneal **opacification** (loss of transparency) may be either reversible or permanent, depending to some extent on whether or not the cause is inherited or acquired, and whether the opacity was present at birth (congenitally) or developed at a later date. Some corneal disorders progress painfully and are easily noticed because the pain produces blinking, tearing, redness and rubbing. Other progressive disorders are silent and painless, thereby preventing an alert to the mounting menace to vision.

Keratitis

Inflammation of the cornea can be divided into **ulcerative** (characterized by a defect or hole in the corneal surface) and *nonulcerative* keratitis. Either form may be superficial or deep, and may be the result of mechanical irritation (traumatic injury) or infectious disease (bacteria, viruses, fungi). Superficial ulcers often heal with little or no scarring, while deeper ulcers may produce large scars and impaired vision. Appropriate veterinary attention can prevent superficial ulcers from becoming deep and complicated. This usually involves culturing and scraping the cornea and applying topical antibiotics. Topically applied **atropine** (a medication for dilating the eyes) is sometimes used to control ciliary muscle spasm and its associated ocular discomfort. Sometimes a protective **Elizabethan collar** is placed on a dog suffering from this ailment to prevent self-mutilation of the cornea. In cases of deep ulcerative keratitis, surgery of various types may be necessary to prevent the cornea from perforating, with resultant vision loss.

An important nonulcerative, noninfectious, inflammatory condition of the canine cornea, called **chronic superficial keratitis (CSK,** or **pannus;** also known as *German Shepherd pannus*), is a highly progressive and potentially blinding disorder. Although it was first noticed in German Shepherd Dogs, it may occur in other breeds as well. The cause is unknown. The disorder commonly begins as a vascularized red patch, often intermixed with dark pigment, in the upper region of the conjunctiva. Unless it is aggressively and persistently treated, this vascularized pigment will gradually spread across the cornea. There is no cure for this condition, only medical or surgical management and control. Therapies include corticosteroid medications, radiation therapy, and surgical intervention by freezing, heating or *excising* (cutting out) the lesion.

Corneal Dystrophy

This is an inherited condition wherein gray-white or silver, crystalline opacities develop in or around the central area of the cornea. The opacities are almost always present in the same area in both eyes (i.e., they are symmetrical in appearance), and there is no accompanying corneal inflammation or systemic illness. No treatment is available, but thankfully the condition is not painful and usually not blinding, with a few exceptions. If the dystrophy affects the deepest corneal layer, as it does in Boston Terriers, Chihuahuas and Dachshunds, it can lead to diffuse corneal swelling and blindness. Most dystrophies are more superficial and circumscribed, such as those seen in Siberian Huskies, Beagles and Cavalier King Charles Spaniels. Affected dogs should not be bred in order to avoid perpetuating the defect.

Corneal Degenerations

These are similar in appearance to corneal dystrophies, except that these white-to-silver, crystalline opacities are not inherited and frequently occur only in one eye. When they occur in both eyes, they often are not symmetrical in appearance. Degenerations occur as a result of secondary changes from metabolic or physical injury to the cornea, leading to the deposit of salts and fats within corneal cells. Corneal degenerations always have an associated vascular response and may ulcerate and become uncomfortable. The condition can be stabilized to eliminate discomfort by using topical antibiotic-corticosteroid combinations or by surgical removal. Although topical medication will usually keep the eye comfortable, it will not eliminate the opacity. A surgical **keratectomy** (removal of the damaged portion of the cornea) can be performed, but will leave behind some degree of scarring. Fortunately, most corneal degenerations remain quiet and require neither mode of therapy. All breeds of dogs are susceptible to this ailment.

DISORDERS OF THE LENS

The lens is second in importance to the cornea as a refractive structure for obtaining a clear, focused retinal image. As it ages the lens may either become hardened (**sclerotic**), change position (**subluxate** or **luxate**), or become opaque (develop a **cataract**).

Nuclear Sclerosis

This is the most common disorder of the lens and is considered part of the normal aging process. As the lens continues its slow, lifelong growth, its central region (nucleus) becomes dense and hard compared to the peripheral (**cortex**) region. This hard, dense, inflexible nucleus is referred to as **nuclear sclerosis,** just as inflexible "hardening of the arteries" is referred to as arteriosclerosis. Nuclear sclerosis makes the pupil area appear hazy gray or blue, and is often confused with cataracts by many dog owners. This condition does not prevent a clear visual examination of the inner portion of the eye as a cataract might, nor does it impair the dog's vision to any recognizable extent. It can be assumed, however, that some degree of sharpness of near-vision is lost, for reading glasses are required to overcome nuclear sclerosis in people, despite the fact that distance-vision remains sharp. No treatment is required for the canine condition (unless the dog is an avid reader!).

Cataract

A cataract is an opacity of any size in the lens. The opacity is usually white, but can have a yellowish tint. It can be singular or multiple, of any size or shape, and may affect the entire lens. The degree of vision impairment is determined by the size and location of the cataract within the lens (although even small cataracts may produce sufficient glare from scattered light to induce squinting). Cataracts are common in dogs and most are inherited, especially in purebreds. Of those that are acquired, most are the result of metabolic injury to the lens protein caused by diabetes mellitus (*see* CHAPTER 32, "THE ENDOCRINE SYSTEM AND METABOLIC DISORDERS"). Congenital cataracts may or may not be inherited and generally do not progress to blindness, although in puppyhood such a cataract may represent a visual handicap. As the lens ages and enlarges, the increasing lens size relative to the nongrowing opacity will diminish the vision-impairing effects of a congenital cataract. Surgical extraction of a cataract is a highly successful procedure using the newest lens-removal technique, **phacoemulsification,** which involves fragmentation of the lens by ultrasonic vibrations. Vision will be returned nearly to normal when the extracted lens is then replaced by a clear plastic intraocular lens.

Luxation and Subluxation of the Lens

The loss by rupture of zonular attachments between the lens and ciliary body will, depending on the number of fibers lost, lead to a slightly altered lens position (**subluxation**) or to total lens displacement (**luxation**) into the anterior chamber or vitreous. Trauma, inheritance, glaucoma, inflammation and aging can be associated with diseases of the zonules contributing directly to changes in lens position. Several breeds exhibit an inherited predisposition to lens luxation, including the terriers (Wire and Smooth Fox, Sealyham, Jack Russell, Tibetan) and Border Collie. Luxated lenses are treated by surgical extraction. Vision can be saved if lens removal is not delayed. A luxated lens is usually painful; an affected eye will be red around the sclera and opaque owing to fluid collection in the cornea or to opacity within the dislocated lens itself. Subluxations of the lens are more subtle in appearance, and can cause mild squinting, redness and tearing. Subluxations can usually be managed medically by controlling the associated inflammation, and by reducing the tension on the remaining intact zonules using ocular medications that must be given for the lifetime of the affected dog.

DISORDERS OF THE IRIS

Disorders of the iris (plural: **irides**) are readily detected because they frequently are manifested by changes in the shape of the pupil or alterations in iris color. **Heterochromia iridis** (difference of color in different areas of the same iris, or between the two irides) may be the sole manifestation of ocular color dilution seen in a number of breeds (Old English Sheepdog, Siberian Husky, American Foxhound, Alaskan Malamute, Shih Tzu). In some cases it may be accompanied by thinning of the iris, holes in the iris, eccentric pupils, or persistent pupillary membranes (*see* below). Other, more severe ocular anomalies may accompany heterochromia iridis in certain breeds (Australian Shepherd Dog, Great Dane, Collie, Dachshund) and can include microphthalmia (undersized eye), cataracts, thinned sclera, **retinal dysplasia** (abnormally developed retina), and **optic nerve hypoplasia** (underdeveloped optic nerve) (*see* below).

Persistent Pupillary Membranes (PPMs)

These tiny strands in the eyes of some juvenile and adult dogs represent remnants of the fetal iris vessels and tissues. The strands may stretch from iris to lens, from iris to cornea, or extend across the pupil from one side of the iris to the other. PPMs are common in dogs and fortunately most do not impair vision. Those that do cause vision loss usually are attached to the back of the cornea or the front of the lens, and can produce corneal opacities or cataracts. PPMs are an inherited condition in some breeds, like the Basenji, in which blindness from severe corneal swelling is not uncommon. Generally, no treatment is needed, although surgery can prevent vision loss if it appears imminent.

Iris Cysts

These appear as freely moving, floating brown spheres or "balloons" within the aqueous humor, or as single or multiple brown bodies poking out from behind the iris into the pupillary space, while remaining attached to the iris near the pupil margin. They can be differentiated from pigmented, internal ocular tumors by their ability to allow light to be transmitted through their entire structure. Generally no treatment is required.

Anterior Uveitis

Inflammation of the anterior uvea (i.e., iris and ciliary body) is a component of most intraocular disease processes in dogs because the uvea, representing the middle, highly vascular layer of the eyeball, is in close proximity to many other internal eye structures. Extension to and from the posterior uvea (i.e., choroid) that lies between the retina and sclera is quite common. A correct diagnosis of this condition is essential for prevention of vision loss. Blood samples, cultures of aqueous humor, and more sophisticated tests (X rays, diagnostic ultrasound) may be required to arrive at the diagnosis. Uveitis can be caused by internal or external sources, and may be the result of an inflammatory process, infectious disease (bacteria, viruses, fungi, parasites), or cancer. When uveitis is present in both eyes it is often the result of disease elsewhere in the body. Clinical signs can range from the subtle to the dramatic, and may include tearing, mild-to-severe squinting, **photophobia** (visual hypersensitivity to light), corneal clouding, iris color change, **hypotony** (decreased intraocular pressure), and vision impairment or loss. Untreated or poorly treated eyes may progress to blindness as a result of glaucoma, cataract formation or retinal detachments. Successful treatment to preserve vision requires high levels of topical and systemic corticosteroids. These may be contraindicated for a brief period of time if an infectious agent is identified as the cause of the uveitis, but should be initiated as soon as the infection is under control. Delay in their use often results in a decrease in vision. In addition to steroids, the arsenal of drugs used to treat uveitis includes antifungals, antiparasitic agents and antibiotics. When cancer is the cause, anticancer drugs and treatment modalities such as **immunotherapy** (use of medications that boost the immune response) or irradiation may be employed. (*See* CHAPTER 38, "CANCER.")

DISORDERS OF THE VITREOUS

The vitreous body or vitreous is a semifluid and transparent hydrogel (watery gel, like gelatin) that occupies three-quarters of the volume of the eyeball. It is limited in its range of reactions to disease because of its relatively simple structure and lack of blood- and lymph-vessel supply. Most of the serious developmental abnormalities seen in the canine vitreous relate to the persistence, long after birth, of the developing eye's internal vascular system (i.e., the fetal hyaloid artery). In dogs, the fetal hyaloid artery should disappear within three weeks after birth. Inflammation and/or infection can lead to **cicatrization** (scar-tissue formation) and vascularization, which become a source of hemorrhage, opacification and retinal detachments.

Persistent Primary Vitreous

This denotes the hyaloid artery's lifelong persistence as a posterior remnant, seen as a red or white "tail" in front of the optic disk and extending a variable distance into the vitreous and as far as the lens. Alternatively, it may persist as a more forward remnant that appears as an opaque dot (**Mittendorf's dot**) on the back of the lens and may be mistaken for a cataract. This condition does not result in vision loss and no treatment is necessary.

Persistent Hyperplastic Primary Vitreous (PHPV)

This is a congenital ocular anomaly caused by failure of the fetal hyaloid artery to regress, accompanied by **fibroplasia** (formation of fibrous tissue) leading to development of a plague of fibrous, vascular tissue on the back of the lens. This causes **leukocoria** (a white pupil) and visual impairment. Lens abnormalities may accompany the condition in more severely affected dogs. Hereditary PHPV has been reported in the Doberman Pinscher and Staffordshire Bull Terrier breeds. Dogs with this condition should not be bred in order to avoid perpetuating the defect. Treatment involves administration of topical atropine every 48 to 72 hours to dilate the pupil and improve the visual field. If severe cataracts are present a cataract extraction procedure with or without vitreous removal (**vitrectomy**) may be necessary.

Vitreous Syneresis

This is a degenerative process occasionally seen in older dogs, but more commonly accompanying glaucoma, lens luxation, infection, or inflammation of the eye. It is characterized by liquefaction (conversion to liquid) of the gel-like structure of the vitreous, predisposing the eye to retinal tears and detachments. In Collies affected with Collie eye anomaly (*see* below), many of the retinal detachments are associated with vitreous syneresis.

Asteroid Hyalosis

This is a common degenerative disorder of the canine vitreous, characterized by the formation of many small, opaque, spherical, refractile bodies composed of calcium and fat. They can be readily observed oscillating slightly with movement of the eyes or head. These can be confused with cataracts by many owners, but they are much less serious for they are not vision-threatening and require no treatment of any kind.

DISORDERS OF THE RETINA

The retina is responsible for converting the light energy entering the eye into electrochemical energy that is then relayed to the brain for processing and image formation. A disease process in one or more layers of the retina can disturb this function and lead to total vision loss or to one or more localized "blind spots" (**scotomas**), depending on the extent of disease involvement. Retinal disease is a complex entity, and it is common for diseases occurring elsewhere in the body to manifest themselves as retinal disorders, particularly abnormalities of the blood. A wide variety of patterns of bleeding in the retina (retinal hemorrhage) may be observed, with profound **septicemia** (presence of bacteria in the blood circulation, accompanied by related clinical signs of disease), **anemia** (low red blood cell count, reduced hemoglobin levels, or reduced volume of packed red cells), **hyperviscosity syndrome** (abnormal thickening of the blood), thrombocytopenia (clotting deficiency caused by low blood platelet levels), or leukemia (cancer of blood cells). Retinal hemorrhage is often the first indicator of systemic **hypertension** (elevated blood pressure) from heart or kidney disease. The diagnosis is based on the history and physical examination, including a thorough ocular examination and laboratory tests. The prognosis depends on the diagnosis, but minimal vision loss will result if treatment of the underlying cause is rapid and complete.

Retinitis (inflammation of the retina) can be caused by infection (bacteria, viruses, fungi, algae, protozoa or other parasites) or by noninfectious means, including trauma, foreign bodies and cancer. Retinitis will lead to spotty or diffuse retinal degeneration, depending upon the extent of injury. The vitreous and/or the underlying choroid may also be involved (**chorioretinitis**). Most infectious causes of retinitis are uncommon, with the exception of certain bacteria and viruses. Infectious causes of retinitis are potentially treatable if identified early. Noninfectious causes should be treated with systemic corticosteroid medication to minimize retinal damage.

Congenital disorders of the retina are common in dogs. Some are breed-specific and inherited as *recessive* traits (*see* CHAPTER 16, GENETICS"). Vision will be affected to varying degrees.

Collie Eye Anomaly (CEA)

This disorder affects smooth- and rough-coated Collies of all coat colors. It is inherited as an *autosomal recessive* trait, which is present in both eyes of affected dogs at birth. (*See* CHAPTER 16, "GENETICS" and CHAPTER 17, "CONGENITAL AND INHERITED DISORDERS.") Published studies report an incidence of CEA in Collies of between 79% and 97%. This incredibly high value indicates that ocular genetic diversity in the Collie breed is quite limited.

The disease involves all three layers of the posterior eyeball. A so-called "pale area" within the middle layer is considered the hallmark lesion of CEA. The characteristic pallor of this lesion is due to the underlying white sclera, which becomes visible owing to the absence of the tapetum, absence of pigment in the lower retina, and the presence of an abnormal formation and distribution of blood vessels in the choroid portion of the uvea. In mildly affected cases the pale area can be masked by pigmentation in the overlying retina. In more severely affected dogs, retinal detachments and/or optic disk defects (**colobomas**), sometimes referred to as "pits," may be present. Mild CEA can result in a large blind spot, which may be clinically undetectable, while large optic-disk colobomas and retinal detachments will lead to overt blindness.

Retinal Dysplasia

This is a congenital disorder characterized by abnormal development of the retina. Retinal dysplasia can result from viral infections (e.g., canine herpesvirus or adenovirus infections), irradiation, certain drugs, vitamin A deficiency, or intrauterine trauma. Inherited dysplasias are the more common and also the more important, because they can be passed on to subsequent generations of dogs. Breeds known to have heritable retinal dysplasia include the Sealyham Terrier, Labrador Retriever, American Cocker Spaniel, Australian Shepherd Dog, English Springer Spaniel and Bedlington Terrier. In some breeds or individuals of a breed, the vision disturbance may be undetectable, while in others the condition leads to blindness. There is currently no effective treatment for this disorder.

A retina that develops normally and is healthy at birth can undergo a process of degeneration at a later stage of life as the result of either inherited or acquired disease. The inherited forms of retinal degeneration are varied and complex, and affect various breeds at different ages with different forms of degeneration. Most are inherited as autosomal recessive traits.

Progressive Retinal Atrophy (PRA).

This is an inherited retinal degeneration that occurs in two basic forms, *central* and *generalized*. The generalized form is the more common and affects the photoreceptor area of the retina. Its presence is indicated by the onset of night blindness. Owners typically will report vision errors in their dogs under dim light conditions. Often, earlier signs will have been observed, but owners may be unable to relate them to the loss of night vision. Earlier signs include an increasing reluctance to cruise the yard widely when let out for the evening toilet, the dog opting instead

to remain near a lighted doorway. Other dogs exhibit a growing tendency to cling to an owner, huddling constantly at his or her feet. Some have a reluctance to climb stairs or clamber onto beds, while performance dogs sometimes experience difficulty marking a moving target or making indoor jumps. Eventually the night blindness progresses to loss of day vision and total blindness. There is no effective treatment at present.

Central Progressive Retinal Atrophy (CPRA) is a similar disorder of the deepest layer of the retina, which lies immediately below the photoreceptor layer. It is inherited in the following breeds: Labrador Retriever, Shetland Sheepdog, Border Collie, Golden Retriever, Irish Setter and English Springer Spaniel. As with PRA, there is no effective therapy.

Hemeralopia.

Also called "day blindness," this condition occurs in Alaskan Malamutes and Miniature Poodles. In Malamutes, it is known to be inherited as an autosomal recessive trait. The fundus appears normal on ophthalmoscopic examination. Dogs with this retinal disorder are blind during the day but have a partial return of vision in dim light. As with PRA and CPRA, there is no effective treatment.

DISORDERS OF THE OPTIC NERVE

Visual impulses are conducted from the retina to the vision relay centers in the brain by the optic nerve. Two important congenital disorders that affect the optic nerve and optic disk in dogs are **coloboma** (localized absence of optic-nerve tissue) and **hypoplasia** (underdevelopment of the nerve). The nerve may also be impaired by inflammation (**optic neuritis**), swelling (**papilledema**), or shrinkage (optic atrophy).

Optic Disk Coloboma

Coloboma ("pits") results from impaired closure of an open fissure in the developing fetus. As an inherited disorder it represents a component of Collie eye anomaly (*see* above), but also occurs sporadically as a noninherited birth defect. In both cases the size of the defect varies from dog to dog. The lesion is nonprogressive and can be found in one or both eyes. Colobomas often make the optic disk appear larger than normal. If the defect is sufficiently large, vision will be compromised or lost. There is no effective treatment and it is best to avoid breeding affected dogs.

Optic Nerve Hypoplasia

In this condition the optic disk appears extremely small because of its underdevelopment. Either eye can be affected by this congenital abnormality, and affected eyes frequently are blind. Because blindness in one eye is compensated by sight in the other, hypoplasia affecting only one eye often will go undetected. Aid in detecting the disorder in such cases is provided by the fact that the pupil of the affected eye will often be larger than the pupil of the normal companion eye. It is best to withhold affected dogs from breeding programs, since the condition is known to be inherited in certain breeds (e.g., Miniature Poodle), while in others it is associated with other inherited ocular disorders. There is no effective therapy.

Optic Atrophy

This is not a single disease, but instead can be the end result of any of several disorders that damage the nerve cells, thereby producing an overall diminution in size of the optic nerve. These disorders include decreased blood flow to the nerve, inflammation, compression, infiltration and loss of the insulating *myelin sheath* of the nerve. On examination, the affected optic disk appears pale, smaller, and more rounded, owing to the loss of **myelin** (a fatty substance forming the outer tunic or sheath around many nerve cells). There may also be an increased reflectivity or brightness surrounding the disk. There is no effective treatment.

Optic Neuritis

This term is used to describe an inflammation of the optic nerve resulting from either an infectious cause (e.g., canine distemper virus) or a noninfectious process (e.g., trauma to the head or orbit). This usually causes a sudden attack of blindness, most frequently in both eyes. The pupils are widely dilated with a sluggish and incomplete response to light. Successful treatment is dependent on an accurate and timely diagnosis. A complete body fluid analysis, including a complete blood count, serum chemistry profile, urinalysis, and cerebrospinal fluid tap and culture should be given. Noninfectious inflammation is treated with prolonged corticosteroid therapy and has a reasonably good prognosis. Infectious causes are treated with appropriate medications, but are given a guarded prognosis.

DISORDERS OF THE EYEBALL AND ORBIT

Disorders of the eyeball are reflected primarily in changes in the size or shape of the globe, while disorders of the orbit usually are manifested by changes in the position of the globe within the orbit. The condition of an oversized eyeball present at birth is referred to as **megalophthalmos,** while the condition of an eyeball that achieves such a state from inadequately controlled glaucoma is called **buphthalmos.** The former condition occurs sporadically in dogs, while the latter is commonly seen, especially in those breeds that develop primary and secondary glaucomas. Likewise, the condition of undersized eyeballs can be congenital (**microphthalmos**) or develop from uncontrolled inflammation of all the internal structures of the eye (**endophthalmitis**). Should the undersized eye still have identifiable internal structures following the attack of inflammation, the shrunken eye is said to be *atrophic* (**atrophia bulbi**), while one that has been so internally scarred as to possess no recognizable structures is said to be *phthisical* (**phthisis bulbi**). Both atrophic and phthisical eyes may result in opaque corneas, which are partially hidden by passive protrusion of the third eyelid. Occasionally, shrunken eyes must be surgically removed because of chronic irritation caused by a number of factors associated with their diminished state. Eyes acquiring buphthalmos, atrophia bulbi, or phthisis bulbi are generally blind. Eyes that are over- or undersized at birth are often sighted, albeit with diminished vision, because they are not the result of elevated intraocular pressure or the ravages of inflammation.

Vision can also be impaired when the globe is

not positioned in its normal place in the orbit. Tumors or severe muscle inflammation (**myositis**) within the orbit can push on the eyeball from behind, leading to **exophthalmos** (protrusion of the eyeball). Sometimes, patients afflicted with exophthalmos are unable to open their mouths fully and may cry out in pain at the attempt. (Normally, a part of the lower jaw called the *ramus* moves forward in the orbit during opening of the mouth, but if its forward motion is restricted by a tumor or inflammation, the mouth will incompletely open and may be extremely painful.) Veterinary attention should be sought immediately. A blood sample should be submitted to the testing laboratory and X rays of the orbit obtained. Treatment is dependent on the underlying cause, and can vary from a medical approach to surgery and/or irradiation or chemotherapy.

On occasion, severe dental disease (tooth-root abscesses) in the bony tooth socket can extend into the fatty tissue (fat pad) of the orbit on which the eyeball rests. Infection of the fat pad may cause shrinkage, resulting in a partial sinking of the eyeball behind the lower eyelid. Tooth and gum disorders play a major role in orbital disease. The teeth and gums should be examined annually by a veterinarian and all recognizable oral disease eliminated. (*See* CHAPTER 21, "CANINE DENTISTRY.")

Because the largest part of the soft-tissue orbit consists of skeletal muscle, uncontrolled myositis can lead to shrinkage and wasting of the muscle, with replacement by fibrous connective tissue. This can result in the eyeball's receding deep within the orbit, a common condition known as **enophthalmos.** Once the muscle has been replaced by connective tissue, no medical or surgical correction is possible. Systemic corticosteroid therapy is necessary to control the myositis before it reaches the fibrous stage.

Occasionally, in the absence of any head movement, an involuntary, repetitive, rhythmic, to-and-fro movement of the eyes known as **nystagmus** may be observed. The movement is either smooth and equal in both directions (**pendular nystagmus**), or alternates between a slow drift and a quick, jerklike movement (**jerk nystagmus**). Pendular nystagmus is usually seen in congenitally blind eyes. One is thus apt to observe this type of nystagmus in breeds, such as Collies, with known congenital, hereditary diseases of the retina and optic nerve. Jerk nystagmus is more dramatic in appearance and often is accompanied by a loss of balance. It is most commonly observed when ear disease affects the balancing apparatus within the inner ear. This often is a serious result of chronic, uncontrolled or untreated outer ear disease that extends into the middle ear following rupture of the eardrum, with continued extension into the inner ear. It is thus important that all ear disorders receive prompt veterinary attention. (*See* CHAPTER 20, "THE EAR AND DISORDERS.")

CHAPTER 20

The Ear And Disorders

by James F. Wilson

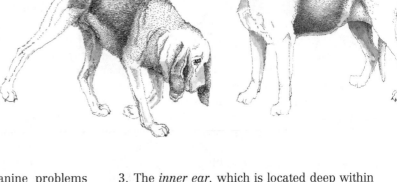

One of the most common canine problems requiring veterinary attention is infection of the outer ear, a condition known as **otitis externa.** Recognizing an ear disorder can be difficult at home, because the narrow ear canal is composed of a long, vertical tube that angles downward from its external opening and then runs horizontally toward the skull. This unique anatomy often conceals ear disease from the owner, making it hard to recognize the nature and seriousness of the problem and, in some cases, difficult for the veterinarian to provide a cure.

Structurally the ear can be divided into three main components:

1. The *outer ear,* consisting of the external earflap (the **pinna**) and the ear canal;
2. The *middle ear,* consisting of the **tympanic membrane,** or **eardrum** (a translucent membrane that vibrates in response to sound vibrations transmitted down the ear canal), and the **auditory ossicles** (tiny bones responsible for transmitting the vibrations of the eardrum to the inner ear);

3. The *inner ear,* which is located deep within the skull and which contains the sensory structures of hearing and balance (the **semicircular canals,** which regulate balance, and the **cochlea,** a curled bone that contains the **organ of Corti,** the actual organ of hearing).

A major benefit of a two-directional ear canal system like that of the dog is to decrease the eardrum's vulnerability to injury. A detriment of the system is that gravity encourages wax, dirt, debris and infectious material to collect at the base of the ear canal. This material, which cannot be shaken out of the ear canal easily, can cause swelling of the canal, allows moisture to accumulate, and diminishes exposure to air, all of which create an ideal environment for infection.

Predisposing Problems

The fact that thick hair grows in the ears of many breeds, thereby preventing proper aeration of the ear canal, contributes to the problem of ear disease in dogs. Poodles, Schnauzers and Old English Sheepdogs are particularly predis-

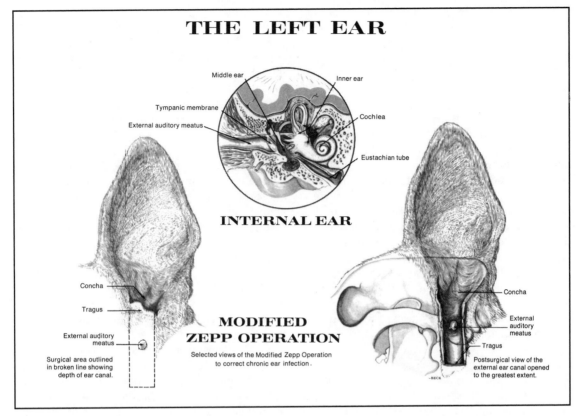

THE LEFT EAR

Middle ear

Inner ear

Tympanic membrane

External auditory meatus

Cochlea

Eustachian tube

INTERNAL EAR

Concha

Tragus

External auditory meatus

Surgical area outlined in broken line showing depth of ear canal.

MODIFIED ZEPP OPERATION

Selected views of the Modified Zepp Operation to correct chronic ear infection.

Concha

External auditory meatus

Tragus

Postsurgical view of the external ear canal opened to the greatest extent.

posed. Dogs that swim or are bathed often may have water left in the ear, another potential source of ear problems.

To complicate matters further, allergies, external parasites, abnormal levels of thyroid or sex hormones, tumors of the ear canal, ruptured eardrums, middle-ear infections and certain skin disorders such as seborrhea all can contribute to ear disease as well. Although not always recognized as such, many ear problems are nothing more than an extension of generalized skin diseases that cause changes in the lining of the ear canal. In these cases, the underlying skin diseases must be diagnosed and treated before the ear disorder can be dealt with successfully.

One of the best ways to protect pets from chronic ear disease is to establish a regular ear-care program with a local veterinarian. Such programs are aimed at preventing ear infections and halting their progress at an early stage. Thus, an effective ear-care program begins with an awareness of possible ear problems, contin-ues with routine veterinary examinations, and concludes with responsible follow-through by owners using the medications and procedures prescribed.

Recognizing the Signs of Ear Disease

The first step in developing an awareness of ear disorders is to recognize their early signs. This helps prevent minor conditions from developing into more serious problems, and serious conditions from producing permanent damage. Listed below are some of the important clinical signs that may indicate ear disease is present:

- shaking the head and ears
- scratching at one or both ears
- a foul odor from an ear
- a yellowish, brown or black discharge from an ear
- inflammation (redness of the earflap or opening to the canal)

- pain when touched around or on the ears
- tilting the head to one side
- lethargy, depression or apparent loss of hearing
- marked swelling of one or both earflaps
- stumbling or circling to one side

If one or more of the above signs is noted, the professional opinion of a veterinarian should be sought. The veterinarian will be likely to ask questions regarding the duration of the problem, whether or not any other veterinarian has provided treatment, and which clinical signs were noted first. The ability to recall which of the signs appeared first and which came second or third can be most beneficial, sometimes even eliminating the necessity for expensive diagnostic testing. If often is a good idea for the dog's owner to poll family members about the sequence of events in order to present the veterinarian with a clear historical picture of the disease course.

DIAGNOSTIC PROCEDURES

The first step in diagnosis may involve taking a sample of material from the ear canal using a cotton-tipped applicator, or peering down the canal with an **otoscope** (a medical instrument equipped with a light for inspecting the ear canal). Some affected pets' ears are so painful that the veterinarian may need to muzzle them or administer a sedative or anesthesia, just to obtain a clear view of the ear canal. In general, the more painful the ear the more likely it is that the eardrum has been ruptured.

Depending on the history of events and the past experience of the veterinarian, it may be beneficial to stain the material retrieved from the ear canal and view it under a microscope. This material should be then be examined for the presence (or absence) of bacteria, white blood cells, yeast or other fungi, unusual cells, or tiny ear mites (*see* below) or their eggs. Sometimes the otoscopic examination may reveal the presence of a foreign body in the ear canal. If so, the veterinarian may attempt to remove the object using a pair of long *alligator forceps.* If the canal is filled with debris, flushing with a bulb syringe sometimes helps to clear it

sufficiently to allow the eardrum to be visualized.

If the ear is too painful, the dog is reluctant to remain still, the eardrum is entirely occluded by debris, or there is a foreign body lodged too deeply in the ear canal to remove without risk of damage to the eardrum or wall of the canal, the veterinarian may recommend the use of general anesthesia. This is for the comfort and safety of the pet, and often helps prevent a dog from fearing its next visit to the veterinary hospital.

One of the primary reasons for using general anesthesia during ear exams is to prevent any sudden movement (as by the dog shaking its head) while a medical instrument such as an alligator forceps is within the ear canal that could cause the eardrum to be punctured. Moreover, because very few dogs understand the words "Hold still for a minute," there often is no other way to inspect the dark, narrow ear canal except with the dog under general anesthesia.

During anesthesia a narrow plastic or rubber tube (a **catheter**) coupled to a syringe may be used to flush fluid into the base of the canal. This allows wax and debris to be removed without injuring the lining of the canal. Alternatively, an instrument called a *curette* may be inserted into the canal to remove large chunks of wax, hair, plant awns, or other foreign material. In some cases, a catheter may have to be placed through a ruptured eardrum deep into the middle ear in order to flush out debris.

Other diagnostic procedures that may be performed include thyroid function tests and bacterial or fungal cultures of the ear canal debris. On occasion, the veterinarian may decide that special X-ray studies of the skull are needed to establish the presence or absence of a middle-ear infection. If a strange growth of tissue is present, a sample of it (a biopsy specimen) may be surgically removed and submitted to a pathology laboratory for evaluation. When an allergy is suspected to be the cause of a recurring ear problem, the veterinarian may recommend *intradermal skin testing* for various inhalation allergies against molds, grasses, trees, newspaper, weeds, shrubs and so on. (*See* CHAPTER 33, "THE IMMUNE SYSTEM AND DISORDERS.")

Some dogs are allergic to certain foods, and this may be expressed clinically by skin and ear disease. Trial feeding periods of several weeks' duration using a **hypoallergenic** (minimizing allergic reactions) diet may be required to determine if the ailing dog will improve. Cocker Spaniels are particularly prone to food allergies and often must be on a hypoallergenic diet for as long as 8 weeks before a food allergy can be ruled in or out as the cause of a chronic ear problem. (*See* CHAPTER 22, "THE SKIN AND DISORDERS.")

If flea allergies appear to be causing or aggravating a chronic skin disease, an intensive flea-control program may be recommended. This often entails the use of baths, dips, sprays, oral or topical medications, household sprays and "bombs," and/or yard sprays. (*See* CHAPTER 23, "EXTERNAL PARASITES.")

Contact allergies caused by medications placed in the ear canal also occur on rare occasions. If a dog improves during the 1st week or so of prescribed medication and then gets worse, with considerable reddening around the opening to the ear canal accompanied by itching, a reaction to the medication should be suspected. The most common culprits causing contact allergies include *neomycin,* an antibiotic present in a number of ear medications, and *propylene glycol,* the normally inert base component of many ear medications.

Ear (Aural) Hematomas

Blood collecting under the skin of the earflap is called an aural **hematoma.** The usual cause is trauma to the ear, resulting in breakage of blood vessels. Dogs suffering from this problem need to have the fluid drained by a veterinarian, using either a needle, surgical opening of the skin, or placement of a drain through the skin. Because hematomas tend to recur after drainage, it usually is necessary for the veterinarian to **suture** (stitch) a temporary support to the ear, insert stitches through the skin and cartilage, or bandage the ear after removing the fluid. Sometimes, an affected dog also has an infection in the ear canal, in addition to the hematoma. In most hematoma cases, however, the rest of the ear is normal.

Mites and Ticks

Mites are minute organisms that, like ticks and spiders, are classified as arachnids (i.e., they are not insects). Several important mites that infest dogs include *Demodex canis, Sarcoptes scabei* var. *canis,* and *Cheyletiella yasguri* (these infestations are discussed in detail in chapter 23, "External Parasites"). The ear canals of dogs and cats are home to another mite known as *Otodectes cynotis.* When these pests are present, a dry, reddish-brown wax often appears at the opening of the ear canal. The cat is the favorite host for most ear mites. Large numbers can create such extensive excrement and wax production that the entire ear canal becomes obstructed with debris. In most canine cases, only small numbers of mites (three to four) are present in affected ear canals. However, even these small numbers can produce a major reaction within the ear and set the stage for secondary infections by yeasts or bacteria.

The spinous ear tick, *Otobius megnini,* is an ugly six-legged tick that attaches itself to the wall of the ear canal and sucks blood from the host. It is found most frequently in the southwestern regions of the United States. It causes considerable itching within the ear canal, and only causes debris to accumulate or secondary infections to occur when owners ignore their dogs' signs of ear discomfort. In most cases, this parasite can be removed by the veterinarian using alligator forceps passed through an otoscope.

COMMON FORMS OF TREATMENT

Once the apparent cause of an ear disorder has been diagnosed, the appropriate treatment can be very simple or very complicated. The simple cases respond well to removal of the underlying cause and the instillation of antibiotic and anti-inflammatory ointments or liquids into the ear canal. More complicated cases require general anesthesia and irrigation of the ear canal with wax solvents, medical-grade detergents, and water or salt solutions via a catheter prior to dispensing any medications.

Some dogs must be muzzled at the veterinary hospital or at home so that veterinarians or owners are not bitten while attempting to place medication into the ear canals. Generally, unless a team effort is established between the veterinarian and the owner, treatment attempts often will result in failure. This can lead to permanent damage of the patient's fragile ear canal, can be expensive, and may cause an owner to move from one veterinary hospital to another because the pet's problem never clears up completely.

Dogs with concurrent **hypothyroidism** (decreased thyroid function, with diminished secretion of thyroid hormone; a condition often associated with skin disorders) may require supplementation with synthetic thyroid hormone. Affected male dogs with concurrent testicular tumors producing an overabundance of the hormone estrogen should be neutered. Occasionally, bitches also can produce excessive amounts of estrogen and may need to be spayed. Pets with underlying food allergies may require restricted diets to control chronic ear disease, while those with inhalation allergies may respond to **hyposensitization** therapy (a regimen of injections intended to reduce an allergic individual's sensitivity).

In most cases, veterinarians will dispense a combination antibiotic/anti-inflammatory ointment or solution to kill or control the growth of bacteria and yeast within the ear canals. To prevent dogs from continuing to scratch their inflamed ears, an injection of an anti-inflammatory medication may be administered at the veterinary hospital, followed by tablets given orally at home. If the eardrum is ruptured or there is a concurrent skin infection, injectable and/or oral antibiotics also may need to be administered at home for 2 to 8 weeks.

In some cases, all efforts to cure an ear disorder fail. The only recourse under such circumstances is surgical removal of the vertical portion of the ear canal (a procedure known as a **Zepp-LaCroix resection**), in order to provide better aeration. Some dogs have extensive and permanent damage to the horizontal canal and/or a ruptured eardrum with a middle-ear infection. When this serious and chronic problem exists, it may be necessary to remove the entire ear canal surgically and open and drain the middle ear, procedures known respectively as total ablation of the ear and a **bulla osteotomy.**

HOME CARE

When ear problems develop, owners of affected dogs need to know how to provide short-term relief for a pet's pain until the pet can be examined by a veterinarian. Knowing how to perform certain simple, beneficial procedures at home can help greatly.

Softening

When a foreign body such as a plant awn (known as a **foxtail** in many Western states and cheet grass in others) or wild oat is suspected to be the cause of an ear disorder, instilling 10 to 20 drops of mineral oil or a viscous ear medication into the ear canal may provide substantial relief. A gentle and thorough massage of the ear usually is required to work the thick, oily material down into the horizontal portion of the ear canal. The goal of this treatment is to soften the foreign body and prevent it from penetrating the eardrum until the pet can be examined at a veterinary hospital. Thus, this is only a temporary measure designed to alleviate distress, and is not intended to cure the ear problem. A thorough ear examination performed by a veterinarian is required to determine the exact cause of the discomfort, and to remove any foreign body that might be occluding the ear canal and that potentially could rupture the delicate eardrum.

Swabbing

When excessive wax, pus or debris is visible at the opening of the ear canal, swabbing this area with a soft facial tissue or cotton ball can be beneficial. Cotton-tipped applicators such as Q-tips should *never* be placed into the ear canal, because their improper or inappropriate use may cause an impaction of wax or foreign material in the horizontal part of the canal, or push the material up against or even through the eardrum.

Flushing

Rapid-acting wax-solvent preparations often are used prior to irrigating the ear canal at the veterinary hospital and may be dispensed for home use as well. When recurrences of copious wax production is a problem, veterinarians may show owners how to medicate a pet's ear canals with wax solvents and detergents and to flush the canals with warm water and a soft rubber bulb syringe. This may be especially important for dogs with chronic **seborrhea** (excessive oily skin). (*See* CHAPTER 22, "THE SKIN AND DISORDERS.")

Many dogs will not tolerate such home treatment, but those that do often benefit greatly from it. One should also be aware that dogs generally shake their heads after water has been flushed into the ear canal, so good clothing should not be worn while home-medicating an ear disorder!

Drying Agents
Drying and/or acidifying agents may be dispensed by the veterinarian for use at home after a dog's ears have been flushed, or after dogs who love to swim have had a cool dip in the pool, river or ocean. In other cases, such medications may be used once or twice weekly to lower the humidity of the ear canal. Lower humidity in the ear canal helps to minimize secondary yeast and bacterial infections. Because of this, some veterinarians routinely dispense drying agents even for floppy-eared dogs, especially in high-humidity regions of the country or during humid seasons of the year. Because hydrogen peroxide leaves the ear canal moist after its application, it should never be used in the ear.

Clipping and Plucking
It is important to clip or pluck the hair around the opening of the ear canal in order to allow air to enter. This is true for all breeds of dogs that have hair lining the canal and do not shed (e.g., Poodles, Schnauzers, Lhasa Apsos, Bouviers and Old English Sheepdogs being representative examples).

The procedure should be performed every 1 to 3 months. In many cases this can be done when the dog is professionally groomed. Otherwise, it can be done at home using one's fingers or an instrument (Kelly forceps) purchased from a pet store or veterinarian. With some fractious dogs, however, the procedure may only be possible at a veterinary hospital.

Cocker Spaniels, Springer Spaniels, and some other droopy-eared breeds will benefit from having the mats of hair that accumulate on their ears clipped every 6 to 8 months. This reduces the amount of weight pulling down on the earflap, thus allowing for better aeration of the ear canal.

These same breeds may develop fewer ear problems if their earflaps are pulled back over their heads or necks and held in place with a piece of tape for a few hours once or twice weekly. In some cases using a blow-dryer to instill modest amounts of warm, dry air into the ear canal may be beneficial. Both of these procedures provide better aeration of the narrow ear canal, lowering the humidity and reducing the likelihood that a chronic ear infection will develop.

FOLLOW-UP
Many ear problems are relatively easy to resolve once a veterinarian has had an opportunity to examine the ear canal, perform appropriate laboratory diagnostic tests, and prescribe treatment. Nevertheless, follow-up appointments are essential because it is impossible to determine if the ear has healed completely without carefully viewing the entire canal with an otoscope. Moreover, because changes to the skin lining the ear canal often develop during months of neglect or incomplete or inappropriate treatment, it often requires months for that skin to recover once the canal has been properly cleaned and effective medications administered. For these reasons owners should not be surprised if the veterinarian is adamant about scheduling the patient for one or more follow-up examinations, in order to be certain that the affected ears are healing properly. In 10–25% of the cases, pets may need to be anesthetized several times so that the entire ear canal can be irrigated and the debris removed, before the eardrum and lining of the canal finally return to normal.

CHAPTER 21

Canine Dentistry

by Leigh West-Hyde

The concept of dental awareness in our pet companions strikes some people as humorous and perhaps even slightly odd. Brush my dog's teeth? Surely, you've got to be kidding! But stop and think: dogs no longer use their teeth in the same fashion as their wild counterparts, nor do they consume similar fare. Moreover, generations of linebreeding have created tremendous variety in the shape and size of the canine head, as the different breed characteristics have been crafted and refined. Regardless of body size, however, each individual dog still has 42 permanent teeth. Because our companion dogs live so closely with us and are living longer owing to improved health care, owners now recognize the benefits of prevention and control of dental disease in their pets.

Veterinary dentistry has experienced an extraordinary expansion in interest by both the pet-owning public and the veterinary profession. The special dental needs of pets are being met by the education of veterinary professionals in the field of dentistry by way of vet school curriculum and postgraduate resident training, by continuing education courses for graduate veterinarians and veterinary technicians, and by the many recent textbooks and journals devoted exclusively to veterinary dental care. The pet-owning public now expects the general practitioner to maintain a standard of excellence in dental care that includes a working knowledge of oral anatomy, oral examination techniques, dental recordkeeping, radiology (X-ray studies), dental **prophylaxis** (disease prevention via thorough cleaning), and diagnosis and treatment of the most common dental problems. Given that veterinary dentistry is today a board-certifiable specialty, the pet owner may justifiably seek specialty dental care for his or her pet companion.

As a client seeking veterinary dental care for your pet, some salient points of inquiry to be made upon seeing the veterinarian include:

Do you take dental X rays?
Do you maintain dental charts?
Will you review the dental X rays with me?
Will you contact me before performing tooth extractions?
Do you scale and polish teeth both above and below the gum line?
What home-care instruction will you give me?
What guidelines do you have for recheck and repeat procedures?

Who will actually perform the dental procedure, and what training does he or she have?

General veterinary practitioners should be aware of any board-certified veterinary dentists in their area for potential referral of dental problems. A pet owner should never hesitate to ask for a second opinion or for referral to a certified specialist.

Tooth Anatomy

GENERAL TOOTH ANATOMY

The basic anatomy of canine teeth is quite similar to that of human teeth. Each individual tooth is composed of a **crown** (the part above the gum line) and a **root** (the part below the gum line). The tooth crown is covered with a hard, calcium-rich substance called **enamel** that functions to resist wear. Underneath the enamel lies the bulk of the tooth, a calcium-based crystalline structure called **dentin.** The root is the portion of the tooth normally embedded in the bone of the jaw and is covered by **cementum,** a specialized type of connective tissue. Different teeth vary in the number of roots present and in the amount of root curvature. Front teeth, for example, have single roots, while **cheek teeth** (the premolars and molars) have two or three roots. The tooth root is physically attached to the bone of the jaw by thousands of tiny fibers referred to collectively as the **periodontal ligament.**

Each tooth may be viewed as having an "inner life" and an "outer life." The "inner life," or endodontic system, refers to the chamber (**pulp chamber,** or **root canal**) within each tooth that contains nerves, blood vessels, lymphatic channels, and cells such as **odontoblasts.** Odontoblasts line the inner tooth chamber and manufacture dentin. Throughout life the interior wall of every tooth increases in thickness, gradually narrowing the root-canal chamber. Blood vessels and nerves make up the **pulp** that fills the root-canal system. Exposure of the pulp, as may occur when the crown of the tooth is fractured, results in bleeding, pain, infection, and eventually partial or total death of the pulp. Teeth with dead pulp are more brittle and prone to fracture than are normal, healthy teeth with living pulp.

The "outer life," or periodontium, of the tooth refers to those structures holding the tooth in the jaw; that is, the gum attachment to the crown and the periodontal ligament attaching the tooth root to the bony socket. The gum-tooth junction is the point where disease of the tooth-holding structures (**periodontal disease**) begins. Periodontal disease attacks the periodontal ligament as well as the bone around each tooth (**alveolar bone**), resulting in abnormal tooth-root exposure, tooth instability and mobility, and eventually tooth loss.

Dogs as meat-eating predators have certain distinct differences in dentition (characteristics of the teeth) when compared to their human companions. Most dogs, for example, have *V*-shaped upper and lower jaws that allow them to open the mouth very wide for grasping and capturing prey. The shape of the different teeth also varies widely, from the nipping front teeth (**incisors**), to the puncturing/grasping fang teeth (**canines,** or cuspids), to the gripping **premolars,** to the shearing/grinding back teeth (premolars and **molars**). **Carnassial teeth** are anatomically defined as the upper fourth premolar tooth and the lower first molar tooth, which interact in a special shearing overlap when the mouth is closed. The forces that dogs can generate when grasping objects with their jaws far exceed human capabilities. Because of this, canine carnassial teeth often experience crown fractures, especially if pets are given inappropriate, nonresilient chew toys.

An additional significant difference in dentition between dogs and human beings is the time sequence of tooth eruption ("teething"). In dogs, eruption of **deciduous teeth** ("baby teeth" or "milk teeth") and *permanent teeth* takes place during the first year of puppyhood. In people, however, this sequence of events is spread out over the first two decades of life.

TOOTH ERUPTION AND REPLACEMENT

Eruption and replacement of deciduous teeth by permanent dentition occurs in the first year and follows the general guidelines given in table 2. A puppy is born without any visible teeth but will erupt its 28 deciduous teeth between approximately 3 and 6 weeks of age. Sequential eruption of the permanent teeth with loss of deciduous teeth occurs between 2 and 7 months of age,

THE SKULL AND TEETH

THE SKULL

1. External auditory meatus
2. External occipital protuberance
3. Mandible (body)
4. Infraorbital foramen
5. Vertical ramus of mandible
6. Ramus
7. Sagittal crest
8. Supraorbital process
9. Tympanic bulla
10. Zygomatic arch

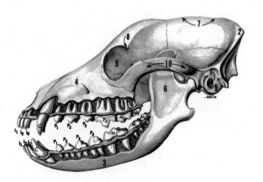

THE TEETH

DECIDUOUS:

$2 (1\tfrac{3}{3}\ C\tfrac{1}{1}\ P\tfrac{3}{3}) = 28$

PERMANENT:

$2 (1\tfrac{3}{3}\ C\tfrac{1}{1}\ P\tfrac{4}{4}\ M\tfrac{2}{3}) = 42$

Normal range for eruption of permanent teeth:

TEETH	MONTHS
Incisor	2 to 5
Canine	5 to 6
Premolar	4 to 6
Molar	5 to 7

starting with the incisor teeth and followed by the cheek teeth and canines. In most breeds, all deciduous teeth should be lost or be very loose by around 6 to 7 months of age, to allow for normal eruption of the permanent teeth. Eruption of the full crown height of a permanent tooth may not be complete until almost a year of age, however. As a general rule, permanent tooth buds erupt toward the inside of the deciduous predecessor. An exception to this rule is the upper canine tooth, which erupts in front of its predecessor.

Variables that may alter tooth eruption time in dogs include:

- general health and nutritional status
- sex (females erupt their teeth earlier than males do)
- breed (large breeds erupt their teeth earlier than small breeds do)
- season of birth (puppies born in summer erupt their teeth earlier)

Permanent tooth eruption (maximal crown-height exposure) is usually complete between 10 and 12 months of age. The mature root length and diameter will be as large or larger than the visible crown of each tooth type. The tooth-wall thickness

---

**Table 1
Canine Dental Formulas**

Deciduous Teeth:

$2 \times (I\ 3/3\ \ C\ 1/1\ \ P\ 3/3) = 28$

Permanent Teeth:

$2 \times (I\ 3/3\ \ C\ 1/1\ \ P\ 4/4\ \ M\ 2/3) = 42$

where
I = incisors
C = canines
P = premolars
M = molars
#/# = upper/ lower

---

increases throughout the life of the animal, but especially during the first 3 years of life, as the result of the deposition of dentin by odontoblasts.

How long should one wait to take action if a puppy has retained one or more deciduous teeth? A general rule is that no two teeth should occupy the same site. Prolonged retention of deciduous teeth can cause permanent teeth to erupt incorrectly, resulting in tooth displacement, overcrowding and an abnormal bite. If deciduous

THE MUSCLES

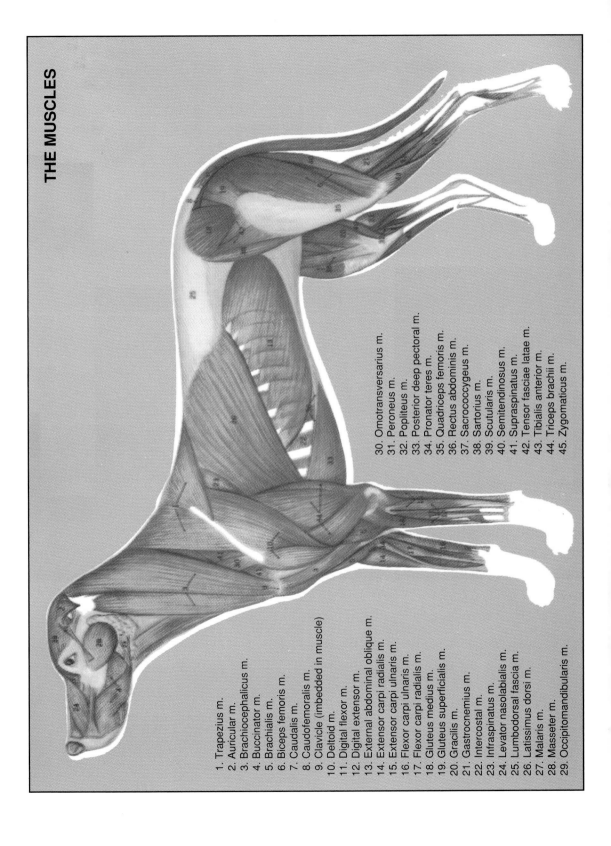

1. Trapezius m.
2. Auricular m.
3. Brachiocephalicus m.
4. Buccinator m.
5. Brachialis m.
6. Biceps femoris m.
7. Caudalis m.
8. Caudofemoralis m.
9. Clavicle (imbedded in muscle)
10. Deltoid m.
11. Digital flexor m.
12. Digital extensor m.
13. External abdominal oblique m.
14. Extensor carpi radialis m.
15. Extensor carpi ulnaris m.
16. Flexor carpi ulnaris m.
17. Flexor carpi radialis m.
18. Gluteus medius m.
19. Gluteus superficialis m.
20. Gracilis m.
21. Gastrocnemius m.
22. Intercostal m.
23. Infraspinatus m.
24. Levator nasolabialis m.
25. Lumbodorsal fascia m.
26. Latissimus dorsi m.
27. Malaris m.
28. Masseter m.
29. Occipitomandibularis m.
30. Omotransversarius m.
31. Peroneus m.
32. Popliteus m.
33. Posterior deep pectoral m.
34. Pronator teres m.
35. Quadriceps femoris m.
36. Rectus abdominis m.
37. Sacrococcygeus m.
38. Sartorius m.
39. Scutularis m.
40. Semitendinosus m.
41. Supraspinatus m.
42. Tensor fasciae latae m.
43. Tibialis anterior m.
44. Triceps brachii m.
45. Zygomaticus m.

SKELETON, LUNGS, DIAPHRAGM

46. Carpals
47. Costal cartilages
48. Diaphragm
49. Femur
50. Fibula
51. Humerus
52. Ilium
53. Ischium
54. Lung
55. Metacarpals
56. Metatarsals
57. Patella
58. Phalanges of forepaw
59. Phalanges of hindpaw
60. Pubis
61. Radius
62. Ribs (13 pairs)
63. Scapula
64. Tarsals
65. Tibia
66. Ulna
104. Atlas
105. Axis
106. Carpals
107. Caudal vertebrae
108. Cervical vertebrae
110. External auditory meatus
111. Fabellae
112. Femur
113. Fibula
114. Humerus
118. Lumbar vertebrae
120. Mandible

121. Maxilla
122. Metacarpals
123. Metatarsals
124. Obturator foramen
125. Orbit
126. Patella
127. Phalanges of forepaw
128. Phalanges of hindpaw
132. Radius
133. Sacral vertebrae
135. Sternum
136. Tarsals
137. Thoracic vertebrae
138. Tibia
139. Trachea
140. Ulna
141. Zygomatic arch

THORACIC AND ABDOMINAL ORGANS (VISCERA)

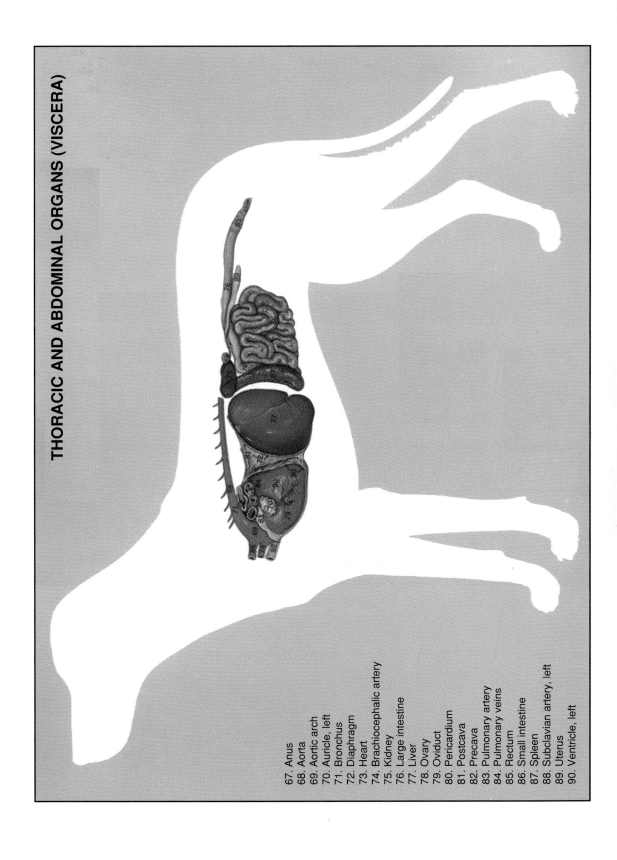

67. Anus
68. Aorta
69. Aortic arch
70. Auricle, left
71. Bronchus
72. Diaphragm
73. Heart
74. Brachiocephalic artery
75. Kidney
76. Large intestine
77. Liver
78. Ovary
79. Oviduct
80. Pericardium
81. Postcava
82. Precava
83. Pulmonary artery
84. Pulmonary veins
85. Rectum
86. Small intestine
87. Spleen
88. Subclavian artery, left
89. Uterus
90. Ventricle, left

THORACIC AND ABDOMINAL ORGANS (VISCERA)

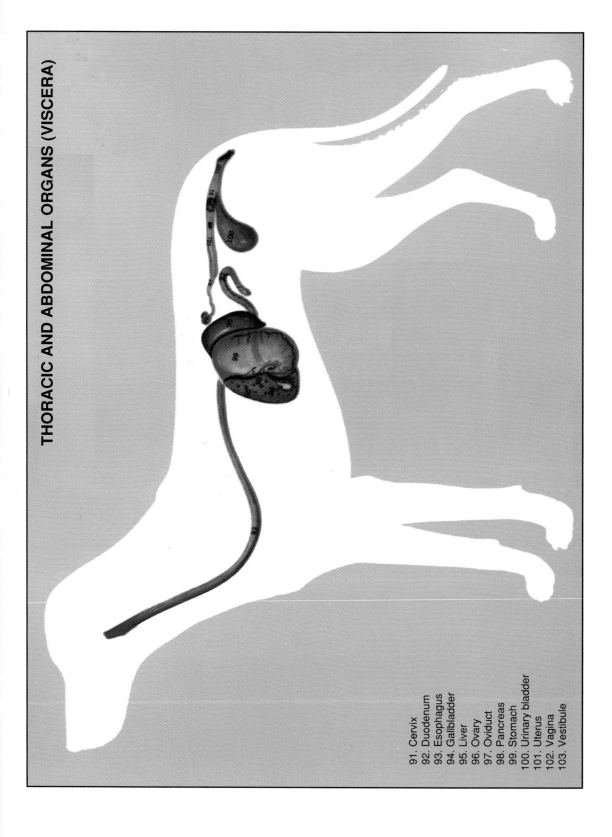

91. Cervix
92. Duodenum
93. Esophagus
94. Gallbladder
95. Liver
96. Ovary
97. Oviduct
98. Pancreas
99. Stomach
100. Urinary bladder
101. Uterus
102. Vagina
103. Vestibule

Table 2
Normal Range For the Eruption of Canine Teeth

	Deciduous	Permanent
Incisors	4–6 weeks	2–5 months
Canines	3–5 weeks	5–7 months
Premolars	5–6 weeks	4–6 months
Molars	None	5–7 months

Note: Eruption time is closely correlated to life span and breed size; i.e., the larger the breed, the shorter the life span, and the earlier tooth eruption occurs.

teeth are still present and not loose by 6 to 7 months of age, their surgical removal is warranted. In general, the toy and miniature breeds are more commonly affected with this problem.

Should one worry about missing teeth in a dog intended to be shown and/or bred? Breed clubs and the American Kennel Club have established what are considered acceptable parameters for dental defects in the individual breeds. (International show events may vary from American breed standards.) These organizations should be consulted directly regarding individual breed stipulations. In general, however, missing teeth are considered a fault that may result in the loss of points or disqualification from an event. Breeding dogs with missing teeth should be discouraged if the offspring are intended for show use. Breeders may request dental X rays in young puppies to document the presence of all permanent tooth buds. Unerupted permanent tooth buds may be detected **radiographically** (by X ray examination) at approximately 9 to 12 weeks of age.

Oral Examination and Occlusion (Bite) Evaluation

ORAL EXAMINATION
Superficial examination of the oral cavity may be performed in most dogs given a few simple guidelines. The outer surface of the teeth and the tooth **occlusion** (bite) pattern are best examined with the mouth closed. Place the animal in a sitting position with its back in a corner, facing you and restrained by an assistant, or with you sitting in a chair and the animal placed between your legs. With the jaws closed, use one hand to cradle the animal's muzzle gently while you use the other hand to lift the lips. Starting at the front of the mouth, you can methodically move through an occlusion checklist (*see* below) by lifting the lips overlying the region of interest.

Open-mouth examination is the most objectionable aspect of oral manipulation for dogs. Dogs object especially to the lower jaw's being grasped, so this maneuver should be reserved for last. For an oral examination in small dogs, the entire head may be grasped with one hand from above, gently tilting the head backward. The opposite hand may then be used to push the lower jaw down gently. For most larger dogs, use one hand to grasp the muzzle behind the nose, then insert the thumb behind an upper canine tooth and use gentle thumb pressure on the hard palate to induce opening of the mouth. Thumb pressure will cause the lower jaw to drop open slightly, allowing oral examination with a flashlight.

OCCLUSION (BITE) EVALUATION
Occlusion evaluation refers to an examination of how the teeth intermesh when the jaws are closed. Abnormal occlusion (**malocclusion**) may indicate an inheritable defect of skull or jaw growth. Breed standards establish what is an "acceptable" occlusion pattern for an individual breed. Some breeds, such as the **brachycephalic** (flat-faced) breeds, have a "normal" malocclusion characterized by an elongated lower jaw, a condition termed **prognathism.**

A common mistake is to look only at how the incisor teeth interact. However, the interaction of all tooth types should be evaluated to determine if there is a problem with skull symmetry or jaw length. The heritability of skull or jaw size, shape and length is supported by the existence of a wide variety of different breeds, the enormous variations among them, and the reproducibility of breed appearance by purposeful breeding.

Occlusion Checklist
Midline match. Viewing the incisor teeth from the front with the jaws closed and lifting the lips,

the upper midpoint between the central incisors should match the lower incisor midpoint. A dog has six upper and six lower incisors, so the midpoint should have three incisors on either side. This checkpoint helps to establish that both sides of the skull/jaw have grown symmetrically.

Incisor overlap (scissor bite). The upper incisors should overlap the lower incisors. This "scissor bite" configuration of the incisors is the most widely recognized occlusion for most breeds.

Canine (cuspid) interlock. The lower canine teeth should fit in the space between the upper lateral (outer) incisor and upper canine tooth. There should not be any contact of tooth surfaces in this interlock.

Premolar interdigitation. The upper premolar teeth **cusps** (points) should aim directly at the spaces between the lower premolar teeth.

Carnassial overlap. The upper fourth premolar should overlap the lower first molar tooth.

The Most Common Malocclusions
When evaluating the bite in all animals, the placement relationships of the incisors, canines, premolars and molars must be considered.

Prognathism. Prognathism refers to a condition wherein the lower jaw is longer than the upper jaw. All brachycephalic breeds "normally" have a prognathic occlusion pattern.

Level bite. This is a mild type of prognathism wherein the incisors meet cusp-tip to cusp-tip, rather than having the uppers overlap the lowers (scissor bite). Due to the abnormal incisor cusp-tip contact, all incisors will experience abnormal crown wear. Individual incisors will also experience a greater frequency of fracture than incisors with a scissor occlusion.

Brachygnathism. This is a condition wherein the lower jaw is shorter than the upper jaw; that is, this malocclusion places the lower incisor teeth farther behind the upper incisor teeth. As a consequence, the lower incisor teeth may trau-matize the soft tissue of the palate. The lower canine teeth are also shifted back, causing crown wearing against the opposing upper canine teeth. More severe forms of brachygnathism may actually place the lower canine teeth behind the upper canine teeth.

Base-narrow. This refers to the lower jaw's being too narrow and/or the lower canine teeth's lacking the proper lean to the outside in order to fit into the space between the appropriate upper teeth. The result of this malocclusion is that the lower canine teeth strike the soft tissue of the palate. Severe cases may actually create a hole through the palate into the nasal cavity, a condition known as an oronasal fistula.

Cross-bite. This implies that the normal tooth-crown overlap is reversed. *Anterior cross-bite* means that one or more of the lower incisor teeth occlude in front of the upper incisor teeth. *Posterior cross-bite* is a rare phenomenon in which the carnassial tooth's overlap is reversed, so that the lower first molar lies outside the upper fourth premolar when the jaws are closed.

Wry bite. This refers to an asymmetric growth of the skull or jaw, resulting in a midline malalignment. It is a form of **unilateral** (one-sided) brachygnathism or prognathism.

Open bite. Open bite is a severe form of wry bite wherein the upper and lower incisors are unable to come together when the jaws are closed.

DENTAL RADIOLOGY
Dental *radiographs* (X rays) should be considered an essential element of a definitive oral examination. Dental radiographs represent a powerful tool for visualizing what cannot be seen on a physical examination of the oral cavity. Pre- and postprocedure dental radiographs serve as pictorial documents that can be readily comprehended by the pet owner. Follow-up dental radiographs are a critical aid for evaluating treatment success or failure, and for dictating the necessity and frequency of further inter-

vention. Coupling the oral examination with dental radiographs provides the basis for staging and treatment planning of dental disease.

Disorders of the Teeth

CARIOUS LESIONS (CAVITIES)

Carious lesions, known more commonly as *cavities* or *dental caries,* are the result of acid demineralization of the tooth surface by oral bacteria, particularly certain streptococci. The acid is produced by bacterial fermentation of ingested sugars. Tooth decay may progress through enamel and dentin with possible infection of the pulp. Fortunately, true carious lesions are an uncommon problem in dogs for several reasons, including the constitution of the diet (low in carbohydrates) and a relatively high salivary pH. When decay does occur, it most often involves the upper or lower molars. A number of restoratives are available for filling cavities in dogs' teeth, including **amalgam** (an alloy of mercury, copper, silver, zinc, tin and other metals), which is commonly used in human dentistry.

CROWDING

Crowding is the result of inadequate space for the teeth in either the upper or lower jaw, resulting in tooth contact or overlap. Crowding occurs especially in dogs that are bred for miniaturization or **brachycephalic** (flat-faced) head characteristics. Retained deciduous teeth or abnormally placed permanent tooth buds can also result in crowding. A secondary effect of crowding is increased retention of plaque (*see* below), with resulting **gingivitis** (inflammation of the gums) and a predisposition to periodontal disease (*see* below).

CALCULUS

Dental **calculus,** or *tartar,* consists of mineralized *concretions* (masses built up over time) of salivary calcium and phosphate salts and tooth surface **plaque.** Plaque is composed of a mixture of oral bacteria, bacterial sugars, salivary proteins, and food and cellular debris. The host response to the presence of plaque is gum inflammation, or gingivitis, usually visible as a reddening of the tissue along the gum line.

Calculus does not directly cause gingivitis; rather, the calculus serves as a spot for plaque to collect and for bacteria to multiply.

The presence of calculus will hamper plaque removal. Plaque cannot be removed by rinsing, but requires mechanical abrasion with a toothbrush or paste. Removal of calculus requires the use of dental instruments. Buildup of dental calculus can be retarded by feeding dogs hard-food diets and by encouraging prolonged chewing of resilient objects such as rawhide. Toothbrushing at home is the safest, most effective method of removing plaque and discouraging calculus formation. Recommendations for frequency of brushing are based on the health of the gums at the time. Brushing three times a week is recommended for dogs having otherwise healthy gums, while brushing seven times a week is recommended for those with alveolar bone loss caused by periodontal disease (*see* below).

DISCOLORED TEETH

Both dogs and cats normally have ultrawhite teeth. Discoloration of the teeth can be caused by either extrinsic (tooth-surface stain) or intrinsic (tooth structure itself) causes. Extrinsic stains, such as those caused by pigment-producing plaque bacteria, are removable with thorough cleaning and polishing. Intrinsic stains may arise from abnormal development pre- or posteruption, acquired disease, or secondary to a dental procedure. Developmental discoloration of teeth may be acquired during tooth eruption as a defect of growth or from incorporation of material into the growing tooth structure. **Enamel hypoplasia** (reduced enamel formation) results in a porous enamel surface and, depending on the severity of maldevelopment, may expose the underlying dentin (which is softer and more porous than enamel). Affected teeth are more receptive to plaque retention and to the uptake of dyes present in some chew toys. Intrinsic tooth stains may also be caused by excessive fluoride ingestion (causing white spotting, brown spots, or enamel pitting), iron ingestion (causing an orange discoloration), or administration of tetracycline antibiotics (causing yellow, brown, gray or blue discolorations) during tooth formation.

Acquired intrinsic stains can result from impact trauma, crown wear, deep decay, or materials used as dental restoratives. Metallic restoratives such as amalgam can cause virtually irreversible discoloration of teeth.

Vital and nonvital bleaching techniques refer to the external or internal application of bleaching materials to alter tooth color. Such procedures are used cosmetically in human beings and occasionally in animals. The success of the treatment relies on proper diagnosis in order to choose the appropriate technique for maximizing the whitening effect.

Enamel Defects

Defects of the enamel may be developmental or acquired and may involve one (focal) or many (generalized) teeth. Enamel hypoplasia (*see* above) can result from damage to the ameloblasts (enamel-forming cells) of the developing, unerupted tooth bud caused by a high fever or by canine distemper virus infection occurring during tooth-bud formation (less than 5 months of age). Tooth discoloration and increased crown wear may be seen despite normal chewing patterns. Severely hypoplastic enamel may even chip off the tooth when explored with dental instruments. Restorative veneering of the teeth may be necessary to decrease plaque retention on the defective enamel and prevent further loss of crown structure. Acquired loss of normal enamel may result from wearing or chipping as a result of adverse or peculiar chewing habits of a dog.

Epulis

Epulis (plural: **epulides**) is the most common benign oral tumor of dogs and arises from the periodontal ligament, the collection of tiny fibers that attach the tooth root to the bone of the jaw. Epulides usually appear as firm enlargements of the gum. As they grow they can displace the tooth of origin and may interfere with mouth closure. Because they are benign, epulides do not spread to other regions of the body.

Biopsy and radiographs will help differentiate epulides from oral neoplasms (tumors), which tend to be aggressive and difficult to cure and require early detection. Early, wide surgical **excision** (cutting out) of the epulis is usually curative. Other effective forms of therapy include **cryosurgery** (a procedure by which local application of intense cold is used to destroy tumor tissue) and **radiotherapy** (radiation therapy).

Fractured Teeth

Teeth may be fractured at either the crown or root. Radiographic evaluation is always warranted when deciding between tooth extraction and tooth salvage. A freshly fractured tooth with exposure of the pulp represents a dental emergency. The preferable option is, of course, to maintain the integrity of the pulp cavity and hence a live tooth. Partial **pulpectomy** (removal of damaged pulp) and protection of the remainder by means of tooth capping can achieve this, provided the pulp remains viable.

The maximal length of time that pulp can be exposed to the oral environment and still be successfully salvaged by capping is controversial. General guidelines for maximal time of pulpal exposure range from 24 to 48 hours for dogs older than 18 months, and longer periods (up to 2 weeks) in dogs under 18 months of age.

Gingival Hyperplasia

Generalized **gingival hyperplasia** (gum enlargement caused by an increase in the number of cells) is a common clinical observation in older dogs. Collies, Boxers and other large-breed dogs are more commonly affected with this condition. Treatment is unnecessary unless there is plaque or calculus retention below the gum line or the overgrown gum tissue is being traumatized by the opposing teeth when the jaws close. Treatment consists of surgical removal of the excess gum tissue. Owners should be aware that this problem may recur.

Gum enlargement also occurs in puppies during the eruption of deciduous (primary) and permanent (secondary) teeth. Gingivitis (gum inflammation) may be superimposed on this normal tissue enlargement due to the mix of teeth in various stages of eruption accompanied by poor self-cleaning mechanisms. The presence of loose or retained deciduous teeth, or mispositioned teeth causing overcrowding, greatly contributes to overlying gingivitis due to increased plaque retention.

Benign or malignant tumors can mimic gingival hyperplasia. The importance of early biopsy and interpretation of any localized gum enlargement should be stressed, given the inability to distinguish clinically between benign and malignant oral growths.

GUM RECESSION

Gum recession refers to the gradual exposure of the tooth-root surface by a loss of the gingiva and the **alveolar crestal bone** (the "collar" of bone encircling the neck of the tooth). The most common causes of gum recession include chronic inflammation (gingivitis, periodontal disease) and aging. Exposed root surfaces promote plaque retention and are more difficult for an owner to keep clean. Exposed root surfaces may result in tooth hypersensitivity due to exposure of dentin and resultant pulpal irritation. Loss of gum tissue between the teeth removes the natural food deflection function of the gingiva and creates an excellent environment for the buildup of plaque, bacteria and food debris. Treatment measures will depend on identification of the underlying cause.

MOBILITY

Increased tooth laxity in the socket is most commonly associated with moderate-to-severe loss of tooth attachment (as seen in periodontal disease), certain types of tooth fractures, erupting permanent teeth that have not completed root maturation and periodontal attachment, malocclusion or chewing trauma, tumors, or metabolic diseases that remove calcium from the bone, such as **hyperparathyroidism** (hyperactivity of one or more parathyroid glands). The underlying cause of the tooth mobility will dictate the treatment measures that need to be taken.

PERIODONTAL DISEASE

Periodontal disease should interest all of us *because it is the most common cause of tooth loss in adult human beings, dogs and cats.* The focus of this disease process at the tooth-crown junction is the transformation of a normal environment, the **gingival sulcus** (the area formed by the junction of the tooth and the gums), into the diseased environment of the **periodontal pocket.** The sulcus is the space bounded by the crown enamel surface, the free gingival margin (the visible edge of the gums opposing the tooth surface), and the microscopic gum attachment to the **cementoenamel junction** (the anatomical junction of the crown and the root).

Periodontal disease represents a continuum, initially involving only gingival soft-tissue inflammation (**gingivitis**) with possible progression to loss of the microscopic gum-tooth attachment and alveolar bone destruction (**periodontitis**). Gingivitis is a completely reversible process involving inflammation of the gum tissue bordering the teeth. Gingival inflammation can range from a slight reddening (caused by increased blood flow) to severe swelling and frank bleeding. Periodontitis is a partially reversible (but controllable) progression to loss of gum-to-tooth attachment and tooth-socket bone support. With microscopic gum-attachment loss, the normal gingival sulcus deepens and is transformed into the abnormal periodontal pocket, conducive to the creation of an oxygen-free microenvironment in which bacteria can proliferate and cause even further tissue destruction.

Periodontal disease progression is episodic or cyclic, with periods of exacerbation and remission. It is important to point out that the progression from gingivitis to periodontitis *is not inevitable;* given an early diagnosis, it can be halted with therapeutic intervention. The primary factor influencing disease progression is the bacterial population of the gingiva. The amount and type of bacteria (plaque population) above and below the gum line and the individual host animal's response to infection are both of great importance in this regard. Plaque is composed primarily of proliferating microorganisms plus food and cellular debris, all embedded in a sticky matrix of salivary proteins and bacterial sugars. One cubic millimeter of dental plaque weighs about 1 milligram *and contains over 300 million bacteria.* Despite the fact that over 300 species of microorganisms reside in the oral cavity, only a few are responsible for the tissue destruction seen in periodontal disease.

In the natural sequence of events in canine periodontal disease in the Beagle dog, gingivitis becomes severe at around 2 years of age and progresses to periodontitis by 4 to 6 years of age. In clinical surveys of pet populations of dogs and cats, periodontitis has been reported to occur at rates *between 60 to over 80% of patients examined.* Without therapeutic intervention, periodontal disease will result in tooth mobility and eventually tooth loss.

Dogs with periodontal disease may or may not exhibit overt signs of oral disease. Owners of animals with periodontal disease most frequently report nonspecific clinical signs in their dogs, such as **halitosis** (bad breath) or behavior changes referable to chronic oral pain, such as poor self-grooming, teeth chatter or grinding, hesitancy to open or close the mouth completely, decreased chewing of toys or treats, pawing at the mouth, facial rubbing, reluctance to perform trained bite behaviors, personality changes (more passive or more aggressive), head- or mouth-handling shyness, or a preference for soft food. Sneezing, one-sided nasal discharge, and incessant nose licking often are seen in dogs with advanced periodontal disease in which an oronasal fistula (*see* above) has developed. Periodontal disease in more unusual cases may be manifested by severe gingival hemorrhage, nasal bleeding, jaw fractures, oral ulcers, tooth displacement into the nasal cavity, or deep bone infection (**osteomyelitis**) of the jaws.

As in human beings, the extent of periodontal disease cannot be fully evaluated without a definitive oral examination that includes a periodontal probe of every tooth and radiographic evaluation of the teeth. Such an examination may reveal tooth abscesses, periodontal pockets (with or without active gingival inflammation), or oronasal fistulas. A definitive oral examination in the dog necessitates that the patient be placed under general anesthesia.

The baseline objective in treatment is to reduce or eliminate disease-producing bacteria from the tooth crown and root surfaces. The starting point of periodontal therapy thus relies on thorough cleaning of the teeth both above and below the gum line; that is, crown and root **scaling** (cleaning) and polishing, with or without surgical intervention. Periodontal therapy goes a step beyond routine dental cleaning, however, having **root planing** as its basis. Root planing involves scaling the root surface of plaque, calculus, and bacterial-laden cementum. Obtaining sufficient access to the depths of the periodontal pocket and exposure of the contoured root surface may require gum surgery.

Root planing without gum surgery is known as *closed root planing,* while planing that necessitates surgical intervention is referred to as *open root planing.* Periodontal pockets in excess of 4–5 mm may require surgical intervention. (Clinically healthy gums should have a maximal sulcus depth of 0–3 mm in the dog.) Root planing attempts to produce a glasslike smoothness to the root surface to discourage redeposition of plaque bacteria, debris, and subsequent calculus formation. Long-term control of periodontal disease progression relies on an oral hygiene home-care program (*see* below), consistent patient follow-up, timely dental **prophylaxis** (preventive measures, such as scaling), and repeated periodontal therapy as needed. Successful periodontal therapy will:

1. produce a healthy gingival attachment to the teeth;
2. diminish periodontal pocket depth;
3. allow access for continued control of plaque on all exposed crown and root surfaces;
4. prolong pain-free tooth retention and function.

PULPITIS

Pulpitis (inflammation of the pulp) can occur following trauma and is characterized locally by increased blood flow, fluid and red blood cell leakage from blood vessels, and pain. Given that the soft-tissue pulp is surrounded by a rigid wall of dentin, there is little available space for swelling within the tooth itself. Discoloration of the crown usually is an indication of pulpitis, the death of odontoblasts (the pulp cells responsible for making dentin), and possibly even death of the pulp itself. Colors ranging from pink, gray, beige and brown are indicative of pulpal hemorrhage.

The pain related to active pulpitis is difficult to evaluate in dogs. Tests of pulp vitality, such as *percussion* (tapping) and hot/cold sensitivity testing are also difficult to perform and interpret in animals. Oftentimes, the only reliable measure of pulp vitality involves sequential radiographs of the tooth and comparison of root-canal diameters over several months of time.

Crown fractures or deep cavities with subsequent exposure of the pulp often result in pulpitis and possibly pulpal death. A common salvage technique used for such problems in human beings, and which is also available for pet dogs, is *root-canal therapy.* The goal of root-canal therapy is to remove the diseased pulp of the tooth while preserving the calcified tooth structure. Root-canal therapy is indicated in situations where the disease of the pulp is considered irreversible. During the procedure the pulpal contents are taken out, the root canal is cleaned and reshaped, and the empty chamber is then sealed and filled with a biocompatible material. In general, teeth that have undergone root-canal therapy become more brittle and thus more prone to fracture than are normal, healthy teeth, regardless of the type of internal reinforcement or crown restoration used. Treated teeth should be reexamined radiographically 6 to 12 months after a root-canal procedure to verify that the underlying disease process has resolved.

In some cases, a live tooth pulp may be maintained by removal of only the damaged portion, a procedure known as a **vital pulpotomy.** Vital pulpotomies are indicated whenever there is a reasonable chance of maintaining pulpal vitality. Because of the extreme stresses placed on dogs' teeth, an endodontically dead tooth is more brittle. A fracture can be the end result of root-canal therapy and would always be less desirable than a living tooth having had only a portion of its pulp removed. It is highly advisable that pulpotomy patients be monitored by periodic radiographic reevaluation in 6 to 12 months to determine if the underlying disease has progressed. Failure of a pulpotomy procedure with death of the pulp will necessitate root-canal therapy.

ROTATED TEETH

A rotated tooth is a tooth that has turned or rotated a variable degree from its normal position. This problem is most frequently observed in the shortened upper jaw of brachycephalic breeds, or among the overcrowded teeth in toy breeds. The first, second and third upper premolars of brachycephalic breeds are most often affected. Rotated teeth are seen sporadically in other breeds that are cultivated for a more "Pug-like" head conformation (e.g., Rottweilers and Labrador Retrievers).

Poor self-cleaning and increased plaque retention predispose rotated teeth to chronic gingivitis, with an increased likelihood for progression to periodontal disease. Malpositioned teeth are harder for an owner to brush. Persistence with regard to oral hygiene is highly encouraged. However, extraction of malpositioned teeth may be necessary to maintain proper oral hygiene.

RETAINED DECIDUOUS (BABY) TEETH

Retained deciduous (RD) teeth do not undergo the normal process of root **resorption;** that is, dissolution of the root with eventual loss of the temporary tooth in order to make way for the permanent dentition. Retained teeth can result in overcrowding, increased plaque retention with secondary gingivitis, and malocclusions. Retained teeth may be either an inherited or an acquired defect. (Inheritance, especially in small and toy breeds, has been implied by clinical experience, but not by definitive breeding studies.) Tibetan Terriers may be affected by retention as well as delayed eruption of deciduous and permanent teeth, while Shetland Sheepdogs have a singular predilection for retention of the upper deciduous canine teeth, with secondary forward deviation of the erupting permanent teeth ("spear" or "lance" tooth).

Treatment of RD teeth consists of careful extraction in order to avoid root fracture and trauma to the erupting permanent-tooth bud. Extraction of RD teeth should take place as soon as the problem is identified (e.g., at 6 months), in order to avoid displacement of the erupting permanent tooth.

Worn Teeth

Excessive crown wearing can be caused by an animal's toy-chewing habits, overaggressive self-grooming, a particular use of the animal (e.g., attack-training), malocclusion-induced contact-rubbing of teeth, overaggressive tooth-brushing, and abnormalities of enamel formation. Slow, chronic crown wearing induces a low-grade pulpitis that stimulates the formation of reparative dentin. Aggressive, acute crown wearing (e.g., self-chewing secondary to flea allergy dermatitis) may result in pulpal exposure. Treatment is strongly influenced by the underlying cause.

Preventive Dentistry

Veterinary Care

Dental prophylaxis (prevention), or teeth cleaning, is a treatment procedure aimed at preventing dental disease from developing. Reduction or elimination of the causative microorganisms from the tooth crown and root surfaces is the only sure way to maintain periodontal health and to treat gingivitis and periodontitis. Given the progressive nature of periodontal disease, early recognition will lessen the degree of surgical intervention required at a later date. This equates to shorter anesthesia time and decreased postoperative pain for the patient, as well as less rigorous dental home care for the owner and increased tooth retention and function.

Major concerns voiced by clients seeking dental care for their pets include the safety of general anesthesia, pain related to oral disease, and frustration with progressive tooth loss and the necessity for further tooth extractions. Given the high level of dental awareness among the general public and the greater safety of the newer anesthetic agents, waiting until a dog's teeth are "really dirty" is no longer a justifiable cause for delaying prophylactic intervention.

Updated standards of care in veterinary dentistry dictate that the baseline preventive cleaning procedure should involve not only the crown of the teeth but the tooth surface below the gum line (**subgingival** tooth surface). The extent of the subgingival tooth surface to be cleaned normally is determined at the time of the definitive oral examination by exploration of the gingival sulcus with a dental instrument called a perioprobe. If the gum attachment level is no longer at the cementoenamel junction, periodontal therapy (i.e., root planing) will be required (*see* above).

Scaling of the teeth with dental instruments removes the plaque and calculus from tooth surfaces. Regardless of the hand or power instrumentation used, the tooth surface will be scratched during the scaling process. Polishing after calculus removal completes the cleaning process by removing debris and tooth discoloration caused by bacterial pigments. Polishing involves the use of a paste containing an abrasive grit that is applied with a rotating rubber cup, or use of a jet stream of water and air containing an abrasive. The two most important reasons for polishing are:

1. to render the tooth surface as smooth as possible to discourage plaque reaccumulation;
2. to remove microscopic plaque debris in order to disrupt the bacterial cycle that leads to gingivitis and periodontitis.

Human dentistry is currently addressing the issue of "selective polishing" because of the cumulative loss of enamel over the human life span. Owing to the shorter life span of dogs and fewer number of prophylactic procedures performed, enamel loss caused by polishing is not a significant problem provided that the proper instrumentation and technique are used. Polishing will *not* remove intrinsic stains that are incorporated into the tooth structure itself (e.g., tetracycline staining). Human dentistry is also particularly concerned about cosmetic treatment of intrinsic tooth discoloration using external or internal "bleaching" techniques. The long-term effects of the bleaching process on teeth are unknown at this time.

Antibiotic therapy in dentistry is used either acutely (within hours) as a prophylactic measure to destroy bacteria that may reach the bloodstream as the result of a dental procedure, or chronically (over days to weeks) to treat a specific dental problem, (e.g., severe periodontal disease). Antibiotic usage in conjunction with routine dental prophylaxis of healthy animals is *not* warranted. Dental procedure-related **bacteremia** (release of bacteria into the blood) is usually of low intensity and transient duration, with the bacteria being cleared from the bloodstream within 15 to 30 minutes after the procedure has been completed. Certain preexisting medical conditions may, however, necessitate the use of prophylactic antibiotics for a dental procedure. These include:

- diseases of the heart valves (**endocarditis**) and certain other cardiac conditions
- immunosuppression
- diabetes mellitus
- chronic kidney disease
- obstructive lung disease
- liver failure

HOME CARE

Dental home care refers to the tasks performed by owners as an aid in maintaining good oral hygiene for their pets. Given the primary role of bacteria in dental disease, the major goal of any home-care program should be plaque control at the gingival margin.

As mentioned earlier, the most reliable method of plaque control is mechanical removal. Significant but incomplete removal of plaque and calculus may be achieved through natural self-cleaning imposed by diets rich in hard foods and through the use of rawhide chew-toys. The self-cleaning action of the tongue also greatly assists in reducing plaque on the inner surface of the tooth crown.

Toothbrushes are the most effective mechanical plaque-removers available for home care. The most "ideal" toothbrush should have soft, multitufted synthetic bristles with rounded bristle tips to minimize tooth abrasion and injury to the gums. Proper toothbrushing technique is essential for the effective removal of plaque from the gingival sulcus. Pet acceptance of the procedure can be enhanced if the jaws are not forced open; instead, the lips are gently rolled back to expose the teeth. The toothbrush should be applied to the gum-tooth interface at a 45° angle to maximize cleaning of the gingival sulcus. The brush is rotated several times in very small circular motions at one site, overlapping several teeth. The final brush stroke consists of vertically dragging the brush head off the tooth crown so that the bristles provide additional plaque removal from between the teeth. The brush is then placed on a new section of teeth and the cleaning continued systematically until all the outer (cheek-side) surfaces of the teeth have been brushed. The inner surfaces are more difficult to clean because the dog will object to having its mouth opened. Pet acceptance of toothbrushing may be increased by incremental introduction of the procedure with the use of interim appliances (i.e., toothbrush substitutes) such as cotton- or foam-tipped applicators, soft rubber finger brushes, or a finger wrapped in soft gauze. Gradually, as the dog becomes accustomed to the procedure, these interim substitutes can be phased out and replaced by the toothbrush itself.

A variety of **dentifrice** (toothpaste) preparations are available for use in brushing pets' teeth. In general, an effective dentifrice will be composed of:

1. an inorganic *abrasive* such as calcium carbonate, calcium phosphate, sodium phosphate or aluminum oxide;
2. a detergent or *surfactant* such as sodium lauryl sulfate or sodium lauryl sarcosinate;
3. a *humectant* (moistening agent) such as glycerin or sorbitol;
4. a *binder* such as carboxymethylcellulose, alginate or amylose;
5. a flavoring agent such as saccharin or malt;
6. preservatives and colorings.

Some dentifrices also contain fluoride in the form of sodium fluoride or stannous fluoride and/or an anti-tartar compound such as pyrophosphate, which interferes with the formation of calculus crystals. Fluoride is widely used in human dentistry for the prevention of cavities and control of tooth hypersensitivity. Fluoride becomes incorporated into dental plaque, where it directly inhibits bacterial enzymes. Stannous fluoride is superior to sodium fluoride in its antibacterial effects. Topical fluoride is available as professionally applied varnishes, foams, and gel concentrates, and as owner-applied dentifrices and gel concentrates. Recommendations for clinical use of fluoride in dogs must take into account the fact that the fluoride will be internally ingested, with some potential for toxicity. Fluoride toxicity (**fluorosis**) affects developing teeth (i.e., in dogs less than 6 months of age) by causing defects in enamel formation that result in weakened, chalky, easily stained enamel surfaces. Thus, fluoride should be used with caution in dogs under 6 months of age. The metabolism of fluoride in the body is quite different for different animal species. Dogs appear to be quite susceptible, with cats less so. Acute, systemic fluoride toxicity can result in sudden cardiac arrest, while chronic administration of lower doses of fluoride can cause calcium deposits in skeletal and cardiac muscle and softening of bone structure. Owners must therefore be cautioned with regard to the use of fluoride-containing dentifrices in dogs.

CHAPTER 22

The Skin and Disorders

**by Peter J. Ihrke
and Jeffrey E. Barlough**

Components of the Skin

The skin, the outer covering of the body and the primary interface between the body and the environment, is made up of three major layers: the **epidermis,** the **dermis,** and the **subcutis.**

THE THREE MAJOR LAYERS OF THE SKIN

Epidermis

The outermost major layer of the skin is the epidermis. It is an avascular (lacking blood vessels), multilayered structure, the exact number of layers varying from species to species and from body area to body area. In general, in any given area there is an inverse relationship between the thickness of the epidermis and the amount of hair present. In haired skin the epidermis is quite thin, consisting of one to four layers of viable cells; in nonhaired skin the epidermis is much thicker.

Three major cell types are found in the epidermis. The majority of cells in the epidermis are **keratinocytes.** These are the cells that produce **keratin,** the insoluble, sulfur-rich protein that represents the principal structural component of skin, hair and nails. The other major cell types in the epidermis are **melanocytes** (cells that produce the skin pigment **melanin**) and **Langerhans cells,** which are important in generating immune responses within the skin.

Keratinocytes. The keratinocytes are arranged in multiple layers. The lowermost layer is referred to as the **basal cell layer.** The basal cells are generally cuboidal in shape and rest on a basement membrane-like structure that separates the epidermis from the underlying **dermis** (the middle major layer of the skin). It is through the multiplication of the basal cells and the subsequent maturation of their daughter cells that the upper layers of keratinocytes are formed. The next several layers above the basal cell layer are referred to as the **prickle cell layer** or **squamous cell layer.** The prickle cells are polyhedral (having many faces or sides) in shape. Above the prickle cell layer is the **granular cell layer,** composed of flattened cells containing many **basophilic** (staining dark blue) granules. The outermost layer is the **horny layer,** which is composed entirely of tightly adherent, dead keratinocytes containing abundant quantities of keratin.

The keratinocytes of the epidermis are not in a static condition, but instead are constantly replacing themselves. As keratinocytes are generated and mature, they progress upward through the several epidermal cell layers, gradually changing from the cuboidal basal cell form to the prickle cell form to the granular cell form, finally transforming into the horny cells comprising the very outermost layer of the skin. How ironic that this outermost layer of skin, which in human beings in particular is the recipient of such lavish attention and so much dutiful care, should in actuality be composed entirely of dead tissue!

Under normal conditions in the dog, it takes about 20 to 25 days for a keratinocyte to progress upward from the basal cell layer to the horny layer; this is known as the **epidermal cell renewal time.** The entire process whereby the keratinocytes mature to form the horny layer is referred to by the general term **keratinization.**

Melanocytes. Melanin is the major pigment present in the skin. Two types of cells are important in melanin production. **Melanoblasts** are the immature melanin-forming cells that originate early in fetal life. During fetal development, the melanoblasts migrate from their point of origin to their point of maturation in the basal cell layer of the epidermis. One out of every 5 to 10 cells in the basal cell is a mature melanin-forming cell, or **melanocyte.** In addition to migrating to the epidermis, some melanoblasts migrate to the roots of the hairs, where they will provide color for the future developing hairs. A few of the melanoblasts do not complete their migration and instead remain in the connective tissue portion of the skin (the dermis).

The ability of melanocytes to produce melanin depends on their ability to synthesize a key enzyme, tyrosinase. Through the action of this enzyme, the amino acid **tyrosine** is converted to melanin. Pigmentation of the epidermis is accomplished when the melanocytes transfer melanin to the surrounding basal cells (i.e., the keratinocytes). The exact mechanism by which this is accomplished is not understood.

The melanin is then dispersed throughout the epidermis by the multiplication and maturation of the keratinocytes.

Langerhans cells. Langerhans cells are part of the immune system and serve the important function of processing **antigens** (substances against which an immune response can be raised) in certain hypersensitivity states, such as allergic contact dermatitis.

Dermis

The dermis is the middle and thickest major layer of the skin and provides the skin with most of its bulk. It is made up of connective tissue fibers and a ground substance. The connective tissue fibers consist of approximately 90% **collagen** fibers, the major protein constituent of the dermis, and approximately 10% *elastic fibers,* which provide the skin with its suppleness and elasticity. The connective tissue fibers are large and densely packed throughout most of the dermis. The fibers are smaller and more loosely arrayed directly under the epidermis and surrounding the **epidermal appendages** (i.e., the hair follicles and skin glands).

A variety of cell types are normally present in the dermis. The most common cell type is the **fibrocyte,** or **fibroblast,** which resembles similar cells found in other areas of the body. The next most common cell type is the **mast cell.** Mast cells are round to spindle-shaped cells and contain large numbers of granules. Within the granules are a variety of noxious chemical substances, including **histamine** and serotonin— important mediators of inflammation that are involved in the production of allergic disorders. (*See* "ATOPY," below, and CHAPTER 33, "THE IMMUNE SYSTEM AND DISORDERS.") Mast cells tend to be concentrated around capillary beds; thus, most mast cells are present in the more superficial dermis and surrounding the epidermal appendages. The final cell type present in the dermis under normal conditions is the **histiocyte.** Histiocytes are tissue **macrophages** (specialized white blood cells that ingest cellular debris and foreign material) originating in the bone marrow. They exist in the dermis in very small numbers.

Subcutis

The innermost major layer of the skin is the sub-cutis (also called the **hypodermis**). It is composed of fat cells and thin strands of **collagenous** (containing collagen) connective tissue. The nerves and blood vessels supplying the skin weave their way through the strands of connective tissue in order to reach the overlying dermis.

THE EPIDERMAL APPENDAGES

The major epidermal appendages include the hair and hair follicles, sebaceous glands, and sweat glands.

Hair and Hair Follicles

Hair has become a rudimentary, vestigial structure in human beings, for whom it is now of little value in protection against the environment but instead serves primarily as ornamentation. The haircoat of animals, by contrast, is of great practical importance to their daily existence. Because of its fibrous and bulky nature, hair is an efficient filter and insulator and affords a defense against cuts, abrasions, injuries due to heat or sunlight, and chemical irritants. Physical trauma also is greatly blunted by the haircoat before it can reach the sensitive surface of the skin.

The basic unit of hair production is the **hair follicle.** Each hair follicle consists of two major components, the **follicular sheath** and the **hair bulb.** The follicular sheath is a long tubelike structure through which the hair passes through the dermis and exits to the skin surface. The hair bulb is the deepest portion of the hair follicle. The cells of the hair bulb (the **hair matrix cells**) and the associated **dermal papilla** are responsible for the actual production of hair.

The hair follicles lie at an oblique angle. Bundles of smooth muscle known as **arrector pili** muscles are present in haired areas of skin. Arrector pili muscles stretch from the dermis to the hair follicles; when they contract, they cause the hairs to "stand up." These muscles may be called into action in response to a perceived threat, fear, a cold environment, or emotional stress. In dogs, the action of arrector pili muscles is particularly prominent along the back, as when a dog gives warning by "raising its hackles."

Types of hair follicles. There are two major types of hair follicles, *simple* follicles and *compound* follicles. In a simple follicle, only a single hair is produced; this type of follicle is found in *herbivores* (plant-eating mammals). In compound follicles, however, many hairs are produced. Bundles of 7 to 15 hairs normally share a common skin opening and a single follicle down to the level of the sebaceous gland (*see* below), where they then separate into individual follicles. In a "normal coat," as is found in German Shepherd Dogs and wild canids such as wolves and coyotes, each compound follicle contains a single large, long, stiff **primary hair** (also called a **guard hair**), which occupies a deeper follicle, together with many fine **secondary hairs** (also called **underhairs;** collectively known as the *undercoat*) with more superficially located follicles; that is, the follicles are closer to the skin surface. Variation in the relative size and number of primary and secondary hairs is responsible for the variety of haircoats observed in different breeds of dogs (e.g., the short, fine coat of Boxers, the fine, long coat of Cocker Spaniels, the coarse coat of terrier breeds).

Hair and Hair Growth. Hair, like the horny layer of the epidermis, is in actuality a lifeless, keratinized structure. Each hair consists of an upper, free portion known as the **hair shaft** and a lower, anchoring structure known as the **hair root.** The hair shaft is composed of three layers. Working from the outside in, the three layers are known as the **cuticle, cortex** and **medulla.** All hairs have a cuticle and a cortex. The degree of development of the inner layer, the medulla, varies according to the animal species and the type of hair. Primary (guard) hairs have a well-developed medulla, while secondary hairs have a narrow medulla.

Hair does not grow continuously, but instead is periodically lost and renewed in a rhythmic fashion. Hair follicles actively produce hair in the **anagen** phase of hair growth. During this phase the hair matrix cells in the hair bulb are actively dividing, the resulting daughter cells **differentiating** (becoming increasingly specialized) to produce the hair shaft. This phase of growth normally alternates with a resting phase known as **telogen.** In telogen the hair matrix cells become inactive. The root of the hair detaches from the matrix cells in the hair bulb, although the hair itself is still retained within the follicular sheath by a structure known as the internal root sheath. After a variable period of time the dormant hair matrix cells reactivate and a new hair begins forming. As the new hair grows and moves up the follicular sheath, the old hair is finally pushed out of the follicle and shed.

In people, the average period of growth of each individual hair is approximately 1000 days, with a range of 2 to 6 or more years. The duration of growth is genetically determined. The resting phase of growth lasts approximately 100 days. Thus, at any given time, about 90% of human hair follicles are in anagen and about 10% are in telogen. Adjacent hair follicles tend to be in different phases of the growth cycle, so that no obvious "shedding" is observed. In animals, however, there is a distinct tendency for hair follicle growth to become synchronized, resulting in seasonal shedding of hair. This is most apparent in wild animals living in colder climates. The most important factor regulating synchronization of hair follicle activity is the length of daylight; environmental temperature plays a much lesser role.

Sebaceous Glands

Sebaceous glands are simple, **lobulated** (divided into small branched lobes, or *lobules*) glands associated with the hair follicles. Each gland is connected to the **lumen** (interior space) of the upper part of its associated follicle by a short **duct** (small tube or passageway). Sebaceous gland cells secrete their product by a **holocrine** type of secretion; that is, each entire cell disintegrates with the cell contents becoming the secretion. The product or secretion of sebaceous glands is known as **sebum.** Sebum is a complex fatty substance whose exact composition varies from species to species. Its primary function appears to be as a skin lubricant, although it also has some inherent **antimicrobial** (killing or suppressing the growth of microorganisms) activity.

Certain hormones, particularly male and female sex hormones, exert an influence on sebum secretion. Very small amounts of male sex hormones (**androgens**) will cause an increase in size of the sebaceous glands and a corresponding increase in sebum secretion. Certain female sex hormones (**estrogens**) have the opposite effect, causing a decrease in size and diminished secretion. It should be stressed, however, that very high (i.e., toxic) doses of estrogens are required to affect sebaceous gland function to any significant extent.

Sweat Glands

There are two types of sweat glands: **apocrine** and **eccrine.** Apocrine sweat glands are coiled structures with a large lumen; they empty their contents into their associated hair follicle. Apocrine sweat glands are found throughout the body and produce a scented, fluid secretion that may play a role as a sexual attractant. Eccrine sweat glands also have a coiled structure, but the lumen is much smaller and the glands empty their contents directly onto the skin surface. They are found in the footpads and nasal pad. In animals, the majority of sweat glands are of the apocrine type. In people, by contrast, most sweat glands are of the eccrine type, with apocrine sweat glands being limited to the armpits and the anal and genital regions.

It should be noted that although domestic animals are abundantly supplied with sweat glands, significant differences exist among the different species as to the function of the glands. In horses, for example, the sweat glands are highly functional and assist in regulating body temperature. In dogs and cats, by contrast, sweat glands appear to exist only as rudimentary structures and are essentially nonfunctional.

Definition of Terms

In addition to the anatomic and physiologic terms described above, there are a number of common medical terms that must be defined as a prelude to discussing the individual skin diseases of dogs. These are terms that veterinary dermatologists use to describe the pathologic changes produced in the skin by different disease processes. Accurate description and identification of such changes are a necessary prerequisite to making a diagnosis.

TERMS OF IMPORTANCE IN THE DIAGNOSIS OF SKIN DISEASE

alopecia. Absence or loss of hair.

bulla. A large vesicle.

comedo (plural: comedones). A blackhead or pimple.

crusts. Residue of dried serum, blood, pus and epidermal, keratinous and bacterial debris.

depigmentation. Localized loss of normal skin color.

dermatitis. Any inflammatory skin disease or simply an inflammation of the skin.

dermatosis. Any skin disease, particularly one without an inflammatory component.

erosion. A superficial denudation of the skin involving only the epidermis.

erythema. Reddening of the skin, due to congestion of the underlying capillaries.

excoriations. Erosions and ulcerations produced by self-trauma.

exfoliation. Peeling of the skin.

fissures. Cracks in the skin secondary to loss of normal skin tone associated with inflammatory processes.

hyperkeratosis. Abnormal overgrowth of the horny layer of the epidermis.

hyperpigmentation. Localized, abnormal darkening of normal skin color.

lesion. Any disease-induced abnormality of tissue structure or function.

lichenification. A leathery thickening of the skin, with exaggeration of normal skin markings.

macule. A discolored area of skin that is not elevated above the skin surface.

nodule. A large papule; small lump.

papule. A minute, firm, well-demarcated elevation of the skin.

patch. A large macule.

plaque. A flat area in the skin.

pruritus. Itchiness.

pustule. A vesicle containing **pus** (fluid produced by an inflammatory process, containing many white blood cells).

scale(s). Accumulated fragments of the horny layer of the epidermis.

symmetrical (bilaterally symmetrical). Occurring simultaneously in approximately the same area on each side of the body.

tumor. A large nodule, or obvious cancerous mass.

ulcer, ulceration. A severe sloughing of the skin surface, extending at least into the dermis.

vesicle. A circumscribed elevation of the epidermis, filled with **serum** (fluid component of blood); a blister.

wheal. A hive; a discrete, well-circumscribed, reddened swelling with a flat top and steep-walled margins, produced by **edema** (excessive fluid in the intercellular tissue spaces) in the dermis; often associated with allergic reactions (i.e., urticaria).

Disorders of the Skin

BACTERIAL SKIN DISEASES

Pyotraumatic Dermatitis

Pyotraumatic dermatitis ("hot spots") is a self-induced, traumatic skin disease commonly seen in dogs. It is believed to be caused by an itch-scratch cycle that results from an underlying itchy (especially allergic) skin disease. The disease most often occurs secondary to flea allergy dermatitis (*see* CHAPTER 23, "EXTERNAL PARASITES").

Affected dogs exhibit rapid development of reddened, well-demarcated, slightly elevated plaques that often ooze. Erosion and ulceration can occur, and sticky debris often mats the surrounding hair. The lesions progress rapidly and may coalesce. They occur mainly along the lower back and on the lateral thighs. The lesions appear to result from licking, chewing, and scratching; that is, they are a result of self-trauma, which then predisposes to secondary bacterial infection.

German Shepherd Dogs, Golden Retrievers, Labrador Retrievers, Collies and Saint Bernards are predisposed to develop pyotraumatic dermatitis. The disease occurs most frequently in warm, humid weather.

Therapy consists of local clipping of the hair, gentle cleansing, and topical or systemic anti-inflammatory medication. The underlying cause (e.g., fleas) should be investigated and treated.

Canine Pyoderma

"Pyoderma" is a general term for any skin disease in which **pus** (fluid produced by an inflammatory process, containing many white blood cells) is formed. The bacterium most commonly implicated in canine pyoderma is *Staphylococcus intermedius.* At least four forms of pyoderma are recognized in dogs.

Impetigo is a common disease in which superficial pustules not associated with hair follicles develop. Pruritus may be either absent or very mild. Underlying causes have not been identified, although inflammation secondary to fecal debris or urine scalding in the anal or groin area has been suggested. Impetigo is seen most often in young dogs. Therapy consists of antibacterial shampoos and systemic antibiotics.

Superficial bacterial folliculitis (also called **superficial pyoderma**) is a very common skin disease. It is characterized by the development of superficial pustules in association with hair follicles. The only canine skin disease seen worldwide with greater frequency is flea allergy dermatitis. (*See* CHAPTER 23, "EXTERNAL PARASITES.")

Most bacterial folliculitis in dogs occurs secondary to coexistent disease or in conjunction with other predisposing factors. Pustules vary greatly in size and may be difficult to identify without a magnifying lens. Owing to their fragile nature they tend to rupture easily, transforming into crusted papules, the most common lesion seen in this disease. Pruritus of variable intensity is also a common feature. Therapy consists of treating the underlying cause (if it can be identified), applying antibacterial shampoos, and administering systemic antibiotics.

Superficial spreading pyoderma may occur alone or more commonly along with superficial bacterial folliculitis. Lesions frequently arise first in the groin and **axilla** (armpit), suggesting that heat retention and moisture, together with the frictional trauma associated with movement, may be important in disease development.

Affected dogs exhibit reddened macules that frequently expand and coalesce. Crusting, hyperpigmentation and alopecia (often in ring-shaped patterns) may be present. Treatment is based on the use of antibiotics and antibacterial shampoos.

Deep bacterial folliculitis and **furunculosis** (also called *deep pyoderma*) together represent a less common form of pyoderma. These two diseases have been grouped together because they commonly coexist, inflammation deep within the hair follicles (**folliculitis**) leading to hair follicle rupture (**furunculosis,** or **boils**). As in the other forms of canine pyoderma, *Staphylococcus intermedius* is the primary cause. Secondary invasion by bacteria such as *Proteus, Pseudomonas* and *Escherichia coli* occurs in deeper infections. Deep pyoderma often occurs as a complication of other diseases, including **demodicosis** (infestation with *Demodex* mites). On occasion, hair follicle trauma may be an initiating factor. Backcombing, clipping, persistent licking, or continued or repeated pressure applied over bony prominences can cause hair follicle rupture and subsequent infection and inflammation.

German Shepherd Dogs, Golden Retrievers, and Irish Setters are predisposed, as are certain short-coated breeds such as Bull Terriers, Dalmatians, Doberman Pinschers and Great Danes. Treatment is based on the use of antibiotics and antibacterial shampoos.

Canine Acne

Canine acne is a common disease of young dogs. The formation of blackheads or pimples on the chin and lips is characteristic. Because canine acne occurs in adolescent dogs, as does human acne in adolescent youngsters, there has been speculation that the underlying causes of the two diseases may be similar; that is, heightened sensitivity of the sebaceous glands and hair follicles to the effects of circulating **androgens** (male sex hormones). The increased production of sebum followed by the breakdown of sebum to free fatty acids may induce inflammation and subsequent comedo formation. Affected dogs exhibit comedones, crusted papules, and pustules, with variable amounts of erythema and alopecia, most often on the chin and less commonly on the skin surrounding the lower lip. The upper lip and lateral muzzle may also be affected in more severe cases. There is usually little itching. The disease occurs most frequently in short-coated breeds (Doberman Pinschers,

Great Danes, English Bulldogs, German Short-haired Pointers, Boxers) and usually coincides with the onset of puberty, between 5 and 12 months of age. It is usually a self-limiting disease, but on occasion may persist into adulthood. Therapy consists of chin compresses, antibacterial shampoos and antibiotics.

FUNGAL SKIN DISEASES

Ringworm

Ringworm (also called **dermatophytosis**) is a common skin disorder of dogs. It is caused by fungi known as *ringworm fungi* or **dermatophytes,** which invade the outer, superficial layers of the skin, hair and nails. Ringworm fungi feed on keratin shed from the dead cells of the horny layer of the epidermis (normally, ringworm fungi cannot survive in living tissue). Some ringworm fungi are residents of the soil, while others are strictly parasitic. Warm temperatures and high humidity are ideal conditions for promoting dermatophyte infections. Dogs less than a year of age are at greatest risk. Older animals with decreased immune function may be at increased risk for a rare, generalized form of dermatophytosis.

Canine ringworm is caused most frequently by *Microsporum canis* (*M. canis*), *Trichophyton mentagrophytes* (*T. mentagrophytes*), and *Microsporum gypseum* (*M. gypseum*). Of these, *M. canis* is most commonly implicated. Transmission of the fungi occurs by direct contact with infected animals or with objects contaminated with hair or scale from affected dogs or cats. Ringworm fungi, such as *M. canis,* that are well-adapted to their host species usually induce little or no host response to their presence, and infected dogs may become inapparent carriers; that is, they harbor the fungi but exhibit no clinical signs. By contrast, infection with poorly host-adapted dermatophytes such as *T. mentagrophytes* or *M. gypseum* usually elicits a greater inflammatory reaction in the host. Soluble substances produced by the fungi must reach the underlying dermis in order for an inflammatory response to occur. These substances can either be *toxins* (i.e., irritants) or *allergens* (substances inducing an allergic response). Reactions to toxins often are milder than reactions to allergens.

Normally, ringworm is a self-limiting condition in healthy dogs because the host inflammatory response eventually eliminates the infection. Dogs with compromised immune systems are at greater risk for chronic or more generalized disease. Ringworm is also a **zoonotic disease,** that is, it can be transmitted from affected animals to people. Infected dogs should be handled with care, keeping this aspect of the disease in mind. (*See* APPENDIX A, "ZOONOTIC DISEASES: FROM DOGS TO PEOPLE.")

Affected dogs often exhibit circular, expanding patches of alopecia, with erythema at the margins, scaling, crusting, variable amounts of pruritus, and an area of central clearing (hence the name "ringworm"). Remaining hairs usually are thickened and broken. Papules or pustules may be seen. The head and forelimbs are common sites for initial infection because these are the areas that interface most directly with the surrounding environment.

Diagnosis relies on the history, clinical signs, and microscopic examination of hair or scale for the presence of ringworm fungi. Scale and hair are collected by scraping the suspected lesions. In some cases a fungal culture, the most definitive means for diagnosing ringworm, may be necessary to identify the fungi.

Treatment is aimed at eliminating the fungus from the patient and its environment. In some cases, because the disease is essentially self-limiting, little or no therapy is given. In more resistant cases, topical or oral antifungal medication may be necessary. Exposed, clinically normal animals in contact with an affected dog should receive topical antifungal medication, since they too may be harboring ringworm fungi. The environment should be thoroughly cleansed using disinfectants and frequent vacuuming. A physician should be consulted if suspicious lesions develop on any individuals, particularly children, in close contact with an affected pet.

Subcutaneous and Systemic Mycoses

The *subcutaneous mycoses* are a group of relatively rare fungal diseases affecting the skin and underlying (subcutaneous) tissues and deeper organs. Occasionally they may spread to involve other regions of the body, including one or more organ systems. By and large, however, they are pathogens of more superficial body surfaces. Among the subcutaneous mycoses affecting the skin of dogs are *sporotrichosis, phycomycosis, phaeohyphomycosis,* and *eumycotic mycetoma.* The *systemic mycoses* are rare fungal diseases (*blastomycosis, histoplasmosis, coccidioidomycosis, cryptococcosis*) in which inhalation (usually) of the causative organism is followed by widespread dissemination to internal organs and other tissues, including in some cases the skin. For pertinent information on these diseases, *see* CHAPTER 36, "FUNGAL DISEASES."

PARASITIC SKIN DISEASES
See CHAPTER 23, "EXTERNAL PARASITES."

ALLERGIC SKIN DISEASES

Urticaria (Hives)
Urticaria, or "hives," is an acute, usually localized swelling of the skin caused by an increase in the **permeability** (leakiness) of capillaries. This results in an outpouring of fluid from the blood into the tissue spaces and a characteristic skin wheal. The overlying hair may stand erect when wheals are present in haired areas. Wheals vary in size from small circular spots to lesions many centimeters in diameter. Individual lesions may expand by coalescing with adjacent wheals. The degree of pruritus of the lesions varies greatly.

Urticaria may be instigated by immunologic or nonimmunologic factors. The most common immunologic causes include drug reactions, food allergies, contact with stinging or biting insects, vaccines, blood transfusions, infections, certain plants, and atopy. Nonimmunologic or physical causes include heat, cold, and sunlight.

Therapy involves elimination of the underlying cause (if identified) and symptomatic treatment with anti-inflammatory medications.

Atopy
Atopy (allergic inhalant dermatitis, atopic disease) is a common, heritable hypersensitivity to pollens or other environmental allergens. It occurs when genetically predisposed individuals inhale, or possibly absorb through the skin, substances to which they are allergic. These substances subsequently initiate specific immunologic reactions in the skin, leading to the release of noxious compounds, including histamine and serotonin, from mast cells. It is these compounds that are responsible for the unpleasant physical sensations of allergy (itching, red runny eyes, scratchy throat, coughing, sneezing). (*See* CHAPTER 33, "THE IMMUNE SYSTEM AND DISORDERS.")

Most of the lesions are caused by self-trauma (i.e., the animal's response to the itchiness and irritation), leading to erythema, alopecia and excoriations. The face, feet and ears are the body sites most frequently affected. Greasiness or **hyperhidrosis** (excessive sweating) may be present, and secondary pyoderma is often observed. Dogs with a light coat color may exhibit staining of the haircoat with saliva. Atopy is manifested initially in most dogs as a summer-to-fall disease, with the clinical course tending to lengthen progressively in each succeeding year.

Predisposed breeds include small terriers (West Highland White Terriers, Wire-haired Fox Terriers, Cairn Terriers, Scottish Terriers), Golden Retrievers, Dalmatians, Boxers, Pugs, Irish Setters, English Setters, Miniature Schnauzers, Lhasa Apsos and Chinese Shar-Peis. Female dogs may have a slightly higher risk. Peak incidence of atopy occurs between 1 and 3 years of age. Clinical signs rarely appear before 6 months or after 7 years of age, although in Chinese Shar-Peis atopy has been seen in animals as young as 3 to 6 months of age.

Treatment involves avoidance of the offending allergen(s), administration of antihistamines, judicious use of anti-inflammatory medications, and possibly **hyposensitization** ("allergy shots") to reduce the patient's sensitivity to the allergen(s).

Food Allergy
Food allergy is an uncommon skin disease believed to result from an allergic reaction to an ingested substance. The immunologic mechanism behind food allergy in domestic animals is unknown. Food allergy is observed more fre-

quently, however, in animals having other allergic conditions. Interestingly, food allergy has been characterized as being both very rare and very common!

As in atopy, most of the lesions appear to be caused by self-trauma. Primary skin lesions, when present, may include reddened papules, wheals, pustules and crusting. Subsequent self-trauma leads to erosions, ulcerations, excoriations and alopecia. Lesions may be generalized, or localized to the face, feet or ears. Breeds possibly at increased risk for developing food allergies include Miniature Schnauzers, Golden Retrievers, West Highland White Terriers and Chinese Shar-Peis. Food allergy in dogs can begin as early as 6 months of age. However, food allergies may develop in dogs of any age.

Diagnosis involves feeding the patient a **hypoallergenic** (minimizing allergic reactions) diet for several weeks and observing for improvement. Protein sources for a hypoallergenic diet may include mutton, cottage cheese, tofu or white fish; rice or potatoes are acceptable carbohydrate sources, and corn oil may be added as a source of fat. The key feature of a hypoallergenic diet is that it does not contain the ingredients that the dog has been eating previously. There is nothing intrinsically "hypoallergenic" about the ingredients suggested; they are simply not part of the dog's usual diet.

If the skin problem worsens when the hypoallergenic diet is discontinued and the dog is returned to the original diet, a diagnosis of food allergy may be made. Therapy consists primarily of avoidance of the offending dietary item(s). Response to medications such as corticosteroids often is disappointing.

Allergic Contact Dermatitis

Allergic contact dermatitis is the least common of the allergic skin diseases. It is caused by a hypersensitivity reaction analogous to that occurring in hikers and backpackers following contact with poison ivy or poison oak. Sensitization to the offending substance may require years to develop, or may occur within several weeks. The disease usually is seen in adult dogs. An increased risk has been reported for German Shepherd Dogs and yellow Labrador Retrievers.

Affected animals exhibit erythema, papules, and vesicles that rapidly progress to crusted lesions. The degree of pruritus often varies. Healing follows quickly if exposure to the offending substance is brief. Gradual expansion of the lesions, with lichenification and hyperpigmentation, result from chronic exposure. Because the haircoat normally protects the underlying skin from contact with most potential allergens (except for liquids and aerosols), lesions tend to occur more commonly in hairless or relatively hairless body areas.

Treatment involves avoidance of the offending allergen, if it can be identified, and symptomatic care. Topical anti-inflammatory medications may provide palliative relief.

AUTOIMMUNE SKIN DISEASES

A number of skin diseases exist whose origins lie in an inappropriate or exaggerated response on the part of the immune system. When this response is directed against the body's own cells and tissues, it is referred to as an autoimmune disease. The underlying cause of such misguided attacks is often unknown. Many different hypotheses have been proposed to account for the development of autoimmune diseases. It is likely that a combination of factors, including genetic predisposition and reactions against foreign substances, initiate and maintain these diseases. Some autoimmune diseases are characterized, at least in part, by clinical signs of skin disease. (*See* CHAPTER 33, "THE IMMUNE SYSTEM AND DISORDERS.")

Discoid Lupus Erythematosus

Discoid lupus erythematosus is a relatively common autoimmune skin disease of dogs. Cases previously diagnosed as *nasal solar dermatitis* ("Collie nose") were most likely cases of discoid lupus erythematosus. It has been postulated that the human form of the disease may be caused by an autoimmune reaction against keratinocytes that have been altered by chronic exposure to ultraviolet radiation (sunlight). Because canine discoid lupus erythematosus is at least sunlight-aggravated if not overtly sunlight-induced, the lesions often are more severe in the summertime and in parts of the world with high solar intensity. Collies, Shetland

Sheepdogs, German Shepherd Dogs and Siberian Huskies exhibit a breed predilection for the disease. As a subgroup, white German Shepherd Dogs are at greater risk.

Clinical signs commonly are restricted to the face. The earliest signs involve a symmetrical pattern of depigmentation, erythema and scaling, often limited to the nose. Loss of the normal "cobblestone" architecture of the **planum nasale** (the tip of the nose) may occur. Lesions may also develop on the top of the muzzle, lips, around the eyes, and on the ears. Rarely, mouth ulcers and lesions on the genitals and extremities have been reported. Alopecia, crusting, erosions, ulcerations and scarring may be seen in severe cases. Long-standing lesions are fragile, easily abraded, and bleed readily.

Diagnosis is based on the history, clinical features, and skin biopsy. Treatment involves restriction of access to sunlight, and application of sunscreens and topical anti-inflammatory medication. Systemic anti-inflammatory drugs should be given only if absolutely necessary.

Systemic Lupus Erythematosus (SLE)

Systemic lupus erythematosus is a rare, *multisystemic* (involving many body systems) autoimmune disorder characterized by a general derangement of certain key immune defense mechanisms. "Lupus" ("wolf") refers to the patchy discoloration and erythema of the face observed in human patients with SLE. Skin lesions are only a single component of the disease, however. In SLE a variety of immune mechanisms begin to attack structural components of the body, some as basic as **deoxyribonucleic acid (DNA)**—the genetic material within the nuclei of cells. Autoantibodies directed against such host-cell components attach to cells in the blood, kidneys, skin and elsewhere, resulting in a widespread immunologic assault on the host.

Canine SLE is more prevalent in Spitzes, Poodles and certain other breeds, including Collies, Shetland Sheepdogs and German Shepherd Dogs. Dogs between 2 and 4 years of age are most often affected. Skin lesions of SLE can include erythema, scaling, crusting, depigmentation and alopecia. Ulcers may develop from ruptured vesicles in the skin, at **mucocutaneous junctions** (areas where mucous membranes and skin adjoin, such as the lip margins), and on mucous membranes. Common sites of involvement include the face, ears, and extremities. Generalized **exfoliative dermatitis** (skin disease characterized by inflammation and peeling), ulcers of the footpads, **panniculitis** (inflammation of subcutaneous fat), and lesions resembling those of discoid lupus erythematosus have been noted. On the face, the lesions may be partially symmetrical—an important diagnostic clue. Lymph node enlargement also is commonly observed. The disease is exacerbated by exposure to light.

The diagnosis is made on the basis of the history, clinical signs, and results of supportive laboratory tests, including the **antinuclear antibody (ANA) test,** which detects autoantibodies directed against DNA. The presence of such autoantibodies is one of the most important diagnostic criteria for SLE in people as well as in dogs. Corticosteroids combined with even more potent immunosuppressive medications represent the cornerstone of treatment. The prognosis is guarded to fair. (*See* Chapter 33, "The Immune System and Disorders.")

Pemphigus Foliaceus

Pemphigus foliaceus is an uncommon autoimmune disease characterized by autoantibody production and the subsequent development of vesicles and pustules in the superficial layers of the skin. The lesions are bilaterally symmetrical and tend to develop in waves; animals may progress rapidly from the total absence of disease signs to the sudden appearance of dozens of pustules, which quickly progress to form thick, adherent crusts with marked exfoliation (peeling). These exfoliative crusts represent a hallmark lesion of pemphigus foliaceus. The top of the muzzle and nose, ears, skin around the eyes, and the footpads are the most common sites of lesions.

Pemphigus foliaceus is seen most often in middle-aged dogs. Bearded Collies, Akitas, Chow Chows, Newfoundlands, Schipperkes and Doberman Pinschers are genetically predisposed to development of the disease. In the Chow

Chow and Akita breeds, facial lesions tend to predominate.

Diagnosis is based on the history and clinical signs, skin biopsy and immunologic testing. Immunosuppressive drug therapy (corticosteroids or other, more potent medications) is the mainstay of treatment. The prognosis is guarded.

Pemphigus Vulgaris

Pemphigus vulgaris is a very rare autoimmune disease characterized by the development of vesicles in the skin. The fragile, irregularly shaped, fluid-filled vesicles tend to develop in small groups. Their dissolution produces erosions that are substantially larger than the original vesicles themselves. Secondary bacterial infection of the lesions results in widespread ulceration.

The most common sites of involvement include the mouth and mucocutaneous junctions of the lips, eyelids, nostrils, anus, prepuce and vulva. At least 90% of affected animals exhibit mouth lesions; indeed, oral ulceration is often the initial clinical sign. The appearance of coalescing ulcers on the tongue, palate and gums should heighten suspicion that the underlying problem may be pemphigus vulgaris. Involvement of the lips usually accompanies extensive oral disease. A thick, ropy, odorous saliva may drip from the mouth. Affected animals may exhibit constitutional signs, including inappetence and depression.

Diagnosis of pemphigus vulgaris is based on the history, clinical signs, skin biopsy and immunologic testing. Immunosuppressive drug therapy (corticosteroids or other, more potent medications) is the primary means of treatment. The outlook for recovery is poor.

Bullous Pemphigoid

Bullous pemphigoid is a very rare autoimmune disease characterized by the production of autoantibodies and the development of vesicles and bullae beneath the epidermis. Because of their location, the vesicles are more often found intact than in some of the other **vesicular** (blister-forming) skin diseases of autoimmune origin. Bullous pemphigoid may be more common in older dogs. Doberman Pinschers and possibly Dachshunds may have an increased risk of developing the disease.

Affected dogs exhibit swollen, distended vesicles that develop rapidly and then rupture, producing the widespread ulceration that is a hallmark of the disease. Generally, the ulcers do not coalesce, remaining essentially the same size as their predecessor vesicles. Secondary bacterial infection and scarring may both occur as complications. Most affected dogs have lesions in and around the mouth and around the eyes; however, lesions almost always are present at other locations as well, including the armpits and groin. Both acute and chronic forms of the disease have been recognized. Dogs severely affected with the acute form may exhibit constitutional signs (fever, inappetence, lethargy, depression).

Diagnosis is based on the history, clinical signs, skin biopsy and immunologic testing. Immunosuppressive drug therapy (corticosteroids or other, more potent medications) is the primary means of treatment. The outlook for recovery, as with pemphigus vulgaris, is poor.

OTHER IMMUNE-MEDIATED SKIN DISEASES

Erythema Multiforme

Erythema multiforme is an uncommon skin reaction with a proposed immunologic basis. The process of cell destruction underlying erythema multiforme occurs when affected cells initiate an apparent "self-destruct" mechanism, probably under the command of immunologic or other factors. Cases in small animals are usually associated with a drug hypersensitivity, with tumors and infections less commonly implicated.

The onset usually is acute, with reddened macules and papules developing rapidly. The early lesions may resemble hives (urticaria). Circular, crusting "target" lesions with an area of central clearing may develop during some stages of the syndrome. Lesions are located most commonly on the trunk and in the groin. Other sites include the mucocutaneous junctions, mouth, ears and armpits. Pain or pruritus may accompany the lesions.

Diagnosis is based on the history, clinical

signs and skin biopsy. Therapy is contingent on the cause. If the disease can be linked to a drug hypersensitivity reaction, the offending medication should be withdrawn. Mild cases tend to resolve spontaneously in a few weeks to a few months. In severe cases, systemic anti-inflammatory medication (corticosteroids) may be necessary.

Toxic Epidermal Necrolysis

Toxic epidermal necrolysis is a rare, severe, life-threatening, ulcerative disorder of the mouth and skin with an apparent immunologic basis. Drug hypersensitivity is the most common underlying cause, although tumors and infections also can cause this syndrome.

Affected dogs usually exhibit an acute onset of fever, inappetence, depression and progressive erythema. The skin becomes tender to the touch. **Necrolysis** (separation or peeling of tissue caused by cell death) results in ulceration as the dead overlying skin layer is shed, peeling off in translucent sheets resembling moist tissue paper. Such peeling may result simply from the dog's being handled. The face, mucocutaneous junctions, and footpads are most commonly affected. Inner body structures such as the pharynx, esophagus, trachea and bronchi may also become involved. The occurrence in some cases of a bloody diarrhea suggests that the intestinal tract also may be a target.

Diagnosis is based on the history, clinical features and skin biopsy. Therapeutic measures are contingent on identifying the underlying cause. If the disease can be linked to a drug hypersensitivity reaction, the offending medication should be withdrawn. Immunosuppressive drug therapy may also be required. Secondary bacterial infection of the lesions may complicate therapy. The prognosis for recovery is poor; the mortality rate is usually high.

Canine Familial Dermatomyositis

Canine familial dermatomyositis is an inherited inflammatory disease of muscle and skin. The cause is unknown. The disease occurs almost exclusively in Shetland Sheepdogs and Collies and their related crossbreeds.

Severely affected dogs experience cyclic recurrences over their lifetime. A transient erythema, progressing to crusted erosions and ulcers, may develop early in the course of the disease (usually by 6 months of age). Bony prominences, especially on the muzzle and around the eyes and ears, are favored areas for the development of initial lesions. As the disease progresses, similar lesions appear on the tips of the ears, nail folds, tip of the tail, and over bony prominences of the extremities and other pressure points. Scarring is a feature of severe, chronic lesions.

Muscle involvement is often subtle in nature, and may be limited to atrophy of certain facial muscles, with subsequent difficulties in chewing and swallowing. Severely affected dogs exhibit stunted growth, **megaesophagus** (enlargement of the esophagus, resulting in chronic regurgitation), lameness and widespread muscle atrophy. **Infertility** (diminished ability to produce offspring) may be an additional feature of severe cases.

Diagnosis is based on the history, clinical features, skin and muscle biopsies, and **electromyography (EMG)** (examination of the electrical activity of muscles and associated nerves). Therapy is purely supportive in nature. Affected animals should not be bred, in order to prevent propagation of the underlying heritable trait.

HORMONAL AND METABOLIC SKIN DISEASES

Hypothyroidism

Hypothyroidism is the most common hormonal disease of dogs and results from a deficiency of thyroid hormone. Thyroid hormone (composed of **thyroxine [T4] and triiodothyronine [T3]**) is necessary for the normal functioning of all cells and tissues. Most cases of hypothyroidism in dogs are the result of either an immune-mediated process (**lymphocytic thyroiditis**) or thyroid **atrophy** (shrinking or wasting) of unknown cause.

Affected dogs are often lethargic, mentally dull, exercise-intolerant and overweight. Other common clinical signs include symmetrical alopecia on the trunk and tail, poor coat quality, a change in coat color, and hyperpigmentation and lichenification of affected skin. Retarded regrowth of hair after clipping may be noted. Secondary seborrhea and pyoderma also are commonly observed.

Many breeds have an apparent increased risk for the development of hypothyroidism (*see* TABLE 1 IN CHAPTER 32, "THE ENDOCRINE SYSTEM AND METABOLIC DISORDERS"). However, hypothyroidism may be seen in any breed. Most affected dogs are between 2 and 6 years of age, but dogs of any age may be affected. Hypothyroidism is treated with a synthetic thyroid hormone supplement, usually given orally twice a day. Supplementation must be provided for the lifetime of the patient. The prognosis for recovery is excellent. (*See* CHAPTER 32, "THE ENDOCRINE SYSTEM AND METABOLIC DISORDERS.")

Hyperadrenocorticism (Cushing's Disease, Cushing's Syndrome)

This is a relatively common hormonal disease of dogs. It results primarily from overproduction of steroid hormones, most notably cortisol, by the adrenal glands. This may be caused by:

- adrenocortical hyperplasia (overgrowth due to an abnormal increase in the number of cells in the **cortex,** or outer layer, of the adrenal glands) secondary to excessive stimulation by the brain's pituitary gland
- a functional tumor of the adrenal cortex

A similar syndrome can also result from overzealous or chronic administration of cortisol-containing medications, such as certain skin cremes, eyedrops or ear medications.

Common nondermatologic signs of hyperadrenocorticism include increased water consumption and urination (**polydipsia** and **polyuria**), excessive eating (**polyphagia**), muscle weakness, malaise, **hepatomegaly** (enlargement of the liver), and neurologic abnormalities. Dermatologic signs can include:

- symmetrical alopecia involving primarily the trunk
- thinning and decreased elasticity of the skin
- aberrations in pigmentation (changes in coat color, hyperpigmentation or depigmentation of the skin)
- scaling, comedones and **calcinosis cutis** (calcium deposits in the skin, producing nodular irregularities)
- bleeding abnormalities (small skin hemorrhages, **hematomas** [localized pockets of collected blood])
- delayed wound healing

The alopecia often commences over bony prominences and other areas of friction (i.e., beneath a collar). The paper-thin, inelastic skin allows the subcutaneous blood vessels beneath to show through. Comedones may be especially prominent around the nipples and genital region. Secondary pyoderma, particularly impetigo, commonly results from the immune suppression induced by corticosteroid overproduction or oversupplementation.

For additional information on clinical signs, diagnosis and treatment *see* CHAPTER 32, "THE ENDOCRINE SYSTEM AND METABOLIC DISORDERS."

Sertoli Cell Tumor

The **Sertoli cells** within the testicular tubules are important for nurture and development of **spermatozoa** (sperm; the mature germ cells of the male). Functional Sertoli cell tumors leading to **hyperestrogenism** (excessive production of the female sex hormone **estrogen**) and **feminization** (development of female sex characteristics) are the cause of an uncommon canine disease with skin manifestations. The severity of the clinical signs often can be correlated with tumor size and duration. **Metastasis** (tumor spread) is seen occasionally. Sertoli cell tumors usually develop in conjunction with **cryptorchidism,** a developmental defect wherein one or both of the testicles does not descend into the scrotum.

Affected dogs initially exhibit symmetrical alopecia or a coat-color change on the flanks. The area of involvement then expands to include the groin, abdomen, chest and neck. Affected hairs are dry, brittle and easily **epilated** (pulled out by the roots). In more advanced cases, spotty hyperpigmentation on the neck or more diffuse hyperpigmentation in the areas of hair loss may be seen. Lichenification may be an accompanying feature. Feminizing signs, including **gynecomastia** (overdevelopment of the male mammary glands), a pendulous **prepuce** (fold of skin covering the penis), and attraction to other male dogs commonly occur.

Boxers, Shetland Sheepdogs, Pekingese, Weimaraners and Cairn Terriers are predisposed to the development of Sertoli cell tumors, with middle-aged or older dogs being affected most often. Treatment involves surgical removal of the testes (**castration**). Because most Sertoli cell tumors are benign, the prognosis for recovery is good. (*See* CHAPTER 14, "REPRODUCTIVE DISORDERS.")

Growth Hormone/Castration-Responsive Dermatosis

This is an uncommon canine hormonal disorder of unknown cause. It is characterized by symmetrical hair loss and hyperpigmentation. Strong breed predilections (Chow Chows, Pomeranians, Keeshonds, Samoyeds, Toy and Miniature Poodles, and related crossbreeds) suggest a heritable basis, although this has not been proven.

The syndrome occurs primarily in male dogs. Clinically, signs usually first develop between 9 months and 2 years of age, near the onset of puberty. However, it has been common to affect dogs as old as 12 years at initial onset. Recent studies suggest that the syndrome, at least in Pomeranians, may be caused by abnormal hormone production by the adrenal glands, resulting in adrenal **hyperprogestinism** (excessive production of the hormone **progesterone**) and **hyperandrogenism** (excessive secretion of male sex hormones).

Affected dogs exhibit symmetrical alopecia that often originates in frictional areas on the neck (i.e., under a collar), on the thighs, or in the groin and genital regions. Occasionally a sparse, woolly coat may remain. Retarded regrowth of hair after clipping may be noted even before the alopecia is evident. The syndrome progresses slowly to involve the entire chest, neck, upper portions of the limbs and tail, and less commonly the ears. The head, feet and tip of the tail are usually spared. Islands of

apparently normal haircoat and underlying skin occasionally may be present on the trunk.

Hormonal function tests, serum biochemical profiles, history, clinical course of the hair loss, and skin biopsy may be helpful in diagnosis. A definitive diagnosis sometimes is made only by observing the patient's response to therapy (i.e., treatment with synthetic human growth hormone). However, human growth hormone is expensive and may be difficult to obtain, and there may be side effects. This disease is purely cosmetic; affected dogs are healthy in every other respect. Consequently, therapy usually is not required. In intact male dogs, however, castration may exert a beneficial effect. (*See* CHAPTER 32, "THE ENDOCRINE SYSTEM AND METABOLIC DISORDERS".)

SCALING SKIN DISEASES

Seborrhea (Keratinization Disorders)

"Seborrhea" is a term that has been used to describe clinical signs of excessive scaling, crusting and greasiness. The terms **seborrhea sicca** and **seborrhea oleosa** are used to delineate the dry, waxy form and the oily form of seborrhea, respectively. Seborrhea has connotations both of specific keratinization disorders (*see* below), as well as of the scaling and greasiness associated with a number of unrelated skin diseases such as hypothyroidism, demodicosis, canine scabies and flea allergy dermatitis.

The term **primary seborrhea** is used in a narrower sense in reference to inherited keratinization disorders occurring in specific breeds of dogs. Keratinization, as described earlier in this chapter, is the series of genetically programmed events by which keratinocytes, the skin cells that manufacture keratin, proceed through an orderly series of developmental stages to produce the outermost layers of the epidermis. Defects in this complicated process can lead to any of several keratinization disorders, including seborrhea sicca and seborrhea oleosa. **Seborrheic dermatitis** represents an additional disorder characterized by severely inflamed lesions of primary seborrhea (*see* below).

Primary seborrhea. Clinical signs include scaling, crusting, dryness, waxiness and greasiness of the skin and haircoat. A waxy **otitis externa** (inflammation of the outer ear) often is an accompanying feature, while a rancid odor is a consistent finding in the greasy forms of primary seborrhea. Erythema and hair loss may be evident in varying degrees as well. The lesions are located most commonly on the trunk, while some locally severe lesions may be found on the ears. Secondary bacterial infections also occur. Local or generalized enlargement of lymph nodes may be present in the more severe cases.

Primary seborrhea occurs usually in adult dogs. Breeds affected by primary seborrhea include Cocker and Springer Spaniels, Basset Hounds, Golden Retrievers and Chinese Shar-Peis (all usually affected with seborrhea oleosa), as well as Doberman Pinschers, Irish Setters, and German Shepherd Dogs (all usually affected with seborrhea sicca).

Diagnosis is based on the history, clinical features, knowledge of breed predilections and skin biopsy. Treatment involves use of antiseborrheic shampoos and medications aimed at altering the pattern of keratinization.

Seborrheic dermatitis. This term has been used to describe visually distinctive lesions seen in some dogs with primary seborrhea. These lesions usually occur in dogs with the greasy, more odoriferous form of seborrhea (seborrhea oleosa). Locally severe areas of abnormal keratinization may encourage inflammation, possibly because of self-trauma resulting from pruritus associated with the lesions. Alternatively, secondary bacterial infections may play an important role. Alterations of the fatty surface film of the skin, with overgrowth of bacteria, may contribute to the clinical signs of seborrheic dermatitis.

Seborrheic dermatitis usually is seen in dogs with generalized seborrhea. Reddened, circular plaques are characteristic. Adherent greasy to waxlike debris frequently mats the surrounding hair. Hair loss, thickening of the skin, and hyperpigmentation may be evident in older lesions. Lesions are located primarily on the trunk, particularly on the lower portion of the chest. Overt pyoderma may also be evident. The degree of pruritus is variable.

Adult dogs are affected most often. The breed predilections parallel those for seborrhea oleosa (*see* above). Seborrheic dermatitis is seen most commonly, and in its most severe form, in Cocker Spaniels. Diagnostic and treatment measures are similar to those for primary seborrhea (*see* above).

Schnauzer Comedo Syndrome

This is a relatively common, usually **asymptomatic** (without clinical signs), skin disease seen exclusively in Miniature Schnauzers and related crossbreeds. This highly specific breed predilection is a likely indicator of heritability of the disorder. The syndrome may be caused by abnormalities in hair follicle development.

Substantial variation in character and severity of the lesions is evident among individual dogs. The lesions may be **palpable** (detectable by touch or feeling) rather than visually distinctive. Occasionally, the principal abnormality is a band of darkly colored or diffusely erect hair along the back. Crusted papules, small nodules, or comedones are seen characteristically in association with hair follicles. The comedones may be very small and require the use of a magnifying lens for proper identification. The more obvious comedones are characterized by inflamed, dilated hair follicles containing dark debris. The hair usually is lost from severely affected follicles. Scaling and erythema are variable. Occasionally, a secondary bacterial **folliculitis** (inflammation of hair follicles) accompanied by reddening and scarring is observed. Lesions occur along the back from the shoulders to the hips, usually within a few centimeters of the spine.

Schnauzer comedo syndrome is a visually distinctive disease. The diagnosis is made on the basis of the history, clinical features, knowledge of the breed predilection, and possibly skin biopsy. Therapy involves the use of antiseborrheic shampoos, together with antibiotics if secondary bacterial infection is present.

Hyperplastic Dermatosis of the West Highland White Terrier (Westie Seborrhea)

This is an uncommon, severe, chronic skin disease with clinical features similar to primary seborrhea and seborrheic dermatitis (*see* above). The restrictions to West Highland White Terriers, coupled with evidence of involvement of related dogs, indicates that the disease is probably hereditary. The cause is unknown; however, an association with a generalized yeast infection has been made by some observers.

This syndrome may be complicated by the frequent coexistence in West Highland White Terriers of allergic skin diseases such as flea allergy dermatitis, atopy and food allergy. Thus, differentiating this syndrome from chronic allergic skin diseases may be difficult, since the severely affected dog is often the end product of several coexistent skin conditions.

The age of onset for the disorder extends from less than a year of age to middle age. Clinical signs commonly commence at less than a year of age in the more severely affected patients. Affected dogs exhibit generalized erythema with hair loss, lichenification and hyperpigmentation. Thickened skin folds develop on the legs and occasionally on the trunk. The skin is often malodorous and may be coated with an adherent, brownish gray, greasy debris. Crusting may also be present. Pruritus and accompanying self-trauma vary in intensity, but are noted frequently. Secondary bacterial infections are common, particularly in the thickened folds of skin. Owners report that lesions often begin on the trunk and rapidly spread over the body. In advanced cases, the lesions may involve virtually all of the haired body surfaces. Local or generalized enlargement of lymph nodes is a consistent clinical feature.

Diagnosis is based on the history, presenting clinical signs, knowledge of the breed predilection, and supportive laboratory tests, including biopsy. Until a definitive cause is uncovered, treatment remains purely supportive in nature. In other words, secondary effects are alleviated but the underlying causes of the disease cannot be addressed. Affected dogs should not be bred.

Sebaceous Adenitis

Sebaceous adenitis (sebaceous gland inflammation) is an uncommon skin disease whose cause remains unknown, although both genetic and autoimmune origins have been proposed. Plugging of hair follicles and scaling probably occur as complications of reduced sebum flow resulting from sebaceous gland inflammation and destruction. Abnormalities of hair follicle maturation may be seen. It is unclear whether a causal relationship exists between the loss of sebaceous glands and abnormal follicular maturation, or if these are simply both features of a common disease process.

Young adult dogs are most often affected. The clinical signs, distribution, and severity of the disease vary substantially among different breeds. Adherent scale is the most common clinical sign. Coat quality diminishes as the disease progresses, leaving behind dull, dry, brittle and broken hairs. In Standard Poodles, adherent scales on the muzzle may be the earliest visible sign. This scaly debris coats affected hairs. Lesions similar to those seen in Standard Poodles may be seen in Samoyeds.

In Akitas the lesions are similar to those of Standard Poodles, but hair loss is more severe. Secondary bacterial infection of affected hair follicles is a prominent feature. Fever, malaise and weight loss occasionally may occur as well. A markedly different clinical presentation has been noted in Vizslas and occasionally in other short-coated breeds. In these dogs, localized, coalescing nodular lesions and plaques with hair loss and adherent scale are seen predominantly on the trunk.

Diagnosis is made on the basis of the history, clinical features and skin biopsy. Treatment is almost purely symptomatic, involving the use of antiseborrheic shampoos. Experimental therapies are currently under investigation. Affected dogs should not be used for breeding.

Nutritional Skin Diseases
See Chapter 10, "Diseases of Dietary Origin."

Physicochemical Skin Diseases

Foreign-Body Reactions
Foreign-body reactions occur commonly in dogs. Lesions are characterized by penetration of the skin by a variety of foreign bodies, many of them of plant origin. Penetrating objects can include

grass awns, cactus spines, porcupine quills and fiberglass fibers. One particular grass awn, the **foxtail,** is the most common penetrating foreign body affecting dogs in North America.

Distinctive sharp structures on the surface of the foxtail pierce the skin or a body orifice after first being retained in the haircoat of the animal. Barbs on the awn prevent the foxtail from backing out of the wound, while forward motion is encouraged by the muscular movements of the dog. The webs of skin between the toes are the most common sites for lesions caused by grass awns, although puncture wounds may be found in almost any location. Multiple lesions are the rule rather than the exception. Secondary bacterial infection along the track of the foxtail through the tissues frequently occurs. Deep penetration of the chest or abdominal cavities by a migrating foxtail and its passenger bacteria can result in severe, life-threatening illness. (*See* CHAPTER 35, "BACTERIAL DISEASES.")

Young hunting and working breed dogs are at greater risk, owing to a greater likelihood of exposure. Diagnosis is based on the history, clinical features, visualization of the foreign body, and perhaps skin biopsy. Treatment involves removal of the foreign body, with antibiotic therapy if required.

Irritant Contact Dermatitis

Irritant contact dermatitis is an uncommon inflammatory skin disease caused by direct contact with an irritating concentration of an offending substance. Immune-mediated mechanisms are not involved; the irritant damages the skin by a direct toxic effect. Irritants include corrosive substances such as strong acids and alkalis, as well as less potent materials such as soaps, detergents, solvents and various other chemicals. Excessive moisture, which retards the normal barrier function of the skin and increases the effective contact area by allowing diffusion of the irritant, is a predisposing factor for irritant-induced skin damage. Preexisting inflammatory skin diseases also will increase susceptibility to irritant contact dermatitis.

Clinical signs and affected sites are virtually identical to those for allergic contact dermatitis (*see* above). However, pain may be more evi-

dent, and pruritus less common, in irritant contact dermatitis. Irritant contact dermatitis is less likely to become chronic owing to the fact that identification and elimination of the irritant can be accomplished more readily.

Diagnosis is based on the history, clinical features and identification of the offending substance. Limiting access to the irritant will effectively cure the problem.

Thermal and Chemical Burns

Thermal and chemical burns are relatively common injuries in dogs. Burns are categorized as either partial-thickness or full-thickness burns, based on their depth of penetration into the skin. Thermal burns are seen more frequently than chemical burns and often cause deeper, more severe injuries. Partial-thickness thermal and chemical burns may be indistinguishable unless residue of the chemical agent is present on the haircoat or underlying skin. Boiling water, electric heating pads, drying cages and fires are the most common causes of thermal burns in dogs. Because lesions may be hidden by the haircoat, burns may be more obvious in nonhaired areas. Progression of the burn lesion beyond the initial area of damage can occur for several days after the burn is first noted.

Pain may be the initial presenting complaint, while a well-demarcated reddening of the skin may represent the earliest visible clinical sign. Resultant erosion and ulceration will vary depending on the depth of injury. In full-thickness burns, the damaged skin becomes firm and dry and may eventually slough. Secondary bacterial infection is a common complication of burn injuries; spread of the infection can result in life-threatening **sepsis** (widespread bacterial infection of the blood and tissues).

For information on the treatment of burns, *see* CHAPTER 42, "HOME EMERGENCY CARE," and CHAPTER 43, "PROCEDURES FOR LIFE-THREATENING EMERGENCIES."

INHERITED SKIN DISEASES

Cutaneous Asthenia (Ehlers-Danlos Syndrome)

"Cutaneous asthenia" is a term used to group multiple rare, heritable, congenital defects of connective tissue. Clinically affected dogs exhibit hyperextensible and fragile skin. In people, many distinct subgroups of cutaneous asthenia (usually termed Ehlers-Danlos syndrome in human medicine) have been documented, and multiple underlying biochemical defects have been delineated. Variability in the clinical signs of cutaneous asthenia suggests that multiple specific collagen defects may exist in dogs as well.

Hyperextensibility and decreased tensile strength of the skin are this ailment's most common features. Hyperextensibility is manifested clinically by a loose attachment of the skin to subcutaneous tissues. The skin is of normal thickness, but may be stretched well beyond what is possible in normal dogs. The decreased tensile strength can lead to lacerations following minor trauma. The large, gaping wounds of cutaneous asthenia have been compared descriptively to "fish mouths." Bleeding is surprisingly minimal. The wounds heal rapidly, although the resultant scars are thin and lack normal tensile strength. Hyperextensibility of the joints has been seen only rarely in dogs.

Signs of cutaneous asthenia generally are noted shortly after birth. The disease has been observed in Boxers, Dachshunds, English Springer Spaniels, Greyhounds, Beagles, Saint Bernards, and mixed-breed dogs.

Diagnosis is based on history, clinical features and skin biopsy. Therapy involves avoidance of trauma in order to minimize damage to the patient's excessively fragile skin. Open wounds should be **sutured** (stitched together) as soon as possible after their appearance. Dogs only mildly affected can lead a fairly normal life. As with all inherited skin diseases, affected dogs should not be bred.

Congenital Hypotrichosis

This is a rare disease characterized by varying degrees of baldness since birth. Affected animals are born with a diminished number of hair follicles. Congenital hypotrichosis may be the only abnormality noted or may be seen in conjunction with other defects such as abnormal teeth or diminished tear production.

Affected dogs lack hair in well-defined areas.

Baldness may vary from partial to complete. The head, ears, trunk and tail are most frequently affected. The exposed skin initially appears normal in the hairless areas, but hyperpigmentation and scaling may be noted subsequently.

Congenital hypotrichosis has been reported in the Poodle, Basset Hound, Rottweiler, Beagle, Labrador Retriever and Bichon Frise breeds. Most reports of this syndrome have been in male dogs; inheritance of the trait is believed to be sex-linked.

Diagnosis is based on the history, clinical features and skin biopsy. There is no effective therapy. Affected animals should not be bred in order to avoid propagating the defect.

Color-Dilution Alopecia (Blue Dog Disease)

Color-dilution alopecia is an uncommon hereditary skin disease seen in color-diluted dogs. Clinically affected dogs exhibit hair loss and poor coat quality. A color-dilution gene may be directly responsible for producing the skin disease. Alternatively, the dilution gene may be linked to another gene coding for the underlying hair follicle abnormalities. Attempts to breed for color dilution without the associated skin disease have not been successful.

Affected dogs gradually develop a dry, dull, brittle, poor-quality coat. Hair shafts fragment and hair regrowth is retarded, resulting in "moth-eaten" hair loss. Hair loss usually is most severe on the trunk. Hyperpigmentation of the skin may also occur. The skin disease is limited to the color-diluted (usually blue) hairs; the tan points are spared. Secondary pyoderma is a common complication in severely affected dogs. The syndrome varies markedly in severity. Dogs with a lighter coat color are more severely affected. Hair loss on the trunk of lighter-colored dogs may be almost complete by the age of 6 years.

The disease occurs most often in the blue Doberman Pinscher, hence the original name, *blue Doberman syndrome*. It also is seen in other breeds with blue color dilution, including Dachshunds, Great Danes, Whippets, Italian Greyhounds, Chow Chows, Standard Poodles, Yorkshire Terriers, Miniature Pinschers, Chihuahuas, Bernese Mountain Dogs, Shetland

Sheepdogs and Schipperkes. Color-dilution alopecia has also been reported in the fawn Doberman Pinscher, fawn Irish Setter and red Doberman Pinscher. Most affected dogs develop signs of disease between 4 months and 3 years of age.

Diagnosis is based on the history, clinical features and skin biopsy. There is no effective therapy, except for treatment of secondary bacterial infections (antibiotics). Affected animals should not be bred in order to avoid propagating the trait. Unfortunately, since the disease often develops after 3 years of age, the animals may have already been used for breeding.

Acquired Pattern Alopecia
(Pattern Baldness)

This is a relatively common skin disease characterized by a gradual, somewhat symmetrical loss of hair on the ears and elsewhere. The striking breed predilection for Dachshunds, coupled with similarities to pattern baldness in human beings, suggests an underlying genetic basis for the disorder.

Affected dogs exhibit a slowly progressive thinning of the haircoat. Hyperpigmentation may be seen in chronic cases. The ears are affected most often, but loss of hair may also be noted behind the ears, on the neck, chest, abdomen and thighs, and around the anus.

Although acquired pattern alopecia occurs primarily in Dachshunds, it has also been seen in Boston Terriers, Chihuahuas, Whippets and Italian Greyhounds. The syndrome is uncommon in dogs less than a year of age.

Diagnosis is based on the history, clinical features, knowledge of breed predilections, and skin biopsy. As in human beings with pattern baldness, there is as yet no truly effective medical therapy to restore normal hair follicular function.

Canine Follicular Dysplasia

Canine follicular dysplasia is an uncommon disease that produces hair loss and alterations in coat quality. Breed specificities of the condition and information obtained from breeders suggest an inherited cause.

Clinical signs vary with the breed affected.

Changes in coat quality and color, loss of guard hairs, or complete hair loss may be seen. Lesions may be generalized, or localized in a somewhat symmetrical fashion. The face and lower parts of the extremities tend to be spared. Although transient partial hair regrowth may be noted occasionally, the disease usually progresses. Additional clinical findings are outlined below for the individual breeds affected.

Siberian Husky. Affected Siberian Huskies lose guard hairs, and a color change occurs in the undercoat hairs to a reddish brown or "rusty" color. Secondary hairs are of poor quality and appear "woolly." More complete hair loss is seen on pressure points and under collars. This syndrome may also occur in Alaskan Malamutes.

Irish Water Spaniel, Portuguese Water Dog and Curly-Coated Retriever. Similar coat problems have been seen in these breeds. Many guard hairs are lost, and the undercoat hair color changes to a dull, lighter shade. Occasionally, abnormally long guard hairs may be seen.

Airedale. Affected Airedales develop a saddle-like configuration of total or almost total hair loss. Skin in the affected areas is hyperpigmented. Islands of normal hair may remain. Cyclical, nonseasonal, partial hair regrowth has been seen.

Boxer, Miniature Schnauzer, English Bulldog and French Bulldog. A localized, partially symmetrical hair loss occurs predominantly on both sides of the trunk. This syndrome is observed most often in Boxers. All or almost all hairs are lost in patches. Partial regrowth of poor-quality hairs may occur in a cyclical fashion.

Follicular dysplasia has also been seen in other breeds, including German Shorthaired Pointers, German Wirehaired Pointers and Chesapeake Bay Retrievers. The age of onset varies considerably; however, the syndrome most commonly begins at less than 3 years of age.

Diagnosis is based on the history, clinical features, knowledge of breed predilections, rule-out of hormonal skin diseases, and skin biopsy. There is no effective therapy. Affected animals should not be bred in order to avoid propagating the defect(s).

Neoplastic Skin Diseases

Tumors (**neoplasms**) of the canine skin occur in a variety of types, both benign and malignant. Basal cell tumors, lipomas, squamous cell carcinomas, mast cell tumors, lymphosarcomas, and malignant melanomas are a few representative examples. (For further information on canine skin tumors, *see* Chapter 38 "Cancer," and Chapter 33, "The Immune System and Disorders.")

Miscellaneous Skin Diseases

Acral Lick Dermatitis (Lick Granuloma)

Acral lick dermatitis, also known by the older name **lick granuloma,** is a relatively common disease in dogs. It is characterized by chronic licking at an area of skin, usually on the lower part of an extremity, resulting in the development of a solitary, firm, oval plaque, with loss of the overlying hair. A central irregular ulcer is surrounded by hyperpigmentation. Staining of the lesion with saliva may be evident in light-coated dogs. Secondary bacterial infection may develop as a complication.

Boredom is usually incriminated in the generation of an itch-lick cycle leading to development of acral lick dermatitis. Less commonly, it may be initiated by a preexisting irritation in the area (infection, trauma, prior surgical procedure, tumor). The syndrome is seen most frequently in large, active breeds that demand constant attention, such as Labrador Retrievers, German Shepherd Dogs, Doberman Pinschers, Great Danes and Irish Setters. However, acral lick dermatitis can occur in any breed. Adult dogs over 3 years of age are most often affected. Male dogs may be more commonly affected.

Diagnosis is based on the history, clinical features, rule-out of other diseases, and skin biopsy. Interrupting the mental itch-lick routine of boredom for an affected dog may be challenging; many cases of acral lick dermatitis are never cured. Spending a greater amount of time playing with the dog, acquisition of a puppy as a new companion, and avoidance of strict confinement may help in breaking the cycle. Tranquilizers or other antianxiety medications may on occasion provide some benefit, particularly during periods of stress for the dog. Other, newer medications that have shown promise in treating acral lick dermatitis are currently under investigation.

Acanthosis Nigricans of Dachshunds

This is a rare disease of unknown cause that is seen exclusively in Dachshunds. It begins with subtle, symmetrical hyperpigmentation in the armpits. The early lesions then progress slowly to lichenification and hair loss. Greasy, odorous debris accumulates in more severely affected dogs. The abdomen, groin, anal area, chest, neck, forelimbs and hocks may all be involved, with pyoderma as a common complication. The disease usually develops in dogs under 2 years of age.

Diagnosis is based on the history, clinical features, knowledge of the breed predilection, rule-out of other similar diseases, and skin biopsy. There is no specific therapy. Affected animals should not be bred in order to avoid possibly propagating the defect, in the event that there is an underlying heritable basis.

Post-Clipping Alopecia

This is a relatively common syndrome seen after hair clipping and involves an arrest of the normal hair-growth cycle. A marked breed predilection (sled-dog breeds) suggests that there may be an underlying genetic predisposition, although this has not been proven. The responsible mechanism is unknown; it may involve a decrease in the blood supply to the affected hair follicles, resulting from constriction of small vessels in skin no longer insulated by the haircoat. The occurrence of post-clipping alopecia predominantly in sled-dog breeds suggests that such a mechanism could represent an adaptive trait for minimizing heat loss during severe winter weather. Alternatively, the normal skin temperature of the affected breeds may simply be higher because of the insulating properties of their heavy haircoats; loss of the coat may produce a drop in temperature sufficient to affect the local blood supply. The importance of altered blood supply as a possible underlying cause of post-clipping alopecia is highlighted by the observation that hair frequently regrows after biopsy, trauma or vigorous brushing—all actions that serve to increase blood flow to the affected area of skin.

Post-clipping alopecia is seen primarily in Siberian Husky Dogs, Alaskan Malamutes, Samoyeds, Keeshonds and Chow Chows. No age or sex predilections have been noted. Regrowth of hair in an area following close clipping of the area for **venipuncture** (taking a blood sample), surgery, or wound management is delayed. The loss of hair usually is complete, although some guard hairs may regrow. Hair regrowth may not be evident for as long as 6 to 12 months after the initiating event. Newly regrown hair may be of a darker hue in "pointed" haircoat breeds such as Siberian Husky Dogs and Alaskan Malamutes.

Diagnosis is based on the history, clinical features, knowledge of breed predilections, rule-out of other causes of impaired hair regrowth (especially hormonal causes), and skin biopsy. There is no effective treatment, but most affected dogs will regrow hair within a year. Post-clipping alopecia has the potential for occurring anytime a dog belonging to a breed at risk is clipped. Consequently, clipping should be performed only when absolutely necessary!

Vitiligo

Vitiligo is an acquired disorder of pigmentation characterized by progressive, usually well-circumscribed, areas of pigment loss in the skin. It is uncommon in dogs. Marked breed predilections suggest that there may be a heritable component (as there is with vitiligo in human beings). The underlying cause of the disorder remains unclear.

Depigmentation develops gradually on the nose, lips, muzzle and elsewhere on the face. The footpads also may be affected. Whitening of the hair (**leukotrichia**) and depigmentation of the nails may accompany the changes in the skin. In some cases, pigmentation may return to the affected areas; in others, the disease may remain static or adopt a waxing and waning course.

A marked breed predilection for vitiligo exists in Belgian Tervuren dogs. Other breeds at increased risk include Rottweilers, German Shepherd Dogs and Doberman Pinschers. Vitiligo also has been observed in Dachshunds, Collies and Old English Sheepdogs. The disease develops most frequently in dogs less than 3 years of age.

There is no effective therapy. Affected animals should not be bred in order to avoid possible propagation of the trait.

Cysts

Cysts are simple, saclike cavities that develop within the skin and usually contain fluid or a semisolid, cheesy or doughy material. They are most often solitary, well-defined, and firm or fluctuant to the touch. Partial hair loss may be present in the skin overlying the cyst.

Cysts come in several different varieties, including follicular (or epidermoid), dermoid, apocrine and sebaceous duct cysts. *Follicular (epidermoid) cysts,* often erroneously called "sebaceous cysts," are commonly observed in dogs and originate within hair follicles in the dermis. There are no recognized site predispositions for solitary follicular cysts. Occasionally, multiple and recurrent cysts may be observed, suggesting a developmental abnormality. *Dermoid cysts* are rare developmental abnormalities that may occur as single or multiple lesions resembling follicular cysts. They often develop along the back (as in Rhodesian Ridgebacks), but may be found at other sites. *Apocrine cysts* are caused by obstruction of sweat gland ducts. They usually occur singly, but multiple cysts may be present. Apocrine cysts exhibit a characteristic blue tint when viewed through the thin, overlying skin. They develop most often on the head, neck and upper areas of the trunk. *Sebaceous duct cysts* are uncommon lesions involving the ducts leading from sebaceous glands to their associated hair follicles. There are no recognized site predilections.

Therapy consists of surgical removal of the cyst. Attempted manual expulsion of cyst contents using **digital pressure** (pressure applied by the fingers) should be strongly resisted, since rupture of the cyst can result in intense local skin irritation and inflammation.

Actinic Keratoses

These are single or multiple, firm, elevated, plaque- or papule-like lesions that result from excessive exposure to ultraviolet light (sunlight). Actinic keratoses are characterized by deranged epidermal cell growth, producing adherent scale and erythema. In dogs, the lesions are found most often on the lower abdomen and inner surface of the thighs in short-coated, white-haired breeds. A predisposition for development of actinic keratoses exists in Dalmatians, Beagles, Basset Hounds, American Staffordshire Terriers, Whippets and Italian Greyhounds. All of these breeds have lightly pigmented skin and thin haircoats, affording very little solar protection.

Although benign in themselves, actinic keratoses are considered precancerous lesions: they can invade the underlying dermis and transform into a malignancy (**squamous cell carcinoma**). *Actinic keratoses are danger signs of overexposure to the sun.* Affected dogs should receive minimal solar exposure. Sunscreens are beneficial. Therapy of existing lesions consists of surgical excision or cryosurgery (removal by local freezing of tissue). (*See* Chapter 38, "Cancer.")

Nevi

A **nevus** (plural: **nevi**) in its broadest sense can be defined as any stable, well-defined lesion of congenital (present at birth) origin affecting any cellular component of the skin. Nevi are often referred to as *birthmarks*. A number of different types of nevi occur in dogs, including *pigmented epidermal nevus, hair follicle nevus* (also called *follicular hamartoma*), and *sebaceous nevus.* Most of these lesions are rare and benign. Treatment consists of surgical excision.

CHAPTER 23

External Parasites

by Peter J. Ihrke
and Jeffrey E. Barlough

A parasite is an organism that lives in or on another organism, from which it draws nourishment and for which it provides no appreciable benefits in return. Parasites come in all shapes and sizes, from microscopic protozoa that are a fraction of a millimeter in diameter, to giant tapeworms whose length can be measured in feet. Parasites can be distinguished from other organisms residing in or on a host—such as the population of bacteria and other microbes normally found within the large intestine—by the fact that parasites, for the most part, are ultimately detrimental to the health of the host.

For our purposes parasites can be classified into either of two very broad groups: endoparasites and **ectoparasites.** Endoparasites, or internal parasites, are found inside the host, chiefly in the gastrointestinal tract, liver and lungs. Ectoparasites, or external parasites, live instead on or within the skin of the host. It is this latter group of organisms—primarily fleas, ticks, mites and lice—that forms the subject of the present chapter.

Fleas and Flea Allergy Dermatitis

FLEAS

Fleas are wingless, brown or black, bloodsucking insects with flattened bodies and three pairs of powerful, jointed legs. There are nearly 2000 recognized species of fleas. Some species are host-specific in their feeding habits (i.e., each host has its own species of flea), while others have preferred hosts but are less specific. The few flea species of importance in domestic animals are primarily host-preferred and host-non-specific; that is, they will feed on more than one species of animal.

The most common flea found on dogs and cats is *Ctenocephalides felis,* also known as the *cat flea.* This is an aggressive, tenacious flea that represents an important and sometimes intractable parasite problem in many parts of the world. Fleas found on human beings include *Pulex irritans* and *Pulex simulans,* both of which are especially common in the southeastern United States, where they are also a component of the canine flea population. *Ctenoce-*

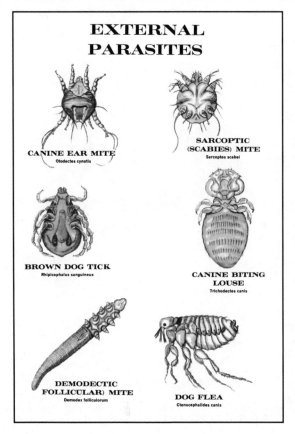

EXTERNAL PARASITES

CANINE EAR MITE
Otodectes cynotis

SARCOPTIC (SCABIES) MITE
Sarcoptes scabei

BROWN DOG TICK
Rhipicephalus sanguineus

CANINE BITING LOUSE
Trichodectes canis

DEMODECTIC FOLLICULAR) MITE
Demodex folliculorum

DOG FLEA
Ctenocephalides canis

phalides canis, the *dog flea,* is a less common variety. Another species, *Echidnophaga gallinacea,* the *sticktight flea* of poultry, occasionally feeds on dogs and cats.

While the adult cat flea spends most of its time on a dog or cat, the majority of the flea life cycle is spent *off* the host, that is, in the environment. The length of the life cycle ranges from 16 days to 21 months, depending upon environmental conditions, particularly temperature and humidity. Ideal temperatures for fleas to thrive range from 65°F to 80°F, ideal humidities from 75–85%. Flea **larvae** (immature forms) and adults do not survive well in extreme temperatures. Relative humidity below 50% and greater than 92% for any considerable time will kill flea larvae. Dog and cat fleas also do not thrive at altitudes above 5000 feet in elevation.

Fleas develop by a process of metamorphosis, in which they undergo a series of transformations through different developmental stages, or instars. Eggs (0.5 to 2 mm in length, white, oval) are laid by the female on the host dog or cat, but readily fall off and thereby are deposited in the environment. Adult female fleas at peak performance can lay 30 to 50 eggs a day, depending on temperature, humidity and other conditions. A female flea thus may lay hundreds of eggs in her lifetime. After an incubation period of 2 to 12 days (2 to 4 days under optimal conditions), the eggs hatch and release larvae. The larvae are 1 to 2 mm in length, white, legless, and maggotlike. They feed on organic matter, including dried blood and flea fecal material. Under optimal conditions the larvae undergo a series of molts (usually three) in 1 to 2 weeks. The third larval stage then spins a thin cocoon and within a few days transforms into a *pupa* inside the cocoon. The adult flea, the final metamorphic stage, may emerge from the cocoon days or months later, depending upon environmental conditions and the presence or absence of local stimulatory vibrations.

Flea eggs, larvae and pupae are usually deposited in areas where the parasitized dog or cat spends most of its time. It has been estimated that for every adult flea on an animal there are 100 to 200 immature fleas in various other stages of the flea life cycle in the local environment.

Under ideal conditions, the life span of an adult flea is approximately 6 to 12 months. Fleas may survive for months without feeding if environmental conditions are optimal. They also may live for weeks to months by feeding on an aberrant host. Depending on the species of flea, some may survive but not reproduce during this time.

Fleas usually feed only once every 1 or 2 days. The adult flea must ingest blood in order to attain sexual maturity. After the ingestion of blood, mating and egg laying occur. The adult male ingests only enough blood for body maintenance and reproduction. The adult female, however, ingests many times the amount of blood necessary in order to produce an adequate supply of blood-enriched fecal matter for the nourishment of the larvae. Fleas are attracted to their hosts by a number of factors including smell, body temperature, carbon dioxide concentration, interruption of light (shadows), and movement toward air currents.

Fleas also serve as intermediate hosts for the common tapeworm of dogs and cats, *Dipylidium caninum*. Dogs frequently acquire tapeworm infections by ingesting fleas carrying one of the immature stages of the worm. (*See* CHAPTER 37, INTERNAL PARASITES.")

FLEA ALLERGY DERMATITIS (FAD)

Flea allergy dermatitis (FAD) is the most common skin disease of animals in the world. It is caused by a hypersensitivity to certain components of flea saliva. Flea saliva is secreted into the skin of the host as the flea feeds. The saliva contains a number of components, including histamine-like substances, enzymes and other proteins, that are believed to be involved in eliciting the hypersensitivity reaction.

The single most telling clinical sign of FAD is **pruritus** (itching) and is most severe on the rear half of the dog. Crusted **papules** (minute, firm, well-demarcated elevations of the skin) usually are found on the lower back, base of the tail, thighs, and **perineum** (region between the thighs, encompassing the anus and genitalia). The severity of the lesions varies markedly. In chronic cases hair loss, **lichenification** (leathery thickening of the outer layer of the skin, usually caused by excessive scratching or rubbing), and **hyperpigmentation** (abnormal darkening of the skin) may be present. Recurrent **pyoderma** (bacterial skin disease characterized by pus formation) may occur as a complication.

FAD develops most often in dogs between 1 and 3 years of age, but may occur at any age. On rare occasions clinical signs may develop in very young dogs (under 6 months of age). In areas of the world experiencing a four-season climate, FAD exhibits a definite seasonality, occurring most commonly in the summer and autumn months. This corresponds in general to the period of greatest flea activity. In areas with milder climates, FAD may occur at any time during the year.

Diagnosis of FAD is based on the history, clinical features (including restriction of the disease process to the rear half of the body), and presence of fleas or "flea dirt" (flea fecal pellets, containing blood) on the dog. Diagnosis may also involve intradermal skin testing (injection of test material into the skin) to confirm an allergic response to flea saliva, and possibly trial therapy. The diagnosis of flea allergy dermatitis by a veterinarian does not require the finding of fleas.

TREATMENT AND CONTROL

Treatment of FAD and of flea infestations in general involves stringent flea control. Major problems in flea control include the fact that fleas are *very* prolific, and that it is only the adult flea that is present on the dog. Eggs, larvae and pupae comprise over 95% of the flea population and are present in the environment, rather than on the animal. Products for use on dogs usually do not kill fleas until the dog has already been bitten, and thus are ineffective for controlling allergy and infestation. Therefore, treatment of the environment is of paramount importance. Fully 95% of flea control involves environmental control. *The local environment (both internal and external), the affected dog, and other dogs or cats that are in contact with the affected dog should be treated simultaneously for fleas.* (FAD is much less common in cats. Unfortunately, cats that go in and out of doors are a common source of flea recontamination, since access to the outside enables them to carry fleas home to reinfest the household environment.)

Commercial flea shampoos are less useful than other types of products because they provide little residual activity once the process of bathing the dog has been accomplished. Pump sprays and rinses (also called dips) are the most effective methods of treatment for use on dogs. Most pump sprays contain either pyrethrins or synthetic pyrethroids as their effective ingredients. Pump sprays are preferred over aerosols for several reasons:

1. The alcohol base in the aerosol can be irritating to dogs
2. Animals often are frightened by the noise of the aerosol spray
3. Pump sprays are more economical

Most rinses contain either organophosphates or synthetic pyrethroids as their effective ingredients. Care should be taken in performing appropriate dilutions. Rinses should be administered outdoors, using a pail and sponge reserved for this purpose only. The person rinsing the dog should wear rubber gloves during the procedure.

Powders have less of an ability to penetrate the external skeleton (*exoskeleton*) of the flea. Flea collars can give owners a false sense of security and are relatively ineffective unless they are used as one small part of a general plan of attack involving treatment of the environment and all in-contact animals. Ultrasonic flea collars and the feeding of brewer's yeast have been shown in published scientific studies to be ineffective in controlling fleas on dogs.

Products containing insect growth-hormone regulators (IGRs), sodium polyborate, or products protected by microencapsulation may offer substantial advantages over the more conventional "bombs" or "foggers" for control of fleas in the environment. The IGRs are particularly advantageous because of their extremely low toxicity for animals and people; usually they are used in conjunction with insecticide spraying of the internal environment.

The key to any successful flea-control program is continuity; that is, *regular and consistent treatment of all animals and of the internal and external environment.* Regular control of the internal environment (i.e., in the house) usually involves thorough vacuuming and spraying with any of several available products for at least 4 to 6 weeks. Local "hot spots" inside the house wherein stages of the flea cycle can be found in abundance include the bedding, rugs and other such materials used by dogs for prolonged periods. In the external environment, fleas can complete their life cycle most effectively in shady, protected spots, such as can be found in garages, beneath bushes or shrubs, or under porches; they do not survive as well in the middle of a sunny lawn. They also require organic debris for optimal breeding efficiency. Areas of the external environment suspected of harboring fleas should first be raked or swept clean of organic debris and then sprayed. As an alternative to these measures, a pest-control company can be contacted to provide thorough treatment of the environment.

Since regional differences occur in the susceptibility of fleas to insecticides, the best source of beneficial products for a particular area of the country is the veterinarian. A veterinarian should always be consulted when devising an overall plan for flea control in an infested household. Animals vary in their susceptibility to side effects seen with flea control. The general health of a dog may be a key feature in resistance to toxicity. Consequently, a general physical examination performed by a veterinarian should precede flea control.

Ticks

Ticks are bloodsucking parasites that, like mites and spiders, are classified as arachnids (i.e., they are not insects). Heavy infestations with ticks can result in severe blood loss and subsequent **anemia** (low red blood cell count). Ticks can also transmit a variety of infectious disease agents, including those causing Rocky Mountain spotted fever, tropical canine pancytopenia, and Lyme borreliosis (*see* CHAPTER 35, "BACTERIAL DISEASES" and APPENDIX B, "ZOONOTIC DISEASES: FROM DOGS TO PEOPLE").

Ticks can be classified anatomically as either **ixodid** ("hard") ticks or **argasid** ("soft") **ticks.** Ixodid ticks are characterized by the presence of a hard protective shield or plate (*scutum*) on the back. The life cycle of ticks includes four successive stages consisting of an egg, a six-legged larva (commonly called a *seed tick*), an eight-legged *nymph,* and an eight-legged adult. Different tick species have different requirements for completing the entire life cycle; that is, they may require one, two, or even three different hosts to reach the adult stage. Most hard ticks are three-host ticks, each stage feeding only once during the cycle. Each tick species has evolved adaptations to survive under different conditions of humidity and temperature. Eggs from some species of tick can survive for 8 weeks or more.

Ticks commonly feeding on dogs include the brown dog tick (*Rhipicephalus sanguineus*) and the American dog tick (*Dermacentor variabilis*). The brown dog tick is widely distributed throughout the world. It is a three-host tick that requires three feedings on dogs to complete its life cycle. As a consequence, brown dog ticks can survive in a household by feeding only on dogs, making them particularly difficult ticks to control in homes and kennels. These ticks can also feed on rabbits, cats, horses and people. By contrast, the larval and nymphal stages of the American dog tick, another three-host tick, must feed on field mice. Dogs become parasitized with the adult stage of this tick when the ticks are transferred to their coats from grass or shrubbery. The American dog tick is found throughout North America, but is most common along the East Coast. The adults can feed also on cattle, horses, wild animals, and people.

Most tick-associated conditions are seen during the spring and summer months, when ticks are most numerous. All animals should be checked for ticks before being allowed indoors. Preventing a tick infestation is far more effective than eliminating one. Ticks are usually found around the head, neck, ears or feet of the dog. They are visually distinctive and thus can be readily recognized. Before removing ticks they should be sprayed with an insecticide that is safe for use on dogs, such as a commercially available flea-and-tick spray. After spraying, the ticks can be removed with forceps or tweezers. The tick's head should be grasped as close to the skin of the dog as possible and the tick slowly and firmly pulled out.

Some of the newer plastic collars designed expressly for tick control may be of benefit for dogs living in heavily tick-infested areas. Recently a new, more effective tick collar has become available that may also prevent transmission of tick-borne diseases such as Lyme borreliosis. The veterinarian should be consulted regarding the efficacy and usefulness of this and other tick-control products.

Mites

Mites are minute organisms that, like ticks and spiders, are classified as *arachnids*. Infestation of an animal by mites is referred to by the general term **acariasis.** There are many species of mites, of which only a few cause medical problems in dogs.

DEMODICOSIS

Demodicosis is a noncontagious skin disease caused by an excessive infestation with the canine follicular mite, *Demodex canis.* Mites of the genus *Demodex* are normal inhabitants of the hair follicles of most species of domestic animals (and also of human beings). Adult *Demodex* mites are small, elongated, cylindrical creatures with four pairs of short legs and a long, tapering abdomen. Their overall "cigar" shape represents a perfect anatomic adaptation to the environment of the long, narrow hair follicle (*see* "Hair and Hair Follicles" in chapter 22, "The Skin and Disorders"). The life cycle, involving eggs, six-legged larvae, eight-legged protonymphs, and the four-legged adults occurs completely on the host. *Demodex* mites are highly host-specific.

Because they are members of the normal population of the skin, canine demodectic mites are present in small numbers on most healthy dogs. Transmission of mites occurs by direct contact from the bitch to the nursing puppies during the first 2 or 3 days after birth. Overt disease usually is seen in young dogs having an overabundance of *Demodex* mites.

Clinically, canine demodicosis (also known by the older name *demodectic mange*) can be divided into a more common *juvenile-onset form,* seen in young dogs, and a less common, acquired, *adult-onset form* that occurs in mature dogs. Both forms may be either localized or generalized. *Localized and generalized demodicosis are very different diseases.* Localized demodicosis is very common and is a mild, self-limiting disease. Generalized demodicosis, by contrast, is a severe and potentially life-threatening illness and usually evolves from the more localized form. It is relatively uncommon in dogs.

In demodicosis, an alteration of the normal protective mechanisms of the skin apparently fosters an overgrowth of the *Demodex* population. It is most likely that a dysfunction of the immune response (which normally keeps the mite population under control) is involved. However, immunologic studies have not as yet provided convincing proof of a specific immunologic defect in canine demodicosis. In cases of juvenile-onset demodicosis, a genetic defect in immune function is the most likely cause, as suggested by recognized breed predispositions and frequent multiple occurrences of the disease in families of dogs. An underlying immunologic basis for demodicosis is further supported by the occurrence of adult-onset demodicosis in dogs with immunosuppressive illnesses (such as hyperadrenocorticism [hyperactivity of the adrenal cortex] or cancer) or in those being given immunosuppressive medication (such as corticosteroids).

Demodicosis is most often a disease of young dogs: 3 to 12 months of age for localized demodicosis, and less than 18 months of age for generalized demodicosis. This juvenile-onset form of demodicosis is reported to be more common in certain purebreds (see TABLE 1). Cocker Spaniels may be at increased risk for adult-onset demodicosis. There is no recognized sex predilection for either form of canine demodicosis.

Table 1
Dog breeds with an apparent increased incidence of juvenile-onset demodicosis

Afghan Hound	Dalmatian
American Staffordshire Terrier	Doberman Pinscher
	English Bulldog
Boston Terrier	German Shepherd Dog
Boxer	Great Dane
Chihuahua	Old English Sheepdog
Chinese Shar-Pei	Pit Bull Terrier
Collie	Pug

Dogs affected with localized demodicosis exhibit one or more well-circumscribed areas or patches of hair loss, **erythema** (reddening of the skin), and scaling. Common sites for these patches to develop include the face, around the eyes or the corners of the mouth, and on the forelimbs. The lesions may or may not be itchy. Plugging of hair follicles and subsequent pimple or blackhead formation may be seen, especially in German Shepherd Dogs. The vast majority of cases resolve without therapy, either by the time the affected dogs reach puberty or by at least 1 year of age.

Dogs affected with generalized demodicosis usually have a history of prior localized demodicosis from which the generalized form has evolved. Diffuse or patchy, generalized hair loss with scaling, crusting and signs of chronic skin inflammation (lichenification, hyperpigmentation) are characteristic. Secondary pyoderma occurs frequently. The feet may be severely affected in generalized demodicosis. Itching, pain and generalized enlargement of lymph nodes are often evident. In some severe cases **septicemia** (presence of bacteria in the blood circulation, accompanied by related clinical signs of disease) may develop.

Diagnosis is based primarily on the history, clinical findings and identification of *Demodex* mites in skin scrapings. Skin scrapings should be performed to rule out generalized demodicosis in all dogs with unidentified skin diseases, pyoderma or **exfoliative dermatitis** (skin disease characterized by inflammation and peeling). Skin biopsies may be required in some cases where suspicion of demodicosis is strong but skin scrapings are consistently negative. Identification of an underlying disease process possibly predisposing to heavy infestation with *Demodex* mites should be attempted in cases of generalized demodicosis.

Treatment of localized demodicosis may not be necessary. If required, a bland ointment containing a **miticidal** (able to kill mites) medication can be applied sparingly once daily to the affected area(s). By contrast, treatment of generalized demodicosis almost always requires administration of miticidal medications. The hair should also be clipped from the entire body of the dog to optimize therapy, which often involves weekly or biweekly dipping with a miticide. Secondary pyoderma should be treated with appropriate antibiotic therapy. Benzoyl peroxide shampoos and whirlpool baths or soaks may be needed. The use of immunostimulants—drugs designed to boost immune responses—has not proven beneficial for treating canine demodicosis. The prognosis for recovery from generalized demodicosis is always guarded. Chances for recovery diminish considerably as the age of the affected dog increases.

Because there is ample evidence indicating that juvenile-onset demodicosis has a heritable component, it has been recommended that dogs with generalized demodicosis be neutered (if that has not already been done) in order to prevent perpetuation of the underlying defect(s).

CANINE SCABIES

Canine scabies (also known by the older name *sarcoptic mange*) is a highly contagious, intensely itchy, transmissible skin disease caused by the burrowing epidermal mite, *Sarcoptes scabei* var. *canis*. This mite is restricted almost exclusively to dogs, but may produce a transient **pruritic** (characterized by itching) disease in other hosts, including cats and people. The intense itching characteristic of scabies results from mechanical irritation caused by the mites as they burrow into the skin, and by their production of toxic and **allergenic** (inducing allergy) compounds. Temporary infestation of human beings with the canine scabies mite is one of the more common *zoonotic* (transmissible from animals to people) diseases of small animals. (*See* APPENDIX A, "ZOONOTIC DISEASES: FROM DOGS TO PEOPLE.") An apparent age predilection for young dogs exists, although this may simply reflect an increased opportunity for exposure of pups in large breeding kennels and pet stores.

Sarcoptic mites are small, oval, whitish, opaque mites. The life cycle includes four stages (egg, larva, nymph, adult). Adult mites have eight legs and live on average for 4 to 5 weeks. Although they spend most of their life on the host, sarcoptic mites can exist for up to 48 hours off the host in the local environment. Transmission occurs by direct contact with an infested dog. When newly fertilized females encounter a new host, they move fairly rapidly onto the warm skin and burrow into its **horny layer** (outermost layer of the skin). The female usually lays her eggs within a few hours after burrowing. The eggs hatch in 3 to 8 days and a new generation of larvae molt, give rise to the nymph stage, and develop into adults.

Clinical signs may develop within a week of contact with an infested animal. Affected dogs exhibit intense itching, small reddened papules with crusting, hair loss, and often severe secondary self-trauma caused by scratching and biting. Lesions are located primarily along the underside of the body, margins of the ears, elbows and forelegs. There may also be a generalized enlargement of lymph nodes. In contrast to generalized demodicosis, secondary pyoderma is uncommon.

Diagnosis is based on the history, clinical features, identification of sarcoptic mites in skin scrapings (it has been estimated that mites can be reliably identified in fewer than 30% of cases, however, even after repeated scrapings), and in some cases simultaneous occurrence of scabies in other animals or people in the household. If mites cannot be identified in scrapings, the clinical response to therapy may provide a tentative diagnosis.

Affected dogs should be temporarily isolated and the premises thoroughly cleansed. Treatment involves the use of shampoos and miticidal dips, the latter being applied every 5 days for a minimum of six treatments. Lime sulfur is particularly safe and effective for puppies. Oral anti-inflammatory medication (corticosteroids) may be administered during the first week of therapy to control itching. *All dogs and cats living on the premises and having had significant contact with the affected dog should be treated as well, since it is possible they may be harboring sarcoptic mites, with or without accompanying clinical signs.*

CHEYLETIELLOSIS

Cheyletiellosis (also called *Cheyletiella* dermatitis) is a mild, contagious, variably itchy, transmissible skin disease of domestic animals, wildlife and people, caused by mites of the genus *Cheyletiella*. These mites live on the surface of the skin and appear to be only partially host-specific. Dogs are thought to be parasitized primarily by *Cheyletiella yasguri*. Cheyletiellosis is seen most often in parts of the world where vigorous flea control either is not necessary or is not practiced, since most *Cheyletiella* mites are sensitive to the same insecticides that kill adult fleas.

Cheyletiella mites are large mites with prominent hooklike mouthparts, and can be visualized by the unaided eye (or a magnifying lens) as small white specks on the dog's skin or in the hair. They have a typical four-stage life cycle (egg, larva, nymph, adult). Cheyletiellosis is considered to be an underreported **zoonosis** (disease that can be spread between animals and people). Although the entire life cycle is completed on the host, adult female mites can survive in the environment for extended periods of time—thus increasing the likelihood of transmission to other animals or to human beings. (*See* Appendix A, "Zoonotic Diseases: From Dogs to People.")

Cheyletiellosis is most often a problem in puppies and young adolescent dogs. Clinical disease is characterized primarily by scaling and crusting (i.e., dandruff) along the back, and sometimes in other areas. Itching may or may not be a prominent feature. Enlargement of lymph nodes can occur.

Infested adult dogs may carry the mites and transmit them without exhibiting clinical signs.

Diagnosis is based on the history, clinical features, identification of mites in skin scrapings or other preparations, and in some cases response to therapy. Treatment involves the use of shampoos and miticidal dips, the latter being applied every 5 days for a total of four applications. All dogs or cats in contact with an affected dog should be treated as well, since some of them may be harboring mites with or without accompanying clinical signs. The premises should be thoroughly cleansed to remove any residual mites.

Ear Mites

Ear mites (*Otodectes cynotis*) can be found in the ear canals of both dogs and cats. For information on ear mites, *see* Chapter 20, "The Ear and Disorders."

Lice

Lice are wingless insects that are spread by direct contact. Lice spend their entire life on the host and usually parasitize only one species of animal. They are uncommon or rare parasites of dogs in North America. It has been suggested that lice are rare in areas where frequent flea control is necessary because anti-flea preparations may kill lice quite readily.

Lice can be classified as either sucking lice or biting lice, depending on their method of feeding. *Sucking lice* move very slowly and have pointed, piercing mouthparts for feeding. There is only one common species of sucking louse affecting dogs in North America, *Linognathus setosus*. Itching and poor haircoat quality are the usual clinical signs. Blood loss can be a serious consequence of infestation with sucking lice, however. Heavily infested dogs can become seriously anemic and may even die. *Biting lice* are smaller than sucking lice and move much more rapidly. They have a more rounded head and biting mouthparts. Hair loss and itching are the major clinical signs of infestation, making biting lice more of a nuisance than a serious health hazard. The biting lice of dogs include *Trichodectes canis* and *Heterodoxus spiniger*.

Female lice attach their eggs (known as **nits**) to the hairs of the host. Lice infestation is normally diagnosed by identification of adult lice and eggs on an affected dog. A magnifying lens and good lighting conditions are required. Treatment of lice infestation involves the use of insecticides. A repeat treatment after an interval of several weeks is usually necessary because the eggs are quite resistant to the insecticidal chemicals; after several weeks, any eggs on the dog will have hatched, at which time the young lice will then be susceptible to insecticidal treatment. In cases of severe infestation, control of lice in the environment may be indicated; usually this is not required, however, owing to the poor survival capacity of lice when off the host.

Spiders

Spider bites can produce an array of skin manifestations in dogs, ranging from localized swelling to life-threatening tissue **necrosis** (tissue death). However, spider bites are only rarely reported in veterinary medicine. This may owe something to the reclusive nature of spiders, which often makes it difficult to connect a spider with the occurrence of a particular skin lesion. Spiders most often implicated in spider bites in North America include the brown recluse spider, black widow spider, red widow spider and the common brown spider. Woodpiles, abandoned structures and undisturbed areas of old buildings represent some of the favorite hideaways of spiders.

Bites by spiders of the genus *Latrodectus* (including the black and red widows) can cause generalized constitutional signs through the release of **neurotoxins** (toxins affecting the nervous system). Bites by spiders of the genus *Loxosceles* (brown recluse spider, common brown spider) produce local tissue damage through the elaboration of necrotoxins (toxins causing localized cell death). The necrotoxin made by brown recluse spiders can produce extensive tissue injury. Other spiders capable of producing such skin lesions include the running spiders, black jumping spiders, golden orb weavers, wolf spiders, green lynx spider, and funnel-web spider.

The brown recluse spider produces small, relatively innocuous puncture wounds in the skin. Reaction to the bite involves the development of a central papule with surrounding erythema. Within 6 to 12 hours a blister forms, followed by localized necrosis. The tissue damage can be extensive, producing a dark, chronic, nonhealing ulcer. The face and forelegs of the patient are most often involved. Rarely, pain or itching may be present. Brown recluse spiders are active primarily between March and October in North America (the spider spends the winter in hibernation).

The bite of a black widow spider produces a minor amount of skin damage, which is usually limited to localized erythema. Subsequent constitutional signs are highly variable, but may include nausea, vomiting, abdominal pain, incoordination, convulsions or paralysis. When present, such signs usually begin developing within 1 to 8 hours after the bite.

Active and inquisitive dogs with access to spider habitats probably are at increased risk for spider bites. Diagnosis is based on the clinical features, history of access to a spider habitat or factual evidence for a spider bite, and the clinical course. Treatment is chiefly supportive in nature.

CHAPTER 24

The Circulatory System and Disorders

by Mark D. Kittleson

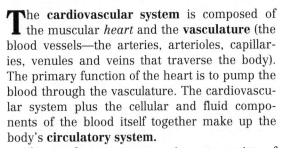

The **cardiovascular system** is composed of the muscular *heart* and the **vasculature** (the blood vessels—the arteries, arterioles, capillaries, venules and veins that traverse the body). The primary function of the heart is to pump the blood through the vasculature. The cardiovascular system plus the cellular and fluid components of the blood itself together make up the body's **circulatory system.**

The circulatory system carries out a variety of important, life-sustaining functions. First and foremost, it delivers inhaled oxygen from the lungs to the **mitochondria,** the specialized structures within body cells that are responsible for producing energy. In the reverse direction, the circulatory system transports *carbon dioxide,* a cellular waste product, from the cells to the lungs, where it is exhaled during **respiration** (breathing). The circulatory system pumps blood through the kidneys and liver, organs where other waste products are either excreted or **metabolized** (chemically altered or broken down). It also transports hormones, **glucose** (blood sugar), **electrolytes** (ions; charged atoms such as sodium and potassium), and other com-

pounds throughout the body in order to maintain the normal "mix" of chemicals in and around cells, and to help regulate the functions of each cell. From this brief description, one can readily understand why "death" historically has been defined as the cessation of heart and, consequently, circulatory system activity.

Normal Structure and Function

THE CIRCULATORY SYSTEM PROPER

The circulatory system, as the name implies, moves blood in a circle through the body. It is divided into two separate circulations, the **systemic** (body) circulation and the **pulmonary** (lung) circulation, which are coupled together in a series (i.e., they form one long continuous loop). The systemic circulation begins in the left side of the heart (also known simply as the left heart), where blood rich in oxygen (which has been returned via the blood vessels passing through the lungs) is pumped out through the **aorta** and into the arteries and arterioles of the body (i.e., systemically), then through the **systemic capillaries** (where the oxygen is extracted by the cells), the systemic venules and veins and the superior vena cava and the inferior vena cava (where the amount of oxygen is approximately 60% of that in arterial blood), and so to the right side of the heart (right heart). The left heart is on the dog's left side and the right heart on the dog's right.

The coupled pulmonary circulation originates in the right heart, which pumps blood into the pulmonary arteries in the lungs, through the pulmonary capillaries (where the blood is exposed to inhaled air and thus receives its supply of precious oxygen), through the pulmonary veins, and so back to the original starting point, the left heart, whence the richly *oxygenated* blood courses back out into the systemic circulation.

THE HEART

The heart is approximately 0.6–0.9% of a dog's body weight. It lies in the chest cavity, with its *base* lying closer to the spinal column (the vertebrae) and its *apex* lying closer to the **sternum** (breastbone) between the dog's front legs. The base of the heart is composed primarily of the receiving chambers (the left and right **atria;** singular: **atrium**) and the great vessels—the aorta and the pulmonary artery. The apex is composed of the bottom of the right and left **ventricles.**

Internally, the heart of a dog is composed of four separate chambers. The two upper chambers are the left atrium and right atrium, which function as receiving chambers for the blood. The two lower chambers are the left and right ventricles. The ventricles are muscular pumping chambers that actually provide the force to push the blood through the circulation. As indicated previously, the heart can also be divided into the right heart (right atrium and right ventricle) and the left heart (left atrium and left ventricle). The atria and ventricles are separated by atrial and ventricular **septa** (dividing walls; singular: **septum**).

Within the heart is a series of one-way valves that force the blood to flow in only a single direction (forward) during normal cardiac function. They are divided into **atrioventricular (A-V)** and **semilunar valves.** The A-V valves separate the atria from the ventricles. They open passively whenever a ventricle relaxes, allowing blood to flow into the ventricle, and close passively when the ventricle contracts, thus preventing backflow of blood into the atrium. The A-V valve on the right side of the heart is known as the **tricuspid valve,** and the corresponding valve on the left side is called the **mitral valve.**

The semilunar valves separate each ventricle from the great artery with which it is connected (either aorta or pulmonary artery). The semilunar valves open passively whenever a ventricle contracts and pumps blood into a great artery, and close passively when the ventricle relaxes, preventing backflow into the ventricle. The semilunar valve on the right side of the heart is known as the **pulmonic valve,** and the corresponding valve on the left side is called the **aortic valve.**

To summarize: When the left ventricle relaxes, it allows blood in the left atrium to flow across the mitral valve and into the ventricle. When the left ventricle subsequently contracts, the mitral valve is squeezed shut and the blood is propelled across the aortic valve into the aorta, where it enters the systemic circulation. As the left ventricle relaxes the aortic valve closes, preventing backward flow; as a result, blood is continually forced through the arteries by the pressure built up during the contraction phase. From the arteries and arterioles the blood percolates through the capillary beds in the tissues, where it discharges its oxygen load, then drains into the systemic venules and veins and so makes its way to the right heart. It enters through the right atrium, crosses the tricuspid valve when the right ventricle relaxes, and is forced out across the pulmonic valve and into the **pulmonary** (lung) circulation when the right ventricle subsequently contracts. In the lungs the blood receives a fresh supply of oxygen, and so is readied for yet another of its countless excursions through the body.

The heart is composed principally of heart muscle called **myocardium.** The myocardium in turn is composed of microscopic, contractile units known as sarcomeres, which are the structures that actually move following the appropriate stimulation to produce muscular contraction.

The cardiac chambers are lined by an inner layer of tissue called the **endocardium,** while the exterior of the heart is surrounded by a layer of tissue called the **epicardium.** The entire heart is enclosed in a membranous sheath known as the **pericardial sac, or pericardium.** The pericardial sac keeps the heart in a relatively stable position within the chest cavity, and contains a small amount of fluid to maintain lubrication.

The heart contracts and relaxes in sequential fashion. The contraction phase is called **systole** and the relaxation phase is called **diastole.** Mechanically, systole begins when the ventricles start to contract and the mitral and tricuspid valves close. Closure of these valves produces the *first heart sound* (the "lub" in "lub-dup"). Systole ends and diastole begins when the heart starts to relax and the aortic and pulmonic valves snap shut. Closure of these valves produces the characteristic *second heart sound* ("dup").

Contraction and relaxation of heart muscle are both controlled by electrical signals within the heart. Normally, the heart's rate of contraction and relaxation (the **heart rate**) is controlled by a *pacemaker* in the heart known as the **sinoatrial (SA) node.** During contraction, this collection of highly specialized cells located at the base of the right atrium first **depolarizes** (changes from a negative to a positive charge), generating an electrical wave. This depolarizes the cells next to the node, which in turn depolarize the cells next adjacent, and so forth, thus propagating the electrical wave through the heart. The wave spreads initially across the two atria, causing them to contract, and then slowly traverses a region electrically connecting the atria and the ventricles and known as the **atrioventricular (AV) node.** The AV node slows the conduction of the depolarization wave so that a short period of time is interposed between atrial and ventricular contractions. Once the electrical wave traverses the AV node it spreads across the ventricles, which contract in response.

Depolarization occurs when specific channels or "gates" in the surface membranes of heart muscle cells are opened, allowing *sodium* to rush in and produce a rapid change in the polarity (net electrical charge) of the cells. The depolarization of the cells in turn causes release of their internal stores of *calcium*. The calcium interacts with the sarcomeres, inducing them to slide past one another; this concerted, microscopic action on the part of the many sarcomeres results in the contraction of the muscle. And so by the interaction of two relatively simple and common elements, sodium and calcium, heart muscle contracts, blood is pumped, oxygen is delivered, and the body lives.

The depolarization rate of the SA node determines the heart rate in the normal heart. The heart rate can be affected by many factors, including **adrenaline** (a hormone produced by the adrenal glands), temperature (fever increases heart rate), sodium and potassium concentration in the blood, and certain medications. The heart rate commonly is as slow as 30 beats per minute in a sleeping, large dog, but can rise to well over 200 beats per minute in an excited, active, small dog.

The heart's *rhythm* reflects whether or not the heart rate is normal, too fast, too slow, regular or irregular. Healthy dogs and small children exhibit a completely normal rhythm known as **sinus arrhythmia,** wherein the heart rate accelerates during **inspiration** (breathing in) and slows during **expiration** (breathing out). Sinus arrhythmia is not a normal finding in adult humans or cats. Fever can cause the SA node to depolarize too quickly, resulting in an accelerated heart rhythm known as **sinus tachycardia.**

There are numerous examples of abnormal heart rhythms, known as **arrhythmias.** One of the more common is **ventricular tachycardia,** wherein damaged or diseased heart muscle within a ventricle begins firing (depolarizing) on its own, which it normally does not do. If it fires at a rate faster than the SA node, it will take over the heart's rhythm. This results in a heart rate that is too rapid and in some instances can predispose an animal to sudden death from **ventricular fibrillation** (rapid, repeated firing of ventricular muscle fibers without coordinated contraction of the muscle).

Heart rhythms are evaluated by recording an **electrocardiogram (ECG).** The electrocardiogram records the size and direction of the waves of depolarization that spread across the heart.

Using an electrocardiogram, the veterinarian can determine the heart rate and whether or not the depolarization wave originates in the SA node or from an abnormal site (such as a ventricle).

THE BLOOD VESSELS

The aorta and the systemic arteries are relatively thick, muscular tubes that can withstand substantial pressure. The systemic arterioles are smaller arteries with well-formed smooth muscle in their walls and can contract and relax in order to increase or decrease the resistance to blood flow. The capillaries are microscopic blood vessels that allow red blood cells to deliver their load of oxygen while flowing through the tissues, one cell at a time.

The systemic venules and veins are larger, more thinly walled vessels that direct the deoxygenated blood back to the right heart. The walls of the pulmonary vessels in the lungs are also relatively thin, because the pulmonary circulation operates at a much lower pressure than does the systemic circulation (the average pressure in the systemic circulation is around 100 mmHg [millimeters of mercury], whereas the pressure in the pulmonary circulation is only about 15 mmHg).

The heart rate and the strength of the pulse in dogs are commonly evaluated by feeling the **femoral pulse.** The femoral artery lies beneath the inner surface of the hind limbs, in the groin region. The artery is easily located in most dogs, although it may be more difficult to find in obese or short-limbed animals. To evaluate the pulse, the tips of the first and second fingers are placed over the femoral artery and pressure is placed on it. The pressure is increased or decreased until the pulse feels the strongest. The number of pulses per minute can then be counted. Healthy, average-sized dogs will have a pulse rate of 60 to 150 beats per minute at rest (larger dogs having comparatively slower rates than smaller dogs).

The pulse strength can be determined by the difference in blood pressure between systole and diastole. Most people have had their blood pressure evaluated by a physician or nurse and know that it normally should be about 120 mmHg over 80 mmHg (millimeters of mercury).

The 120 mmHg is the **systolic blood pressure** that occurs when the heart contracts and pushes blood into the arterial system, increasing the pressure. The 80 mmHg is the **diastolic blood pressure** that occurs when the heart is not pumping any blood into the system, resulting in a decrease in blood pressure. When one feels the pulse, one is actually feeling the **pulse pressure,** which is the difference between systolic and diastolic pressure—in this case 40 mmHg. The pulse pressure may be falsely weak when the individual evaluating it performs the examination incorrectly (e.g., places too little or too much pressure with the fingers over the femoral artery). Pulse pressure can be truly decreased, however, in patients in **shock** (e.g., with severe blood loss resulting in too little blood for the heart to pump) or in those in heart failure (the heart is too weak to pump the normal amount of blood).

Canine blood pressure readings in general are similar to those for human beings, except that the upper end of the systolic pressure range is higher, because most dogs' pressures are taken when the animals are quite excited. Normal diastolic pressure in dogs should still be < 90 mmHg, however.

Disorders and Diseases

CIRCULATORY SHOCK

Circulatory shock is a common abnormality in critically ill or injured veterinary patients. **Shock** is defined as circulatory collapse in which oxygen delivery to the cells is grossly inadequate, forcing the cells to switch from using oxygen as their main source of energy generation (**aerobic metabolism**) to other energy sources not requiring oxygen (**anaerobic metabolism**). Anaerobic metabolism produces toxic by-products such as *lactic acid.* The end result is that the entire circulatory system grows further and further deranged until complete collapse and death occur. (*See* CHAPTER 41, "PROCEDURES FOR LIFE-THREATENING EMERGENCIES.")

Forms of shock include **hemorrhagic shock, septic shock** and **cardiogenic shock.** In hemorrhagic shock, severe bleeding (usually caused by trauma) results in depletion of blood from the circulatory system, so that less blood, and so less oxygen, is transported from the lungs to the tissues. In septic shock, the body and circulatory system are invaded by bacteria. The bacteria produce substances that injure the cells so that they cannot utilize oxygen. These substances also commonly injure the heart and the blood vessels. In cardiogenic shock the heart itself is diseased, becoming so dysfunctional that it cannot pump enough blood to the body. Cardiogenic shock is the terminal stage of *heart failure* (*see* below).

The diagnosis of shock is usually based on the clinical signs (poor mucous membrane color [indicative of decreased blood flow], weak femoral pulse, etc.). Diagnosing the cause of hemorrhagic shock may only require knowledge of the precipitating event (e.g., a dog's owner reports that the dog was hit by a car). The diagnosis of septic shock, on the other hand, may be difficult to make. Affected dogs may not resemble other shock cases clinically because they may have very pink mucous membranes. Recovering the causative bacteria from the bloodstream is important for the diagnosis but requires time (often 24 to 48 hours or longer). The diagnosis of cardiogenic shock requires an in-depth evaluation of heart function.

Treatment of shock cases often is dictated by the underlying cause. In hemorrhagic shock, intravenous fluids or fresh whole blood may be administered to restore blood volume. In septic shock, fluids and drugs to support heart function are usually administered along with antibiotics. In cardiogenic shock, drugs to support heart function are of greatest importance.

SIGNS OF HEART DISEASE

The signs of heart disease can be as varied in dogs as they are in other species. Chronic heart failure is usually manifested by fluid retention, either **edema** or **ascites.** Edema (fluid accumulation in tissues) develops in the lungs (**pulmonary edema**) and creates signs of respiratory distress (cough) when the left heart fails. When the right heart fails, fluid accumulates in the abdominal cavity (ascites), although it will sometimes accumulate beneath the skin (**subcutaneous edema**) or in the space between the lungs and the chest

wall (pleural effusion). Other signs of heart disease include poor growth (in puppies), exercise intolerance, weakness, **cyanosis** (bluish discoloration of the skin and mucous membranes), collapse, and sudden death.

A **heart murmur** is another common sign of heart disease. Heart murmurs occur when the blood flows too rapidly through a portion of the heart or the blood vessels. When blood moves too quickly its flow becomes chaotic, generating turbulence that creates the sound referred to as a murmur. Blood flows too rapidly when it is forced through an orifice or a vessel whose diameter is too narrow. Leaky heart valves, narrowed valves, and abnormal communications (openings) between heart chambers or between blood vessels are the most common causes of increased flow velocity and resulting heart murmurs. Heart disease is suspected in dogs most often when a heart murmur is detected. In some cases the nature of the cardiac abnormality may be identified simply by listening to the murmur. In most instances, however, a chest X ray, an electrocardiogram and a cardiac ultrasound are needed to make an accurate diagnosis and to assess the severity of the disease.

Within the last decade cardiac ultrasound (**echocardiography,** the use of reflected sound waves to visualize the position and motion of the heart walls and internal structures) has become an extremely valuable tool for the diagnosis and assessment of heart disease in veterinary medicine. With echocardiography, the veterinarian can inspect the entire heart and assess the size of the individual chambers as well as the thickness of the chamber walls, noting any abnormal structures or defects. The technology has recently advanced such that the direction and velocity of blood flow within the heart and great vessels can now be directly examined (**Doppler echocardiography**). With **color flow Doppler echocardiography,** a veterinary cardiologist can actually see the regions of abnormal blood flow that develop in association with most common cardiac abnormalities.

CONGENITAL HEART DISEASES

Congenital diseases are those that are present at birth. Congenital diseases may or may not be *hereditary* (genetically passed on from one or both parents). The incidence of congenital heart disease seen in veterinary hospitals is quite low (fewer than 1% of puppies born). The actual incidence is probably much higher, though, because pups with very severe defects may not survive very long after birth. Certain congenital heart defects are more commonly observed in specific breeds of dog.

Patent Ductus Arteriosus (PDA)

Patent ductus arteriosus is one of the most common congenital heart defects of dogs. It is seen more frequently in Miniature Poodles (in whom it is inherited) and in German Shepherd Dogs. The **ductus arteriosus** is a vessel normally present during fetal life that allows blood to bypass the lungs, which are nonfunctional *in utero.* The ductus normally closes shortly after birth. In dogs with PDA, the ductus remains open due to lack of smooth muscle in the vessel wall. Blood then flows from the higher-resistance, systemic arterial side (the aorta) through the **patent** (open) ductus and into the lower-resistance, pulmonary side. To compensate for this "leak," the left ventricle must pump more blood in order to maintain normal blood flow to the body.

The diagnosis of PDA is usually made by **ausculting** (listening to) the heart and detecting a murmur that is present in both systole and diastole (**continuous heart murmur**). The diagnosis can be confirmed by examining a chest X ray and evaluating the heart on an echocardiogram.

Left heart failure is a complication of PDA that results in pulmonary edema with ensuing respiratory difficulty. Dogs with heart failure are initially treated with a **diuretic** (medication that promotes urination) to remove excess fluid. Surgical closure of the patent ductus usually results in a complete and permanent cure.

Pulmonic Stenosis

Pulmonic stenosis is another common congenital heart defect, and is observed most often in the smaller breeds. Pulmonic stenosis is a narrowing (**stenosis**) of the connection between the right ventricle and the pulmonary artery. This narrowing increases the resistance to blood flow, making it more difficult for the right ventricle to pump blood (i.e., it must generate a higher pressure). The right ventricle responds by enlarging and thickening the muscle tissue in its walls (myocardial hypertrophy), in much the same way that body muscle grows in response to an activity such as weight lifting. This compensatory mechanism is extremely efficient and generally results in the right ventricle's pumping a normal amount of blood. Consequently, even dogs with severe pulmonic stenosis often exhibit few or no discernible clinical signs. In contrast to patent ductus arteriosus, heart failure secondary to pulmonic stenosis is an extremely rare complication.

Pulmonic stenosis is usually first suspected when the veterinarian detects a systolic murmur. The diagnosis may be confirmed with a chest X ray and an electrocardiogram. A definitive diagnosis and an assessment of the severity of the stenosis are made by evaluating the thickness of the right ventricular wall and determining the velocity of blood flow through the narrowing with an echocardiogram, or by measuring the difference in pressure on either side of the narrowing with an intravenous catheter (**cardiac catheterization**). The latter procedure is performed with the patient under general anesthesia.

Dogs with severe pulmonic stenosis are candidates for treatment. Treatment consists of a procedure known as a **balloon valvuloplasty,** wherein a catheter with a large, stiff balloon attached is inserted into the heart through a peripheral blood vessel and placed across the narrowing. The balloon is then inflated to widen the stenosis. Balloon valvuloplasty is successful in restoring normal function approximately 70% of the time. Alternative procedures involving surgery generally are less successful and entail greater risks for the patient. Dogs that do not respond to balloon valvuloplasty, however, may have to undergo surgery.

Aortic Stenosis

Aortic stenosis is another common congenital defect. It occurs most often in larger breeds such as Newfoundlands, Rottweilers and Golden Retrievers. Aortic stenosis is an abnormal narrowing of the connection between the left ventricle and the aorta. It usually is caused by scarlike tissue that forms a ring just beneath the aortic valve. This ring is very strong and thick. As in pulmonic stenosis, the heart compensates quite well for the abnormality. Affected dogs may have few or no clinical signs, or may exhibit exercise intolerance or weakness and collapse upon exercise. About 20% of dogs with aortic stenosis will die suddenly, sudden death being the major complicating factor for this abnormality. Up to 70% of dogs with *severe* aortic stenosis die suddenly within the first 3 years of life.

The diagnosis is made and the severity of the abnormality is assessed in the same manner as described for pulmonic stenosis above. Unfortunately, balloon valvuloplasty has been unrewarding in the treatment of aortic stenosis. Open-heart surgery with **cardiopulmonary bypass** (wherein a heart-lung machine oxygenates and pumps blood while the heart is stopped) is the treatment of choice. However, this procedure is available only at a few veterinary schools. It is also risky and quite expensive.

Ventricular Septal Defect (VSD)
In this uncommon congenital abnormality, a defect (a hole) exists in the wall or septum separating the left and right ventricles. Because the resistance to flow is lower through the pulmonary circulation than through the systemic arterial system, blood tends to flow through the hole from the left ventricle to the right ventricle and out into the pulmonary vessels. The left ventricle enlarges to pump more blood in compensation for the leak. The amount of blood streaming through the pulmonary circulation is increased in direct relation to the size of the defect. If the defect is large enough, the heart cannot compensate adequately and heart failure ensues.

This problem is usually first identified when a murmur is detected. A definitive diagnosis generally cannot be established without resorting to an echocardiogram or cardiac catheterization.

Generally only large VSDs are treated. A mild to moderate, artificial pulmonic stenosis can be created to increase the resistance to pulmonary blood flow and so decrease flow through the defect. Open-heart surgery using cardiopulmonary bypass can be performed, but can be risky and is costly.

Atrial Septal Defect (ASD)
This rare congenital defect is characterized by a hole between the left and right atria. Blood flows from the left atrium to the right atrium, in most cases, because the right ventricle is thinner and less stiff than the left ventricle and so will accommodate a greater blood volume during diastole. Consequently, the right ventricle enlarges to accommodate for the increased amount of blood it must pump.

The diagnosis of this defect is difficult to make and generally requires an echocardiogram or a cardiac catheterization. Therapy is usually attempted only if the defect is large and causing clinical signs. Treatment consists of open-heart surgery, either under **hypothermia** (cooling of the body to slow metabolism) or using cardiopulmonary bypass.

Tetralogy of Fallot
This is the most common defect causing *cyanosis* (bluish discoloration of the skin and mucous membranes; "blue baby"). The Keeshond breed is predisposed to developing this abnormality. Congenital heart defects associated with cyanosis share the common characteristic of having a certain amount of venous (low-oxygen) blood flowing into the systemic arterial (high-oxygen) circulation. In tetralogy of Fallot, affected dogs have a ventricular septal defect (VSD) and severe pulmonic stenosis together with an abnormally placed aorta. The severe pulmonic stenosis increases resistance to flow in the pulmonary circulation, so much so that the pulmonary resistance is actually higher than the resistance in the systemic circulation. This results in right ventricular (deoxygenated or venous) blood surging across the VSD into the left ventricle and aorta.

Normal, healthy dogs have a partial pressure (pressure exerted by a component of a gas mixture) of oxygen of about 100 mmHg (millimeters of mercury) in arterial blood and 30 mmHg in venous blood. Most severe cases of clinically affected tetralogy of Fallot have an arterial partial pressure of oxygen in the 30 mmHg range. Such dogs commonly exhibit cyanosis at rest or following mild exercise. They often have an excessive number of red blood cells (**polycythemia**), which renders their blood thick and viscous. The increased numbers of red blood cells are produced by the body in an attempt to compensate for the low oxygen pressure. A heart murmur is usually but not always present with this abnormality. Affected dogs often are exercise-intolerant and may exhibit stunting of growth.

A presumptive diagnosis can be made based on the history, clinical signs, arterial blood gas measurements (levels of oxygen and carbon dioxide), chest X rays, electrocardiogram, and **packed cell volume** (a measure of red blood cell numbers). A definitive diagnosis is based on echocardiography or cardiac catheterization.

Treatment may consist of **phlebotomy** (bloodletting) to decrease red cell numbers, surgical formation of an artificial patent ductus arteriosus in order to increase blood flow through the lungs (**Blalock-Taussig shunt**), or open-heart surgery on cardiopulmonary bypass to repair the defects.

ACQUIRED HEART DISEASES

Acquired heart diseases are not present at birth, but instead develop gradually over time. They can be degenerative, infectious, immune-mediated, traumatic, cancerous or biochemical in nature. Some diseases that are now generally considered to be "acquired" will certainly have to be reassessed and possibly reclassified in the future as underlying genetic causes are discovered.

Mitral Regurgitation

Many diseases affecting the mitral valve and its supporting structures result in partial backflow of blood through the valve (**regurgitation**). The most common primary disease of the mitral valve is **valvular degeneration,** which is seen most often in older dogs of the smaller breeds. In this disease, the leaflets or cusps comprising the valve contract and curl back on themselves, allowing the valve to leak. Mitral regurgitation can also occur secondary to an infection on the valves (**endocarditis**), or as a congenital lesion in which the valve is malformed at birth. Mitral regurgitation can also occur secondary to **dilated cardiomyopathy** (*see* below).

In mitral regurgitation, blood leaks back from the left ventricle into the left atrium. To accommodate for this increased quantity of blood, the left atrium enlarges. The left ventricle grows larger (it **hypertrophies**) so that it may pump a larger quantity of blood to compensate for the leak. In primary mitral regurgitation, the amount of regurgitation correlates directly with the size of the left atrium and ventricle. Severe mitral regurgitation can produce a tremendous increase in left heart size together with varying degrees of **congestive heart failure.** Congestive heart failure is manifested by fluid accumulation in the lungs (pulmonary edema) caused by high pressure in the left atrium backing up into the pulmonary capillaries.

The diagnosis of primary degenerative mitral regurgitation is usually made based on the size, age and breed of the dog and the presence of a typical heart murmur. The severity of the illness can be assessed on a chest X ray. An echocardiogram is often useful to document the severity of the problem and to assess the function of the heart muscle.

Therapy is usually initiated when clinical signs of heart failure become evident. Attempting to manage the underlying problem with a low-salt diet *before* the actual onset of clinical signs has not proved beneficial, while use of *angiotensin converting enzyme (ACE) inhibitors* such as captopril or enalapril prior to the onset of heart failure remains a controversial issue. In human beings, these medications have been shown to decrease the number of hospital visits required but not to affect survival time.

The most common signs of left heart failure include an increased respiratory rate, **dyspnea** (labored breathing), and cough. Medications used in the treatment of heart failure include diuretics, angiotensin converting enzyme inhibitors, **vasodilators** (drugs that expand blood vessels), and *digoxin*. Digoxin is administered to improve the performance of the heart muscle, but its use is controversial in primary mitral regurgitation. Because myocardial performance usually is not depressed in small dogs with mitral regurgitation, digoxin often may not be needed. In larger dogs with mitral regurgitation the heart muscle is weakened and so digoxin would seem to be indicated, but unfortunately in these dogs it does not often produce the desired effect of improving myocardial performance. A drug such as *hydralazine* is generally employed when other medications have failed or when heart failure is **acute** (of sudden onset) and very severe in nature.

Bacterial Endocarditis

If bacteria gain access to the bloodstream they may be capable of infecting the heart. Bacterial infections of the heart almost always localize on the heart valves (**bacterial endocarditis**). In dogs, infection usually involves the mitral or aortic valves, with valvular regurgitation as the result.

A presumptive diagnosis of bacterial endocarditis is based on clinical signs of fever and evidence of infected blood clots broken off from the affected valve circulating throughout the septum (lameness being a common manifestation), along with the presence of a new heart murmur. A definitive diagnosis must be based on identification of lesions on the affected valve using echocardiography. Blood cultures are usually attempted in order to identify the causative bacterium or bacteria and to select appropriate antibiotic therapy.

Treatment consists of antibiotics to combat the infection and medications to ameliorate the consequences of the failing heart valve. Infection of the aortic valve is usually more serious, because it often results in severe and intractable heart failure.

Dilated Cardiomyopathy

Dilated cardiomyopathy is a disease of the heart muscle itself. The term "dilated cardiomyopathy" probably encompasses several different diseases, each having, however, the same end result: the heart muscle gradually becomes dysfunctional over time. Dilated cardiomyopathy has been recognized in a number of species,

including dogs, cats and human beings (artificial heart transplant recipient Dr. Barney Clark had this disease). In cats, dilated cardiomyopathy is due primarily to a dietary deficiency of the amino acid *taurine*. In dogs, the cause of the disease is generally unknown but the disease itself is highly breed-specific, being observed most commonly in Doberman Pinschers, Boxers, Great Danes, Irish Wolfhounds, Saint Bernards, Cocker Spaniels, Golden Retrievers and German Shepherd Dogs. More than 90% of cases of canine dilated cardiomyopathy are confined to these eight breeds. Dilated cardiomyopathy occurs only rarely in mixed-breed dogs. The disease is most likely genetic in origin, although this has not been proved and the mode of inheritance has yet to be documented.

Dilated cardiomyopathy has been studied most thoroughly in Doberman Pinschers. In this breed it appears that the disease is of relatively early onset (2 to 5 years of age), after which it progresses slowly and insidiously over the ensuing several years. Only an echocardiogram or a 24-hour recording of an ECG (**Holter monitor**) can identify the illness at this early stage. On an echocardiogram, the walls of the left ventricle usually exhibit an impaired ability to contract. A Holter monitor often will reveal an increased number of **premature ventricular contractions (PVCs),** which are produced by the diseased heart muscle. As the illness progresses the affected heart muscle grows weaker and weaker, while the left ventricle compensates by enlarging. In male dogs, dilated cardiomyopathy usually becomes severe between 5 and 8 years of age. Females often show no clinical signs until they are about 9 to 12 years of age. The signs themselves often appear suddenly, as if the affected animal has become ill only within the last few days; in reality, the dogs by this time have already progressed through the early stages of the disease and are now in severe heart failure.

Heart failure often can be controlled by medication (diuretics, ACE inhibitors, digoxin). If the disease is very severe, however, an affected dog may not survive the initial hospitalization. Even if the illness is initially controlled, the long-term prognosis is poor; most affected Dobermans will die within 1 to 6 months. The prognosis in other breeds can be somewhat better, but in almost all cases the disease is ultimately fatal. Exceptions to the rule are some Cocker Spaniels that are taurine-deficient and respond to the administration of taurine and **carnitine** (an amino acid required for energy production), some Boxers (and rarely other breeds) that may respond to carnitine, and a few dogs that are taurine-deficient and that may respond to taurine therapy.

Heartworm Disease

The term "heartworm disease" is actually a misnomer. The disease is caused by a parasitic worm, Dirofilaria immitis, which lives, in most cases, in the pulmonary arteries rather than in the heart itself. During the life cycle the adult worms reproduce and pass a minute, prelarval stage (the **microfilaria**) into the bloodstream. The many microfilariae are subsequently ingested by mosquitoes that feed on the dog. In the mosquito, the organisms mature to an infective stage and are then deposited on the skin when the mosquito feeds on another dog. The parasites enter the new host through the feeding wound and migrate through the body. Eventually (2 to 4 months later) they penetrate a systemic vein and are carried into the lungs by flowing blood. The capillaries in the lungs are too narrow for the parasites to pass through; consequently they lodge in the pulmonary arteries, where they mature and begin to reproduce.

Once the adult worms are in place, the body launches an immunologic assault against them. The more vigorous the attack and the greater the number of worms present, the more severe is the resulting disease. As a consequence of the immunologic reaction, the pulmonary arteries become enlarged and the lungs surrounding the affected area are infiltrated by white blood cells. Some dogs actually appear to be allergic to the worms and develop severe illness, even in the presence of only a small number of worms.

Dogs with large numbers of worms and dogs that are highly allergic usually develop clinical signs of heartworm disease. The most common signs include coughing, respiratory distress, weight loss, **hemoptysis** (coughing up blood), and right heart failure creating fluid buildup in the abdomen (ascites).

The diagnosis of heartworm infestation is based on either the identification of microfilariae in the blood or detection of proteins shed by the adult worms into the bloodstream (*heartworm antigen test*). Both tests should be used to screen a dog for heartworm disease. About 30% of dogs with heartworm infestation do not have identifiable microfilariae in the blood, necessitating the use of an antigen test to detect them. Conversely, dogs carrying only 2 to 5 worms may not be positive by the antigen test but still may have microfilariae in the blood, so an antigen test alone is not sufficient for making the diagnosis either. Moreover, some dogs with only a few worms may be negative on both tests! Usually, such a small number of worms would create no clinical problems. However, dogs that are highly allergic to heartworms may become symptomatic (exhibit clinical signs) even if they are carrying only a few worms. Chest X rays can be used in this situation to identify the characteristically enlarged pulmonary arteries, thus making the diagnosis.

Prior to therapy, affected dogs should be evaluated with a chest X ray and blood tests. The veterinarian can use the X ray to assess the severity of the disease. Blood tests can identify potentially complicating abnormalities in other organ systems. Dogs with severe heartworm disease are more prone to develop heart failure as a result, and are also more prone to develop complications following therapy.

Treatment to kill the adult worms consists of the administration of **thiacetarsamide** (*Caparsalate*), an arsenical compound that is given intravenously twice daily for 2 days. The drug is very toxic to tissue, and if accidentally injected into the tissues around the vein (i.e., given perivascularly) it will produce a large wound. Thiacetarsamide is also toxic to the liver, although this is usually not a severe-enough problem to cause clinical signs. Some dogs will not tolerate the drug and may stop eating or begin to vomit and develop **jaundice** (yellow discoloration of the skin and mucous membranes). Under such circumstances treatment should be halted for a month, after which time affected dogs will usually tolerate the treatment.

The adult heartworms begin dying 5 to 10 days after therapy is initiated. Treated dogs normally should not be hospitalized after drug treatment, but instead should be taken home by their owners *and strictly confined.* Exercise or excitement increases blood flow in the pulmonary arteries and heightens the probability that a large mass of worms will be carried into the lungs all at once. If the worms die slowly—which is the desired situation—they will gradually pass into the lungs, where they will be degraded by the host's immune defenses. If a large worm mass is delivered to the lungs, however, pulmonary blood flow may be compromised and a severe reaction will likely ensue. Such affected dogs may develop a cough and fever, usually 1 to 4 weeks after therapy. Treatment for this complication consists of the administration of antibiotics and corticosteroids. Recovery is generally prompt, but additional complications may occasionally develop.

Approximately 4 to 6 weeks after the adult worms have been treated, a second medication is administered to kill the microfilariae. The most common drug in current use is **ivermectin,** but either levamisole or dithiazanine may be given as an alternative. Once the microfilariae are killed or a dog tests negative for heartworm, a preventive drug should be administered if the dog is living in an area where heartworm infestation is prevalent. Either ivermectin or milbemycin oxime can be administered once a month for this purpose. **Diethylcarbamazine** also is effective in preventing heartworm disease, but must be given on a daily basis.

Thiacetarsamide usually kills only about 70% of the adult worms present. In general, if a dog has a positive antigen test prior to treatment of the adults, another antigen test should be performed 3 months later to determine if a significant number of worms are still alive. The dog may require another course of therapy if the antigen test remains positive and there is clinical or X-ray evidence that the disease is still active.

Pericardial Disease

The most common problem affecting the pericardium is the accumulation of fluid in the pericardial sac (**pericardial effusion**); that is, the space between the sac and the heart fills with fluid. This is most often the result of inflammation affecting the pericardial sac itself, or infection or cancer involving the outer surface of the heart. Pericardial effusion causes an increase in pressure within the pericardial sac, putting pressure on the heart. This in turn increases the pressure in the heart when the heart is relaxed (i.e., during diastole). The pressure then backs up and produces edema. Because the right ventricle is thinner than the left ventricle, it is less able to compensate for this change. Consequently, dogs with severe pericardial effusion usually develop signs of right heart failure; that is, fluid buildup in the abdomen (ascites).

The diagnosis of pericardial effusion can usually be made by observing a large, round heart silhouette on a chest X ray. The diagnosis can be confirmed and the cause of the effusion surmised using echocardiography. The echocardiogram can be used to identify the presence or absence of tumors. The two most common tumors in such circumstances are **hemangiosarcoma** and **heart base tumor.**

Hemangiosarcomas usually are found on the right atrium. They are highly malignant (cancerous) tumors of blood vessels and associated tissue, and portend a poor prognosis. Heart base tumors grow around the great vessels. They do not generally spread and grow rather slowly, displacing the normal anatomic structures and producing fluid. **Mesothelioma** is a less common malignant tumor that grows along the pericardial sac and epicardium. It *cannot* be identified using an echocardiogram, but instead is diagnosed during exploratory surgery or at **necropsy** (autopsy). If no tumor can be found on an echocardiogram, the diagnosis of **idiopathic** (of unknown cause) pericardial effusion is usually made, although a mesothelioma may still be present.

Initial treatment of pericardial effusion consists of draining the sac by placing a catheter into it and withdrawing the fluid. Analysis of the cells in the fluid generally is not helpful in arriving at a diagnosis. Withdrawal of the fluid is still of benefit, however, for it can produce a prompt and dramatic improvement in the way the dog acts and feels.

Hemangiosarcomas are usually not treated and consideration must be given to euthanasia. Surgical removal of the pericardial sac may provide several months of relief to a dog with a heart base tumor. Occasionally a skilled surgeon will attempt to remove a large portion of the tumor itself. Dogs with idiopathic pericardial effusion are treated by removing the fluid—this procedure can be repeated two to three times if fluid accumulation recurs. If there is a third recurrence, however, surgical removal of the sac and exploration of the region are recommended.

Arrhythmias

Abnormal heart rhythms (**arrhythmias**) can cause clinical problems in dogs. **Tachycardias** (fast heart rates) originating from the atria can increase the heart rate to 300 to 350 beats per minute and cause severe weakness and collapse. Digoxin, **beta blockers** such as *propranolol,* and **calcium channel blockers** such as *verapamil* or *diltiazem* are used to slow the heart rate. Tachycardias originating from the ventricles can be very benign (i.e., cause no problems) or can result in collapse and sudden death. They are commonly observed following trauma to the chest and after *gastric dilatation-volvulus* or bloat (*see* CHAPTER 30: "THE DIGESTIVE SYSTEM AND DISORDERS"). Tachycardias are also often observed in primary myocardial disease (e.g., dilated cardiomyopathy) where they are more likely to cause ventricular fibrillation, leading to cardiac arrest and sudden death. Drugs such as lidocaine, procainamide, quinidine, propranolol, tocainide, and mexiletine are used to stop such tachycardias and prevent sudden death (often they are not successful in the latter).

Bradycardias (abnormally slow heart rates) can produce clinical signs of weakness, fainting, or collapse. The most frequent causes are degeneration of the sinoatrial (SA) node or the atrioventricular (AV) node. SA nodal degeneration is called *sick sinus syndrome,* whereas a nonfunctional AV node produces *third degree AV block.* The recommended treatment for symptomatic dogs with either condition is implantation of an artificial pacemaker. Pacemaker generators (devices that produce electrical impulses) are procured from pacemaker companies by veterinarians and are usually donated for veterinary use. The battery often will last for 3 to 5 years, and since most dogs that require pacemakers are in older age groups this length of time is very adequate. The lead (covered wire) that connects the generator to the heart is either implanted surgically or placed inside the heart by advancing it carefully down a vein in the neck (*endocardial placement*) under fluoroscopic (X-ray) guidance. Although both procedures require general anesthesia, endocardial placement is generally safer and avoids the additional risks and complications of major surgery. The generator is connected to the lead and then buried beneath the skin or sometimes placed in the abdominal cavity.

CHAPTER 25

The Muscles and Disorders

**by Jeffrey E. Barlough
and George H. Cardinet III**

The Muscular System and the Motor Unit

The muscular system of the dog is composed of the muscles and their surrounding connective tissue structures, and the blood vessels, nerve endings, and lymphatic channels that supply them. Individual muscles are composed of muscle fibers (**myofibers**), each of which consists of bundles of **myofibrils,** slender threadlike structures protected by a delicate cell membrane known as the **sarcolemma.** Myofibrils are composed, in turn, of even smaller threadlike elements, the **myofilaments.** It is these myofilaments, constructed chiefly of two vital proteins, **actin** and **myosin,** that are responsible for the ability of muscles to contract. Around the sarcolemma of muscles are wound layers of connective tissue, which ultimately become continuous with the **tendons,** the fibrous tissue that connects muscles to bone, or with the **fasciae,** sheets of fibrous tissue that ensheath the muscles and define their shape.

The body has several different types of muscle. **Skeletal muscle** is under the dog's voluntary control and composes most of the muscles of movement attached to the skeleton. **Smooth muscle,** by contrast, is not under voluntary control of the will. Smooth muscle is found in the walls of blood vessels and in the major internal organs. **Cardiac muscle** is a specialized type of muscle tissue found only in the heart. Contractions of cardiac muscle occur without conscious control and are responsible for maintenance of the heartbeat.

The basic functional and anatomical organization of **neurons** (nerves) and myofibers within skeletal muscle is referred to as the **motor unit.** Each motor unit is composed of a single **motoneuron** (nerve cell that supplies myofibers in skeletal muscle), **neuromuscular junctions** (the intimate connections between the muscle and nerve cells, representing a specialized extension of the sarcolemma), and the myofibers supplied by the motoneuron. Each motoneuron is composed of a *cell body* located in the **central nervous system** (brain or spinal cord) and an **axon,** the fingerlike extension of the cell which passes to a given muscle within its respective **cranial** or peripheral nerve. (*See* CHAPTER 28,

"THE NERVOUS SYSTEM AND DISORDERS.) Along its course the axon becomes enveloped by a row of **Schwann cells** that form a myelin sheath around the axon. The myelin sheath serves to facilitate the conduction of nerve impulses along the axon. Within a muscle the axon branches into variable numbers of **axon terminals,** which form neuromuscular junctions with the myofibers supplied by the motoneuron. The size of individual motor units (i.e., the number of myofibers supplied by a single motoneuron) can vary from fewer than 100 to more than 1000 myofibers per motoneuron.

When nerve impulses arising in the cell body reach each axon terminal, a chemical called **acetylcholine (ACh)** is released from the terminal and diffuses across the **synaptic cleft** (the space between the axon terminal and the myofiber it supplies), where it is captured by specific ACh-receptor sites located on the sarcolemma of the myofiber. The formation of ACh-receptor complexes on the sarcolemma causes an inflow of sodium and potassium, creating a wavelike **muscle action potential**—essentially an electrical impulse—that spreads throughout the muscle and triggers the events leading to muscle contraction. The contraction of each myofiber is accomplished by the sliding of actin and myosin myofilaments, the energy for this process being provided by molecules of **adenosine triphosphate (ATP).** The activity of the released ACh is regulated by its diffusion away from ACh-receptor sites and its destruction by a specific enzyme (**acetylcholinesterase**) present in the synaptic cleft. This regulatory loop prevents overstimulation of myofibers and thus serves as a braking control on muscular contraction.

Diagnosis of Muscle Diseases

ELECTRODIAGNOSTIC TESTING
Electrodiagnostic testing represents a valuable adjunct to the clinical evaluation of motor-unit disorders in dogs. The techniques employed provide information about the functional integrity of myofibers, nerve fibers and neuromuscular junctions. Most of these procedures must be performed with the patient under deep, general anesthesia.

Electromyography (EMG)
Electromyography (EMG) is the examination of electrical activity within a muscle at rest or during voluntary or evoked muscular contractions. The examination involves insertion of a recording electrode into a muscle for the detection of electrical impulses (muscle action potentials).

Motor Nerve Conduction Velocities
Evaluation of **motor nerve conduction velocities** provides information about the integrity of nerve fibers, principally the fastest-conducting motor nerve fibers. In essence, the procedure measures the elapsed time between the initiation of an electrical stimulus to a nerve at different sites along its course and the subsequent contraction of the muscle fibers supplied by the nerve.

Evaluation of Compound Muscle Action Potentials
With this technique the characteristics of the electrical impulses responsible for causing contraction of a muscle can be collectively evaluated and screened for abnormalities.

BIOPSY EXAMINATION
The findings of the clinical examination and electrodiagnostic testing can provide extremely useful information about the integrity of motor units; however, they only rarely provide complete information about the nature of the underlying disease process. The direct evaluation of motor unit components through **biopsy** examination (examination of tissue samples) offers the most definitive means of identifying the cause of a muscular abnormality.

In the past, demand for and usefulness of muscle biopsy examination have been limited because conventional tissue-processing techniques (fixing, staining, etc.) often do not reveal essential features required for a definitive diagnosis. Over the past 30 years, newer preparative and staining techniques have been introduced for the evaluation of human and animal neuromuscular diseases. During the ensuing years the application and extension of these techniques have greatly enhanced the recognition of neuromuscular diseases in both human and veterinary medicine.

The biopsy procedure should follow and be coordinated with the electrodiagnostic examination for which the patient has been anesthetized. Coordination of the procedure aides in selection of the biopsy site and limits the number of times anesthesia needs to be induced; however, muscle biopsy alone can be performed using local anesthesia. The preferred method is the "open" biopsy technique in which the skin and overlying fascia of the muscle to be biopsied are incised to expose the muscle itself. Techniques for "needle" or "punch" biopsies have been described, but they are less favored because of the small samples obtained and because of various technical difficulties.

EXAMINATION OF SERUM

Evaluation of the patient's serum can be employed for a variety of organ-function tests, the detection of specific antibodies and toxins, and the determination of abnormal values of a number of other serum components. (*See* APPENDIX C, "DIAGNOSTIC TESTS.") Measurement of muscle-specific enzymes in serum, particularly **creatine kinase (CK),** is useful in distinguishing between **neuropathies** (neurologic disorders) and muscle disorders. Elevations in serum CK are indicative of **myonecrosis** (muscle-cell death) and the extent of the elevation is approximately proportional to the extent of the myonecrosis. Since myonecrosis is not a usual feature in neuropathies, elevated CK levels are not commonly observed in neuropathies.

Disorders of the Motor Unit

Disorders of the motor unit can be divided into four major groups: **neuropathies** (disorders of the neuron), **junctionopathies** (disorders of the neuromuscular junction), **myopathies** (disorders of the muscle fiber), and **neuromyopathies** (disorders of both neurons and muscle fibers). Disorders involving the neuron (neuropathies and neuromyopathies) are described in chapter 28, "The Nervous System and Disorders." The remaining disease groups, junctionopathies and myopathies, are discussed below.

JUNCTIONOPATHIES

Myasthenia Gravis (Acquired)

Acquired **myasthenia gravis (MG)** is caused by a deficiency of ACh-receptors on the myofiber membrane. Acquired MG results from destruction of the ACh-receptors by antibodies of the host's immune system. The inciting cause is unknown. Acquired MG affects numerous breeds of dogs, with most dogs being older than 1 year at the time clinical signs appear. Incidence of the disease is highest between 2 and 4 and 9 and 13 years of age. Signs of muscular weakness may be *focal* (localized; e.g., affecting only facial or swallowing muscles), or *diffuse* with signs of generalized muscle weakness. It has been estimated that 25% of cases of **megaesophagus** (enlargement of the esophagus, caused by paralysis of the esophageal musculature) are caused by focal MG. (*See* CHAPTER 30, "THE DIGESTIVE SYSTEM AND DISORDERS.")

Signs of generalized muscle weakness can vary enormously, from some degree of exercise intolerance that resolves with rest to acute **tetraplegia** (paralysis of all four limbs). Patients with focal or generalized signs and megaesophagus often develop pneumonia caused by the aspiration of foreign material into the lungs.

Diagnosis is based on the history, physical examination and results of supportive laboratory examinations, including electrodiagnostic testing; immunologic testing of biopsy tissue to search for antibodies bound to the patient's neuromuscular junctions; immunologic testing of serum for antibodies to ACh-receptors; and pharmacologic testing, involving the intravenous administration of a short-acting *cholinesterase* inhibitor, edrophonium (the **"Tensilon test"**). Cholinesterase inhibitors slow the breakdown of ACh and thereby prolong the action of ACh at the neuromuscular junction. A presumptive positive test with a cholinesterase inhibitor will result in marked, transient improvement in clinical weakness and exercise intolerance. Treatment involves improving neuromuscular transmission through the long-term use of an oral cholinesterase inhibitor and/or suppression of the immune response with corticosteroids.

The prognosis in general is good, unless pneumonia is present.

Myasthenia Gravis (Congenital)

Congenital (present at birth) MG is an uncommon hereditary disorder characterized by a deficiency of ACh-receptors at the neuromuscular junctions. It has been reported in Jack Russell Terriers, Springer Spaniels, Airedales, and Smooth Fox Terriers. The disease usually becomes apparent at 6 to 8 weeks of age, with signs of generalized muscular weakness associated with exercise. The weakness then grows progressively more severe, leading to tetraplegia and death. Diagnostic testing includes pharmacologic and electrodiagnostic tests used in acquired MG. The prognosis for hereditary MG is poor. Treatment with a cholinesterase inhibitor may be helpful, however, and some cases have been maintained for 1 to 2 years. The disease appears to be inherited as an *autosomal recessive* condition (*see* CHAPTER 16, "GENETICS"). Affected dogs should not be bred in order to avoid propagating the genetic defect.

Botulism and Tick Paralysis

Botulism is a rare disease caused by a bacterial toxin that affects neuromuscular activity by preventing the release of ACh. Botulism is contracted either by ingestion of preformed toxin in improperly canned food, raw meat or decomposing carcasses, or by contamination of a wound with the causative bacterium (*Clostridium botulinum*), which subsequently produces the toxin in the damaged tissue ("wound botulism"). (*See* "BOTULISM" IN CHAPTER 35, "BACTERIAL DISEASES.")

Tick paralysis is a reversible paralysis of motor function associated with an infestation by ticks (*Dermacentor, Ixodes* or *Amblyomma*). The ticks secrete a toxin in their saliva that in a sense mimics the toxin of botulism by preventing the release of ACh. Clinical signs are usually observed within a week after attachment of ticks and include incoordination of the hindquarters, reduced respiration, an altered bark, vomiting and difficulty swallowing. These signs then progress to forelimb paralysis and complete recumbency without loss of consciousness. Treatment measures include removal of the causative ticks, administration of antiserum, and general supportive care. The prognosis for recovery is good.

MYOPATHIES

Myopathies are relatively uncommon in dogs and are encountered less frequently than either junctionopathies or neuropathies. Myopathies may be subdivided into *noninflammatory* and *inflammatory* myopathies. The noninflammatory myopathies include *X-linked muscular dystrophy* and the *metabolic muscle disorders,* while the inflammatory myopathies include *masticatory muscle myositis, polymyositis* and *canine familial dermatomyositis.*

X-Linked Muscular Dystrophy

The muscular dystrophies represent a large and widely varied class of muscle disorders in human beings, but in dogs they have been only infrequently reported. *X-linked muscular dystrophy* is a rare hereditary myopathy of dogs (and cats) characterized by a deficiency of **dystrophin,** a cell protein associated with the inner surface of the sarcolemma and whose exact role in muscle-cell function remains unclear. The disorder is referred to as "X-linked" because the defective gene is located on the X chromosome, the female sex chromosome (*see* CHAPTER 16, "GENETICS"). The inheritance of X-linked disease-producing genes exhibits a pattern of expression that matches the pattern of transmission of the sex chromosomes. Thus males (having one X and one Y chromosome) inheriting a defective gene will be clinically affected, while females (with two X chromosomes, one from either parent) can act as healthy carriers because the chromosome with the normal copy of the gene can compensate for the chromosome with the defective gene. The events underlying X-linked muscular dystrophy in dogs appear to be identical to those of *Duchenne muscular dystrophy,* the well-known muscular dystrophy that affects young male children.

Canine X-linked muscular dystrophy has been best recognized and characterized in

Golden Retrievers. (Other breeds that can be affected include Rottweilers, Samoyeds and Irish Terriers.) Clinical signs usually become apparent between 8 and 10 weeks of age and include generalized muscle weakness; a crouched posture, with a stiff-limbed, short-strided, shuffling gait; splaying of the paws; some reduced mobility of the jaws; and difficulty chewing and swallowing associated with excessive salivation. The signs are relentlessly progressive, with affected dogs developing muscle wasting and spinal curvature. Cardiac muscle may also be moderately involved in the disease process.

Diagnosis relies on the history and physical examination, together with the results of appropriate laboratory tests such as, markedly elevated serum CK levels, abnormal findings on an EMG examination, and reduced levels (or absence) of dystrophin in the patient's muscle cells. There is no effective treatment. The life span of affected dogs often is shortened owing to secondary complications. Future research advances in this disease will undoubtedly provide benefits for both dogs and people with muscular dystrophy.

Metabolic Muscle Disorders

These are relatively uncommon disorders of carbohydrate, fat and oxygen metabolism that involve deficiencies in the production of energy (ATP) needed to sustain muscular contraction and other cellular functions with a high energy requirement. One example, **phosphofructokinase deficiency,** has been reported in English Springer Spaniels. It is an inherited disorder characterized by **hemolytic anemia** (anemia caused by destruction of red blood cells), lethargy and weakness after exercise. The underlying cause is a red blood cell enzyme deficiency. A laboratory test can be used to confirm the diagnosis and to distinguish carriers from normal animals.

Masticatory Muscle Myositis

This is an inflammatory myopathy of unknown cause and is limited to the muscles of **mastication** (chewing). The onset may be acute or chronic. Cases with an acute onset often exhibit swelling of the *temporalis* and *masseter* muscles on both sides of the head, and possibly **exophthalmia** (eyeball protrusion) due to swelling of the *pterygoid* muscles. Fever, **conjunctivitis** (inflammation of the mucous membrane lining the eyelids), enlargement of the tonsils and lymph nodes, and **splenomegaly** (enlargement of the spleen) may also be seen. **Trismus** (lockjaw) is frequently present, and affected dogs often exhibit pain when the jaws are manipulated or the mouth is forced open.

In chronic cases the disease either develops slowly and insidiously, or represents repeated bouts of acute myositis. The chewing muscles may be markedly shrunken or wasted, creating a "skull-like" appearance. Trismus usually is present.

Diagnostic aids include CK levels (may or may not be helpful), EMG examination (may be difficult to perform in severely wasted muscles), muscle biopsy, and serologic tests for detection of antibodies to muscle fibers. Treatment usually is directed at suppressing the immune response with corticosteroids.

Polymyositis

Polymyositis refers to a varied collection of generalized inflammatory myopathies that can be caused by several different infectious disease agents (*Toxoplasma, Leptospira, Neospora*), as well as by ill-defined immunologic mechanisms. Widespread inflammatory lesions are present in the muscles, with the severity of localized pain and swelling varying markedly. Elevations in CK levels are usually marked and muscles biopsies may be helpful in identifying an infectious agent. Treatment must be based on the underlying cause.

Canine Familial Dermatomyositis

This is an inherited disorder affecting Collies and Shetland Sheepdogs almost exclusively. **Dermatitis** (inflammation of the skin) can affect the face, ears and lower extremities. Muscle lesions have been described in the chewing muscles and some of the limb muscles. The underlying cause is unknown. (*See* CHAPTER 22, "THE SKIN AND DISORDERS.")

CHAPTER 26

The Skeleton and Disorders

by Robert L. Leighton

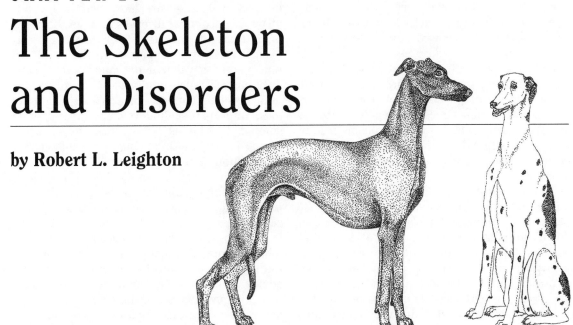

The Skeletal System

The skeletal system is composed of the bones, joints and **ligaments** (strengthening bands of fibrous tissue for stabilizing joint structures) that make up the supporting and protective portions of the body and that provide for rigidity and bodily movement. The **skeleton** represents the bony frame upon which the soft tissues depend for support. However, the skeletal system does much more than just support the body and protect its delicate internal structures. For example, the bones comprise an essential storage system for important minerals such as calcium, magnesium, phosphorus and fluoride. Moreover, the bone marrow (composed of **cancellous bone**) deep within the long bones represents the ultimate source of all the blood cells—both red cells as well as white cells—that are essential for the functioning of the body.

Living bone is provided with blood vessels, nerves, and lymphatic channels and undergoes continued renewal in the form of **resorption** (loss) and subsequent replacement. A thin covering sheath of sensitive tissue, the **periosteum,** provides for the nutrition, growth, repair and protection of the underlying bone, particularly in the young growing phase. Bone cells normally respond to a variety of nutritional and hormonal stimuli, including **estrogens** (female sex hormones), **parathyroid hormone (PTH)** (hormone secreted by the parathyroid glands that regulates the metabolism of calcium and phosphorus), growth hormone (produced by the brain's pituitary gland), **calcitonin** (calcium-regulating hormone produced by the thyroid gland), and vitamin D. (*See* CHAPTER 32, "THE ENDOCRINE SYSTEM AND METABOLIC DISORDERS.")

In the developing fetus, bones arise by the mineralization of an underlying matrix of **cartilage. Cartilage** is a specialized type of connective tissue that is important not only in bone growth but also in the formation of joints (where it is called **articular cartilage**). Areas of bone deposit and change within bones are known as **calcification centers** and can be readily observed on X-ray films.

It is usually convenient to divide the skeletal system into two major parts: the **appendicular skeleton** (composed of the bones forming the limbs and pelvis) and the **axial skeleton** (the bones forming the skull, vertebrae, ribs and sternum). In the dog there is also a **penile bone,** located within the penis of the male. The long bones of the appendicular skeleton grow from growth plates, or **physes,** located between the **epiphysis** (the part that will form the end of the bone) and the **diaphysis** (the long central portion of the bone). Growth normally continues until maturity, which occurs anywhere from about 7 months of age in the smaller breeds of dogs, to as long as a year or more in the giant breeds.

There are three types of joints in the body. Fibrous joints are the connecting "seams" between the bones of the skull, and are also found forming the special type of joint that anchors the teeth in their sockets. Cartilaginous joints are found in the vertebral column, while synovial joints are found in the limbs. **Synovial joints** are enclosed in a **joint capsule** and are lubricated by **synovial fluid,** which facilitates essentially frictionless movement of one cartilage surface against another. As indicated earlier, the actual contacting surfaces of the bones within a synovial joint are lined with articular cartilage, which receives its nutrition from the synovial fluid. When **tendons** (fibrous tissues attaching muscle to bone) glide over the surfaces of bone near bone ends, they are often protected by a small bone known as a **sesamoid,** which is embedded within the muscle tendon itself. Examples of sesamoid bones include the **patella** (the kneecap), and smaller structures in the knee (called **fabellae**) and in the foot.

Skeletal Disorders

Diseases affecting the skeletal system are described according to their cause, if such is known. Bone diseases may be congenital or hereditary, metabolic, infectious, inflammatory, neoplastic or traumatic in origin. In some cases, the diagnosis may be readily apparent to the veterinarian; in other cases, a clinical and laboratory workup may be required in order to uncover the cause of illness.

CONGENITAL AND HEREDITARY DISEASES
Congenital diseases are those that are present at birth. Congenital diseases may be the result of intrauterine accidents, maternal disease, exposure to toxic compounds in the uterus, or unexplained developmental failures. This category includes such things as failure of normal limb development, presence of extra limbs or toes, improper skull development, and other similar deformities. *Hereditary* diseases are those due to an individual animal's genetic constitution. Many hereditary skeletal diseases are of interest because of the deleterious effects of the resulting abnormalities. Such diseases include hip dysplasia, osteochondrosis dissecans (*see* "DISEASES INVOLVING THE GROWTH PLATES," BELOW), elbow dysplasia, cervical vertebral deformities (deformities of vertibrae in the neck), **lumbosacral** malarticulation (cauda equina syndrome, a lumbosacral instability which involves spinal cord complications in the lower back), **patellar luxation** (dislocation of the knee), intervertebral disk degeneration, overshot and undershot jaws, atlanto-axial malarticulation (abnormal movement between first and second vertebrae), Legg-Perthes disease (osteochondrosis of the head of the femur), odontoid process dysplasia (abnormal formation of the projections on the vertebrae). In fact, there are at present more than *forty* recognized or strongly suspected genetic skeletal diseases of dogs, only the most important of which can be discussed here. Many other suspected hereditary skeletal disorders have not been thoroughly investigated as yet because of the high cost of selective breeding, the long observation time required, and the paucity of good, reliable breeding records. (*See* CHAPTER 16, "GENETICS," and CHAPTER 17, "CONGENITAL AND INHERITED DISORDERS.")

Some hereditary disorders are not looked upon as representing disease or deformity, but rather as traits to be sought for. One example of these is **achondroplasia,** the condition of dwarfism that is perpetuated in the Dachshund and Basset Hound breeds. Such a condition would, of course, be deemed undesirable in the Alaskan Malamute.

The foreshortened head seen in English and French Bulldogs, Pugs, Boston Terriers, Brussels Griffons, Pekingese, Japanese Spaniels, Lhasa Apsos and Boxers is another aberrant hereditary trait that is considered desirable. The same applies to screw tails, short tails, absent tails, and variations in hair structure such as are seen in the Rhodesian Ridgeback. In attempting to develop desired specific breed characteristics, unfortunately, some harmful deformities may be accentuated.

Hip dysplasia is an important hereditary developmental disease that is seen in almost all of the canine breeds, particularly the larger ones. In hip dysplasia the "ball-and-socket" joints of the hips develop abnormally. Either the sockets are too shallow, or the ligaments and/or muscles do not exert enough control over the movement of the joint, allowing the "ball" end of the **femur** (thighbone) to separate from the hip joint. The failure of the development of the hip joints may vary from slightly abnormal joints to complete joint dislocation. The poorly developed hip is frequently (but not always) painful, and interferes with proper gait and activity. Although hip dysplasia is caused primarily by an hereditary defect, the severity of the disease is influenced by rapid growth, overfeeding and excessive exercise.

Dysplastic dogs are born with normal hip joints which subsequently undergo changes as the dogs mature. The customary diagnosis is made by X rays taken at maturity, when the dogs are about 1 year of age. Some cases of hip dysplasia can be diagnosed much earlier, while others may not exhibit disease until 2 years of age.

Elimination of the disease is a difficult undertaking, relying upon X-ray diagnosis, accurate breeding records, and breeding of only the best proven sires to proven dams. The treatment chosen for damaged hips depends upon the severity of the deformity. **Excision arthroplasty** (removal of the head of the femur), **pelvic rotation** (a surgery in which the hip socket is moved outward to provide more coverage of the head of the femur), and *total hip replacement* are options for therapy. Of these three, total hip replacement is the most consistently successful procedure.

METABOLIC DISEASES

Metabolic diseases of bone are those that are caused by either an excess or a deficiency in one or more substances regulating body growth, development or maintenance of the normal physiological state. The exact chain of events that occurs often is very complex and interdependent on various stimuli and responses; bone may be only one of the many parts of the body affected. Some metabolic disorders are dietary in origin, having their cause in an imbalance in certain nutrient, mineral or vitamin levels. Others may be secondary to an underlying problem such as cancer or kidney failure. Some metabolic diseases produce serious physical abnormalities that cannot readily be corrected. The diagnosis often relies upon clinical and laboratory procedures to identify or confirm the nature of the metabolic imbalance. (*See* CHAPTER 10, "DISEASES OF DIETARY ORIGIN" and CHAPTER 32, "THE ENDOCRINE SYSTEM AND METABOLIC DISORDERS.")

Pituitary dwarfism seen in German Shepherd Dogs results from a lack of growth hormone, which is normally produced by the pituitary gland at the base of the brain. **Hyperparathyroidism** (hyperactivity of one or more parathryoid glands, resulting in excessive parathyroid hormone secretion and release of calcium from the bones) is often induced secondarily by secretions stimulated by a pituitary tumor. *Renal secondary hyperparathyroidism* is associated with several types of kidney dysfunction. In this disease, the damaged kidneys cannot excrete phosphorus in a normal fashion. This leads to an increase of phosphorus levels in the bloodstream (**hyperphosphatemia**), which in turn causes a drop in blood calcium (**hypocalcemia**). This stimulates the parathyroid glands to compensate by increasing the withdrawal of stored calcium from the bones, thus weakening their structure. From just this single example, it is evident how strikingly interdependent are the various metabolic processes of the body.

Corticosteroids are hormones (such as **cortisol** and **corticosterone**) produced by the adrenal gland that elevate blood sugar levels, increase fat and protein breakdown, and exert an anti-inflammatory effect on conditions such as arthritis and **dermatitis** (inflammatory skin disease). Elevated levels of corticosteroids (either from prolonged steroid therapy or from a pituitary or adrenal gland tumor) can also cause **osteopenia** (loss of bone calcium), resulting in bone weakness and even fracture and collapse under stress. This effect is due to a direct effect of corticosteroids on the cells associated with bone resorption and regeneration.

Overzealous supplementation of the diet with certain vitamins, particularly vitamin D, can induce harmful bone changes—exactly the opposite of what an owner may be striving for. Lengthy feeding of an all-meat diet can induce **nutritional secondary hyperparathyroidism,** resulting in bone decalcification. This disease is essentially a calcium deficiency; because meat is so high in phosphorus (and so correspondingly low in calcium), the parathyroid glands (by secreting parathyroid hormone) begin pulling calcium out of the skeleton in order to compensate for the imbalance. Overfeeding a high-energy diet to induce the fastest and greatest growth, coupled with a hereditary predisposition for large size and rapid growth, has been shown to increase the severity of certain genetic diseases such as hip dysplasia and osteochondrosis dissecans.

Metabolic diseases of the joints are rare. **Hemophilic arthropathy** is an inherited blood-clotting disorder that causes bleeding into the joints. Hypertrophic osteoarthropathy is a proliferative disease affecting mainly the long bones and their joints. It is usually associated with lung tumors or other masses in the chest, and only rarely with tumors located elsewhere in the body. Hypertrophic osteoarthropathy is characterized by a slowly progressive thickening and proliferation of the surfaces of the long bones and the digits, and is thought to be caused by changes in blood flow to the affected bones. The function of joints such as the *carpus* (equivalent of the human wrist) and *hock* (equivalent of the human ankle) is compromised (often severely) by the new deposits of bone tissue around the ends of the affected bones and joints.

Bones and joints may also be damaged by disuse (**disuse atrophy**), with loss of calcium and subsequent weakness. In joints the articular cartilage is liable to detach from the underlying bone as the joint becomes stiff and eventually dysfunctional, owing to *adhesions* (fusion of surfaces) in and around the affected joint.

INFECTIOUS/INFLAMMATORY DISEASES

Just as people do, dogs suffer from "arthritis," an all-inclusive term that covers inflammatory and degenerative changes in the articular cartilage. *Degenerative* arthritis (also known as osteoarthritis or *degenerative joint disease*) is usually considered the result of the normal aging process, but it can also be caused more acutely by traumatic injury to bone, cartilage or ligaments. It is the most common form of arthritis affecting dogs and is manifested chiefly by lameness, which typically is exacerbated by cold, damp weather conditions and by exercise. Osteoarthritis is not really a disease itself, but rather the secondary result of damage (either short-term or long-term) to joint structures. (*Note:* osteoarthritis should not be confused with **rheumatoid arthritis,** a disease with an immune-mediated basis.) The damage may be caused by hip dysplasia, rupture of internal or external ligaments, partial or total joint dislocation, poor anatomical alignment of a fracture site, or pressure from a disparity of growth of component bones. Naturally, the severity of the disease depends upon the extent of the damage that has occurred. It can vary from the relatively simple stretching of a ligament (known as a **sprain**), to a joint's being torn open and smashed in an automobile accident.

Inflammatory arthritis may be the result of either infection or immune-mediated disease (*see* CHAPTER 33, "THE IMMUNE SYSTEM AND DISORDERS"). Infection may arise from the entry of bacteria into the joint through puncture wounds, contamination during surgery, or via the bloodstream from an infectious focus elsewhere in the body. Joints in the limbs as well as those of the intervertebral discs within the spinal column may be involved. One example of the latter occurs in *brucellosis,* caused by the bacterium *Brucella canis* (*see* CHAPTER 35, "BACTERIAL DISEASES").

Immune-mediated arthritis is seen in **rheumatoid arthritis,** a chronic, progressive, ulcerative arthritis with joint changes very similar to those seen in people with this debilitating illness. In an immune-mediated arthritis, antibodies and/or cells of the immune system are involved in producing the underlying inflammatory response that leads to the destructive arthritic lesions. Another example is **systemic lupus erythematosus (SLE),** a rare disease that often is manifested by *polyarthritis* (inflammation of one or more joints). Both rheumatoid arthritis and SLE will exhibit recognizable changes on X ray, but the actual diagnoses are dependent on sophisticated laboratory tests such as the **antinuclear antibody (ANA) test** (*see* APPENDIX C, "DIAGNOSTIC TESTS"). Treatment of immune-mediated arthritis relies on anti-inflammatory drug therapy. (For additional information on immune-mediated arthritis, *see* CHAPTER 33, "THE IMMUNE SYSTEM AND DISORDERS.")

NEOPLASTIC DISEASES

Bones, like other tissues of the body, are subject to the development of tumors (*see* CHAPTER 38, "CANCER"). One of the most common bone tumors in dogs is **osteosarcoma,** or **osteogenic sarcoma,** which tends to occur more frequently in the larger breeds. Some breed lines are apparently more susceptible than others to osteosarcoma. A highly destructive tumor, osteosarcoma is malignant and thus capable of spreading from the site of its development, particularly to the lungs. The syndrome of hypertrophic osteoarthropathy (*see* above) can be produced by spread of osteosarcoma to the lungs. More than half of the osteosarcomas in dogs arise in the long bones. Osteosarcomas have been reported to occur in areas of chronic irritation—for example, at sites where bone plates, pins or wires have been used for fracture repair (*see* below). Faulty implantation appears to be the cause, rather than the implants themselves. Clinical signs at the tumor site can include local pain and swelling, deformity and lameness. X rays of the tumor area and chest as well as biop-

sies are usually required to confirm the diagnosis. Treatment may require surgical amputation of an affected limb, perhaps combined with chemotherapy. If spread to the lungs has already occurred at the time of diagnosis, however, the prognosis must be considered poor.

The second most common bone tumor is the **chondrosarcoma,** a malignant tumor of cartilage-producing cells. Chondrosarcomas grow more slowly than osteosarcomas and have a predilection for flat bones such as are found in the nasal **turbinates** (thin, scroll-shaped bones found at the rear of the nasal passages). These tumors can arise in the long bones and spine as well. Therapy depends upon the extent of tumor invasion of local tissue and whether or not spread has taken place.

Fibrosarcomas, malignant tumors of connective tissue cells, frequently affect the jaw and skull, but can arise in other areas as well. **Multiple myeloma** is a rare malignant tumor of **plasma cells** (white blood cells that produce antibodies) arising from the bone marrow. The signs of the disease are many and varied, but can include local swelling, pain, lameness and fractures at the tumor site. (For additional information on multiple myeloma, *see* CHAPTER 33, "THE IMMUNE SYSTEM AND DISORDERS.")

Joints are the site of some specific tumors affecting the synovial lining membrane, such as **synovial sarcoma.** A malignant tumor, synovial sarcoma has the capability of spreading to other regions of the body. Treatment of this tumor is difficult and often impossible; the prognosis is considered poor.

DEEP BONE INFECTIONS (OSTEOMYELITIS)

Bone is subject to infection, as are other body tissues. Sources of infection may be the bloodstream, infections elsewhere in the body, bite wounds, fractures that rupture through the overlying skin, penetrating foreign bodies, or the results of contaminated surgery. Many infections remain in and around the bone site and may be quite resistant to antibiotic therapy. Some eventually discharge pus through a sinus or draining tract in the skin.

Bacterial cultures of the infectious material

are taken in order to identify the causative organism and to select the most effective antibiotic. Fragments of dead bone (**sequestra**) may be found within the site of infection and must be removed surgically.

Diseases Involving the Growth Plates

The growth plates at the ends of the long bones (**epiphyses**) are particularly affected by hormonal, genetic, metabolic, nutritional and biomechanical factors. As indicated above, decreased growth hormone production can result in *dwarfism,* which is seen occasionally in German shepherds. An excess or deficiency of steroid hormones, including male or female sex hormones, will also affect bone; however, such conditions are relatively rare.

When the bones that arise from the growth plates are affected, as in achondroplasia, they fail to develop properly, while the other bones of the body continue to develop normally. The result is a dwarf such as a Dachshund, with its normal body and shortened legs. A hereditary interference with cartilage production at the growth plate is seen as a rare dwarfism in the Alaskan Malamute, Norwegian Elkhound, and English Pointer. Impairment of normal growth also may occur in vitamin D deficiency. This is rarely seen today, however, owing to the fortification and supplementation of commercial pet foods.

Osteochondrosis is a disturbance of the germinal cells (cells capable of dividing and differentiating) within cartilage. When the condition is present in the growth plate, it results in a retained cartilaginous core that is associated with arrest of lengthwise growth. This is seen particularly in the forelegs of large-breed dogs. With a disturbance of the germinal layers under the articular cartilage of joint surfaces, degeneration of these tissues occurs. If associated with trauma, the overlying articular cartilage may crack and produce a loosened fragment, which may even break free into the joint. This condition is called **osteochondrosis dissecans (OCD)** and is a problem in young, fast-growing, active dogs of medium and large breeds.

Injury to the growth plate, as in a dislocation or fracture, may not be sufficient to cause cessation of bone growth. Such fractures may be **reduced** (set) and further growth continue without complication. If, however, the injury is sufficiently severe, or the repair holds the growth plate together too firmly, fusion (closure of the growth plate) can occur and the bone will no longer expand in length from that area. If the shortened bone is part of a pair, as in the *radius* and *ulna* of the forelimb (*see* Chapter 18, "Anatomy"), severe developmental changes can occur. Premature fusion of the ulna will cause a marked distortion of the associated radius, which continues to grow, and the resulting pressures bring about damage to the elbow.

Fractures along the cartilaginous division between an epiphysis and the bone to which it will become attached are seen in several bones, including the scapula, humerus, femur and tibia, as well as in the radius and ulna. In some breeds the anconeal process, a segment of the ulna located in the elbow, has such a cartilaginous growth plate. Pressure from uneven growth affecting the elbow may cause this portion of the bone to separate from the ulna proper.

Fractures

Of all the diseases affecting the skeletal system, the most common by far are fractures. Among the most frequent causes are unexpected leaps or falls, encounters with automobiles, and gunshot wounds. A few fractures occur spontaneously at the site of tumors (such as multiple myeloma), or secondarily to other conditions that weaken bone (e.g., hyperparathyroidism; *see* above). Some bones are more susceptible to fractures than are others, the pelvis being the most frequently affected, followed by the femur, tibia, radius and ulna, humerus, mandible, spine and ribs (*see* Chapter 18, "Anatomy").

The extent of injury may vary from a barely visible crack to a severe fracture, and more than a single bone may be affected at one time. When joints are involved, it is essential that the joint surfaces be set carefully because uneven healing of the joint surface will result in interference with function, inflammation, pain, osteoarthritis and disuse atrophy.

The diagnosis of a fracture may be quite obvious or may be surprisingly obscure. A tentative diagnosis can be made in some instances by

palpation (feeling with the hands), but it is usually necessary to obtain a good diagnostic X ray. This will allow the veterinarian to assess the location, extent and type of fracture involved. Using this information, coupled with the physical examination, the veterinarian can then design an appropriate treatment and anticipate possible complications. Based on these findings, an estimate of the probable results of treatment (the **prognosis**) can also be made. Often the probable outcome may represent no more than an educated guess, however, for other factors can alter the course of the injury. Damage to the surrounding tissue, hemorrhage, infection, bone loss, age, physical status, and concomitant diseases are all potentially confounding variables that must be taken into consideration.

Selection of the course of treatment is dependent upon a number of factors, including the type and location of the fracture(s), size and age of the dog, facilities and instrumentation available to the veterinarian, the extent of his/her technical training in fracture repair, and cost. Basic treatment involves immobilization of the fracture site to allow the broken bones to heal together. Some fractures can be treated simply by confining the injured dog for a specified period of time, as with some minor pelvic injuries. Partial fractures, often referred to as **greenstick fractures**, may be nicely immobilized with a simple splint. More complicated fractures can be immobilized by several different means:

1. **Intramedullary pinning,** which consists of the insertion of a stainless-steel rod (*intramedullary pin*) down the central, marrow cavity of the fractured bone in order to realign the broken pieces, like threading spools on a pencil.
2. **External fixation,** in which small pins are inserted through the skin and muscle tissue into the underlying bone fragments. The protruding ends of the pins are attached to a connecting bar, which holds all the fragments together until healing takes place.
3. **Bone plating,** which consists of replacing the bone fragments in their original location and holding them in position with a perforated metal plate (*bone plate*). The bone plate

is fastened to the several fragments by small screws and can be custom-contoured to "mold" to the shape of the underlying bone. This method requires that the bones be exposed surgically (a procedure called **open reduction**).

All three major methods of fracture repair have specific body locations and fracture types for which they are best suited. In addition to setting a fracture a portion of the broken bone may be removed, as is done with a severely damaged head of the femur in the smaller dogs, forming a quite satisfactory "false joint" at the hip. A portion of the bone may also be replaced, as in a total hip replacement. Here, the ball-and-socket joint of the hip is replaced with metal and plastic. Hip replacement is a quite satisfactory procedure today in middle- and large-sized dogs. Defects in fractured bone may also be "filled in" with *bone grafts* obtained from the patient's own body or from a donor.

In some cases fractures may actually be created by the veterinary surgeon in order to correct deformities, such as those caused by premature fusion of the radius and ulna. Others are made to widen a narrow pelvis or to increase the coverage of the hip joint, as in a triple pelvic **osteotomy** (surgical cutting of bone) for improvement of hip dysplasia.

In joints, dislocations can be replaced and repairs can be made to realign broken fragments and hold them in place until healing occurs. Torn ligaments can be replaced with tissue grafts or strong *sutures* (stitching material). Spinal joints (**intervertebral disks**) that have ruptured or become distended, placing pressure on the spinal cord and compromising nerve function, often must be removed surgically.

Severely damaged joints, or those that have failed to develop properly, can be fused (made to grow together) by a procedure known as an arthrodesis. The fresh bone surfaces are brought together and held in position with screws, plates, pins or wires until the surfaces fuse, effectively "locking" the joint in place. In the process joint function (movement) is lost, but the joint is no longer painful and reasonable overall use of the affected limb is restored.

Failure of development may occur in the stifle, wherein the **patella** (kneecap) does not arise in the correct location. Surgical correction can provide for more proper function. In some cases, fragments of bone or cartilage may become loose or free in a joint (so-called "joint mice") and must be removed surgically. Parts of some joints have cushioning cartilages called *menisci* which, if damaged, may require removal or repair.

With so many disease conditions and such a multiplicity of treatments, it can be appreciated that the field of fracture repair today constitutes a specialty in veterinary medicine.

CHAPTER 27

The Urinary System and Disorders

by Larry D. Cowgill,
Donald G. Low and
Jeffrey E. Barlough

The Urinary System

The primary functions of the urinary system are to filter metabolic waste products from the bloodstream and to regulate the chemical and fluid composition of the blood. The chief functioning components of the urinary system are the paired, bean-shaped **kidneys** (located in the lower back region, on either side of the *aorta*); the paired **ureters** (hollow tubes connecting the kidneys to the bladder); the urinary bladder (a muscular sac that serves as a reservoir for *urine*); and the **urethra** (the hollow tube leading from the bladder to the exterior of the body). (*See* CHAPTER 18, "ANATOMY.") In cross section the kidneys are composed of two major zones, an outer **cortex** and an inner **medulla,** each containing several hundred thousand microscopic nephrons, the functioning units that actually produce the urine. Anatomically, the urinary system can be further subdivided into an *upper urinary tract* and a *lower urinary tract,* the upper tract being composed of the kidneys and ureters, the lower tract being composed of the urinary bladder and urethra. For our purposes here, the **prostate gland** of the male can also be considered as a component part of the lower urinary tract.

Waste products of protein metabolism, such as the nitrogen-containing compounds **urea** and **creatinine,** are generated from the breakdown of ingested nutrients. As these wastes build up they must be removed in order to avoid toxic reactions in the host. It is the prime function of the kidneys to filter these and other wastes from the blood. Blood enters the kidneys through the *renal arteries* and passes into the nephrons, where it is filtered through microscopic tufts of blood vessels called **glomeruli** (singular: **glomerulus**) that separate the cellular and fluid components of the blood. The resulting cell-free filtrate of blood is passed through the microscopic renal tubules where the toxic materials are excreted, while essential ions, amino acids, organic acids and bases, and water molecules are either excreted or reabsorbed, depending upon the current needs of the body. The waste products removed by each kidney are passed out through the **renal pelvis** (a "collecting funnel" deep within each kidney into which the tubules drain), move down the ureter and are stored in the bladder as urine, and are eventually eliminated from the body through the process of *urination.*

Urination may be defined as the storage and conscious elimination of filtered waste fluid from the body. Voluntary control of urination is initiated in the higher centers of the brain. Filling of the bladder with urine causes the bladder wall and the **detrusor** (smooth muscle layer of the bladder wall) to stretch. Sensory nerve fibers within the *pelvic nerve* detect this stretching and send nerve impulses to the brain, which commands the detrusor muscle to contract. Concomitant relaxation of the **external urethral sphincter** (a circular band of muscle surrounding the junction between the bladder and urethra) results in voiding of the urine.

In addition to filtering wastes from the blood, the kidneys also play a role in the secretion of essential hormones such as **erythropoietin** (which stimulates the production of red blood cells) and renin (which is involved in the control of blood pressure), as well as other physiologically active substances such as **prostaglandins** and the active form of *vitamin D.*

The ability of the kidneys to accomplish their essential daily tasks can be examined in a number of different ways. Two of the most common laboratory tests used to evaluate kidney performance are the **blood urea nitrogen (BUN)** and **creatinine** assays. Both tests can be readily performed on blood samples and provide the veterinarian with a measure of the ability of the kidneys to remove nitrogen-containing wastes from the body.

Diseases of the Upper Urinary Tract

CONGENITAL KIDNEY DEFECTS

Congenital defects are those that are present at birth, and may or may not be inherited. Congenital kidney defects represent the result of abnormal maturation of the kidneys in the developing fetus. Although they are not common, congenital renal defects do occur from time to time in dogs. Among those that may be seen are **renal hypoplasia** (underdevelopment of one or both kidneys), **renal aplasia** (absence of one or both kidneys), and polycystic kidneys, wherein nonfunctional, cystic structures are found replacing normal kidney tissue.

KIDNEY FAILURE

It is important to distinguish between *kidney disease* and *kidney failure.* Kidney disease can be defined as any deviation from normal function or normal anatomic structure, and can be classified as either progressive, arrested or healed. Kidney disease usually causes no detectable loss of kidney function unless the disease process is extensive, resulting in the loss of 65–70% or more of functional tissue in *both* kidneys—at which point the kidneys can be considered to be in failure. Thus the terms "kidney disease" and "kidney failure" are *not* synonymous, because kidney disease does not always result in kidney failure.

Acute Kidney Failure

Acute kidney failure is the rapid-onset inability of the kidneys to perform their normal functions. It is characterized by **oliguria** (reduction in the amount of urine excreted) or **anuria** (complete cessation of urine production), reduced blood flow to the kidneys with a concomitantly reduced **glomerular filtration rate** (rate at which the kidney glomeruli filter the blood passing through them), and the clinical and biochemical consequences of these changes. Rapid increases in BUN and creatinine levels as well as acid-base disturbances are laboratory evidence of kidney failure.

Acute kidney failure is a tenuously reversible state, and must be diagnosed quickly and treated aggressively. Failure to initiate therapy in a timely manner will result in irreversible damage to kidney tissue and ultimately death. The causes of acute kidney failure are many and varied, but may be divided broadly into three major categories.

1. *Hemodynamically Mediated.* In these conditions the blood flow to the kidneys is impaired, either because of low blood pressure, low blood fluid volume, circulatory system collapse, or renal **hypoperfusion** (reduced blood flow to the kidneys owing to

damage within the kidneys themselves). Conditions predisposing to hemodynamically mediated acute kidney failure include shock, adrenal gland insufficiency, heat prostration and prolonged anesthesia.

2. *Nephrotoxic.* Toxins that damage kidney tissue are important causes of acute kidney failure. Included among these are ethylene glycol (commercial antifreeze), arsenic, mercury and certain antibiotics.

3. *Miscellaneous.* Other causes include **leptospirosis** (an infection caused by bacteria of the genus *Leptospira; see* CHAPTER 35, "BACTERIAL DISEASES"), excessive vitamin D intake, and elevated blood calcium levels secondary to **lymphosarcoma** (a tumor of the lymphatic system; *see* CHAPTER 33, "THE IMMUNE SYSTEM AND DISORDERS").

Dogs in acute kidney failure appear depressed and exhibit **uremia** (high levels of urea nitrogen and other nitrogenous waste products circulating in the blood), low blood pressure, and often a lowered body temperature. The respiratory rate frequently is elevated, the heart rate may be slow and irregular, and the pulse often is weak. Convulsions may occur in the terminal stages of the disease as a consequence of the uncontrolled buildup of toxins in the bloodstream.

Treatment often includes intravenous fluids and **diuretics** (drugs that promote urine flow). In patients whose fluid and other metabolic disturbances are unresponsive to such conservative measures, **peritoneal dialysis** represents a viable alternative. In this procedure a special fluid is instilled into the peritoneal cavity (inside the abdomen), which draws waste material out through the peritoneal lining. After a period of time the waste fluid is removed and fresh fluid is added. In this way the peritoneal lining temporarily takes on the function of the kidneys, drawing waste material out of the blood and removing it from the body. Once instituted, peritoneal dialysis becomes a major undertaking with rigid time demands if it is to prove either useful or successful. The availability of **hemodialysis,** in which the blood is actually filtered through a special apparatus (an "artificial

kidney"), is limited at present to a small number of veterinary teaching hospitals.

Chronic Kidney Failure

Chronic kidney failure is caused by single or multiple (cumulative) injuries to the kidneys that result in the irreparable loss of functioning kidney tissue. It has been conservatively estimated that approximately 0.5% of the 52 to 53 million pet dogs in the United States develop chronic, progressive renal failure each year, making it one of the most important disease entities of companion animals.

Clinical signs exhibited by dogs in chronic kidney failure range from no signs at all, when the loss of function can still be accommodated, to a severely disordered state wherein normal kidney function has effectually vanished and the disease process is at an end stage. Uremia develops when the residual functioning kidney mass is insufficient to meet the needs of the body. At each stage of the disease process, the clinical signs of kidney failure are sufficiently stereotyped to stage the extent of disease and to direct an appropriate course of therapy.

Once it has progressed beyond certain ill-defined thresholds, the deterioration of kidney function progresses steadily to an end stage and death. This "autodestruction" proceeds on course, whether or not the ultimate inciting cause is still active. The causes of kidney failure are multiple in nature and incompletely understood, but involve factors both intrinsic and extrinsic to the failing kidneys themselves.

Intrinsic factors that promote progression to kidney failure include increased blood pressure and blood flow within the kidneys; **proteinuria** (overflow of filtered protein into the urine); and increased kidney production of ammonia. Extrinsic factors involve certain dietary constituents (protein, phosphate, fats and sodium), increased systemic blood pressure (**hypertension**), and elevated levels of fat in the bloodstream (**hyperlipidemia**).

Management of chronic kidney failure in the dog is targeted at ameliorating the clinical, metabolic, hormonal and biochemical aberrations of failure. The physical and laboratory findings will vary with the degree of failure, the rapidity of its onset, the nature of the underlying injury to the kidney tissue, and the nature of any previous therapy. Dogs whose disease is still compensated for (i.e., dogs with enough kidney tissue remaining to support normal function) usually exhibit few clinical signs, and the diagnosis is usually established by laboratory tests. By the time clinical signs become apparent, the disease has already progressed to an advanced stage.

Dietary Management of Chronic Kidney Failure

Dietary therapy is the foundation of the conservative medical management of chronic kidney failure. Dietary manipulations can counter many of the metabolic excesses and deficits that result from failure of the kidneys to perform their normal functions. Diets must be formulated to minimize the signs and metabolic disorders of uremia and simultaneously provide adequate nutrition. Appropriate dietary changes can both alleviate the clinical signs of failure and retard its progression.

Proteins are the most "harmful" dietary constituent and their restriction in the diet must be considered mandatory. The use of protein-restricted diets is generally correlated with improvements in clinical signs and prolonged survival. The provision of an adequate caloric intake with a formulated or prescription diet is also essential. Although diets for patients with chronic kidney failure may be assembled from their component parts by an owner, it is more common (and much more practical) to purchase any of the several commercial prescription diets for kidney failure that are currently available from veterinary sources.

The use of sodium chloride (table salt) in the management of chronic renal failure has undergone a considerable evolution in the past decade. Previous recommendations advocated dietary sodium supplementation, based on the premise that uremic dogs lose sodium in the urine and thus require additional sodium in the diet. Recent research concerning the metabolic adaptations of the body to progressive kidney failure have altered this recommendation; in fact, dietary sodium supplementation is now considered not only inappropriate but potentially harmful. Thus, judicious restriction of salt intake is currently recommended, particularly in light of the elevation in blood pressure that develops concurrently in dogs with chronic kidney failure.

Glomerulonephritis

Injury to the renal glomeruli may result in either no clinical signs or in profound clinical manifestations. Glomerular lesions that are progressive or unresolved damage the renal blood supply, kidney tissue, and kidney tubule cells and promote end-stage **nephrosclerosis** (scarring of kidney tissue). At this stage, glomerular disease is irreversible and indistinguishable from other causes of renal scarring. Nephrosclerosis is a principal cause of the normal, progressive deterioration of kidney function that accompanies aging.

Glomerular injury has a decidedly immunologic basis. The precise cause for activation and subsequent immune-mediated tissue injury is unknown, however. Inciting causes of diverse chemical composition and biologic reactivity may participate in the production of glomerulonephritis. Such causes can include bacteria (as in pyometra, bacterial endocarditis, or foxtail granulomas), viruses (canine adenovirus type 1), parasites (heartworm), and host body components (as in cancer or systemic lupus erythematosus [SLE]. Indeed, any infectious, inflammatory, cancerous or degenerative process capable of sustained stimulation of the immune system can produce immune-mediated glomerular damage. In most clinical situations, however, the underlying cause remains unknown.

Damage to the glomeruli results in proteinuria and is the signature of glomerular injury. The magnitude of the protein loss directly influences the subsequent clinical course of the disease. Small or moderate urinary protein losses may be compensated for by dietary supplementation, increased protein production by the liver, or decreased protein breakdown and may result in few if any recognizable clinical signs. Moderate to massive proteinuria (7 to 20 grams of protein lost per day) will exceed all compensatory mechanisms, and can result in the

nephrotic syndrome, which is characterized by fluid retention either as **edema** (swelling of the tissues) or **ascites** (fluid accumulation in the abdomen). Dogs are less prone than people, however, to develop either generalized or localized edema or ascites.

A careful and detailed history and physical examination are required to evaluate patients with glomerular disease. Its diverse causes (especially cancer) and nonspecific signs may make a clinical diagnosis difficult. Affected patients usually exhibit weight loss, inappetence, weakness, depression and listlessness. There is no apparent age or sex predilection. All ages of dogs are affected, but the incidence increases in those over 5 years of age. The manifestations of the disease are influenced by the length of time the disease has been present and by its severity and the degree of kidney failure. Vomiting, diarrhea, **polydipsia** (excessive thirst), **polyuria** (excessive urination), **nocturia** (excessive urination at night), and oral ulcerations may be predominant clinical features if kidney failure is advanced. Hypertension is also a consistent finding in dogs with either acute or chronic glomerulonephritis, and represents an important factor perpetuating glomerular damage.

The clinical diagnosis is supported on the basis of routine urinalysis by persistent proteinuria and by other laboratory tests. The excretion of greater than 1.5 g of protein per day is not likely to be caused by genital or lower urinary tract disease and suggests significant glomerular abnormalities. Therapy of glomerular disease is divided into efforts to alter the course of the disease and supportive measures to provide relief from clinical signs. The most obvious means to alter the course of an immune-mediated disease is to remove the specific inciting cause; rarely, however, can the cause be identified and even more rarely can its source be controlled or eliminated. If a source of chronic infection, parasitic infestation, or cancer is found, its removal may halt progression of the disease. There is evidence, however, that some forms of chronic glomerulonephritis are perpetuated through autoimmune mechanisms that may take over even after the inciting cause has been eliminated

(i.e., the chronic stimulation has induced the body to begin attacking its own components).

A second course of action more readily implemented, but of uncertain efficacy, is the use of anti-inflammatory medications (corticosteroids or cytotoxic drugs) to modulate the immune response and subsequent tissue destruction. Use of such medications for glomerulonephritis remains controversial, however, with the possible exception of glomerular disease mediated by systemic lupus erythematosus (*see* CHAPTER 33, "THE IMMUNE SYSTEM AND DISORDERS).

Supportive therapy is intended to correct nutritional inadequacies, edema, hypertension and the generalized manifestations of kidney failure that may accompany glomerular disease. In general, supportive therapy has no effect on the primary renal injury and should be applied to the individual patient as clinical circumstances dictate. Such supportive measures in general are quite similar to those described for management of chronic kidney failure, as outlined above.

PYELONEPHRITIS

Pyelonephritis refers to any infection of the kidney involving the renal pelvis. The infection is often *ascending* in nature, that is, it arises at a lower point in the urinary tract (often the bladder) and migrates slowly upward until the kidneys become involved. However, pyelonephritis may also occur secondarily to infections extrinsic to the urinary tract itself. Malaise, weight loss, pain in the area of the affected kidney(s) and fever are clinical signs that may be exhibited. Treatment (including appropriate antibiotics) must be applied promptly to avoid extensive damage to kidney tissue.

AMYLOIDOSIS

Amyloidosis is a disease process characterized by deposition of an insoluble protein substance (**amyloid**) in various tissues of the body, including the kidneys. Renal amyloidosis may be found in the glomeruli as well as in the kidney tissue proper. In dogs, amyloidosis may be complicated by generalized **thrombosis** (formation of blood clots resulting in blood vessel obstruction) in the lungs, heart, spleen, kidney and elsewhere. Kidney failure eventually results as damage to the tissues and tubules increases. The rate of progression of the disease may vary from dog to dog. The cause is unknown, and the prognosis is poor.

Diseases of the Lower Urinary Tract

Urinary Tract Infections

Bacterial infection of the urinary tract is the most common infectious disease of dogs. At least 10% of all dogs seen by veterinarians *for any reason* have a urinary tract infection (UTI) in addition to the problem for which they were presented. Fever, lethargy, backache, **dysuria** (painful or difficult urination), and **pollakiuria** (increased frequency of urination) often accompany episodes of UTI in human beings, but dogs only rarely exhibit clinical signs that would alert an owner or veterinarian that a UTI is present. The diagnosis therefore must be made in the laboratory by examination and bacterial culture of urine.

The consequences of UTI in dogs are similar whether clinical signs are present or not. Inflammation of the kidney and the renal pelvis (*pyelonephritis*), with subsequent scarring and eventual kidney failure, is a potential consequence of a long-standing or chronic, recurrent UTI. Infection caused by certain bacteria (*coagulase-positive staphylococci*) is the principal causal factor in the formation of **struvite** (magnesium-ammonium-phosphate) stones in the bladder in dogs. In male dogs, UTIs frequently extend to the **prostate gland** (gland surrounding the neck of the bladder and urethra, important in the production of semen) and are the most common cause of inflammation of that structure (**prostatitis**). From this site, bacteria may reinfect the urinary tract, may spread to distant areas of the body, or may cause an acute or chronic infection locally within the prostate itself, with or without eventual **abscess** (a walled-off lesion filled with pus) formation. Infections of the urinary tract may extend to the testicles of male dogs and may be a cause of infertility in both sexes. (*See* Chapter 14, "Reproductive Disorders.") Because UTIs are so common in both sexes of dogs, and because the serious consequences of UTI are nearly always preventable, proper diagnosis and management of canine UTI are of great practical importance.

The most common cause of therapeutic failure in canine UTI is the acquisition of drug resistance by the causative bacteria. The terms "sensitive" and "resistant" are used daily by veterinarians in discussions of antimicrobial therapies. A clear understanding of what these two terms mean is basic to the successful use of antibiotics in the treatment of infectious diseases.

"Sensitive" and "resistant" are relative terms. They have been defined simply as the ability ("resistant") or inability ("sensitive") of a specific bacterium to grow in the presence of a certain concentration of a specific antibiotic. The goal of antibiotic therapy is to provide an appropriate antibiotic at the site of infection in excess of the quantity needed to inhibit the growth of (or directly to kill) the infecting organisms. Although achieving this goal in actual disease situations in animals is often impractical in many organs of the body, even with modern-day antibiotics, it is not difficult to achieve in the urinary tract. This is because many of the antibiotics useful for treating UTI concentrate at very high levels within the urine. These urine concentrations of active antibiotic *may be as high as 100 times the corresponding level in the blood* because of the rapid filtration of the drug through the kidneys and accumulation in the urinary bladder. It is highly desirable to make use of this phenomenon in treating a UTI, because antibiotic concentrations in urine have been shown to be the most important factor (along with bacterial sensitivity) in success or failure of UTI therapy.

Management of Selected Types of Urinary Stones

Struvite or Struvite/Apatite "Infection Stones"
Infection of the urinary tract with bacteria such as coagulase-positive staphylococci or *Proteus mirabilis* is the principal causal factor in the formation of **struvite** (magnesium-ammonium-phosphate) urinary stones. Virtually *all* struvite-containing stones in dogs are induced by staphylococcal UTI. Because struvite-containing

"infection stones" are by far the most frequently occurring **calculi** (stones) in dogs, culturing the urine of animals with urinary stones, or direct culture of the stones themselves, identification of the isolated bacteria, and (if necessary) antimicrobial susceptibility testing of the isolates represent important clinical aids in treatment and in prevention of recurrence.

For most dogs, management of urinary stones *of any type* should begin with complete surgical removal of the stones themselves. Proper antimicrobial therapy should be given if UTI is present. Penicillin is the antibiotic of choice for all UTI caused by coagulase-positive staphylococci. The urine should be recultured at the time of *suture* (stitch) removal (10 to 14 days postoperatively). If the urine is negative for bacteria at this time, it is recommended that *a 6-month regimen of long-term/low-dose antibiotic therapy* be initiated. If the urinary tract can be maintained in a bacteria-free state, "infection stones" (e.g., struvite-containing calculi that formed in conjunction with staphylococcal UTI) usually should not form again. Dogs that form infection stones seem to be individually more susceptible than "normal" dogs to staphylococcal UTI throughout their lives, and thus are more likely to experience another stone-forming episode months to years after the 6-month period of low-dose antimicrobial therapy has been completed.

The use of a low-protein, low-*ash* (calcium, magnesium and phosphate), high-salt commercial dog food has been recommended as an aid in the medical dissolution of struvite urinary stones. When deciding whether to attempt dietary dissolution of the stones using a **calculolytic** (stone-dissolving) diet rather than surgical removal, several points need to be considered.

The dietary efficacy claim is made *only* for calculi that are composed of struvite.

About 75% of all "infection stones" in dogs are actually mixtures of struvite and apatite (calcium-phosphate), struvite and *uric acid,* or struvite and oxalate (salt of oxalic acid), components (other than struvite) that are not affected by this diet.

Therefore, a large percentage of mixed struvite stones may not dissolve at all, or may incompletely dissolve.

The concurrent use of antibiotics is important and should be continued on a full-dose basis until the stones have disappeared or until it becomes evident that they will not dissolve.

The calculolytic diet is not palatable for many dogs and owners may react to this by supplementing the diet with other high-protein foods. Dogs on a stone-dissolving diet *must not be supplemented with protein from any other source, or with calcium and magnesium from any source (mineral tablets, tuberous vegetables).*

Supplementation of any sort may negate the beneficial effect of the controlled protein and mineral concentrations and the **diuretic** (fluid-losing) effect of the high-salt concentration in the diet.

Surveillance X rays should be taken every 3 weeks to monitor the progression of stone dissolution.

Dietary dissolution of urinary calculi should not be undertaken in *male* dogs unless it is well understood that the calculi may decrease in size to a diameter that will allow them to pass into the urethra. *If this happens, acute urinary obstruction may occur, resulting in the need for emergency surgical intervention.*

A calculolytic diet is not recommended for use as a *preventive* measure in any dog. It should not be used in pregnant or lactating bitches, in growing dogs, working dogs, or in dogs that are ill for any reason. Restriction of the diet to *female* dogs alone is also recommended.

Uric Acid Calculi in Dalmatian Dogs

Dalmatian dogs have the highest incidence of uric acid (*urate*) stones. In all other breeds of dogs, uric acid is normally converted in the liver to **allantoin,** a highly soluble (and ultimately excreted) end product of purine (a class of nucleic acid) metabolism. In Dalmatians, however, uric acid is variably, but incompletely, converted to allantoin, so that the filtrate from the glomeruli contains large amounts of uric acid compared to that found in non-Dalmatians.

The amount of dietary purine protein *greatly* influences the concentration of uric acid in the urine of Dalmatians, as well as the amount of uric acid excreted in the urine per day. Following surgical removal of urate calculi, therefore, it is advisable to standardize the dog's daily food intake with a high-quality, low-purine prescription diet that is palatable to the dog and that an owner is willing to feed on a long-term basis (years).

Allopurinol is a medication that helps to decrease the amount of uric acid in urine and represents an important adjunct to dietary therapy. Affected Dalmatians must receive allopurinol for life.

Urinary Incontinence

Urinary incontinence is defined as the unconscious escape of urine (usually manifested by dribbling or spotting) during the storage phase of urination. Incontinence may be constantly evident or only intermittent in nature, and the volume may be large or small, depending on the underlying cause. Incontinence may be *congenital* (present at birth) or *acquired,* and each of these may be further subdivided into *neurogenic* incontinence (the underlying cause lying in the nerve supply) and *nonneurogenic* incontinence. In dogs, acquired neurogenic incontinence is seen in old German Shepherd Dogs with spinal nerve degeneration, and in dogs suffering trauma to the spinal cord or intervertebral disk rupture. Medical therapy generally is *not* effective in treating neurogenic disorders of urination, although it may prove useful as adjunct therapy. Correction of these problems, if correction is possible, nearly always relies on surgical intervention.

Congenital, nonneurogenic causes of incontinence usually are associated with abnormalities of detrusor muscle or ureter formation. Surgical correction of the abnormality is far more successful than any medical therapy. However, both medical and surgical intervention may be required in an individual patient.

Fortunately, incontinence caused by acquired, nonneurogenic causes is by far the most common type of incontinence encountered in dogs. Perhaps 85–90% of such cases can be successfully managed without surgery. Acquired nonneurogenic incontinence is the most common disorder of urination in spayed female dogs. Dribbling usually (but not always) occurs after lying down for a period of time. Treatment with *diethylstilbestrol (DES)* or other drugs is very effective in managing this condition.

Infections of the Prostate Gland

Infections of the prostate gland are an important source of bacteria for infection of the urinary tract and represent the principal source of bacterial reinfection in male dogs following therapy for UTI. Bacteria from an infected prostate gland can cause **septicemia** (bacteria in the bloodstream accompanied by clinical signs of disease) in dogs following high doses of corticosteroid drugs or other immunosuppressive medications. Bacteria spreading from the prostate can also caused **discospondylitis** (inflammation of an intervertebral disk) as well as **bacterial endocarditis** (infection of the heart valves and the lining of the heart), and have been known to reduce the production of sperm in the male. There is good reason, therefore, for prompt recognition and proper treatment of bacterial **prostatitis** (inflammation of the prostate gland) in dogs.

Bacterial prostatitis occurs particularly in the larger breeds. Clinical signs accompanying infection of the prostate can include fever, painful defecation, blood or pus oozing from the tip of the penis, an abnormal gait in the rear limbs, guarding of the abdomen, and exhibition of pain during rectal examination. Unfortunately, more often than not prostatitis in dogs is **asymptomatic** (without clinical signs). It may be very difficult, therefore, to establish a diagnosis of prostatitis in dogs that have no clinical signs of infection or physical findings referable to the prostate gland. The index of suspicion may be quite low and a history of recurrent UTI may be the only indication that the prostate is infected. Bacterial prostatitis should *always* be suspected in male dogs exhibiting recurrent episodes of UTI.

Specific diagnosis relies on isolation and identification of the causative bacteria in prostatic fluid. (The veterinarian can collect a sample of prostatic fluid by manual ejaculation of the dog. The prostatic fluid represents the final portion of the ejaculate, following the sperm-rich fraction. If a prostatic abscess is suspected, a direct aspiration sample can be obtained with a needle and syringe.) The bacteria that cause infection of the prostate are generally similar, in species makeup and incidence, to those that cause UTI. The most common cause is *Escherichia coli,* followed in descending order of incidence by coagulase-positive staphylococci, streptococci, *Klebsiella* and *Enterobacter.* *Proteus mirabilis* and *Pseudomonas,* frequent causes of UTI, are uncommon causes of prostatitis.

Selection of an antibiotic for use in prostatic infection must be limited to those drugs capable of concentrating to high levels in prostatic tissue and prostatic fluid. Once the dog has been placed on treatment, follow-up examinations at frequent intervals (about every 3 weeks) should be performed until the bacteria can no longer be cultured from the prostatic fluid. Antibiotics *must* be given until the prostatic fluid is negative for bacteria; *this may require 6 to 9 weeks or more of therapy.* When the prostatic fluid has been found negative twice in succession, treatment may be decreased to long-term, low-dose therapy (similar to that for chronic UTI) in order to prevent recurrence of infection.

CHAPTER 28

The Nervous System and Disorders

by Cleta Sue Bailey

The canine nervous system is composed of a complex interwoven network of specialized cells. These cells have the unique ability to respond to environmental stimuli (e.g., light, sound, touch, pain, cold, heat) and to convey their responses to other cells within the nervous system, to muscle cells, or to cells of certain glands, through a series of connections known as **synapses.** Such capabilities allow the dog to receive and integrate information about its environment and to respond in a proper manner to that environment. The responses may be *involuntary* or *voluntary.* Involuntary responses, also known as **reflexes,** are relatively stereotyped reactions to specific stimuli. The quick, involuntary withdrawal of a paw from a painful stimulus, such as the clipping of a nail too short, is one example of a reflex. Voluntary responses involve the perception of an environmental cue, followed by the conscious planning and execution of any number of possible actions. Thinking of biting, and then acting to bite, the nail clippers or the owner's hand following the reflex response to pain, would be an example of a voluntary response.

Basic Structure of the Nervous System

The nervous system classically has been divided into two major masses of complex circuitry, the **central nervous system (CNS)** and the **peripheral nervous system (PNS).** The CNS is composed of the brain and spinal cord, while the PNS is composed principally of the cranial, spinal and peripheral nerves and their connections to muscle (for motor nerves) or sensory receptors (for sensory nerves).

The brain, spinal cord and peripheral nerves are each composed of subdivisional structures that have specific functions. The forward and largest part of the brain, for example, is known as the **cerebrum** and is composed of four lobes. The cerebrum is the site of "higher" neural activity such as consciousness, awareness of surroundings, sensory perception (sight, hearing, taste, smell, touch), learning, decision making, and the initiation of voluntary movement. A lower portion of the brain, the **cerebellum,** or "little brain," is responsible for the coordination of movement, producing smooth actions that start and stop precisely where the dog intends.

The **hypothalamus** is a small area of the brain that modulates behaviors related to appetite and thirst, regulation of body temperature, sleep cycles, reproduction and responses to danger. The hypothalamus also produces hormones that affect growth, thyroid function, reproductive cycles and stress responses.

The basal portion of the brain contains sensory nerve fibers that enter the brain and motor nerve fibers that leave the brain to connect with distant muscles. For this reason, and because of its relatively cylindrical shape, this part of the brain is known as the **brain stem.** The brain stem also contains centers that control heart rate, respiratory rate and pattern, and the level of consciousness. The brain stem also gives rise to most of the twelve **cranial nerves** that control the facial muscles and certain specialized activities of the head (sight, smell, hearing).

Within the brain are several cavities, or **ventricles,** that are filled with a watery liquid called **cerebrospinal fluid (CSF).** Cerebrospinal fluid is produced within the ventricles and flows through ventricular apertures into the space surrounding the brain and spinal cord. This fluid has several functions, including removal of metabolic waste products and physical cushioning of the brain and spinal cord.

The **spinal cord** consists primarily of nerve fibers connecting the PNS with the brain. These nerve fibers carry sensory information to the brain and motor impulses from the brain to muscles. The nerve cells and fibers that form the neural networks for reflexes are also located within the spinal cord.

The brain and spinal cord are covered by layers of tissue called the **meninges.** The meninges, together with the CSF that fills the space between meningeal layers, support and protect the neural structures. The brain and spinal cord are further protected by the bones of the skull and spinal column, which encase them. The spinal column is composed of blocklike bones called **vertebrae.** Typically, a dog has 7 **cervical** (neck) vertebrae; 13 **thoracic** (chest) vertebrae, each with a pair of ribs; 7 lumbar (lower back) vertebrae; 3 sacral (pelvic) vertebrae that are fused to form a single bone, the sacrum; and a variable number of **caudal** vertebrae in the tail. The vertebrae are held together in a row by **ligaments** (strengthening bands of connective tissue) and spinal muscles. Between most of the vertebrae are the **intervertebral disks,** fibrous and gelatinous "pillows" that cushion the vertebrae and absorb the stresses and shocks of movement. Each vertebra is penetrated by a central hole, so that the spinal column somewhat resembles a bony pipe composed of many small segments, the spinal cord and its meninges running through the center of the pipe.

Pairs of **spinal nerves** arise from the spinal cord and leave the spinal column, exiting between the vertebrae. These spinal nerves form the *peripheral nerves* of the PNS. Most of these nerves contain both sensory and motor fibers, but some nerves are composed solely of sensory fibers, while others are composed only of motor fibers. The sensory fibers receive information about the world from specialized sensory receptors (e.g., temperature and touch receptors in the skin). The motor fibers supply the muscles by which the dog moves in response to sensory input, or simply as a result of a conscious decision to move.

Diagnosis

APPROACH TO THE DIAGNOSIS OF NEUROLOGIC DISORDERS

When dealing with a canine patient in need of medical attention, the veterinarian asks the owner a number of questions (termed "taking the history") regarding the pet's current illness, as well as any previous illnesses or injuries, vaccinations, diet and environment. The veterinarian then does a complete physical examination of the animal. If historical or physical evidence suggesting the possibility of neurologic disease is uncovered, a complete neurologic examination is then performed.

The neurologic examination consists of a number of observations (e.g., the animal's gait) and manipulations (e.g., tapping tendons to elicit reflexes). The objective is to determine whether neurologic disease is present and, if so, the location of the disease within the nervous system. Initially the veterinarian will attempt to localize the disease to one of the major areas of the nervous system, such as the brain, spinal cord, or PNS. An attempt is then made to localize the disease more precisely (i.e., to a portion of the brain or spinal cord, or to particular peripheral nerves). This initial localization process represents a slightly different approach from that utilized for diseases of other organ systems, and is necessary in order to select the most appropriate diagnostic procedures. If the disease is localized to the brain, for example, then **radiographs** (X rays) of the skull would be indicated while radiographs of the spinal column would not. Occasionally, precise localization of the disease process is not possible. Moreover, in some cases the disease may be present in more than one location, necessitating diagnostic procedures that can examine several different components of the nervous system.

DIAGNOSTIC PROCEDURES FOR EXAMINING THE NERVOUS SYSTEM

Although the nervous system is not available for direct examination—as is, for example, the skin—a number of diagnostic procedures are available by which the veterinarian can examine its structure and function.

The structure of the nervous system can be examined using techniques that produce images or pictures of certain parts of the nervous system. The most common of these procedures is **radiography** (the taking of X-rays). Other available techniques include **myelography** (X-ray study of the spinal canal using dye-injection techniques), **computerized axial tomography** (**CAT scan;** an X-ray technique that produces cross-sectional images of the inside of the body), and **nuclear magnetic resonance imaging** (**NMR** or **MRI;** a technique for visualizing internal structures of the body using an external magnetic field). (*See* APPENDIX C, "DIAGNOSTIC TESTS.")

Procedures to evaluate neurologic function generally investigate the ability of the nervous system to respond to stimuli and convey the responses to the appropriate neural centers. These procedures are known as *electrodiagnostic procedures* because they use electrodes and electrical equipment to record neurologic responses, which are themselves electrical in nature. Examples of electrodiagnostic procedures include **electroencephalography** (**EEG;** "brainwave" recording), peripheral nerve conduction velocity determination, and **electromyography** (**EMG;** recording of muscle electrical activity).

Another type of diagnostic procedure involves the acquisition of fluid (CSF) or tissue from the nervous system for analysis. A sample of CSF can be **aspirated** (withdrawn with a needle and syringe) from various sites and analyzed by several procedures. A sample of neural tissue can be acquired using *biopsy* procedures and examined in the laboratory by microscopic or chemical techniques.

In order to provide minimal discomfort and anxiety to the patient, as well as maximal safety and diagnostic accuracy, most of the procedures mentioned above require that the dog be heavily sedated or anesthetized. Prior to sedation or anesthesia, and as part of the search for the underlying cause of disease, certain basic tests will be performed to ensure that the patient's organ systems are functioning adequately. Sedation and anesthesia have inherent risks, even for healthy animals; therefore, the general health of a patient must be evaluated in order to minimize the enhanced risk involved in anesthesia of an ill animal. These basic tests usually include red blood cell and white blood cell counts, several chemical tests of the blood that screen liver and kidney function, and an analysis of urine. Many other tests are available as well and may be recommended by the veterinarian if the patient's condition warrants them. (*See* CHAPTER 40, "SURGERY AND POSTOPERATIVE CARE," and APPENDIX C, "DIAGNOSTIC TESTS.")

RECOVERY FROM NEUROLOGIC DISEASE OR INJURY

Because of the disabling effects of neurologic disorders and the long-held belief that the nervous system does not regenerate, neurologic disease has traditionally been viewed with horror and hopelessness. In fact, clinical improvement and even recovery occur commonly in animals and people afflicted with neurologic disorders. Experimental and clinical observations have yielded information regarding the mechanisms of neurologic recovery, as well as clues to the development of more effective therapies. Under appropriate conditions damaged components of the nervous system can regenerate, while undamaged portions can reorganize at the cellular and chemical level to assume some of the functions of the disabled tissue. Additional factors influencing recovery include the patient's age (the younger, the better) and the rate of development of the disease (the slower, the better). An appropriate environment and physical rehabilitation can also have a profound effect on recovery. Of course, appropriate therapy cannot be instituted without a correct diagnosis of the underlying disorder; perhaps the most important factor in achieving a satisfactory recovery is early and prompt diagnosis and treatment.

Signs of Neurologic Disease

Neurologic diseases can cause a myriad of structural and functional changes in an animal. These changes, or clinical signs, are what gain the attention of the owner and prompt the initial visit to the veterinarian. (See CHAPTER 39, "CLINICAL SIGNS OF DISEASE.") For this reason, most of the remainder of this chapter is organized according to disease signs. The most common signs of neurologic disease are addressed, the discussion of each sign covering the most common diseases causing that particular sign. Another reason for organizing the discussion in this manner is the knowledge that different diseases can produce identical neurologic signs if the disease processes affect the same neurologic structure. For example, a traumatic fracture of the spine can produce exactly the same clinical signs as a tumor of the spine in the same location. Therefore, when an animal is initially examined and neurologic disease is detected and localized, the veterinarian usually can provide only a "short list" of the most likely diseases causing the neurologic problem. The definitive diagnosis requires additional, specialized tests of the types already described above.

SEIZURES

Seizures (fits, convulsions) are relatively brief episodes of neurologic derangement caused by abnormal bursts of electrical activity within the brain. The episode may last a few seconds, a few minutes, or less commonly an hour or more. Abnormalities observed may include rigidity or jerking of the body or limbs; anxiety, hysteria, or unconsciousness; vocalizing; and salivation, drooling, urination and defecation. Seizures may occur once in a dog's life and never occur again, or may recur at varying intervals ranging from a few minutes to several months. A dog exhibiting recurrent seizure episodes should be examined by a veterinarian to determine the cause of the seizures. Even though the dog may seem perfectly normal before and after a seizure, serious and progressive disease may be present. Despite this fact, and the disturbing appearance of a seizure, animals rarely die during seizure episodes. The individual seizure is not usually life-threatening in and of itself; however, seizure episodes repeated rapidly without intervening periods of consciousness are life-threatening and require emergency veterinary care. This condition of rapidly repeated seizure episodes is known as **status epilepticus.**

Although seizures are the result of transient brain dysfunction, the dysfunction may be caused by diseases originating outside the nervous system, such as liver or kidney disease, blood sugar abnormalities, or toxins. The veterinarian will look first for such causes by examining the dog and performing specific blood tests. If disease external to the nervous system is not evident, the veterinarian will then search for a cause within the brain, such as infection or cancer. Seizure-causing disorders located within the nervous system itself are investigated using the electrodiagnostic tools, imaging techniques, and CSF analysis described above.

Common acquired causes of seizures in dogs include:

- metabolic disorders such as low blood sugar levels (**hypoglycemia**)
- infectious diseases such as canine distemper
- brain injury
- toxins such as lead
- brain tumors

A genetic seizure condition also occurs in dogs. This condition is termed inherited or idiopathic **epilepsy.** The term **idiopathic** ("of unknown cause") refers to the fact that the examination of a dog with an inherited seizure disorder may reveal no recognizable abnormality; the cause of the seizures is therefore unknown and an inherited condition is assumed, based on the dog's age, breed and absence of evidence of other disease. Breeds known or suspected to have inherited seizures include the Beagle, Belgian Tervuren, Cocker Spaniel, German Shepherd Dog, Golden Retriever, Irish Setter, Keeshond, Labrador Retriever, Poodle and Saint Bernard Dog.

The treatment of seizure disorders is usually a two-pronged effort, aimed at treating the underlying disease (infection, injury, tumor, etc.) and at decreasing or eliminating the seizure episodes. Treatment of the underlying disease usually involves specific medication. In some disorders, such as brain tumors, surgery and radiation therapy may be indicated. The treatment of seizures requires an *anticonvulsant* medication such as *phenobarbital.* Anticonvulsants are often prescribed together with specific disease therapy because the seizures themselves are debilitating and may continue even if the underlying disease has been eliminated. Anticonvulsant therapy must be given under the guidance of a veterinarian and should not be altered or halted without additional veterinary consultation.

DEAFNESS

Deafness is a particularly disturbing problem because it eliminates the major line of communication between a dog and its owner. The primary causes of deafness in dogs are congenital (present at birth) deafness, ear infections, and drug toxicities. Rarely, head trauma or tumors may cause deafness. Congenital deafness is caused by failure of the sound-receptor cells in the ear to form (neural deafness). This condition is predominately associated with the merle or piebald gene (*See* CHAPTER 16, "GENETICS") and is known or suspected to be inherited in several breeds. A few of the affected breeds are: Australian Shepherd Dog, Boxer, Bull Terrier, Collie, Dalmatian, English Setter, Old English Sheepdog and Shetland Sheepdog. Affected puppies are deaf from birth, although owners may

not be aware of the problem until they attempt voice training when the puppy is several weeks or months of age. Some affected dogs are able to hear sound waves of certain frequencies and may respond to dog whistles. The condition is not progressive, nor is it treatable. Attempts to fit deaf dogs with hearing aids have been largely unsuccessful.

Severe ear infections (**otitis**) can cause deafness by destroying the bone and tissue structures of the ear that conduct sound (conduction deafness) or by destroying the neural receptor cells. Otitis is most common in dogs with hanging, floppy ears and dense coats. Drugs and certain topical antiseptics used to treat otitis can cause deafness, including some antibiotics, such as *streptomycin.* With otitis or toxicity, the onset of deafness may be sudden or may develop slowly. Deafness in only one ear may not be noticed by the owner.

Hearing loss can be confirmed by electrodiagnostic procedures, such as a **brain stem auditory evoked potential recording.** This test is technically easy to perform and does not require anesthesia; however, interpretation of the test should be made by a veterinarian with specialized, advanced training. Treatment of otitis involves identification of the organism causing the infection and administration of appropriate antibiotics, as well as careful cleansing of the ear. Overly vigorous cleansing can damage the delicate ear structures, which could also produce deafness or loss of balance. In the case of drug toxicity, administration of the offending drug should be discontinued. With either syndrome treatment may eliminate the primary underlying cause, but the damage to the ear structures, and therefore the deafness, may be permanent.

INCOORDINATION AND LOSS OF BALANCE

Balance and proper orientation of the body with respect to gravity are governed by nerves in the ear, brain and spinal cord that together form an interconnected network called the **vestibular system.** The clinical signs associated with vestibular system disease include constant, uncontrollable tilting or turning of the head; circling; leaning or rolling; and abnormal position or movements of the eyes.

Disease processes may also involve adjacent nerves controlling other neurologic functions, producing other signs such as incoordination and weakness of muscles of the head or body. Common causes of vestibular dysfunction include otitis, infections or tumors of the brain, and brain trauma. A disorder of elderly dogs, **old dog vestibular syndrome,** is characterized by a very sudden onset of severe vestibular signs. The cause is unknown, but fortunately the signs usually abate within a week even without treatment.

Coordination of movement is governed by the portion of the brain known as the **cerebellum.** An animal with cerebellar disease can move voluntarily and the movements are strong, but they are jerky and often excessive. The animal may sway when standing, stagger and fall, pick its feet up too high when walking (high-stepping), and quickly bob its head up and down when attempting to eat. A portion of the cerebellum is actually part of the vestibular system; therefore, animals with cerebellar signs may also have vestibular signs. The same disease processes that cause vestibular disorders may also cause cerebellar disorders, that is, infections, tumors, trauma.

Some puppies are born with an incompletely formed cerebellum (**cerebellar hypoplasia**). Incoordination appears at several weeks of age when the pup begins to walk or run. Puppies of this age are normally incoordinated, however! Therefore, the pup may not appear overtly abnormal until it is several months of age. Cerebellar hypoplasia is not a progressive condition and no treatment is available.

Cerebellar abiotrophy, a degenerative condition of the cerebellum that produces progressively worsening clinical signs, occurs in several breeds of dogs. The cerebellar nerve cells apparently form in a normal fashion, only to degenerate and die prematurely. Signs become apparent at a few weeks to a few months of age and can progress either slowly or rapidly, progressively disabling the dog. The cause is unknown but the disorder is known or suspected to be inherited in several breeds, including the Kerry Blue Terrier, Rough-coated Collie, and Gordon Setter. There is no effective treatment.

PARESIS OR PARALYSIS OF ONE LIMB

The term **paresis** refers to a diminished ability to move a muscle or a body part voluntarily. **Paralysis** is the total absence of voluntary movement. An animal with a *paretic* (affected by paresis) limb can move the leg, but may drag the toes on the ground, stumble, and "knuckle over" on the paw when walking, and be unable to extend the leg fully when standing on it. A paralyzed limb will simply be dragged along the ground or hang limply when the animal walks.

Paresis or paralysis of one leg is most commonly caused by injury to the nerves supplying the leg or to a tumor constricting those nerves. The most common injury in dogs involves damage to the nerves supplying a front leg, often caused by falling out of a pickup truck or being struck by an automobile. The condition is referred to as **brachial plexus avulsion.** In some cases, the damage may be only moderate in severity, so that normal function is regained with time. More commonly, however, the damage is irreversible and the leg may need to be amputated. The degree of damage can usually be determined by physical and neurologic examination, but electrodiagnostic tests may also be required.

The most common tumor affecting the nerves to a single limb is the schwannoma, or **neurofibroma.** This tumor arises at one spot along the length of a nerve, then spreads up and down the nerve and along any other nerves that join the original affected nerve. The earliest sign is not weakness in the leg, but pain caused by the tumor pressing on the nerve. Responding to the pain, the dog favors or limps on the leg rather than dragging it. Because pain and limping are the most common signs of disorders of the bones and muscles of a leg, schwannomas are very commonly mistaken for a bone or joint disease. This has serious ramifications because an early diagnosis is essential if the affected limb, or even the life of the dog, is to be saved. At the present time the only effective therapy for this tumor is surgical removal. If not detected promptly the tumor will grow so large and affect so many nerves that surgical removal becomes impossible without also amputating the leg. If complete surgical removal is not feasible, or if diagnosis is delayed, the tumor may invade the spinal cord and produce severe pain and weakness in other legs. At this stage, **euthanasia** (putting the dog to sleep) is usually the only viable option.

PARESIS OR PARALYSIS OF THE HIND LIMBS OR ALL FOUR LIMBS

Paresis or paralysis of the hind limbs is usually caused by a disorder affecting the spinal cord, which contains the motor and sensory nerve fibers that connect the brain with the peripheral nerves. The causes of spinal cord disorders (**myelopathies**) are numerous and varied. The location of the disease along the spinal cord, as well as the specific clinical signs and their mode of progression, depends on the nature of the underlying disorder. Paresis or paralysis may develop very suddenly, as with a fractured spine, or may have a slower and more insidious onset, as with a spinal tumor. Sudden onset or rapid progression of paralysis is always a medical emergency.

Common causes of spinal cord disorders in dogs include herniated intervertebral disks (also called **slipped** or **protruded** disks), spinal trauma, or cancer of the spinal cord or adjacent tissues. With herniated discs, one of the most common spinal cord disorders of dogs, degeneration of the supporting tissue of the spinal column causes an intervertebral disk to shift out of place and press on the spinal cord, resulting in inflammation and paresis. Less common causes of spinal-cord disease include infections of the spinal cord or adjacent tissues, congenital malformations, blockage of blood vessels supplying the spinal cord (fibrocartilaginous emboli), and degeneration of the spinal cord (e.g., **German Shepherd Dog** degenerative myelopathy).

Treatment of spinal cord disease depends on the nature of the underlying cause. Although specific medical therapy may be sufficient in some cases, many of these disorders require surgical intervention. Many dogs with spinal cord disease recover amazingly well, particularly if given enough time and appropriate care. For the degenerative diseases, however, no effective therapy is available.

Paresis or paralysis of all four limbs (quadriparesis, quadriplegia) can be caused by the spinal cord disorders mentioned above if the disease is localized to the neck region. However, brain disease and disorders of the PNS may also cause quadriparesis or quadriplegia. The same types of brain diseases that cause seizures may also produce quadriparesis (e.g., infections, trauma, cancer or degenerative diseases). Usually, however, other signs suggestive of brain disease are also present, such as seizures, abnormal behavior, incoordination, loss of balance or blindness.

Diseases affecting most or all of a dog's peripheral nerves (polyneuropathies) are much more prevalent today than they were ten years ago, probably due to advances in veterinary diagnostic procedures, or possibly to genetic influences within breeds or environmental factors, such as toxins. Polyneuropathies usually have an insidious onset and a slowly progressive course; often a voice change, **regurgitation** (involuntary return of undigested food to the mouth after swallowing), or **dysphagia** (difficulty swallowing) are the earliest clinical signs. The known causes of polyneuropathies include:

- degenerative diseases, several of which are breed-specific and known or suspected to be inherited, such as spinal muscular atrophy of Brittany Spaniels, giant axonal neuropathy of German Shepherd Dogs, demyelinating myelopathy of Miniature Poodles, and hereditary myelopathy of Afghan Hounds
- dysfunction of the immune system
- metabolic diseases such as diabetes mellitus
- drug or heavy-metal toxicity (e.g., lead)
- cancer

Unfortunately, the specific cause of a polyneuropathy in many dogs may not be identified despite a thorough diagnostic investigation, including nerve biopsies. In such cases attempts at therapy remain empirical and are often fruitless. Clearly, this particular area of canine neurology requires a great deal of further experimental and clinical study.

CHAPTER 29

The Respiratory System and Disorders

by Philip A. Padrid

The Respiratory System

The canine respiratory system is composed of a series of branching, semiflexible tubes of various lengths and widths, which terminate within the lungs in thin-walled blind sacs called **alveoli.** These tubes or conducting airways include the **trachea, bronchi** and **bronchioles,** and serve to connect elements from the outside atmosphere with the blood circulatory system. During inhalation the inspired air travels through these tubes until it reaches the lungs, at which point the oxygen in the air is transported across the alveoli and into the blood. During exhalation carbon dioxide, a by-product of body metabolism, is transported in the reverse direction, moving from the blood across the alveoli and into the airways, and so passes out of the body.

For convenience the respiratory system may be divided into three continuous anatomical areas: the upper airway, the lower airway, and the **pulmonary** (pertaining to the lungs) region. The lower airway and the pulmonary region both lie within the chest cavity, while the upper airway lies above the chest cavity and outside of it.

THE UPPER AIRWAY

The upper airway consists of the nose and nasal cavity, mouth opening and oral cavity, hard and soft palate, sinuses, **larynx** ("voice-box"), and approximately the upper one-third of the trachea. The palate is divided into a "soft" portion near the larynx, and a "hard" portion commonly referred to as the "roof" of the mouth. The soft and hard palates are continuous with each other. The soft palate divides the **pharynx** (area extending from the rear of the oral cavity and nasal passages to the larynx and esophagus) into an upper region (**nasopharynx**) and a lower region (**oropharynx**).

The nasal cavity is composed of a series of delicate, scroll-like bony structures called **turbinates.** The turbinates have a very well-developed nerve and blood supply and contain both fluid- and mucus-secreting glands. This makes the nasal area extremely sensitive to irritation and is responsible for the reflex action recognized as sneezing. In response to irritation or injury the glands of the turbinates release variable amounts of clear fluid and mucus. If the tissue is more severely damaged (as by ulceration or erosion), the mucus may be mixed with or replaced by blood. As the nasal passages become swollen or blocked by fluid and mucus, sniffling will occur. If the obstruction becomes severe, an affected dog may begin to breath through the mouth (open-mouth breathing). This will be readily apparent during periods of exercise, stress, or excitement.

The nose is divided into two compartments called **nares** by a vertical dividing wall known as the **nasal septum.** Specialized cells that are continuous with the **olfactory** nerve (the nerve that feeds sensory information concerning the sense of smell to the brain) are found in the turbinates, the nasal septum, the sinuses, and parts of the bony nasal cavity. These nasal chambers filter, humidify and warm the incoming air. The three **paranasal sinuses** of the dog (frontal, maxillary, and sphenoid) are actually holes in the skull that empty directly into the nasal cavity.

The larynx can be considered the "gateway" to the respiratory system and is instrumental in protecting the lower respiratory tract from contamination during swallowing. The larynx is composed of five cartilage-containing structures and forms a boxlike configuration within the rear portion of the pharynx. The larynx functions in swallowing, vocalization and passage of air from the pharynx to the trachea. During swallowing the **vocal folds** (vocal chords in people) close completely to prevent aspiration of food or fluid into the trachea. During inhalation the vocal folds open, then partially close during exhalation, although during stress or heavy exercise the vocal folds remain open during exhalation, predisposing dogs to accidental aspiration of such foreign bodies as blades of grass or grass awns (foxtails).

THE LOWER AIRWAY

The trachea is a relatively noncollapsible tube, C-shaped in cross section, and extends from the larynx to a point inside the chest cavity where it divides into right and left main-stem bronchi. The main-stem bronchi then branch into the smaller airways known as bronchioles.

The air passageways from the trachea to the bronchioles are covered by specialized lining cells with tiny hairlike projections known as **cilia.** A major function of these cells is to power the so-called **mucociliary escalator,** a coordinated and forceful wavelike movement of cilia that is essential for the normal removal of mucus, inhaled particulate material, and inhaled environmental bacteria. The cough reflex and the mucociliary escalator are the two major factors responsible for clearing foreign debris, bacteria and mucus from the trachea and preventing such material from entering the lungs.

THE PULMONARY REGION

The pulmonary region is composed of the respiratory bronchioles (the smallest branches of the bronchial system) and lung tissue. The respiratory bronchioles **arborize** (branch) much like the veins in the leaves of a tree and eventually terminate in the saclike alveoli. The alveoli are microscopic, bubble-like structures and are surrounded by a very intricate blood supply composed of tiny vessels called **capillaries.** The alveoli are lined by a single layer of cells, which represents the only barrier between the inspired air and the adjacent blood capillaries. When air is inhaled it collects within the alveoli, where it is exposed to the blood vessels. It is at this point that the inspired oxygen is transferred to the blood circulatory system. Conversely, carbon dioxide is transferred from the blood to the alveoli, from where it is passed up the airways and exhaled. Specialized cells lining the alveoli make **surfactant,** a soaplike substance responsible for decreasing the pressure (surface tension) within the alveoli. Without surfactant the pressure tending to collapse the alveoli would be enormous, making it exceedingly difficult for a dog (or a person) to take even a single breath.

Disorders of the Upper Airway

VIRAL AND BACTERIAL DISEASES

Many different infectious disease agents can disrupt the normal functions of the upper airway. In general, infections of the nasopharynx can produce such clinical signs as sneezing, nasal discharge, sniffling, **snuffling** (abnormal breathing sounds), nose-rubbing, and facial deformity (in severe cases). Infections are usually of sudden onset and occur most commonly in newborn or young dogs. While certain clinical signs associated with upper-airway disease may be physically objectionable to the owner, they do not usually constitute a significant health threat for the pet. The disease agents responsible for these infections are discussed in CHAPTER 34, "VIRAL DISEASES," and CHAPTER 35, "BACTERIAL DISEASES," and will not be reviewed here.

CLEFT PALATE

Under normal circumstances the hard palate closes completely before birth. However, in some cases the two sides of the hard palate do not fuse together, leaving an abnormal opening between the upper chamber (nasopharynx) and lower chamber (oropharynx) of the pharynx. Food or other foreign material may pass from the oral cavity into the nasal cavity through this defect, leading to chronic nasal inflammation and discharge. Conversely, excessive nasal secretions may enter the oropharynx and be aspirated into the lungs. Affected puppies or newborns have difficulty eating and suckling and will not grow as quickly or as large as their littermates. The diagnosis is made by visual inspection of the defect. The problem can often be completely corrected by surgery.

BRACHYCEPHALIC UPPER-AIRWAY SYNDROME

Certain breeds, most commonly short-nosed (**brachycephalic**) breeds such as Boston Terriers and Bulldogs, are born with abnormally small openings to the nares and relatively long soft palates. Because dogs prefer to breathe through the nose and it is difficult to inhale through the small openings, affected animals must increase their respiratory effort even at rest. Any increase in demand for oxygen results in an exaggerated breathing effort. When stressed or forced to exercise, affected dogs find it almost impossible to inhale sufficient amounts of air and must resort to open-mouth breathing. Over time negative pressure within the nasopharynx causes swelling of the soft palate and adjacent structures at the rear of the pharynx, further obstructing the flow of air.

Dogs with this abnormality tend to avoid exercise and will become short of breath following any mild exertion or stress. This may be evident after even the slightest increase in activity, although it is usually most apparent during vigorous exercise or excitement. Abnormal, noisy breathing commonly occurs when the pet becomes excited, as when the owner returns home from work or an extended absence. Since dogs normally dissipate heat through panting, those with brachycephalic upper-airway syndrome are much less tolerant of heat and often refuse to walk in hot weather. Many affected dogs also snore loudly while asleep. The condition is often debilitating and may be life-threatening if dogs are encouraged or forced to exercise too strenuously or in hot weather. They may become cyanotic (turn blue) and even collapse under such extreme circumstances.

Diagnosis is based on the history, physical examination, visual inspection of the soft palate, and recognized breed predisposition. Some animals can be significantly helped by surgical intervention to enlarge the openings to the nares and shorten the long and swollen soft palate. Surgery is often most helpful if performed while the animal is still under a year of age. Dogs suffering from respiratory difficulty due to heat stress, excitement or overexertion can become seriously ill in a short period of time. If the breathing effort does not return to normal within 5 to 10 minutes an affected dog should be transported immediately to the nearest veterinary hospital for treatment.

INJURIES

Because of its prominent location the nasal area is particularly prone to blunt trauma and bite wounds. The resulting clinical signs will depend on the nature and extent of the injury, and can include a bloody discharge from the nostrils (**epistaxis**) and noisy breathing caused by airflow obstruction. In more serious cases the structures making up the nasopharynx or even the skull may be damaged, resulting in facial deformity.

The clinical signs and a history of trauma are usually all that is required for making the diagnosis. More serious cases may require X rays and **rhinoscopy** (visual examination of the inner nasal passages) to assess the extent of the damage.

Most cases are self-limiting and require no specific therapy. Severe or prolonged epistaxis may require packing of the nostrils with soft tissue paper or instillation of nasal drops designed for human use. If these interventions fail to stop the bleeding, the dog should be taken to a veterinary hospital for further care.

Foreign Bodies

Inhalation of plant material, including blades of grass and grass awns (foxtails), is a very common phenomenon in certain regions of the country, especially during the spring and summer months. Typically, an owner will relate that the dog has recently been romping through a grassy field when it suddenly develops an explosive sneeze. Other signs can include nose-rubbing, pawing at the nose, and occasionally epistaxis (nosebleed). If the foreign material is blown out of the nose, or passed to the rear of the pharynx and swallowed, the clinical signs will soon disappear. If it remains in the nasal cavity, however, signs may persist for several days. Eventually the object is walled off by the inflammatory defenses of the body. *However, this is not a cure.* If left untreated, there will frequently be a chronic nasal discharge. If inhaled, the foreign body may cause serious lung and chest complications.

A history of recent exposure to plant material is very important for making the diagnosis. Definitive diagnosis and treatment often require that the dog be anesthetized so that specialized viewing instruments can be passed into the nasal cavity to visualize the foreign material and remove it.

Fungal Rhinitis

Inflammation of the nasal passages (**rhinitis**) with destruction of large parts of the turbinates and nasal septum can occur as a consequence of infection by fungi, most commonly members of the *Aspergillus* group. Although the condition is not life-threatening, it often results in severe clinical signs, such as an extensive foul-smelling nasal discharge, chronic sneezing, and frequent pawing and rubbing at the face. (For a complete discussion of this problem, *see* "Aspergillosis and Penicilliosis" in chapter 36, "Fungal Diseases.").

Non-infectious Rhinitis of Unknown Cause

Chronic rhinitis can occur in the absence of any specific or recognized cause. In some cases it may represent an allergy to something in the local environment, or an inherited defect of one or more components of the normal defense mechanisms of the upper airway. The clinical signs can include nasal discharge and occasional sneezing, and may mimic some of the more specific diseases already mentioned. There is some evidence that Irish Wolfhounds may be particularly susceptible to this condition.

The diagnosis is based on long-standing clinical signs of rhinitis and by ruling out other causes of nasal disease, such as fungal infection and cancer. Because the cause is unknown, treatment can only be directed toward the clinical signs. Individual dogs may respond positively to many different kinds of drugs, including antibiotics, corticosteroids and antihistamines. No one treatment has been proven to be more effective than another, however, so therapy should be tailored to the individual animal.

Nasal Tumors

Cancer of the nasal cavity is not a frequent cause of nasal discharge and sneezing in dogs. However, once the more common causes of these clinical signs have been ruled out, the possibility of a nasal tumor should be considered. Typically, nasal tumors are a problem of older dogs, usually greater than 8 years of age and rarely less than 6 years of age. Any breed may be affected although long-nosed (**dolichocephalic**) breeds such as Collies may be particularly prone. Clinical signs are similar to those of other diseases of the nasal cavity and include sneezing, nasal discharge and noisy breathing. Nasal tumors tend to cause epistaxis more frequently than do other, less serious nasal disorders. Deformity of the nose and adjacent areas may become obvious as the disease progresses. Nasal tumors do not commonly spread to other organs.

To confirm the presence of a nasal tumor, the veterinarian will usually recommend X rays and a **biopsy** (sampling of tissue for laboratory studies) of the affected area. The patient must be placed under general anesthesia for these procedures. Treatment usually requires the consultation and guidance of a veterinarian specializing in cancer therapy (*veterinary oncologist*). In general, the most successful approach seems to be radiation therapy. Without therapy many affected dogs will die from complications of the condition within 6 months of diagnosis. Even with aggressive therapy, however, the long-term prognosis is poor. (*See* CHAPTER 38, "CANCER.")

REVERSE SNEEZE

Many owners report that a dog will occasionally snort and exhibit severe, forced exhalations through the nose. Such episodes are generally sporadic and unpredictable in nature, lasting from a few seconds to a few minutes. Affected dogs are otherwise completely healthy and have no other signs of nasal disease. The cause is unproven but is thought to result from a temporary misalignment of the soft palate in the region of the larynx.

The diagnosis is based on clinical signs of occasional transient snorting in an otherwise healthy pet. The condition disappears as mysteriously as it appears, and usually no treatment is required. In severe cases surgical intervention to repair a misaligned soft palate may be helpful.

LARYNGITIS

Acute inflammation of the laryngeal region (**laryngitis**) may occur in dogs with a viral infection of the upper respiratory tract. It also occurs commonly for the first 24 to 48 hours following any surgical procedure for which a dog has had a breathing tube in place. Prolonged barking is another common cause. Clinical signs include a sudden change in the quality of the bark, coughing and gagging.

Confirmation of the diagnosis, if not evident from the history and physical examination, can be made using a quick-acting anesthetic and direct visualization of the larynx (**laryngoscopy**). Laryngitis is usually a self-limiting condition for which no therapy is required. Rest and avoidance of stimuli that cause the pet to bark will hasten recovery.

LARYNGEAL EDEMA

Laryngeal **edema** (swelling) is a severe consequence of laryngitis. Occasionally, however, it can result from an allergic reaction to insect bites or drugs. In mild cases laryngitis and laryngeal edema produce identical clinical signs. When the swelling is more advanced it can obstruct a portion of the airway and reduce the amount of air entering the trachea (and hence the lungs). Clinical signs in severe cases include a loud, strained noise on inhalation (**stridor**). In the most serious cases the dog will become frantic as it tries to breath against a closed airway. This constitutes a medical emergency and requires immediate veterinary attention.

Laryngeal edema should be suspected whenever stridor is heard. Treatment is based on the severity and progression of the clinical signs. In mild cases rest may be all that is required, while in more severe cases sedation and anti-inflammatory medication may be necessary. In the most seriously affected animals, the veterinarian may surgically create a temporary opening through the skin and into the trachea below the level of the obstruction (a procedure known as a **tracheostomy**), to allow for the insertion of a breathing tube.

LARYNGEAL PARALYSIS

Normally, the vocal folds open during inhalation and partially close during exhalation. In laryngeal paralysis the vocal folds either do not move at all or move out of time with the phases of respiration. One or both vocal folds may be affected. This syndrome has been reported as a *congenital* (present at birth) problem in the Bouvier des Flandres, Siberian Husky and Dalmatian breeds. It also occurs commonly in older dogs of the sporting breeds, such as Labrador Retrievers. It was once thought that laryngeal paralysis was linked to an underactive thyroid gland (**hypothyroidism**). Instead it is now believed that laryngeal paralysis probably occurs as a component of a more serious inflammatory disease involving either the neurologic system, the muscular system, or both. Clinical signs tend to develop gradually over a long period of time, and depend on the severity of the paralysis and the resulting obstruction to airflow through the larynx. The earliest sign is often a change in the quality of the bark. Affected dogs are easily fatigued, sensitive to heat, and pant excessively. In severe cases the condition can be life-threatening.

Confirmation of the diagnosis can be made by direct visualization of the vocal folds with the dog under light anesthesia. Because laryngeal paralysis commonly occurs as part of a generalized neuromuscular disorder, affected dogs should have a thorough neurologic evaluation performed by a veterinarian who is skilled in this type of procedure.

In general, treatment is similar to that for laryngitis or laryngeal edema. Correction may be attempted by surgically attaching one or both vocal folds to the outer sides of the larynx so that the larynx will remain open on inhalation and exhalation. While this often results in resolution of the clinical signs, it predisposes the dog to aspiration of foreign bodies and even food and water into the lungs. The prognosis often depends on the progression of the underlying inflammatory disorder.

LARYNGEAL TUMORS

Tumors of the larynx are very uncommon in dogs. Clinical signs are the same as for laryngeal edema and laryngeal paralysis. Laryngeal tumors tend not to **metastasize** (spread). Direct visualization of the larynx will suggest the presence of a tumor, and the diagnosis can be confirmed by biopsy. Therapy involves surgical removal of the tumor, followed by chemotherapy or radiation therapy. These cases are best managed by veterinarians specializing in cancer therapy.

Disorders of the Lower Airway

CANINE INFECTIOUS TRACHEOBRONCHITIS ("KENNEL COUGH")

Acute **tracheobronchitis** (inflammation of the trachea, larynx and bronchi), known commonly as "kennel cough," has been recognized in dogs for many years. It is a disease of multifactorial origin; that is, a virtually identical clinical syndrome can be produced by several different infectious disease agents, either alone or in various combinations, the most important of which are the bacterium *Bordetella bronchiseptica,* canine parainfluenza virus, and canine aden-

ovirus type 2. (For a complete discussion of this condition, *see* CHAPTER 34, "VIRAL DISEASES.")

TRACHEAL HYPOPLASIA

Dogs with this condition are born with a narrow, underdeveloped trachea that does not provide sufficient airflow even during normal breathing at rest. The disorder occurs most often in short-nosed (brachycephalic) dogs and is especially common in the English Bulldog breed. The clinical signs include exercise/stress intolerance leading to an early onset of fatigue, and even collapse after more strenuous tasks or excitement. Because tracheal hypoplasia often occurs in conjunction with other congenital problems in brachycephalic breeds, it may be difficult to determine what proportion of the clinical signs is due to the narrow trachea alone.

The condition is most commonly uncovered when a dog has an X ray taken for some other suspected condition, or when **intubation** (insertion of a breathing tube into the trachea) with a normal-diameter tube prior to routine spay or neuter surgery reveals an unexpectedly narrow tracheal opening.

There are no current treatments available to correct this anatomic problem. Owners of affected dogs should not encourage their pets to exercise forcefully or allow them to become overly excited. If clinical signs of respiratory difficulty become apparent, the animal should be taken to a veterinarian as soon as possible.

TRACHEAL TRAUMA

The canine neck contains many powerful and well-developed muscles. Because the trachea is surrounded by these muscles, it is usually shielded from trauma. For example, when a dog on a leash running at full speed toward another dog or person is brought up short by the leash, it rarely suffers any significant damage to its neck or underlying structures. Trauma to the trachea usually is the result of a bite wound resulting from a confrontation with another dog or cat. If the trachea is punctured, air and/or bacteria can leak out into the surrounding tracheal tissues and cause air bubbles to form either in the skin (**subcutaneous emphysema**) or in the chest (**pneumothorax, pyothorax**).

The latter condition, involving bacterial infection and pus formation in the chest, can cause significant respiratory distress and can even be fatal.

Diagnosis is based on inspection of the neck area combined with a history of recent fighting or roaming free in the neighborhood. Confirmation of a tracheal puncture may require visualization of the inside of the trachea using an endoscope (a small viewing tube inserted into an orifice or body cavity) and with the animal under light anesthesia.

Veterinary assistance is generally required when breathing difficulty occurs or when air bubbles accumulate under the skin. Surgery is needed to close any puncture wounds in the trachea. If a small amount of air has leaked into the chest cavity, it can often be quickly removed with a needle and syringe. More persistent air leaks may require that a tube be temporarily placed within the chest cavity for drainage.

FOREIGN BODIES

Tracheal foreign bodies can include plant fragments, twigs, rocks, sewing needles, fishing gear, or just about anything else that is smaller in diameter than the opening of the canine larynx. The presence of a foreign body in the trachea will immediately elicit a harsh strenuous cough that may continue with little interruption for hours. If the object blocks the trachea or opening of the bronchi it can cause serious respiratory distress. If left untreated, the dog may cough up the foreign body. More commonly, however, the object will migrate deeper into the bronchi and smaller branches of the respiratory tract.

Bronchial foreign bodies begin as tracheal foreign bodies. Objects that migrate down the respiratory tract as far as the bronchi are only rarely coughed up. Instead they either lodge within the bronchi and are walled off by the resulting inflammatory response, or migrate still further into the lung. In either case the most prominent clinical sign continues to be coughing, perhaps accompanied by the production of a bloody mucus. If the foreign body enters the lung pneumonia may result (*see* below). If the object migrates still further, passing out of the lung and into the chest cavity, it can result in infection and fluid accumulation (pleural effusion) (*see* below).

The diagnosis is suspected whenever there is an acute onset of a harsh, continuous cough. Confirmation requires direct visualization of the trachea and bronchi using an endoscope, with the patient under light anesthesia.

If the presence of a foreign body is recognized early, removal of the object during the endoscopic examination is curative. Surgery is required only rarely. If the foreign material penetrates the lung, causing pneumonia, antibiotic therapy may be required for long periods of time (years, perhaps even for life).

TRACHEITIS

Noninfectious inflammation of the trachea most commonly is the result of persistent coughing due to any cause. Less often it can occur after routine surgery if the animal has had a breathing tube in place. The most serious cause of tracheitis is smoke inhalation or inhalation of any irritating gas. The primary clinical sign is a harsh cough.

Tracheitis should be suspected whenever there is a recent history of having a breathing tube in place for surgery, or following inhalation of any irritating gas or smoke. Veterinary assistance usually is not required. In advanced cases, prescription cough suppressants are usually very effective. With tracheitis caused by smoke inhalation, there often are other pulmonary complications that will require intensive veterinary care. If the tracheitis is the result of persistent coughing, treatment should be based on resolution of the preexisting problem.

TRACHEAL AND BRONCHIAL TUMORS

Tumors of the trachea or bronchi are very uncommon in dogs. Clinical signs usually depend on the size and position of the tumor within the airway and range from an occasional cough to severe exercise intolerance, stridor, and collapse during or after exercise. Such signs are similar to those produced by other disorders of the trachea. X rays of the trachea and direct visualization of a mass with the patient under light anesthesia may provide a tentative diagnosis. Definitive diagnosis requires analysis of tissue obtained from the tumor during endoscopic examination.

Surgical removal of the tumor is usually indicated. The specific tumor type and growth pattern will determine whether additional therapy is required. As with other tumors of the respiratory system, this condition is best managed by, or in consultation with, a veterinary cancer specialist.

TRACHEAL COLLAPSE

Tracheal collapse refers to a syndrome most commonly recognized in aging small- and toy-breed dogs, such as Poodles and terriers, in which the normally rigid structure of the trachea is weakened, making the trachea easily collapsible by external or internal pressures. In mild cases, clinical signs of cough and exercise intolerance occur only during periods of strenuous exercise or excitement. In more advanced cases signs may occur during normal breathing or during periods of the mildest excitement. Dogs with severe tracheal collapse are unable to exercise and routinely exhibit harsh coughing fits that end in retching, gagging or vomiting. Occasionally, affected dogs collapse during periods of excitement. Tracheal collapse may occur alone or in combination with other airway diseases, most commonly chronic bronchitis (*see* below).

A history of a chronic, honking cough in an otherwise healthy small- or toy-breed dog is strongly suggestive of tracheal collapse. The diagnosis may be made by observation of a narrowed trachea on X ray, or by direct visualization during endoscopic examination.

Mild cases usually respond to cough suppressants and efforts to minimize daily stress and excitement. Many affected dogs lead relatively normal and happy lives. More severe cases can progress to life-threatening respiratory distress. If only a small segment of the trachea is affected, surgical removal and replacement of the affected portion is sometimes curative. It is important to emphasize, however, that tracheal collapse often occurs in combination with other airway disorders. In these cases treatment must be directed as well toward the other disorders.

ASTHMA

Asthma is a severe, possibly allergic reaction resulting in bronchial airway obstruction and life-threatening respiratory distress. Although it is common in human beings, allergic asthma is not known to occur in dogs, possibly because of differences in the tissue distribution of **mast cells** (specialized granule-containing cells that play a central role in the development of allergy) between the two species.

CHRONIC BRONCHITIS

Chronic bronchitis refers to long-standing inflammation of the bronchial airways that results in a chronic cough and an increase in the production and accumulation of mucus within the respiratory tract. The cough may resemble the harsh cough of tracheal collapse. This is a problem of older dogs and may be especially common in small dog breeds including Poodles, Beagles and terriers. There is no proven cause of chronic bronchitis in dogs, and no strong evidence that infectious disease agents contribute to the problem in any way. Because dogs do not **expectorate** (spit), the excessive mucus produced in the airway may cause gagging or retching, especially at the end of a long bout of coughing. In all other respects dogs with chronic bronchitis are healthy, although with advanced disease they may be unable to exercise for long periods without becoming fatigued.

Diagnosis is based on a chronic cough in a dog that is otherwise healthy. Other diseases that can produce coughing—including heart failure, heartworm infection and cancer—should be ruled out before a diagnosis of chronic bronchitis is made. Additional studies needed to confirm the diagnosis may include X rays and an endoscopic examination.

Mild cases may not require veterinary assistance. Cough suppressants are usually not indicated because they retard the expulsion of mucus. When the cough is continual or is awakening the dog or owner from sleep, the advantages of cough suppressants may, however, outweigh their potential for harm. Severe clinical signs are most effectively controlled by long-term administration of low doses of anti-inflammatory medication (corticosteroids). Some dogs respond positively to **bronchodilators,** drugs that cause expansion of the vital airways and allow for improved respiration. In rare cases, bacterial infections may complicate and worsen the condition. If an infection is suspected, bacterial cultures should be obtained from the airway and the appropriate antibiotic prescribed.

Disorders of the Pulmonary Region

PNEUMONIA

Pneumonia is an inflammatory condition of the lung that can result from bacterial, viral or fungal infection, inhalation of harmful gases, or aspiration of material from the oral cavity. Occasionally pneumonia may be caused by invasion of lung tissue by inflammatory cells even when infection is not present. The primary viral agent responsible for pneumonia in dogs is canine distemper virus. Many bacteria can cause pneumonia by themselves or can complicate the lung inflammation initiated by a virus such as distemper virus. Fungal agents responsible for pneumonia in dogs include *Histoplasma capsulatum, Blastomyces dermatitidis,* and *Coccidioides immitis.* These fungal infections are almost always limited to certain geographic regions of the country, such as the Midwest, South and Southwest. (For a full discussion of the diseases caused by these microbial agents, *see* CHAPTER 34, "VIRAL DISEASES"; CHAPTER 35, "BACTERIAL DISEASES"; and CHAPTER 36, "FUNGAL DISEASES".)

Pneumonia is primarily a problem of young dogs under 2 years of age and older dogs greater than 8 years. Regardless of the underlying cause, pneumonia results in essentially the same set of clinical signs; that is, cough, depression and fever. Often pneumonia is not recognized in its earlier stages until the pet over time "wastes away" and slowly loses weight and condition.

Aspiration pneumonia usually results from some condition in which the normal function of the larynx is disturbed. Most commonly this occurs when an animal is anesthetized, has undergone surgery for laryngeal paralysis, or has a specific disorder of the muscular or nervous system or a chronic debilitating disease.

Accidental inhalation of material from the oral cavity may produce a sudden bout of coughing and retching, similar to signs of a foreign body. Lung involvement then leads to pneumonia.

Inhalation pneumonia most often occurs when a pet is exposed to noxious fumes during a house or forest fire. Clinical signs may not become apparent for 24 to 48 hours. The clinical course is extremely variable, ranging from a mild, self-limiting condition to a serious and potentially fatal disruption of the respiratory tract.

Pneumonia is usually suspected in dogs with chronic coughing and depression. The diagnosis can be confirmed by X rays of the chest. To determine the underlying cause, samples of lung secretions must be obtained for bacterial and fungal culture, using either local or general anesthesia. In some cases, surgical removal of a small piece of lung tissue for microscopic examination (biopsy) may be required.

Treatment is basically supportive, and includes intravenous or **subcutaneous** (beneath the skin) fluid administration, maintenance of normal body temperature, and rest. It is important that the pet be encouraged to get up and walk a few times each day to stimulate the cough reflex. Specific treatments such as antibiotics or antifungal drugs usually will be prescribed based on the culture results.

LUNG TUMORS

Lung tumors may arise within the lungs themselves (primary tumors) or result from spread of a cancerous condition elsewhere in the body (secondary or *metastatic* tumors). Primary lung tumors are uncommon in dogs. When they do occur, the clinical signs may include coughing, depression and wasting. Unfortunately, such signs are similar to those of many other respiratory conditions, so that by the time a diagnosis is made the tumor often is quite advanced.

A lung tumor may be suspected on the basis of X-ray studies of the chest. Confirmation of the presence and type of tumor requires microscopic evaluation of lung tissue. This sometimes can be obtained by inserting a needle through the chest wall and into the lungs, using local anesthesia. More commonly, surgical exploration of the chest cavity may be required.

Treatment is based on the type of tumor, whether it is primary or secondary, and its stage of progression at the time of diagnosis. Patients with a lung tumor are best managed in consultation with, or directly by, a veterinarian specializing in cancer therapy.

Disorders of the Chest Cavity

PLEURAL EFFUSION

Pleural effusion refers to an accumulation of fluid within the **pleural cavity,** the potential space between the **visceral pleura** (a thin transparent membrane covering the surface of the organs in the chest cavity) and the **parietal pleura** (the membrane that forms the inner lining of the chest cavity). If the fluid is clear it is most likely the result of either heart failure, low body stores of protein (**hypoalbuminemia**), or excessive intravenous fluid administration. Because pleural fluid accumulates and surrounds the lungs, a significant volume of fluid can limit the lungs' ability to expand normally during inhalation. When the fluid contains microorganisms (a condition known as **pyothorax**) they can spread to the lungs or bloodstream and threaten the life of the patient.

Clinical signs of pleural effusion may be inapparent or may include rapid, shallow breathing and panting. If the fluid accumulation is the result of heart failure or infection, the pet may also be depressed and unwilling to move. The diagnosis is usually suspected on the basis of the clinical signs, difficulty in hearing the normal lung sounds with a stethoscope during routine physical examination, and abnormalities seen on X rays of the chest. Confirmation of the diagnosis is made by removal of fluid from the chest, using a needle and syringe. Specific treatment must be based on the underlying cause of the fluid accumulation.

CHAPTER 30

The Digestive System and Disorders

by Donald R. Strombeck

The Digestive System

The *gastrointestinal (GI) tract*—composed essentially of a hollow tube running through the body from stem to stern—is concerned with the digestion and absorption of nutrients. The individual functions of the GI tract include **motility** (movement within the walls of the tract), secretion and absorption. Each function is precisely regulated so that it integrates with similar functions elsewhere in the digestive system. The functions of the GI tract as a whole also are integrated with functions elsewhere in other body systems.

The digestive functions that begin in the hindmost portion of the **pharynx** (area extending from the rear of the mouth and nasal passages to the larynx and esophagus) with the initiation of swallowing are **reflex** events, and thus are not under voluntary control of the will. From swallowing on, the only conscious control exerted over the digestive tract is at the **external anal sphincter,** the valve that discharges fecal waste from the body. The functions of the pharynx and **esophagus** (muscular tube extending from the pharynx to the stomach) are entirely motor in

nature, and directed to the movement of food to the stomach. These actions are controlled by nerves that have their origins in the brain stem. As food passes from the pharynx to the stomach, **sphincters** ("valves" that partition different sections of the GI tract), also under involuntary nervous control, open and shut at the upper and lower ends of the esophagus.

The stomach serves as a food reservoir and as a mixing vat where the digestion of food begins. **Gastric** (pertaining to the stomach) control of motility allows the stomach to relax when food enters, and also initiates movement to push food out of the stomach when the time is appropriate. Emptying of the stomach is controlled by the **pyloric sphincter** between the stomach and **duodenum** (the first part of the small intestine) and by events occurring in the duodenum. The latter can inhibit motility and hence gastric emptying, in order to prevent overloading of the digestive and absorptive capacities of the intestinal tract. The stomach responds to a meal by secreting *hydrochloric acid (HCl)* and **proteolytic** (capable of breaking down protein) enzymes. The stimuli for secretion are quite specific, the presence of protein in the stomach and distension of the stomach wall being the most significant. Both the nervous system and specialized hormones regulate motility and secretion in the stomach.

The small intestine is concerned with digestion and absorption of food. The efficiency of these **enteric** (pertaining to the small intestine) processes is determined by the speed with which food passes through the small intestine. That speed is determined by intestinal motility that is primarily under the control of the nervous system. There are two major types of motility in the intestinal tract:

1. *Rhythmic segmentation,* in which the tract "squeezes down" at intervals to promote thorough digestion and absorption of the intestinal contents by slowing passage of food through the tract
2. **Peristalsis,** which causes food to be moved longitudinally through the intestinal tract

Between meals there is little motility in the intestine. Rhythmic segmentation increases when food enters, however, serving to delay the passage of intestinal contents until digestion and absorption have been completed. Peristalsis is not as important as rhythmic segmentation in determining the rate of passage of food through the small intestine.

The digestion of food is essentially a chemical process. The amounts and types of both enzymes and food within the intestine and the conditions under which enzymatic reactions take place determine the rate of digestion. The pancreas and the intestinal **mucosa** (inner surface lining) secrete enzymes and an alkaline fluid into the intestine. This secretion is stimulated by acid contents and food entering from the stomach. The nervous system and hormones control the secretion. The alkaline fluid provides a high pH under which the digestive enzymes function best. The digestive process proceeds to completion unless nutrients are sequestered by fiber, or secretion or motility within the intestine have been disrupted by disease.

Carbohydrate digestion is dependent on normal pancreatic enzyme secretion and on also secretion of digestive enzymes from the surface cells of the intestinal mucosa. Fat digestion and absorption are dependent on normal pancreatic secretions and normal **bile** (digestive fluid produced by the liver, stored in the gallbladder, and released into the intestine through the bile ducts) release from the gallbladder. Protein digestion and absorption also require normal pancreatic enzyme secretion, but assimilation of protein can be adequate even with a marked deficiency of pancreatic enzymes. The absorption of nutrients is an unregulated event. It is dependent on the surface area of the intestinal mucosa, the integrity of the mucosal surface cells, and the absence of disease in the mucosal tissues and in the blood and lymphatic vessels that supply the tissues.

The rate of blood flow to secreting organs dictates their rate of secretion, since the circulation must provide both the fluid and **electrolytes** (molecules that dissociate into ions in solution) needed to form secretions and the energy required for their production. The rate of blood flow is also important in the intestine, where it influences the absorption of nutrients and electrolytes. Both the nervous system and hormones regulate the rate of blood flow in the GI tract. Some cases of diarrhea result from a disturbance of that regulation.

A vast, complex system of microorganisms (primarily bacteria) lives within the confines of the GI tract. Normally, dog and microorganisms live together in harmony, but only as a result of maintenance of the balance within the GI tract. Overgrowth of microorganisms is prevented by acid secretions of the stomach, by normal peristalsis, and by the immune system. Gastrointestinal function is optimal when the intestinal microorganisms are intact and properly ordered in their respective locations within the tract. When the balance of this delicate ecology is upset, major clinical signs of disease appear.

Clinical Signs of Gastrointestinal Tract Disease

Dysphagia, regurgitation and vomiting are considered primary clinical signs associated with problems in the pharynx, esophagus, stomach and upper small intestine.

Dysphagia is difficult or painful swallowing, wherein the dog is either reluctant to swallow or makes a number of swallowing attempts before the food is swallowed. **Regurgitation** is the retrograde expulsion of ingested food from the esophagus or pharynx. It most often results from esophageal disease. Regurgitation can occur from minutes to hours after ingestion of a meal. It is *not* associated with other signs such as **retching** (abdominal contractions, such as are seen with vomiting), and the food is disgorged from the mouth almost spontaneously. Food is regurgitated from the esophagus when the dog's body position allows for gravity to push it back out through the mouth. **Vomiting,** by contrast, is the forceful ejection of stomach contents following stimulation of a nervous system reflex. Vomiting is accompanied by pronounced contractions of the muscles of the **diaphragm** (the large muscle used for breathing, and which separates the abdominal and chest cavities) and abdomen. Vomiting is always preceded by indications of nausea, such as restlessness, depression, excessive salivation, lip licking, frequent swallowing, and retching. Certain drugs known as **antiemetics** may be effective in controlling vomiting, but no drug is effective in controlling regurgitation.

DISEASES OF SWALLOWING

Swallowing disorders are caused by motility problems of the pharynx, esophagus, or the sphincters between the pharynx and esophagus (**pharyngoesophageal sphincter**) or between the esophagus and stomach (**gastroesophageal sphincter**); by **esophagitis** (inflammation of the esophagus); or by obstruction of the esophagus.

Pharyngeal-esophageal Motility Problems

Oral or **pharyngeal dysphagia** are uncommon problems characterized by regurgitation. They are caused by the dysfunction of nerves from the brain to the structures involved. Such diseases are usually not treatable.

Cricopharyngeal dysphagia (or **achalasia**) is an uncommon neurologic disease resulting in failure of the pharyngoesophageal sphincter to open and close properly. Clinical signs include dysphagia and regurgitation. A surgical treatment that involves cutting to cut the muscles forming the sphincter is usually successful.

Megaesophagus (enlargement of the esophagus) is a relatively common problem resulting in paralysis of part or all of the esophagus. This most often affects puppies and involves a congenital or inherited form of megaesophagus. However, an acquired form of megaesophagus can also be seen in adult dogs of any age. The congenital form is most frequent in larger breeds such as Great Danes, German Shepherd Dogs and Irish Setters. Clinical signs include regurgitation that can occur immediately after eating or a number of hours later. Most affected dogs are underweight and exhibit a voracious appetite. The diagnosis is made by X rays of the chest, with or without an X-ray contrast medium such as **barium** to highlight the structure and function of the esophagus. Some dogs develop a loss of normal motility because of esophagitis, but such a problem is usually not a complete paralysis and is reversible. The cause of megaesophagus is unknown. In some cases other neuromuscular problems such as **myasthenia gravis** (a neuromuscular disease) or certain toxicities may be the root of the acquired form of the disease.

There is no treatment for the congenital form of megaesophagus other than feeding the affected dog with the food placed in an elevated position, so that the dog remains standing while eating. The esophagus in any case remains paralyzed and affected animals are at risk for developing a complication such as **aspiration pneumonia** (pneumonia caused by inhalation of food material into the lungs). Most affected pups are euthanatized. If a known treatable cause can be identified in dogs with the acquired form, the problem may be treatable. In general, however, the overall prognosis is poor.

Esophagitis

Inflammation of the esophagus is most commonly caused by the ingestion of a substance that damages the mucosal surface of the esophagus as it passes through. **Reflux** (backflow) of acid contents from the stomach is another cause. Clinical signs of esophagitis include inappetence and regurgitation. Dogs with reflux esophagitis exhibit slightly different clinical signs, in that they often vomit during the early morning hours after arising. They usually will eat if fed then and will not vomit until the next morning.

The diagnosis of esophagitis is difficult to make because most laboratory tests and X-ray studies will reveal no abnormalities. Inflammation of the esophagus can cause the esophagus to appear **dilated** (enlarged), however, as is seen with megaesophagus. The diagnosis can be confirmed by biopsy of the esophageal mucosa, which can be performed by **endoscopy** (procedure wherein a small tube [endoscope] is inserted into the GI tract, for the purpose of examining and/or sampling its internal structure). Treatment consists of a variety of measures implemented in the evening hours, which include the giving of antacids, or treating with a drug that inhibits gastric acid secretion. Reflux esophagitis is usually treated by feeding the dog suffering from it a low-fat, high-protein diet.

Esophageal Obstruction

Obstruction of the esophagus is most commonly caused by foreign bodies such as bones, fishhooks, stones, chunks of food or pieces of fabric. Less commonly, obstruction is caused by inflammation resulting in **stricture** (narrowing of the diameter of the esophagus) formation; esophageal tumors; or **congenital** (present at birth) defects of structures adjacent to the esophagus. In addition to exhibiting regurgitation, affected dogs are usually inappetent (lacking appetite) and some will show signs that suggest pain. The diagnosis is usually made with X-ray studies of the chest, with or without barium. The diagnosis is sometimes made during an **endoscopic** examination of the esophagus.

Esophageal foreign bodies represent a serious problem. Removal of the foreign body is not always successful and complications can develop. Removal is performed either by endoscopy or surgery. Strictures can be treated surgically, while tumors are not treatable. Some forms of obstruction caused by congenital defects can be treated by surgery.

GASTRITIS

The stomach's functions as both a reservoir and mixing vat that delivers partially-digested food at a programmed rate to the small intestine can be disrupted by disease. The clinical signs that signal the loss of function include vomiting, which is an indication that the stomach's reservoir function has been lost. **Bloat** (gastric distention) is a sign that the stomach is retaining food to an abnormal degree, and that stomach emptying is delayed. Acute or chronic **gastritis** (inflammation of the stomach) can cause a loss of both of the stomach's primary functions.

Vomiting is not always caused by a disease process in the stomach. In fact, most dogs presented to veterinarians for vomiting have a problem in an organ system outside the GI tract. For example, diseases of the kidneys, **endocrine** (hormonal) organs (causing diabetes mellitus or Addison's disease), liver, pancreas and uterus; infectious disease agents such as canine distemper virus and canine parvovirus type 2; toxicities resulting from the ingestion of poisons; and certain drugs—can all cause vomiting as a primary clinical sign. Most cases of vomiting caused by gastritis are caused by dietary indiscretions or by food allergies.

Acute gastritis consistently causes vomiting and usually also results in complete inappetence and depression. The **vomitus** (vomited material) usually contains mucus, is often bile-stained, and small amounts of blood may be seen. Other signs such as pain, **borborygmus** (gurgling noises caused by the rapid movement of gas through the intestines), **halitosis** (bad breath), shivering, **polydipsia** (excessive thirst), and fever sometimes occur. Physical examination usually reveals no abnormalities. Laboratory tests are often performed, especially if the cause is suspected to be in an organ system external to the GI tract, or if complications such as dehydration are found. X-ray studies are generally not useful unless the dog is suspected to have swallowed a foreign body.

The diagnosis is based on the history, presenting clinical signs, physical examination, and the results of laboratory tests. Treatment consists of fasting the dog for at least 24 hours. A vomiting dog often craves water and allowing free access to water will cause the vomiting to continue. The dog's thirst can be alleviated at least in part by allowing it to lick ice cubes. Many affected dogs require intravenous fluid therapy to replace lost fluids. A drug to prevent vomiting is not always necessary and some such medications can actually cause depression and worsening of the condition in patients with a lowered blood pressure secondary to fluid loss from vomiting. Other treatments may include inhibitors of gastric acid secretion, antacids or antibiotics. None of these is usually necessary, however, unless the problem appears to be chronic in nature.

After at least 24 hours of fasting, feeding can be resumed by providing small meals at frequent intervals. A very bland diet is recommended. The ideal diet to feed is one prepared by the owner and consists of either cottage cheese or tofu as the source of protein, and either boiled rice or tapioca as the source of carbohydrate. After a week or more, attempts can be made to return the dog to its usual diet. If the vomiting stops but any secondary signs continue, it is an indication that the dog has not recovered completely and that dietary management should continue.

Persistent vomiting can signal chronic gastritis. The laboratory and X-ray findings in chronic gastritis are usually normal. Proof of chronic gastritis can be obtained only with a biopsy of the gastric mucosa. Biopsies can be obtained during endoscopy, or by a surgical procedure that is more involved and invasive but that provides larger and more diagnostic pieces of tissue. Chronic gastritis is managed with a controlled diet as described above. It is often necessary to feed the diet indefinitely. Many causes of chronic gastritis are really a form of chronic inflammatory bowel disease (see below) and may be treated successfully with corticosteroid medications. In most cases the controlled diet is the most important management factor and must be continued alongside corticosteroid therapy. Antacids or inhibitors of gastric acid secretion are sometimes useful in managing chronic gastritis, at least during the early phase of therapy.

GASTRIC RETENTION

Abnormal retention of gastric contents occurs in acute gastritis, when inflammation, stress, and loss of body salts results in a reduction of normal stomach motility. Abnormal retention also occurs in chronic diseases that affect the stomach wall by a long-standing inflammatory or neoplastic (tumorous) process. A similar problem occurs when chronic inflammation affects the duodenum. Disease of the pyloric sphincter, the "valve" between the stomach and duodenum, has the same effect in a problem called *pyloric stenosis* (**stenosis:** a narrowing). Pyloric stenosis is a unique form of gastric retention that occurs congenitally in certain breeds such as Boxers and Boston Terriers.

Clinical signs of gastric retention include vomiting, which can occur soon after eating but in many cases is delayed for up to 24 hours after a meal. Normally, the stomach should be completely empty within 7 to 8 hours after the ingestion of food. Thus the vomiting of food eaten 24 hours previously is essentially diagnostic for a gastric retention problem. In gastric retention bloating is also frequently observed after consuming a meal. In most cases the appetite remains normal although affected dogs are often underweight.

Gastric retention can be diagnosed by X-ray studies showing delayed gastric emptying of food or liquids. Disease of the pyloric sphincter can be treated surgically with good results if the underlying cause does not involve cancer. Such cancers often have spread by the time they are discovered and so treatment is not attempted. Diseases of the gastric wall that interfere with normal motility are usually difficult to manage. Attempts can be made to treat them with drugs such as metoclopramide, but the overall prognosis is poor.

GASTRIC DILATATION-VOLVULUS

Acute *gastric dilatation-volvulus* (bloat) is a serious, life-threatening problem primarily affecting large-breed, deep-chested dogs such as Great Danes, German Shepherd Dogs, Saint Bernards, Irish Setters, and Doberman Pinschers. Bloating occurs after eating and appears to develop because of an accumulation of air and fluid in the stomach that cannot be expelled by **eructation** (burping) or vomiting. The underlying basis for the disease, however, is not completely understood.

Clinical signs include abdominal distension, depression, retching without vomiting, and excessive salivation. X rays are usually taken to confirm the diagnosis and to determine if the stomach has rotated in position. Management consists of passing a stomach tube to release air and fluid from the stomach. If the tube cannot be passed or if X rays reveal rotation of the stomach, then surgery must be performed. Affected dogs require intensive care with fluids and medications to control shock. Mortality rates in gastric dilatation-volvulus can be as high as 30–60%. For dogs that recover, proper management of the diet to prevent a recurrence of the problem is essential. This involves the feeding of small meals more often than once a day, with moistening of the food. Restriction of water consumption and exercise after feeding is also recommended. (*See* CHAPTER 40, "SURGERY AND POSTOPERATIVE CARE.").

SMALL AND LARGE INTESTINAL DISEASES

Diarrhea is the most consistent manifestation of intestinal disease. Diarrhea can be defined as a change in the frequency, consistency, or volume of bowel movements. Bowel movements may exhibit other abnormalities, including the presence of fresh blood, mucus, malassimilated nutrients, and **melena** (dark, pitchy stool due to bleeding into the GI tract). Problems involving the **colon** (large intestine) and **rectum** (lowermost portion of the large intestine) are often associated with straining to defecate. The production and accumulation of abnormal amounts of gas in the GI tract can produce abdominal distension, borborygmus, eructation, **flatus** (expulsion of gas), halitosis, discomfort and pain. Salivation and shivering are seen consistently when smooth muscles of the intestine are stretched or in spasm. The appetite may vary from complete inappetence to **polyphagia** (excessive eating). Water consumption also frequently increases, while weight loss develops following disruption of normal food intake. Thus, diseases of the

intestinal tract can have a number of manifestations beyond, or in lieu of, diarrhea.

Acute Diarrhea

The acute onset of diarrhea, with or without vomiting, is a very common problem in the canine species. There are an extensive number of possible causes, which may be classified as infectious, parasitic, or toxic in nature. The specific cause of acute diarrhea in an individual dog is seldom identified, however, because the transient nature of the disease precludes extensive diagnostic evaluation. The most common cause is thought to involve a dietary change; that is, *food intolerance,* or *food allergy.* Viral infectious agents causing diarrhea include distemper virus, canine coronavirus, and canine parvovirus type 2 (*see* CHAPTER 34, "VIRAL DISEASES"). Bacterial causes can include *Campylobacter, Escherichia coli, Salmonella,* and possibly *Clostridium perfringens.* Many of these bacteria cause no disease in some animals. In others, they populate the intestinal tract because the dog has an underlying problem that has lowered its resistance to the organisms, or an antibiotic has been given that allows the bacteria (which are resistant to the antibiotic) to colonize sites previously occupied by normal bacteria that have been eliminated by the antibiotic therapy (*see* CHAPTER 35, "BACTERIAL DISEASES"). The most likely parasitic causes of acute diarrhea include *Giardia,* coccidia, hookworms and whipworms; roundworms and tapeworms are unlikely to cause diarrhea (*see* CHAPTER 37, "INTERNAL PARASITES"). Many toxins can cause diarrhea; usually, however, a toxic cause cannot be proven in any individual case.

Acute diarrhea is managed with **symptomatic therapy;** that is, therapy aimed at alleviating the clinical signs of a disease rather than treating its underlying cause, which may not be known. In many cases of acute diarrhea, nothing needs to be done except to withhold all food for 24 hours. Intravenous fluid therapy will be of importance in cases where the diarrhea has caused dehydration, however. For some causes, such as parvovirus infection, fluids are essential for survival.

Most cases of acute diarrhea do not require

the use of antibiotics. Antibiotics may be given in cases when the diarrhea continues despite the withholding of food. In some cases, antibiotics are essential to prevent secondary bacterial infection, as in parvovirus infection. The most effective antibiotics with the fewest side effects are the penicillins, given orally or by injection. Newer antibiotics are often used but offer no advantage over the penicillins. The feeding of live cultures of the bacterium *Lactobacillus acidophilus* to dogs with acute diarrhea is of no benefit.

Symptomatic therapy can include medications that alter the motility of the intestinal tract. The most effective of these medications (and the one with the fewest side effects) is Imodium (loperamide). **Antispasmodic** drugs (drugs to prevent spasms within the GI tract) are contraindicated in treating diarrhea. A variety of locally acting drugs is also available. These contain combinations of kaolin, pectin, bismuth compounds and astringents; all are essentially worthless. Antacids containing aluminum or calcium have a constipating effect, however, and may be of some value in therapy.

The primary goal in treating acute diarrhea is to rest the GI tract. Following a fast of at least 24 hours, feeding can be resumed. The mucosa of the digestive tract will still be healing at this time—a time when the dog is susceptible to the development of food intolerance or food allergy—so foods should not be given to which the dog could become sensitive (i.e., commercial dog foods). An owner-prepared diet is recommended, and can be prepared using either cottage cheese or tofu as the protein source, and either boiled rice or tapioca as the carbohydrate source. Nothing else should be fed, including dog biscuits or treats, or toys such as rawhides, which contain chemicals that could result in prolongation of the diarrhea. The primary disadvantage of such a diet is its poor palatability and hence its sometimes poor acceptance by the patient.

Acute hemorrhagic enterocolitis and gastroenteritis (bleeding and inflammation in the gastrointestinal tract) is a disease with no apparent cause. The problem occurs in small breeds with a greater than expected incidence in Miniature Schnauzers, Dachshunds and small Poodles. It is seen in dogs that have been restricted to their home environment and that have had no contact with other animals. Such dogs usually have received the best care, have followed a regular routine in their eating habits, and live in an environment that is remarkably constant from day to day. The chief clinical sign is bloody diarrhea; the feces often are said to resemble raspberry jam. Affected dogs are depressed and may exhibit signs of shock. The problem can be very serious and requires immediate veterinary attention. The most important factor in management is the administration of intravenous fluids to counteract the effects of shock. Antibiotics given by injection are also always used. Supplemental therapy is similar to that for treating acute diarrhea. With proper management affected dogs usually recover, but some may have recurrent bouts of the disease.

Chronic Diarrhea with Weight Loss

Chronic diarrhea accompanied by weight loss or an inability to gain weight in the small intestine usually indicates **malassimilation.** Malassimilation—the defective transport of one or more nutrients from the intestinal contents to the body fluids—is caused by faulty digestion (**maldigestion**) or faulty absorption of nutrients by the intestinal mucosa (**malabsorption**). Clinical signs are essentially the same as described above—diarrhea, with a variety of secondary signs. None of the secondary signs except weight loss can be used to determine whether the problem is in the small or large intestine.

Maldigestion. Maldigestion is caused by a deficiency of pancreatic enzyme secretion or activity in the small intestine, or by a deficiency of digestive enzymes produced in the small intestine itself. Pancreatic enzyme insufficiency (**pancreatic exocrine insufficiency**) is most common in dogs less than 2 or 3 years of age, with German Shepherd Dogs being most often affected. (*See* "PANCREATIC ATROPHY" IN CHAPTER 31, "THE LIVER, PANCREAS AND DISORDERS.") Affected dogs exhibit a ravenous appetite but fail to gain weight. The volume of feces produced by these dogs is always very large. The feces also contain excess fat owing to the maldigestion of dietary fats. The fat can be identified by staining fecal smears. The feces can be stained also for starch granules (indicative of undigested carbohydrates) and muscle fibers (undigested protein, if the dog is eating a diet containing muscle meat). The diagnosis can be confirmed only by conducting a blood test measuring **trypsinogen-like-immunoreactivity,** a measure of an enzyme produced in the pancreas that normally leaks into the blood in small quantities. No other laboratory tests or X-ray studies are useful for identifying this problem. Management of pancreatic enzyme insufficiency requires the addition of pancreatic enzymes to the diet. Enzyme powder (*not* tablets) must be used, and optimum results will be achieved if a high-quality, easily digested diet is fed in place of commercial dog food. In proven cases the response to treatment is excellent, but it is important to understand that life-long dietary therapy will be required.

Malabsorption. Malabsorption can be caused by many problems affecting the small intestinal mucosa such that proper absorption of nutrients is diminished. The clinical signs are similar to those for maldigestion. The feces also contain excess fat, but in this case it is mostly in the form of fatty acids, which are found as fatty-acid soaps. The fatty acids can be demonstrated on fecal smears, but only after treating them with an acid before they are stained. The results of most other tests are normal, including X-ray studies. There are no reliable, easy-to-perform tests to prove malabsorption; the diagnosis requires a biopsy of the small intestinal mucosa. There are also no readily available tests to indicate that biopsy is clearly the next best step in the diagnostic workup. If available, measurement of **breath hydrogen** can be useful in documenting both bacterial overgrowth (a complication of many intestinal problems) and malabsorption of carbohydrates in the small intestine. The breath hydrogen test provides the information needed to justify intestinal biopsy as the next logical step.

There are limits, however, to the information a biopsy can provide. Three general types of

diagnoses can be expected from the results of an intestinal biopsy. First, the biopsy may reveal no abnormalities, even when it is known that the dog has a small intestinal problem causing malabsorption (e.g., an intestinal cancer such as lymphoma, adenocarcinoma or leiomyoma). The second is **lymphangiectasia,** a disease of the intestinal lymph vessels. The third includes all forms of *inflammatory bowel disease.* Biopsies obtained by endoscopy are physically limited to the beginning portion of the small intestine, and often are too small in size to allow an accurate diagnosis to be made. Biopsies taken during surgery are adequate for making a diagnosis, but the procedure is more invasive and the recovery period longer.

Management of malabsorption involves, most importantly, the feeding of a controlled diet. The cottage cheese/tofu and boiled rice/tapioca diet can be utilized and in the case of malabsorption it is likely that this diet must be fed indefinitely. After 3 weeks the diet should be supplemented with vitamins and minerals.

Inflammatory Bowel Diseases
Inflammatory bowel diseases are a group of disorders characterized by persistent clinical signs of gastrointestinal illness, associated with biopsy evidence of inflammation of undetermined cause in the mucosa of the small or large intestine. These diseases are classified according to the type of inflammation present, and the area of the intestinal tract in which the inflammation predominates. A number of diagnoses fall into this classification, and all are treated similarly. They include: *lymphocytic-plasmacytic enteritis/colitis; eosinophilic granulomas; hypereosinophilic syndrome; histiocytic enteritis/colitis; granulomatous enteritis/colitis; transmural granulomatous colitis;* and *suppurative colitis.* The different descriptions are not an indication that they are all different diseases; rather, they may be the same disease with different responses because of individual variation.

The cause or causes of inflammatory bowel disease remain unknown. Proposed causes include defective immunoregulation of the intestinal immune system; genetic, *ischemic* (caused by loss of blood supply resulting from constriction or obstruction of blood vessels), bio-chemical and psychosomatic disorders; infectious or parasitic agents; defects in permeability of the intestinal wall; dietary allergies; and adverse drug reactions. Whatever the cause, the consensus is that the problem involves hypersensitivity responses to substances in the bowel **lumen** (interior) or mucosa. Management of the problem involves elimination of the offending substance (by feeding a controlled diet) and attempts to block immune system effects (by the use of corticosteroid drugs or other agents that can suppress immune responses).

Inflammatory bowel disease of the small intestine affects dogs of any age but is more common in middle-aged animals. Breeds more likely to be affected include German Shepherd Dogs, Rottweilers, Chinese Shar-Peis, Basenjis and Lundehunds. Inflammatory bowel disease of the large intestine occurs more commonly in Boxers and German Shepherd Dogs. The disease in Boxers is unique in that the pathologic changes involve **histiocytes** (tissue macrophages) rather than the lymphocytes, plasma cells, and eosinophils that are usually found. All of these diseases are diagnosed by means of biopsy of the intestinal mucosa. In general, the results of all other testing will be normal unless the disease has produced a complication such as **anemia** (low red blood cell count) due to blood loss, or **hypoproteinemia** (low level of plasma proteins in blood) due to the loss of plasma proteins in the diarrhea.

Management of inflammatory bowel disease involves the feeding of a controlled diet. Corticosteroids or other immunosuppressive medications are used when necessary; they often fail to help, however. Management of **colitis** (inflammation of the large intestine)—never small intestinal problems—can also include the use of drugs that inhibit the formation and action of molecules that fuel inflammation. These drugs are often used only when the controlled diet fails to produce a complete recovery. Additional fiber in the diet is sometimes recommended, although in some cases it can worsen the diarrhea. It is important to remember that affected animals are never cured; at best, management allows a dog to remain virtually free of clinical signs, despite having a chronic, underlying problem.

Motility Disorders of the Intestinal Tract

Irritable bowel syndrome, nervous colitis, spastic colitis, and *mucus colitis* are terms used to describe a motility disorder in human beings that remains poorly understood. It is unknown whether such an entity truly exists in the canine species. There is no doubt that stressful situations can precipitate acute diarrhea in dogs. There is no evidence, however, that similar situations can produce chronic or persistent diarrhea. A thorough and in-depth investigation usually will identify a treatable and understandable cause for diarrhea in a dog suspected initially of having the so-called "irritable bowel syndrome."

Intestinal Obstruction

Obstruction of the small or large intestine is caused most commonly by a foreign body that the dog has swallowed. Other causes include constriction of the intestinal wall by tumors, and loss of normal intestinal motility (**ileus**).

A wide variety of foreign bodies can be ingested by dogs. Foreign objects that commonly lodge in the intestine include bones, corncobs, stones, fruit stones, tampons, fabrics, food wrappings, chew toys, children's toys, bottle caps, plant material, hair, fishhooks and sewing needles. Small-diameter and smooth foreign bodies usually pass through uneventfully; larger ones will usually lodge in the small intestine and cause obstruction. Some sharp foreign bodies will pass through while others penetrate the intestinal wall and lead to infection. Ingested zinc and lead objects can release amounts of metal that can be toxic when absorbed. Obstruction can also be caused by a swallowed string that becomes fixed at one point, and by passing through the remainder of the small intestine results in the bunching up of the intestinal loops like an accordion.

Intestinal obstruction usually causes vomiting and often causes diarrhea. If the obstruction is in the small intestine shortly beyond the stomach, it is more likely to result in vomiting soon after eating or drinking. With obstructions at the lower end of the small intestine, diarrhea may be more likely than vomiting; if vomiting is seen it may be delayed for 6 to 8 hours after eating.

Intestinal obstructions are often identified on physical examination of the abdomen (*palpation*). The diagnosis is made by X rays of the GI tract. Often a contrast medium such as barium will be required for the X-ray study. Occasionally, an obstruction will be difficult to visualize even with good X-ray films. Surgery is usually required for the management of intestinal obstruction due to any cause except ileus.

The diagnosis of ileus is made with X-ray studies. Ileus (decreased bowel motility) can be caused by stress (as following surgery) or by loss of potassium through vomiting or diarrhea. Management of ileus involves replacement of potassium losses, and sometimes administration of a drug to stimulate intestinal motility.

CHAPTER 31

The Liver, Pancreas and Disorders

by Donald R. Strombeck

The Liver

The liver is the largest organ in the body. It has a highly **vascularized** (well-supplied with blood vessels) structure, receiving **venous** blood (blood from veins) from the spleen and gastrointestinal organs through the portal vein and returning that blood to the circulation through the inferior vena cava. In addition, the liver receives arterial blood as its source of energy through the hepatic artery.

The liver is located just below the diaphragm above the stomach, spleen, pancreas and intestines (*see* CHAPTER 18, "ANATOMY"). Anatomically it is divided into a number of sections, or lobes, each of which in turn is composed of many thousands of minute structural and functional units called lobules. The many functions of the liver enable it to participate in carbohydrate, fat and protein metabolism; temperature regulation; regulation of circulation, **detoxification** (reduction in toxic properties of compounds) and excretion of useless substances; storage of nutrients; and certain host defense activities.

CLINICAL SIGNS OF LIVER DISEASE

Many dogs' clinical histories contain some information suggesting the possibility of **hepatic** (liver) disease. None of the clinical signs of liver disease is diagnostic for hepatic problems, however—even such signs as **jaundice** (yellow discoloration of the skin and mucous membranes), which is more often caused by a **hemolytic** (red blood cell-destroying) disease, and **ascites** (accumulation of fluid within the abdominal cavity), which is more frequently a sign of heart disease. With liver disease, ascites or jaundice usually do not appear until the disease process is well advanced and severe, and even then they are not observed consistently. The other nonspecific signs offer few clues for suspecting hepatic illness. Liver disease should be suspected, however, when any of these nonspecific signs cannot be explained by another underlying problem.

Few clinical signs are found consistently in hepatic disease. The only specific signs indicating the possibility of hepatic disease are ascites, jaundice, and abnormalities in liver size.

Laboratory procedures must be performed to

obtain information necessary for the identification, management and prognosis of hepatic problems. Most patients with liver disease are presented with clinical signs that are not specific for any particular problem. In some cases the signs are not even suggestive of hepatic illness; it is only when the different organ systems are surveyed with clinical laboratory procedures that a liver problem is identified. Laboratory test results can help determine the type of disease process involved, the clinical management of the problem, and the overall prognosis.

Laboratory procedures used to investigate a suspected hepatic problem include biochemical tests and **morphologic** (pertaining to shape and structure) evaluation of the liver. Biochemical tests (**blood chemistry panel**) include measurement of the plasma activities of enzymes originating in the liver. The most important of these is **alanine aminotransferase (ALT).** Following liver cell damage, the activity of ALT in the plasma increases. With all forms of liver disease, ALT activity increases in 60–100% of cases, but the magnitude of the increase varies greatly from one disease to another. With diseases such as **hepatitis** (inflammation of the liver) and **liver cell necrosis** (cell death) due to a toxin, the activity of plasma ALT can increase from 5 to 100 times normal. On the other hand, with diseases such as a **portasystemic shunt** (abnormal persistence of an embryonic blood vessel within the liver) or cancer that has spread to the liver, the magnitude of the increase for ALT is often only 2 to 5 times greater than normal. The results of many other tests can be found on a blood chemistry panel, but abnormalities in these tests are not specific for liver disease. (*See* APPENDIX C, "DIAGNOSTIC TESTS").

Biochemical tests for liver disease also include a liver function test, which is important to perform if the results of the chemistry panel are normal. One function test that is easy to perform is measurement of **plasma bile acids** (steroid acids made from cholesterol). This test is not very sensitive, however. Bile acid measurement is most widely used for screening patients for portasystemic shunts, but its results

are abnormal (elevated) in no more than 75% of dogs with that problem. With other liver diseases the results of this test are abnormal in no more than 50% of diseased dogs. Measurement of blood ammonia levels provides a much more reliable test for identifying dogs with liver disease. It is the only function test that provides abnormal results in nearly 100% of dogs with liver disease that are exhibiting clinical signs. It is the only test that can determine whether clinical signs of central nervous system dysfunction can be attributed to liver disease (**hepatic encephalopathy**). Of all the signs of liver disease, **anorexia** (reduced food intake) is the first to appear and it too is a sign of hepatic encephalopathy.

Most forms of liver disease cannot be diagnosed by morphologic evaluation of the liver. Morphologic evaluation can be performed grossly with X rays of the liver, but judgments on liver size are unreliable and usually provide little useful information. A normal dog can have a small liver or a large liver, either of which may reflect no pathologic changes. Most importantly, morphologic evaluation of the liver can be performed with a liver **biopsy** (microscopic examination of tissue). With one exception, biopsy is the only means to gain a definitive diagnosis of what is occurring in the liver. Abnormalities in a blood chemistry panel or liver function test results cannot be used to define the disease process in the liver. Biopsy can identify all the problems in the liver except for a portasystemic shunt, which can be diagnosed with another imaging technique that employs either X-ray (**angiography**) or nuclear medicine ("scan") procedures.

With strong evidence for hepatic disease, it is often not important or even necessary to biopsy the liver to understand the pathologic process. The liver is at the center of many normal and disease activities in the body. In addition, the liver consists of some of the body's most sensitive tissue, in that many diseases external to the liver will nevertheless produce disease changes in the liver. The liver can therefore be thought of in many cases as an "innocent bystander." If it can be judged that some other disease is responsible for liver changes that are causing abnormalities in laboratory findings, it is often not necessary to perform a liver biopsy. Examples of nonhepatic diseases that regularly cause abnormalities in liver tests include **endocrine** (hormonal) diseases such as diabetes mellitus and Cushing's syndrome; circulatory diseases such as congestive heart failure, anemia, and **thromboembolic** (blood-clot) problems; cancer; gastrointestinal disease; pancreatitis (inflammation of the pancreas); kidney disease; and generalized or local infection. In addition, many drugs produce changes in the results of liver tests. These drugs include such commonly prescribed medications as corticosteroids, sulfa drugs and other antimicrobial agents, aspirin, acetaminophen, and some drugs used to control seizures. Thus, it is important that the patient be carefully evaluated for a nonhepatic cause of liver test abnormalities before the liver is biopsied.

DISEASES OF THE LIVER

Chronic Hepatitis

Chronic hepatitis (inflammation of the liver) is the most common liver disease in dogs. It develops most often in dogs 6 to 8 years of age, but can be seen in dogs as young as 1 year old. It affects all breeds, with the Doberman being the only breed more susceptible than the others. In most cases (two-thirds) the specific cause of the disease is unknown. In this primary form the cause is presumed to be a virus, drug or immune-mediated response. In the remaining one-third of cases, hepatitis can be attributed to another problem such as infection, cancer, gastrointestinal disease, kidney disease or another generalized cause. The clinical signs are nonspecific, with inappetence being the earliest and most important. Most cases of chronic hepatitis will exhibit abnormalities in a blood chemistry panel. The disease can be definitively diagnosed only with a liver biopsy. Treatment involves removal or correction of any underlying cause (such as discontinuing any nonessential medications), and management with corticosteroids

and a controlled diet (*see* below). Approximately one-third of dogs with hepatitis will die within 1 week of presentation to a veterinarian, despite all efforts at treatment. The remaining two-thirds will survive longer if treated with corticosteroids.

Hepatic Necrosis

Hepatic necrosis (cell or tissue death) is usually a manifestation of disease elsewhere in the body or the result of a drug or toxin. In only 20% of cases is the problem a reflection of a disease process originating in the liver. Clinical signs are usually due to the primary disease. Management consists of treating the primary problem, with management of the hepatic damage being based primarily on feeding a controlled diet (*see* below).

Hepatopathy, Vacuolar Hepatopathy, Hepatic Lipidosis

Hepatopathy refers to degenerative changes in the liver for which the underlying cause is unknown. **Vacuolar hepatopathy** refers to degenerative changes in which the cause in over half of the cases is generalized, such as an infection, or is located in another body organ. **Hepatic lipidosis** is a more severe degenerative change wherein the body is unable to transport fats out of the liver. The cause is usually known, with complete anorexia, diabetes mellitus, gastrointestinal disease, pancreatitis and cancer being the most important. The management of these three forms of hepatic degeneration most importantly involves the feeding of a controlled diet (*see* below). If the primary problem outside the liver is managed successfully, the liver can return to its normal state.

Portasystemic Shunts

Portasystemic shunts (also known as **portacaval shunts**) are abnormal communications between the portal vein coming from the gastrointestinal tract and the posterior vena cava, which carries blood back to the heart. The communications are normally present during fetal life and then close off shortly after birth. When the communications fail to close properly, the vessels serve as shunts so that portal blood flow does not pass through the liver for processing (detoxification, etc.) before being delivered to the rest of the body. Many different breeds can have this problem, with small breeds such as Yorkshire Terriers and Miniature Schnauzers being the most commonly affected. Clinical signs appear at a young age, usually before 1 year. Most importantly, they include neurologic signs of hepatic encephalopathy: depression, seizures and **ataxia** (incoordination), in addition to vomiting, **polydipsia** (excessive thirst), and retarded growth. Blood chemistry panel results usually are normal. Performing an ammonia tolerance test is the most reliable means of determining that the signs are caused by a hepatic abnormality. The diagnosis can be confirmed by an X-ray imaging study. Most cases can be treated successfully by partial surgical closure of the shunt. Dietary management (*see* below) will help alleviate clinical signs in dogs not treated surgically.

Hepatic Tumors

Dogs only infrequently develop primary tumors of the liver. The liver is often involved, however, in cancers that have spread from elsewhere in the body. In both cases, dogs may exhibit signs of other forms of liver disease. Treatment is usually not attempted in most cases. An exception is **lymphoma** (malignant tumor of lymphocytes), which is sometimes treated with success. (*See* CHAPTER 33, "THE IMMUNE SYSTEM AND DISORDERS.")

DIETARY MANAGEMENT OF LIVER DISEASE

The liver is able to heal if the patient is provided with a diet that supports an optimal return to normal function. The liver cannot heal if the patient does not eat; thus, it is important to ensure an adequate food intake. The diet must be based on protein from milk and/or soybean; healing is impaired when the protein source is meat. The diet should be prepared by the person feeding the dog; no commercially prepared foods are acceptable. In general, the diet is formulated with cottage cheese and/or tofu (as a source of protein), a source of starch such as boiled rice, a source of

fat (animal fat is acceptable and is more palatable than vegetable fat), and a vitamin-mineral mixture to balance the diet. It is important to ensure that adequate vitamin C and zinc are added. In some cases the diet should be low in copper because of copper's accumulation and toxicity in some forms of liver disease. Since vitamin A can be toxic to the liver, any amount added to the diet should be minimal. Vitamin E is protective to the diseased liver and can be added in greater than usual quantities.

The Pancreas

The pancreas is a small organ lying next to the lower part of the stomach and the beginning of the small intestine. It functions both as an endocrine and an exocrine organ. As an **endocrine** organ it produces and secretes a variety of hormones directly into the bloodstream, the most important of which is **insulin.** As part of its **exocrine** function the pancreas produces and secretes digestive enzymes through ducts into the digestive tract. Disease develops with inflammation (pancreatitis), atrophy (**pancreatic exocrine insufficiency** and/or diabetes mellitus), or tumors of either the exocrine or endocrine portion of the pancreas.

DISEASES OF THE PANCREAS

Acute Pancreatitis

Acute **pancreatitis** (inflammation of the pancreas) is most commonly a disease of middle-aged dogs that are well cared for. Clinical signs usually include inappetence, depression, vomiting, diarrhea and abdominal pain. In a few cases pain and vomiting may not be observed. Weakness and difficulty breathing are sometimes seen. Physical examination usually reveals fever, pain on **palpation** (feeling with the hands) of the abdomen, rapid heart rate and dehydration. About one-third of pancreatitis cases are primary, wherein there is no known cause; in such instances it is usually believed that the problem was precipitated by ingestion of a fat-rich meal, garbage, offal (butchers' scraps), etcetera. In the remaining two-thirds, the disease is related to a primary problem elsewhere in the body, such as kidney disease, corticosteroid use, gastrointestinal disease, liver disease, systemic infection, blood-clotting disorders, or cardiovascular disease. In either case, the development of pancreatitis remains a poorly understood phenomenon.

Laboratory evaluation of **acute** (rapid-onset) pancreatitis is most importantly performed using a blood chemistry panel that reports plasma activity of the enzyme **lipase.** This enzyme is normally produced in the pancreas and is released to the circulation in greater than normal amounts when the pancreas is inflamed. With a finding of elevated lipase activity, the probability of a dog's having acute pancreatitis is approximately 75%. The causes of elevated lipase in the other 25% of cases include liver disease, kidney problems, tumors and a variety of other disorders. No other test results are useful for the diagnosis of acute pancreatitis. Amylase activity in plasma was once used for this purpose, but is now recognized as unreliable because amylase activity increases in many different gastrointestinal as well as other diseases. The diagnosis of acute pancreatitis can be confirmed using **ultrasonography** (a noninvasive diagnostic technique for visualizing internal structures of the body using sound [echo] reflections; **ultrasound**). In normal dogs, the pancreas cannot be seen during an ultrasound examination; when acute pancreatitis occurs, the organ becomes visible. Thus, a high lipase value together with a visible pancreas on ultrasound examination usually will confirm the diagnosis of acute pancreatitis.

Acute pancreatitis can be a diagnostic challenge because it can manifest itself clinically in a variety of ways. In addition, acute pancreatitis can cause many very serious complications. These include secondary damage to the heart, lungs, kidneys, liver and brain; blood clotting abnormalities; and infection. Many of these complications are responsible for the high mortality rate associated with acute pancreatitis.

Management of acute pancreatitis involves, most importantly, the administration of intravenous fluids. If this therapy is neglected, an affected dog is unlikely to recover. During acute pancreatitis blood flow through the pancreas is compromised. Fluid therapy is essential to restore normal pancreatic circulation so that recovery from inflammation will occur. Fluid therapy is also important to minimize complications. Fluids help restore normal circulation to the kidneys and liver and assist in their recovery. Fluids also assist in recovery from clotting disorders.

Antibiotics are also important for the treatment of pancreatitis. Affected dogs are at risk of both generalized and localized infection in the pancreas. The latter can lead to abscess formation, a life-threatening complication that is usually difficult to treat. Acute pancreatitis is also treated by fasting the patient for up to 5 days. Many other treatments have been tried and found wanting. No other treatments can improve on the combination of fluid therapy, antibiotics and fasting.

After recovery, the dog can be fed a low-fat, high-quality diet. If certain table foods or commercial dog foods are suspected to have caused the problem, they should of course be avoided in the future.

Chronic Pancreatitis

Dogs that recover from acute pancreatitis often develop a chronic form of the disease. There may be no overt clinical signs, and blood chemistry results may be normal. On ultrasound, however, the pancreas will appear abnormal. No treatment other than the feeding of a low-fat, controlled diet is recommended. These dogs are at high risk for eventually developing complications of diabetes mellitus and/or pancreatic exocrine insufficiency.

Pancreatic Tumors

Pancreatic tumors of the exocrine cells (**adenocarcinomas**) cause clinical signs similar to those of pancreatitis. When identified, they have usually already spread and are essentially untreatable. Tumors of the endocrine cells (**insulinomas**) produce signs of insulin excess so that the affected dogs develop low blood sugar levels (**hypoglycemia**).

Pancreatic Atrophy

Pancreatic atrophy develops usually secondary to destruction of exocrine cells by pancreatitis, or because the exocrine tissue never developed fully or atrophied early in life. The latter problem (**pancreatic exocrine insufficiency**) is most commonly observed in the German Shepherd Dog breed. Clinical signs include weight loss and usually diarrhea. The problem is diagnosed using a blood test (**trypsinogen-like-immunoreactivity test**). Treatment consists of replacement by the addition of pancreatic enzymes to the diet. (*See* "Maldigestion" in Chapter 30, "The Digestive System and Disorders.")

Diabetes Mellitus

(For a full discussion of diabetes mellitus, *see* Chapter 32, "The Endocrine System and Metabolic Disorders.")

CHAPTER 32

The Endocrine System and Metabolic Disorders

**by Richard W. Nelson
and Edward C. Feldman**

The Endocrine System

Endocrinology is the study of hormones and hormone-producing glands. **Hormones** are regulatory or "messenger" molecules that are secreted into the bloodstream and carried to a distant site, where they interact with the tissue at that site to modify its function. Hormone-producing glands include the pituitary gland, thyroid gland, parathyroid glands, pancreas, adrenal glands, ovaries and testes. Diseases of the *endocrine system* typically result from excessive or deficient production of a hormone by an endocrine gland. Some of the more common endocrine disorders affecting dogs are the subject of this chapter. (For information on hormone-related disorders of the reproductive system, *see* CHAPTER 14, "REPRODUCTIVE DISORDERS.")

Disorders of the Pituitary Gland

The **pituitary gland** is often called the "master" endocrine gland because it controls the functions of almost all other endocrine glands. Several different hormones are produced by the pituitary, including antidiuretic hormone (ADH), growth hormone (GH), adrenocorticotropic hormone (ACTH), thyroid-stimulating hormone (TSH), follicle-stimulating hormone (FSH), and luteinizing hormone (LH). Excessive or deficient secretion of certain pituitary hormones are responsible, either directly or indirectly, for most of the endocrine disorders affecting dogs.

DIABETES INSIPIDUS
Antidiuretic hormone (also called **ADH** or **vasopressin**) is the hormone that controls water resorption by the kidney, urine production and concentration, and water balance. Defective synthesis or secretion of ADH, or an inability of the kidneys to respond to ADH, is the cause of a syndrome known as **diabetes insipidus** (not to be confused with **diabetes mellitus,** a disease involving the hormone **insulin**). In dogs, the underlying cause of diabetes insipidus usually is not known. A voluminous increase in water consumption and urination is the hallmark of the disease.

Clinical signs can develop at any age, although the disorder most commonly affects puppies or young adult dogs. The diagnosis is established by ruling out other causes for increased water consumption and urination and by demonstrating a lack of production or effectiveness of ADH. The latter is usually accomplished by performing a modified water deprivation test, or by evaluating the response to ADH replacement therapy; that is, by determining whether water consumption and urination decrease following administration of ADH.

Treatment of diabetes insipidus involves the daily administration of synthetic ADH, usually in the form of eye drops. Therapy can be quite expensive and must be given for the remainder of the dog's life. The clinical signs usually are ameliorated in dogs given appropriate therapy, and with proper care affected animals have an excellent life expectancy.

Growth Hormone-Responsive Dermatosis

Growth hormone-responsive dermatosis is a poorly defined skin disorder affecting adult dogs. The cause is unknown. **Growth hormone (GH)** is a pituitary hormone responsible for regulation of the body's growth rate. In most affected dogs the concentration of GH in the blood is low and does not increase following artificial stimulation of the pituitary gland (*see* below). The clinical signs are believed to be caused by a deficiency of GH. Although the disease has been reported in many breeds, Chow Chows, Pomeranians, Toy and Miniature Poodles, Keeshonds and Samoyeds are overly represented, suggesting a possible genetic basis for this disorder. Male dogs also seem to suffer from this disease more often than female dogs.

Clinical signs usually develop in young animals 2 to 5 years of age and consist entirely of symmetrical hair loss on the trunk, neck, ears, tail and thighs. The skin gradually turns black in areas affected by the loss of hair. The dogs are otherwise normal.

A diagnosis of GH-responsive dermatosis is based on documenting GH deficiency with a GH stimulation test as well as demonstrating a beneficial response to GH replacement therapy. In the GH stimulation test a compound (either **clonidine** or **xylazine**) known to produce an increase in circulating GH levels in normal dogs is injected into the patient. This is then followed by measurement of GH levels in the patient's blood at various time intervals (15, 30, 45, 60, 90 minutes) after injection, to see if a response has occurred.

Treatment relies on administration of synthetic human GH. Unfortunately, human GH is quite expensive and can be difficult to obtain. Regrowth of hair is used to assess response to therapy, which usually occurs within 4 to 6 weeks of initiating treatment. (*See* Chapter 22, "The Skin and Disorders.")

Acromegaly

Persistent, excessive secretion of GH in adult dogs results in **acromegaly,** a chronic disease characterized by overgrowth of connective tissue, bone, and **viscera** (the large interior organs of the body). Acromegaly can result from:

- spontaneous GH overproduction by a pituitary tumor.
- stimulation of GH secretion after prolonged administration of progestogens, especially medroxyprogesterone acetate (**progestogens** are compounds with progesterone-like activity, i.e., their primary function is to prepare the uterus for pregnancy; in dogs they also stimulate GH secretion)
- stimulation of GH secretion during the *diestrus* phase of the estrous (heat) cycle in intact older bitches, owing to the dominance of progesterone secretion

Chronic GH stimulation has both **catabolic** (causing the breakdown of body molecules) and **anabolic** (causing the buildup of more complex body molecules) effects. The anabolic effects are caused by increased concentrations of **somatomedins** (small proteins produced mainly in the liver) and include proliferation of bone, cartilage and soft tissues, and enlargement of body organs (e.g., heart, kidneys). The catabolic effects of GH are a direct result of anti-insulin effects of GH on tissues, which cause the development of diabetes mellitus (*see* below).

Acromegaly typically develops in older, intact female dogs. The most consistent clinical signs are difficulty breathing, exercise intolerance, fatigue and frequent panting. Additional clinical signs include:

- an increase in body size, most frequently manifested as enlargement of the limbs, feet, head and abdomen
- broadening of the head with prominence of the jowls, a protruding lower jaw, and an increase in the **interdental spaces** (spaces between the teeth)
- degenerative arthritis

The diagnosis is based on recognition of the appropriate clinical signs together with identification of diestrus in the affected older female dog or a history of chronic progestogen administration. Treatment involves withdrawal of progestogen therapy (if this is the likely underlying cause) or **ovariohysterectomy** (spay operation). Most of the clinical signs are reversible following treatment; however diabetes mellitus, if present, may or may not resolve.

Disorders of the Thyroid Gland

The **thyroid gland** consists of two lobes located on either side of the **trachea** (the "windpipe"). (Because of its bilobed structure, the thyroid *gland* is sometimes referred to as the thyroid *glands*.) The thyroid gland secretes two major hormones, **thyroxine** (T_4) and **triiodothyronine** (T_3), which together are referred to as **thyroid hormone.** Secretion of thyroid hormone is under the control of the pituitary gland, by way of the pituitary hormone known as **thyroid-stimulating hormone (TSH).** Thyroid hormone acts to regulate the overall metabolism of almost all cells in the body. Problems with the thyroid gland affect all organs and can produce many different clinical manifestations. The thyroid gland also produces another important hormone, **calcitonin,** which lowers blood calcium levels. Calcitonin thus acts as an antagonist to **parathyroid hormone (PTH)** produced by the parathyroid glands, which raises blood calcium levels by drawing calcium out of the bones (*see* below).

HYPOTHYROIDISM

Hypothyroidism is the most common hormonal disorder affecting dogs and results from a deficiency of thyroid hormone. Canine hypothyroidism is usually caused by destruction of the thyroid gland, either from an immune-mediated process (**lymphocytic thyroiditis** [inflammation of the thyroid gland, involving lymphocytes]), atrophy, or cancer. The genetic makeup of the host is believed to play a role in the development of lymphocytic thyroiditis.

Clinical signs usually appear at between 2 and 6 years of age. Some breeds have an apparent increased risk for the development of hypothyroidism (*see* TABLE 1). There is no recog-

Table 1 Dog breeds with an apparent increased incidence of hypothyroidism	
Afghan Hound	Golden Retriever
Airedale	Great Dane
Beagle	Irish Setter
Boxer	Irish Wolfhound
Brittany	Malamute
Chow Chow	Miniature Schnauzer
Cocker Spaniel	Newfoundland
Dachshund	Pomeranian
Doberman Pinscher	Poodle
English Bulldog	Shetland Sheepdog

nized sex predilection.

Most dogs with hypothyroidism exhibit some degree of mental dullness, lethargy, exercise intolerance or unwillingness to exercise, and a propensity to gain weight without a corresponding increase in appetite or food intake. These signs are often gradual in onset, subtle, and may not be appreciated until they are contrasted with the animal's improved state after thyroid hormone replacement therapy has begun.

Additional clinical signs of hypothyroidism typically involve the skin, reproductive system, or neuromuscular system. Alterations in the skin and haircoat are common and include symmetrical hair loss on the trunk and tail; a dull, dry and easily **epilated** (epilate: to pull out hairs by the roots) haircoat; slow regrowth of hair; scaly skin; "puffiness" of the skin (i.e., **myxedema**); **seborrhea** (oiliness caused by excessive production of sebum, the secretion of the sebaceous glands); and bacterial infections. Deleterious effects on the reproductive system include prolonged interestrus intervals or failure to cycle in the bitch, and lack of libido, atrophy of the testicles, and low sperm counts in the male. Neurologic signs that have been reported in hypothyroidism include seizures, "drunken" gait, circling, head-tilt, and facial nerve paralysis.

Hypothyroidism in the juvenile dog causes **cretinism.** The most glaring abnormalities in hypothyroid pups are related to the skeletal and central nervous systems. Dogs with cretinism appear physically disproportionate, with large broad heads, thick protruding tongues, wide square trunks and short limbs. Cretins are mentally dull and lethargic and lack the typical playfulness seen in normal pups. Persistence of the "puppy haircoat," hair loss, inappetence, delayed eruption of the teeth, and **goiter** (enlarged thyroid gland) are additional clinical signs.

The diagnosis of hypothyroidism requires careful assessment of the history, physical findings, clinical pathology, and serum cholesterol and thyroid hormone concentrations, usually serum thyroxine (T_4) concentration. A normal level of circulating thyroid hormone usually indicates normal thyroid gland function in most dogs. Low serum thyroid hormone concentration in conjunction with increased blood cholesterol levels and appropriate clinical signs supports a diagnosis of hypothyroidism. Definitive diagnosis must then rely on response to trial therapy with thyroid hormone supplementation.

Hypothyroidism is treated with synthetic thyroid hormone, usually given orally twice a day. Treatment must be continued for the remainder of the dog's life. With appropriate therapy the clinical signs should resolve. The prognosis for recovery is excellent.

HYPERTHYROIDISM

Functional thyroid tumors that secrete excess thyroid hormone into the blood can cause a clinical syndrome known as **hyperthyroidism.**

Clinical signs include a ravenous appetite, weight loss, increased water consumption and urination, hyperactivity and aggressive behavior. Thyroid tumors causing hyperthyroidism may be small benign masses or, more commonly, malignant tumors—usually large, solid masses that frequently extend into the esophagus and trachea and into the surrounding musculature, nerves and thyroidal blood vessels. Distant **metastases** (the spread of the tumor) to the lungs and lymph nodes are common.

The average age for development of thyroid tumors, benign or malignant, is 10 years, with a range of 5 to 15 years. Although any breed can be affected, Boxers, Beagles, Golden Retrievers and German Shepherd Dogs may be at increased risk. There is no recognized sex predilection.

The diagnosis requires documentation of increased circulating levels of thyroid hormone and **histologic** (microscopic examination of tissue) evaluation of a biopsy specimen obtained from the mass. Benign tumors and small malignant tumors that have not spread are usually treated surgically. The prognosis is good following surgical removal. Large malignant masses that have extensively invaded surrounding tissues or that have spread to other areas of the body can be treated with a combination of surgery, chemotherapy, radioactive iodine and radiation therapy. The prognosis for these tumors is poor, however.

Disorders of the Parathyroid Glands

Adherent to the two lobes of the thyroid gland are the four small **parathyroid glands,** one pair associated with each thyroid lobe. The parathyroid glands secrete **parathyroid hormone (PTH, parathormone),** which is responsible for maintaining calcium and phosphorus concentrations in the blood. Normally PTH acts to increase blood calcium levels (and thereby lower blood phosphorus levels) by drawing calcium out of the bones and by increasing calcium absorption in the intestine as well as calcium retention in the kidneys. The activities of PTH are normally kept in balance by its antagonist hormone, calcitonin, which is produced by the thyroid gland (*see* above).

PRIMARY HYPERPARATHYROIDISM

Primary hyperparathyroidism (PHP) is a disorder resulting from excessive, relatively uncontrolled secretion of PTH by one or more abnormal parathyroid glands. Excessive secretion of PTH produces an abnormal increase in blood calcium levels (**hypercalcemia**) and a corresponding decrease in blood phosphorus levels (**hypophosphatemia**). The most common cause is a benign parathyroid gland tumor. PHP occurs in older dogs (average age, 10 years). Keeshonds, German Shepherd Dogs and Norwegian Elkhounds appear to have a predisposition for this disorder, suggesting a role for genetics in its development in these breeds. There is no recognized sex predilection.

Clinical signs of PHP are caused by hypercalcemia and include increased water consumption and urination (**polydipsia** and **polyuria**), lethargy, inappetence, vomiting and weakness. In the mildest form of PHP clinical signs may not be evident; the elevated level of blood calcium is often an unexpected finding on a serum chemistry panel performed by the veterinarian for another reason. Hypercalcemia can be caused by other disorders as well, which must be ruled out before a diagnosis of PHP can be established. Measurement of serum PTH levels will help to confirm PHP.

Surgical removal of the abnormal parathyroid tissue is the cornerstone of treatment. Failure to treat PHP will ultimately lead to kidney failure. Abnormally low blood calcium levels (**hypocalcemia**) frequently develop after surgery but can be managed with oral vitamin D and calcium supplements. These supplements can gradually be discontinued in most dogs after a period of two to four months. The prognosis for recovery is excellent, unless concurrent kidney failure is present.

PRIMARY HYPOPARATHYROIDISM

Primary hypoparathyroidism develops because of an absolute or relative deficiency in secretion of PTH, causing a decrease in blood calcium levels and a corresponding increase in blood phosphorus levels. The cause of the disease is unknown, although immune-mediated destruction of parathyroid tissue is suspected in most cases. Primary hypoparathyroidism usually occurs in young adult dogs (those less than 6 years of age) and is seen disproportionately more often in females. There is no apparent breed predisposition.

Clinical signs are caused by the hypocalcemia and include nervousness, generalized seizures, localized muscle twitching, rear-limb cramping or **tetany** (muscle spasms), a "drunken" gait and weakness. Additional signs include lethargy, inappetence, intense facial rubbing and panting. The onset of clinical signs tends to be abrupt and severe. Signs appear more frequently during exercise, excitement or episodes of stress.

Diagnosis of primary hypoparathyroidism is based on a finding of low levels of PTH in a dog with persistently low blood calcium levels. Treatment involves the daily oral administration of vitamin D and calcium supplements, the goal being to maintain blood calcium in the normal range. Most dogs with primary hypoparathyroidism require at least the vitamin D therapy for the remainder of their lives. With appropriate therapy, the prognosis is excellent.

Disorders of the Endocrine Pancreas

The *pancreas* consists of two distinct parts: an **exocrine** part whose cells secrete digestive enzymes through ducts into the intestinal tract for the digestion of nutrients, and an **endocrine** part whose cells secrete hormones into the blood to process those nutrients once they have been absorbed from the gut. (*See* CHAPTER 30, "THE DIGESTIVE SYSTEM AND DISORDERS," and CHAPTER 31, "THE LIVER, PANCREAS AND DISORDERS," for information on the pancreas's exocrine function.) The endocrine cells of the pancreas are found in clusters called the **islets of Langerhans** that are dispersed, like small islands, throughout the exocrine portion of the pancreas. The most important hormone of the endocrine pancreas is **insulin,** which is secreted by cells called **beta cells** within the islets of Langerhans. Insulin is responsible for regulating the blood concentration of **glucose** (blood sugar), the most important "fuel molecule" of the body.

Diabetes Mellitus

Diabetes mellitus (not to be confused with diabetes insipidus) results from a deficiency of insulin. The hallmark of diabetes is an abnormal increase in blood glucose concentration (**hyperglycemia**), which is responsible for most of the clinical signs and long-term complications. The most common clinically recognized form of diabetes in dogs is **insulin-dependent diabetes mellitus** (IDDM), wherein the body is unable to utilize blood glucose because inadequate amounts of insulin are produced by the pancreas. The cause of canine IDDM remains unknown, but it is likely that many factors are contributory. Genetic predisposition, infection, insulin-antagonistic diseases and drugs, immune-mediated disease, and *pancreatitis* (inflammation of the pancreas) have been identified as inciting factors in the development of human IDDM. Regardless of cause, the end result is loss of beta cell function, resulting in insulin deficiency, hyperglycemia, and eventual spillage of blood glucose into the urine (**glucosuria**).

Clinical signs of diabetes mellitus include increased appetite and water consumption, increased frequency and volume of urination (polydipsia and polyuria), and weight loss. If these clinical signs go unnoticed, sudden blindness may occur because of **cataract** (opacity of the lens of the eye) formation, or diabetic ketoacidosis (*see* below) may develop, resulting in systemic signs of illness including lethargy, inappetence and vomiting.

A diagnosis of diabetes mellitus is made on the basis of the history, physical examination, and results of supportive laboratory tests (i.e., persistently elevated fasting blood glucose level together with glucosuria). Treatment, which includes insulin injections, dietary management, regular exercise, and avoidance or control of concurrent illness, is required for the life of the dog. The primary goals of therapy are elimination of the clinical signs and avoidance of the chronic complications of diabetes. Common complications of canine diabetes include blindness with cataracts, ketoacidosis, infections, weight loss and pancreatitis.

Dietary therapy should be aimed at correcting obesity, maintaining consistency in the timing and caloric content of meals, and furnishing a diet that minimizes fluctuations in blood glucose level after consumption of a meal. Canned and dry kibble foods containing increased quantities of fiber are recommended. The increased fiber helps promote weight loss, slows glucose absorption from the gastrointestinal tract, reduces blood glucose fluctuations, and enhances control of blood glucose concentration.

Commonly used insulins for the long-term management of diabetic dogs include isophane (also called NPH), lente, and ultralente insulins. Commercially available insulin preparations include a combination of beef and pork insulin, pork insulin, or synthetic human insulin. All of these preparations are effective in diabetic dogs. Beef/pork lente insulin is recommended initially, with the other insulin types reserved for use only if problems with lente insulin evolve.

Most dogs require **subcutaneous** (beneath the skin) insulin injections twice a day to control blood glucose concentration. Treatment must be individualized for each patient. This often requires frequent evaluations of blood glucose levels during the initial regulation of therapy. Changes in dosage or type of insulin are often necessary to obtain proper control of the disease. Assessment of insulin and dietary therapy is required periodically in order to reevaluate control of the diabetes.

Diabetic Ketoacidosis

Diabetic ketoacidosis (DKA) is a serious, life-threatening complication of untreated or poorly treated diabetes mellitus. When insulin is deficient, glucose cannot enter the cells of the body to be used for energy. The body compensates by producing **ketone bodies** (also called **ketones**) from the breakdown of fat, which are used in place of glucose to power the body's cellular machinery. On a short-term basis, ketone bodies do no harm. However, if the insulin deficiency persists for too long, ketones will be produced faster than they can be used up and will begin to accumulate in the blood. As they accumulate the ketones cause the blood to become acidic, which, in turn, produces illness. If the insulin deficiency continues still further, death from severe **acidosis** (buildup of acid in the blood and tissues) will ensue.

Diagnosis of DKA is made by laboratory identification of ketones in the urine (**ketonuria**) of a diabetic dog. DKA is a serious medical illness that requires intensive insulin and fluid therapy to correct. With appropriate therapy DKA is reversible; however, the prognosis is guarded and dependent on the severity of illness at the time the diagnosis was established.

BETA CELL TUMORS

Tumors arising from the insulin-producing beta cells of the pancreas are often functional, secreting excessive amounts of insulin into the blood regardless of blood glucose concentration. Because insulin promotes the movement of glucose into cells, excessive quantities of insulin from a beta cell tumor result in low blood glucose levels (**hypoglycemia**). Beta cell tumors are almost always malignant; the most common sites of **metastasis** (spread) include the liver, lymph nodes and tissues surrounding the pancreas.

Beta cell tumors usually occur in middle-aged to older dogs, with an age range of 4 to 14 years. A breed predisposition may exist in Standard Poodles, Boxers, Fox Terriers, German Shepherd Dogs and Irish Setters. There is no recognized sex predilection.

The clinical signs are related to the hypoglycemia and include intermittent episodes of weakness, collapse and seizures. Fasting, excitement, exercise and eating may be predisposing factors in the development of clinical signs. Dogs with beta cell tumors often appear outwardly normal, although some gain weight.

The diagnosis of a beta cell tumor requires initial confirmation of low blood glucose levels, followed by documentation of inappropriate insulin secretion and identification of a pancreatic mass, using **ultrasonography** (**ultrasound:** a technique for visualizing internal structures of the body by means of sound [echo] reflections) or exploratory surgery.

The only chance for a cure lies in surgical removal of the tumor, if it is still localized as a solitary mass. Medical management of chronic hypoglycemia is initiated when surgery is not

performed or when inoperable or *metastatic* (having spread) cancer results in recurrence of clinical signs. Medical therapy is designed to reduce the frequency and severity of clinical signs and to avoid the sudden development of hypoglycemia. Medical therapy is aimed at increasing the absorption of glucose from the intestinal tract by means of frequent feedings and at interfering with the glucose-lowering action of insulin through the administration of certain medications, usually glucocorticoids and diazoxide. Owing to the extremely strong likelihood of malignancy in any dog with a beta cell tumor, the long-term prognosis is guarded to poor at best. The mean survival time for dogs treated medically is approximately 1 year from the onset of clinical signs of hypoglycemia to death.

Disorders of the Adrenal Glands

Adjacent to each kidney is one of two tiny **adrenal glands.** The adrenal glands secrete several very important hormones involved in:

- control of blood potassium and sodium concentrations
- water metabolism
- protein, fat and carbohydrate metabolism
- stress response
- regulation of blood pressure
- sex hormone levels (to a lesser extent)

The outer portion of each adrenal gland is known as the **cortex** and produces steroids known, appropriately, as **corticosteroids.** Among these are **cortisol, corticosterone,** and **aldosterone.** Corticosteroids such as cortisol that are involved in the metabolism of carbohydrate, fat and protein are referred to generally as **glucocorticoids.** Corticosteroids such as aldosterone that are involved in regulation of mineral and water balance are called **mineralocorticoids.** The inner portion of each adrenal gland is known as the **medulla** and produces **epinephrine** (**adrenaline**), which acts by raising blood glucose levels and increasing blood pressure and cardiac output. By far the most common endocrine disorders affecting the adrenal glands result from an excess or deficiency of glucocorticoids or aldosterone.

Hyperadrenocorticism (Cushing's Disease)

Hyperadrenocorticism (HAC) results from the excessive secretion of glucocorticoids, most notably cortisol, by the adrenal cortex. HAC is also called **Cushing's disease** (or **Cushing's syndrome**) in reference to the Boston surgeon who first described it in people. HAC is usually caused by an underlying benign and often microscopic tumor in the pituitary gland, which secretes excessive quantities of ACTH (*see* "Disorders of the Pituitary Gland," above), the hormone normally responsible for stimulating cortisol secretion by the adrenal glands. Approximately 80% of dogs with HAC have this form of the disease, its origin lying in the brain. The remaining 20% of dogs with HAC have a functional adrenal gland tumor **autonomously** (uncontrollably) secreting excessive amounts of cortisol into the bloodstream. Adrenal gland tumors can be either benign or malignant. HAC can also occur secondary to overzealous or chronic administration of cortisol-containing medications, such as certain skin creams, eyedrops and ear medications. This form of HAC is called *iatrogenic HAC* (**iatrogenic:** arising as a complication of medical treatment).

HAC typically develops in dogs 6 years of age or older, but has been seen in dogs as young as 1 year of age. Boxers, Boston Terriers, Dachshunds, Miniature and Toy Poodles, and possibly Beagles have an increased risk for developing HAC. The most common clinical signs include:

- increased water consumption and urination (**polydipsia** and **polyuria**)
- symmetrical hair loss primarily on the trunk
- abdominal enlargement ("pot-bellied" appearance)
- thin skin
- excessive panting
- weakness

Diabetic dogs with HAC develop insulin resistance and loss of control of their diabetes. Neurologic signs may be present in some dogs with HAC as a result of growth of the pituitary tumor in the brain. Typical neurologic signs include stupor, head-pressing, pacing, circling, behavioral alterations, seizures and a "drunken" gait.

Diagnosis of HAC and determination of the site of dysfunction (i.e., pituitary vs. adrenal tumor) require evaluation of specific diagnostic tests of the pituitary-adrenocortical system by a veterinarian. These tests include the ACTH stimulation test, low- and high-dose **dexamethasone** (a synthetic glucocorticoid) suppression test, and measurement of **endogenous** (originating within the animal) ACTH concentration.

The method of treatment is dependent on the location of the underlying tumor. Adrenal tumors can be removed surgically. HAC caused by a pituitary tumor is usually treated medically with the drug o,p'-DDD (Mitotane). Medical therapy can control the clinical signs of HAC but it does not affect the pituitary tumor itself, and therefore must be given for the remainder of the dog's life. Radiation therapy has been used successfully in some dogs when the pituitary tumor has grown sufficiently to produce neurologic signs.

Surgical removal of either a benign adrenal tumor or a malignant adrenal tumor that has not yet spread carries an excellent prognosis for recovery. A malignant adrenal tumor that has spread to other sites carries a poor prognosis, with most dogs succumbing to the disease within a year of diagnosis. The prognosis for dogs with HAC caused by a pituitary tumor is dependent, in part, on the age and overall health of the dog, and owner's commitment to therapy. The mean life span following diagnosis is 2 years. Younger dogs may live considerably longer (i.e., 6 to 8 years). Many dogs ultimately die from, or are put down because of, geriatric disorders such as kidney failure or heart failure.

Hypoadrenocorticism (Addison's Disease)

Hypoadrenocorticism results from deficient secretion of both glucocorticoids (most notably cortisol) and mineralocorticoids (chiefly aldosterone) from the adrenal cortex. Hypoadrenocorticism is also called **Addison's disease** in reference to the 19th-century

English physician who first described it in people. The cause of the disease is unknown, although immune-mediated destruction of the adrenal gland is suspected in most cases. The loss of adrenal gland function is usually a gradual process, first leading to a partial deficiency syndrome with relatively mild clinical signs, often occurring only during periods of stress (e.g., boarding, travel, after surgery). As destruction of the adrenal glands progresses, hormone secretion becomes inadequate even under non-stressful conditions, and a true metabolic crisis without any obvious inciting event then ensues.

Hypoadrenocorticism is typically a disease of young to middle-aged female dogs (average age, 4 years). No breed predilection has been described. The most common clinical manifestations are related to the gastrointestinal tract and include inappetence, vomiting and lethargy. Weakness is also a common clinical sign. Initially the patient experiences a waxing and waning of the clinical signs, which become more persistent and severe as the adrenal glands are progressively destroyed. Eventually vomiting, diarrhea and dehydration develop, leading to shock, a moribund state, coma and death.

Abnormally elevated blood potassium levels (**hyperkalemia**) and decreased blood sodium and chloride concentrations (**hyponatremia and hypochloremia**) represent the "classic" alterations in hypoadrenocorticism and are perhaps the most important clues in making the diagnosis. Confirmation of the diagnosis requires an evaluation of the ability of the adrenal glands to secrete cortisol following stimulation with ACTH (*see* "HYPERADRENOCORTICISM," ABOVE). Affected dogs exhibit low baseline plasma cortisol concentrations without any appreciable increase following ACTH administration; that is, their decimated adrenal glands are nonresponsive to ACTH, the hormone normally responsible for stimulating cortisol secretion.

Treatment includes fluid therapy and glucocorticoid and mineralocorticoid replacement. Hormone replacement is accomplished by daily oral administration or by monthly injections of the appropriate medications. Mineralocorticoids and, for approximately one-half of affected dogs, glucocorticoids must be given for the remainder of the patient's life. The prognosis for recovery, however, is excellent.

PHEOCHROMOCYTOMA

The cells of the adrenal medulla secrete a number of important substances called **catecholamines,** the most notable of which is **epinephrine (adrenaline). Pheochromocytoma** is a catecholamine-producing tumor derived from these cells. This tumor typically occurs in older dogs (mean age, 11 years). There are no apparent breed or sex predispositions.

Clinical signs are usually vague and nonspecific in nature, and easily associated with other disorders. The most common signs include weakness, lethargy, inappetence, vomiting, weight loss and increased respiratory rate. An increase in blood pressure may be seen in some cases.

Diagnosis requires identification of an adrenal mass in a dog exhibiting appropriate clinical signs, and subsequent confirmation by microscopic examination of the surgically removed tissue (surgical removal is the treatment of choice). The prognosis for recovery depends on the presence of any significant concurrent disease, whether invasion of the mass into surrounding tissues has occurred, and whether the tumor has spread to distant body sites.

CHAPTER 33

The Immune System and Disorders

**by Jeffrey E. Barlough
and Niels C. Pedersen**

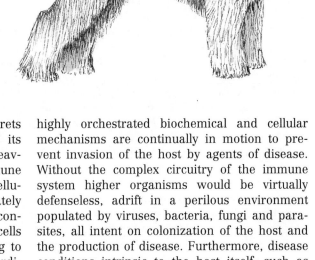

The immune system still holds many secrets waiting to be discovered. Because of its innate intricacy and its extraordinary interweaving of structure and function, the immune response—its individual components, both cellular and molecular—has proven an inordinately elusive target for scientific study. Imagine a constantly changing panorama of circulating cells and molecules, all signaling and responding to one another and the host in intricately coordinated patterns, so that when called upon to meet an invader they will provide just the right response, in just the right manner, and in just the right degree. Multiply this by the vast repertoire of potential disease agents that may be encountered at any time in the environment, all of which the immune system must be able to recognize and respond to, and one will gain some notion of the enormity of the task.

A smoothly functioning immune system is essential to the health and well-being of all higher living organisms. From humming fruitflies to sea urchins, to the big yellow Labrador in pursuit of the perfect Frisbee, to the human being casting said Frisbee skyward—within all, highly orchestrated biochemical and cellular mechanisms are continually in motion to prevent invasion of the host by agents of disease. Without the complex circuitry of the immune system higher organisms would be virtually defenseless, adrift in a perilous environment populated by viruses, bacteria, fungi and parasites, all intent on colonization of the host and the production of disease. Furthermore, disease conditions intrinsic to the host itself, such as cancer, would more often than not gain the upper hand were it not for the complex interplay of molecules and cells that comprises the immune response.

It has been said that the immune system oversees some of the most powerful molecular and biological "explosives" in nature. When unleashed against an aggressor, the firepower of the immune response would surely be the envy of any microbiological field commander. Thus, one can see the importance of maintaining firm and uncompromising control over such an arsenal, for if turned against the host itself—as in *autoimmune diseases* (*see* below)—the consequences can be devastating. It is a tribute to the marvelous efficiency and balance of this control system that most infections by potential disease agents result in only very mild clinical signs, or in no demonstrable signs at all.

What will be discussed in this chapter, in relation to dogs, are among the more well-accepted aspects of the anatomy and physiology of the immune response, with descriptions of some canine diseases whose origins lie within the immune system itself. Readers with a deeper interest in these topics are referred to any of several excellent texts available in veterinary or human immunology. It should be noted that, in general, the introductory discussion of anatomy and physiology and factors influencing immune responses may be readily applied to the human immune system as well.

Anatomy and Physiology of the Immune System

The immune system is composed of a complicated network of cells and molecules, all precisely balanced in their individual functions, and which act as both "detectors" and "effectors" of the immune response: cells and molecules, some cells so modest and unassuming in appearance that their origins and functions for decades went unrecognized; molecules, some of which are found in significant quantities in the blood, others in vanishingly small amounts. The immune system is closely allied to two other body systems, the blood circulatory system and the lymphatic system. The blood circulatory system is chiefly responsible for transporting oxygen and other vital nutrients to the tissues and for removing metabolic waste products. Among the materials transported are some of the most important constituents of the immune system: **Antibodies** are specialized proteins able to recognize molecules and cells foreign to the host; **lymphocytes** and **monocytes** are white blood cells capable of responding to the presence of such foreign material; and **cytokines** are "messenger" molecules by which cells of the immune system signal and instruct one another and, in some cases, direct other activities occurring in body tissues. Among the more important cytokines are **gamma-interferon** and the (at

least) ten known **interleukins**. In addition, the spleen acts as an important immunologic filter to trap and destroy foreign material as well as host cellular debris (dead or dying red blood cells, for example) that happens to pass through the spleen by way of the blood circulation.

The lymphatic system is composed of a highly specialized, interconnected lacework of delicate vessels that transport a viscous fluid called **lymph** from body tissues back to the blood circulatory system. Lymph consists of a clear admixture of tissue fluids, various proteins, **solutes** (dissolved substances) and other minor constituents. Many lymphocytes circulating within the lymph fluid itself traffic regularly between the system's lymph nodes and blood circulatory system and back again. **Lymph nodes** are the small specialized structures within the lymphatic system that act as barrier filters for the removal of foreign material, which is then subjected to destruction by the effector arm of the immune response. The lymph nodes' immunologic filtering of lymph can be considered analogous to the spleen's immunologic filtering of the blood.

The end result of all this filtration and circulation is the creation of a highly desirable network of immune surveillance, wherein the cells and molecules of the immune system constantly "scan" the blood and lymph for signs of foreign intruders, abnormal cellular components (tumor cells or virus-infected cells, for example), and host cellular debris, all of which are appropriate targets for immunologic attack.

The tissues or organs comprising the immune defenses of the body can be classified in either of two convenient categories: the **primary lymphoid organs** and the **secondary lymphoid organs**. Primary lymphoid organs are those in which the production and maturation of lymphocytes take place. In mammals, primary lymphoid organs consist of the **bone marrow**, the **mucosal-associated lymphoid tissue** (MALT; lymphoid tissue found lining the digestive, respiratory and urogenital tracts), and the **thymus**, an organ located in the chest cavity that regulates the maturation of specialized lymphocytes known as **T lymphocytes**, or simply **T cells**. Secondary lymphoid organs are those in which

antigens (substances capable of being recognized by the immune response) are trapped and destroyed by immune system cells. Secondary lymphoid organs consist of the lymph nodes, spleen, and portions of the bone marrow and MALT.

Antigens (which can occur as component parts of bacteria, fungi, viruses, parasites, toxins, or altered host body cells) are normally ingested (through a process known as **phagocytosis**) by specialized white blood cells called **macrophages,** which can be found in large quantities in secondary lymphoid organs. Following ingestion of the antigen, the macrophage, by means of cytokines and other molecules, begins signaling local lymphocytes—those which have already detected the antigen's presence—to mount a highly specific immune response against the antigen.

A subset of T cells known as **helper T cells** assists other lymphocytes, known as **B cells,** to produce antibody against the antigen. (The cells that actually secrete the antibody are end-stage B cells called **plasma cells.**) The mounting of an antibody response to an antigen is referred to as a **humoral immune response.** Helper T cells also assist in the maturation of another subset of T cells known as **cytotoxic T cells.** Cytotoxic T cells are responsible for tracking down and eliminating altered or infected body cells (for example, a cell infected with a virus, or a tumor cell carrying altered surface molecules that the body interprets as foreign or "nonself"). Also important in destroying such cells are the macrophages themselves, which not only aid in directing the immune defenses of the body but also inactivate many ingested antigens. (Other white blood cells known as **neutrophils** can ingest and destroy foreign substances, particularly bacteria, but they do not "direct" the activities of lymphocytes quite the way macrophages do.) A population of specialized lymphocytes known as **natural killer cells,** or **NK cells,** also is important in detecting and eliminating tumor cells and virus-infected cells. The mounting of a cytotoxic T cell/macrophage/NK cell response to an antigen is referred to as a **cellular (or cell-mediated) immune response.**

The net effect of these two interrelated immune responses, humoral and cellular, is to attack the inciting antigen simultaneously from several different angles in order to enhance the probability of its successful immunologic destruction. Such a multipronged fail-safe strategy is desirable also because of the varied nature of the different antigens with which the immune defenses may be confronted. Not all immune mechanisms perform as efficiently against all antigens (an enveloped virus vs. a roundworm parasite, for example); hence, the greater the number and variety of immune defenses alerted and activated, the greater the chance for a favorable outcome. In some cases, antigens even stimulate preferentially the precise immune mechanisms that are the most effective against them—a tribute to the marvelously wily and adaptive capabilities of the immune system.

Antibodies, also known as **immunoglobulins,** produced by plasma cells, are vital players in a number of different immune mechanisms. Several different types or *classes* of immunoglobulins exist. The most common class, immunoglobulin G (IgG), circulates in the blood and tissue fluids and in human beings is able to cross the mother's placenta into the circulation of the developing fetus (this does not happen to such an extent in dogs or cats). A second class, IgM, is a much larger molecule than IgG and is found almost exclusively in the bloodstream. IgM is the first immunoglobulin type to be produced in the blood following initial exposure to an antigen. A third type, IgA, is the major immunoglobulin found in the mucous secretions that constantly bathe the surfaces of the body's mucous membranes—primarily the linings of the digestive, respiratory and urogenital tracts. These surfaces are frequent first sites of contact between antigens and the immune system; IgA plays a crucial role in patrolling these surfaces and preventing potential disease agents from gaining deeper access to the body. (This IgA-mediated surface-monitoring system is often referred to as the *secretory immune system.*) A fourth immunoglobulin type, IgE, exists in vanishingly small quantities in the blood but is also found adhered to the surface of **mast cells** and **basophils,** cells found in tissue. These cells and IgE (along with a type of white blood cell known as an **eosinophil**) are important in protecting the body against invasion by certain parasites. Unfortunately mast cells, basophils and IgE are also largely responsible for the annoying signs and symptoms of allergy. The final immunoglobulin type, IgD, still remains something of a mystery, being found only on the surface of certain lymphocytes where it seems to function mainly as a *receptor* or "sensor" for the detection of antigens.

Antibodies are "detectors" and do nothing more than attach to or "tag" antigens; they have no power in and of themselves to destroy them. Antibodies are merely a subgroup of complex messenger molecules with which the immune system is replete. Attachment of antibody to an antigen sets into motion a chain of events that results ultimately in the antigen's removal by other, so-called "effector" mechanisms. In the case of IgG and IgM, the presence of these antibodies adherent to the surface of an antigen is a signal to certain cell types—macrophages, neutrophils, eosinophils, some lymphocytes—that a foreign antigen is present and requires elimination. In addition antigen-antibody complexes, known as **immune complexes,** act as attractants for components of a specialized series of blood proteins known as the **complement system,** whose major role is to disrupt the surface structure of microbes and altered body cells, resulting in their destruction.

The immune system can be said to possess two vital characteristics: *specificity* and *memory.* "Specificity" refers to the ability of antibodies and lymphocytes to recognize specific, individual antigens. Each individual antibody molecule recognizes *one and only one* antigen; the same is true for each individual lymphocyte. In other words, the receptors present on each antibody or on each lymphocyte are each specific for only a single antigen. When a particular antigen appears in the body, only those lymphocytes carrying the proper receptors for that antigen are stimulated, and only those antibody molecules capable of binding to it are bound, so that humoral and cell-mediated immune responses to the antigen are produced. In this way the energies of the immune system are focused very specifically on the inciting antigen.

"Memory" refers to the fact that exposure of lymphocytes to an antigen results in the production of a population of *memory lymphocytes,* which continue to circulate once the antigen has been eliminated. Should that particular antigen again be introduced into the body, memory lymphocytes in conjunction with macrophages will very quickly trigger a vigorous immune response. It is for this reason that, with many infectious disease agents (measles virus, for example), a single, symptomless exposure to the agent or a single bout with the disease is sufficient to produce a solid, long-lasting immunity.

Maternal immunity is a form of temporary immunity that is passed from mother to offspring *in utero* (in the uterus) and/or after birth. Maternal immunity, primarily in the form of antibody, serves to protect the neonate until its own immune system becomes fully operative. In dogs, most maternal immunity is transferred in the **colostrum** (first milk) delivered to the suckling pups during the first 24 to 48 hours after birth. This initial "transfusion" of antibody is taken up from the small intestine and passed into the blood circulation, where it serves to protect the pups temporarily against serious systemic infections. Soon after this, the intestinal tract becomes impermeable to the absorption of maternal antibody. Instead, antibody that is passed in the milk during subsequent feedings serves to coat the tonsils, associated lymphoid tissue, and intestinal tract and thus protect the pups against invasion by many types of disease agents. In this way the pups are shielded against the microbial agents prevalent in their environment until a few months of age, by which time the pups' maternal antibody levels will have decayed and their own fledgling immune systems will have begun to take over.

It is at this point, when maternal immunity is waning, that the standard series of immunizations ("puppy shots") is normally administered. Prior to this time, the presence of maternal antibody will interfere with vaccine administration by complexing with the individual components of the vaccine and quickly removing them, the mother's antibodies make it impossible for the pup's own immune system to produce a response. *Thus, if a vaccine is administered too early in a pup's life it will not immunize.* This is the reason for the multiple injections given over several weeks during the puppy series—to assure that the vaccine is not given too soon, in which case its effect would be blocked by maternal antibody, yet still soon enough after maternal immunity begins to wane so that the pups will be able to protect themselves. Because maternal immunity decays at different rates in different animals, being dependent primarily on the initial amount of antibody that was transferred in the colostrum, pups become susceptible at different times. By giving several injections sequentially, chances are optimal that pups will be vaccinated at the proper time. (*See* Appendix B, "Vaccinations.")

Factors Influencing the Immune Response to Infection

Veterinarians and dog owners are frequently confronted with infectious disease masquerading in a variety of disguises. Unfortunately, we are usually aware only of the most severe manifestations of a given infection. This severe form is often described in textbooks as the "classical" or "typical" form of that particular disease. In reality, the severe form of the disease usually is *not* the most common form occurring in nature. Animals and human beings have evolved over time with their corresponding disease agents to the point that, following exposure, the host often experiences only a mild, self-limiting, or even clinically inapparent (**asymptomatic**) infection. As a general rule, severe illness usually occurs only when host, disease agent and environmental factors are particularly unfavorable. At such time, not only is the primary illness apt to be severe, but the proportion of individuals developing a persistent infection will be increased; aberrant or chronic forms of the disease will be more prevalent; and overall mortality rates will be higher.

Factors influencing the outcome of an individual infection are many and varied, and include most of the following.

Host Factors
Host factors include age at time of exposure; developmental or inherited abnormalities of the immune system; the inheritance of still poorly defined genetic resistance factors; presence or absence of maternal immunity; intercurrent disease; and nutritional status.

Age Resistance
Age resistance is an extremely important phenomenon. As an example, 2- to 4-week-old puppies lacking sufficient maternal immunity will develop a rapid and invariably fatal disease following infection with canine distemper virus. If they are infected at 8 to 12 weeks of age, the resulting disease is of a more chronic nature, the clinical signs are different, and the mortality rate is lower. If the animals are infected as adults, the effects of the disease will be even less dramatic. Age resistance is also evident for another canine viral disease, neonatal herpesvirus infection, which is highly fatal only in pups 2 weeks of age or younger.

Developmental or Inherited Abnormalities
Developmental or inherited abnormalities of the immune response can cause the host to be born or become deficient in cell-mediated immunity, deficient in the ability to make all or only certain antibody classes, or a combination of the two. Fortunately such defects are rare in dogs. One uncommon example is the development of fatal post-vaccinal (after vaccination) distemper in pups born with an inherited immunodeficiency syndrome. In such a case it is the live vaccine virus that actually causes the disease. Although modified (**attenuated**) such that it produces immunity rather than disease in normal pups, the vaccine's weak effects are nevertheless sufficient to overwhelm an immunodeficient immune system.

Far more important are the *undefined genetic resistance factors,* which can greatly influence the host's response to disease agents. As an example, a group of pups may be born with seemingly intact immune systems; by every conceivable test of immune competence the pups appear normal. In spite of this, one or more of the litter may respond to a particular infectious disease agent in a very different manner from the rest. Following exposure some of the group may suffer severe or fatal illness, while others exhibit virtually no clinical signs.

For example, about one-half of pups exposed naturally to canine distemper virus will produce sufficient immunity within the first 10 days to abort the infection, exhibiting only mild and transient signs of illness. In contrast the remaining half of the pups fail to mount an effective immune response within the same amount of time. In these animals the infection will proceed to its secondary stage and respiratory, gastrointestinal, and neurologic disease signs may be exhibited. Most of the severely affected puppies will die. As a second example, many German Shepherd Dogs, following exposure to the **tropical canine pancytopenia** agent *Ehrlichia canis,* develop a progressive and ultimately fatal illness. Beagles, on the other hand, exhibit only mild primary signs of illness after exposure and usually do not develop the progressive, fatal form of the disease.

When selecting breeding stock, undefined genetic resistance factors need to be given equal or primary importance to selecting for traits such as coat color, body conformation, and size. Inbreeding is one means of lowering the overall immunologic resistance of a breed or species to infectious disease.

Maternal Immunity

Maternal immunity can be divided into two general types: *passive systemic immunity* and *passive local immunity*. Passive systemic immunity consists of the antibodies that the newborn pup receives from the mother, primarily through the **colostrum** ("first milk" produced by mother). It provides the pup with protection during the critical first weeks of life, when its own fledgling immune system is still developing, but ultimately the young animal is left to combat infection on its own. Fortunately, maternal immunity does not disappear until the pup's own immune system has nearly matured (approximately 14 to 16 weeks after birth). Anything that prevents adequate transfer of maternal antibody to the newborn will cause the young animal to become prematurely susceptible to infection. The failure of a pup to receive sufficient colostrum from its mother can contribute to the development of a severe or even fatal infection in the pup during the neonatal period.

Passive local immunity consists of antibodies present in the milk of the mother and is continually available for as long as the pup nurses. These antibodies act to prevent infection of the tonsils, associated lymphoid tissue, and intestinal tract—areas where many ultimately systemic infections are initiated. Weaning of the pup terminates this form of passive immune protection. Not all mothers provide adequate milk antibodies for the entire nursing period.

Intercurrent Illness

Whether due to an infectious or other cause, intercurrent illness can greatly influence the capacity of the host to resist infection. Disease saps the body of essential nutrients and in the case of some diseases such as canine distemper or human measles, the disease agent itself can depress the host's immune system. In other cases, infection with one microorganism may predispose the host to subsequent infection with another. Intercurrent illnesses are particularly important in breeding kennels, where large numbers of young animals are raised in close proximity to older animals, and where pups of all different ages are in contact with one another.

Nutritional Status

The nutritional status of an animal is very important in determining its resistance to infection. The components of the immune response are made largely of protein, and proteins are produced only in healthy, well-nourished tissues. Nutritional problems are particularly noticeable in young animals. The caloric requirements per unit of body weight of a young animal are several times greater than those of an adult, and the need for specific nutrients such as protein, vitamins, and minerals are much different in the young (*see* CHAPTER 8, "CANINE NUTRITIONAL REQUIREMENTS" and CHAPTER 9, "FEEDING DOGS"). Malnutrition exists in some enterprises where large numbers of young animals are being reared.

DISEASE AGENT FACTORS

These include the virulence (disease-causing capacity) of the disease agent; dose of the agent delivered to the host; and the route of exposure (oral, venereal, inoculation, etc.).

Virulence

The virulence of the infecting agent is of prime significance. Individual strains of many different infectious disease agents can be found that cause severe disease, while other strains of the same agents can be found that cause no disease at all.

Dose

The dose of the agent received by the host is also critical. The age-related resistance to many disease agents can be overcome in large measure by exposure to higher and higher doses of the agent. In general, all other factors being equal, the higher the dose of the disease agent, the higher the infection rate, the more severe the resulting disease, and the greater the mortality rate.

Route of Exposure

Besides these, the route of exposure often is an important consideration. For example, some viruses will not produce any illness when injected into an animal. However, if delivered to the ocular or nasal mucous membranes, characteristic illness will occur. This particular phenomenon occurs because certain viruses do not **replicate** (reproduce) efficiently at core body temperature, preferring instead the cooler temperature of the superficial mucous membranes of the eyes and upper respiratory tract.

ENVIRONMENTAL FACTORS

Environmental factors include population density (crowding) and the maintenance of proper hygiene; the interchange of individuals from one population to another; environmental temperatures and humidity; and "stress".

Population Density

Population density is one of the most important factors in determining the course a particular disease will take within a population and among individuals within that population. A high population density increases the spread and severity of infection by increasing the number of **carriers** (infected animals) of the disease agent; increasing the proximity of susceptible animals to animals harboring the contagion; increasing contamination of the environment (food, water, air, soil) with the disease agent; increasing the dose or amount of disease agent passed from infected to susceptible animals; and increasing stress and competition for food resources.

The deleterious effects of increased population density can be counteracted, at least in part, by improved ventilation (to dilute airborne contamination), and better removal of **excreta** (feces, urine). These steps become more time-consuming, labor-intensive, and expensive as the population density increases.

Interchange of Animals

The interchange of animals between populations spreads disease, especially when it occurs between populations of high density. Each population of animals has its own viral, bacterial, parasitic and protozoal **flora** (the range of microorganisms normally present within that population). Because there is greater severity of disease in high density populations, many of the animals are carriers of these agents. An animal taken from one population to another is more likely to spread new strains and types of infectious disease agents to the second population, and is itself exposed to a myriad number of new organisms. Once a new type of infection is introduced into such a population, any unfavorable environmental or host factors will insure its rapid spread.

Temperature and Humidity

Environmental temperature and humidity are significant factors in infection by themselves. Many species of animals have temperature and humidity requirements that are optimal for good health. Sudden fluctuations of either temperature or humidity can be just as deleterious as unfavorable static conditions. There is no question that changes in temperature and humidity can influence disease, as evidenced by temperature-related outbreaks of respiratory and enteric disease in human beings and animals. Temperature may influence disease directly by stressing the mucous membranes or by other more subtle means. For instance, during sudden changes in temperature or humidity, animals or people are often stressed by being brought together into crowded, often poorly ventilated quarters (cattle and horses brought into barns or corrals, dogs into kennels, cats into catteries, children into schoolrooms, etc.).

Stress

"Stress" is a nebulous term in and of itself and a difficult variable to measure. There is no doubt, however, that stresses of many kinds—innate, environmental or social—can contribute to susceptibility to disease.

In summary, infectious diseases and infectious disease agents do not exist in a vacuum. Many intrinsic and extrinsic factors serve to influence the final outcome of an infection. *Moreover, many infectious disease problems must be viewed from the standpoint of the herd or group in question.* One cannot manage wisely the health and welfare of animals in a kennel environment without an appreciation for the underlying basis for problems occurring in such an environment.

Disorders of the Immune System

In certain instances the immune defenses of the body may go awry, so that harmful side effects deriving from the immune response become more serious than those produced by the inciting antigen itself. In such cases it is actually the inappropriate response of the immune system that leads to disease.

This section will discuss briefly some of the consequences of an improperly functioning immune response. Some of the following topics are covered in greater detail in other chapters.

ALLERGY, ATOPY AND ANAPHYLAXIS

True allergies are the result of an inappropriate reaction on the part of IgE, mast cells, and basophils to relatively innocuous antigens, e.g., house-dust mites, molds, pollen, dander, or other environmental substances. Contact with such sensitizing **antigens** (referred to as **allergens**) results in massive **degranulation** (release of granules) of IgE-coated mast cells and basophils lying beneath tissue surfaces. The granules released from these cells contain an armory of noxious compounds that include **histamine,** serotonin and **leukotrienes.** In any given individual, the degree of sensitivity to an allergen is directly proportional to the quantities of these compounds released by the cells.

In many cases the tendency toward the development of allergies is inherited; this tendency is referred to as **atopy,** and an animal (or person) with such an inherited predisposition is said to be *atopic.* In human beings, allergies commonly are manifested by signs of irritant respiratory disease (reddening and tearing of the eyes, scratchiness of the throat, sneezing) or, less commonly, skin disease. In dogs, skin lesions predominate as common manifestations of atopy (for a full discussion of allergy-related skin diseases in the dog, *see* CHAPTER 22, "THE SKIN AND DISORDERS").

Many sensitizing allergens are acquired by inhalation. Occasionally, food hypersensitivities may occur and be manifested by an allergic skin condition. Treatment of allergic disease problems relies on accurate identification of the underlying cause of the allergy, followed by avoidance of the allergen, dietary modification, and possibly therapeutic intervention.

Allergic Rhinitis

Allergic rhinitis (allergic inflammation of the nasal passages) is the most common allergic disorder of human beings, but is only infrequently recognized in dogs. It is caused by a reaction to inhaled pollen, danders, dusts, molds, certain cosmetics, cigarette smoke, or other miscellaneous irritants. Clinical signs may occur seasonally in the case of allergens such as pollen. Inhalant allergens in dogs are more commonly associated with **atopic dermatitis** (allergic skin disease; *see* CHAPTER 22, "THE SKIN AND DISORDERS") than with rhinitis, while the opposite is generally true for people. This is caused by differences in the tissue distribution of sensitized mast cells in dogs and human beings.

Sneezing and **snuffling** (reverse sneezing) are the most common presenting clinical signs. During the allergic period the signs are usually intermittent rather than persistent. The nasal discharge is scanty and normally of a clear, watery consistency. In severe cases, however, sneezing and nasal discharge may be quite pronounced. **Conjunctivitis** (inflammation of the conjunctiva, lining of the eyelid), with reddening of the eyelids and a watery ocular discharge, is an uncommon accompanying manifestation.

Careful examination of the nasal passages is indicated if the signs are severe or chronic. Microscopic examination of the nasal discharge often will demonstrate both eosinophils and neutrophils. Bacterial cultures of nasal flushes will often be sterile or nearly sterile.

Allergic rhinitis is often diagnosed in a patient responding to hospitalization or other changes in environment after identifying eosinophils in a nasal flush sample (their presence in large numbers is often indicative of allergic reaction), and by ruling out other possible causes. A positive response to therapy will also provide a clue.

Treatment is aimed at identifying the underlying cause of the allergy and removing it from the dog's environment. If this is not possible, low-dose treatment with **corticosteroids** (hormones secreted by the adrenal gland cortex) may be required. Treatment should be limited to times of the year when the rhinitis appears.

Allergic Bronchitis

Allergic bronchitis (allergic inflammation of the bronchi) is more common in dogs than in other domestic species. Allergic bronchitis is only infrequently associated with a defined allergen; presumably it is caused by inhalation of the same types of substances that are associated with allergic rhinitis. Clinical signs are usually chronic in nature and persistent for most of the year, however.

A chronic, dry, honking-type of cough (somewhat similar to that associated with kennel cough; *see* CHAPTER 34, "VIRAL DISEASES") is the most frequent clinical finding. The cough is easily elicited by massaging the dog's trachea and often can be evoked by exercise, drinking of water, excitement, or pulling on the leash. The cough is usually dry, but may occur in **paroxysms** (sudden bouts) that end with a drawn-out gag or retch. The underlying cause is allergic stimulation of the tracheal and bronchial mucosal cells which secrete a thick, tenacious mucus that is very irritating and difficult for the animal to clear. The cough results from chronic, low-grade irritation and from the animal's attempts to clear the mucus from the airways.

The diagnosis is fairly easy to establish. Other causes of chronic bronchitis can usually be eliminated by the history, physical examination, and by chest X rays. Once other causes have been ruled out, the diagnosis can be confirmed by analysis of a tracheal wash sample. The wash is usually bacteriologically sterile and contains many eosinophils.

Canine allergic bronchitis can be treated with **expectorants** (medications that aid in coughing up mucus and other secretions) and **bronchodilators** (drugs that open up the airways), or with corticosteroids to suppress inflammation, or both. Mild cases often respond well to expectorants or bronchodilators alone.

Allergic Pneumonitis (Pulmonary Infiltrates with Eosinophilia [PIE] Syndrome)

Allergic pneumonitis (PIE syndrome) is relatively common in dogs and probably has many causes; as such it is not really a single disease but instead can be considered as a manifestation of several different disease conditions. It is a subacute or chronic allergic inflammation of the small bronchioles and alveoli in the lungs and is associated with a profound eosinophilia (increased numbers of eosinophils in the blood). Most cases in dogs are **idiopathic** (of unknown cause) but are probably associated with inhalant allergens or with heartworm infestation.

The clinical signs can include fatigue, exercise intolerance, **dyspnea** (respiratory difficulty), and a soft cough. The chronic form of the condition may be associated with weight loss.

Diagnosis is made by characteristic findings on chest X rays and by the presence of eosinophilia and large numbers of eosinophils in a tracheal wash.

In heartworm-endemic areas the diagnosis should be directed at identifying an underlying heartworm infestation. Occasionally, it may be possible to associate the condition with particular environmental allergens, in which case it is best to place the dog in a new environment or to alter the existing environment to minimize exposure. In many cases, however, the cause remains unknown and environmental control is not feasible. Treatment with corticosteroids for several weeks or more will usually provide a rapid resolution of clinical signs. The disease often does not recur following treatment.

Allergic Gastritis

Allergic gastritis (allergic stomach inflammation) is recognized in dogs and is associated with the ingestion of dietary allergens (food allergies). Clinical signs include vomiting of a bile-tinged mucus several hours after eating. The vomiting episodes may be periodic (two or three times a week) or more constant (several times a day). Weight loss and a poor hair coat are common in cats with this disease, but less so in dogs.

There are no specific tests to diagnose food allergies in either dogs or cats. The diagnosis of allergic gastritis is usually made by ruling out other causes of vomiting and by demonstrating an improvement following institution of a **hypoallergenic** (reduced likelihood of inducing allergy) diet. A useful hypoallergenic diet for dogs can be made by mixing cottage cheese or tofu with rice. (*Note:* Some dogs are allergic to milk proteins, so cottage cheese may not always be hypoallergenic.) The hypoallergenic diet should be fed for at least 2 weeks. If there is no improvement in the dog's condition, an alternative hypoallergenic diet should be tried for 2 more weeks. If there is still no improvement, then the diagnosis of food allergy should be called into question. If dramatic improvement is evident, a multivitamin and mineral supplement should be added to the hypoallergenic diet and the diet continued for several weeks more. After this other foods can be slowly reintroduced, one at a time every 1 or 2 weeks.

Allergic Enteritis

Allergic enteritis (allergic intestinal inflammation) is a related condition characterized by intermittent or chronic diarrhea associated with the ingestion of dietary allergens. Bowel movements usually are normal in frequency and amount but the stools are loose, watery and foul-smelling. In severe cases the animals may become emaciated and the haircoat dry and lacking in luster. Diagnosis and treatment are approached in much the same manner as for allergic gastritis. Thus the diagnosis ultimately is confirmed by demonstrating a positive response to treatment (i.e., institution of a hypoallergenic diet).

Eosinophilic Enteritis

Eosinophilic enteritis is characterized by a pronounced eosinophilia, poor haircoat quality, a more or less persistent diarrhea and weight loss. Stools usually assume a "cow-pie" consistency, but are normal in frequency. Affected dogs are thin and have a poor-quality haircoat. The diagnosis is made by ruling out more serious causes of chronic inflammatory or infiltrative bowel disorders, such as lymphosarcoma, lymphangiectasis, pancreatic exocrine insufficiency, and others (*see* CHAPTER 30, "THE DIGESTIVE SYSTEM AND DISORDERS"). Treatment consists of a hypoallergenic diet combined with corticosteroid therapy.

Allergic Colitis

Allergic colitis (allergic inflammation of the colon) is uncommon in dogs. It is really a form of allergic enteritis, wherein the colon is more severely affected than the upper intestinal tract. When the disease occurs it is characterized by diarrhea and blood in the stools accompanied by weight loss. Colitis of *non*-dietary origin is fairly common in dogs; therefore, other more serious conditions need to be ruled out when making the diagnosis. Treatment consists of dietary modification beginning with a hypoallergenic diet.

Anaphylaxis

Anaphylaxis or an anaphylactic reaction represents a rare but extreme example of an IgE-mediated response gone awry. Massive release of histamine and other unpleasant substances from mast cells and basophils produces a range of deleterious effects, such as constriction of airways and blood vessels within the lungs and contraction of smooth muscle in the walls of the digestive tract and bladder. The release of histamine also causes an intense itching about the face and head. The changes within the lungs—constriction of breathing passages and reduced outflow of blood—result in sudden respiratory distress. Affected dogs will salivate profusely, urinate, become uncoordinated, seem dazed, may attempt to vomit, and ultimately collapse. Death when it ensues usually occurs within the first few minutes. An anaphylactic reaction is a life-threatening emergency that arises abruptly following contact with the inciting allergen. The treatment of choice is **epinephrine (adrenaline)**, which must be administered immediately. Causes of anaphylaxis in dogs include the protein components of certain vaccines, medications such as penicillin, pollens, molds, insect bites and bee stings. (Persons sensitive to bee stings frequently carry a supply of epinephrine with them as a safeguard against possible exposure.)

Anaphylaxis is an inappropriate overreaction of an idiosyncratic nature; not all substances induce anaphylaxis in dogs, nor are all dogs sensitized to the extent that anaphylaxis will occur. Anaphylactic reactions are relatively uncommon occurrences.

Autoimmune Hemolytic Anemia

Autoimmune hemolytic anemia (AIHA) is a disease condition in which broadly cross-reactive **autoantibodies** (antibodies directed against "self," i.e., against the body) called **hemagglutinins** attach to red blood cells, resulting in their immunologic destruction and thereby producing **anemia** (reduction in red blood cell numbers). The cause or causes of AIHA are unknown, but the disease is often associated with other conditions occurring simultaneously in the same animal, such as blood **platelet** (clotting cell) disorders. It is thought that many cases of AIHA are the result of exposure to drugs or viruses that bind to the surface of red blood cells, allowing for the attachment of antibodies with subsequent removal and destruction of the antigen/antibody-coated cells by the immune system. Other cases are associated with underlying chronic disease processes such as cancer. In general AIHA is one of the most common immune-mediated diseases seen in dogs.

The hemagglutinins in dogs with AIHA may be of two distinct types, called **warm agglutinins** and **cold agglutinins.** Warm agglutinins are by far the more common type. These autoantibodies are usually of the IgG class and attach to the red cells more avidly at body temperature than at lower temperatures. Cold agglutinins, which occur only rarely in dogs, are usually of the IgM class and attach themselves to red cells more vigorously at lower temperatures.

The onset of AIHA in dogs may be sudden or gradual, and in general the clinical signs exhibited by affected animals can be quite variable in nature. Based on the progress of the disease course, canine AIHA can be divided into three main types: peracute, acute or subacute, and chronic.

Peracute AIHA

This form occurs more commonly in larger dogs of the shepherd type that are from 2 to 6 years of age. Peracute AIHA accounts for 10–20% of the cases of AIHA in dogs. The onset is extremely rapid and the anemia is usually quite severe. Affected dogs often exhibit lethargy, malaise, and sometimes fever 1 to 3 days prior to the actual disease episode. At the time of hospitalization the dogs are obviously depressed, have pale mucous membranes and an increased respiratory rate (both indicative of anemia), and there may be a marked reddening or darkening of the urine ("port wine urine") caused by the excretion of **hemoglobin** (the red blood cell pigment that carries oxygen) released from damaged red cells. As the disease progresses both the urine and serum may assume a yellowish discoloration (icterus or **jaundice**) also due to the released hemoglobin. Blood clotting anomalies and a drop in blood platelet levels sometimes accompany the peracute form of AIHA, and may be manifested clinically by neurologic signs (loss of balance, blindness, dementia), cardiac and respiratory dysfunction (respiratory distress, arrhythmias), or kidney disease.

Diagnosis of peracute AIHA is made on the basis of the history, clinical signs and results of appropriate laboratory assays, particularly hematologic and clotting tests. The hemagglutinins responsible are usually of the warm (IgG) type.

Treatment of the disease relies upon the use

of corticosteroids or other more potent immuno-suppressive drugs to suppress the immune-mediated phenomena that are at the heart of the problem. In some cases blood transfusions may be required, although their use is somewhat controversial. Gradual improvement usually will occur within 2 to 4 days of initiating therapy. Full restoration of blood counts to normal may require months, however.

Unlike the other forms of AIHA, the prognosis for the peracute form has to be considered only fair to poor. If not treated quickly and aggressively, almost all affected dogs will succumb. Even with the best treatment, the mortality rate may be 50% or greater. The prognosis becomes generally more favorable if the dog successfully negotiates the first few days of therapy.

Acute or Subacute AIHA

This is the most common form of AIHA in dogs. It is usually caused by warm agglutinins but the onset is more gradual than in the peracute form. There is a distinct predilection for females and the disease occurs in Cocker Spaniels at a higher than expected frequency. Many of the clinical signs are similar to those in the peracute form, but generally of slower onset and milder nature. When cold agglutinins are present, if the affected dog is exposed to very cold weather, an acute episode of **hemolysis** (red blood cell destruction) may occur, owing to the higher efficiency of the IgM agglutinins at lower temperatures. In addition to hemolysis, cold agglutinins manifest themselves by causing **necrosis** (tissue death) of the ear tips, toes, or tip of the tail (i.e., the colder parts of the body).

Diagnosis of acute or subacute AIHA is made using similar criteria as for the peracute form. Treatment is directed against the underlying cause (if identifiable), and also involves the use of corticosteroids or other immunosuppressive medications. The prognosis is fair to good. If cold agglutinins are present, affected animals should be kept warm and not be exposed to cold weather conditions.

Chronic AIHA

This is an uncommon form of AIHA in dogs. The presenting clinical signs include lethargy,

fatigue, and pallor of the mucous membranes. There is a distinct predilection for the smaller breeds of dog. Treatment consists of corticosteroids or other immunosuppressive therapies. In general, therapy for the less acute forms of AIHA may need to be extended for a lengthy period of time (months to years) to avoid disease recurrence; in others, medication can be slowly withdrawn after a short period. The disease course is extremely unpredictable; some dogs experience only a single attack, others are subject to recurrent bouts, while still others suffer from a chronic disease course necessitating life-long therapy. Because the underlying cause is almost always unidentified, it is difficult to provide more specific therapeutic guidelines.

AUTOIMMUNE THROMBOCYTOPENIA
Autoimmune thrombocytopenia (decreased blood platelet numbers), like AIHA, is one of the most common immune-mediated diseases seen in dogs. It is more common in females than in males by a 2-to-1 ratio, and there is a distinct breed predilection toward Poodles. It can occur in the postestrus period in intact female dogs. The disease is often idiopathic, but like AIHA it can occur secondarily to drug administration, infectious diseases, or as a consequence of systemic lupus erythematosus (SLE) (*see* BELOW).

The blood platelets are indispensable for normal blood clotting and thus signs of deficiency are manifested as a bleeding syndrome. The most common clinical signs consist of small hemorrhages appearing as pigmented spots in the skin and mucous membranes. The hemorrhagic areas often are noticed during or after hair clipping. **Epistaxis** (nosebleed), **melena** (dark, pitchy stool due to bleeding into the digestive tract), **hematuria** (blood in the urine), and **hyphema** (ocular hemorrhage) may be observed in more severely affected animals. In such cases there may be substantial blood loss and anemia may be an accompanying feature. Often it may be difficult in anemic and thrombocytopenic animals to determine whether the primary problem is autoimmune thrombocytopenia with secondary hemorrhage, autoimmune thrombocytopenia and AIHA at the same time, or a massive blood clotting disorder.

Diagnosis is made on the basis of the history, clinical findings, and the results of specific laboratory tests. The presence of low numbers of blood platelets and red cells together with blood clotting abnormalities will usually suffice to make a good clinical diagnosis. The diagnosis often is confirmed on the basis of the animal's response to appropriate therapy.

In animals with minor, small hemorrhages but without severe blood loss, corticosteroids alone usually will provide effective treatment. In some cases more powerful immunosuppressive medications may be required. Animals with severe blood loss should also receive one or more transfusions of blood or platelet-rich plasma in addition to immunosuppressive drug therapy. The prognosis for recovery is fair to good, provided that therapy is quickly and aggressively applied. As with AIHA, some dogs will experience only a single episode of disease, while others will endure recurrent bouts. A small number of affected dogs develop a more chronic form of disease necessitating lifelong immunosuppressive medication.

AUTOIMMUNE NEUTROPENIA

This disease is seen more commonly in dogs than in other species, and is characterized by an acute onset of high fever, depression and profound **neutropenia** (decreased levels of circulating neutrophils, predisposing dogs to bacterial infections). The disease onset may be associated with previous drug therapy, particularly therapy with antiseizure medications and sulfa drugs. There is usually a good response to long-term corticosteroid treatment.

SYSTEMIC LUPUS ERYTHEMATOSUS

Systemic lupus erythematosus (SLE, lupus) is a rare, **multisystemic** (involving many body systems) disorder characterized by a general derangement of certain key immune defense mechanisms. It is considered to be the prototypic immune-mediated disease. "Lupus" ("wolf") refers to the wolflike patchy discoloration and reddening of the skin observed in human beings with SLE. Skin lesions are only a single manifestation of this disease, however; in people, virtually every organ system in the body may be

affected. In SLE a variety of immune mechanisms begin to attack basic structural components of the body, some as basic as the **deoxyribonucleic acid** (DNA)—the genetic material within the nuclei of cells. Autoantibodies directed against such host-cell components attach to cells in the blood, kidneys, skin and elsewhere, resulting in a widespread immunologic assault upon the host.

The ultimate cause of SLE in dogs and human beings has not been determined, although there is some evidence that a latent virus infection may be involved. Hyperactivity of the B-cell system, possibly resulting from abnormalities in T-cell regulation, is thought to be a key underlying defect. The genetic makeup of the host is also believed to play a role in determining susceptibility to the disease. In people, at least 25 different medications have been shown to produce a lupus-like syndrome. This drug-induced form of SLE differs from "naturally occurring" SLE in a number of important features, however.

Canine SLE is more prevalent in Spitzes and sporting breeds, including Spaniels, Pointers, Retrievers, German Shepherds, and Dobermans. Dogs between 2 to 4 years of age are most often affected. A common feature of SLE in dogs is a cyclic fever unresponsive to antibiotic therapy, accompanied by one or more organ-specific signs:

1. *Polyarthritis* (inflammation occurring simultaneously in several joints) occurs in most dogs with SLE and is the most common presenting clinical sign. Most dogs exhibit generalized stiffness, difficulty in rising or lying down, or a shifting lameness in one or more limbs. The arthritis may be associated with **polymyositis** (inflammation of muscles) and **neuritis** (nerve inflammation) in 25% or more of the cases.

2. *Skin disease* is the second most common presenting sign of SLE in dogs. Lesions appear as small, reddened, crusty, sometimes ulcerating areas, usually on the face (bridge of the nose, above the eyes, on the ears, margins of the lips). Ulcerating lesions of the palate and toes can also occur, along with polyarthritis manifesting as lameness.

3. *Kidney lesions* (**glomerulonephritis**) are often present as an accompanying feature of SLE in dogs but may result in few if any clinical signs. A **urinalysis** (examination of the urine) may reveal some loss of protein in the urine. Canine SLE is much less likely to produce severe kidney failure than is either human or feline SLE.

4. *Neurologic disease* may include a rapid-onset **meningitis** (inflammation of the lining membranes of the brain and spinal cord). Affected dogs exhibit depression and fever, and may also display signs of dementia, generalized stiffness and neck pain, and occasionally seizures. Neurologic disease is uncommon in SLE, however, and when present is usually accompanied by polyarthritis.

The diagnosis of SLE is made on the basis of the history, clinical signs, and results of supportive laboratory tests, including the **antinuclear antibody (ANA) test,** which detects autoantibodies directed against the DNA in cell nuclei. The presence of such autoantibodies is one of the most important diagnostic criteria for SLE in human beings as well as in dogs and is considered a hallmark of the disease.

The initial attacks of the disease tend to be the most severe and must be treated aggressively. Once the disease has been brought into remission, it can be kept under control with a minimal amount of drug therapy. About 50% of animals may be withdrawn completely from therapy after 6 months to a year, while the remainder must remain on therapy indefinitely. Corticosteroids combined with more potent immunosuppressive medications represent the cornerstone for treating the disease. The prognosis is always guarded to fair, but tends to improve the longer a remission lasts.

IMMUNE-MEDIATED ARTHRITIS

Arthritis (joint inflammation) is the most common manifestation of a general phenomenon known as **immune-complex** disease—a syndrome wherein antigens joined together with their specific antibodies into antigen-antibody complexes are filtered out of the circulation and deposited in certain vulnerable tissue sites such as the joints, kidneys, or the walls of small blood vessels. The trapped complexes attract white blood cells and related components of the immune system, which interact to produce destructive inflammation and secondary tissue damage. The term polyarthritis frequently is used to describe arthritis occurring simultaneously in several joints.

A number of different classifications of immune-mediated arthritis have been described in dogs, including **idiopathic polyarthritis, plasmacytic-lymphocytic synovitis, enteropathic** and **hepatopathic arthritis,** and **rheumatoid arthritis.**

Idiopathic Polyarthritis

Idiopathic polyarthritis (polyarthritis of unknown cause) is commonly observed in dogs, most often (but not exclusively) among sporting breeds (Retrievers, Pointers, German Shepherds, Dobermans) and toy breeds (Poodles, Terriers). The age at onset may be 6 months to 8 years or more; however the majority of cases are diagnosed in dogs between about 2 and 4 years of age. Clinical signs include a cyclic fever that does not respond to antibiotic therapy, stiffness, and lameness. Visual swelling of the joints themselves is an uncommon feature but is frequently observed on X-ray examination.

The key to making a diagnosis is the discovery of inflammatory cells within joint fluid (**synovial fluid**), the material that lubricates the joint surfaces. Fluid samples should be obtained from several of the larger joints, because the inflammatory process may not be present in all of them. In some dogs the polyarthritis may be accompanied by muscle or nerve inflammation (**polymyositis, polyneuritis**).

The disease is treated through a combination of corticosteroids and other anti-inflammatory or immunosuppressive drugs. The prognosis for recovery in almost all cases is good.

Plasmacytic-lymphocytic Synovitis

Plasmacytic-lymphocytic synovitis (inflammation of the lining membranes of joints, with infiltration by plasma cells and lymphocytes) has a particular predilection for the **stifle** (knee) **joints.**

Acute or chronic lameness in one or both hind limbs is the major presenting sign, with or without arthritic disease. Because of the nature of the signs and the location of the inflammation, this disease is sometimes mistaken for rupture of the cruciate ligament of the stifle joint, a common injury in dogs. Plasmacytic-lymphocytic synovitis tends to occur in larger breeds of dog and is more insidious in onset than are normal cases of cruciate ligament rupture. Conventional cruciate ligament ruptures tend to occur in older, obese, small to medium-sized dogs, and are usually characterized by an acute, non-weight-bearing lameness of the affected leg.

The presence of lymphocytes and plasma cells in samples of joint fluid usually will confirm the diagnosis of plasmacytic-lymphocytic synovitis. Treatment measures are the same as for idiopathic polyarthritis (see ABOVE).

Enteropathic and Hepatopathic Arthritis

Enteropathic and hepatopathic arthritis are arthritic conditions associated with concomitant inflammatory intestinal disease (more commonly) or liver disease (less commonly). Cases have been associated most commonly with chronic **ulcerative colitis** (ulcerating inflammation of the colon) and occasionally with *chronic active hepatitis* (inflammation of the liver). The underlying cause is probably attributable to an increase in absorption of foreign antigens through a damaged bowel (as in colitis), or deficient clearance of antigens by a damaged liver. Therapy should be directed at the primary cause—i.e., the intestinal or liver disorder—rather than at the secondary arthritis itself.

Rheumatoid Arthritis

Rheumatoid arthritis occurs primarily in toy breeds of dog, usually in young to middle-aged animals. It resembles idiopathic polyarthritis (see above) in its earlier stages, but deviates significantly in that in rheumatoid arthritis the joints are almost completely destroyed as the disease progresses. There is a definite predilection for joints closer to and including those of the paws—i.e., the joints near the ends of the limbs.

The diagnosis is made by microscopic examination of joint fluids and by X-ray studies of the affected joint structures. The earliest X-ray changes include swelling of the local soft tissues and **periarticular osteoporosis** (decreasing density of the bones bordering the joints); with time there is eventual collapse of the joint structures themselves. Tests for **rheumatoid factor** (an autoantibody found in rheumatoid arthritis and some other autoimmune diseases, and which is believed to play a prominent role in disease development) are inconsistently positive in dogs with rheumatoid arthritis, a situation quite unlike that for people with rheumatoid arthritis, in whom over 90% are rheumatoid factor-positive.

Treatment requires aggressive therapy with corticosteroids and other immunosuppressive medications to alleviate the immune-mediated destruction of the joint structures. The prognosis is usually guarded, particularly in long-standing cases. Surgical *arthrodesis*—fusion and stabilization of damaged joint structures by surgical means—may be attempted once the disease has been brought into remission, depending upon the severity of the individual case.

IMMUNE-MEDIATED MENINGITIS

Immune-mediated **meningitis** (inflammation of the lining membranes of the brain and spinal cord) has been recognized in dogs. A similar condition in human beings is recognized and is known as **periarteritis nodosa**. Immune-mediated meningitis is usually seen in adolescent or young adult Beagles, Boxers, German Shorthaired Pointers and Akitas. The clinical signs include cyclic bouts of fever, severe neck pain and rigidity, reluctance to move, and depression. Each attack may last from 5 to 10 days, with intervening periods of complete or partial normalcy lasting a week or more. The underlying cause is unknown. The causative lesion is an **arteritis** (inflammation of arteries) primarily of the vessels of the **meninges** (the lining membranes of the brain and spinal cord), but occasionally of vessels in other organs as well. The disease is often self-limiting over a period of several months. **Glucocorticoid** (form of corticosteroid excreted from adrenal gland cortex) therapy usually will minimize the severity of the attacks. In some animals the disease assumes a chronic form and is only partially amenable to therapeutic intervention.

A more severe form of immune-mediated meningitis is seen in young Bernese Mountain Dogs. The disease course is variably cyclical, but there is less resolution of signs in the intervening periods than in the same disorder in other breeds. The condition is less likely to be self-limiting and often requires long-term high doses of glucocorticoids to maintain animals in a comfortable state.

A syndrome of meningitis associated with polyarthritis has been seen in Akitas as young as 12 weeks of age. Affected dogs exhibit severe bouts of fever, depression, neck pain and rigidity, and generalized stiffness. They tend to grow at a slower rate than their siblings and often have an unthrifty appearance. The condition responds only poorly to glucocorticoid and combination immunosuppressive drug therapy; most animals are euthanatized as young adults. A milder and more drug-responsive form of the condition has been recognized in older Akitas.

AUTOIMMUNE SKIN DISEASES
Autoimmune skin diseases observed in dogs include **pemphigus vulgaris, pemphigus foliaceus,** pemphigus vegetans, pemphigus erythematosus, **bullous pemphigoid, discoid lupus erythematosus,** and **panniculitis.** *See* CHAPTER 22, "THE SKIN AND DISORDERS."

LYMPHOSARCOMA
Lymphosarcoma (LSA) is one of the more common malignancies of dogs. Lymphosarcomas consist primarily of solid masses of proliferating lymphocytes no longer responsive to the inhibitory signals that normally halt cell division. The net result is runaway growth. This is compounded by the fact that many LSA tumor cells closely resemble the normal cells from which they were derived, and hence may evoke little response from the immune system.

The cause of canine LSA remains unknown. The feline leukemia virus is the causative agent of most LSA tumors in cats; to date no analogous canine **oncogenic** (tumor-inducing) virus has been shown to cause LSA in dogs.

Several different forms of canine LSA have been delineated, based principally on variations in the anatomic distribution of the tumor masses. The three most common forms follow.

Multicentric LSA
This is by far the most commonly encountered form of LSA in dogs. It is characterized by primary involvement of many lymphatic tissues of the body, accompanied by invasion of other organ structures such as the liver, spleen, kidneys or lungs. Common presenting signs can include **inappetence** (loss of appetite), weight loss, wasting, depression, generalized **lymphadenopathy** (enlargement of lymph nodes), tonsillar enlargement, **hepatosplenomegaly** (enlargement of the liver and spleen), and **polydipsia** (excessive thirst).

Alimentary LSA
The alimentary (digestive tract) form of LSA is the second most common type. It is characterized by tumor-cell infiltration of the digestive tract and other organs, including the associated lymph nodes, liver and spleen. Clinical signs can include inappetence, weight loss, wasting, vomiting and diarrhea. The examining veterinarian frequently will be able to detect the enlarged lymph nodes lining the gastrointestinal tract by *palpating* (feeling with the hands) the affected dog's abdomen.

Cutaneous LSA
The cutaneous (skin) form is the third most common form of LSA in dogs. It is characterized by the presence of few to many nodules and ulcerated masses infiltrating the skin, which may develop a scaly or oily appearance in the affected areas. Frequently the tumors become infected with bacteria and ooze a malodorous pus. Cutaneous LSA may assume a chronic course of extensive duration, gradually progressing to involve more and more of the skin surface while at the same time slowly infiltrating internal organs.

Diagnosis of canine LSA is usually made on the basis of the history, presenting clinical signs, and results of appropriate laboratory tests, including serum chemistries, X-ray studies, blood counts, and others. Microscopic examination of the tumor cells themselves provides the most definitive diagnosis, and together with other diagnostic information also allows the veterinarian in some cases to *stage* the tumor—i.e., to determine how far down the road of disease progression the particular tumor has traveled.

A variety of chemotherapeutic and radiation therapy regimens have been developed and in certain cases these can produce clinical remissions. Combination chemotherapy, using several anticancer agents that attack the tumors in different ways, provides the most effective means of obtaining a remission. Dogs in remission may continue in a reasonably healthy state for a period of weeks to months, or sometimes longer. It must be remembered, however, that these are only remissions, and not necessarily cures (although apparent cures do occur on occasion). The drugs that are used are quite potent and their effects must be monitored carefully during the period of treatment. The prognosis is always guarded.

Multiple Myeloma

Multiple myeloma is an uncommon malignant tumor of **plasma cells** (the cells that make antibody) arising from the bone marrow. Clinical signs of the disease are many and varied, but can include local swelling, generalized pain, lameness, and bone fractures at the tumor site (the most common sign). The most frequent sites for myelomas to arise in dogs include the vertebrae (particularly in the **lumbar** [lower back] region), pelvis and skull. The cause is unknown.

Multiple myelomas grow through and destroy the normal architecture of bone, and this is the underlying cause of the more common clinical signs. The cancerous plasma cells often produce sizable quantities of immunoglobulins or fragments of immunoglobulins that can be detected in blood and sometimes urine, where they are known as **Bence-Jones proteins.** In some cases an increase in the viscosity of the plasma occurs, producing a **hyperviscosity syndrome** characterized by dementia, depression, or ocular disease.

The diagnosis of multiple myeloma is made on the basis of the history, clinical signs, blood counts, X rays (which may graphically reveal the extent of bone destruction caused by the tumor), and microscopic examination of the tumor cells themselves, usually derived from a bone marrow aspirate or biopsy. On occasion small numbers of tumor cells will be found in blood smears.

Treatment attempts rely primarily upon combination chemotherapy using corticosteroids and other immunosuppressive agents. The prognosis is always guarded.

Immunodeficiency Syndromes

Important immunodeficiency syndromes have been reported in a number of animal species. Such syndromes often represent **congenital** (present at birth) conditions that do not become apparent until maternal immunity has waned considerably. The most widely known of these disorders is the combined immunodeficiency (CID) syndrome seen in Arabian foals. Other immunodeficiency states are acquired sometime after birth—the AIDS-like syndrome of cats caused by feline immunodeficiency virus being one prominent example.

Immunodeficiencies that have been reported in dogs follow.

Cyclic Hematopoiesis of Gray Collies

This is an inherited condition wherein the bone marrow's blood cell-producing machinery shuts down at periodic intervals, creating cyclic deficiencies of white blood cells important in immune responses, particularly neutrophils. Affected dogs suffer repeated bacterial infections due to the neutrophil deficiency and to impaired neutrophil function, and usually do not live for more than a few years at most. Blood platelet levels may also drop precipitously, resulting in bleeding episodes.

Selective IgA Deficiency

This uncommon disease is characterized by an

inability to produce sufficient quantities of IgA, which is important in guarding mucosal surfaces against microbial invasion. Recurrent respiratory tract infections seem to predominate, suggesting that the levels of IgA being produced are insufficient to protect against respiratory pathogens.

Canine Granulocytopathy Syndrome

This is a rare disease of Irish setters, wherein neutrophil counts are actually *elevated,* but the neutrophils themselves are apparently poorly functional or completely nonfunctioning. Affected dogs suffer from acute bacterial infections that often are life-threatening.

PART VI

Infectious Diseases and Cancer

There's an old cliche, "Sick as a dog." After you have seen as many sick dogs as I have, you realize it's more truth than cliche. A dog who hurts can't reason that he has felt bad before and recovered to chase cats. He can't comfort himself that this too will pass. He doesn't even care whether the doctor, the nurse or the other patients in the waiting room think he's a coward. He's sick as a dog.

—JAMES R. KINNEY
"Most of My Patients Are Dogs"
written with Isabella Taves,
McCall's, December 1957

CHAPTER 34

Viral Diseases

**by Jeffrey E. Barlough
and Niels C. Pedersen**

In the complex world of the microbes, viruses and certain closely related agents occupy a unique niche: they infect and parasitize living hosts, *yet they themselves are not alive.* To us as human beings such a mode of existence may be quite difficult to imagine. Viruses, for example, do not ingest or process nutrients. They do not respire. Because they have no independent metabolism they do not excrete waste products. They are incapable of movement, nor do they "sense" their environment in any way comparable to our own powers of sensation. Their sole purpose for existence is the perpetuation and dissemination of their own species. From a broad evolutionary perspective, such is the ultimate purpose of all nature's creatures, and so in this a virus is not very different from a bacterium, or a dinosaur, or a dog. But the way viruses go about it provides a rare and fascinating glimpse of biochemistry hovering at the threshold of life.

In essence, a typical virus is composed of a segment or segments of **nucleic acid**—the virus's genetic material, equivalent to the chromosomes of living cells—that is encased in a protective shell of protein known as a capsid. The genetic material is made of either **ribonucleic acid (RNA)** or **deoxyribonucleic acid (DNA)**—either one or the other, never both. By contrast, the genetic material of living cells is composed of DNA, while different types of RNA in the cell carry out important regulatory and protein-synthetic functions.

In some viruses the protein shell is itself encased in a soft outer envelope which conveys certain additional properties to the virus. Some viruses also carry with them a packet of **enzymes** (proteins that speed chemical reactions) to assist in the viral replication (reproduction) cycle. A virus must rely upon living cells of a suitable host for its reproduction. Outside a cell a virus is simply an inert bit of particulate matter. Once taken inside, however, the virus proceeds to commandeer the cell's biosynthetic machinery, converting the cell into a "biotechnology factory" for the construction and subsequent release of countless new virus particles.

Many viruses destroy their host cells through their activities, often producing disease and usually initiating an attack by the host's immune defenses. In some cases the immune response may become particularly aggressive and produce unwanted side effects that can be more severe than the virus disease itself. Other viruses cause very little damage to host cell machinery and provoke little if any reaction; some may remain in a dormant or *latent* form for years. Most virus infections by far appear to be **asymptomatic** in nature—that is, the infections are so mild and the host response so effective that clinical signs of disease never become apparent.

Very few diseases caused by viruses respond clinically to specific antiviral medication. Usually it is the secondary effects of a virus infection that are addressed, in order to stabilize the patient and protect against bacterial or fungal infections while an immune response to the virus is developing (bacteria and fungi can act as opportunistic disease agents in tissues damaged by virus infection). Despite great progress in our understanding of the immune system and the various mechanisms underlying disease, it remains true that most successful attacks against viral invasion are carried out by the body itself.

The most effective therapy for any virus disease is prevention (i.e., immunization through vaccination). Antibiotics (which are active against bacteria and some fungi) and antifungal drugs in general have no appreciable effect on virus replication, while clinically useful medications having direct antiviral activity remain few in number and are restricted almost exclusively to some very specific virus infections. In people, viruses for which some type of antiviral therapy is available include several of the herpesviruses, Lassa fever virus, and human immunodeficiency virus (HIV), the cause of human AIDS.

Canine Distemper

Canine distemper, also known as *Carré's disease,* is the most important viral infectious disease of dogs. Although the causative virus (**canine distemper virus, CDV**) was identified only in the early years of the present century, the disease itself has been recognized clinically for much longer. Canine distemper is characterized initially by acute upper respiratory disease signs and fever, and later by more severe respiratory disease (pneumonia), vomiting, diarrhea and neurologic signs. Canine distemper is a highly contagious disease, the virus spreading rapidly from infected to susceptible animals by aerosol and direct contact. Moreover, the dog is only one of a vast array of species susceptible to infection with CDV.

The Cause

Canine distemper virus is a member of the Paramyxoviridae family of viruses. The genetic material of paramyxoviruses is composed of a single strand of RNA, coiled into a lengthy and complex tubular structure. Paramyxoviruses have an outer envelope and so as a group are relatively sensitive to most common household detergents and disinfectants. Routine measures for disinfection and decontamination of kennels and veterinary hospitals are usually considered sufficient to inactivate CDV.

Occurrence and Transmission

Canine distemper virus infects an astonishingly broad panorama of carnivorous species—dogs, coyotes, wolves, foxes, ferrets, jackals, hyenas, weasels, raccoons, mink, skunks, badgers, **binturongs** (raccoon-like mammals related to the civet, found in Asia) and otters, among others. There has even been a report of fatal CDV infection in a Bengal tiger. In 1988 approximately 18,000 harbor seals in northwestern European seas succumbed to fatal infection with a previously unknown paramyxovirus that appears to be closely related to CDV.

Canine distemper virus is excreted in the saliva, respiratory secretions, urine and feces, and can be transmitted from dog to dog by aerosol (airborne droplet contamination) and by direct contact. Because the virus does not survive for extensive periods in the environment, infected and susceptible animals usually must be in close proximity for the infection to spread efficiently.

Pathogenesis

Within a day after exposure to a virus-laden aerosol, CDV can be identified in the tonsils and local lymph nodes. By the second or third day a **viremia** (presence of virus in the bloodstream) develops, with the virus contained within circulating **phagocytic cells** (white blood cells that engulf and ingest foreign material). In this way the virus is carried to more distant sites where it replicates rapidly, primarily in lymph nodes and related tissues. It is during this initial period of virus growth and expansion that a fever first develops. It is also at this point that the developing immune response of the host will determine the ultimate clinical outcome of the infection.

Dogs that develop a sufficiently strong immune response by day 8 or 9 postinfection will terminate further spread of the virus and clear it from most tissues. Dogs with an intermediate level of immunity will eliminate or suppress the spread of CDV to the respiratory and intestinal tracts, but not to the eyes, nervous system, or footpads. These latter animals often develop neurologic disease without manifesting respiratory or diarrheal signs. Dogs unfortunate enough to develop only a poor immune response to the virus by day 8 or 9 postinfection will be completely overcome by the infection, with spread of virus throughout the body. Animals with this form of chronic distemper will exhibit varying degrees of pneumonia and diarrhea followed (if they survive long enough) by neurologic disease.

CLINICAL SIGNS

Most infections with CDV appear to be asymptomatic or very mild in nature, reflecting the variable virulence of different CDV strains and the widespread immunity or partial immunity in the canine population, resulting from previous exposure to CDV and, of course, routine vaccination. When severe, generalized distemper does occur it can assume a number of different clinical forms, some of which may be difficult to diagnose. In general, clinical distemper most often affects younger dogs. The major clinical manifestations are outlined as follows.

"Kennel" Form of Distemper

Canine distemper virus can produce an overwhelming **hemorrhagic enteritis** (inflammation and bleeding in the intestinal tract) that can have a rapidly fatal outcome in very young puppies. The most significant death losses in kennels occur in pups 5 to 7 weeks of age. Overcrowding and unfavorable hygienic conditions in the kennel are believed to predispose pups by providing a high level of virus exposure that overwhelms the pups' level of maternal immunity (characteristically, the disease strikes during the time when maternal immunity is waning, but before active immunization with vaccines has begun). Affected puppies often exhibit a low-grade fever, depression, coughing and a mild to moderately severe diarrhea. They fail to respond to treatment and slowly waste away, dying within 1 to 3 weeks. Often a diagnosis of distemper may be discounted because the clinical signs are atypical of "classical" distemper, and because of a mistaken belief that maternal immunity will protect all pups of this age against CDV. If many litters of pups are being raised in the affected kennel, the infection may spread from litter to litter as maternal immunity wanes sufficiently for the infection to take hold. Pup losses can approach 75% or more in some kennels.

Pups 9 to 12 Weeks of Age

This is a common age group in which to see distemper in dogs, particularly puppies obtained from humane shelters, pounds, or local pet stores. Often these animals are incubating the infection at the time of purchase and break with disease signs several days or weeks after arrival in a new household. Approximately 6 to 9 days after exposure to CDV, a transient fever appears which is associated with initial spread of the virus through the body. **Inappetence** (lack of appetite), slight depression, ocular or nasal discharges, and tonsillitis may be noted. Once this stage has passed, the disease may take any one of the three major courses previously mentioned, depending upon the level of immune response that develops. Spread of virus to the lungs and upper respiratory tract will lead to pneumonia and an inflammatory response in the nasal passages (**rhinitis**) and mucus membranes of the eyes (**conjunctivitis**). Intestinal spread leads to diarrhea and fluid loss. Skin involvement is manifested initially by a measles-like eruption and later by **hyperkeratosis** (thickening of the skin) of the nose and footpads ("hardpad disease"). The inflammatory response in the respiratory and digestive tracts is frequently complicated by secondary bacterial infections, which may serve to enhance the disease process.

Although the respiratory and intestinal disease signs can be severe and debilitating in themselves, it is the neurologic manifestations of distemper that are pivotal in determining the outcome in treated cases. Respiratory, intestinal, or other disease manifestations may have been of only minor importance or even unobserved for several weeks before the onset of neurologic disease. Neurologic signs observed in distemper can include circling, head-tilt, **nystagmus** (rapid eye movements), **paresis** (partial paralysis), paralysis, convulsions and dementia. **Myoclonus** (involuntary rapid, jerky twitching or contraction of muscles) and convulsions preceded by so-called chewing-gum movements of the mouth are considered virtually diagnostic for distemper.

There appears to be a strong positive correlation between the development of hardpad disease and central nervous system spread of CDV. A low-grade fever that persists after the initial mild upper respiratory signs have disappeared is also a strong indicator of virus persistence and eventual nervous system involvement. *A dog is not "out of the woods" with regard to distemper for at least 6 weeks after the initial mild fever and respiratory and intestinal signs have first appeared.* This is a critical point, because the early stages of distemper can mimic a number of other canine diseases, particularly those with respiratory system involvement such as kennel cough. Canine distemper virus causes a profound **atrophy** (shrinking or wasting) of the thymus gland and certain areas of the lymph nodes and spleen—all tissues of great importance to the immune system. This can lead to a profound suppression of immune responses. Dogs with chronic distemper thus are very sensitive to bacterial pneumonia, lung abscesses, systemic spread of *Toxoplasma gondii, Nocardia* septicemia, and other microbial or parasitic diseases.

Older Dogs with Partial Immunity

Older dogs, even if they have been vaccinated against CDV, can occasionally develop distemper after severe exposure. The disease in older dogs is atypical in that it manifests primarily as an **ascending myelitis** (inflammation of the spinal cord), either with or without signs of brain dysfunction. The disease often is self-limiting after several weeks. Residual central nervous system impairment following resolution of the disease may be evident.

Postvaccinal Distemper

A **fulminating** (explosive) distemperlike disease is occasionally seen in puppies following vaccination. These animals are either **congenitally immunodeficient** (i.e., born with an inherent immune system defect) or for some reason have a selective lack of resistance to CDV.

ANCILLARY COMPLICATIONS

In addition to these several major forms of distemper, a number of ancillary complications resulting from distemper have also been recognized. Among them are:

Old Dog Encephalitis

Encephalitis (inflammation of the brain) caused by CDV may be seen in some older dogs. It is a distinct disease entity from the acute encephalitis that may develop shortly after infection with the virus. Thus the disease represents a delayed manifestation of an earlier mild or even inapparent infection with CDV. Most of the brain lesions are probably caused by the immune response to the virus rather than by the virus itself; thus the disease is considered to be **immune-mediated.** It is interesting to note that human measles virus, which is closely related to CDV, has a partial counterpart to old dog encephalitis in *subacute sclerosing panencephalitis (SSPE),* a delayed (and devastating) neurologic manifestation in children and adolescents and resulting from an earlier, persistent measles virus infection.

Enamel Hypoplasia

Canine distemper virus has a preference for the enamel-forming cells of the tooth bud. If infection occurs during the time that the enamel layer of the tooth is being laid down, the mature tooth will develop irregularities of the dental surface characteristic of **enamel hypoplasia** (underdevelopment or incomplete development of the enamel). Fortunately, the underlying **dentin** layer of dogs' teeth is very hard and resistant to decay, and affected teeth usually function quite well.

Residual Neurologic Damage
Dogs infected with CDV that recover from severe neurologic distemper may nevertheless retain certain of the neurologic abnormalities, such as chewing-gum movements, muscle twitching (**myoclonus**), intermittent seizure episodes, partial paralysis (**paresis**), or abnormalities of balance.

Ocular Abnormalities
In some cases of distemper there may be complications involving the eyes. Healed areas of inflammation may be found in the area of the retina at the back of the eye, or the cornea may be affected by **keratoconjunctivitis sicca** ("dry eye") secondary to CDV infection of the tear glands.

DIAGNOSIS
Diagnosis of CDV infection most often is made on the basis of history and clinical signs, and to some extent supportive laboratory findings. Virus in cells (white blood cells, tracheal washings, footpad biopsies, cells scraped from the surface of the conjunctiva) sometimes can be identified by special staining techniques, although the virus usually disappears from these sites after antibody appears. The presence of CDV in these cells is so variable that in most cases a negative test cannot rule out a diagnosis of distemper. Virus isolation and serology today are little used in clinical practice because of a number of limitations.

TREATMENT
No curative therapy for canine distemper currently exists. Treatment instead is aimed at supporting the patient and preventing secondary complications, by using antibiotics for bacterial infection; fluid replacement to counter the effects of prolonged diarrhea, inappetence and vomiting; antidiarrheal medications; and anticonvulsive therapy should seizures occur. Treatment of the neurologic complications of distemper is perhaps the least successful owing to the relatively frequent persistence of certain abnormalities, such as myoclonus. A number of supposed miracle "treatments" for distemper have been touted in the past, including ether inhalation and megavitamin C supplementation. To date there is no published scientific evidence that any of these are of benefit to affected dogs.

PREVENTION
There are a number of excellent vaccines available to immunize dogs against CDV. These vaccines are quite effective and produce long-lasting immunity. Because distemper is a highly preventable disease, one cannot overemphasize the importance of proper immunization. Modified-live CDV vaccine is recommended for puppies every 3 to 4 weeks between 6 to 16 weeks of age. As an alternative combined distemper-measles virus vaccine may be given as the initial dose at 6 weeks of age, if CDV vaccine interference by residual maternal immunity to CDV is anticipated; this should then be followed by regular CDV inoculations at the appropriate time intervals. The measles virus fraction of the vaccine can provide pups with limited immunity against clinical (manifestation of observed signs) distemper but not distemper virus infection, in the presence of residual low levels of **maternal antibody** (antibody that ordinarily would interfere with standard CDV vaccine). Annual booster CDV vaccinations are usually recommended.

Infectious Canine Hepatitis

Infectious canine hepatitis (ICH), also called *Rubarth's disease,* has long been confused clinically with canine distemper. It occurs not only in dogs but also in several other species, most notably foxes. The disease was first recognized in the 1920s in silver foxes, in which signs of encephalitis (inflammation of the brain) were most prominent. It was known as early as 1927 that the fox virus was highly contagious to dogs.

The natural disease in dogs, in its more common form of **hepatitis** (inflammation of the liver), was subsequently described in the 1940s.

The Cause

This disease is caused by an *adenovirus* called **canine adenovirus type 1 (CAV-1)**. The nucleic acid is composed of DNA. Adenoviruses have no outer envelope and so are more resistant to the effects of many common detergents and disinfectants. Disinfectants active against the virus include iodine, sodium hydroxide and chlorine bleach (diluted 1:32 in water).

Occurrence and Transmission

The virus is distributed worldwide in dogs and foxes. It is particularly widespread in the canine population and can be found wherever dogs exist. CAV-1 also can infect coyotes, timber wolves, skunks and bears. A closely related virus, called **canine adenovirus type 2 (CAV-2)**, is a respiratory pathogen of dogs that is involved in the "kennel cough" complex and is also important in the formulation of the newer vaccines against ICH.

A significant percentage of dogs develops antibodies to the virus by the age of 1 or 2 years. This supports the view that CAV-1 is quite prevalent in nature and that the mortality rate following infection is very low. Transmission appears to be by direct contact spread between dogs, rather than by aerosol infection (as is common in distemper). The disease is seen most often in unvaccinated dogs less than a year old, but it can occur in dogs of any age.

Pathogenesis

Following inhalation or ingestion of CAV-1, the virus localizes in the tonsils from where it disseminates to local and more distant lymph nodes before gaining access to the bloodstream. Once in the blood the virus is showered throughout the body, targeting certain specific tissues such as the liver, kidneys, eyes, and **vascular endothelium** (cells lining the inner surface of blood vessels). Once an antibody response arises (usually within 5 to 7 days of infection) the virus is rapidly cleared from most areas of the body but persists for some time in the kidneys, from where it is excreted into the urine.

Dogs that survive CAV-1 infection, particularly those experiencing severe clinical illness, may develop a transient clouding of the **cornea** (the transparent outer coat of the eye) known colloquially as "blue eye." This is caused by an immunologic reaction involving antibodies and virus that occurs in the deeper regions of the **uvea** (cellular layer within the eye that contains the iris and blood vessels). The origin of this reaction lies in residual virus that persists within uveal vessels and that subsequently interacts with circulating antibody to produce localized swelling and cloudiness of the cornea. The blue-eye reaction is self-limiting and usually dissipates within a few weeks.

Clinical Signs

Several clinical forms of ICH in dogs are recognized.

Subclinical ICH

In many instances the only clinical sign of CAV-1 infection is a transient fever lasting 24 to 48 hours. Occasionally, a second fever spike may follow within a few days. A fall in the white blood cell count (**leukopenia**) usually accompanies the fever. Lethargy, malaise and inappetence often are not very pronounced. There may be slight enlargement of the tonsils and a reddening of the membranes of the mouth and **conjunctiva** (membrane lining the inner surface of the eyelids).

Peracute ICH (Extremely Rapid Onset)

In very young puppies (2 to 6 weeks of age) ICH can assume a highly virulent form, with death occurring within a day or less. The initial clinical signs of fever, tonsillitis, **colic** (acute abdominal pain) and reddening of the membranes of the mouth and conjunctiva are rapidly superseded by shock and death. In many cases the veterinarian is presented with puppies that were reportedly normal one day and in shock the next. Often the owner believes the animals have been poisoned. The puppies may respond initially to standard therapy for shock (fluids, corticosteroids, antibiotics), only to experience a relapse and die a few hours later.

Acute ICH

This is the "classical" form of ICH that is most often described in veterinary textbooks. Although it can occur in adolescent and mature dogs, it is most often seen in puppies between 6 and 10 weeks of age. The early clinical signs of fever, lethargy, malaise, reddening of the membranes, enlargement of lymph nodes of the head and neck, and tonsillitis are often quite pronounced. Colic and **hepatomegaly** (enlargement of the liver) may also be present; **jaundice** (yellowing of the mucous membranes), however, is uncommon. In fortunate cases recovery occurs within 4 to 7 days. In the less fortunate, a bleeding syndrome (**hemorrhagic diathesis**) develops between the 2nd and 5th day of illness. Small hemorrhages may be noted in the skin and on the mucous membranes, and the blood fails to **coagulate** (clot) in standard clotting tests. Blood may be discharged from the nose, mouth, rectum, and urinary tract. Central nervous system signs including seizures, blindness, or **dementia** (mental dysfunction) may occur secondary to liver disease and hemorrhage and swelling in the brain.

The cause of the bleeding disorder is the widespread infection of blood vessel walls by the virus. As a result of the widespread vascular damage—the virus produces lesions in blood vessels in many tissues—the clotting factors essential for the cessation of bleeding are rapidly depleted. This depletion is aggravated by the fact that the liver, which is responsible for the synthesis of many of these clotting factors, is also under heavy attack by the virus. Thus, it is actually the widespread activation of the blood clotting system (and thus the consumption of clotting factors) that leads to the bleeding syndrome. This syndrome of excessive blood clotting that results ultimately in a bleeding tendency is known by the general term **disseminated intravascular coagulopathy (DIC)**.

DIAGNOSIS

Diagnosis of ICH is often made indirectly through a combination of the history and presenting clinical signs and supportive laboratory test findings. Among the findings that may be noted are an elevation in liver enzyme levels in **serum** (clear liquid in blood), hematologic changes and abnormal blood clotting tests. Only rarely is diagnosis made by isolation of the causative virus or by **serology** (detection of antigen or antibody). A tentative diagnosis may be supported by obtaining a biopsy specimen, with demonstration of characteristic virus inclusion bodies in liver cells.

TREATMENT

There is no curative therapy for ICH. Treatment is aimed instead at minimizing the effects of shock and hemorrhage, management of neurologic disease, and prevention of secondary bacterial infection; thus the need often for aggressive intravenous or **intraperitoneal** (into the body cavity surrounding the primary abdominal organs) fluid therapy, corticosteroids, blood transfusions and antibiotics.

PREVENTION

Modified-live vaccine using CAV-2 (which cross-protects against CAV-1 but does not induce the "blue eye" phenomenon) is available for the routine immunization of puppies and adult dogs. The vaccine usually is given in concert with distemper vaccine and so the vaccine schedule usually reflects the schedule for immunization against CDV. As a minimum, puppies should receive at least two injections of ICH vaccine. Annual booster vaccinations are usually recommended.

Rabies

The specter of rabies has haunted Europe and Asia since before the dawn of recorded history. The first identifiable account of it may be found in the law tablets of ancient Mesopotamia: "If a dog is vicious and the authorities have brought the fact to the knowledge of its owner, (if nevertheless) he does not keep it in, it bites a man and causes (his) death, then the owner of the dog shall pay two-thirds of a mina of silver . . . "

Rabies was well-known to the ancient Greek people, among them Aristotle and Xenophon, who recorded instances of its occurrence in their writings. In today's world rabies exists on all continents except Australia and Antarctica. It is a disease primarily of bats and carnivores, the latter including the domestic dog and cat. Despite the availability of effective rabies vaccines for both animals and human beings, rabies remains a persistent cause of concern, particularly in the developing nations of the earth.

In the Western industrialized world, vaccination programs aimed at domestic dog populations have virtually eliminated human cases of rabies. In the United States rabies cases among both dogs and cats continue to be reported at a relatively low frequency. Although the numbers of cases still remain relatively small, their occurrence serves as a constant reminder of the presence of this scourge from the earliest days of antiquity.

THE CAUSE

Rabies is caused by a bullet-shaped virus in the family Rhabdoviridae. The nucleic acid of rhabdoviruses is composed of RNA. Rhabdoviruses have outer envelopes and thus are relatively easily destroyed by common household soaps, detergents and disinfectants.

OCCURRENCE AND TRANSMISSION

Rabies virus cycles in nature through wild and domestic carnivores and through certain other wildlife species. Geographic variation exists in the pattern of hosts in different areas of the world. In the United States, skunks play a major role in transmitting the disease, particularly in the Midwest, where they are now the main reservoir of rabies virus infection. In the southeastern states raccoons are important in spreading the infection and have recently begun moving it northward along the eastern seaboard. Wild foxes are very important reservoir hosts in Europe and to some extent in North America as well. In the Caribbean islands and much of the Americas, bats are important reservoirs of infection. In the Latin American countries, vampire bats are particularly notorious for spreading rabies to herds of cattle. The mongoose is another well-known reservoir host in certain regions, including South Africa and the Caribbean. Of the many rodent species in the United States, only the woodchuck, sometimes

called the groundhog, appears to be of importance in rabies virus transmission, particularly in the mid-Atlantic and Midwest regions. Rats, mice, squirrels, chipmunks, guinea pigs, etcetera are not involved to any great extent.

Of the domestic species, only the dog and cat are important carriers of rabies virus. In most of the developing nations, domestic dogs remain the primary reservoir hosts for rabies and the principal source of human exposure to the virus. Rabid animals excrete large quantities of rabies virus in their saliva, which accounts for the primary mechanism by which the virus is transmitted; that is, by the bite of an infected animal.

PATHOGENESIS

The **incubation period** (time between exposure and the onset of clinical signs of disease) for rabies may be quite variable, ranging from a week to as long as a year. This variability apparently reflects the amount of time the rabies virus is retained within muscle cells at the site of inoculation (usually a bite wound). Following this early stage of infection, the virus crosses the **neuromuscular junctions** (connections between muscle cells and adjacent nerve cells) and advances boldly into the nervous system, traveling directly up the nerve bodies until it gains access to the spinal cord and eventually the brain. Invasion of the brain is followed by virus spread—again within the nerve bodies themselves—to additional sites important for subsequent transmission of the virus, such as the salivary glands, respiratory system and digestive tract. Of greatest importance from a veterinary and public health standpoint is the excretion of large quantities of virus from the salivary glands into the saliva. Salivary shedding of virus in dogs can begin as much as one or two weeks *before* the actual onset of clinical signs. Once clinical signs have developed the outcome is inevitably fatal, although the precise cellular mechanism by which the virus causes death remains unidentified.

CLINICAL SIGNS

The clinical signs of rabies are similar overall in the different animal species, but the signs observed in individual cases can vary widely. In general, two forms or manifestations of rabies are recognized: the excitatory, or "furious" form (the more well-known, and the more graphic), and the paralytic, or "dumb" form. In actuality, most cases of rabies exhibit one or more manifestations of both forms. The paralytic form always represents the terminal stage of the disease; however, some animals die during convulsive seizures while in the furious stage without progressing to the final, paralytic stage. Some animals show few or no signs of excitement or "madness," the clinical picture reflecting instead the effects of **paresis** (partial paralysis) or paralysis. Occasionally rabid animals die suddenly without exhibiting any recognizable clinical signs whatsoever.

In dogs the furious stage of rabies may last anywhere from 1 to 7 days. It is characterized by restlessness, nervousness and a developing viciousness. Affected dogs may snap at imaginary objects and try to bite any animal or human that approaches. Initially this behavior is directed toward strangers, but as the disease progresses a dog may turn on its owner. Excitability, a heightened sensitivity to being touched, and **photophobia** (visual hypersensitivity to light) may also be manifested. If restrained, a rabid dog may chew viciously on its leash or on the bars of its cage. It may break its teeth, lacerate its mouth and gums, and drool a ropy slobber tinged with blood and teeming with rabies virus particles. A heavy, rapid respiration through the mouth may cause frothing of the saliva—providing the classic, characteristic picture of the rabid animal.

Affected dogs frequently appear oblivious to pain or other discomfort. They may utter weird, howling cries or hoarse yowls because of the advancing paralysis of the muscles of the **larynx** (voice box). **Hydrophobia** (aversion to water), which is common in human beings with rabies, seems to occur only rarely in canine rabies. Instead, there is a growing loss of interest in food, although there may be some spastic attempts at swallowing. Sometimes an affected dog will attack and swallow strange objects, such as wooden sticks, pebbles, gravel or fecal material. An advancing facial paralysis may prevent the dog from closing its eyes. The corneas then become dry and dull, and the pupils may dilate widely, producing a characteristic staring or "faraway" look.

Within a very short time signs of excitement (when they occur) give way to the final, paralytic stage of the disease, which typically lasts for only a day or two. The paralytic stage is much less spectacular than the excitatory stage, and may be difficult to diagnose when it represents the sole clinical manifestation of the disease. The paralysis usually appears initially in the muscles of the head and neck, the most characteristic sign being difficulty in swallowing. An affected dog cannot chew or swallow its food, or does so only with great difficulty. An owner, imagining that perhaps a bone or other foreign object has lodged in the dog's throat, may attempt to examine the animal's mouth. In so looking for an object that is not there, the owner may be exposed to the rabies virus by scraping hands or fingers on the dog's teeth, bathing the abrasions in the virus-laden saliva. Signs of localized paralysis are succeeded quickly by more generalized paralysis, with coma and death following shortly thereafter.

For both dogs and humans, rabies is an inevitably fatal illness once clinical signs have appeared. To date only a handful of human survivors are recorded in the medical literature, although humans can be treated before clinical signs appear. Utmost caution must be observed if one suspects that a pet has been exposed to rabies virus. (For a particularly vivid account of canine rabies, readers are referred to the famous scene in chapter 10 of Harper Lee's novel, *To Kill a Mockingbird*.)

DIAGNOSIS

The clinical signs of rabies, although characteristic of the disease, are not in and of themselves sufficient to make the diagnosis; a definitive diagnosis can be made only by laboratory examination of brain tissue. In cases involving human exposure to a possibly rabid dog or other animal—taking into account the grave prognosis for recovery once clinical signs are apparent—the accuracy of the diagnosis in the suspect animal assumes paramount importance.

Currently there are three methods available

for the laboratory diagnosis of rabies:

1. immunofluorescence microscopy, the most rapid and accurate method and the one most recommended, in which brain tissue is directly examined for the presence of rabies virus, using special antibodies and a fluorescent microscope;

2. **histopathology,** in which sections of smears of brain tissue are examined for the presence of **Negri bodies,** intracellular inclusion bodies that are formed in the brain in many (but not all) cases of rabies;

3. mouse inoculation, which is often used to confirm positive results or to investigate further any strongly suspected rabies cases that have tested negative by other methods.

Guidelines for the control of rabies virus infection in animals are available from the National Association of State Public Health Veterinarians, Inc. (NASPHV). Each year, usually in January, updated NASPHV guidelines are published in an issue of the *Journal of the American Veterinary Medical Association,* together with a compendium of currently licensed rabies vaccines for use in domestic animals. It is these guidelines in part that serve as the basis for the recommendations that follow.

Any wild or domestic mammal that has bitten a human being and is exhibiting clinical signs consistent with a diagnosis of rabies should be humanely destroyed. The head should be submitted to a qualified rabies diagnostic laboratory where the brain will be examined for the presence of rabies virus. *Regardless of clinical signs,* any bat or wild carnivorous mammal (including offspring of wild animals crossbred with domestic dogs and cats) that has bitten a human being should be destroyed and the head submitted for diagnostic testing (this is because of the variable period of salivary shedding of rabies virus that can occur *before* clinical signs are manifested). Any bat that has bitten a human being should be presumed rabid until confirmed negative by laboratory examination. *Any healthy dog or cat that has bitten a human being should be confined for at least 10 days and observed for the development of clinical signs of rabies.*

An *unvaccinated* dog or cat that has been bitten by or exposed to a known rabid animal should either be destroyed, or quarantined for 6 months and vaccinated for rabies 1 month before release. *A rabies-vaccinated dog or cat that has been bitten by or exposed to a known rabid animal* should be given a rabies booster immunization immediately and kept under observation for 90 days. If clinical signs of rabies should appear during the observation period, the animal should be humanely destroyed and the brain examined to confirm the diagnosis.

TREATMENT

Owing to the potential risk of exposing human beings to rabies virus, attempted treatment of animals suspected of having rabies is *not recommended.* Treatment of human beings exposed to a known or suspect rabid animal, however, must be aggressively applied. Any person bitten by a wild animal should immediately report the incident to his or her physician, who can evaluate the need for antirabies therapy. Treatment should consist of *thorough flushing and cleansing of the bite wound with soap and water* (the importance of this simple measure cannot be overemphasized); administration of rabies virus antiserum to exposed individuals who have no previous history of rabies virus immunization; and administration of human diploid-cell rabies vaccine in five doses, given on days 0, 3, 7, 14 and 28 postexposure. Further details regarding preexposure and postexposure rabies prevention and vaccine administration can be found in the current recommendations of the Immunization Practices Advisory Committee (ACIP) of the U.S. Public Health Service. These recommendations are available from state health department offices.

PREVENTION

In the United States and most other countries, highly effective rabies virus vaccines are available for use in domestic species. Mass immunization programs for dogs have been employed for many years to control rabies virus spread by creating an "immunological barrier" between wildlife reservoirs of the disease and human beings (dogs frequently acquiring the infection from wildlife hosts and then subsequently transmitting it to human contacts). Such measures have succeeded in reducing the annual number of laboratory-confirmed cases of canine rabies in the United States from 6,949 in 1947 to 130 in 1993. Some nations, notably Japan, England, Iceland and the Scandinavian countries, have eradicated rabies by implementing control programs and stringent quarantine regulations. Despite such successes, however, canine rabies remains a significant public health hazard in many developing regions of the world.

Immunization of dogs and cats remains the best deterrent to the spread of rabies to human populations. *All dogs and cats should be vaccinated for rabies at 3 months of age, again 1 year from the initial inoculation, and then revaccinated every 3 years or as required by individual vaccine specifications.* In comprehensive rabies control programs, only vaccines with a 3-year duration of immunity should be used.

The response of wild animal species to rabies vaccines licensed for use in domestic animals has often been erratic and unpredictable. For this reason it was recommended for many years that wild animals not be vaccinated for rabies, even with inactivated (killed) virus preparations. Hybrids (offspring of wild animals bred with domestic dogs or cats) are generally considered wild animals and as such were included under this recommendation. Recently, a new genetically engineered oral rabies vaccine for distribution in fish meal baits has become available to vaccinate wild populations (primarily raccoons) in selected areas of the United States.

PUBLIC HEALTH SIGNIFICANCE
The clinical signs and course of rabies in human beings are similar to those of animal victims of the disease. Both excitatory and paralytic symptoms may be apparent. The incubation period, as in animals, may vary in length—from about 2 weeks to as long as a year—but usually averages between 3 and 6 weeks. Once symptoms appear

the course of illness is brief—only a few days— *and the mortality rate is essentially 100%.* The risk of rabies developing in an exposed individual varies with many factors. For their own safety and the safety of other human beings and their pets, dog and cat owners should see to it that their animals are regularly vaccinated against this most deadly and uncompromising of viral diseases.

Canine Parvovirus Enteritis

A worldwide outbreak of a severe and sometimes fatal **hemorrhagic gastrointestinal** (intestinal hemorrhaging) disease of domestic dogs was recognized in 1978, and subsequently shown to be caused by a wholly new canine pathogen, *canine parvovirus type 2 (CPV-2).* The virus is now widespread in canine populations throughout the world. (Canine parvovirus type 1 [CPV-1], known as the *minute virus of canines,* also is widespread in the dog population, but its exact significance as a cause of disease remains to be determined.) Studies indicate that CPV-2 came into existence in about 1976, since canine serum samples collected before that year are universally negative for CPV-2 antibodies. Although it has not been proven, current thinking suggests that CPV-2 arose as a mutation of either feline parvovirus (feline panleukopenia virus) or a related parvovirus of wildlife.

THE CAUSE
CPV-2, like other members of the Parvoviridae family, is a very small DNA virus and lacks an outer envelope. It is one of the most highly resistant viruses known, easily surviving in the environment for as long as 5 months or more. The virus is resistant to the action of most common household detergents and disinfectants, but is susceptible to chlorine bleach.

OCCURRENCE AND TRANSMISSION
Within months of its identification in 1978, CPV-2 had already spread to dog populations throughout much of the world. In addition to infecting dogs, CPV-2 also infects coyotes and several other canids, including three from South America: the bush dog, maned wolf and crab-eating fox. It

seems likely that many other canid species also are susceptible to CPV-2 infection and disease.

Transmission of CPV-2 occurs primarily by the fecal-oral route; that is, the virus is ingested, replicates in the intestinal tract, and then is excreted in large quantities in the feces. Although infected animals may carry and shed the virus for short periods, the general hardiness of the virus and its persistence in the environment are believed to be of greater importance in perpetuating the disease.

Pathogenesis

The virus usually gains entry through the oral cavity, with the initial infection occurring primarily in the tonsils. From there the virus threads its way through the local lymphatic channels to reach the bloodstream, by which means it is disseminated throughout the body. Replication of CPV-2 occurs exclusively in actively dividing cells; nondividing cells are resistant. Actively dividing (**mitotic**) cells can be found in notable supply in the intestinal tract, bone marrow, thymus and lymph nodes—not surprisingly, all sites of preference for CPV-2 attack. (As expected, clinical signs observed in acute CPV-2 disease mirror quite closely the roster of susceptible cell types infected and destroyed by the virus.) In the intestinal tract, CPV-2 produces **necrosis** (death) of rapidly dividing crypt cells that are essential for maintaining the nutrient-absorptive lining of the small intestine. Loss of these cells, together with the accompanying inflammatory response, impairs the normal absorption of nutrients from the gut with resultant signs of diarrhea and fluid and weight loss. Within a week of infection, massive quantities of new virus particles are being generated in infected intestinal cells and released into the feces, contaminating the environment. By 2 weeks postinfection the immune defenses normally succeed in suppressing the infection and virus shedding ceases. Rapid regeneration of affected tissues usually occurs in concert with suppression of virus replication.

In the thymus, bone marrow and lymph nodes CPV-2 targets a number of cell types that are essential for the generation of immune responses, leading to the suggestion that the virus is a cause of immunosuppression. This remains a somewhat controversial aspect of CPV-2 pathogenesis, particularly with regard to its significance for the outcome of infection. Most authorities today seem to hold that any effect of the virus on immune responsiveness is negligible. Although there is a transient depression of circulating white blood cell numbers during the peak of acute illness, the decrease is not nearly as severe nor as clinically significant as it is with feline parvovirus infection (panleukopenia) of cats (*see* The Cornell Book of Cats, Chapter 29). Moreover, dogs that recover from canine parvovirus **enteritis** (inflammation of the small intestine) are solidly immune against subsequent clinical disease.

Amidst the initial excitement attendant upon the discovery of canine parvoviral enteritis in the late 1970s were unusual reports of outbreaks of **myocarditis** (inflammatory heart-muscle disease) among litters of parvovirus-infected pups. Two clinical forms of disease leading to either acute or chronic heart failure and death were observed. It was subsequently demonstrated that CPV-2 replicating in heart-muscle cells was indeed the cause of this unexpected disease manifestation. Further, it was shown that myocarditis developed only if pups were infected in the uterus or shortly after birth. This is because the virus's target cells in the heart have reduced their rapid rate of division by the time pups are about 2 weeks of age; myocardial injury thus is produced only if CPV-2 infection occurs before this time.

Myocarditis occurs mainly in pups from nonimmune bitches. Evidence suggests that infection usually takes place during the last week or so of gestation. Following this there is systemic spread of the virus from the bitch to the fetuses or newborns. Clinical signs of heart failure usually are delayed until pups are at least 3 to 8 weeks of age. Today, outbreaks of acute parvoviral myocarditis are relatively rare owing to the fact that most bitches of breeding age now are immune to CPV-2 infection, either through past natural infection or routine vaccination.

Clinical Signs

Clinical signs of CPV-2 infection are most severe in pups 6 to 14 weeks of age. In this age group the mortality rate, even if pups receive veterinary attention, can approach 20%. Although the disease course tends to be milder in older animals, fatal infections nevertheless have been observed in dogs of all ages. Clinical disease in general is less frequently observed in older animals.

Canine parvovirus infection may be difficult to differentiate from a severe coronavirus infection (*see* "OTHER CANINE VIRUS INFECTIONS," BELOW). Dual infections with both viruses may occur in up to 20% of cases. Most of the severe cases of CPV-2 infection have been recorded in kennels, pet stores, animal shelters and the so-called puppy mills. The disease is less frequently seen in the more general pet population.

Peracute (extremely rapid-onset) parvovirus enteritis exhibits some clinical similarities to feline parvovirus infection (feline panleukopenia). Pups first exhibit **colic** (abdominal pain), depression and lethargy, then proceed rapidly into shock and die before other clinical signs are evident. The **acute** (rapid-onset) form of the disease represents a far more common clinical presentation, however. The earliest signs often are fever, depression and colic. These are rapidly followed in most cases by vomiting and diarrhea. In milder cases the stool is semisolid, and there may be a slightly increased frequency of defecation. In more severe cases, the stool becomes watery and has a characteristically fetid odor. The most severe cases exhibit a bloody diarrhea (**hemorrhagic enteritis**). Shock caused by fluid and electrolyte (electrically charged substances in the circulatory system) loss in the diarrheic feces is a serious and life-threatening complication.

These severe forms of parvovirus enteritis have gradually become less common as the canine population has become more immune. A chronic (1 to 2 weeks) diarrheal form of the disease is now being diagnosed with increasing frequency in dogs having some prior immunity to CPV-2. This form is much more easily managed and usually not fatal if supportive care is delivered promptly.

As indicated previously, sudden death in pups from acute or chronic heart failure secondary to parvovirus-induced myocarditis has been a complicating factor of CPV-2 infection. When parvovirus myocarditis occurs, up to 80% of an individual litter may be involved. Just prior to death pups often exhibit inactivity, coughing, crying, respiratory distress, foaming at the nostrils and mouth, retching and, in some cases, convulsions. Sometimes the slightest stress is sufficient to precipitate a fatal crisis. Some pups are found dead without having exhibited any recognizable signs at all. Fortunately, for both dogs and dog owners, parvovirus myocarditis is a much less common problem today.

DIAGNOSIS

A presumptive diagnosis of canine parvoviral enteritis can be made by the veterinarian on the basis of the history, clinical signs, and the results of supportive laboratory tests, the most important of which is the stool test for detection of CPV-2 excreted in feces. Several methods are available for identifying the virus in fecal samples, including the *ELISA* and *hemagglutination* tests and *electron microscopy*. Samples for testing often must be submitted to a diagnostic laboratory, although some "in-house" test kits for use in veterinary hospitals have become available in recent years. These tests all exploit the observation that massive numbers of virus particles are shed in stool samples during the acute phase of illness. In consequence, testing for CPV-2 antibodies (which are widespread in the canine population) and detection of depressed white blood cell counts (which are found in only about a third of the cases, as well as in **enteric** [pertaining to the small intestine] diseases due to causes other than parvovirus) are of significantly less value in making an accurate clinical diagnosis. (*See* APPENDIX C, "DIAGNOSTIC TESTS.")

TREATMENT

There is no specific antiviral therapy for CPV-2 infection. Instead, veterinary care is aimed at preventing dehydration and secondary bacterial infections (pneumonia, **septicemia** [presence of bacteria in the bloodstream, with associated clinical signs]). The primary objective is to stabilize the patient until the normal immune defenses can clear the infection and initiate a recovery. Fluid and electrolyte solutions and to a certain extent **parenteral** (injectable) antibiotics thus have become mainstays of therapy. All food should be withheld for at least 24 to 48 hours to allow the intestinal tract time to rest. Both food and water should be withheld if bouts of severe vomiting or retching are evident. Once signs of enteritis have subsided food can be slowly reintroduced. A bland diet consisting of cottage cheese and rice or one of several commercially available prescription diets, given in multiple small feedings, is excellent for this purpose. As the patient improves over the succeeding several days the normal diet may be gradually reinstated **ad libitum** (at the animal's choice).

One cannot overemphasize the importance of fluid therapy, either oral or by injection, in the treatment regimen for parvovirus enteritis. It is the massive fluid and electrolyte loss that can occur in diarrheic stool, more than any other single factor, that is most contributory to an unfavorable outcome. Dehydration of the patient must be prevented at all costs if a successful recovery is to be achieved.

PREVENTION

Dogs that have recovered from CPV-2 infection acquire a solid and long-lived immunity. Apart from such natural infection, **active immunization** (vaccination) using any of several commercially produced vaccines is the most practical and efficient means for preventing parvovirus enteritis. Of the several different vaccine types available, modified-live CPV-2 vaccines seem to provide the most effective barrier against infection and disease. Annual boosters are usually recommended.

Residual **maternal immunity** (antibodies derived from the mother's colostrum and milk) can have a profound interfering effect on vaccination against canine parvovirus (this is particularly true for killed virus vaccines, less so for modified-live). If pups are vaccinated at too young an age, when their levels of maternal antibody are still significant, the antibody may "soak up" the vaccine virus and so prevent the pups from developing their own active immune response (a common cause of so-called vaccine failures). In general, the higher the antibody titer (level) in the bitch when the pups are born, the higher the titer subsequently transmitted to the pups and the longer it will take for that titer to fall sufficiently to permit effective vaccination. As a complicating factor, low levels of maternal antibody *insufficient to prevent infection* should the pup be exposed to CPV-2 *may still interfere with active immunization.* Thus, as maternal titers in pups fall over the first few months of life, a transient "window of opportunity" opens up during which pups are susceptible to natural parvovirus infection, but yet are incapable of responding to vaccination. (*See* CHAPTER 33, "THE IMMUNE SYSTEM AND DISORDERS.")

Once infection with CPV-2 has occurred in a kennel or household, the virus may persist for months or even years. The extraordinary resistance of CPV-2 to environmental inactivation necessitates thorough cleansing and disinfection of kennels and runs before the introduction of new dogs. It is recommended that the premises first be washed down thoroughly with hot soap and water to remove organic debris, and then disinfected with a 1:32 dilution of chlorine bleach to destroy residual virus. Kennels should be designed so that each run can be hosed down without contaminating the adjacent runs. Animals from one household should not be mixed with dogs from other areas, if possible. Newly acquired pups and adult dogs should be current on parvovirus vaccinations before they are introduced to a kennel or household where CPV-2 infection has occurred.

Canine Infectious Tracheobronchitis ("Kennel Cough")

Acute **tracheobronchitis** (inflammation of the **larynx** [upper throat], **trachea** [tube from larynx to bronchi], and **bronchi** [tubes leading to each lung]), known colloquially as "kennel cough," has been recognized in dogs for many years. It was not until the late 1960s, however, that the multifactorial cause of the disease began to be appreciated.

THE CAUSE

Kennel cough is a disease of multifactorial origin; that is, a virtually identical clinical syndrome can be produced by several different infectious disease agents, either alone or in various combinations. Among the agents involved are the following, the most common being listed first:

Bordetella bronchiseptica, which is believed to represent the most important disease agent in the kennel cough complex. This bacterium can cause a highly severe tracheobronchitis in and of itself without the assistance of other microorganisms.

Canine parainfluenza virus (CPIV), a member of the Paramyxoviridae (RNA viruses with outer envelopes), the virus family to which canine distemper virus also belongs. Canine parainfluenza virus is frequently isolated from cases of upper respiratory disease in dogs. It can produce a mild to moderately severe tracheobronchitis.

Canine adenovirus-2, which can produce severe tracheobronchitis, with about 10–20% of affected dogs also developing a pneumonia.

Mycoplasmas are microorganisms closely related to bacteria and are ubiquitous inhabitants of the respiratory and genital tracts of dogs. They appear to contribute to some extent to the total disease syndrome in kennel cough. Under rare circumstances some mycoplasmas (such as *Mycoplasma cynos*) may also initiate respiratory tract disease themselves.

Canine distemper virus, which more often produces a more severe and systemic illness. The initial stages of distemper may be difficult to distinguish from kennel cough.

Canine herpesvirus, a DNA virus, which produces a mild to inapparent respiratory tract infection. It has been associated with more severe tracheobronchitis in a few outbreaks.

Pasteurella multocida, a frequent bacterial inhabitant of the upper respiratory tract.

Many of the respiratory viruses, particularly CPIV, can cause rapid and sometimes complete denudation of the **cilia** (hairlike projections) lining much of the upper respiratory tract. These minute, hairlike cellular processes generate rhythmic beating movements by which, in concert with the overlying layer of mucus, they effect the removal of debris and other foreign material from the respiratory tract. Damage to ciliary cells severely limits the host's ability to clear irritants from the respiratory tract, allowing resident bacteria and other microorganisms to descend into deeper regions of the tract (bronchi, bronchioles, lungs). Certain insidious organisms, such as *Bordetella bronchiseptica* and *Mycoplasma cynos,* can actually attach themselves to the respiratory cilia and thus escape clearance by the normal removal mechanism.

OCCURRENCE AND TRANSMISSION

Kennel cough is a highly contagious disease and occurs worldwide wherever dogs are allowed to congregate. Clinical illness often follows boarding, showing, or sometimes field trials. In kennel situations (the most common occurrence), dogs not only are being subjected to stress, owing to the unfamiliar environment, but simultaneously are being placed in close proximity to other dogs, some of which may either be actively exhibiting respiratory disease or acting as asymptomatic carriers of one or more kennel cough agents. Kennels are often poorly ventilated, and this, along with the high density of crowding and other stresses, can lead to severe respiratory infections; exposures of such magnitude and duration may simply overwhelm whatever weak immunity a dog may have. Moreover, the stresses of kenneling may temporarily depress immune system function, enhancing susceptibility to new viral or bacterial infections or allowing for the activation of preexisting infections.

PATHOGENESIS

Clinically ill or asymptomatic carrier animals will excrete kennel cough disease agents in oronasal secretions and aerosol droplets, an efficient mechanism for transmission to other dogs in close vicinity. Following an incubation period of 4 to 6 days, an acute tracheobronchitis with its peculiar, high-pitched "honking" cough develops in susceptible, exposed animals. The major viruses and *Bordetella bronchiseptica* are particularly important for initiating this first phase of the disease. Some dogs will recover from the acute phase in a week or two, while others may develop secondary bacterial or mycoplasmal infections that can produce a chronic, low-grade tracheobronchitis lasting for many weeks. It is this latter chronic phase of illness, with its seemingly endless bouts of harsh coughing, that has given kennel cough its particularly unpleasant reputation among breeders and owners.

The immunity that occurs following infection with these respiratory agents is a local phenomenon, due primarily to IgA (a specific antibody; *see* CHAPTER 33, "THE IMMUNE SYSTEM AND DISEASES.") Systemic antibodies may prevent spread of the infection to the rest of the body, but it is local immunity on the surfaces of the respiratory tract that actually contains infection and prevents recurrence. Following recovery, small numbers of disease agents may persist on the mucous membranes for weeks, months, or even indefinitely. Local immunity is notoriously short-lived (6 months or less in many cases), and it has no "memory" (i.e., once local immunity wanes, infection with the same disease agent again can result in another bout of disease, rather than protection). Although reinfection can occur it is seldom as severe, however, as the initial disease.

CLINICAL SIGNS

Clinical signs of kennel cough may vary somewhat, depending upon the disease agents involved in each particular case. The following, therefore, is a general clinical picture, and not necessarily reflective of the extremes of the disease.

About 4 to 6 days after exposure an infected dog begins to cough. Fever, ocular and nasal discharges, lethargy, malaise, or inappetence are usually *not* seen. When they are evident, however, the disease may superficially resemble early canine distemper. In the beginning stages (first several days) the cough may be moist and productive, with a white foam exuding from the margins of the mouth. The tonsils and **oropharynx** (back of the throat) may be reddened from inflammation and layered with foam. Within

several days the cough becomes dry, harsh and "honking" (this probably due to laryngitis and swelling of the vocal folds). This is the characteristic sign of "classical" kennel cough. The cough is not very productive at this stage, and often occurs in **paroxysms** (sudden bouts) that end in a long, drawn-out gag or retch. Coughing can easily be induced by excitement, drinking water, or by digital pressure on the trachea. The cough usually persists for 1 to 2 weeks, but in some cases may continue at a chronic low level for as many as 5 or 6 weeks, severely testing an owner's chronic annoyance level.

DIAGNOSIS

The diagnosis is made on the basis of the history (evidence of recent kenneling or other exposure to strange dogs) and clinical signs, particularly the characteristic honking cough. Very few laboratory findings will be abnormal in uncomplicated cases of kennel cough. Isolation of *Bordetella bronchiseptica* from the respiratory tract may be attempted in order to confirm the presence of this major member of the kennel cough complex.

TREATMENT

Treatment of kennel cough is both specific and supportive. Enforced rest and avoidance of stressful, cough-inducing situations (i.e., leash-walking) are important during the first few weeks of illness. Specific and supportive treatment measures may include one or more of the following:

• antibiotics in cases with lung involvement or secondary bacterial infections
• cough suppressants (**antitussives**), to break the "cough/tracheal irritation/cough again" cycle
• **bronchodilators** (drugs to help widen clogged airways)
• glucocorticoid hormones, to aid in cough suppression by ameliorating inflammation
• aerosol therapy (**nebulization**), to help break up mucous secretions within the airways and to deliver antibiotics directly to the site of infection
• fluid therapy to maintain normal hydration, if required

PREVENTION

Immunization measures against kennel cough suffer from some of the same disadvantages as immunization against the "common cold": there are many different disease agents involved, the local IgA immunity to natural infection is often transient or incomplete, and many poorly defined "stress" factors apparently play a role in susceptibility to infection. Many different vaccines against the most important of the kennel cough agents (*Bordetella bronchiseptica*, CPIV, CAV-2), either alone or in combination, are currently available. Some of the products are for parenteral use (by injection) while others are designed for intranasal administration. Intranasal vaccines are aimed at stimulating local IgA immunity—the primary effector of protection against the kennel cough agents—within the upper respiratory tract. Annual or more frequent booster vaccinations are frequently recommended. Field experience with the various products suggests that:

- CPIV/CAV-2 vaccine decreases the incidence of kennel cough by about 25% or less
- *Bordetella bronchiseptica* intranasal vaccine reduces the incidence of kennel cough much more than CPIV/CAV-2 vaccine
- vaccines combining all three agents seem to provide greater protection than either CPIV/CAV-2 or *Bordetella bronchiseptica* vaccines alone

Cleansing of the environment to remove pathogenic viruses and bacteria is particularly important in kennel situations. Benzalkonium chloride, chlorhexidine, and chlorine bleach (diluted 1:32 in water) are all effective disinfectants for most of the important agents of kennel cough.

Neonatal Canine Herpesvirus Infection

Canine herpesvirus (CHV) is the cause of a "fading" or sudden-death syndrome in puppies, particularly those less than 3 or 4 weeks of age. The syndrome itself was known for many years before the actual discovery of the causative virus in the 1960s. Antibody (serologic) studies indicate that CHV infection is common in dog populations the world over.

THE CAUSE

Canine herpesvirus is an alpha-herpesvirus, just one of a large and diverse group of herpesviruses causing very important diseases in many species, including human beings. Herpes simplex virus (the cause of "cold sores"), Epstein-Barr virus (a cause of infectious mononucleosis), and cytomegalovirus (an important cause of birth defects) are among the herpesviruses of greatest significance in people. Herpesviruses contain DNA as their genetic material and have prominent outer envelopes, and so are inactivated by many common household soaps, detergents and disinfectants.

OCCURRENCE AND TRANSMISSION

Canine herpesvirus can be recovered from the respiratory and genital tracts of healthy adult dogs. The virus can persist for an indefinite period in a latent (dormant) form in the nasal mucous membranes and genital tract, even in the face of an active immune response. Such latent infections are a common characteristic of many herpesviruses. Subsequent shedding of virus can occur intermittently, often following a period of stress. Transmission occurs primarily by ingestion or inhalation. Newborn puppies can acquire infection during passage through the birth canal, from the oronasal secretions of the bitch, or from contact with infected siblings. Infection of the fetus *in utero* (in the uterus) is apparently a less common occurrence. The stress of late pregnancy and **parturition** (giving birth) may be in part responsible for reactivating a latent herpesvirus infection in the bitch (and thus causing an episode of virus shedding), or perhaps for accentuating a new, active infection. If the pups are born with an adequate supply of maternal immunity, they usually will be protected against the most severe effects of the virus.

PATHOGENESIS

Following infection, the virus replicates first in the tonsils and nasal cavity, then enters the bloodstream by being carried inside certain types of white blood cells. This cell-associated

viremia (virus in the blood) allows the virus to spread to other areas of the body over the next several days. In susceptible pups a second wave of virus replication then occurs in many target organs, including lymph nodes, spleen, kidneys, liver, lungs, gastrointestinal tract, adrenal glands and brain. In these sites the virus produces cell death and localized hemorrhaging. Hemorrhages may in part be caused by a drop in the numbers of blood **platelets** (cell fragments essential for blood clotting).

Body temperature and its regulation are important in the pathogenesis of infection. The optimal temperature range for replication of CHV is 35–36°C, with a dramatic inhibition of growth beyond either end of this narrow window. Although the core body temperature of the normal adult dog (38–39°C) exceeds this range, neonatal pups are not yet capable of properly controlled temperature regulation; that is, their body temperature frequently corresponds with that for the optimal growth of CHV. Moreover, certain protective mechanisms of the immune response are less active at lower body temperatures. Thus, temperature sensitivity most probably explains in large part the marked age-resistance of dogs to CHV disease.

Clinical Signs

In puppies over about 5 weeks of age, canine herpesvirus produces only a mild or inapparent respiratory tract infection. A mild **rhinitis** (inflammation of the nasal passages) occurs within 48 hours of infection and lasts from 4 to 8 days. Fever, malaise and inappetence usually are not apparent. Most severe cases occur in pups less than 3 to 4 weeks of age, with most fatalities restricted to those less than 1 to 2 weeks of age. In pups in this latter age group, the virus produces a severe and often fatal illness affecting many organ systems. The disease is characterized by the sudden death of apparently healthy pups after only a brief period of illness. Affected pups are depressed and lethargic, stop nursing, and pass a soft, odorless, yellow-green stool. They often cry persistently and exhibit abdominal pain and tenderness. There may be a nasal discharge and a rash on the belly. Neurologic signs may become prominent

prior to death. Animals surviving severe infection may exhibit residual neurologic abnormalities, such as blindness or **ataxia** (incoordination). At necropsy widespread hemorrhage and **necrosis** (cell death) are usually evident in many organs. Especially characteristic are the kidney hemorrhages, which appear grossly as multiple, bright red spots on a gray background of dying kidney tissue ("speckled kidneys").

Diagnosis

A presumptive diagnosis of canine herpesvirus infection in a group of neonates can be made based on the history, clinical findings, and characteristic pathologic alterations in necropsy tissues. In pups that survive, virus isolation and serology may be helpful in pinning down the diagnosis, should it remain in doubt. In older animals the infection may pass altogether unnoticed.

Treatment

Because of the rapidly fatal course of the disease, treatment of the most severely affected pups is often an exercise in futility. Moreover, pups that do survive frequently have residual lesions and all are chronically infected carriers of the virus. To date there is little evidence to support the notion that artificially raising the body temperature of affected pups (i.e., with heating pads, heat lamps, incubators, etc.) will in any way modify the disease course.

Prevention

Owing primarily to the sporadic nature of the disease, there has been relatively little medical or financial incentive to market a canine herpesvirus vaccine. Several experimental inactivated and modified-live virus vaccines have been developed in Europe and the United States, each exhibiting varying shades of efficacy. To date there is no available vaccine that appears to be universally protective.

Other Canine Virus Infections

Canine Viral Papillomatosis

Young dogs are occasionally troubled by a syndrome of multiple infectious **papillomas** (warts) that usually arise in the mouth, but may occur also on the cornea, conjunctiva, eyelids or skin. Multiple canine papillomas are benign tumors of the upper skin layers and are caused by *papillomaviruses,* members of the Papovaviridae family of double-stranded DNA viruses. Oral papillomas often are found in large numbers in proliferative patches or bunches along the surface of the gums, palate, lips and lip margins. Transmission of papillomaviruses from dog to dog occurs probably by means of direct contact.

Diagnosis is based on the history and clinical findings, most importantly on the physical appearance of the tumors themselves. Most infectious papillomas, particularly those affecting the mouth, spontaneously regress without treatment within several months of appearance. They can, however, be surgically removed in order to relieve patient discomfort or because of their unsightly appearance. Surgery, **electrosurgery** (cauterization) or **cryosurgery** (freezing) may be used, depending on the tumor site(s), number of tumors present and the clinical expertise of the consulting veterinarian. Treatment is often discouraged if only a few tumors are present. The prognosis in virtually all cases is good to excellent. "Wart vaccines," often recommended in the past, are probably of questionable value in preventing papillomavirus infection and disease in dogs.

Canine Coronavirus Enteritis

Coronaviruses are enveloped RNA viruses that can be isolated from a wide variety of animals in nature. Coronavirus infections are characterized in general by mild to moderately severe respiratory or gastrointestinal disease signs. One exception is the feline infectious peritonitis virus (FIPV), which causes a multisystemic, highly fatal immune-mediated disease in cats (*see* THE CORNELL BOOK OF CATS, CHAPTER 29).

Canine coronavirus (CCV) was first isolated in Germany from an outbreak of diarrheal disease in military dogs. The significance of CCV infections was not widely appreciated until 1978, however, when outbreaks of CCV-associated diarrhea were diagnosed concurrent with the discovery of canine parvovirus enteritis. Dogs of all ages and breeds are susceptible to infection, as are coyotes. Infection is acquired primarily by ingestion of virus following direct contact with infected animals or their feces.

Infections range in severity from inapparent to fatal, the latter being extremely uncommon. Younger animals are more severely affected. Clinical signs may include inappetence, malaise, vomiting, diarrhea and dehydration. There may be mucus or blood in the feces. Stools are loose, often yellow-orange in color, and characteristically fetid. In most instances, recovery without treatment usually occurs within 7 to 10 days. Occasionally, the diarrhea may persist for several weeks.

A tentative diagnosis in most cases is made on the basis of the history, clinical signs, and sometimes by identification of coronavirus particles in stool samples by electron microscopy. Mixed infections with other agents (such as canine parvovirus type 2) must be considered as well. Treatment is purely supportive in nature and should be directed at the control of vomiting and fluid loss from diarrhea in severely affected pups. A vaccine is available. Because asymptomatic CCV infections appear to be very common, however, vaccines may have limited utility and the cost and risk of vaccination may outweigh other potential benefits.

Canine Rotavirus Enteritis

Rotaviruses are members of the Reoviridae family of viruses and contain several segments of double-stranded RNA as their genetic material. The name *rotavirus* is derived from the "spoked-wheel" appearance of the viral particles, which are non-enveloped but surrounded by a unique double-layered capsid that provides significant protection against environmental inactivation. Rotaviruses are causative agents of diarrheal disease in many species, including dogs, cats, cattle, pigs, horses, sheep, mice, antelope, monkeys and human beings.

Rotaviruses cause disease in animals and humans of any age, although disease is most common and most severe in the young, particularly in the immediate post-weaning period. In dogs, canine rotavirus can produce diarrhea and dehydration in very young pups (those less than about 2 weeks of age). Most natural infections appear to be mild or completely asymptomatic, however. There are no good diagnostic tools currently available for diagnosis of canine rotavirus infections, but all information thus far suggests that rotavirus is a relatively insignificant pathogen in dogs. Treatment measures for affected pups are purely symptomatic and similar to those for parvovirus and coronavirus infections.

PSEUDORABIES

Pseudorabies, also known as *Aujeszky's disease* or *mad itch,* is a disease primarily of pigs and is caused by an alpha-herpesvirus (enveloped DNA virus). Most mammals, except for human beings and certain apes, are susceptible to pseudorabies virus infection. The virus is distributed worldwide in the swine population, which represents the primary reservoir of infection. Infections in swine are usually asymptomatic, but are often fatal in other susceptible species, including the dog. Dogs in rural areas near swine-production facilities are at greater risk of developing pseudorabies. Fortunately, cases of pseudorabies in dogs (and cats) are of only sporadic occurrence.

Dogs acquire pseudorabies virus infection by ingesting material contaminated with the virus, most often raw pork scraps. The virus enters sensory nerve endings in the oral cavity or tonsils and travels up the nerve bodies to the brain, in a manner similar to that for rabies virus. The course of the disease is short, often lasting only 2 or 3 days, and the outcome invariably fatal. Infected dogs usually exhibit behavioral changes, a growing uneasiness, drooling, respiratory difficulties, and an intense **pruritus** (itching) that affects primarily the head and ears. Affected dogs will scratch madly at their muzzle and ears, the degree of irritation often leading to self-mutilation. They may shake their heads and rub them against hard surfaces such as the floor or walls. Occasionally signs of pruritus are completely absent, with lethargy and depression being the predominant clinical signs. Death occurs following paresis, paralysis or coma.

Diagnosis in the living animal is made most commonly by an evaluation of the history and clinical signs. After death a definitive diagnosis may be made by identification of the causative virus in tissues such as the brain and tonsils.

There is no effective treatment for pseudorabies in dogs. Trials of pseudorabies virus vaccines for use in dogs have been reported, but at present there is no commercially available product. Avoidance of feeding raw pork scraps or related offal (waste from butchering) to dogs remains the most effective means of prevention.

CANINE CALICIVIRUSES

Caliciviruses are small, non-enveloped RNA viruses with a characteristic "soccer-ball" appearance and are moderately resistant to environmental conditions. There are a few reports of caliciviruses recovered from dogs with enteric disease and from both male and female dogs with **vesicular** (blistering) lesions of the genitalia. Although caliciviruses are well known for the diseases they produce in cats, pigs and seals, to date their importance as pathogenic agents in dogs remains ill-defined.

CANINE ASTROVIRUS

Astroviruses are a cause of diarrhea of the young of several animal species. Astroviruses or astroviruslike particles have been identified in feces of both healthy and diarrheic dogs. Whether astroviruses are an actual cause of diarrhea in dogs, however, has not been ascertained.

CANINE RETROVIRUSES

Several reports over the years have suggested that one or more retroviruses (enveloped RNA viruses) associated with certain cancers may be present in the canine population. Retroviruslike particles have been described in several cases of **lymphosarcoma** and lymphocytic leukemia (both cancers of the lymphoid system). To date, however, the role, if any, of such viruses in canine tumor development remains undetermined.

CHAPTER 35

Bacterial Diseases

by Jeffrey E. Barlough and Niels C. Pedersen

Bacteria are a diverse group of single-celled microorganisms whose family tree can be traced back to the very roots of life on earth. These minute, versatile microbes surround us in our everyday lives—living not only in our environment but living also on us and even inside us—and yet remain essentially invisible to the unaided human eye. Bacteria (singular: bacterium) are complex, sophisticated, metabolizing, self-reproducing, living organisms, and thus are quite unlike the inanimate, particulate, **subcellular** (smaller than cells) biochemical entities known as viruses (*see* CHAPTER 34, "VIRAL DISEASES"). Moreover, bacteria contain both types of nucleic acid, both **deoxyribonucleic acid (DNA)** and **ribonucleic acid (RNA)**, whereas a typical virus contains only one or the other. Bacterial cells are surrounded by a cell wall and have a central nucleus that lacks a delimiting membrane. Most bacteria multiply by **binary fission**—that is, the parental cell dividing into two approximately equal daughter cells.

Taxonomic classifications for bacteria are identified primarily by the genus, whose first letter is capitalized, followed by the species which

is entirely in lowercase. Both are always in italics. After the bacterium is named formally, it is thereafter identified by the initial of the genus and the species name.

Many bacteria exist as free-living inhabitants of the biosphere and through their multifarious biochemical activities are instrumental in maintaining local and global ecosystems. Other bacteria occur on the skin and in the digestive and reproductive tracts of higher organisms, where they often exist in harmonious balance with the host, from whom they derive nourishment and for whom they often provide a beneficial presence. One example of this is the large intestine's extensive and rather heterogeneous population of bacteria (its "normal flora"), which aid the digestive processes of the host and also synthesize certain important vitamins. On occasion, if provided with the proper conditions, many of these otherwise harmless bacteria can gain access to the deeper, normally sterile tissues of the host and produce disease.

Another large and somewhat specialized group of bacteria can be classified as true **pathogens**—agents of disease. These are bacteria that for the most part have a much greater potential for harming the host; they are able to colonize tissue and for some period of time can evade the host's immune defenses. In many cases they are not part of the normal bacterial flora and if present are almost always associated with a disease process. These organisms are the primary bacterial disease agents of importance to veterinarians, their clients and their canine patients.

The **rickettsiae** represent a group of specialized bacteria that differ from more "conventional" bacteria in a number of important features. Rickettsiae multiply only within host cells (being somewhat virus-like in this requirement), and usually are transmitted to animals and human beings by lice, ticks, fleas or mites. Some examples of rickettsial pathogens include *Rickettsia rickettsii,* the cause of Rocky Mountain spotted fever; *Ehrlichia canis,* the cause of tropical canine pancytopenia (canine ehrlichiosis); *Ehrlichia platys,* the cause of infectious cyclic thrombocytopenia; and *Neorickettsia helminthoeca,* the cause of salmon disease.

Included among the many bacterial diseases are a broad spectrum of infections that may develop at any time in a dog's life. During the neonatal period pups receive their initial exposure to the bacterial population of their immediate environment. Should the maternal immunity the pups received in their mother's colostrum and milk prove insufficient, or should the pups be exposed to a pathogen during the time that maternal immunity is waning but before their own immune defenses are fully operational, serious infections may occur. In later years some bacterial infections may be promoted, at least in part, by **immunosuppression,** (i.e., by a compromised immune system). Certain drugs, inherited tendencies, or viruses (an example being canine distemper virus) can to one degree or another interfere with the normal functional mechanisms of the immune response and predispose the host to bacterial infection.

Fortunately, many bacteria are sensitive to the action of substances known generically as **antibiotics.** As a guiding definition, antibiotics are chemical substances that are produced by microorganisms and that are capable of inhibit-

ing or killing other microorganisms. Antibiotics thus are actually a form of defense that some microbes use to protect themselves from other microbes! Although microbial cultures represent important sources of antibiotics, many of today's front-line products are chemically synthesized in the laboratory, or are chemically modified from antibiotics obtained from laboratory cultures.

Antibiotics act in a number of ways, either by killing bacteria directly or by inhibiting their multiplication. Some antibiotics act by targeting essential metabolic reactions of bacteria, while others interfere with the chemical synthesis of important constituents of the bacterial cell wall. Antibiotics in common use in canine medicine today include penicillin, ampicillin, amikacin, cephalexin, chloramphenicol, gentamicin, kanamycin and the tetracyclines.

Unfortunately, resistance to antibiotics has arisen among many bacterial species. The survival of antibiotic-resistant bacteria through Darwinian modes of *natural selection* has been enhanced by the use of antibiotics—the antibiotics "selecting" for those bacteria able to survive in their presence, by suppressing or killing their antibiotic-sensitive rivals and allowing the resistant strains to flourish. Control of antibiotic resistance among bacteria is dependent upon two important elements: the identification of new and unique antimicrobial substances to overcome resistance; and greater restraint in the clinical use of available antibiotics to preclude the development of new resistant strains.

Leptospirosis

Leptospirosis is a **zoonotic disease** (disease transmissible from animals to human beings) that is worldwide in occurrence. The causative bacteria, known generically as **leptospires,** are maintained in nature in a number of wild and domestic animal reservoir hosts. Leptospires are classified as **spirochetes** (filamentous, spiral-shaped bacteria) and are carried and shed in the urine of healthy reservoir hosts. Animals that have recovered from leptospirosis often continue to excrete the organisms in urine for periods of months to years. Leptospires are not long-lived outside the body except under circumstances of ideal temperature and humidity. They frequently contaminate water supplies where livestock and wild rodents tend to congregate. Susceptible animals acquire the infection most often by direct contact with infected carriers or by ingesting organisms suspended in water contaminated with urine.

Leptospira canicola (*L. canicola*) is the most common leptospire causing leptospirosis in dogs, which are the main reservoir host for this particular **serovar** (variant or subspecies of leptospire). The majority of *Leptospira* infections of dogs are clinically inapparent—i.e., no clinical signs are produced or the signs are so mild that they pass unnoticed by the pet owner. When disease occurs, *L. canicola* infection most often produces an acute **nephritis** (kidney inflammation) without lasting kidney damage; less commonly, it is associated with a more generalized, systemic illness. *Leptospira icterohaemorrhagiae* (reservoir host: rats) is a less frequent cause of canine leptospirosis, and is usually associated with a serious, generalized, hemorrhagic (bleeding) illness that also involves the liver and kidneys. *Leptospira pomona* is primarily a pathogen of large animal species (cattle, pigs) but nevertheless can cause a severe nephritis in dogs. Canine *L. pomona* infections occur more often in farm dogs, and often in warm rainy weather when pastures are dotted with pools of freestanding water contaminated with cattle urine. Other *Leptospira* serovars reported to cause canine leptospirosis include *L. grippotyphosa* (reservoir host: voles [small rodents]) and *L. bataviae* (reservoir hosts: rats, mice, dogs).

The most common manifestation of leptospirosis in dogs is a localized kidney disease. Male dogs tend to be affected more often than females. Dogs may exhibit signs of mild to moderate malaise and depression, a low-grade fever, vomiting, and **hyperemia** (reddening) of the mucous membranes and conjunctiva. The blood urea nitrogen (BUN), a measure of kidney function, is moderately elevated, and there may be a **leukocytosis** (elevated numbers of circulating white blood cells). In cases of more generalized disease, other signs of pneumonia, **hepatitis** (liver inflammation) or **enteritis** (intestinal

inflammation) may be evident. Liver enzymes may be elevated, there may be **jaundice** (yellowish discoloration of the mucous membranes), and the blood platelet (clotting cell) count may be depressed.

Complications of leptospirosis include a more chronic, progressive form of kidney disease (**chronic interstitial nephritis**), which may follow one or more mild attacks of primary nephritis, or may occur in dogs improperly or insufficiently treated for the initial infection.

Diagnosis is based on the history, physical examination, and results of supportive laboratory tests. Laboratory evidence of kidney disease with or without concurrent signs of liver damage may be found. In dogs infected with *L. icterohaemorrhagiae,* blood-clotting abnormalities together with **thrombocytopenia** (decreased numbers of circulating blood platelets) may be evident. Serum from a suspect case may be submitted to a diagnostic laboratory for the **microscopic agglutination test (MAT),** a standard serologic assay for the detection of antibodies to leptospires. A **serologic** (antigen-antibody) diagnosis of leptospirosis in a dog exhibiting suspicious clinical signs can be made by demonstrating a fourfold or greater increase in antibody **titers** (levels) in paired serum samples, one taken at the time of active disease and the second approximately 2 to 4 weeks later. Isolation of the causative leptospires from blood, urine, or tissue (liver, kidney) may be attempted in cases where the diagnosis is difficult to achieve by other means.

Supportive care of dogs with leptospirosis involves replenishment of fluid and electrolyte loss (from vomiting and diarrhea) and the prevention of shock and complications of kidney or liver dysfunction. The presence of mucous membrane or skin hemorrhages, or other indications of blood loss or clotting abnormalities, may necessitate a transfusion with fresh whole blood. **Diuretics** (drugs promoting urination) may be required to treat the early stages of kidney failure. The antibiotic penicillin should be administered immediately to inhibit the leptospires and thus prevent further kidney or liver damage. Antibiotic therapy (penicillin together with dihydrostreptomycin) should be maintained for at least several weeks following the reinstitution of normal kidney function, in order to eliminate remaining leptospires.

Leptospire **bacterins** (inactivated bacterial vaccines) containing primarily serovars *L. canicola* and *L. icterohaemorrhagiae* are available in combination vaccine products for use in dogs. These products are effective in reducing the occurrence and severity of leptospiral disease *but they do not prevent infection;* that is, vaccinated dogs may still acquire and shed leptospires. Moreover, the duration of protection following vaccination is probably no more than about 6 months. Immunity to leptospires is also serovar-specific; hence, the commercial bacterins will not protect against serovars other than those included in the individual product. Given these and other considerations, it is clear that more inclusive and more highly effective leptospiral vaccines for use in dogs are needed.

Owners of clinically affected dogs should be cognizant of the fact that leptospirosis is a disease of public health significance and that the leptospires excreted in the urine of an infected dog represent a potential health hazard for human beings. Human infections with *Leptospira* can be severe and may persist for a lengthy period of time. Thus, owners must be especially cautious and observe strict hygienic measures while caring for any pet suffering from leptospirosis. Fortunately, leptospirosis today is a relative uncommon problem in dogs. (*See* Appendix A, "Zoonotic Diseases: From Dogs to People.")

Salmonellosis

Salmonellosis is a primarily diarrheal disease caused by members of the genus *Salmonella.* These bacteria, representing nearly *2 thousand* different member types, are ubiquitous in the environment and infect a wide variety of wild and domestic host species. Infection is usually acquired by ingestion of food or water contaminated by *Salmonella*-laden feces. Healthy carriers of *Salmonella* as well as clinically affected animals or people can serve as sources of infection.

The vast majority of infections in dogs are inapparent. The development of overt disease is probably dependent upon a number of factors, including dose and strain of the infecting bacterium, immune competence of the host, concurrent infections, and long-term antibiotic therapy (which may suppress much of the normal intestinal flora and allow *Salmonella* to thrive).

The most common clinical signs observed in infected dogs include inappetence, lethargy, fever, weight loss, vomiting, colic and a watery to bloody diarrhea. Many strains of *Salmonella* have the potential for invading deeper tissues of the body and producing serious systemic illness. Clinical signs of severe systemic salmonellosis often are related to the sudden onset of shock or central nervous system dysfunction.

Diagnosis is made on the basis of the history, clinical signs, and identification of the causative bacterium. Isolation of a *Salmonella* from the feces of a dog exhibiting signs of diarrheal disease often suggests, but may not prove, that the organism is responsible for the illness, because it is always possible that its presence is coincidental. In severe systemic illness, however, recovery of a *Salmonella* from a normally sterile body fluid or tissue, such as the blood, is usually considered diagnostic for salmonellosis.

Treatment of uncomplicated salmonellosis should be directed at minimizing fluid and electrolyte loss resulting from chronic diarrhea.

Good nursing and supportive care are essential for a complete recovery. In order to minimize possible selection for a more aggressive, antibiotic-resistant *Salmonella* (and also to avoid killing many of the normal intestinal bacteria that act as a shield against more harmful microorganisms), antibiotics should *not* be administered unless it is evident that the organisms have spread beyond the intestinal tract and are producing severe, life-threatening systemic illness.

Owners of clinically affected dogs should be aware that salmonellosis is a zoonotic disease and that the organisms excreted in the feces of an infected dog represent a potential health hazard for human beings. Salmonellosis today is a disease of great public health significance. Human infections with *Salmonella* can be particularly severe and in some cases may persist for many months. Thus, owners must be especially cautious and observe strict hygienic measures while caring for any pet suffering from salmonellosis. Hands should be washed often, especially after handling the ill animal, its food dishes or toys, or other possibly contaminated materials. Disinfectants such as chlorine bleach (diluted 1:32 in water) should be used to wash floors or other surfaces where the affected dog may eat or sleep. Food and water bowls should be cleaned as often as possible. Young children, older adults and individuals taking an **immunosuppressive medication** (such as a corticosteroid) or antibiotics should be kept away from the affected dog, especially for the first few weeks after infection, until the numbers of bacteria excreted in the feces have declined. Should any individual in the household develop diarrhea, severe abdominal pain (**colic**), and fever, the family physician should be consulted immediately and the possibility of salmonellosis presented. It is recommended that the physician contact the attending veterinarian for specific details about the case and the particular *Salmonella* involved. (*See* APPENDIX A, "ZOONOTIC DISEASES: FROM DOGS TO PEOPLE.")

Enteric Campylobacteriosis

Enteric campylobacteriosis is a diarrheal disease caused by members of the genus *Campylobacter.* These bacteria are widespread in the environment and in animal and human populations, and are considered part of the normal flora of the intestinal tract in many species. Many infected animals thus act as healthy carriers, excreting the bacteria in their feces. Although campylobacteriosis is rare in dogs, in human beings it is considered one of the major bacterial causes of infectious diarrhea. Individuals acquire infection in any of several ways: direct contact with a carrier animal; contact with contaminated fecal matter; contact with contaminated food, water or inanimate objects; or contact with human carriers. Major food sources of human infection include poultry, pork and milk. (*See* APPENDIX A, "ZOONOTIC DISEASES: FROM DOGS TO PEOPLE.")

The most common *Campylobacter* causing disease in dogs is *Campylobacter jejuni* (*C.*

jejuni). Fecal contamination of food or water is the usual means of spread. Most infections in adult dogs are very mild or completely **asymptomatic** (without clinical signs). Overt disease usually occurs only in young pups, probably because they have not been previously exposed and lack protective immune responses. Clinical signs in pups can include fever, partial inappetence and watery stools covered with mucus. The disease is normally self-limiting, the diarrhea lasting for 1 to 2 weeks before spontaneously resolving.

Diagnosis is made by an evaluation of the history and clinical signs, and by identification of the causative bacterium, either by direct microscopic examination of the feces or by culture of the organism from fecal or rectal swabs.

Most mild cases of campylobacteriosis in dogs are self-limiting and thus do not require treatment. Others, however, may require symptomatic therapy to guard against excessive fluid loss resulting from the diarrhea. Antibiotic therapy probably is not warranted unless the clinical signs are unusually severe, or unless there is some indication of spread of the organisms beyond the intestinal tract.

Enteric campylobacteriosis is a zoonotic disease and thus *C. jejuni* shed in the feces of infected dogs represents a potential health hazard for human contacts. Human infections with *C. jejuni* can result in severe gastrointestinal illness characterized by vomiting, diarrhea, abdominal cramping and fever. Owners of clinically affected dogs thus need to observe strict hygienic measures while caring for their pets. (*See* "SALMONELLOSIS," ABOVE, for more details on hygienic precautions.)

Streptococcal Infections

Streptococcal bacteria often are involved in causing local or generalized **pyogenic** (pus-forming) infections in dogs. They may act alone or in concert with other bacteria in mixed bacterial infections. Streptococci are frequently classified into several major groups (designated A, B, C, D, E, G, L, and M), based on differences in the sugar components of their cell walls.

People are the usual reservoir hosts for *group*

A streptococci, which cause a number of significant human diseases such as scarlet fever, rheumatic fever, diplococcal pneumonia, tonsillitis and "strep throat." The organisms are normally carried in the tonsils and **pharynx** (area extending from the rear of the mouth and nasal passages to the larynx and esophagus), from which locations they can be readily transmitted in oral and respiratory secretions. Some individuals are chronic carriers of group A streptococci, harboring them for long periods in the absence of any clinical signs and serving as a constant source of infection for others. The greatest percentage of group A infections occurs in young children.

In recent years it has been found that both dogs and cats are susceptible to transient infection with group A streptococci acquired from their human contacts. Infected animals exhibit no clinical signs and if separated from the source of infection will clear the organisms in a few weeks. Before clearance, however, the animals represent a potential source of infection for human beings. Thus, it is important when treating individuals in a household for group A streptococcal infection that any pet dogs or cats in the household receive treatment as well.

Group B and *group C* streptococci have been reported to cause disease only sporadically in dogs. Disease signs can include **septicemia** (bacteria in the bloodstream, accompanied by systemic illness), kidney disease, pneumonia, genital tract disorders, and neonatal death ("fading puppies"). Group C streptococci have also been associated with a specific septicemia/pneumonia syndrome in racing Greyhounds. *Group G* streptococci comprise a significant portion of the normal bacterial flora of canine skin and superficial mucous membranes, but if given the opportunity can cause a variety of disease conditions, including abscesses and other skin infections, **polyarthritis** (inflammation occurring simultaneously in several joints), **mastitis** (inflammation of one or more mammary glands), and neonatal death.

Diagnosis of streptococcal infections is made on the basis of the history, clinical signs, and identification of the causative bacteria. Group-typing of the bacteria usually is performed by a diagnostic laboratory, although several kits are now commercially available for "in-house" testing. Fortunately, most streptococci remain susceptible to penicillin or penicillin-group antibiotics.

Staphylococcal Infections

Staphylococci are a widely distributed group of bacteria that cause disease in human beings and many animal species, including dogs. Staphylococci are ubiquitous in nature and are more resistant than many other bacteria to drying and the action of disinfectants. Staphylococcal bacteria are often found on the skin and mucous membranes; many of them represent members of the normal bacterial flora of the host. Staphylococci are opportunistic **pathogens** (agents of disease) and usually cause illness only if presented with suitable conditions. Strains of staphylococci carrying the enzyme **coagulase** (*coagulase-positive staphylococci*) are the more virulent members of the genus and are more frequently implicated in disease processes. The major species of staphylococci involved in canine diseases are *Staphylococcus aureus* and *Staphylococcus intermedius.*

Staphylococci often cause infections of the skin, eyes, ears, respiratory tract, bladder and reproductive tract. Such infections are among the most common of all bacterial infections of dogs. Localized infections of the skin often begin with a superficial scratch or puncture wound that progresses to form an abscess or staphylococcal **pyoderma** (pus-producing skin infection). Hair follicles may also become infected, resulting in inflammation (**folliculitis**). Scratching or trauma can lead to a deeper local infection and subsequent spread of the causative staphylococci to adjacent tissues. A **boil** may result when a folliculitis progresses to form a deep, firm nodule filled with pus. A **carbuncle** is an even deeper infection characterized by interconnected pockets of pus. The carbuncle is the most severe of the staphylococcal skin infections and has the potential to rupture and seed the bloodstream with bacteria, producing **bacteremia** or **septicemia** (bacteria in the bloodstream, accompanied by clinical signs). Ear infections, **dis-**

cospondylitis (inflammation of inter-vertebral discs within the spinal column), and **urolithiasis** (development of stones within the urinary tract) are other disease processes with which staphylococci have been associated.

Diagnosis is made on the basis of the history, the presenting clinical signs, and identification of the causative bacteria.

Treatment of uncomplicated local infections such as an abscess usually involves hot-packing the lesion, followed by puncture of the abscess and drainage of pus, and instillation of a disinfectant or antibiotic solution. Deeper infections may require hospitalization for additional therapy and for antibiotic therapy to be instituted and monitored. Unlike streptococci, many strains of staphylococci have developed resistance to the action of penicillin and penicillin-group antibiotics. Cephalosporins and trimethoprim-sulfa drugs are frequently used in their place in order to treat staphylococcal infections.

Actinomycosis and Nocardiosis

Bacteria belonging to the genera *Actinomyces* and *Nocardia* are filamentous (threadlike) organisms that cause pus-forming infections in human beings and in a number of animal species. *Actinomyces* bacteria are widespread in the environment but are also part of the normal bacterial flora of the mouth, while bacteria of the genus *Nocardia* are primarily inhabitants of the soil. Trauma and puncture wounds, and occasionally inhalation or ingestion, probably allow these organisms to gain access to normally sterile tissues of the body.

Actinomycosis occurs most often in the larger breeds of dog, particularly those that spend a good deal of time outdoors. Most infections remain localized, and frequently the *Actinomyces* organisms are present in conjunction with other bacteria as a mixed infection. Lesions include abscesses and draining tracts, often in the neck and head region. Yellow-colored **sulfur granules** (clumps of bacteria mixed with dead and dying cells) can be seen in the pus draining from these lesions. Direct extension of a more superficial skin infection into an internal body cavity such as the abdomen (pro-ducing *peritonitis*) may occur when the contaminating bacteria are carried in on a migrating foreign body—a grass awn (foxtail), for example—which because of its shape and surface characteristics can be forced deeper into the tissues by the muscle and body movements of the dog. Empyema (accumulation of pus in a body cavity, usually the chest cavity) is another possible manifestation of infection.

Nocardiosis is similar in many ways to actinomycosis, but in nocardial infection there is a greater likelihood of lymph node involvement and systemic spread of disease. Nocardial empyema closely resembles empyema caused by *Actinomyces*. There is also a disseminated form of nocardiosis that progresses from a relatively simple respiratory infection to a generalized systemic disease that in some cases can be mistaken for canine distemper.

Diagnosis of either disease is based on the history, clinical signs, and identification of the causative organism in fluid or tissue samples, followed by laboratory culture. Cases presenting as simple abscesses in the skin usually require only drainage and flushing with a disinfectant solution. If there is involvement of the deeper tissues, however, prolonged antibiotic therapy together with repeated flushing of the affected body cavity (chest, abdomen) must be aggressively employed. Five to 10 days of intensive flushing and cleansing may be required to stabilize severely affected patients. Surgery may be required to search the infected body cavity for the source of infection. In such cases antibiotic therapy will need to be continued for at least 4 to 6 weeks after surgery, and sometimes longer. The prognosis in all but the more superficial skin infections is guarded.

Tetanus

Tetanus is an acute, often fatal disease caused by a **neurotoxin** (toxin targeting the nervous system) produced by the bacterium *Clostridium tetani* (*Cl. tetani*), and is characterized by violent muscle spasms and contractions, hyperreflexive responses, and "lockjaw." It is not a common disease of dogs, but occasionally cases are seen.

The causative bacteria are normal residents of the soil, but may also be found in small numbers among the bacterial population of the large intestine. Special conditions must be present for the organism to induce disease, however. In general, bacterial contamination of dead or dying tissue in a penetrating wound is the most common means by which tetanus is produced. Spores of *Cl. tetani,* which are widely present in the soil, **germinate** (grow into mature bacterial forms) soon after entering the wound. Germination is followed by production of the neurotoxin, called **tetanospasmin,** which affects neuromuscular responses in different areas of the body. The toxin blocks nerve impulses that normally inhibit muscular contractions. As a result the large muscle groups are trapped in a state of contraction, which is often accompanied by prolonged, painful spasms.

The clinical signs of tetanus in dogs are a reflection of sustained muscle contraction: stiffness of the limbs resulting in a so-called "sawhorse" stance; outstretched tail; wrinkling of the forehead, erection of the ears, and contraction of the corners of the mouth, producing a "sardonic smile"; extrusion of the third eyelid; swallowing difficulties, together with rigidity of the chewing muscles ("lockjaw"); and usually fever (secondary to prolonged tensing of the muscles). Painful spasms resembling convulsions (except that the dog remains totally conscious), **dyspnea** (respiratory difficulty), and **dysuria** (difficult urination) occur in more severely affected animals. Most untreated dogs with tetanus will die. Death is usually the result of **respiratory insufficiency** (suffocation).

The diagnosis in most cases is fairly straightforward, based on the history and the rather characteristic physical appearance of the patient. Therapy must be applied quickly and aggressively. *Thorough cleansing and disinfection of the wound to remove dead and dying tissue as well as the clostridial organisms is an absolutely necessity.* The antibiotic penicillin is then infiltrated directly into the wound area to kill any remaining bacteria, and is also given systemically. Tetanus antitoxin (antibodies against the neurotoxin) to "soak up" unbound toxin may also be administered. Following these initial critical measures, recovery will depend on good nursing and supportive care. Several days may pass before any improvement in the animal's condition is noted; complete recovery may require weeks of therapy, and there may be unforeseen complications. The prognosis is always guarded and is directly related to the speed of onset of disease; that is, the more quickly clinical signs develop following injury, the poorer is the prognosis for recovery.

Botulism

Botulism is a rare disease caused by a neurotoxin (**botulinal toxin**) produced by the bacterium *Clostridium botulinum,* and is contracted either by ingestion of preformed toxin in improperly canned food, raw meat, or decomposing carcasses, or by contamination of a wound with the bacteria, which subsequently elaborate the toxin in the damaged tissue ("wound botulism").

Botulinal toxin is one of the most potent biological toxins known in nature. It targets the neuromuscular nerve endings, producing a flaccid paralysis of affected muscle groups. Clinical disease is characterized by vomiting or regurgitation, abdominal pain, dryness of the mucous membranes, hind leg weakness ("bunny hopping"), reduced or absent neurologic reflexes, difficulty swallowing, and a growing generalized **paresis** (partial paralysis) that progresses to paralysis. Death is usually the result of paralysis of the respiratory musculature.

The diagnosis is not always as clear as it is with tetanus. The history and clinical signs may or may not provide a high index of suspicion for botulism. The only available laboratory test involves detection of the toxin in gut contents, vomitus, feces, serum, or in a suspect food source (if available). One key difference between botulism and some of the other canine diseases producing flaccid paralysis is that, in botulism, the muscles of the head are also involved in the disease process.

Antibiotic or antitoxin therapies are of little benefit in botulism; treatment is almost entirely supportive. The patient must be kept alive and free of secondary infections or other complications until the toxin is naturally cleared from the body. As much as a week may pass before signs of improvement are seen. The prognosis is always guarded and is directly related to the speed of onset of disease; that is, the more quickly clinical signs develop following exposure, the poorer is the prognosis for recovery. Fortunately, botulism is observed only rarely in dogs.

Canine Brucellosis

Brucella canis (*B. canis*), the causative agent of canine brucellosis, was first identified in the mid-1960s. Since then it is has become clear that *B. canis* is distributed worldwide among canine populations. General estimates indicate that approximately 1% of pet dogs and approximately 5% of stray dogs are infected with the organism, although there is significant geographic variability. *B. canis* is relatively sensitive to environmental conditions and does not survive for lengthy periods outside the host.

Canine brucellosis is seen most commonly among dogs in kennels. Transmission occurs most efficiently during breeding, the highest incidence of infection being found in animals mated to chronic carriers of the organism. In bitches, *B. canis* is present in greatest concentration in the placenta and vaginal secretions, while in males it is excreted in the semen. Kennel runs and other surfaces can become contaminated with organisms shed from uterine discharges or aborted fetuses, thus providing a ready source of infection for other animals.

Following ingestion or venereal transmission of the organism, there is a period of initial growth and multiplication in local lymph nodes (nodes of the head and neck after ingestion, those of the pelvic region after genital exposure). This is followed soon thereafter by a chronic bacteremia. The bacteremia can last from several months to as long as 2 years or more. It is during the bacteremia phase that the organism spreads and then localizes in the placenta of the pregnant uterus of the female, or in the prostate and testicles of the male.

The level of bacteremia remains fairly steady during the first few months of infection, becom-ing somewhat more variable as time progresses. Bacteremia is usually not associated with fever or other signs of illness, although there may be a slight enlargement of the lymph nodes (lymphadenopathy) or spleen. Lymph nodes near the site of entry of the organism will exhibit the greatest degree of enlargement. Occasionally, infected dogs may exhibit some malaise, weight loss, worsening of condition, loss of libido, or fatigue. As the time of infection lengthens, the animal gradually acquires immunity to the organism. Once immunity develops the bacteremia slowly wanes; eventually the organisms hidden in lymph nodes or other organs also succumb to the host's immune defenses.

The primary disease signs associated with canine brucellosis are referable to the genital tract. These may include:

Abortion (occurring late, usually at 6 to 8 weeks of gestation), or the birth of dead pups at term or near term, or birth of weak ("fading") pups that die shortly after birth. Uncommonly, pups may survive to carry the illness into later life.

Infertility (diminished ability to produce offspring) in the male, usually attributable to inflammation and **atrophy** (shrinking or wasting) of the testicles, lowered sperm count and the production of abnormal sperm. Affected males may become completely sterile.

Inflammatory diseases of the testicle (**orchitis**) or prostate gland (**prostatitis**), leading to the development of draining tracts from the **scrotum** (dependent pouch of skin holding the testicles).

Discospondylitis (inflammation of intervertebral discs within the spinal column), usually in the lower back area.

Canine brucellosis is usually diagnosed on the basis of the history, presenting clinical signs, and the results of laboratory tests. Because infected dogs remain bacteremic for months to years after infection, culture of the organism from the blood provides the most definitive means of diagnosing the disease. However, blood cultures are expensive and time-consuming, particularly if a large number of animals must be screened. Measurement of antibody **titers** (levels) to *B. canis* provides an alternative means of achieving a diagnosis. The *rapid slide agglutination test* can be used as a quick screening test for the detection of antibodies. The test has a high negative predictive value; that is, a *negative* test indicates that there is essentially a 99% chance that the animal is truly free of infection. *A positive test can be falsely positive in roughly 33–50% of cases, however.* Positive tests should be confirmed using a more specific brucellosis assay such as the *tube agglutination test* or *agar gel immunodiffusion test.*

Bitches aborting as a result of infection with *B. canis* usually do so only during the pregnancy immediately following infection, or possibly in the second or third succeeding pregnancy if they are rebred quickly and the bacteremia is still present at the time. After 10 to 24 months most infected dogs will recover, as evidenced by the disappearance of the bacteremia. Once recovery has occurred, dogs appear to be immune to reinfection with *B. canis.*

In kennels, a test-and-removal program for infected dogs, followed by periodic retesting of animals is the usual means of eliminating the organism. Vigorous screening of bitches and studs brought in from other sources is an essential part of this program. Many combinations of antibiotics have been explored in an attempt to clear the infection in individual dogs. Several antibiotics have been found effective in clearing the bacteremia for the period that they are administered; because the organisms remain sequestered in tissues, however, the bacteremia usually returns once the antibiotics have been withdrawn. There is no vaccine available.

Brucella canis has been recovered from human beings on a number of occasions. Some infections have been the result of laboratory exposure, some from contact with infected dogs (primarily bitches experiencing abortion), and some could not be associated with an obvious source of the organism. This rate of infection is relatively low compared to the numbers of people exposed to *B. canis.* Thus, although its potential transmissibility to human contacts must be kept in mind, canine brucellosis in general is not considered to represent a major human health risk at the present time.

When *B. canis* infection does occur in people, the resulting disease may be manifested by localized abscesses (often in lymph nodes), or by a protracted course characterized by intermittent fever, headache, lymph node enlargement, chills, weakness, joint pains, weight loss, malaise, cold sweats and sore throat. Fortunately, antibiotics are usually effective in controlling the infection in human beings. (*See* APPENDIX A, "ZOONOTIC DISEASES: FROM DOGS TO PEOPLE.")

Lyme Borreliosis (Lyme Disease)

Lyme borreliosis is named for the town of Old Lyme, Connecticut, located a short distance inland from Long Island Sound. In the 1970s, physicians in the area noticed an unusual pattern of transient, recurrent **arthropathies** (joint diseases) that occurred mainly in children during the summer and early autumn months. After a period of intense investigation a new spirochete called *Borrelia burgdorferi* was implicated in the causation of the disease. Lyme borreliosis (or more simply, Lyme disease) has now been recognized in people throughout the world, and there is some evidence that it is increasing in incidence. This may be due to the increased urbanization of rural woodlands in endemic areas—i.e., by the growing encroachment of human civilization upon the woodland reservoirs of infection.

The majority of cases of Lyme borreliosis reported each year in the United States are from the northeastern and mid-Atlantic regions of the country. The causative bacterium is carried and transmitted by **ixodid** (hard) **ticks,** different tick species serving as carriers in different geographical areas. In the Northeast and Midwest, the deer tick *Ixodes scapularis* (previously referred to as *Ixodes dammini*), a tiny tick that infests wooded areas, is the primary **vector** (transmitter of infection). Typically, 25–50% of *I. scapularis* ticks in the Northeast are infected with the spirochete. The primary reservoir of *B. burgdorferi* infection in the wildlife population of the Northeast is the white-footed mouse, upon which the deer tick feeds, injecting spirochete-laden saliva through the bite wound and thereby perpetuating a cycle of infection that assures transmission of the organism to successive generations of mice. This tick also bites human beings and dogs and is considered the major vector for transmission of the spirochete to these species as well. Free-roaming dogs in endemic areas are more likely to be infected than are the human beings resident in such areas, probably owing to their greater contact with the outdoors and subsequently greater exposure to infected ticks.

In California the primary vectors are *Ixodes pacificus,* the western black-legged tick, and a second ixodid tick, *Ixodes neotomae,* both of which feed on a wildlife reservoir, the dusky-footed wood rat (also called the pack rat). *The California cycle is unique in that both ticks are required to perpetuate the disease in the human population.* Typically only 1–5% of *I. pacificus* ticks are infected with the Lyme spirochete, while approximately 15% of *I. neotomae* are infected. This latter tick does not feed on human beings, however, but seems to be more important in sustaining the infection among wood rats—hence its relatively high frequency of infection. It is the western black-legged tick (which *does* feed on people) that apparently plays the important role of transmitting the infection from the wood rat cycle to human beings.

LYME BORRELIOSIS IN PEOPLE

The spirochete multiplies at the site of infection for a period of several weeks of more. This local multiplication is followed by the appearance of a typical skin reaction called **erythema chronicum migrans (ECM)** at the site of the bite. It begins as a small red spot that then expands in a circular fashion with an area of central clearing. The appearance of ECM in humans is usually associated with varying degrees of fever, chills, malaise, fatigue, vomiting, headache, **lymphadenopathy** (enlargement of lymph nodes), and neck stiffness. These signs are probably caused by systemic spread of the spirochete and the immune responses directed against it. The ECM usually undergoes expansion for several weeks, clears in the center, and then fades. Skin lesions sometimes appear to spread to other areas of the body; this probably is due not to subsequent tick bites but to further systemic spread of the preexisting spirochete infection.

Weeks to months after the primary ECM lesion has faded, a small proportion of infected individuals develop signs of chronic Lyme borreliosis. Neurologic complications are observed in about 15% of affected people, while heart problems are seen in about 8%. The most common complication, present in over 60% of affected individuals, is a polyarthritis that occurs as a series of attacks lasting for several weeks to months, with subsequent recurrences developing over a period of years. This novel association of a specific infectious disease agent with chronic arthritis has spurred much promising new research into the causes (and possible cures) of arthritic ailments in people.

LYME BORRELIOSIS IN DOGS

In contrast to the current picture in the human medical field, the significance of Lyme borreliosis for canine medicine is less clear. Between 25 and 50% or more of free-roaming dogs in highly endemic areas have antibodies to *Borrelia burgdorferi* and yet exhibit no signs of disease. The same is often true of cats, livestock and wildlife. Although an acute, self-limiting polyarthritis has been seen in some dogs following both natural and experimental infection with the spirochete, there is little evidence that the organism causes a chronic disease analogous to that observed in people. The acute disease in dogs is characterized by fever, inappetence, malaise, lethargy, lymph node enlargement, joint pain and lameness. One major difference from the human acute syndrome is the total absence of the ECM lesion.

There are no specific hematologic or biochemical markers of infection; thus, serologic tests to detect antibodies to the Lyme spirochete are heavily relied upon for making a diagnosis of Lyme borreliosis. Antibodies are usually present at a low level during the acute, polyarthritis illness seen in naturally infected dogs, rising to very high levels (greater than 1:256) during subsequent weeks. A diagnosis of Lyme borreliosis in a dog exhibiting clinical signs can be made by demonstrating a fourfold or greater increase in antibody titers in paired serum samples, one taken at the time of onset of fever and polyarthritis, and the other approximately 1 to 2 months later.

In cases where serologic testing does not provide a firm diagnosis, a course of tetracycline antibiotic therapy may provide suggestive evidence that the disease in question is Lyme borreliosis. However, it must be remembered that acute borreliosis in dogs resembles certain other canine infectious diseases (such as tropical canine pancytopenia) that may also respond to tetracycline antibiotics. Attempts can also be made to culture the Lyme spirochete from blood, urine, or joint fluid collected during the acute fever/polyarthritis stage of infection, although the rate of recovery of the organism is usually low. The organisms are rapidly cleared from blood and urine following recovery from the acute illness.

An inactivated *Borrelia burgdorferi* vaccine has recently been introduced for use in dogs. It is given by intramuscular injection in two doses spaced several weeks apart. The vaccine reportedly protects for a period of at least 6 months. The absolute need for such a vaccine remains questionable given the high rate of asymptomatic infection, the self-limiting nature of the acute disease and the extremely low incidence of chronic complications in dogs. Nevertheless, the vaccine is available in areas of the country where the incidence of Lyme borreliosis in people is high. The vaccine is not marketed in states where local health officials feel the disease is not a serious human health problem.

There is some public health concern regarding dogs that have come into contact with the Lyme spirochete. Dogs may physically transport infected ticks adhered to their bodies into gardens, backyards or homes, although the importance of this passive carriage in spreading the infection to people is not known at present. Available evidence suggests that acutely infected dogs may shed the organism in urine; however, the organisms appear to be much less virulent when transmitted from one animal to another, than from a tick to an animal—suggesting that the greater danger to human beings is being bitten by infected ticks rather than being exposed to an infected dog. Currently, the public health authorities of the United States do not view animals in and of themselves as major factors in Lyme borreliosis transmission.

Tuberculosis

Tuberculosis is an ancient scourge, its varied symptoms and disease course having been familiar to medical practitioners since the dawn of recorded history. The causative bacteria remained unidentified until barely a century ago, however, when the great German microbiologist Robert Koch presented his now-famous paper on the subject before the members of the Physiological Society of Berlin. In the relatively brief period since then, much additional information has been gathered concerning the cause, cure, transmission and prevention of tuberculosis in both human beings and animals.

The term "tuberculosis" derives from the multiple small nodules of inflammatory tissue ("tubercles") that are characteristic of the disease in some species. Tuberculosis is caused by several members of the genus *Mycobacterium,* including *Mycobacterium tuberculosis, Mycobacterium bovis* and *Mycobacterium avium* (known collectively as "tubercle bacilli"). Today it is estimated that at least *one-third* of the world's human population is or has been infected with *M. tuberculosis,* the primary causative agent of tuberculosis in people. In the United States, between 22,000 and 25,000 new human cases of tuberculosis are being diagnosed annually, and this number is on the increase owing to the prevalence of human immunodeficiency virus (HIV) infection. Global morbidity and mortality figures now reflect *8 million* new human cases and approximately *3 million human deaths* each year. Any notion of human tuberculosis as a "disease of the past" must be seriously questioned in light of such statistics.

Human beings are susceptible to infection with all three main types of tubercle bacilli. Dogs are equally susceptible to infection with either *M. tuberculosis* or *M. bovis,* but seem to acquire the infection more often through contact with tuberculous people who are actively shedding the bacteria in respiratory secretions (so-called open cases of tuberculosis). Most canine infections produce no clinical signs, the immune system of the dog actively suppressing the bacteria. When disease does occur, affected dogs most often exhibit clinical signs referable to the respiratory tract, such as coughing, retching and dyspnea. Fever, inappetence, weight loss and lymph node enlargement are common accompanying features. In some cases the disease may disseminate to other sites such as the heart, liver, spleen, bones or brain.

Local public health authorities should be notified immediately if a diagnosis of tuberculosis is suspected. The best methods for obtaining a definitive diagnosis of tuberculosis include isolation of the causative bacterium (a lengthy procedure, requiring weeks) and microscopic identification of the organisms in tissue biopsies or lesion smears (much faster, although both false-negative and false-positive results may occur). Biopsy of enlarged lymph nodes is probably the most rapid method of obtaining a reliable diagnosis in the living animal. In all cases, biopsy should always be accompanied by bacteriological culture so that the infecting strain can be classified (this will facilitate identification of the source of infection). Skin testing (**tuberculin testing**) and serologic testing (detection of antibodies) are too unreliable in dogs to provide an accurate assessment of infection.

Treatment of canine tuberculosis using several standard antituberculosis medications has been reported. However, the required therapy is prolonged and dogs undergoing treatment represent a potential disease threat to people and animals with which they come into contact. For this reason *treatment of tuberculous in dogs is not recommended.* A search for the source of infection, if unidentified, should be instituted as soon as a definitive diagnosis has been made. Vaccination of dogs against tuberculosis is not currently feasible.

Tyzzer's Disease

Tyzzer's disease is an extremely rare and highly fatal disease caused by a spore-forming bacterium, *Bacillus piliformis,* and is characterized primarily by acute liver dysfunction in young pups. The organism is a normal inhabitant of the intestinal tract of mice, and dogs are thought to acquire infection by ingesting fecal matter contaminated with bacterial spores. Alternatively, it is possible that dogs themselves harbor the organism, which for some reason causes fatal illness in only a small percentage of infected animals.

Clinical signs include inappetence, malaise, abdominal pain, and **hepatomegaly** (enlargement of the liver). The course of the disease is extremely short, often lasting only 1 to 2 days; consequently the diagnosis is usually made after death, by identifying the characteristic bacteria in samples of liver tissue. Death is usually attributable to massive liver failure. There is no effective treatment or vaccine.

Tropical Canine Pancytopenia (Canine Ehrlichiosis)

Tropical canine pancytopenia (TCP) is a tick-borne disease that was first reported in the 1950s in dogs in the Netherlands Antilles, and thereafter in the Caribbean, Central and South America, and North America. A tremendous explosion in knowledge about the disease resulted from outbreaks among military dogs that occurred in Southeast Asia during the Vietnam conflict. The disease occurs worldwide wherever the brown dog tick (*Rhipicephalus sanguineus*), which transmits the infection, is found. Besides the areas mentioned, the disease has also been recognized in southern Europe, the Middle East, India and Africa. Infection has been reported from dogs in virtually every state of the United States, but is most prevalent in those states south of an imaginary diagonal line drawn from central California to Maine. Most cases are observed in dogs from the Gulf coastal region of Texas and the southern states.

The causative organism *Ehrlichia canis* (*E. canis*) is classified as a *rickettsia,* a member of a specialized group of bacteria that multiply only within host cells and that are transmitted to animals and people by **arthropods** (invertebrate organisms with a hard outer skeleton and a segmented body; examples include ticks, fleas and lice). The primary reservoir for *E. canis* is the brown dog tick, which excretes the organism in its saliva. The organism normally multiplies in the tick and enters the dog at the point of feeding, probably by contamination of the bite wound with the tick's saliva.

The outcome of infection with *E. canis* can vary considerably, depending upon the breed of dog (German Shepherd Dogs reportedly are much more susceptible than are Beagles or mongrels), concurrent stress (military dogs are apt to show disease), and geographic origin of the organism (North American isolates of *E. canis* appear to be less virulent than isolates from Southeast Asia). The organism enters through the tick-bite wound and is carried to the local lymphatic tissue, where multiplication occurs in white blood cells (monocytes and macrophages). Within 5 to 15 days the rickettsiae enter the bloodstream and spread to lymphatic tissues elsewhere in the body, including the spleen, liver, and lymph nodes.

Two major clinical phases of disease are usually observed, acute and chronic. The *acute phase* may be completely inapparent or quite severe, depending on the circumstances. This phase is characterized by a fever lasting for 3 to 7 days, often accompanied by a mild to moderate generalized lymphadenopathy, mild ocular and nasal discharge, malaise, stiffness and inappetence. Some degree of pneumonia may be present on X-ray examination of the chest, but usually no clinical signs resulting from this are evident. Blood counts show a drop in blood **platelet** (blood-clotting cell) levels (*thrombocytopenia*). Muscle twitching and vague neurologic signs may be evident in some dogs. The acute stage of the disease often lasts from 2 to 4 weeks, following which the affected dog either recovers or proceeds to the second, chronic stage of illness.

The chronic stage of TCP lasts for many months and is caused by an imperfect immune response to the organism, resulting in increasingly severe impairment of blood-cell production within the bone marrow. Thus the chronic stage is manifested by cyclical, progressive decreases in the numbers of platelets, red blood cells, and white blood cells (**pancytopenia**). Platelet counts are the most consistently decreased, although it is usually apparent that all bone marrow elements are affected to some degree. There is usually a progressive increase in serum **gamma globulins** (blood proteins that include most of the antibody classes) that tends to be spread over a wide range of protein types and is known as a **polyclonal gammopathy.** Fever, enlarged lymph nodes and other constitutional signs evident during the acute phase of illness are usually absent or minimally evident in the chronic phase. Kidney disease ranging from mild **proteinuria** (loss of protein in the urine) to progressive **glomerulonephritis** (inflammatory disease involving the capillaries of the kidney glomeruli) is evidenced in many animals and may become more serious with time, sometimes culminating in kidney failure. Signs of bone marrow suppression include epistaxis, small hemorrhages in the skin and mucous membranes, **melena** (dark, pitchy stool due to bleeding into the digestive tract), **hematuria** (blood in the urine), fatigue, and pallor of the mucous membranes (a consequence of anemia). A small percentage of dogs may exhibit signs of ocular or neurologic disease or polyarthritis.

Diagnosis of canine ehrlichiosis is made on the basis of the history, clinical signs, and the results of supportive laboratory tests. Any dog exhibiting signs of chronic bone marrow suppression (pancytopenia) accompanied by fever, polyclonal gammopathy, enlarged lymph nodes or other systemic signs, should be examined further for the presence of *E. canis*. This can be done by identifying the organism in monocytes and macrophages in blood or tissue smears, or by testing the suspect animal for antibodies to *E. canis*. Because antibody titers are maintained only while the organism persists in the dog's body, the presence of such antibodies is essentially diagnostic for infection. Recovered dogs tend to be immune or to develop only a mild disease course upon reexposure. It varies from dog to dog.

Treatment is most successful in the early stages, at which time several days of therapy with tetracycline antibiotics will bring about a rapid resolution of signs. Six weeks or more of therapy may be required for dogs that have progressed to the early chronic stage. Antibodies to *E. canis* usually disappear from the blood over a 3- to 9-month period following treatment. No amount of therapy is likely to be successful in dogs with long-standing disease, especially if the bone marrow has been severely depleted of its blood-cell production capability. Some dogs with chronic disease may require months of therapy before a significant response is seen. In general, dogs should be treated continuously until their blood counts have returned to normal. The prognosis in chronic cases is guarded, but is particularly poor if no response is evident after 2 to 4 months of intensive therapy. There is no available vaccine.

Infectious Cyclic Thrombocytopenia

An infectious, cyclic *thrombocytopenia* (decreased number of blood **platelets** [blood-clotting cells]) caused by a rickettsia was first recognized in dogs in Florida in the late 1970s. Cases have now been diagnosed throughout the southeastern states from eastern Texas to the Atlantic seaboard. The causative agent is *Ehrlichia platys,* which to date cannot be artificially cultured in the laboratory. The organism is apparently transmitted by ticks, but the species of tick is not known. The existence of dual infections with *E. platys* and *Ehrlichia canis* (the agent of tropical canine pancytopenia, *see* ABOVE) suggests that the brown dog tick, *Rhipicephalus sanguineus,* which transmits *E. canis,* may be an important reservoir of infection for *E. platys* as well.

The rickettsiae enter the dog through a tick bite and parasitize mature blood platelets. The initial wave of platelet infection and rickettsemia (presence of rickettsiae in the blood) occurs 1 to 2 weeks following exposure and usually lasts for about 3 or 4 days. A dramatic decrease in the numbers of circulating blood platelets occurs 2 to 3 days following the rickettsemia. This in turn is followed by an equally rapid rebound in the platelet count as the organisms are extracted from the bloodstream by the immune defenses of the host. Subsequent waves of rickettsemia usually occur at 1- to 2-week intervals over the succeeding several months. Organisms become more difficult to locate within blood platelets during these subsequent rickettsemic episodes. Eventually the rickettsemias cease altogether or are no longer detectable in blood smears.

Most infections produce no clinical signs of disease. In rare instances dogs may exhibit signs typical of immune-mediated thrombocytopenia (nosebleed, hemorrhages in the skin and mucous membranes, blood in the stool or urine, etc.). More severe disease has been associated with concurrent infections with *E. canis* or *Babesia canis* (a protozoan blood parasite of dogs). The thrombocytopenia often is detected incidentally in dogs having blood counts performed for other reasons.

The diagnosis is made by identifying the organism microscopically in platelets found in blood smears during the 2- to 3-day periods of rickettsemia. During the initial episode up to 30% of platelets may harbor the organism. This percentage rapidly declines with each succeeding episode; subsequent attacks may be associated with levels of infection of only 1% or less. Detection of antibodies to the organism in blood samples will also confirm the presence of infection.

Treatment is not often necessary, owing to the fact that the vast majority of infections are asymptomatic. Tetracycline antibiotics would be the drug therapy of choice in dogs exhibiting signs of disease.

Salmon Disease ("Salmon Poisoning")

Salmon disease has been recognized as a specific entity of dogs and related members of the family Canidae since the early years of this century. Salmon disease occurs exclusively in the Pacific Northwest region of the United States, as far north as Alaska and as far south as San Francisco. It is most prevalent on the western slopes of the far northern California and Oregon coastal forests.

Salmon disease is an acute, rapidly progressive and frequently fatal **enterocolitis** (inflammation of the small intestine and colon) that occurs shortly after an affected dog has fed on infected raw salmon or trout from coastal rivers and streams. Cases have also been associated with ingestion of hatchery-reared fish planted in inland reservoirs.

Salmon disease is caused by one or both of two rickettsial bacteria, *Neorickettsia helminthoeca* and the *Elokomin fluke fever (EFF)* agent (the latter organism most probably being a variant of *N. helminthoeca*). Of the two, *N. helminthoeca* produces the more severe disease, but dual infections are common.

In salmon disease, as in most rickettsial diseases, invertebrate hosts represent important vectors of infection. The geographic distribution of salmon disease corresponds closely with the range of an aquatic snail, *Oxytrema silicula*, that inhabits stream waters of the northern Pacific coastal forests. The snail in turn is the intermediate host for a fluke called *Nanophyetus salmincola*. The fluke leaves the snail and penetrates the tissues of fish of the salmonid family (salmon, steelhead, trout), where it forms cysts in muscles and organs. After the infested fish is eaten by a dog or other canid (fox, wolf, coyote), the encysted flukes are released into the intestinal tract and rapidly become egg-laying adults within 5 days. The flukes burrow partly into the surface of the dog's upper small intestine, but cause no overt disease by themselves. The fluke eggs are shed in the feces and hatch in the environment, where they penetrate into the snail and so continue the life cycle. Humans and black bears can be infected with the fluke if they eat infested raw fish; however, they do not develop disease from the bacteria.

When the rickettsial bacteria causing salmon disease are present in the fluke, they are associated with the entire life cycle and are present in all of the fluke's life stages. About 5 to 7 days after ingestion of the infested fish, rapid multiplication of the rickettsiae occurs in the dog's lymphatic system. This is accompanied by a high fever that persists for several days, the temperature falling to subnormal prior to death. The rickettsiae spread into the bloodstream and proliferate in lymphatic tissue throughout the dog's body. Resulting clinical signs include inappetence, depression, nasal and ocular discharge, generalized enlargement of lymph nodes (lymphadenopathy), weight loss, weakness and a progressively severe enterocolitis.

The gastrointestinal signs are manifested initially as vomiting, with a rapid progression to diarrhea. The stools are loose at first, but subsequently become more fluid and copious. Blood-laden stools are associated with the development of **necrotizing** (causing tissue death) inflammation within the digestive tract. These signs may clinically resemble those observed in canine parvovirus enteritis and may confuse the diagnosis. With more severe gastrointestinal disease and its concomitant fluid and electrolyte loss, affected dogs rapidly develop shock and die.

Jaundice (yellowish discoloration of the skin and mucous membranes) is a rare manifestation in severe cases. An atypical disease course also may be seen, wherein affected dogs show vague signs of illness and gastrointestinal disease signs for 1 to 2 weeks before breaking with more florid clinical signs.

Diagnosis is made on the basis of the history, presenting clinical signs, and identification of either fluke eggs or rickettsiae in affected dogs. The rickettsiae often may be identified microscopically within monocytes or macrophages (white blood cells) in lymph node smears. The soft brown eggs of the fluke begin to appear in feces within 5 to 8 days of an affected dog's ingesting a fluke-infested fish. Because the incubation period of the disease is often the same, however, the eggs usually are present at the time a dog becomes ill. Although fluke infestation does not in and of itself signal infection with one or both of the rickettsiae, the presence of fluke eggs in feces of a dog exhibiting clinical signs consistent with a diagnosis of salmon disease provides a high index of suspicion.

Supportive care is essential for successful therapy of salmon disease. Treatment measures include the use of fluid and electrolyte solutions to maintain proper water and electrolyte balance and to combat the dehydration resulting from diarrhea; whole blood or plasma if blood loss is severe; and antibiotic therapy (principally tetracycline antibiotics) to combat the causative rickettsiae.

There is no available vaccine. Prevention chiefly involves reducing a dog's potential exposure to infected fish. Freezing fish will considerably lower its infectivity, as will proper smoking.

Rocky Mountain Spotted Fever

Rocky Mountain spotted fever (RMSF) was often encountered by early American settlers traveling westward through parts of the Rocky Mountains in the Colorado and Montana territories. The name is really a misnomer, however, because the infection is much more prevalent in other regions of the United States. Cases in people have occurred in almost all states, but the hardwood and softwood forest regions of the central United States from Colorado to the Atlantic coast are the areas of greatest incidence. The highest rates of animal and human infections occur in the states of the mid-Atlantic seaboard.

The disease is caused by a rickettsia called *Rickettsia rickettsii*. The organism is carried and transmitted by several species of ticks, in particular *Dermacentor andersoni* (wood tick) and *Dermacentor variabilis* (American dog tick). The wood tick is the principal reservoir and vector of *R. rickettsii* in the Rocky Mountain region and in the western Sierras and Cascades, while the American dog tick is the principal vector in areas east of the Mississippi River.

The vast majority of canine infections with *R. rickettsii* appear to be mild or completely asymptomatic. When serious clinical cases arise they usually occur between the months of March and October, largely corresponding to the seasonal feeding period of the tick hosts. The rickettsiae enter the tissues of the dog following a tick bite and readily reach the lymphatic system. They then multiply in *endothelial* cells in the walls of the smaller blood vessels, initiating a destructive inflammatory reaction around the vessels (**vasculitis**) that subsequently produces blood-clotting abnormalities and damages adjacent organ tissue.

In dogs RMSF occurs in acute and chronic stages. The acute stage is often asymptomatic, as judged by the large numbers of dogs in endemic areas carrying antibodies to the organism. The clinical signs of infection in animals that become ill can vary from mild to severe. Mild signs resemble those described for the acute phase of tropical canine pancytopenia (*see* ABOVE); i.e., fever, depression, lethargy, inappetence, vomiting, diarrhea, ocular and nasal discharge, enlarged lymph nodes, muscle or joint pain, and thrombocytopenia. In more severe cases there is often **edema** (swelling) of the lower limbs, lips, jaw, ears, scrotum and penile sheath, owing to the disruptive effect of the organisms on blood vessel walls and the subsequent outpouring of fluid. Edematous areas rapidly become bruised

in appearance due to hemorrhage. Multiple small hemorrhages may appear on the oral or genital mucous membranes of some dogs with RMSF.

Multisystemic signs may develop within 1 to 4 weeks in dogs surviving the acute stage of illness. Sloughing of tissue due to **gangrene** (tissue death from loss of blood supply, followed by bacterial invasion and subsequent tissue decomposition) may occur in areas of severe edema and hemorrhage. Ocular (eye) abnormalities may involve the cornea, uveal tract, or retina. Neurologic signs including confusion, stupor, convulsions, **hyperesthesia** (heightened sensitivity to touch), paresis, **ataxia** (incoordination), and coma may be seen in some animals. Kidney failure is a terminal sign in a proportion of affected dogs. This chronic phase of RMSF in dogs can last for weeks and either follows the acute phase of the illness or appears without any preceding signs.

Diagnosis is made on the basis of the history, season of the year, clinical signs, and results of appropriate laboratory tests. Rickettsial organisms often are identifiable within monocytes and macrophages in lymph node or spleen aspirate smears, but not in blood or bone marrow. The organisms are most apparent during the acute phase of illness, becoming more difficult to identify in the chronic phase. Platelet counts may be decreased but not markedly so.

Antibody titers can be of help in diagnosing the infection. A diagnosis of RMSF in a dog exhibiting suspicious clinical signs can be made by demonstrating a fourfold or greater increase in antibody titers in paired serum samples, one taken at the time of active disease and the second approximately 1 to 2 months later. Immunodiagnostic testing of skin biopsies for the presence of the rickettsiae early in the course of infection is also a possibility.

Treatment consists of supportive care for the prevention of shock and severe clotting disorders, together with the administration of tetracycline antibiotics for at least 1 to 2 weeks. There is usually a rapid response to therapy in dogs treated early in the course of the disease. Dogs recovering from RMSF appear to be resistant to reinfection with the causative rickettsia. Currently there is no available vaccine for dogs.

CHAPTER 36

Fungal Diseases

**by Jeffrey E. Barlough
and Niels C. Pedersen**

The general term "fungus" encompasses the yeasts and molds, mushrooms, smuts and rusts, all of which are found normally in the environment. Fungi as a group are characterized by the presence of a rigid cell wall and the absence of chlorophyll, the green pigment used by plants, algae and certain bacteria to convert sunlight into useful energy. The primary life function of fungi is decomposition—i.e., the breakdown of inert organic material. Fungi are thus of great importance ecologically because their digestive processes release the nutrients trapped in organic debris and recycle them back to the biosphere.

A yeast is a unicellular, budding fungus that forms bud-shaped spores. A mold is a **filamentous** (threadlike) fungus. Some fungi, such as those causing sporotrichosis or the systemic mycoses, are classified further as **dimorphic,** meaning that they are able to exist in either of two different physical forms: in the environment they exist as free-living molds, while in the body of the host they convert to a parasitic yeast form.

Many fungi, if given the proper opportunity and conditions, are able to produce disease in animals and human beings. Often, fungal dis-eases occur because of some underlying defect in the immune defenses of the host, e.g., congenital absence or deficiency of immune system components, or acquired defects produced by immunosuppressive virus infection or long-term administration of an immunosuppressive medication. In other cases, such as ringworm, infection occurs commonly in a normal host, but usually is transient in duration—once the immune system has been alerted, the fungus is gradually eliminated. Fungal diseases in the latter category can be managed fairly easily; those in the former may be resistant to treatment and threaten the life of the host. The side effects observed to antifungal medications are dependent upon the individual antifungal drug being administered. In general, side effects of systemic antifungal therapy can include kidney failure, anemia, hemorrhage, diarrhea, vomiting and liver inflammation (hepatitis).

Ringworm (Dermatophytosis)

Ringworm is one of the most common fungal diseases of dogs and cats. The highly contagious ringworm fungi (**dermatophytes**) invade the most superficial outer layers of the skin, nails, and hair, subsisting on **keratin,** an insoluble, sulfur-rich protein derived from shed skin cells. Although ringworm is most often a self-limiting disease, with spontaneous remission occurring within 1 to 3 months of onset, treatment of some resistant cases may be long and costly. (*See* Chapter 22, "The Skin and Disorders.")

Aspergillosis and Penicilliosis

The genera *Aspergillus* and *Penicillium* encompass a large group of fungi that are widely disseminated in the environment—in the air, soil, decaying vegetation, hay, straw and animal feeds. These fungi are opportunistic invaders with a preference for tissues of the respiratory tract. Some *Aspergillus* species found in moldy feed produce **aflatoxins,** poisonous compounds that can cause serious injury to the liver if ingested. Species of *Penicillium* are well known not so much for the diseases they cause as for the lifesaving antibiotics they manufacture, the **penicillins.** Of the two genera, *Aspergillus* is by far the more common **pathogen** (disease-producing agent) in dogs.

Canine aspergillosis presents most often with signs of respiratory disease localized to the nasal passages and sinuses; rarely, a disseminated form of the disease is observed. Several long-nosed breeds such as Collies and German Shepherds Dogs may have an enhanced susceptibility to the nasal form. It is suspected that underlying immune defects, either inherited or acquired, represent an important determinant of susceptibility.

A watery nasal discharge tinged with blood, nasal pain, ulceration of the nose and nostril area, and **epistaxis** (nosebleed) are common presenting signs of nasal aspergillosis and penicilliosis in the dog. The discharge may flow from one or both nostrils. The signs are referable to growth of the fungus within the nasal passages, with invasion and destruction of local bone and tissue.

The diagnosis may be a difficult one to make. **Radiographs** (X rays) of the head to demonstrate bone destruction by the fungus, **rhinoscopy** (visual examination of the inner nasal passages), **serology** (detection of serum antibodies to the fungus), and laboratory culture of the organism from nasal swabs or flushes may all be necessary to reach a firm diagnosis. In some cases, surgery to inspect the extent of damage to the inner nasal passages and to obtain biopsy samples may be required.

A combination of medical and surgery therapies has often been used to treat the nasal form of these two fungal infections. Recent evidence suggests that surgical excavation at the site of fungal growth may be of little benefit to the patient and may even be detrimental to the outcome. A more conservative approach involves the placement of temporary drains through the frontal sinuses and into the nasal passages, for use in flushing the affected areas with antifungal medication. Flushing may need to be performed twice daily for several weeks. Oral antifungal medication given for a period of 6 to 8 weeks may be used in conjunction with this topical form of therapy. The prognosis is guarded.

Candidiasis

Candidiasis in dogs is a relatively uncommon yeast infection of the skin and mucous membranes of the oral cavity, respiratory tract and genital area. Yeasts of the genus *Candida* are members of the normal microbial population residing in the digestive and reproductive tracts. With lowered host resistance caused by prolonged **maceration** of skin (softening or dissolution of skin cell layers by soaking), long-term antibiotic therapy, immunosuppressive drug medication, or by certain diseases such as diabetes mellitus, serious localized or systemic *Candida* infections may occur. In human beings, *Candida* is a recognized cause of superficial oral lesions in children and the elderly ("thrush") and chronic vaginal infections in women.

Localized infections in dogs may be characterized by ulcerations, moist **dermatitis** (skin inflammation), or a whitish discharge from the genital tract. Clinical signs observed in systemic infections vary considerably, depending upon the organ systems involved. Fever, generalized pain, abscesses, lymph node enlargement, blockage of small blood vessels, and widespread skin lesions have been reported in cases of systemic spread.

A definitive diagnosis is made by culture of the organism in the laboratory and by microscopic identification of the fungus within affected tissues. Superficial lesions usually can be treated with any of several topical antifungal medications. Serious disseminated infections require aggressive therapy with systemic antifungal drugs, all of which can be toxic to the patient. The prognosis for disseminated infections is generally unfavorable.

The Systemic Mycoses

The systemic mycoses (blastomycosis, histoplasmosis, **coccidioidomycosis,** and cryptococcosis) are a group of rare fungal diseases in which inhalation (usually) of the causative organism is followed by widespread dissemination of the fungus to internal organs or other tissues. The fungi causing most of these diseases exploit specialized ecological habitats and so their distribution in the environment is often geographically restricted. In the vast majority of cases (with the possible exception of blastomycosis), exposure to these organisms results in the production of strong immunity in the host rather than disease. In a small percentage of infections, however, the fungi are not checked by the immune response and proceed instead to engineer a serious (often fatal) illness. It appears that certain inherited or acquired defects in the immune defenses of the host may underlie susceptibility to these fungal disease agents.

An important feature of the fungi causing the systemic mycoses is their *dimorphic* nature. In the environment they exist as filamentous fungi (i.e., molds). However, upon inhalation or inoculation the filamentous form converts into a parasitic yeast that, unlike the mold form, is capable of growing in tissues of the host. One significant consequence is that, in general, infected animals or human beings are not directly contagious to others because the yeast form in their tissues is not infective. (*One caveat:* under certain circumstances, there may be reversion to growth of the filamentous form on or within bandages placed over a draining tract or other fungal lesion, or in contaminated stalls containing an abundance of straw or other bedding. The potential for reversion from noninfective yeast to infective mold can be greatly decreased by frequent bandage changes and removal of litter.)

The change from the filamentous mold form to the parasitic yeast form is apparently an adaptation to survival in an unfavorable environment (in this case, the body of the host) and confers little additional advantage to the fungi. Diseased animals or people in essence are "dead-end" hosts who have accidentally become involved in a minor sidetrack of the fungal life cycle. Growth in dead-end hosts is wholly irrelevant to the maintenance and propagation of these fungal species in nature.

BLASTOMYCOSIS

Blastomycosis is caused by *Blastomyces dermatitidis,* a presumed soil fungus that is found along the mid-Atlantic seaboard and in the north-central states and Ohio/Mississippi river valley regions. Unlike *Histoplasma* and *Coccidioides* (*see* BELOW), *Blastomyces* cannot routinely be recovered from soil in areas where blastomycosis is prevalent. Following outbreaks of blastomycosis wherein the mold form of the organism has been identified in the soil, it often cannot be recovered again in subsequent years, suggesting that growth of the fungus occurs sporadically and only in isolated ecological niches. When it can be recovered, *Blastomyces* usually is associated with moist, rotting organic debris, often enriched with bird droppings and protected from direct sunlight. Infection of dogs, cats or human beings occurs when they encroach unknowingly upon one of these isolated areas of fungal growth.

Blastomycosis is much more common in dogs than in either cats or people. This may be a consequence of the tendency of dogs to nose about aggressively in soil and underbrush, thus perhaps exposing themselves to far larger doses of the organism. Alternatively, there may be an inherent susceptibility of dogs that favors growth of the parasitic yeast form of *Blastomyces* in their tissues. Younger male dogs of the larger (often sporting) breeds constitute a significant percentage of blastomycosis cases.

Following inhalation (or, more rarely, inoculation through the skin), the organism can disseminate from the lungs to other areas of the body, producing respiratory disease, skin and bone lesions, ocular disease, and central nervous system abnormalities. In dogs, the respiratory form of blastomycosis is by far the most common and is characterized by generalized pneumonia, coughing, **dyspnea** (labored breathing), exercise intolerance, lymph node enlargement, inappetence and weight loss. Lameness is a frequent feature of the disease when bone involvement occurs. Skin lesions can occur alone or in association with lesions in other organs, particularly the lungs or lymph nodes. Lesions are common on the face, limbs, between the toes, and sometimes on the tongue. Skin lesions appear usually as thickened, ulcerated areas that exude fluid. Many dogs with blastomycosis also have ocular abnormalities, usually a **uveitis** (inflammation of the middle coat of the eye containing the iris), which may be manifested by changes in the anterior chamber of the eye and **photophobia** (visual hypersensitivity to light).

Clinical diagnosis of blastomycosis is made by microscopic identification of the thick-walled, budding *Blastomyces* yeast forms in biopsy or other lesion material. In most cases, the organism can be found in great abundance and its presence will be sufficient to establish a firm diagnosis.

Therapy consists of systemic antifungal medication, which has side effects and which must be given numerous times over a several-week period that may stretch to several months. Many dogs can be cured of blastomycosis if they receive aggressive treatment and if the disease has not progressed beyond a critical point. Relapses following treatment may occur, however, most often in dogs exhibiting very severe lung involvement at the initiation of therapy. Dogs that are still healthy 1 year after completion of therapy in most cases will remain free of disease. The prognosis for recovery from blastomycosis is always guarded except in the case of the more superficial skin infections, which often respond quite favorably to antifungal therapy. Spontaneous recovery from severe disseminated blastomycosis without treatment is considered an extremely rare event.

HISTOPLASMOSIS

Histoplasmosis is caused by *Histoplasma capsulatum,* a soil fungus common in the midwestern and eastern United States and in Central and South America. Areas of highest incidence in the United States include the Mississippi, Missouri and Ohio river valleys. The organism prefers moist, humid climates and has a predilection for chicken, bat and wild bird droppings, in which the filamentous mold form grows profusely. Unlike *Blastomyces,* the causative agent of blastomycosis, *Histoplasma* can easily be recovered from soil in regions where disease is prevalent. *Histoplasma* is especially common in soils on which chickens have been raised. Contaminated sites will continue to yield viable organisms in the soil for as long as 3 to 6 years after they have been abandoned.

Following inhalation of the organism, mild signs of respiratory disease may be observed (low-grade fever, lethargy, cough). Alternatively, the infection may be **asymptomatic** (no clinical signs apparent). This initial disease often lasts for a week or two. In a high percentage of infected dogs, the organism may persist in walled-off lesions in the lungs and regional lymph nodes for months to years. In such cases, the organism is kept under firm control by the host immune response and no further progression to disease occurs.

In a small percentage of cases (usually younger dogs), the organism may shrug off its immunologic shackles and disseminate to other sites within the body. Often it first spreads widely throughout the lungs, producing a pneumonia. Affected dogs may exhibit signs of fever, wasting, lethargy, a chronic productive cough, **hemoptysis** (coughing up blood), and mild anemia. In many dogs, however, clinical signs of gastrointestinal disease come to predominate. Watery to bloody diarrhea, straining to defecate, and mucus in the stool are commonly observed. Dissemination may progress to involve the liver, spleen, bone marrow, or (more rarely) the central nervous system. **Hepatosplenomegaly** (enlargement of the liver and spleen), anemia, **jaundice** (yellowish discoloration of the skin and mucous membranes), and **ascites** (accumulation of fluid within the abdominal cavity) represent additional clinical manifestations of disseminated histoplasmosis that may be seen in affected dogs.

Clinical diagnosis can be made by identification of the small *Histoplasma* yeast bodies within infected cells in lesion, scraping or biopsy material. Visualization of the intracellular yeast forms is usually sufficient to provide a firm diagnosis.

Therapy consists of systemic antifungal medication, which has unavoidable side effects and which must be given numerous times over a minimum period of 4 to 6 months. Aggressive treatment is required to effect a remission or cure, because the prognosis for animals with disseminated histoplasmosis is poor. Relapses following apparently successful therapy may occur. The prognosis is slightly better for dogs with disease that is largely restricted to the lungs.

COCCIDIOIDOMYCOSIS

Coccidioidomycosis (also called "San Joaquin Valley fever," or simply "valley fever"), the most severe and life-threatening of the systemic mycoses, is caused by *Coccidioides immitis.* This fungus resides in soil of the dry cactus country of the southwestern states from California to central Texas, particularly in areas where the creosote bush is common (an ecological niche known as the Lower Sonoran life zone). It is also found in Central and South America. The organism grows several inches deep in the soil, where it is aided in its spread by the activities of burrowing rodents. Following a period of wet weather, wind and dust storms whipping up the surface soil may spread the filamentous mold forms, called **arthrospores,** across great distances. The fungus is normally dormant in the summer and is killed by freezing temperatures. In most cases, inhalation of the infective arthrospores is followed by either an absence of clinical signs or by a very mild influenza-like illness characterized by fever, lethargy, partial inappetence, coughing, and sometimes joint pain or stiffness ("desert rheumatism" in people). The majority of dogs and human beings become solidly immune following initial infection.

Fewer than 10 inhaled arthrospores are sufficient to cause disease in susceptible dogs. "Susceptible" refers to the small percentage of infected dogs in whom dissemination of the infection beyond the lungs occurs. In these dogs the organism frequently spreads to long bones and joints, eyes, liver and kidneys. Clinical signs may include chronic fever nonresponsive to antibiotics, harsh coughing, inappetence, lethargy and weight loss. Bone swelling and joint enlargement may give rise to lameness, ulcers and draining tracts located over areas of infected bone, and neurologic signs caused by impingement of the disease process on the local nerve supply or by direct extension into the nervous system. Severe neurologic disease is the result of growth of *Coccidioides* organisms in the brain or spinal cord.

In human beings the skin is a frequent site of primary spread, but in dogs this more superficial form of the disease is not common; rather, skin involvement in dogs usually is reflective of widespread dissemination of the organism. *Coccidioides* may also be introduced into the body through a penetrating wound. Following this mode of inoculation the infection usually remains localized; recovery is common but often prolonged.

Clinical diagnosis is made by microscopic identification of the large **spherule** form (the parasitic tissue stage) of the organism in lesion or biopsy material. Visualization of spherules is usually sufficient to provide a firm diagnosis.

Treatment consists of systemic antifungal medication, which has side effects and which must be given repeatedly over a minimum period of 6 to 12 months. *An aggressive course of therapy is required to effect a remission.* Coccidioidomycosis is the most deadly of the systemic mycoses and the prognosis in the disseminated form of the disease, particularly if there is multiple bone involvement, is always guarded at best. Relapses following apparently successful therapy occur. The prognosis is slightly better for dogs with disease that is largely restricted to the lungs. The prognosis in cases of central nervous system involvement, however, is grave.

CRYPTOCOCCOSIS

Cryptococcus neoformans is an encapsulated, yeastlike fungus that exhibits a preference for tissues of the central nervous system. *Cryptococcus* organisms (cryptococci) are surrounded by a thick capsule that is in part responsible for the organism's ability to produce disease. Unlike other dimorphic fungi such as *Blastomyces* and *Histoplasma, Cryptococcus* retains its yeastlike appearance even when cultured outside an infected host (this in spite of the fact that a filamentous or mold form of the organism has been identified in nature).

Cryptococcus is found commonly in bird droppings, particularly those of pigeons, and in the soil. Pigeon excreta represent a highly favorable culture medium for *Cryptococcus,* although the organism is not an inhabitant of the pigeon's digestive tract. If protected from sunlight and drying, cryptococci may remain viable in contaminated droppings for as long as two years. Warm, humid climates are the most favorable for growth and proliferation of the organism.

Cryptococcosis is a relatively rare disease in dogs. Most clinical cases have been reported in younger dogs of the larger breeds, and appear to result from inhalation of the yeastlike form of the organism. This, again, is in contrast to the other systemic mycoses, wherein the filamentous mold form represents the primary infective stage (the infectivity of the mold form of *Cryptococcus* has not been intensively investigated; it is possible that *both* forms of this organism are infective).

Canine cryptococcosis is manifested most often by disseminated central nervous system and ocular disease. Neurologic signs that may be observed include a head-tilt, **nystagmus** (rapid, involuntary, rhythmic eye movements), circling, disorientation, head-pressing, varying degrees of paralysis or **paresis** (partial paralysis), incoordination and seizures. Dilation of the pupils and blindness secondary to lesions in the retina are among the characteristic ocular lesions induced by *Cryptococcus*. Skin lesions with ulcerations have also been reported in infected dogs.

Clinical diagnosis is based on identification of cryptococci, usually by means of an India ink preparation, in smears of nasal discharge, tissue smears, **cerebrospinal fluid** (fluid bathing the surfaces of the brain and spinal cord), ulcerated skin scrapings, or biopsy samples. The organisms are often present in considerable numbers. Visualization of the characteristic budding yeast forms is usually sufficient to make a firm diagnosis. In some samples (particularly cerebrospinal fluid) the organisms may be more difficult to find, in which case laboratory culture of the organism will be required.

Treatment of cryptococcosis in dogs is frequently disappointing. The disease is not as responsive to antifungal medication as it is in cats and, in general, is more frequently disseminated in canine cases. Moreover, the primary site for dissemination in dogs, the central nervous system, is inordinately sensitive to insult and not particularly amenable to therapeutic intervention.

One must keep in mind that cryptococcosis differs from the other systemic mycoses in that the tissue form of the organism appears also to be an infective form; that is, it is *potentially* transmissible from an infected animal to human beings. *Although there has never been a single documented case of transmission of cryptococcosis from an affected dog or cat to a human being,* it is the authors' belief that prudence dictates caution whenever handling an animal suffering from cryptococcosis.

The Subcutaneous Mycoses

The subcutaneous mycoses (**sporotrichosis, phycomycosis, phaeohyphomycosis, eumycotic mycetoma,** and **rhinosporidiosis**) represent a group of relatively rare fungal diseases affecting primarily the skin and underlying (**subcutaneous**) tissues. Occasionally they may spread to involve other areas of the body, including one or more organ systems. By and large, however, they are pathogens (disease agents) of more superficial body surfaces.

SPOROTRICHOSIS
Sporotrichosis is an uncommon chronic, pus-forming infection caused by *Sporothrix schenckii.* This fungus is widely distributed worldwide and can be found in soil, decaying vegetation, sphagnum moss, on rosebushes, tree bark and other natural sources. In the environ-

ment *Sporothrix* exists as a mold, but transforms to a parasitic yeast at the higher temperatures of body tissues (i.e., it is a dimorphic fungus). Infection usually occurs by implantation following a penetrating wound, as by a thorn or wood splinter. Inhalation and ingestion are alternative (and probably less common) means by which the fungus gains access to the body.

Sporotrichosis is most often seen in the hunting breeds. The infection usually remains localized to the skin and underlying tissues, but on rare occasions can spread systemically (spread to internal organs is more common in cats than in dogs). Lesions (nodules, ulcers, abscesses, draining tracts) are found most commonly on the head, trunk, or on a single extremity. It is not unusual for the infection to spread from the initial site into lymphatic vessels, eventually reaching the local lymph node, which may become enlarged.

A diagnosis of sporotrichosis may be difficult to make. *Sporothrix* often is difficult to identify microscopically in tissues, pus or fluid; it may require a number of attempts to locate the characteristic "cigar-shaped" yeast forms in the lesions. The most reliable (but also the most time-consuming and expensive) diagnosis is made by **culturing** (growing) the organism in the laboratory.

Systemic antifungal medication is the recommended treatment. The prognosis in most cases is guarded.

One must always keep in mind that sporotrichosis is also a **zoonosis**—i.e., it is potentially transmissible from an affected animal to human beings. Most cases that have been documented have involved cats; dogs appear to be less effective at transmitting the infection. Caution is recommended when handling an animal infected with *Sporothrix*.

Phycomycosis (Zygomycosis and Oömycosis)

"Phycomycosis" is a general term describing diseases caused by several different organisms, the diseases being classified into two separate groups, **zygomycosis** and **oömycosis** (or **pythiosis**).

Zygomycosis is caused by fungi belonging to the genera *Rhizopus, Absidia* and *Mucor,* and is characterized by inflammation and blockage of small blood vessels. The causative fungi are classical molds—*Rhizopus* frequently found coating the surface of old, moist bread—and only occasionally produce disease in animals, usually as opportunists (invading only if host defenses are compromised). Oömycosis is caused by members of the genus *Pythium,* organisms that are superficially similar to (but quite distinct from) the fungi causing zygomycosis.

Lesions of phycomycosis are frequently located on the extremities but may be found anywhere on the body. Swellings, skin ulcerations, lymph node enlargement and draining tracts characterize many of the lesions. Often there is internal involvement of the digestive tract, with resultant inappetence, weight loss, vomiting and diarrhea. Male dogs of the larger breeds tend to be affected more commonly.

Diagnosis is made by examination of appropriate tissues or draining fluids. The prognosis is equally grave for both zygomycosis and oömycosis.

Unless the affected tissues can be completely excised, there is little hope for a cure. Moreover, antifungal medication often is unsuccessful in eliminating the causative fungi.

Phaeohyphomycosis

Phaeohyphomycosis is an uncommon chronic infection of the subcutaneous tissues and is caused by dark, pigmented fungi known as **dematiaceous fungi.** These organisms normally live in soil and on vegetation, but on occasion can act as opportunistic pathogens, gaining access to tissues usually by means of a penetrating wound. Dematiaceous fungi can often be found in the home, contaminating grout, toilet bowls, shower curtains and other bathroom surfaces. Some of the fungal genera involved in phaeohyphomycosis include *Drechslera, Phialophora* and *Alternaria.* The disease is more common in cats than in dogs.

Lesions usually consist of skin nodules, abscesses or ulcers within which the causative fungus can be found growing. Often there will be an actively draining discharge loaded with pus. The disease tends to be chronic and progressive in the absence of treatment. In some instances, the infection may spread from its initial site to other areas of the body, in which case the prognosis for recovery is poor.

Diagnosis is made by microscopic identification of a dark, pigmented fungus in pus, tissue scrapings, or a biopsy sample. Treatment of small localized lesions usually consists of surgical removal; recurrence following surgery is not uncommon, however. Local or systemic antifungal medication may be required to obtain resolution of the infection in some cases.

EUMYCOTIC MYCETOMA

"Mycetoma" is a general term for a swollen, progressing, tumorlike skin lesion caused by either fungi or bacteria; "eumycotic" refers to those mycetomas produced exclusively by fungal species. Eumycotic mycetomas in animals are caused often (but not exclusively) by dark, pigmented (dematiaceous) fungi (*see* "PHAEO-HYPHOMYCOSIS," ABOVE) and are sometimes referred to colloquially as "fungal tumors." Fungal genera that may be involved include *Curvularia* and *Drechslera*. These fungi normally are found in the soil or on vegetation, but on occasion can act as opportunistic **pathogens** (disease agents) in animals and human beings.

Eumycotic mycetomas caused by dematiaceous fungi (so-called black-grain mycetomas) often are located on the extremities and are usually the result of fungal contamination of a penetrating wound. The causative fungi can be found within the lesions in the form of grains or granules, which represent microcolonies of the organism. The presence of these granules is a primary differentiating feature between eumycotic mycetoma and phaeohyphomycosis (also caused by dematiaceous fungi).

A nodular or tumorlike swelling, draining tracts, and the presence of grains or granules within the draining fluid are characteristic of many fungal mycetomas. In general, such findings are sufficient to provide a fairly confident diagnosis. When the lesion is located on the foot or lower limbs, lameness may be an additional presenting sign. Eumycotic mycetomas caused by fungi other than the pigmented variety (so-called white-grain mycetomas) often occur in abdominal organs, possibly the result of contamination from the digestive tract following intestinal surgery.

The treatment of choice in most instances is surgical excision of the mycetoma. Recurrence following surgery is not unexpected, however. Antifungal medication may be required in addition to surgery in order to eradicate the fungus. The prognosis for recovery is fair to good, except in cases with extensive involvement of internal organs.

RHINOSPORIDIOSIS

Rhinosporidiosis is an uncommon disease caused by an as yet poorly characterized fungus, *Rhinosporidium seeberi*. Rhinosporidiosis in animals and human beings is **endemic** (native to) in parts of Asia and South America, but occurs only sporadically elsewhere. In the United States, most reported canine cases have involved large-breed dogs living in southern states.

Canine rhinosporidiosis is a chronic, localized infection characterized by the formation of **polyps** (small fleshy masses protruding from the surface of a mucous membrane) in the nasal passages. Infection probably occurs when dogs nose about in pools of stagnant water, which probably contain the infective stage (**sporangiospore**) of the fungus (the complete life history of this fungus is still relatively obscure, however). The fungus actively proliferates in the mucous membranes of the nasal cavity, inducing development of the tumorlike polyps.

Clinical signs in affected dogs include sneezing and a bloody nasal discharge, usually from only a single nostril. Because of the chronic nature of the infection, signs may be evident for weeks to months before a diagnosis is reached. The diagnosis is made by microscopic identification of the causative organism in a smear of the nasal discharge or in a biopsy sample of an **excised** (surgically removed) polyp.

Treatment consists of surgical removal of the polyps (which may recur, necessitating more than a single surgical procedure). Medical therapy may in some cases aid in preventing recurrence.

Protothecosis

Protothecosis is a rare disease caused by a ubiquitous, colorless alga called *Prototheca*. (For convenience, *Prototheca* is frequently included in discussions of fungal diseases.) Algae such as seaweed and many **unicellular** (single-celled) freshwater plants are among the most important of earth's organisms because they are responsible for producing the majority of the oxygen present in the atmosphere.

Prototheca is an inhabitant of wastewater sewage and animal waste, from which it contaminates food and water sources available to animals and human beings. Some species of *Prototheca* are capable of invading tissue and causing disease, either superficial infections of the skin and underlying subcutaneous tissues or more widespread systemic illness. In dogs, *Prototheca* produces gastrointestinal disease affecting primarily the colon, from which site the organism is probably disseminated to other areas of the body. It seems likely that an inherited or acquired defect in immune function in the host may underlie susceptibility to dissemination of *Prototheca* infection.

Bloody diarrhea is the most common presenting sign in dogs. Inappetence, weight loss, central nervous system signs, ulcerative skin lesions, urinary dysfunction and ocular disease (including blindness) may also occur. Superficial skin infections as a sole clinical sign are uncommon in dogs.

Diagnosis is made by a combination of clinical findings (particularly, bloody diarrhea combined with ocular disease) and identification of the organism in appropriate smear or tissue samples. *Prototheca* can also be *cultured* quite readily in the laboratory.

Treatment of disseminated prototecosis in dogs has not been successful, even with high doses of systemic antifungal medication. The disease at present is essentially incurable.

Pneumocystosis

Pneumocystosis is caused by a poorly characterized organism called *Pneumocystis carinii*. Previously classified as a protozoan, the organism exhibits characteristics of both protozoa and fungi. Recent genetic analyses indicate that the organism is indeed a fungus, but elements of its life cycle bear a striking similarity to those of certain protozoa. The organism is ubiquitous in the environment and can infect a wide variety of species, including human beings. *Pneumocystis* pneumonia represents the most common disease complication in individuals infected with the human immunodeficiency virus (the agent of AIDS).

Pneumocystosis is an extremely rare disease of dogs. The vast majority of infections are inapparent; under normal conditions, host immune defenses effectively suppress the organism. As with prototecosis and many other diseases discussed in this chapter, some perturbation of host immune control is likely a prerequisite to the development of clinical illness.

Infection occurs probably by inhalation. The primary site of infection is the lung and clinical signs are thus reflective of respiratory difficulty. Gradual weight loss also occurs, often despite a normal appetite. Diagnosis requires demonstration of the causative organism in lung tissue or respiratory fluids (dissemination of *Pneumocystis* to other areas of the body is unusual). A regimen of combination chemotherapy is available for dogs that is similar to that used by AIDS patients. The prognosis is guarded, although clinical remission has been reported. It is likely that long-term therapy will be required, in light of the probable immune defect predisposing to illness. In the absence of treatment the disease is inevitably fatal.

CHAPTER 37

Internal Parasites

**by Charles H. Courtney,
Patricia A. Conrad,
Walter M. Boyce and
Jeffrey E. Barlough**

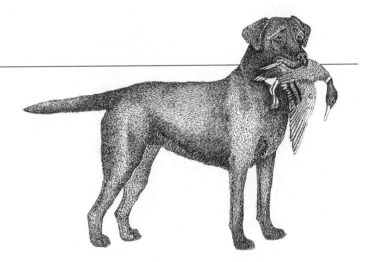

Parasites can be defined as organisms that exist in or on other living organisms, from which they draw nourishment and for which they provide no benefit in return. Parasites come in all shapes and sizes, ranging from microscopic, single-celled protozoa to giant intestinal tapeworms whose length can be measured in feet. Parasites can be distinguished from many other microbes residing in or on a host—such as the large population of bacteria and other microorganisms that are normal inhabitants of the large intestine—by the fact that parasites for the most part are ultimately detrimental to the health of the host.

For the purposes of this chapter, parasites can be classified into either of two very broad categories: *external parasites* and *internal parasites*. External parasites are those found on or within the skin of the host, while internal parasites live within the host, chiefly in the gastrointestinal tract, liver and lungs. It is this latter group of parasites—the roundworms (**nematodes**), tapeworms, flukes and protozoa—that forms the subject of the current chapter.

Definition of Terms

Before proceeding further, a number of common scientific terms must be defined as a prelude to discussing the individual internal parasites of dogs. These are terms that veterinary parasitologists use routinely to describe various features of the parasites, their life cycles, and their hosts. It should be noted that many of these terms are not absolute and that there may be considerable overlap among them.

host. The living organism in or on which the parasite resides.
definitive host. The host in or on which the parasite reaches sexual maturity or undergoes sexual reproduction. If there is no sexual reproduction in the life of the parasite, the host of greatest importance to human infections is considered to be the definitive host.
intermediate host. A host that (usually) is essential to the parasite's life cycle and in which it undergoes development to juvenile but not mature stages. The definitive

host may eat an intermediate host to acquire the infection, or a juvenile parasite stage may be released from the intermediate host and reach the definitive host by other means.

vector. A term usually applied to insects, ticks, and mites that carry disease-causing microorganisms from an infected animal to a non-infected animal. A vector is often, but not always, an intermediate host as well.

biological vector. Vector wherein a developmental stage of the parasite necessarily occurs.

mechanical vector. Vector that merely serves physically to transport a parasite from one host to another.

paratenic host. An optional host in a parasite's life cycle in which juvenile stages may persist but do not develop.

transport host. An animal in which part of the immature phase of the parasite's life cycle is spent, but no development occurs; in contrast to a paratenic host, the **larvae** (immature forms of the parasite) in a passive state may be shed at any time.

reservoir host. An animal from which infection may be passed to domesticated stock or to human beings.

abnormal host. A host infected with a parasite normally found in another host species.

obligatory parasite. A parasite whose life cycle cannot be completed without a parasitic phase at some stage.

facultative parasite. A parasite whose life cycle can be completed without a parasitic phase, but which may optionally include a parasitic phase under certain circumstances.

life cycle. The life story of a parasite's development.

direct life cycle. A cycle that can be completed without the participation of an intermediate host.

indirect life cycle. A cycle that can only be completed with the participation of an intermediate host.

infective stage. The specific stage in the life cycle of a parasite that is able to initiate an infection in a definitive or intermediate host.

free-living stage. A stage in the life cycle wherein the parasite exists freely in the general environment and not in or on a host animal.

prepatent period. The time elapsing between the initiation of infection of a definitive host and the appearance of the products of parasite reproduction, e.g., eggs, larvae, etc.

incubation period. The time elapsed between the initiation of an infection and the onset of disease.

patent infection. Infection in a definitive host that results in the appearance of products of parasite reproduction.

route of infection. The means by which a parasite gains entry to a host, e.g., ingestion, skin penetration, injection, etc.

route of migration. The path certain parasites follow in the body of the host after they have gained entry but before they have developed to maturity.

Taxonomic classifications for microorganisms are identified primarily by the genus, whose first letter is capitalized, followed by the species when used which is entirely in lowercase. Both are always in italics. After the organism is named formally, it is thereafter identified by the initial of the genus and the species name.

How Internal Parasites Cause Disease

Veterinarians are interested in parasites for their ability to cause disease. Disease represents the outcome of a complex interplay of both host and parasite factors. Parasites may be **pathogenic** (disease-inducing) in certain circumstances but not in others. One crucial determining factor is the *number of infective-stage parasites to which the host is exposed.* Nearly all parasitic organisms are pathogenic if present in overwhelming numbers. Another factor is the *competency of the host's immune defenses.* If the host's response to infection is compromised by malnutrition, stress, immunosuppressive drug medication (e.g., corticosteroids), or the presence of other infections, the potential for disease, even by a normally innocuous organism, may be enhanced. (*See* CHAPTER 33, "THE IMMUNE SYSTEM AND DISORDERS.") Some parasitic organisms capitalize on such situations; they are referred to as **opportunistic parasites**. Because the defenses of the newborn are generally less well-developed and effective than those of an adult, a parasitic infection tends to represent a more serious threat to puppies than to adult dogs.

Some animal species have a natural, inherited immunity to certain parasites and this immunity or innate resistance limits in part the normal host-range of a parasite. If the immunity is incomplete, however, disease may arise from the parasite's invasion of an abnormal host. In addition, some parasites are more host-specific than others, regardless of the host's immune status, so that only certain hosts are susceptible to infection. Parasites may also migrate to abnormal locations in their normal host, sometimes with dire consequences.

In general, the basis for the pathogenic effects of an internal parasite can involve one or more of the following:

- competition for, and absorption of, essential nutrients intended for the host
- interference with proper absorption of nutrients by the host
- loss of host body fluids (blood, lymph, or tissue fluid)
- production of anemia in the host by destruction of red blood cells
- mechanical obstruction of hollow organs, ducts and vessels
- tissue **necrosis** (cell death) through the exertion of pressure on surrounding tissue
- physical and chemical damage to tissue during parasite migration through the body
- acute chemical injury resulting from the action of toxins or other secreted substances
- direct or indirect, delayed tissue injury resulting from irritation or chemical effects
- infliction of wounds or disruption of body continuity, predisposing the host to secondary infections
- transmission of other infectious disease agents
- stimulation of abnormal immune or allergic reactions
- debilitation and/or interference with normal growth and development of the host
- inflammatory responses induced in the host by death and decomposition of the parasite

Nematode Parasites

With the exception of insects, there are probably more **nematodes** (roundworms) in the world than any other type of animal. Nematodes can be described generally as elongated, cylindrical, unsegmented, cream-colored worms. Nematodes exhibit extreme variation in size from one species to another. In addition, **sexual dimorphism** (size differences between the sexes) is the rule, with the female being larger than the male. The body of the parasite is normally sheathed in a thick, noncellular covering called a cuticle, which is flexible but not elastic and quite resistant to environmental insults. Various ornamentations may adorn the cuticle, including hooks, spines, bosses (blisterlike swellings), and others.

Nematodes undergo five larval stages, designated L_1 through L_5. The L_5 stage is equivalent to a young adult. Between each larval stage the organism molts and sheds its cuticle:

$$\text{egg} \rightarrow \text{embryo} \rightarrow L_1 \xrightarrow{\text{molt}} L_2 \xrightarrow{\text{molt}} L_3 \xrightarrow{\text{molt}} L_4 \xrightarrow{\text{molt}} L_5 \rightarrow \text{adult}$$

The definitive host usually acquires a nematode infection by being exposed to one of the larval stages. The infective larval stage differs with different nematode parasites. Potential routes of transmission of nematodes include ingestion of an egg, larva, and/or infected intermediate host; direct penetration of the skin (L_3 larval stage); bite of an infected vector; **transplacental** transmission (from mother to fetus across the placenta); and **transmammary** transmission (in **colostrum** ["first milk"] or milk to the neonate). The nematodes perhaps best known to dog owners include ascarids, hookworms and heartworms.

ASCARIDS

Ascarids are among the most common and important gastrointestinal parasites of dogs. The ascarids infecting dogs include *Toxocara canis* and *Toxascaris leonina,* the latter infecting cats as well. Of the two, *Toxocara canis* is the more common and the more important.

The routes of transmission vary with the different worms. For *Toxocara canis* there are four routes:

1. Transplacental
2. Transmammary
3. Ingestion of eggs from the environment
4. Predation on paratenic hosts, such as birds and mice

Of these four, the two most important clinically are transplacental transmission and ingestion of eggs.

Virtually all puppies are born infected with *Toxocara canis* (the L_3 larvae are already in the liver at birth) and shed eggs of this parasite in the feces by 3 weeks of age. Age resistance represents an important phenomenon; the outcome of the ingestion of ascarid eggs is influenced by a pup's age at the time. In puppies less than 3 months of age, a high proportion of the larvae that hatch in the intestine from ingested eggs will migrate through the liver to the lungs, where they are coughed up and swallowed, returning to the intestine for the completion of their maturation. The prepatent period is approximately 4 to 5 weeks.

In older puppies, an increasing proportion of the L_3 larvae become arrested in their migration in various tissues, including muscles, kidneys, eyes and brain. These arrested larvae are at a "dead end" in males, spayed bitches, and intact bitches that never become pregnant. In pregnant bitches, however, arrested larvae become reactivated at about the 42nd day of **gestation** (pregnancy), when host immunity is suppressed by normal hormonal changes related to pregnancy. These larvae then cross the placenta to infect the fetus. Less commonly, the larvae migrate to the mammary gland and subsequently are shed in the bitch's milk. In addition, any new ascarid eggs ingested by the bitch during the period of immunosuppression normally associated with pregnancy may complete the liver-lung migration and develop to a patent infection.

Lactating bitches and their litters from about 3 weeks **postpartum** (after birth of the pups) onward shed vast numbers of *Toxocara canis* eggs in their feces and thus represent a major source of environmental contamination. Like nearly all ascarid worms, the eggs of *Toxocara* and *Toxascaris* are fairly resistant to environmental extremes, and infection can persist in a contaminated environment for years.

Mature dogs (including lactating bitches) may develop a heavy infection and shed large numbers of eggs in feces following ingestion of worms spontaneously shed in the stool of heavily infected puppies. (*Note:* Bitches commonly lick the anus of young puppies to stimulate defecation, then swallow the feces as a way of keeping the nest box clean.) These heavy infections (actually reinfections in the case of lactating bitches) are usually controlled by the bitch's immune system as soon as the pups are weaned and her resistance to the parasite returns to normal. Nonlactating, mature dogs may develop a minor patent infection with low numbers of eggs shed in the stool by ingesting paratenic hosts (most commonly small rodents, birds, earthworms or cockroaches) containing arrested L_3 larvae. In such instances, the larvae develop to maturity without undergoing a liver-to-lung migration and are therefore less affected by the host's immune responses. Similarly, if an adult dog ingests a very small number of ascarid eggs, the developing larvae may not stimulate a sufficiently intense immune response and thus survive to establish a minor patent infection.

Toxascaris leonina is primarily a cold-climate parasite. It does not undergo a liver-to-lung migration following the host's ingestion of eggs, so infection by transplacental and transmammary routes cannot occur. Ingestion of eggs thus is the clinically important means of transmission for this parasite. Some small L_4 larvae may persist in an arrested state in the wall of the digestive tract for up to a year, and can resume their development and repopulate the intestine after the expulsion of adult worms by deworming medication. Paratenic hosts may be another source of infection, particularly in older dogs. Host immunity appears to be less effective against this ascarid than against *Toxocara canis,* and there is no significant age-related resistance.

Clinical signs of ascarid infection generally are more severe in puppies; mature dogs seldom exhibit any clinical signs of infection. Migrating *Toxocara canis* larvae may cause **verminous pneumonia** (inflammation of the lungs due to worms), but this condition is often difficult to diagnose in a live animal. Larvae acquired in the uterus may, in this manner, be a significant cause of early mortality in pups during their first few days of life. Beyond this time emaciation resulting from the effects of maturing and adult worms on the intestinal tract may be a major cause of death, with peak mortalities occurring at 2 to 3 weeks of age. The typical ascarid-ridden pup exhibits a pot-bellied appearance, with a rough haircoat and meager musculature. Vomiting and diarrhea are common signs, and owners often become alarmed when adult worms are vomited up or voided in the feces. Convulsions may occur with heavy infections, usually because of **hypoglycemia** (abnormally low blood-sugar levels) or other metabolic imbalances, but *not* because of larvae migrating through the brain. Occasionally there may be an obstruction or even rupture of the intestine, **intussusception** ("telescoping" of one section of bowel into an adjoining section), or blockage of the **bile duct** (duct that discharges digestive fluids from the liver into the small intestine).

Diagnosis of ascarid infection is usually made by identification of the characteristic worm eggs in feces or by observing the adult worms in vomitus or feces. The method used for identifying eggs in feces is known as *fecal flotation.* With this technique the eggs are selectively induced to float upwards through a special solution, and then are deposited on a glass microscope slide for subsequent examination. (*See* APPENDIX C, "DIAGNOSTIC TESTS.")

There are considerable public health concerns regarding *Toxocara canis* infection of human beings. Heavy infections of young children may lead to **visceral larva migrans** (*see* APPENDIX A, "ZOONOTIC DISEASES: FROM DOGS TO PEOPLE"), while lighter infections may result in **ocular larva migrans** (migration of the parasites through the eyes). Control programs for *Toxocara canis* were actually designed chiefly to prevent human infection, with control of the parasite in puppies representing a side benefit. Control is aimed at preventing the long-lived, highly resistant eggs from being shed into the environment. The Centers for Disease Control and Prevention (CDC) now recommend that the bitch and her litter be wormed with an appropriate deworming medication at 2, 4, 6 and 8 weeks after the pups are born, *regardless of whether or not fecal examinations are positive for eggs.* Newly purchased, weaned pups should be wormed at least twice at a 2-week interval. CDC recommends further that, after weaning, puppies be placed on a heartworm preventive medication that also controls ascarids and hookworms until the pups are a year of age. Older dogs of all ages should be wormed on the basis of a positive fecal exam or observation of worms in vomitus or feces. Control programs for *Toxascaris leonina* likewise involve treatment based on the result of fecal exams.

Sanitation will do much to prevent ascarid infection. A general rule of thumb is that feces should be picked up from lawns at least once weekly, unless rainy weather or insect activity would likely break up or scatter the feces sooner. Human infection can be prevented by this simple procedure, plus the following additional measures:

1. Enforcement of leash laws and aggressive stray-dog control
2. "Doggie bag" laws requiring fecal pickup in public areas
3. Banning dogs from areas where young children play
4. Enactment of laws requiring owners to pick up dog feces on their own property

HOOKWORMS

Hookworms are found in the small intestine of a number of domestic animal species, including dogs. The hookworms of dogs include *Ancylostoma caninum, Ancylostoma braziliense*

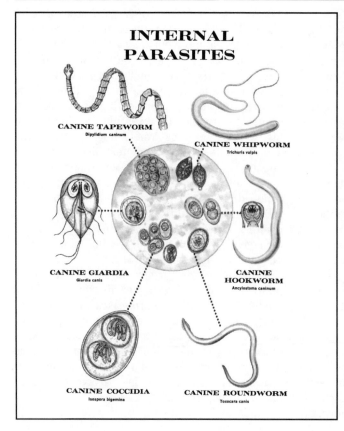

INTERNAL PARASITES

CANINE TAPEWORM
Dipylidium caninum

CANINE WHIPWORM
Trichuris vulpis

CANINE GIARDIA
Giardia canis

CANINE HOOKWORM
Ancylostoma caninum

CANINE COCCIDIA
Isospora bigemina

CANINE ROUNDWORM
Toxocara canis

In older dogs that have acquired a degree of immunity, larvae do not enter the airways but remain in the circulation and are deposited in various tissues, particularly muscle, where their development is arrested. Orally ingested larvae can either penetrate through the lining of the upper digestive tract, behaving like larvae acquired by skin penetration, or pass directly into the small intestine and develop in the intestinal wall. Larvae arrested in muscle and other tissues of bitches will migrate to the mammary glands (and, to a much lesser extent, the uterus) during pregnancy.

Tissue-arrested larvae may also resume their development if an existing infection of adult hookworms in the intestine is removed by **anthelmintic** (deworming) treatment. This is the so-called muscle leak phenomenon, which can frustrate attempts to clear hookworm infections from some dogs. Apparently, larvae are constantly "leaking" from the muscle reservoir, but in the immune host with a small population of adult worms they usually are killed before reaching maturity. If the adult worms have been removed, however, the larvae will mature and eggs will appear in feces after about 4 weeks.

Anemia (low red blood cell count) is the chief clinical sign of hookworm disease. As they feed, the adult worms suck plugs of intestinal tissue into their mouth structures. Certain hookworm species, including *Ancylostoma caninum,* are voracious bloodsuckers and can cause hemorrhage as well. Two severe forms of hookworm disease may appear in young pups. In *acute hookworm disease,* massive infection (usually obtained from the environment) may lead to development of many adult worms in relatively nonimmune puppies. These pups become profoundly anemic, with a bloody to black, tarry diarrhea. Many hookworm eggs can be identified in their feces by flotation techniques. Such animals usually die if they are not treated promptly. *Peracute hookworm disease* is very

in warm climates, and *Uncinaria stenocephala* in cool climates. By far the most important and most pathogenic of these is *Ancylostoma caninum.* Hookworms are of much less importance in dry, arid regions than in warm, humid climates.

Depending upon the species, hookworms can be transmitted in several different ways. Transmammary transmission and infection acquired from the environment by skin penetration or oral ingestion of L_3 larvae are the clinically important routes of infection. Following direct penetration of the skin, larvae enter the blood circulation and migrate to the small intestine by way of the lungs. (Unlike *Toxocara canis* larvae, hookworm larvae do not migrate through the liver.) Entry of larvae into the airways in the lungs may produce a verminous pneumonia, as described for *Toxocara.* The normal prepatent period for infection by skin penetration or oral ingestion is about 2 weeks.

similar, except that eggs are not found in the stool (because the hookworms are too young to lay eggs) and infection occurs via the transmammary route.

Some adult dogs, through either poor diet, filthy environment, less effective immunity, or massive exposure to worm eggs, may suffer *chronic hookworm disease.* In such cases adult hookworms populate the intestine in sufficient quantities to produce mild clinical signs, including diarrhea or vomiting and perhaps a low-grade anemia. *Decompensated chronic hookworm disease* can develop if a severe stress or malnutrition breaks down what little immunity remains. Affected dogs become severely anemic and shed a relatively large number of eggs in the feces, resembling in many ways a pup with acute hookworm disease.

A substantial immunity develops following repeated infections with *Ancylostoma caninum,* although it is not as complete as immunity to *Toxocara canis.* Young pups are highly susceptible to hookworm infection, whereas adult dogs in good health can resist all but the most severe challenges (i.e., there is an age-related resistance). Immunity is maintained in adult dogs by the presence of a few adult worms in the small intestine, a phenomenon known as **premunition.** Apparently, immunity also markedly reduces the bloodsucking activities of adult worms, making them much less pathogenic.

Diagnosis of hookworm infection is usually accomplished by identification of hookworm eggs in a fecal flotation. A number of anthelmintic medications are effective against hookworms. As indicated earlier, however, if hookworms are removed by anthelmintic therapy the intestinal tract will be quickly repopulated by the resumed development of arrested larvae, with a few eggs once again appearing in the feces. Considerable time and expense often are expended on such "nuisance infections" in otherwise healthy dogs, which probably do not even require anthelmintic therapy. Good sanitation (regular pickup of feces) to prevent muscle accumulation of arrested larvae is perhaps the best control method for most cases of hookworm infection in healthy dogs.

Chronic hookworm disease normally requires anthelmintic therapy, but for proper control the underlying cause of the animal's reduced immunity should be identified and treated, if possible. Sanitation and attention to diet and housing are the best preventive measures for chronic disease.

Following heavy exposure to hookworm larvae in older, somewhat immune dogs, an intense hookworm **dermatitis** (skin inflammation) may develop at sites where the larvae have penetrated the skin, particularly on the footpads (a condition known as **pododermatitis,** inflammation of the footpads). Affected feet become swollen, painful and hot and the footpads soft and spongy as a result of the body's reaction to larvae invading through the skin. Separation of the pads and nail deformities may soon follow, with the footpads becoming thick, dry and cracked. Treatment involves removal of the animal from the infected environment, good sanitation, deworming to remove the intestinal worm population, and topical treatment of affected body sites with an anthelmintic paste to kill larvae remaining on the skin.

Acute and peracute hookworm disease causing severe anemia are medical emergencies requiring hospitalization and three-pronged therapy:

1. Physiological support (usually a blood transfusion)
2. Fast-acting anthelmintic medication to kill larvae quickly
3. Follow-up prevention as the host's tissues probably are filled with migrating larvae that will soon mature

Because peracute hookworm disease is usually milk-borne, the bitch should be kept under hygienic conditions that will prevent her exposure to larvae. Anthelmintic therapy prior to **whelping** (giving birth) should also be given since it will have some efficacy against larvae migrating in the tissues. Most infections in pups can be prevented by anthelmintic treatment given at 1, 2, 4, 6 and 8 weeks after birth.

In the environment, hookworm eggs hatch into free-living larvae. Unlike ascarid and whipworm larvae, hookworm larvae are relatively short-lived. They can survive on grass for only about 2 months under ideal conditions (warm, wet weather) and cannot tolerate freezing, *Uncinaria* being an exception. Since larvae exit the fecal mass after 6 days' development, stools should be picked up at least twice a week to prevent environmental contamination. Dry kennel runs exposed to direct sunlight will contain much fewer larvae than shaded, moist runs. Bleach (1% solution) applied daily to concrete runs may help reduce larval populations. Existing L_3 populations on sand or gravel (but not grass) can be destroyed by application of borax or rock salt.

Human infections can occur, resulting in cutaneous larva migrans, an itchy, creeping skin eruption that is seldom serious and that is most commonly associated with *Ancylostoma braziliense* infection. (*See* APPENDIX A, "ZOONOTIC DISEASES: FROM DOGS TO PEOPLE").

WHIPWORMS

Adult whipworms are normally found in the **colon** (large intestine), where the female worms lay eggs that pass out in the feces. The eggs require 3 or more weeks to develop to infective L_1 larvae (the larvae remaining inside the egg during this time). Eggs containing infective larvae are then ingested by the definitive host (dog), hatch in the intestine, and mature to adults in 70 to 90 days.

Most species of *Trichuris* (including *Trichuris vulpis,* the canine whipworm) are blood-feeders. The adults tunnel into the intestinal wall, using their mouthparts to lacerate blood vessels. Light infections usually do not cause any clinical signs, but heavy infections can produce acute or chronic inflammation with diarrhea, anemia, unthriftiness and weight loss.

Clinically significant infections of dogs with *Trichuris vulpis* are common, and once established on the premises can be very difficult to eradicate. The transmission is direct by ingestion of eggs from the environment, and there appears to be little immunity to reinfection. The prepatent period for the canine whipworm is 90 days, but clinical signs of disease can appear as early as 60 days postinfection; thus, clinical signs may appear up to a month before any eggs are shed in the feces.

Affected dogs exhibit diarrhea, vomiting, anemia and weight loss. Because the eggs may survive for up to 5 years in cold climates (but are more rapidly killed in warm climates), whipworm infection may be more common and severe in northern parts of the country. There is little risk of human infection with the canine whipworm; reports of such infections are extremely rare and in some cases identification of the parasite is highly suspect.

One of the greatest difficulties with whipworm disease lies in diagnosis. Because clinical signs can appear before eggs are shed in the feces, diagnosis is sometimes made based on the response to anthelmintic treatment. Once the infection is patent, eggs are often shed only in small numbers and at irregular intervals, and may be absent from the stool for a week at a time. This difficulty can be overcome by performing repeated fecal examinations over a period of several weeks.

Only a few anthelmintic medications are effective against whipworms. Once a medication has been selected, treatment is relatively straightforward. Some authorities recommend routine retreatment of all whipworm-infected dogs after 3 weeks and again after 3 months, on the hypothesis that developing larvae may not have been killed by the initial treatment. The problem of persistent disease-causing infection is particularly relevant if the environment is heavily contaminated with eggs. In such cases, dogs should be routinely treated every 2 months for at least a year, while the owner implements an intensive fecal pickup program. Alternatively, affected dogs may be placed on a heartworm preventive medication that also controls whipworms. If dogs are kept on concrete runs, careful use of a horticultural flame gun will destroy worm eggs on raw concrete surfaces (*Note:* Be aware that some painted surfaces may catch fire.) There is no known method for destroying whipworm eggs on grass surfaces, although regular tillage of bare soils may bury sufficient numbers of eggs to be of benefit.

Control of whipworm infections relies on good sanitation (regular fecal pickup), routine (twice-yearly) fecal examination and, if indicated, anthelmintic treatment. The primary objective of control is to prevent large numbers of whipworm eggs from accumulating in the pet's environment.

THREADWORMS

Threadworms exhibit two types of life cycle, a free-living cycle and a parasitic cycle. In the parasitic cycle, the females are pathogenic and live in the surface tissues of the small intestine. In most species, eggs laid by the female are passed out of the body of the host, but in the major species affecting dogs the eggs hatch in the intestine so that it is the L_1 larvae that are excreted in the feces. In the soil, the L_1 larvae may develop into one of two forms:

1. An L_3 larva that is infective for a new host
2. An L_3 larva that is noninfective and that continues its development in the soil to produce free-living male and female worms

In order to reach the host's intestine, infective L_3 larvae must undergo a migration via the blood circulation to the heart and then the lungs, where they are coughed up and swallowed. *The L_3 larvae must first penetrate the skin in order to enter the blood circulation.* Even though larvae may enter through the mouth and be swallowed, they do not travel directly to the intestine; rather, they must penetrate the surface lining of the oral cavity or **esophagus** (the muscular tube extending from the throat to the stomach), and then undergo the same circuitous migration as do larvae entering through the skin.

Under suitable environmental conditions, free-living larvae that hatch from eggs develop directly in the soil into free-living adult males and females. In turn the females lay eggs, which develop into either free-living larvae or infective larvae. There may be several successive free-living generations, although some threadworm species show a regular alternation between free-living and parasitic cycles.

The major species of threadworm infecting dogs is *Strongyloides stercoralis.* Infections are more prevalent in warm rather than cold climates, but in either locale infections usually are quite rare. Only the female worms parasitize dogs, reproduction in the host occurring by **parthenogenesis** (a mode of reproduction wherein the female produces off-spring without the need for fertilization by a male). Sexual reproduction occurs only among the free-living adults in the soil.

The worms may be pathogenic for young pups, causing a cough (from larvae migrating through the lungs) followed in a few days by a bloody, **mucoid** (containing mucus), or watery diarrhea. Pododermatitis may also occur. Disease is most frequently seen as a kennel outbreak during hot, humid summer weather. Occasionally, infections characterized by an intractable diarrhea are reported in individual dogs.

Diagnosis is made by identification of larvae, and occasionally the small larvated eggs, in a fresh fecal smear. Treatment consists of high doses of anthelmintic medication. Several courses of treatment at regular intervals may be required to rid a kennel of a threadworm infestation. In addition, the environment should be meticulously cleansed using the methods previously described for the control of ascarids, hookworms and whipworms.

LUNGWORMS

The term "lungworm" is used to denote nematodes whose adult stages are found in the airways of the respiratory tract, in **pulmonary** (lung) tissue, and/or in pulmonary blood vessels. Lungworms of the genus *Filaroides* are occasionally found in dogs. The life cycle of these worms is direct. Adults living in the respiratory tract lay eggs that quickly hatch to the L_1 stage. These are coughed up and swallowed. *The L_1 stage is immediately infective by ingestion.* Commonly, the larvae are passed in the saliva as the infected bitch cleans her pups, by fecal contamination of food, or by regurgitative feeding.

The prepatent period is about 10 weeks. As the infection progresses, adults of *Filaroides osleri,* the most important species of lungworm in dogs, localize in wartlike gray nodules up to $3/4$" diameter, which develop at the branching of the **bronchi** (the larger air passages leading from the **trachea** [windpipe] and branching into the lungs). In severe infections this results in a **bronchitis** (inflammation of the bronchi) characterized by episodes of harsh, dry coughing that can be induced by placing pressure on the dog's throat. Inappetence and emaciation may occur.

The mortality rate can reach 75% in some infected litters.

Diagnosis of *Filaroides osleri* infections is made by fecal examination. Unfortunately, there is at present no highly effective anthelmintic medication for use against this parasite.

Dogs may also be infecte with another nematode lungworm, *Capillaria aerophila.* Because of the close resemblance of this parasite's egg to those of whipworms, many cases of Capillaria infection are misdiagnosed as "whipworms." The adult worms live in the nasal passages, trachea, and larger bronchi. Most infections are asymptomatic (producing no clinical signs), but occassionally, heavy infections may produce sneezing and a harsh cough. Earthworms serve as intermediate hosts. Dogs become infected bu ingesting earthworms containing infective larvae. The prepatent period is about 33 days.

Diagnosis is usually made by identification of eggs in a fecal flotation, and occasionally by identification of eggs in a **transtracheal wash** (flushing of material from the trachea and bronchi by needle puncture and aspiration through the skin and tracheal wall). Treatment, if required, may involve one or more doses of an anthelmintic medication.

HEARTWORM

Heartworm disease is a serious problem of dogs caused by *Dirofilaria immitis.* This parasite occurs worldwide throughout the tropics and subtropics, where its presence is limited only by the range of its mosquito vectors. It is also quite prevalent in temperate climates wherever suitable mosquito vectors are abundant, its northern distribution being limited by a requirement for mild temperatures for proper development within the vector. In North America, *Dirofilaria immitis* is most abundant along the Gulf and Atlantic coasts and throughout the Mississippi River valley. It is less common in the more arid states west of the Mississippi.

Dirofilaria immitis is classified as a *filarial* or *filarid* nematode. These are long, threadlike worms with small mouths, the males having coiled tails. Filarids do not lay eggs, but instead release special embryos or prelarval stages called **microfilariae,** which are sometimes encased in a thin sheath called an *egg membrane.* Microfilariae circulate in blood and tissue fluids, where they are available for ingestion by a blood-feeding mosquito (the intermediate host). At times of the day corresponding to the feeding periods of the mosquitoes microfilariae tend to be present in the blood in highest numbers. They develop to infective L_3 larvae in the intermediate host, and gain access to a definitive host (a dog) through mosquito bites.

The large adult heartworms live primarily in the pulmonary arteries, where the female worms expel numerous microfilariae into the bloodstream. When a mosquito takes a blood meal it ingests the microfilariae. In the mosquito they migrate to the **malpighian tubules** (organs located at the midgut-hindgut junction of the mosquito) and undergo two molts to the L_3 form within 1 to 3 weeks. When the mosquito next bites a dog, the L_3 penetrate the bite wound and the infection cycle is complete. In the dog the larvae develop in the **subcutaneous** (beneath the skin) tissues near the site of the bite for about 2 months, molting to the L_4 stage and then migrating through the subcutaneous tissues and eventually entering the bloodstream. Once in the circulation they are carried to the smaller branches of the pulmonary arteries, where they eventually lodge. By 6 months postinfection the worms have grown to maturity in the larger branches of the pulmonary arteries and right side of the heart and are producing microfilariae. The prepatent period thus is about 6 months. Adult heartworms have an expected life span of up to 5 years.

The adult worms are the primary cause of the clinical signs of heartworm disease (*see* CHAPTER 24, "THE CIRCULATORY SYSTEM AND DISORDERS"). An inflammatory response to the worms develops in the pulmonary artery and its branches. This in turn leads to pulmonary **hypertension** (elevated blood pressure in the pulmonary circulation), producing an enlarged pulmonary artery, enlargement of the right side of the heart, and congestion (blood accumulation due to backup) in the liver. Pulmonary **embolism** (sudden blockage of a vessel) may result from dead and decaying worms or from **thromboemboli** (blood clots). Immunologically mediated disorders can develop as a consequence of the immune response to the parasite, affecting particularly the kidneys. Microfilariae may also damage the kidneys directly by causing obstruction of **capillaries** (the smallest blood vessels). Sometimes an antibody response to the microfilariae develops that is of sufficient magnitude to clear the parasites from the circulation. The "newborn" microfilariae become coated with antibody as soon as they are expelled from the female worm and are immediately taken up by certain white blood cells (**eosinophils**) in the capillary beds of the lungs, leading in some cases to a **pneumonitis** (inflammation of the lungs).

The clinical signs of heartworm infection vary with the severity of the infection. (The severity of heartworm disease is affected by the number of worms present and the amount of exercise a dog receives; with either factor, "more is worse.") Most cases of heartworm infection, however, are asymptomatic. When clinical signs do occur, they can include:

- loss of stamina
- weight loss
- coughing on exercise
- **syncope** (fainting spell)
- congestive heart failure (only in severe cases)

Generally, complete blood counts and serum chemistry panels alone will not provide a diagnosis of heartworm disease. Definitive diagnosis rests on identifying microfilariae in the blood. The simplest test is a direct smear of fresh whole blood, but this will miss many light infections. Only the blood-concentration tests are considered valid, including the modified **Knott's test.** X-ray studies indicating enlargement of the pulmonary artery are an important component of the diagnostic workup in dogs with advanced heartworm disease.

Once microfilariae have been found it is necessary to differentiate microfilariae of *Dirofilaria immitis* from microfilariae of other, nonpathogenic filarial species that may infect dogs. *Dipetalonema reconditum* and *Dirofilaria striata* are two apparently harmless microfilarial forms that may occur in dogs. The anatomic characteristics of the three worms are quite important for making a proper identification of the heartworm parasite.

Not all infections with *Dirofilaria immitis* result in the presence of microfilariae in the circulation. So-called occult infections usually result from one of four major causes:

1. presence of sexually immature worms;
2. presence of only a single sex of the parasite;
3. drug-induced sterility of adult worms;
4. clearance of microfilariae by antibodies.

Only rarely is the reverse observed—i.e., microfilariae in the blood but no adult worms. Causes of this can include:

1. microfilariae crossing the placenta to the fetus (rare);
2. spontaneous death of adult worms;
3. medical treatment of the adult worms without a follow-up course of treatment for the microfilariae (*see* BELOW).

Occult heartworm infections are apparently much more common than was previously supposed, and in some situations (e.g., racing Greyhounds) occult infections may be more common than patent infections. Diagnosis of occult infection is made by X-ray studies and/or *immunodiagnosis* (diagnostic tests based on immunologic methods). In recent years immunodiagnosis has become a widely accepted method. Two general approaches have been taken:

1. detection of antibodies to the parasite; and
2. detection of circulating worm components (antigens)

The latter approach has proved the more successful, and most commercially available tests now detect circulating antigens. These tests can be used to:

1. diagnose occult infections in dogs exhibiting clinical signs;
2. screen healthy dogs for heartworm infection;
3. confirm the successful removal of adult

heartworms following medical treatment;

4. estimate the mass of worms present (and therefore the likelihood of severe disease following medical treatment);

5. confirm the presence of adult heartworms in healthy dogs with microfilariae in the blood prior to treatment.

The results of these tests should *always* be interpreted in light of other clinical and laboratory evidence of heartworm infection.

Treatment of heartworms is a four-step process involving:

1. thorough clinical workup prior to treatment;

2. treatment with an adulticide (drug to kill the adult worms);

3. subsequent treatment with a **microfilaricide** (drug to kill the microfilariae);

4. preventive medication after the worms have been eradicated, to guard against reinfection.

A pretreatment workup is necessary because the medications used to kill heartworm parasites are toxic to the liver and kidneys. In addition, the large adult worms as they die and disintegrate may block blood vessels within the lungs. The workup usually involves a thorough physical examination, X rays, complete blood count, urinalysis and serum chemistries.

The only effective adulticide available is thiacetarsamide, an arsenic-containing compound. It is given intravenously twice a day for 2 or 3 days. The worms begin to die after a few days, and worm deaths will continue to occur for about 3 weeks. During this time the dog must be kept quiet with absolutely no exercise, in order to minimize complications resulting from the death of the worms. If the number of worms present is sufficiently large, a fever and cough may develop during adulticide treatment.

Some 3 to 6 weeks later, depending on the severity of the reaction to the adult worms, a course of microfilaricide therapy is given. Drugs now approved for this use include ivermectin and milbemycin oxime. In certain cases microfilariae cannot be cleared from the bloodstream,

even after repeated courses of therapy with different microfilaricides. When this occurs it suggests that adult worms are still present in the dog and that the adulticide treatment should be repeated.

After successful elimination of the microfilariae, dogs should be placed on a preventive program. Diethylcarbamazine (DEC) given daily provides complete protection from reinfection and is available in a variety of formulations. Care must be taken not to give this drug to microfilaria-positive dogs because a fatal reaction may result. In the southern parts of the United States the drug should be given all year. In colder climates, it should be given from the beginning of the local mosquito season until 2 months after the end of the mosquito season. Ivermectin and milbemycin oxime, given monthly, represent two superior alternative medications for preventing heartworm infection.

OTHER NEMATODES AFFECTING DOGS

The following nematode parasites are found only rarely in dogs.

Spirocerca Lupi

This parasite occurs primarily in tropical climates and in the southern part of the United States. It grows in adult form in thickened nodules within the wall of the esophagus or stomach, passing larvated eggs into the feces. These are ingested by a dung beetle, in which the infective L_3 form develops. The infective form can also develop within a paratenic host that ingests an infected beetle. The beetle or paratenic host is ingested in turn by a dog. In the dog, the larvae migrate through blood vessel walls, finally reaching the vicinity of the **aorta** (the great vessel arising from the left ventricle of the heart, that feeds blood through the arterial system into the body), esophagus and stomach. The prepatent period is 5 to 6 months.

The nodules in the esophagus may cause obstruction of the esophagus and induce the formation of **sarcomas** (tumors arising from connective-tissue cells). Vomiting, **dysphagia** (difficulty swallowing), and weight loss are common clinical signs. Migration of the larvae also can result in **aortic stenosis** (narrowing of the aorta) or even aortic rupture. Nodules can also obstruct the trachea and produce upper respiratory tract signs.

Diagnosis is based on the history, clinical signs, and identification of eggs in a fecal preparation. Treatment of the infection involves the administration of an appropriate anthelmintic preparation.

Physaloptera

These parasites are usually found in the stomach or upper portion of the small intestine. Eggs passed in the feces are ingested by an intermediate host (beetle, cricket, cockroach). A paratenic host (rodent, bird, snake) may ingest the intermediate host. Larvae mature to adults in the stomach of the dog after it eats either an intermediate or paratenic host. The adult worms are bloodsuckers and can cause **gastritis** (stomach inflammation), **enteritis** (inflammation of the intestine), anemia (in puppies), and vomiting. Worms present in the vomitus can easily be mistaken for ascarids unless they are carefully examined.

Diagnosis is based on the history and clinical signs and identification of eggs in a fecal preparation. Treatment, if required, involves the use of an appropriate anthelmintic medication.

Giant Kidney Worm

The giant kidney worm *Dioctophyma renale,* one of the largest of all nematodes, is found in a number of species including mink (the major definitive host), dogs, swine and (rarely) human beings. Adult females in the kidney pass eggs into the urine, which require watery conditions in order to develop further. After a period of time the eggs containing infective larvae are ingested by an *annelid* (segmented) worm, such as an earthworm, which serves as an intermediate host. The L_4 larvae that develop in the annelid worm are infective for dogs. Fish and frogs can act as paratenic hosts, carrying the L_4 form in their tissues after eating an infected worm.

In the dog the worm passes into the abdominal cavity and penetrates the kidney. Often, for reasons that are not completely understood, only one kidney is infected. Once inside the kidney the worms grow, displacing and destroying the normal tissue architecture. Kidney function

is gradually lost. Nonpatent infections can occur if larvae mature outside the kidney in the abdominal cavity. Aberrant infections within the abdomen can cause chronic **peritonitis** (inflammation of the internal lining of the abdomen) and **adhesions** (a fusion or sticking together of organ surfaces), particularly involving the liver. When only one kidney is infected, there often are no resulting clinical signs because the normal kidney can compensate for the damaged one.

Diagnosis is based on the history and clinical signs, and identification of characteristic eggs in urine. Surgical removal of the affected organ is the only effective therapy. At surgery the huge red worms (35 to 100 cm in length) can be found inside the affected kidney.

Cestode (Tapeworm) Parasites

Cestodes, commonly known as tapeworms, are highly adaptive internal parasites found in all groups of aquatic and terrestrial vertebrates. Typical tapeworms are long, flattened, ribbonlike, segmented worms. They have no digestive tract, nor is there any respiratory or circulatory system. The surface of the tapeworm is covered with a biochemically active, complex cuticle. Absorption of nutrients and some excretory functions occur through this cuticle.

The body of a tapeworm can be divided into three main regions:

1. the **scolex,** or "head," of the organism, armed with hooks or suckers and used for attachment and locomotion
2. the neck, a highly active region from which the individual tapeworm segments grow
3. the remainder of the body, called the **strobila,** which is comprised of a chain of segments called **proglottids** (proglottids grow from the neck and are pushed back as they mature, so that those farthest from the scolex are also the oldest)

Each mature tapeworm segment is an **hermaphrodite** (i.e., it contains both male and female reproductive organs). Segments wherein both sets of genital organs are fully developed are called mature **proglottids.** As eggs are produced and fertilized, they accumulate in the uterus of the proglottid. When the uterus contains large numbers of eggs, the proglottid is termed a gravid proglottid.

Dipylidium Caninum

This is by far the most common tapeworm infecting dogs throughout much of the United States, probably because it is transmitted by the ubiquitous flea (and, less commonly, by biting lice). Indeed, without good flea control measures, control of this worm is nearly impossible; reinfection will cause tapeworm segments to reappear in the stool in as little as 3 weeks after **cestocidal** (tapeworm-killing) treatment. The mature tapeworm segments contain egg capsules having up to 20 eggs. These are ingested by the intermediate host (flea larvae or lice), which is then eaten by the dog. Rarely, young children may become infected in this same manner. Adult tapeworms in the small intestine of a dog may attain lengths of 50 to 75 cm.

Fortunately this tapeworm is virtually harmless to its host, although owners may be disturbed by the sight of the rice grain-like tapeworm segments, which are capable of independent movement, crawling about in their pet's bedding, on the pet's hind end, or in its stool. Heavy infections, particularly in young animals, may induce some nonspecific gastrointestinal signs. Irritation of the **perineum** (region between the thighs encompassing the anus and genitalia) due to the crawling segments may cause the dog to "scoot" (drag its hind end along the ground).

Diagnosis is made by finding the typical tapeworm segments in the stool or bedding. The segments can be confirmed as belonging to *Dipylidium caninum* by microscopic examination. Egg capsules may also be seen on fecal flotation. Treatment involves an appropriate cestocidal medication, such as praziquantel, and aggressive flea control, involving both the pet and the environment. (For flea-control measures, *see* Chapter 23, "External Parasites.")

Taeniids

Taeniid tapeworms live in the intestine of carnivores and human beings. All mammals can act as intermediate hosts. The taeniid tapeworms

are much less common in dogs than is *Dipylidium caninum*. In their intermediate hosts the taeniid tapeworms are found as larvae in a variety of locations, including the liver, muscle and peritoneal cavity. A predator-prey relationship must exist for completion of the life cycle. Dogs can serve as definitive hosts and pass eggs in their feces. The intermediate hosts become infected by ingesting eggs, with the larval forms encysting in their tissues. Dogs can then acquire new infections by eating tissues containing cestode larvae. The two most important taeniid tapeworms for dogs are *Taenia pisiformis* and *Echinococcus granulosus*.

In the United States, *Taenia pisiformis* (rabbits are the primary intermediate hosts) is the most common species affecting dogs. The worms are generally harmless but their presence is undesirable. Diagnosis is made by identification of the characteristic segments. Treatment involves cestocidal medication and preventing reinfection by controlling the dog's predatory behavior.

Echinococcus granulosus is the cause of **hydatid disease** and is found in adult form in the small intestine of dogs and wild canids. Sheep serve as the intermediate hosts in which the larvae encyst. In the canine intestinal tract the gravid proglottids disintegrate and release eggs in the feces. Following ingestion of the eggs by sheep, the larvae migrate throughout the body and slowly mature into **hydatid cysts**. These brood structures can grow to tremendous sizes and contain literally thousands of infectious tapeworm offspring in different stages of development. (A closely related worm, *Echinococcus multilocularis*, exists in a fox-rodent cycle and is emerging as a potential threat to people and dogs in the midwestern United States.) Usually, these tapeworms cause no recognizable disease in dogs. However, hydatid disease may occur in domestic and wild intermediate hosts, depending on the location of the cysts (e.g., eye, brain, spinal cord, liver). Hydatid disease is an important **zoonotic disease** (transmissible from animals to people), with human beings acting as intermediate hosts. Pressure on the surrounding tissues by the growing cyst results in loss of function and ultimately death of the tissue. (*See*

APPENDIX A, "ZOONOTIC DISEASES: FROM DOGS TO PEOPLE.")

Diagnosis of infection in dogs is based on identification of eggs in feces. Treatment involves periodic treatment with an anthelmintic medication having activity against *Echinococcus granulosus* or *Echinococcus multilocularis,* such as praziquantel.

PSEUDOPHYLLIDEANS

The pseudophyllidean tapeworms *Diphyllobothrium latum* and *Spirometra mansonoides* are occasionally found in dogs. The former can be found in the Great Lakes region of the United States, while the latter is especially abundant in peninsular Florida.

Adults of *Diphyllobothrium latum* reside in the small intestine. Eggs are passed in the feces and must reach water to develop further. From each egg a larval form known as a coracidium develops. While swimming about the coracidium is ingested by the first intermediate host, a **copepod** (a minute aquatic crustacean), in which it develops to a **procercoid** form. The copepod in turn is eaten by a freshwater fish, in whose muscles the procercoid develops into a **plerocercoid.** The plerocercoid infection may be passed through several fish via predation until the infected fish is ingested uncooked by a definitive host (such as a dog or a person), in which the adult form is reached. In human beings this parasite can cause anemia by taking up large quantities of vitamin B_{12} in the intestine, thus depriving the host of this vital nutrient. The disease potential for dogs is less well understood.

The life cycle of *Spirometra mansonoides* is similar to that of *Diphyllobothrium,* except that the second intermediate host may be a frog, snake, bird or mammal. Dogs usually acquire the infection by predation. Adult *Spirometra* rarely cause disease, but the larval plerocercoid stage is pathogenic for human beings. Most canine infections appear to be asymptomatic.

Diagnosis of either infection is made by finding the small, characteristic eggs on fecal flotation. Treatment involves cestocidal medication. Prevention is by control of predation (*Spirometra*) and avoidance of feeding raw fish to dogs (*Diphyllobothrium*).

Trematode (Fluke) Parasites

Flukes are flattened, elongated to oval, wormlike parasites that are found in a wide variety of animal species. Some are external parasites, existing on the skin of fish, amphibians and reptiles. Others are internal parasites, living in organs such as the liver or intestine. Most of the flukes of veterinary importance lie in this latter category. Fortunately, flukes as a group are not especially common or important parasites of dogs.

The body of a typical fluke is covered by a cuticle which often is ornamented with scales or small spines. In most species two suckers are found on the underside of the fluke. The vast majority of flukes are hermaphroditic, with both male and female reproductive organs present in each individual.

Most flukes require an aquatic environment, although a few flukes are primarily terrestrial. There may be more than a single intermediate host in the life cycle. In all instances the first intermediate host is a mollusk, usually a land or water snail. In cycles involving a second intermediate host, it is usually either an invertebrate (snail) or a vertebrate. Early stages of the life cycle are highly host-specific, while the adult stage often parasitizes several definitive host species.

Most flukes lay eggs, from which (usually) five larval stages develop before the adult stage is reached:

egg → miracidium → sporocyst → redia → cercaria → metacercaria → adult

The **miracidium** hatches from the egg and swims about in water, but it must find a snail within 24 hours or it will die. (In terrestrial flukes the egg containing the miracidium has to be swallowed by a snail.) In the snail the **sporocyst** is formed. The sporocyst is essentially nothing but a bag of reproductive cells. In certain fluke species it may give rise to daughter sporocysts, while in others it proceeds to the next larval stage, the **redia.** (If daughter sporocysts are formed, the redia is omitted from the life cycle.) The redia shows some characteristics of the adult fluke. Again, depending upon the species, daughter rediae may arise from the first redial forms. The redial form gives rise to the **cercaria** form, which is a tadpole-like larva that then leaves the snail. Depending on the species of fluke, the cercaria may:

1. directly penetrate the skin of a definitive host;
2. lose its tail and encyst on a plant as an infective **metacercaria,** awaiting ingestion by a definitive host;
3. penetrate a second intermediate host, encyst as a metacercaria and await ingestion by a definitive host.

Alaria

This is the most frequently identified gastrointestinal fluke of dogs in the United States. The adults, usually less than 2 mm in length, are found in the small intestine. Eggs are passed in the feces, hatch, and release miracidiae which penetrate aquatic snails. The resulting cercariae exit the snails and penetrate a second intermediate host (tadpoles and frogs). A paratenic host (frogs, snail, mouse, bird) may ingest the second intermediate host. The dog then ingests either the second intermediate host or the paratenic host. The flukes migrate to the lungs, are coughed up and swallowed, and return to the intestine.

Most infections appear to be asymptomatic. Clinical signs of heavy *Alaria* infections may include respiratory distress and diarrhea. Diagnosis is based on the history, clinical signs, and identification of fluke eggs in a fecal specimen. Treatment, if required, involves administration of an appropriate anthelmintic medication.

Nanophyetes Salmincola

This fluke occurs in the small intestine of dogs that have ingested the metacercarial form in the tissues of infected salmonid fish (salmon, trout). The fluke alone causes little or no problem; however, it often serves as the vector for the rickettsial bacterium *Neorickettsia helminthoeca,* a cause of **salmon disease** ("salmon poisoning") of dogs in the Pacific Northwest region of the United States. (For a complete discussion of salmon disease, *see* Chapter 35, "Bacterial Diseases.")

Paragonimus Kellicotti

This fluke may occasionally be found within cystlike cavities in the lungs of dogs. It is a medium-sized fluke, adults reaching up to 15 mm in length. The first intermediate host is a snail. Dogs acquire the infection by eating crayfish (the second intermediate host) containing encysted metacercariae. Juvenile flukes migrate from the gastrointestinal tract to the lungs where they mature within cysts. The resulting eggs are coughed up, swallowed and passed in the feces.

Mustelid carnivores (mink, otters, etc.) are the normal hosts, with dogs only becoming accidentally infected. Although many infections are asymptomatic, serious disease can occasionally occur. Migrating juvenile flukes may cause peritonitis or **pleuritis** (inflammation of the thin, transparent membrane covering the lungs and lining the chest cavity). Adult flukes and eggs in the lungs can cause chronic respiratory distress and pneumonia. Rarely, **pneumothorax** (collapsed lung) results from infection with this parasite.

Diagnosis is made by identification of the eggs on fecal examination. Less commonly, the cystic cavities in the lungs are discovered on X-ray examination. Treatment with anthelmintics is relatively straightforward, without complication, and usually successful. Infections can be prevented by not permitting dogs to hunt along creek banks where infected crayfish may be found.

Protozoan Parasites

Protozoa are among the simplest **unicellular** (single-celled) members of the animal kingdom. They are microscopic organisms with internal structures that are referred to as **organelles** rather than organs (organs, as in mammals, being composed of cells, and organelles instead representing specialized portions of a single cell). There are organelles to carry out all of the vital functions of the protozoan, including respiration, excretion and locomotion. Many protozoa are free-living in the environment and most are beneficial. Only the parasitic protozoa, which cause important diseases of domestic animals, are of great significance to veterinary medicine.

Parasitic protozoa that are not transmitted to a new host by means of an intermediate host often develop a cyst form, which results from the laying down of a wall around the entire organism. The cyst form enables the parasite to survive in an inhospitable environment (drying, variation in temperature, lack of oxygen or tissue juices of the host), until a suitable host arrives.

Reproduction in protozoa may be either asexual or sexual. The most common type of asexual reproduction is called binary fission, wherein an individual organism divides into two. Another type of asexual reproduction is called **multiple fission,** or **schizogony.** In this form, the nucleus of the organism divides several times before the remainder of the cell divides. The dividing cell is known as a **schizont,** or **meront.** The daughter cells are referred to as **merozoites.** Merozoites may also be formed by a process called **endodyogeny,** wherein two similar daughter cells are formed within the parent cell. Another form of asexual reproduction is known as **budding,** in which the cell divides into two unequal parts, the larger part being considered the parent and the smaller one the bud. Sexual reproduction by **gametogamy** or **syngamy** involves the formation of **gametes** (reproductive cells) which fuse to form a **zygote.** The zygote may or may not then divide by multiple fission to form a number of **sporozoites.**

COCCIDIA

The *coccidia* (singular: *coccidium*) are some of the most important parasites causing economic losses in domestic and wild animals. Fortunately, coccidia are not especially significant parasites of dogs. Coccidia generally are intracellular parasites and have complex life cycles. Both asexual and sexual reproduction may occur in the same host. In other instances, sexual reproduction occurs in one host (the **definitive host**) and asexual reproduction in another (**intermediate host**).

Of the protozoal diseases encountered in small animal practice, one of the more puzzling is intestinal coccidiosis. The most common coccidia infecting dogs are those belonging to the genus *Isospora*. Egg forms of the organism, known as **oocysts,** are generated in the intestinal tract of infected dogs and are easily demonstrated by fecal flotation. Coccidia may be associated with diarrhea, but can also be found in the feces of dogs not exhibiting clinical signs.

Signs of coccidiosis are more common in puppies, particularly under conditions of crowding (i.e., in kennels, pet shops, "puppy mills," animal shelters, etc.), where an increased chance of infection exists through food or water contaminated with oocyst-laden feces. In such an environment young animals may also be stressed and less capable of rapidly mounting a protective immune response.

The extent to which intestinal coccidia actually cause disease in dogs remains controversial, because attempts to reproduce the clinical signs experimentally have not been consistently successful. It is possible that the clinical syndrome attributed to "coccidiosis" might actually involve a synergism between coccidia and one or more other intestinal microorganisms. Nevertheless this syndrome as it occurs in pups, whatever its cause, can be treated successfully with sulfa drugs and/or antiprotozoal medication, such as amprolium, and good nursing care. Treatment is indicated for clinically ill pups, although the benefit from sulfa drugs may actually result from suppression of secondary bacterial invasion of the damaged intestine rather than from any specific anticoccidial effect. Treatment of healthy puppies shedding occasional oocysts may not be necessary, except for very young pups or severely stressed individuals.

Prevention of coccidiosis in kennels involves:

• thorough sanitation, including fecal pickup and disposal
• cleansing of the environment with a strong ammonium hydroxide solution (coccidia are resistant to many common disinfectants)
• heat-treatment of surfaces with steam or a flame gun

Other coccidia (*Sarcocystis, Hammondia*) can infect dogs on occasion, although disease associated with such infections tends to be quite limited. Dogs are the definitive hosts for these coccidia, while cattle, sheep, goats, swine or horses serve as intermediate hosts. Most infections in dogs are self-limiting, although a mild diarrhea may occur. Infections usually arise when farm pets are fed raw meat or **offal** (waste parts from butchering) from livestock species raised on the farm. Nearly all livestock harbor modest numbers of *Sarcocystis* organisms in their tissues. Upon primary infection dogs fed tissues containing these organisms can contaminate pastures, stables, or barnyards with vast numbers of oocysts or sporocysts shed in feces, leading to disease outbreak in the livestock. Control involves preventing dogs from eating raw meat and keeping them out of areas where livestock are fed or grain is stored.

TOXOPLASMA

Toxoplasma gondii, the causative agent of **toxoplasmosis,** is a protozoan parasite that infects a wide range of mammalian species, including human beings. Cats, both domestic and wild, are the definitive host for *Toxoplasma gondii.* They can acquire the infection by ingesting any of the three infective stages of the parasite:

1. tissue cysts (containing **bradyzoites**), usually acquired by ingesting infected prey animals or other raw meat
2. oocysts shed in feces (present in contaminated soil or water)
3. **tachyzoites** (actively dividing forms present in the tissues of infected prey or other raw meat)

The ingested parasites invade cells of the small intestine and undergo cycles of asexual and sexual reproduction. Oocysts are formed in 3 to 10 days and are generally shed for approximately 1 to 2 weeks. Some of the parasites may invade extraintestinal organs and undergo development as described below for intermediate hosts. Clinical signs of toxoplasmosis only rarely develop in cats. However, enteritis, ulceration, pneumonia, and neurological and ocular signs have been reported.

In dogs and other intermediate hosts, a generalized infection may be established as the parasites travel through the body and invade tissue cells. On entering a host cell the parasites multiply by endodyogeny, forming 8 to 16 banana-shaped tachyzoite forms per cell. In most cases the host's immune response during this acute phase limits the invasiveness of the tachyzoites. Cysts containing bradyzoites (a dormant form of the parasite) develop in the tissues. The slowly growing bradyzoite cysts usually remain in a latent stage. If immunity is severely suppressed, however, the bradyzoites may become invasive.

Clinical toxoplasmosis is only rarely observed in dogs. When it occurs, signs can include **dyspnea** (difficult breathing), fever, coughing, neurologic dysfunction, gastrointestinal disturbances and sudden death. Diagnosis is made on the basis of rising antibody levels or by identification of the parasite in body tissues.

There is no completely satisfactory treatment for clinical toxoplasmosis. Sulfa drugs and pyrimethamine are the two drugs most widely used for therapy. They are most effective during the acute stage when the parasites are rapidly multiplying.

NEOSPORA CANINUM

This is a recently identified protozoan that is very similar in appearance to *Toxoplasma gondii.* Tissue stages (i.e., bradyzoite cysts and tachyzoites) have been identified in dogs; however, oocysts have not been discovered and the life cycle of the organism has yet to be determined. The only documented route of natural transmission is transplacental; that is, from the bitch to her offspring in the uterus.

Clinical signs are related primarily to the nervous and musculoskeletal systems, with encephalomyelitis (inflammation of the brain and spinal cord), **paresis** (partial paralysis), paralysis, **dysphagia** (difficult or painful swallowing), **myositis** (muscle inflammation), stiffness, and/or muscle atrophy being observed in affected dogs. Clinical signs are usually more dramatic in puppies than in adults. Signs develop at 3 to 6 weeks of age and usually involve limping or favoring of the limbs. Several pups in a litter may be affected. Unlike toxoplasmosis, successive litters of an infected bitch may have affected pups. Many infected dogs, particularly adults, may exhibit no clinical signs. Currently it is unknown whether signs developing in adult dogs are caused by reactivation of an infection acquired before birth or a recently acquired infection.

The prevalence of *N. caninum* infections has not been documented; however, the incidence of the disease appears to be low. At the present time diagnosis is difficult, owing to the scarcity of widely available diagnostic tests. An indirect fluorescent antibody test using *N. caninum* tachyzoites has been described for detecting specific antibodies. Rising antibody levels in paired serum samples probably are indicative of a recent infection. However, more information about the immune response to this parasite is required to determine the appropriate use of such a test for the diagnosis of clinical illness.

Disease caused by *N. caninum* is progressive and frequently fatal. There is no proven effective therapy for dogs with severe paralysis. However, dogs with early signs of limb weakness may be treated with a combination of trimethoprim, sulfadiazine and pyrimethamine.

GIARDIA

Giardia are found in many vertebrate hosts. Although many species of *Giardia* have been named based on the host in which they are found, there may really be far fewer species, each having a wide host range. *Giardia* infections are usually acquired by ingestion of the cyst form of the parasite. Motile feeding forms called **trophozoites** reproduce in the small intestine by means of binary fission. The trophozoite is the pathogenic stage of the organism and attaches to surface cells, primarily in the small intestine, by means of a cup-shaped "sucker" located on the underside of the parasite. Cysts eventually are formed in the intestine and are passed out, along with some trophozoites, in the feces.

In dogs, *Giardia* appears to cause a mild enteritis and a chronic or intermittent diarrhea, particularly in pups. The type of stools in which both trophozoites and cysts may be found are often loose, light-colored, and occasionally contain mucus. Mild to severe diarrhea may also

occur in human beings infected with *Giardia.* To date it is still unclear whether the species of *Giardia* infecting dogs can also infect people; hence the zoonotic potential of this parasite remains a controversial issue. Water-borne epidemics of giardiasis have been attributed to contamination of drinking water with cysts from the feces of infected wild animals (e.g., beavers), domestic animals or human beings.

Diagnosis is confirmed by identification of trophozoites or cysts in feces. A direct smear of fresh feces should be examined to identify the motile trophozoites, whereas a fecal flotation should be performed to recover cysts. Because cysts are shed more commonly than trophozoites in the feces of dogs with giardiasis, fecal flotation is the preferred diagnostic technique. *Giardia*-specific fluorescent antibody or enzyme immunoassay tests are also used in some laboratories for diagnosis. It should always be kept in mind that the presence of a few *Giardia* cysts does not necessarily indicate that the organism is the primary cause of the disease under consideration. Many dogs are symptomatic carriers. (*See* APPENDIX C, "DIAGNOSTIC TESTS.")

Treatment involves administration of a course of antiprotozoal medication, usually metronidazole. Recent studies indicate that an anthelmintic medication, albendazole, may be a safer and more effective alternative to metronidazole for the treatment of giardiasis.

LEISHMANIA

Leishmaniasis, the disease caused by protozoa of the genus *Leishmania,* occurs primarily in Asia, the Middle East, southern Europe, northern Africa, and parts of South America. An area of canine infection has been reported in Oklahoma where dogs that have never left the United States have developed leishmaniasis. Most canine cases, however, occur in dogs that have lived or traveled outside the United States. (*See* APPENDIX A, "ZOONOTIC DISEASES: FROM DOGS TO PEOPLE.")

In the vertebrate host, *Leishmania* is found in **macrophages** (specialized white blood cells that ingest foreign material and play an important role in the immune response to pathogens) and related cells in the skin, spleen, liver, bone marrow, lymph nodes and other organs. The organisms also are present in white blood cells circulating throughout the bloodstream. When blood of an infected host is consumed by a sand fly vector, the protozoa subsequently undergo a series of maturation steps in the insect. The infective forms are then injected into a new definitive host at the sand fly's next blood meal.

There are two principal forms of leishmaniasis. Visceral **leishmaniasis** in human beings and dogs is characterized by anemia, diarrhea, emaciation, bloating of the abdomen (due to enlargement of the liver and spleen), and ultimately death (70–90% of untreated cases are fatal). Cutaneous **leishmaniasis** is characterized by discoloration and ulceration of the skin, and possibly emaciation and anemia. Cutaneous leishmaniasis is usually a chronic, nonfatal illness, although acute fatal cases have been reported. The incubation period in dogs may be months or years.

Diagnosis is based on identification of the organisms in smears or aspirates of affected lymphoid tissue or in skin scrapings. Treatment of infected dogs is generally not recommended for two reasons:

1. the prognosis is extremely poor despite long-term, expensive treatment
2. the parasite *may* be transmitted from dogs to human beings in the presence of the appropriate sand fly vectors (there is controversy, however, as to whether the canine *Leishmania* present in the United States is transmissible to people)

If treatment is being considered, the attending veterinarian is advised to contact the Parasitic Diseases Branch of the Centers for Disease Control and Prevention in Atlanta, Georgia to discuss the particular case in question and to obtain available medication.

TRYPANOSOMA CRUZI

Protozoa of the genus *Trypanosoma* occur in all classes of vertebrates. In general they are considered parasites of the circulatory system and tissue fluids. However *Trypanosoma cruzi,* which occurs in the New World, is predominantly an intracellular parasite. Most trypanosomes are transmitted by bloodsucking insects. Although most trypanosome species appear to be harmless, the pathogenic trypanosomes are responsible for some of the world's most important diseases of domestic animals and human beings in tropical areas, including sleeping sickness, **nagana** (tsetse fly disease in Africa), **dourine** ("covering disease" in donkeys and horses), **mal de caderas** (a South American disease in horses, mules and dogs), and Chagas' disease.

Trypanosoma cruzi is the cause of **Chagas' disease,** also known as **American trypanosomiasis.** Chagas' disease is a major human health concern in the southern Americas, affecting millions of human beings. Bloodsucking bugs of the family *Reduviidae,* known variously as "conenose," "assassin," or "kissing" bugs, are responsible for transmitting the trypanosome through their feces. Several species of bug known to harbor *Trypanosoma cruzi* are present in the southern and southwestern United States. Infections in wild and domestic animals are known to occur in the United States. Wild animals, notably armadillo, opossum and wood rats, serve as reservoirs. (*See* APPENDIX A, "ZOONOTIC DISEASES: FROM DOGS TO PEOPLE.")

During a blood meal on a susceptible host the bug defecates at the site of feeding. The irritation caused by the bite often induces the host to scratch at the area, thereby rubbing the trypanosome-contaminated feces into the bite wound. Flagellated (having flagella, whiplike projections used for movement) forms of the parasite enter the blood and tissues and invade white blood cells and muscle cells. In these cells the parasites develop into **amastigote** forms and multiply by binary fission. Most of the parasites remain intracellular; however, some may reenter the bloodstream where they are then picked up by an insect vector as it feeds.

Acute or chronic disease may develop, depending on the strain of parasite and the host. Puppies are more susceptible to disease than are adult dogs. The parasites can invade a variety of cell types, especially heart and other muscle cells, resulting in destruction of those cells. Clinical signs in infected animals can include enlarged lymph nodes, swellings, anemia, fever, diarrhea, weight loss, **ataxia** (incoordination), irregular heartbeat and general malaise. If nerve cells are invaded, paralysis of the related musculature may ensue. The disease is relentlessly progressive and ultimately fatal.

Diagnosis is based on the history, clinical signs, and identification of the organism in blood or tissue samples (most readily accomplished during the acute phase of the illness). In some cases blood tests that detect antibodies to the parasite may be helpful in diagnosis. There is no satisfactory treatment. As with leishmaniasis, veterinarians may contact the Parasitic Diseases Branch of the Centers for Disease Control and Prevention in Atlanta, Georgia for advice on medications currently available for restricted use in treating Chagas' disease.

Some control may be effected by insecticidal elimination of the vector bugs from dwellings and old woodpiles, where they are often found. The potential for transmission of the parasite to human beings in contact with an affected dog should always be kept in mind.

BABESIA

Protozoa of the genus *Babesia* cause disease in cattle, sheep, goats, horses, swine, dogs and occasionally human beings. In addition, many wild mammals are probably infected and serve as reservoir hosts. *Babesia* are parasites of red blood cells and are transmitted by ticks. Sexual reproductive stages occur in the tick vectors, while asexual reproduction occurs in the vertebrate host. Ticks inject the infective sporozoite stage of the parasite into the mammalian host. The parasites enter the red blood cells where they multiply by binary fission, or schizogony. After division, merozoites invade other red blood cells. The ticks become infected by ingesting red blood cells containing babesial parasites.

Two species of *Babesia* are highly pathogenic for dogs: *Babesia canis* and *Babesia gibsoni.* Peracute, acute, chronic, or inapparent *Babesia* infections may occur. Puppies are more susceptible to disease caused by *B. canis* than are adult dogs, while *B. gibsoni* can cause fatal illness in dogs of all ages.

Fever, malaise, listlessness and/or inappetence are often the first clinical signs of babesiosis. Anemia develops owing to red blood cell destruction caused by the parasites as well as by the animal's own immune response to the parasites. Some dogs, particularly those infected with *B. gibsoni,* also develop **thrombocytopenia** (decreased levels of blood platelets). In some cases with severe anemia, darkening of the urine caused by **hemoglobinuria** (presence of the red blood cell pigment hemoglobin in the urine; "red water") may be apparent. Death may occur 4 to 8 days after the appearance of clinical signs.

Most cases of canine babesiosis are seen in Asia, Africa, Latin America and some parts of Europe. However, both *B. canis* and *B. gibsoni* are found in the United States, with clinical cases occurring most commonly in the southern regions of the country.

Diagnosis is made on the basis of the history, clinical signs, and identification of *Babesia* in the blood of acutely infected dogs. Babesiosis is often misdiagnosed as **autoimmune hemolytic anemia (AIHA)** (*see* CHAPTER 33, "THE IMMUNE SYSTEM AND DISORDERS"). Accurate diagnosis is dependent upon careful examination of stained blood smears. If blood is sent to a diagnostic laboratory, the veterinarian should specifically request that the laboratory search for *Babesia* parasites within red blood cells. *Babesia* parasites may, however, be present in such low numbers in the blood of chronically infected dogs that they are undetectable. In such cases antibody tests may be more useful for diagnosis. Several antiprotozoal medications have proven effective in treating canine babesiosis, although to date none of them is available for routine use in the United States without special approval from the Food and Drug Administration.

CHAPTER 38

Cancer

by Bruce R. Madewell

Few diseases of companion animals cause as much alarm for the animal owner as cancer. Indeed, several surveys have indicated that cancer represents the group of diseases most feared by pet owners. Although tumors are important, serious illnesses, treatment methods are available for many cancer types, and the results of treatment often are very satisfactory in terms of providing meaningful prolongation of useful life for the animal.

The Warning Signs of Cancer

Early recognition, accurate diagnosis and carefully planned therapy are vital to the successful management of an animal patient with cancer. The veterinary profession, under the auspices of the Veterinary Cancer Society, has delineated a series of warning signs of cancer that are applicable to pet dogs. These signs (*see* TABLE 1) are meant to alert the responsible pet owner to the possibility that a physical or physiological disturbance might be a sign of cancer. No single clinical sign is an absolute indication of cancer, however, and careful examination of the animal may reveal a cause or causes for the disturbance other than cancer. Prompt recognition of a suspicious clinical sign by the astute owner, followed by appropriate reaction to that warning sign by the veterinarian, can ensure that an early, rapid and accurate diagnosis of cancer will be established at a time when effective therapy can be offered.

Delay in Diagnosis

Delay in seeking veterinary medical advice for a serious clinical sign can result from many factors. Delay leading to late diagnosis may be attributed to the fact that the earliest signs of cancer simply were not detected by the animal owner or veterinarian. Long haircoats, for example, can effectively hide tumors of the skin. Tumors may not be observed in pendulous or fat mammary glands, especially in dogs that have whelped previously and nursed puppies. Many pet owners are not in the habit of examining their dog's mouth, and dogs housed outdoors often are not observed carefully enough for changes in normal bladder or bowel habits to be noticed.

Table 1
The Warning Signs of Cancer

1. Abnormal swellings that continue to grow, especially in the lymph nodes

2. Sores that do not heal

3. Bleeding or discharge from the mouth, nose, urinary tract, vagina, or rectum

4. Offensive odor

5. Difficulty eating and/or swallowing

6. Difficulty breathing

7. Difficulty urinating or defecating

8. Hesitation to exercise, or loss of energy

9. Loss of appetite; weight loss

10. Persistent lameness or stiffness of movement

11. Lumps in the breast area

12. Abnormality or difference in size of testicles

Other factors may influence the reaction of an animal owner to the possibility of cancer in a pet. Delay in consulting professional advice for cancer is not due solely to ignorance, but rather to complex interactions of anxiety, fear, rationalization, and conscious and subconscious denial. Denial is a common response to cancer. It represents a defense mechanism; the owner protects him/herself from the truth by simply negating an unpleasant fact and acting as if it were not real. Denial may be a dangerous response to an unpleasant situation when it contributes to delay in seeking medical advice. Further, although cancer authorities recognize the problem of (human) patient delay in seeking medical advice for cancer, it also is clear that a component of this delay can be ascribed to the attending physician, perhaps as a consequence of his or her own insensitivity or pessimism concerning prognosis, or as a consequence of the physician's particular skills, resources, equipment or medical interests.

Epidemiology of Cancer in the Dog

It is sobering to realize that one in four dogs will develop cancer during its lifetime, and that almost one-half of dogs over the age of 10 years will die from cancer. There are several sources of data regarding the occurrence of tumors in dogs, including pathology collections from veterinary teaching hospitals and a limited number of true epidemiologic studies. Most of the data are compilations of cases seen at veterinary schools in the United States and Canada.

An often quoted source of information regarding cancer in pet animals was derived from an epidemiologic study of cancer in Alameda and Contra Costa counties in California during the 1960s and early 1970s. The data collected in this study represent the closest approximations to date of the incidence of cancer in dogs. In the report, the researchers described the numbers and types of microscopically confirmed tumors occurring in a known population of dogs in a defined geographical area over a specific period of time. Although these data are still referred to today, it is prudent to note that more than 30 years have elapsed since these cases were studied, and the cause(s) of cancer in pet animals may very well have changed over the years as the environment has changed. In the study, the overall incidence rate for cancer in dogs was estimated at 213 cases per 100,000 population at risk.

Among the domestic animal species, dogs are at risk for the greatest variety of tumor types and anatomic sites affected with cancer. The most important sites for cancer in the dog include the skin and mammary glands, lymph nodes and other blood-forming organs, mouth, and bones. Virtually any anatomic site in the dog, however, may give rise to a **benign** (not capable of spreading) or **malignant** (capable of spreading) tumor. The most frequently encountered tumor types in the dog include **adenocarcinomas** (malignant tumors derived from glandular tissue), malignant **lymphomas** (malignant tumors of lymphocytes), **lipomas** (benign fat tumors), **osteosarcomas** (malignant bone tumors), and a myriad of benign and malignant tumors derived from components of the skin.

EFFECTS OF AGE ON THE
OCCURRENCE OF CANCER
Age is the most important risk factor for the development of cancer in dogs, for it is aging

that permits the long-term events leading to tumor development and progression to occur. For most tumor types, the risk for cancer increases with increasing age. However, some apparent increases in specific incidence rates for cancer that have been noted in recent years may simply be a reflection of the gradually increasing age of the population in general. The longer life expectancy of a pet dog today can be attributed to overall improved care as well as to improvements in nutrition, vaccination against infectious disease, and leash laws.

There are some tumors associated with the **neonatal** or **perinatal periods** (periods shortly before and after birth), and others that occur early in life. Tumors of the young exhibit a different spectrum of affected anatomic sites and tissue types than do those arising in adult patients. In dogs, tumors occurring in the first 6 months of life are principally derived from the blood-forming organs, brain and skin. It is likely that tumors occurring in young animals are influenced by different factors than are those in adults. The occurrence of tumors in the young suggests prior exposure to a **carcinogenic** (cancer-causing) agent, or a spontaneous mutation occurring *in utero* (during development in the uterus) or in early life.

EFFECTS OF SEX AND BREED

Other than for sex-dependent tumors (e.g., mammary gland cancer in the bitch, prostate cancer in male dogs), few appreciable sex predilections for specific tumor types are recognized in dogs. The **perianal gland** tumor affects primarily male dogs, and this excess risk is known to be associated with the effects of male sex hormones in aging animals (perianal glands are modified sebaceous glands located around the anus and are rarely found in animals other than dogs). In some studies, male dogs were reported to have a higher risk for malignant lymphoma than female dogs, while female dogs are at increased risk for lipomas.

Breed predilections for specific tumors have been described in most of the popular animal species. Examinations of breed predilections are of importance in terms of understanding the genetic influences of cancer. Familial tendencies

for cancer within certain breeds of dogs further support the notion of an hereditary influence. Factors other than genetics per se may influence the risk for cancer, however, and these factors must also be examined so as not to derive erroneous data from breed predilections.

Knowledge of breed predilections may serve to alert the veterinarian to a clinical sign that may be attributable to an underlying cancer. There are several good examples of breed predilections for particular tumor types. For example, Boxers and Scottish Terriers are at increased risk for malignant **melanoma** (a malignant tumor of pigmented skin cells). Large and giant breeds are at high risk for malignant bone tumors, while German Shepherd Dogs have an increased risk for **hemangiosarcomas** (malignant tumors derived from blood vessels) of the spleen. In the sporting breeds, an increased risk for tumors of the mammary glands has been recognized.

Beyond the specific breed predilections, certain families or bloodlines within particular breeds may be at greater risk for tumor development. Examples include an increased risk for osteosarcoma in families of Saint Bernards, for malignant lymphoma in families of English Bullmastiffs, and for certain rare blood disorders in families of Bernese Mountain Dogs.

ENVIRONMENTAL EPIDEMIOLOGY

Clinical observations and epidemiologic and laboratory studies have provided some information regarding the influence of environmental factors on the development of cancer in dogs. These studies have provided some evidence to suggest that asbestos exposure may contribute to development of a respiratory tract tumor (**mesothelioma**) in dogs, although this tumor remains quite rare. There are also data to suggest that exposures to industrial pollutants might influence the development of cancers of the canine urinary bladder, but these too are relatively uncommon tumors. There are also studies suggesting that cancer of the tonsil in dogs may be linked to environmental pollutants. Exposure to certain herbicides has been linked (weakly) to the development of canine malignant lymphoma, and there are other weak associations between exposure to environmental tobacco smoke and cancer of the lung. A tumor affecting the genital region (canine **transmissible venereal tumor**) is a sexually transmitted tumor that is found commonly in some areas of the world and is linked to exposure to free-roaming affected dogs.

Most of the environmental influences on canine cancer have probably not been identified. Dogs avoid many of the industrial exposures that serve to increase the risk for cancer in human beings. Dogs also do not partake of certain social habits that appear to influence the development of cancer in people. In this regard it is particularly interesting that dogs exhibit very low incidence rates for such common cancers of human beings such as cancer of the lung, colon, pancreas, prostate and uterine **cervix** (entrance to the uterus).

Diagnosis

The diagnosis of cancer in dogs is based on the clinical history, physical examination, and the results of supportive laboratory studies. The mainstay of cancer diagnosis remains the **biopsy,** wherein samples of cells or tissues are collected for microscopic examination. The importance of this relatively simple diagnostic procedure cannot be overemphasized. Despite years of clinical experience, most veterinarians cannot consistently and accurately distinguish among many developmental, inflammatory and tumorous conditions of the dog on the basis of physical examination alone. When one considers the potential ramifications of a diagnosis of cancer in a pet animal, it is clear that the diagnostic process must be accomplished as expeditiously and accurately as possible.

With a lesion considered suspicious for cancer, it is not acceptable practice to "watch and wait" to see how the lesion evolves; if there is a remote possibility that the lesion represents a tumor, biopsy is mandatory. Although there has been controversy over the years regarding the potential for spreading tumor cells from the primary site by the biopsy procedure itself, it is now agreed that the risks associated with the procedure are quite small when compared to the

potential harm caused by an inaccurate diagnosis. Furthermore, there are data showing that the collection of a small biopsy specimen does not negatively influence disease outcome if the biopsy is followed quickly by definitive treatment.

Another consideration for the animal owner is the occasional necessity for the veterinarian to repeat a biopsy. This may occur if microscopic examination of the first biopsy specimen does not support the diagnosis of cancer in a highly suspicious lesion. This circumstance is not uncommon when biopsy specimens are collected in an effort to diagnose bone cancer or tumors of the mouth.

For small lesions, the entire specimen may be removed at the time of biopsy. This is referred to as an **excisional biopsy.** For larger tumors, or those affecting complex anatomic sites such as the head and neck, a small tissue specimen might first be collected from the edge of the lesion (**incisional biopsy**) to determine if the lesion is indeed a tumor, and if so, what type of tumor it represents. These findings can then be used to plan the most effective therapy possible. In some veterinary institutions diagnosis can be made by a **frozen-section biopsy,** which allows rapid identification of the tumor while the animal is still under anesthesia, so that definitive therapy can be instituted at once.

Once the biopsy specimen has been collected, examination of the specimen by the veterinary pathologist can provide information regarding the type of tumor present and also an indication as to whether the tumor was entirely removed by the surgeon (the pathologist looks for evidence of normal tissue completely surrounding the tumor biopsy). Finally, the pathologist provides information as to the degree of **differentiation** (development of cellular specialization) of the tumor. Well-differentiated tumors generally are associated with a more favorable treatment outcome than are those considered poorly differentiated or undifferentiated.

The Decision Process Regarding Treatment Options

Once a diagnosis of cancer has been established, dialogue between the animal owner and the veterinarian will serve to determine the disposition of the patient. For some tumors, curative therapy can be offered. For other tumors, if a cure is unlikely, **palliation** (alleviation) of the clinical signs may be the aim of treatment.

Poor long-term prognosis, patient debility, financial considerations, or a host of other personal factors may influence an owner not to pursue treatment for a pet afflicted with cancer. For the patient, additional diagnostic endeavors then become unnecessary, and the owner-veterinarian interaction at this stage should be aimed at providing short-term, palliative therapy for the animal. In some cases, **euthanasia** (putting the animal to sleep) might be considered for humane reasons if the patient is clearly suffering.

If treatment is considered a viable option, a series of additional laboratory tests designed to *stage* the disease is usually performed, and the suitability of the patient for the contemplated therapy is then determined. Clinical staging is used by the veterinarian to judge the overall extent of the cancer. The process of staging generally requires blood tests, sometimes a bone marrow examination, and imaging studies. Imaging methods include **radiography** (X-ray examination), ultrasound examination, special imaging procedures such as computerized axial tomography (CAT scan) and nuclear magnetic resonance imaging (NMR, MRI), and radionuclide scans. (*See* Appendix C, "Diagnostic Tests.") These studies provide estimates of total tumor volume, including size and anatomic location(s) of the cancer. The clinical stage assigned will then be used to plan treatment and to provide an assessment of prognosis.

Treatment

Surgery

Surgery is the primary method for treating most solid tumors in the dog. It is the quickest, most effective, safest and generally least expensive cancer treatment method. Indeed, it is the surgeon who has the greatest opportunity to achieve a cancer cure. For the cancer patient, the surgeon must bring to the clinical situation experience, technical skills and sound judgment. Most veterinarians in clinical practice have surgical capabilities; however, for difficult procedures such as those required for the removal of many tumors, the advice and assistance of a veterinarian with additional surgical training, and preferably certified by the American College of Veterinary Surgeons, are recommended.

Surgical treatment of cancer is based on the premise that malignancies remain localized at the point of origin for a long time, before progressing systematically to invade adjacent local structures, blood vessels and regional lymph nodes. The curative operation involves removal of the primary tumor together with its usual routes of spread. Although past practice has generally involved wide-field, tissue-sacrificing surgical procedures to remove all tumor tissue, modern surgical practice often employs less radical procedures. Historical analysis of treatment failures has shown that in such cases the tumor had already spread far outside the surgical field at the time of the operation, thus making even wide-field excision a virtually hopeless endeavor.

In elderly cancer-bearing patients consideration must be given to the risks associated with surgery and anesthesia, the severity of the underlying illness, and the degree to which the surgery will disrupt normal functioning of the patient.

Radiation Therapy

Radiation therapy (**radiotherapy**) is another established and time-honored method of cancer treatment. Most schools or colleges of veterinary medicine in North America, as well as some private veterinary practices, offer radiation therapy for their patients. The overall number of radiation therapy facilities for animals in the United States remains limited, however.

Radiation therapy delivered to animals is essentially similar to human radiation therapy. In veterinary practice, however, sedation or anesthesia is usually needed for immobilizing the patient so that a concentrated beam of radiation can be directed to the tumor target. This form of radiotherapy, using an external beam, is referred to as **teletherapy.** The actual exposure time usually is measured in minutes, and most patients can be recovered quickly enough to return home the same day. However, delivery of an entire course of radiation therapy often requires a series of treatments, usually 10 to 12 or more. The treatments are given either on a daily basis (usually five days per week) or on a Monday-Wednesday-Friday schedule.

Radiation therapy, like surgery, is a localized form of treatment; it is used therefore to provide local tumor control. It is often used for treatment of tumors affecting anatomic sites that are difficult to reach surgically, or in situations where surgical removal might compromise normal function. Tumors of the mouth or nasal passages are often treated with radiotherapy; indeed, for tumors of the nasal passages and associated sinuses radiation therapy is the treatment of choice. There is a theoretical advantage in treating expansive areas of tissue, including not only the primary tumor site but also adjacent tissues wherein small (microscopic) accumulations of tumor cells may have lodged. In some cases radiation therapy is employed after a surgical treatment has already been performed, the goal being to irradiate residual tumor cells that may have been left behind after surgery.

Another form of radiation therapy is termed **brachytherapy.** In brachytherapy, a radioactive device is actually inserted into the tumor and left in place for a period of time (usually several days). Although there are theoretical advantages to this technique, few veterinary centers in the United States have active programs of brachytherapy for animals. This is essentially a reflection of the personnel hazards associated with implanting, monitoring and removing the radioactive devices. New technologies, however, should markedly expand the application of brachytherapy in veterinary patients in coming years.

Still another method of radiation therapy involves the use of **radioisotopes** (radioactive elements). For example, hormonally active tumors of the thyroid gland can be treated using ^{131}Iodine. Because the thyroid gland utilizes iodine normally in its metabolic functions, the radioactive ^{131}Iodine will accumulate in that organ and exert its effects locally on the tumor cells. Radioactive iodine therapy is used commonly in veterinary practice today for treating feline patients with **hyperthyroidism** (hyperactivity of the thyroid gland). (*See* CHAPTER 27, "ENDOCRINE SYSTEM AND METABOLIC DISORDERS," in *The Cornell Book of Cats.*)

Side effects of radiation therapy are dose-dependent and usually involve sloughing of the tissues (frequently skin or mucous membranes) in the area that has been irradiated. In most cases these changes are transient in nature.

CHEMOTHERAPY

Chemotherapy—treatment with medication—is a continually evolving method for dealing with cancer in animals. Chemotherapy is usually reserved for the treatment of patients with widespread or disseminated tumors, those that are no longer amenable to more localized methods of therapy like surgery or irradiation. At present, the tumors most responsive to chemotherapy include those derived from lymphoid tissues, although certain solid tumors may also respond to chemotherapy.

The decision to treat an animal patient with chemotherapy should not be made casually. Chemotherapy requires a substantial commitment on the parts of both owner and veterinarian. A program of chemotherapy requires adherence to a defined schedule, periodic patient monitoring (usually in the form of repeat blood tests), and attention to the everyday needs of the patient. Although a cancer cure is certainly one goal of therapy, more often than not an animal with advanced cancer will be given chemotherapy for the purpose of ameliorating clinical signs and effectively prolonging the patient's useful life.

Another application of chemotherapy is termed **adjuvant chemotherapy.** In adjuvant chemotherapy, anticancer drugs are used following surgical or radiation treatments in an effort to destroy residual (microscopic) tumor cells that may have been left behind. Adjuvant chemotherapy has proven of value in prolonging survival time for dogs with malignant bone tumors following surgical removal of the primary tumor. Certain other tumor types also appear to respond favorably to adjuvant chemotherapy.

Side effects of chemotherapy are dose-dependent and differ for the individual medications. Signs that may be seen include inappetence, vomiting, bloody diarrhea, weight loss, fever, **hematuria** (blood in the urine), suppression of blood cell formation, neurologic dysfunction, hair loss and sloughing of mucous membranes.

OTHER TREATMENT METHODS

A variety of other technologies, some new and quite innovative, are now used in certain veterinary practices or veterinary teaching institutions for the treatment of cancer in animals. Most of these technologies require specialized equipment and a trained staff dedicated to the use of that equipment.

Cryosurgery

Cryosurgery involves the application of intense cold (freezing) that is lethal to tumor tissue. The **cryogen** (substance producing cold) usually employed is liquid nitrogen. Cryosurgery is a localized method of cancer treatment and is not tumor-specific. Careful monitoring of both tumor and normal tissue temperatures is required for a successful outcome. Cryosurgery has been used most often in veterinary practice for the treatment of superficial tumors of the skin or mucous membranes, especially tumors located in the mouth or **perianal** (near the anus) region.

Hyperthermia

Hyperthermia is a method of heating tumors to lethal temperatures. At the proper temperature, selective destruction of tumor cells occurs with preservation of normal tissue. Hyperthermia is used most commonly in concert with other treatment methods, such as radiation therapy, in an effort to enhance the effect of the other treatment.

Laser Therapy

Lasers (*l*ight *a*pplication by *s*timulated *e*mission of *r*adiation) have a variety of applications in medicine, including cutting or welding tissue, clotting blood, and heating to the point of vaporization. Lasers may be used for tumor removal in an effort to minimize local contamination of the surgical site and to decrease the potential for spreading tumor cells. Lasers may also be used in a specialized form of cancer treatment known as **photodynamic therapy** (PDT). In PDT, a **photosensitizing** (sensitizing to the effect of light) drug is first injected into the cancer patient. After a period of time (usually 24 to 48 hours) the tumor is irradiated with light, activating the photosensitizing drug and resulting in local destruction of tumor tissue.

Immunotherapy

A variety of innovative treatment methods have been developed over the years in an effort to enhance the patient's own immune or biological responses to cancer. Most methods of **immunotherapy,** or biological therapy, in animals are still considered investigational, although it seems likely that true cancer cures will ultimately emerge from these strategies, either to prevent the development of cancer or to treat already established malignancies. **Biological response modifiers** (substances that modify immune responses) are now being evaluated in veterinary patients and are expected ultimately to improve overall patient management and increase the potential for cancer cures. (*See* Chapter 33, "The Immune System and Disorders.")

Tumor Types in Dogs

In the remainder of this chapter the commonly occurring tumors of dogs will be highlighted, together with information regarding treatment methods and overall prognosis. The tumors will be categorized by anatomic site or body system.

Tumors of the Skin and Subcutaneous Tissues

The skin represents a complex organ, virtually every component of which can give rise to benign or malignant tumors. There are also nontumorous conditions of the skin that can mimic cancer; biopsy is required to distinguish such developmental or inflammatory lesions from true tumors.

Benign tumors derived from the surface structures of the skin include *epidermal cysts,* **papillomas** (warts), benign tumors of the sweat or sebaceous glands (**adenomas**), or benign tumors of certain other superficial skin cells (**basal cell tumors**). The suffix "-oma" is used to designate a tumor; benign tumors of the deeper structures of the skin or **subcutaneous** (beneath the skin) tissues are then named according to the type of tissue represented. For example, a benign tumor derived from fat is termed a **lipoma,** one from fibrous tissue a fibroma, a tumor from smooth muscle a **leiomyoma,** one from the blood vessels an **hemangioma,** etc.

By contrast, malignant tumors derived from surface components of the skin are categorized as **carcinomas.** An especially common malignant tumor of the skin is the **squamous cell**

carcinoma. Malignant tumors of glandular structures within the skin are termed **adenocarcinomas,** while malignant tumors derived from deeper or supportive structures of the skin or subcutaneous tissues are termed **sarcomas,** with a prefix indicating the tissue of origin. Thus a malignant tumor derived from fibrous connective tissue is termed a **fibrosarcoma,** one derived from fat a **liposarcoma,** one derived from blood vessels an **hemangiosarcoma,** etcetera.

Some tumors are derived from specialized components of the skin such as the **melanin** (dark pigment)-producing cells. These tumors are termed benign or malignant **melanomas.** Another specialized component of the skin is the **mast cell,** a granule-containing cell that plays a central role in the development of allergies. Mast cells can give rise to either benign or malignant mast cell tumors. A list of the commonly observed tumors of the skin of dogs is presented in Table 2.

Benign tumors of the skin generally grow slowly, are well demarcated from surrounding tissues, and are easily removed surgically. By contrast, malignant tumors of the skin or subcutaneous tissues often grow rapidly, infiltrate adjacent tissues, invade blood vessels of the skin, and **metastasize** (spread) to local lymph nodes (via the lymphatic vessels) or to distant organs such as the liver or lungs (via the bloodstream).

The majority of skin tumors are treated surgically. However, virtually all of the currently available treatment options have a place in the management of malignant tumors of the skin, the choice of the most appropriate therapy being made on the basis of the tumor type, size and site(s) of involvement.

TUMORS OF THE MAMMARY GLANDS

Tumors of the mammary glands are among the most frequently described tumors in dogs. Mammary gland tumors are almost unique to the female dog, occurring most often in intact bitches. There is good evidence that **ovariohysterectomy** (spay operation) performed early in life (6 months of age) almost completely eliminates the risk for development of mammary cancer; some protection also results from ovariohysterectomy performed between 6 months

---

Table 2
Skin Tumors of Dogs

Tumors of the Surface Structures
cysts
warts (papillomas)
keratoacanthoma
squamous cell carcinoma
basal cell tumor
sebaceous gland adenoma/carcinoma
sweat gland adenoma/carcinoma
perianal gland tumor
ceruminous gland adenoma/carcinoma
Meibomian gland adenoma
trichoepithelioma
hair matrixoma

Tumors of Melanin-Producing (Pigment) Cells of the Skin
benign or malignant melanoma

Tumors of the Deep Structures of the Skin
mast cell tumor
fibroma/fibrosarcoma
neurofibroma
hemangiopericytoma
histiocytoma
transmissible venereal tumor
hemangioma/hemangiosarcoma
lymphoma (cutaneous type)
mycosis fungoides
leiomyoma/leiomyosarcoma
lipoma/infiltrative lipoma/liposarcoma
rhabdomyoma/rhabdomyosarcoma
myxoma/myxosarcoma
undifferentiated sarcoma

---

and 2 years of age. If ovariohysterectomy is delayed beyond 2 years of age, there is no protective benefit against the development of mammary gland cancer.

Approximately one-half of tumors of the canine mammary gland are malignant. It is usually not possible to determine whether a mammary gland tumor is benign or malignant by physical examination alone. In general, however, large tumor size, rapid growth rate, evidence of infiltration of surrounding tissues, and involvement of the regional lymph nodes are characteristic features of malignant mammary cancers, which are usually carcinomas or adenocarcinomas.

There are also some unique benign tumors of the canine mammary glands that are termed **benign mixed mammary tumors.** Occasionally, sarcomas may arise in the canine mammary glands. There are also precancerous conditions of the mammary glands that increase the risk for later development of malignant tumors. Thus, it is good practice to biopsy or remove all suspicious lesions of the breast. It is important to remember that the mammary glands undergo normal physiological changes during the dog's **estrus** (heat) period; examination is best carried out, therefore, during the **anestrus** period (the sexually inactive period between two estrus cycles).

Once cancer of the mammary glands has been diagnosed, a further evaluation is usually performed to determine whether the tumor has spread. Malignant mammary gland tumors can spread to lymph nodes in the **axilla** (armpit) or **inguinal** (groin) regions, or invade the bloodstream and spread to other organs such as the lungs. An X ray of the chest is thus a necessary prerequisite for dogs with tumors of the mammary glands.

Complete surgical removal remains the treatment of choice for cancer of the canine mammary gland. The veterinary profession has not optimized surgical treatment for these tumors, and a variety of procedures may be used including simple **excision** (surgical removal) of a nodule or mass (**nodulectomy** or **lumpectomy**), removal of a gland (**mammectomy**), removal of a series of glands (**regional mastectomy**), or removal of the entire chain (or chains) of mammary glands (**unilateral** or **bilateral mastectomy**). The **axillary lymph nodes** (lymph nodes located in the axilla) are removed only if they are determined to contain tumor cells. The superficial **inguinal lymph nodes** (lymph nodes in the groin region) are removed if they contain tumor cells, or often are removed routinely because of their intimate association with the fifth mammary gland. In the hands of a skilled surgeon, whichever procedure ensures complete removal of the tumor is considered adequate. Ovariohysterectomy performed at the time of surgical removal of the mammary tumor has not

been shown to influence the overall survival time for dogs with malignant mammary tumors.

Treatment methods beyond surgical removal have also not been optimized in veterinary practice. Chemotherapy or radiation therapy, or the use of biological response modifiers, often are considered for adjunct therapy following surgical removal of malignant tumors, or for those animals not considered good candidates for surgical treatment. These additional treatment methods are generally patterned after experience gained in human medicine. Although some individual animals have been shown to benefit from such therapies, there are no statistically reliable data to show that these measures are of proven value for the management of breast cancer in dogs. It is important for the animal owner to come to a complete understanding with the veterinarian regarding the rationale and aim of investigational therapies applied after mastectomy, so that expectations of treatment outcomes remain realistic.

TUMORS OF BONE

Tumors of bone are derived principally from the long bones of the limbs and flat bones of the skull; vertebrae, shoulders and pelvis are affected less frequently. Although the majority of bone tumors are considered primary, some tumors of the skeletal system represent extensions of soft tissue tumors that have spread to bones from other sites.

The clinical signs of bone tumors are often of acute onset, and can include progressive lameness, pain and swelling. Tumors occur primarily in the large and giant breeds, most commonly affecting the ends of long bones. For example, a progressive lameness of the forelimb in an adult Saint Bernard with pain localized to the shoulder would have a high probability of being a malignant bone tumor.

Primary bone tumors in dogs are more often malignant than benign. Tumors derived from bone-forming cells (osteosarcomas) are the most frequently encountered type. Osteosarcomas evolve rapidly and can cause extensive bone destruction. They also have a high probability of spreading by way of the bloodstream to other body sites, most commonly the lungs. Other malignant tumors arising in bone include **chon-**

drosarcomas (tumors of cartilage), fibrosarcomas and hemangiosarcomas.

Proper diagnosis of bone cancer requires X-ray examination of the affected bone(s) and of the chest. In some cases, other imaging techniques such as radionuclide scans (bone scans) of the skeleton will be performed in an effort to determine the number of sites involved. Biopsy is required for confirmation of the diagnosis.

Surgical removal of the tumor is the principal treatment method. For tumors of long bones of the extremities, amputation of the limb is advised. In veterinary patients, amputation generally involves sacrifice of the entire limb. The great majority of dogs, even the large and clumsy breeds, fare surprisingly well after amputation. An advantage of complete surgical removal is that the dog is rendered almost immediately free of the chronic pain associated with the tumor. Some specialized veterinary schools and centers will offer limb-sparing surgical procedures for treatment of bone tumors of the limbs. These procedures usually involve removal of the affected portion of the bone and replacement of that segment with an **allograft** (bone collected from another dog). **Prostheses** (artificial limbs) are also used in some cases.

Owing to the high probability of spread of bone cancer to other body sites, surgical treatment alone is not considered adequate therapy. Although postoperative medical treatment may not be curative, there are considerable data to show that dogs given chemotherapy after amputation or limb-sparing surgical procedures have longer postoperative survival times than do dogs not treated with chemotherapy. Considerable advances have been made in recent years in the treatment of bone cancer in dogs, utilizing innovative and sometimes aggressive surgical procedures together with the routine application of chemotherapy.

TUMORS OF LYMPHOID TISSUES

Malignant lymphoma, also termed **lymphosarcoma**, is the most frequently recognized tumor of the blood-forming system. In contrast to the situation in cats with feline leukemia virus, a viral agent has not been identified as the causative agent of malignant lymphoma in dogs.

Although virtually any site or organ of the body may develop malignant lymphoma, most cases reflect involvement of the external lymph nodes of the body. The animal owner may suddenly notice unusual swellings or enlargements, most often in the lower neck region of the dog. Physical examination reveals that virtually all the lymph nodes of the body are enlarged. Although the dog may not seem ill in the early stages of disease, malignant lymphoma nevertheless is a relentlessly progressive illness that eventually leads to the physical decline of the patient, with lethargy, weight loss, fever and other serious signs preceding death.

Diagnosis of malignant lymphoma requires cytologic and biopsy methods, blood tests, bone marrow examination, and imaging studies of the chest and abdomen. The diagnosis is made from the cytologic and biopsy specimens; the other studies are needed to stage the disease—i.e., to determine the site(s) of involvement and the magnitude of the tumor. These findings are then used to design optimal therapy and to provide some estimation of the prognosis for that particular animal.

Treatment of malignant lymphoma involves the use of anticancer drugs. Although there are several published methods for treatment of malignant lymphoma, most of the effective regimens use combinations of anticancer drugs. These drugs are similar to those used for management of human patients with malignant lymphoma, and include vincristine, cyclophosphamide, L-asparaginase, doxorubicin, methotrexate and prednisone. Effective treatment of malignant lymphoma in the dog requires a considerable commitment on the part of the animal owner and veterinarian to ensure that the drugs are given at specifically determined intervals and to decrease the likelihood of adverse reactions to therapy. Average survival times of 1 year or more are now routinely obtained for dogs with malignant lymphoma that responds to chemotherapy. Malignant lymphoma is a tumor that has been the subject of considerable scientific investigation in veterinary medicine. Substantial improvements in treatment methods and outcome can be anticipated in the years ahead.

Tumors of the Mouth

Another important site for cancer in dogs is the mouth. This might appear surprising, given that dogs are not routinely exposed to some of the recognized risk factors for human oral cancer—i.e., alcohol and tobacco. Most oral growths in middle- to old-aged dogs are malignant. The most frequently encountered tumor types include squamous cell carcinomas, malignant melanomas and fibrosarcomas. There is also a spectrum of tumors or tumorlike lesions referred to by the general term **epulis.** Although epulis does not spread, it can cause considerable local tissue destruction and must be treated definitively.

The clinical signs of oral cancer include odor, bleeding from the mouth, apparent pain associated with eating or drinking, facial deformity, an enlarged lymph node in the neck, or **palsy** (paralysis) of the facial musculature. Tumors of the oral cavity can take on a proliferative appearance, forming definite mass lesions, or may present as chronic, nonhealing ulcers.

The diagnosis of oral cancer requires biopsy. X-ray studies of the bony components of the lower jaw (**mandible**) or upper jaw (**maxilla**) are usually required to ascertain if bone has become involved. Malignant melanomas, squamous cell carcinomas, and less frequently fibrosarcomas, will spread to distant sites; thus, X-ray examination of the chest should be a routine component of the diagnostic process.

Treatment of cancer of the oral cavity generally involves surgery and/or radiation therapy. Aggressive surgical procedures are required to ensure complete removal of the tumor; this may involve sacrificing portions of the mandible or maxilla if these bony components are involved. Dogs recover quite rapidly from such procedures, however, and in general are cosmetically and functionally sound. Radiation therapy often is used with certain tumors, such as squamous cell carcinomas, in an effort to spare important structures of the mouth. Tumors located in the front part of the mouth are treated with greater success than are tumors located deep in the oral cavity or throat. Tumors derived from the tonsils are especially difficult to manage effectively. Tumors with the greatest chance of treatment success are those that are recognized early (i.e., while they are still small and confined), are noninvasive of bone, and have no evidence of spread to lymph nodes.

Tumors of the oral cavity pose a considerable problem because they are often not recognized by the animal owner until they have become invasive. Many owners are now in the habit of brushing their pet's teeth on a daily basis. This is really a simple procedure and is enjoyed by the dog. A program of regular oral hygiene for a pet will ensure that the oral cavity is inspected routinely so that tumors can be detected at an early stage.

Throughout the 1950s, 1960s, and even into the early 1970s, the study of cancer in animals was based primarily on compilations of tumor types from pathology collections. In recent years greater attention has been given to understanding the biology of cancer in animals, and new methods of diagnosis and treatment have been introduced. Indeed, companion animals have benefited significantly from the efforts expended in human medicine to identify the causes of cancer and to devise effective treatment methods. Many of the diagnostic and treatment methods developed for use in human cancer patients are directly applicable for use in dogs. Although the costs of new equipment, supplies and procedures often are prohibitive for veterinary practices, over time new methodologies have been and are continuing to be introduced into veterinary medicine. Veterinary medicine has also benefited considerably from the advances in biotechnology. The biotechnology revolution has provided training for young veterinary scientists whose knowledge and skills will impact favorably on the companion animal with cancer. Perhaps most importantly, the public has accepted well the responsibilities of pet ownership, and providing quality health care for that most favorite of companion animals—the dog.

PART VII

Home Care

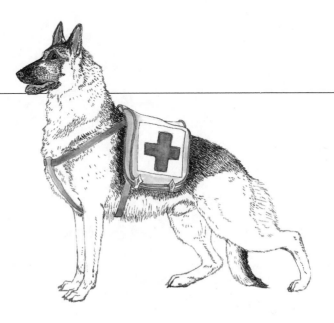

'Mid pleasures and palaces though we
 may roam,
Be it ever so humble, there's no place
 like home.

—JOHN HOWARD PAYNE
"Home, Sweet Home"
from the opera *Clari, the Maid of Milan*

CHAPTER 39

Clinical Signs of Disease

by Janet Aldrich

Disease is a state wherein normal body structure or function is altered. Disease therefore can be defined as the malfunction of any body part. A disease can be a broken leg, poisoning, kidney failure, cancer, infection, an inherited defect, or any of hundreds of other conditions that interfere with normal structure or function. Some known causes of disease include trauma, infection, diet, environment and heredity. However, the cause of many diseases is unknown.

Persons suffering from disease will recognize in themselves any changes from the normal state and report them as **symptoms**. In veterinary medicine the term **clinical signs** is used instead of symptoms, to indicate that what is being reported is based on observation of the patient by someone else (often the owner), and not on a direct report from the patient.

The dog owner recognizes disease as a change in the dog's normal state. The more skilled an owner is at recognizing the normal state, the more likely it is that changes from normal will be detected early in the course of disease. Skills in recognizing the normal state are gained through experience and study.

Opportunities for gaining such experience include living and working with dogs at home, and in specialized situations in the many activities wherein dogs and people work together. Experience with many different dogs over long periods of time, especially when efforts are made to be an accurate and objective observer, can result in the gain of considerable skill at recognizing both normal and abnormal states. Many owners gain additional information about the normal state by reading books and articles dealing with dogs; through discussions with other dog owners, especially those who have special interests and experience with dogs; and through discussions with veterinarians and members of the veterinary staff, especially during visits for routine health care.

Activity level, appetite, water intake, urination and defecation are frequently altered when disease is present. Normal activity includes greeting, investigating, guarding, playing and sleeping. Most activity is spontaneous, but some is encouraged by owners, such as going for walks, training or playing. Dogs that are suffering from disease tend to withdraw from their usual activities and to spend more time resting and sleeping. The more closely the owner lives and works with the dog, the more likely it is that changes in activity level will be recognized.

The body has only a limited number of ways of responding to disease-causing agents; thus, the clinical signs of disease are much fewer than are the causes of disease. Clinical signs are useful as an indicator that disease is present, but usually are not specific enough to define the underlying cause of the disease. For example, one of the responses to a bacterial infection is fever, but not all fevers are due to bacterial infection. Other causes of fever include cancer, immune-mediated disease, inflammation, and infectious agents other than bacteria (viruses, fungi, parasites). Thus, fever is a sign of disease but not a specific indicator of the origin of the disease, or even of the particular body system involved. In other cases the body system involved is obvious, but the cause of the disease is not. For example, seizures indicate that the brain is involved, but do not indicate whether there is a primary disease in the brain or whether the brain is simply being affected secondarily by disease in another organ (such as the liver). The benefit of recognizing the clinical signs of disease lies in the opportunity to alter the natural course of the illness, either by effecting a cure (if a cure is possible) or by implementing appropriate therapy to ameliorate the severity of the disease.

In this chapter, some of the common clinical signs of disease will be described, and their significance in terms of body systems involved—as well as some possible causes—will be summarized. The list of possible causes should not be considered complete, but represents rather a sampling of some of the many causes of disease in dogs.

Pain

Research has verified that animals feel pain to the same extent as human beings. Pain sensation originates either in the skin, the deep tissues such as bone, joint and muscle, or in the internal organs. Pain is evidenced by decreased use of the painful part, possibly by overall decreased activity. Dogs may cry out in pain,

especially if the pain is intermittent and sharp in nature; they may not cry out even when in severe pain if the pain is dull, aching and continuous. Thus the absence of crying, whining, or groaning is not an indication that pain is absent. Better indicators of the presence of pain include:

- attempts to decrease use of the painful part, such as by limping
- reluctance to move the neck or back
- reluctance to change body position or to assume any particular body position (refusing to lie down or to stand or sit up)
- withdrawal from all unnecessary activity

Touching a painful area may elicit signs of resentment, such as motion away from the touch, tightening of the muscles in the area (**splinting**), or aggressive behavior such as growling or biting. Some dogs, however, may be so tractable or stoic in nature that it is difficult to elicit signs of pain even when pain is undoubtedly present.

Pain may be useful in localizing the disease process to a particular body part, but it does not provide much information regarding the cause of the pain. Pain is mainly used as an indicator that further diagnostic investigation is required so that the underlying cause may be identified and if possible treated.

Because animals feel pain to the same extent as human beings, pain control is desirable when pain is moderate to severe. A great deal of research has been conducted in the area of pain control, especially over the past 10 years, and effective and safe means of pain control are available. However, pain control should not be used as a substitute for appropriate diagnostic efforts to identify the cause of the pain.

Lethargy

Lethargy can be defined as an abnormal state of drowsiness or dullness. A dog's usual response to disease is to withdraw from normal activities and to spend more time resting and sleeping. Lethargy is easily recognized by the observant owner and is one of the most commonly reported signs of disease in dogs.

Lethargy is nonspecific with regard to the cause of the illness, but is important as an indicator that the dog is unwell and that further investigation is warranted.

Changes in Appetite and Body Weight

The brain contains specific centers (collections of nerve cells) that regulate hunger and **satiety** (the opposite of hunger—a feeling of sufficiency or satisfaction with regard to food intake). These brain centers are influenced by:

1. information from the rest of the body regarding the overall state of nutrition;
2. blood levels of **glucose** (blood sugar), protein and fat;
3. short-term stimuli, such as a feeling of fullness in the stomach;
4. the effects of various diseases that suppress or stimulate the hunger and satiety centers.

Body weight is determined by the total amount of energy taken in and by its relation to the total amount of energy used. Energy is taken in as food, which must then be digested, absorbed and converted to usable energy within the cells of the body. The total amount of energy used varies with age, activity, state of health and environmental conditions. **Metabolism,** or the metabolic rate, refers to the sum of all the processes within the body which make energy available to sustain life. The metabolic rate is used to determine how much energy must be provided for the usual dog under ordinary conditions. This is the basis for charts suggesting how much food to feed dogs of a certain size and age. These charts are only an estimate, however; dogs, like people, exhibit wide variation in the number of calories needed to maintain a stable weight.

The significance of a change in appetite must be evaluated in light of its association with any expected weight loss or gain. Many diseases cause an increased need for nutrients, and in such situations an increase in food intake may be entirely appropriate to compensate for the increase in metabolic requirements. There is, however, some difficulty in determining whether appetite changes are actually causing weight gain or loss. Most dog owners do not regularly weigh their dogs, and evaluation of body weight by inspection is a skill that a dog owner may not possess. On the other hand, most dog owners feed a known quantity on a regular schedule and so are more likely to recognize changes in the amount of food eaten, rather than the more progressive alterations in body weight that may follow a change in appetite.

DECREASE IN APPETITE

A decrease in appetite (**anorexia**) can be partial or complete. Dogs, like people, are not inclined to eat when they feel unwell; however, a decrease in appetite is not specific for disease in any particular body system. The ability of the owner to recognize the normal state accurately is essential. Occasionally, owners believe that a dog should eat more than is normal for that particular dog, and so misinterpret the dog's normal appetite as inadequate and therefore a sign of disease.

Over the long term (months to years), appetite is adequate if a dog eats enough to maintain a normal and stable body weight. However, over a period of days to weeks changes in body weight may not be readily apparent. A sudden decrease in appetite is likely to be abnormal, and often is an early and very important sign of disease despite its lack of specificity. A change to a more palatable type of food may temporarily correct partial anorexia, but may also mask the presence of an underlying illness. It is also important to verify that the decreased food intake is actually due to a decreased appetite and not to difficulty in the act of eating or swallowing. Painful diseases of the mouth or chewing muscles may make the act of eating too painful for a dog to tolerate.

INCREASE IN APPETITE

An increased appetite may be a normal response to an increased need for nutrients. Exercise, cold environmental temperatures and pregnancy are examples of normal states that require increased nutrition. Many diseases also create increases in nutritional needs, but most of these are associated with poor appetite because the patient does not feel well. Some diseases do not cause a feeling of illness, especially early in the disease course, but may interfere with the way in which food is digested, absorbed, or converted to usable energy, or may increase the rate at which energy is utilized. Such diseases include:

- diabetes mellitus
- diseases causing increases in hormones secreted by the adrenal glands or pancreas
- hyperthyroidism (which increases the body's metabolic rate)
- diseases of the intestinal wall that interfere with food absorption
- diseases of the brain that affect the hunger or satiety centers

In addition, certain medications—especially corticosteroids and some of the anticonvulsants—can produce an increase in appetite as a side effect of their use in therapy.

WEIGHT GAIN

Weight gain may represent a gain of fat, muscle, or fluid. Dogs having more body fat than is required for normal function are by definition overweight. **Obesity** is a synonym for being overweight, both terms indicating that the amount of body fat is greater than normal. Obesity may be mild, moderate or severe. Like people, dogs tend to gain weight over time, especially if their activity level is decreased. If food is quite palatable and especially if it is associated with social interactions, dogs are likely to eat more food than they need to maintain body weight.

Obesity is a disease, and its effects usually worsen the problems associated with other diseases. For example, dogs with joint problems (hip dysplasia or diseases of the knee joints) usually experience increased difficulties if they must carry additional body weight on the already diseased joints. Obese dogs with heart disease have an additional strain placed on the heart as it circulates blood to the increased body mass. Dogs with respiratory disease, especially those with collapsing trachea, can have their condition substantially worsened by the pressure of increased fat on the trachea and lungs. Increase in muscle weight, by comparison, is usually a healthy condition brought on by increased exercise and appropriate increases in appetite.

Corticosteroid hormones from the adrenal gland (hormones such as **cortisone** and **cortisol**) regulate many metabolic processes. Overproduction of these hormones (as in **Cushing**'s **syndrome**) or their administration as therapy for certain diseases can produce a change in the way body fat is distributed. They also can produce enlargement of the liver (**hepatomegaly**) and a loss of muscle mass or strength. This combination of effects produces a "pot-bellied" appearance that may be interpreted as weight gain.

Fluid gain can be caused by accumulation of fluid in the abdominal or chest cavities, or by excessive fluid in the tissues under the skin. Fluid in the abdomen is usually not noticed until it causes a marked increase in abdominal size (*see* "CHANGES IN ABDOMINAL SIZE OR SHAPE," BELOW). Fluid in the chest cavity causes a change in respiratory rate or effort (*see* "CHANGES IN BREATHING PATTERN," BELOW). The accumulation of fluid in the tissues under the skin, called **edema,** can be caused by:

- heart failure
- loss of protein due to intestinal, liver, or kidney disease
- restriction of blood and lymph circulation from the area

WEIGHT LOSS

Weight loss may represent a loss of fat, muscle, or body water. When healthy dogs lose weight because they are exercising more and eating less, the weight loss is due to fat loss. Fat loss continues until body stores of fat are used up, after which time muscle will be used for energy. This is the normal, orderly progression in healthy dogs. If underfeeding continues until body fat stores are too low for normal function, then weight loss becomes a disease because it represents a state in which body function has been compromised. Its cause in this case is incorrect management.

In some diseases affecting metabolic processes, the normal progression of weight loss is changed and muscle is broken down to supply energy even though the body possesses fat stores that have not yet been depleted. Affected dogs often feel ill and do not eat normally. The combination of decreased food intake and presence of a disease causing muscle breakdown can result in a sudden and dramatic loss of muscle mass.

This type of weight loss is a sign of disease, but is not specific for any particular disease.

Muscle **atrophy** is a decrease in muscle mass not due to underfeeding, but due to disease. The owner may recognize the loss of muscle because the bones in the area become more prominent. Muscle mass may be lost because of disuse (**disuse atrophy**), such as when a painful elbow joint causes a dog to stop using the affected limb. Some nerve or muscle diseases also cause a loss of muscle mass owing either to decreased use or to direct destruction of nerve or muscle tissue.

Loss of body water is called **dehydration.** It occurs when the intake of water is not sufficient to cover water losses. (*See* "CHANGES IN WATER INTAKE," BELOW.)

Fever

Normal body temperature for dogs ranges from 100°F to 102.5°F, with the higher end of the temperature range usually found in smaller dogs. Increases in temperature above the normal range can be caused by increases in environmental temperature, exercise, excitement, or by disease.

HIGH ENVIRONMENTAL TEMPERATURES

Dogs regulate their body temperature by panting, during which they move air over moist membranes in the mouth and thus cool themselves by evaporation. This regulatory system is fairly easy to overwhelm with high environmental temperatures, particularly when combined with high humidity. Under such conditions dogs can readily overheat and experience severe and life-threatening rises in body temperature, often to levels greater than 108°F. This is a condition known as *heatstroke* and the rise in temperature can occur within a few minutes. One of the more common causes of this is confinement in a car during hot weather. The consequences of a severe elevation of body temperature include structural alterations of body proteins and interference with normal cell metabolism, which is designed to operate only within a fairly narrow temperature range. Treatment of heatstroke includes cooling the patient to return body temperature to normal, but this strategy alone is rarely sufficient. (*See* CHAPTER 43, "PROCEDURES FOR LIFE-THREATENING EMERGENCIES.")

FEVER

Fever too is characterized by a rise in body temperature, but the cause is instead a change in the thermoregulatory set-point in the brain. Instead of trying to cool off to bring body temperature down, as is the case in heatstroke, the patient with fever is trying to warm up and will conserve body heat by seeking a warm environment, by assuming body positions that conserve heat, and by shivering. With fever, the magnitude of the rise in body temperature is usually well below a level that would be considered dangerous. In fact, fever is thought to be beneficial; the body's natural processes of fighting disease may be enhanced by a moderate increase in body temperature. The underlying causes of the change in the thermoregulatory set-point are natural body substances released following infection, immune-mediated disease, cancer, or inflammation.

Vomiting

Vomiting is the forceful ejection of contents of the stomach and upper small intestine through the mouth. Vomiting is caused by stimulation of a portion of the brain called the **vomiting center.** Vomiting usually is easy to recognize, but it sometimes can be confused with coughing or with the expulsion of **phlegm** (a viscous secretion produced by the respiratory tract). Sometimes vomiting is very mild and self-limiting, perhaps due to a mild stomach irritation. Dogs are often observed to eat grass and then vomit shortly thereafter. They may do this in order to induce vomiting because of a need to evacuate the contents of the stomach. At times, the vomiting may not give relief and so a dog will continue to eat grass and vomit. There is no benefit in allowing this behavior to continue once the stomach contents have been ejected. However, dogs that are not ill will also eat grass, apparently because they enjoy the taste, and they may ingest it without vomiting.

Persistent vomiting is a sign of severe disease, especially when it is seen in combination with other signs such as lethargy, inappetence, pain or fever. The vomiting may be due to diseases within the abdomen, particularly those causing irritation, distension or inflammation. Common causes include:

• **gastric** (pertaining to the stomach) or intestinal foreign bodies, especially if they are producing obstruction
• ingestion of toxic substances that are directly irritating to the lining of the stomach and intestines, or that are absorbed into the bloodstream where they produce generalized toxic effects
• distension of the stomach or intestine with gas or fluid
• loss of blood supply to abdominal organs
• infectious agents causing inflammation, such as canine parvovirus type 2
• dysfunction of other abdominal organs such as the pancreas, liver or kidneys, resulting in local irritation as well as accumulation of toxins in the body

Causes of vomiting originating outside the abdomen include:

• drugs of many types that have a direct action on the vomiting center
• alterations in normal **electrolyte** (molecules dissociating into ions, such as sodium or potassium) concentrations
• anxiety or fear

Vomiting is an important clinical sign both because it indicates that disease is present and because it can in itself worsen disease by producing losses of water and electrolytes.

Diarrhea

Diarrhea is an increase in the fluid content, volume or frequency of bowel movements. Comparison with the normal condition for each individual dog is necessary because stools vary widely in color and consistency among dogs, the result primarily of diet. Diarrhea may be chronic or of sudden onset. Diseases of the intestinal tract that interfere with nutrient or water absorption (and therefore cause diarrhea) include:

• sudden changes in diet
• ingestion of toxins, such as garbage
• intestinal parasites

• infections such as canine parvovirus type 2
• intolerance to certain foods

Other abdominal organs with functions essential to proper digestion and absorption of nutrients include the pancreas and liver. Diseases whose origins lie primarily outside the intestines can also cause diarrhea because of circulating toxins or by interference with blood supply to the intestinal tract.

Changes in Water Intake

Thirst is governed by sensors in the blood vessels and other areas that monitor blood volume and tissue water. Conditions causing the membranes of the mouth to become dry can also stimulate thirst. It is important to note that panting does not cause a dog's mouth to become dry, as it would in people. In dogs, panting serves a thermoregulatory function and the oral tissues must be wet with saliva in order for panting to have the desired cooling effect. Water intake varies with environmental temperature, exercise, and composition of the diet. If the diet contains a large amount of water (as in canned foods and moistened kibble), dogs will drink correspondingly less. Hot weather and vigorous exercise increase water requirements. Most dog owners do not measure the amount of water provided for their pets, so that changes in water intake may be quite substantial before they are noticed.

DECREASES IN WATER INTAKE
In cold climates, water intake may be drastically and involuntarily reduced because the water provided to dogs housed outdoors freezes. This reduction in water intake is not a sign of disease, but rather a management problem. If the decrease in water availability is not corrected, dogs will become dehydrated—a situation that can lead to serious illness.

Voluntary decreases in water intake are usually associated with other signs of disease such as lethargy, vomiting and diarrhea, or fever. Some dogs will quickly follow a vomiting episode with the drinking of water, which then may be followed by more vomiting. In this situation the net amount of water taken in is represented by the amount of water the dog drinks minus the amount lost in the **vomitus** (vomited material). Decreased water intake in such a setting is not specific for any particular disease. The vomiting itself can make the signs of disease worse by causing dehydration and electrolyte abnormalities. Dehydration, if severe, is a life-threatening condition. (*See* CHAPTER 43, "PROCEDURES FOR LIFE-THREATENING EMERGENCIES.")

INCREASES IN WATER INTAKE

Thirst is a closely regulated function and dogs do not normally take in more water than they need. If water intake appears to be increased, the first step is to look for natural causes such as hot weather, exercise, or a need to replace losses sustained by concurrent vomiting or diarrhea. Increased water intake is sometimes noted only because of an associated increase in urine production, which the owner observes as increased frequency and amount of urination.

Most increases in water intake are caused by diseases that alter the ability of the kidneys to conserve water. The kidneys' conservation of water may be affected by kidney disease or by alterations in various hormones and electrolytes. Diseases in this latter category include:

- diabetes mellitus
- diseases of the adrenal glands resulting in decreases or increases in adrenal hormone levels
- uterine infections with accumulation of pus in the uterus (**pyometra**)
- changes in calcium or potassium concentrations in the blood
- liver disease

Changes in Urination Patterns or Urine Color

Urine is produced to carry waste products out of the body and to keep the body's internal environment balanced. The amount of urine produced by a normal dog is related to the amount needed to excrete dissolved waste products and to protect blood volume, **pH** (acid-base), and electrolyte concentrations in the body. In order to achieve this, the fluid portion of the blood with its dissolved constituents is filtered through the kidneys. It is the job of the kidneys to process this filtrate, excreting waste products and reabsorbing most of the water. (*See* CHAPTER 27, "THE URINARY SYSTEM AND DISORDERS.")

The pattern of urination is the combination of acts that forms the characteristic urination behavior of dogs. Patterns of urination include factors such as:

- frequency of urination
- amount of urine passed with each urination
- total amount of urine voided
- ease of passing urine
- awareness that urine is being voided

Urination is a complex process requiring a structurally intact urinary system with appropriate neurologic and muscular controls. It is under both voluntary and involuntary control. Urination not only serves to eliminate waste products, but also assumes a behavioral function by allowing scent-marking of territory.

The normal pattern of urination is different for male and female dogs. Male dogs urinate small amounts frequently within a short period of time because of the need to scent-mark their home range. Female dogs are more likely to empty their bladders in a single urination, but sometimes they too engage in scent-marking.

Both male and female dogs should urinate without any evidence of pain or straining. The bladder serves as a reservoir to collect urine from the kidneys until it can be voided. This allows most adult dogs approximately 8 hours between urinations, although they will urinate more frequently if given the opportunity. If opportunities to urinate are too infrequent, the bladder will become overfilled and overstretched. This condition, if chronic, can lead to damage within the bladder wall and to an increased risk of urinary tract infections.

INCREASED FREQUENCY OF URINATION

An increase in the frequency of urination is much more likely to be noticed in dogs that are closely supervised, such as those that live indoors with the family. Once it has been determined that the frequency of urination is increased, it is important next to ask whether the total daily amount of urine produced is normal or increased.

Increase in Daily Amount of Urine Produced

An increase in the total daily amount of urine produced will, of course, require more frequent emptying of the bladder. Although the actual total volume of urine produced is rarely measured at home, the owner may note that each urination seems to produce a large, rather than a small, amount of urine. Increased urine production will be accompanied by increased water intake (*see* ABOVE).

Increase in Frequency of Urination without an Increase in the Daily Amount of Urine Produced

Increased frequency of urination, when it is not a reflection of normal scent-marking behavior, may be caused by sensations of pain or irritation in the bladder, **urethra** (membranous tube that carries urine from the bladder to the exterior of the body), or genital tract. It may not be obvious that the dog is experiencing pain or discomfort, only that it is urinating small amounts of urine very frequently.

DIFFICULT OR PAINFUL URINATION

Painful or difficult urination is recognized because the dog strains to urinate, takes an unusually long time to complete urination, or produces a small or intermittent urine stream. The origin of this change in urination pattern can be irritation of the bladder, urethra or genital tract, or obstruction of the bladder or urethra. Underlying causes include infection, urinary stones, or masses such as cancer of the bladder or urethra. Neurologic or muscular diseases may result in an inability to perform the complex process of urination.

DISCOLORED URINE

Urine is normally yellow in color, but the depth of color can vary depending on the amount of water and pigment in the urine. Urine may be discolored by the presence of blood or by an excess of pigment obtained from the breakdown of red blood cells elsewhere in the body. Uncommonly, pigment obtained from the breakdown of muscle may appear in the urine. Blood

in the urine may originate anywhere within the urinary or genital tracts. Causes of bleeding include stones, infection, cancer, trauma, and urinary tract parasites. Additionally, hemorrhage due to a primary bleeding disorder such as ingestion of rat poison, **von Willebrand's disease** (inherited coagulation abnormality), or immune-mediated diseases attacking blood **platelets** (blood cell fragments that are an integral part of the clotting mechanism), may produce bleeding anywhere within the body, including the urinary and genital tracts.

URINARY INCONTINENCE

Urinary **incontinence** is the loss of voluntary control over urination. Incontinence differs from increased frequency of urination in that incontinence occurs without any effort to urinate. It is often brought to the attention of the owner when wet spots of urine are found in places where a dog has been sleeping.

Urinary incontinence occurs much more commonly in females than in males. It is not a behavioral problem because the dog is unaware that it is passing urine. Urinary incontinence must be differentiated from the behavioral problem of **inappropriate urination,** wherein the dog voluntarily urinates but in places of which the owner disapproves. (*See* CHAPTER 7, "MISBEHAVIOR.") Urinary incontinence is most common in middle-aged to older female dogs. Although the exact cause has not been determined, it is usually a treatable condition.

In order to keep urine in the bladder, there must be both neurologic and muscular control. Loss of these controls can be caused by neurologic or muscular diseases such as spinal cord or brain disease, or diseases that irritate, infect or destroy the nerves and muscles of the urinary tract.

Coughing

A cough may have a harsh, dry quality or it may be moist. The time of day or the type of activity with which the cough is associated should be noted. The time of day *during which the dog is observed* must also be considered. If the dog is alone during the day and only with the owner at night, it will be difficult to distinguish nocturnal coughing from coughing that is intermittently distributed throughout the day and night.

Causes of coughing include infections, allergies, structural abnormalities, parasites, trauma, cancer within the respiratory system and heart failure. While a cough suggests disease affecting the respiratory tract, all respiratory tract diseases do not cause a cough. Therefore, the absence of a cough cannot be used to exclude the possibility of respiratory tract disease.

DRY COUGH

Dry cough is associated with diseases of the **trachea** (a cartilage-lined tubular airway that descends from the larynx into the chest) or **bronchi** (larger air passages leading from the trachea and branching within the lungs), allergies, and irritation of the **pharynx** (the area extending from the rear of the mouth and nasal passages to the larynx and esophagus) and **tonsils** (masses of lymphoid tissue at the rear of the mouth). Common causes include viral infections, allergic reactions, and occasionally foreign bodies such as plant material within the pharynx, tonsillar area, trachea, or esophagus.

In some dogs the trachea is quite small, soft, and subject to collapse, which produces irritation and stimulates a dry cough. In mild cases the collapse occurs only with forceful respiratory efforts and is mostly associated with excitement or with direct pressure on the trachea from a collar. Obesity worsens the problem of tracheal collapse by increasing the pressure on the trachea from the surrounding fatty tissues. In severe cases the cough may be nearly continuous. (*See* CHAPTER 29, "THE RESPIRATORY SYSTEM AND DISORDERS.")

MOIST COUGH

Moist cough is indicative of the accumulation of fluid in the mouth, airways, or lungs. The fluid may be edema secondary to heart failure, pus from an infection, or blood from trauma or a blood-clotting disorder. Coughing that occurs primarily at night can indicate congestive heart failure.

Changes in Breathing Pattern

The purpose of breathing is to provide oxygen to the body and to eliminate the waste gas carbon dioxide. Breathing also serves a thermoregulatory function. Normal breathing involves the **inspiration** (inhalation) of air through the nose and mouth into the trachea and from there through the bronchi and into the lungs. The action of inspiration requires movement of the muscles of respiration; that is, the **diaphragm** (the large muscle separating the abdominal and chest cavities) and the muscles attached to the ribs. In the lungs, the inspired air comes into contact with red blood cells, to which the inspired oxygen is transferred for delivery throughout the body. With **expiration** (exhalation) the waste gas carbon dioxide (an end product of cellular metabolism) is eliminated.

The components of the normal breathing pattern are rate, rhythm and effort. When the normal breathing pattern is altered, it is usually due to an increase in the breathing rate or to a state of labored breathing, or both. Breathing is under both voluntary and involuntary control, and patterns of breathing should be evaluated with the dog at rest and in a cool environment. Because breathing rate, rhythm and effort are supervised by control centers in the brain, diseases affecting the brain can also affect breathing in the absence of primary respiratory tract disease. Head trauma, pain, fever and shock all can affect the breathing pattern.

INCREASE IN RATE

An increase in the breathing rate without difficulty in breathing may be caused by exercise, high environmental temperature, or anxiety. If these have been eliminated as causative factors, then a persistent and marked increase in breathing rate should be considered a clinical sign of disease even if there is no apparent difficulty in breathing. An increase in the breathing rate is often the earliest clinical sign of a respiratory tract disease that is due either to primary disease in the respiratory tract itself or to the effects of heart failure and resulting **pulmonary edema** (noninflammatory buildup of fluid in the tissues and airways in the lungs).

Anemia (low red blood cell count) is another cause of an increase in the breathing rate. Decreased numbers of red blood cells result in a decreased oxygen-carrying capacity of the blood. The compensatory response of the body is to increase the breathing rate to make more oxygen available to the diminished number of circulating red cells.

DIFFICULTY BREATHING

Difficulty in either inspiration or expiration may be characterized by noisy breathing or by deep, forceful respiratory efforts, or both.

Noisy Breathing

Noisy breathing is caused by an obstruction in the nasal passages, mouth, or **larynx** (muscular structure containing the vocal cords). The dog will make vigorous efforts to inhale or exhale (depending on the type and location of the obstruction) against the obstruction. The condition may be continuous or intermittent. It is a common condition in the **brachycephalic** (flat-faced) breeds, such as the Bulldog and Pug, and is especially prevalent during hot weather when breathing rates are increased because of the need to regulate body temperature. This rapid breathing rate may cause some swelling of the tissues around the larynx and, in dogs with an anatomic predisposition, can result in airway obstruction. Occasionally, diseases within the lungs can produce noisy breathing owing to constriction of the smaller airways. This is heard as a wheezing sound and can be caused by allergic reactions or chronic bronchitis (inflammation of the bronchi).

Deep, Forceful Breathing

Deep, forceful respiratory efforts without signs of airway obstruction can be caused by disease in the chest, either in the lungs (pneumonia, bleeding, cancer, heartworms, **fibrosis** [formation of fibrous tissue]) or in the space between the lungs and interior chest wall (**pleural cavity**). Accumulation of air or fluid within the pleural space compromises the ability to expand the lungs and the dog responds by making increased efforts to inspire and/or expire. Air accumulation in the chest (**pneumothorax**) is caused by a rupture of the lung, which allows air to leak into the pleural space. The cause is usually traumatic, but may be due to infection, cancer, or to spontaneous rupture of a weakened area in the lungs. Fluid in the pleural space may be caused by:

- pus from an infection
- blood due to trauma or a blood-clotting disorder
- lymph from a severed lymphatic vessel
- congestive heart failure
- cancer

Expansion of the lungs can also be compromised by rupture of the diaphragm, with movement of some of the abdominal contents into the chest cavity (**diaphragmatic hernia**). A similar effect occurs with large masses in the pleural space.

DECREASE IN BREATHING RATE OR EFFORT

Severe decreases in breathing rate or effort are usually associated with shock and are indicators of impending respiratory arrest. Because breathing requires muscular work (by the diaphragm and the muscles attached to the ribs), decreases in breathing rate and effort may also occur following paralysis of the breathing muscles. This usually occurs secondary to a toxin or to an acquired neuromuscular disease.

Changes in Mucous Membrane Color

Mucous membranes are the lubricating membranes lining the internal surfaces of body cavities such as the mouth. Blood vessels running very close to the surface of these membranes impart a normal pink color to them. The mucous membranes themselves can have pigment within them that will prevent observation of the blood vessels underneath. Some dogs have totally pigmented (i.e., black) mouths and tongues, so that mucous membrane color cannot be determined easily. Alternatively, one may examine other mucous membranes, such as the internal portion of the lower eyelid, the vulva in the female, or the penis in the male. Because the usual pink color is a reflection of the local blood supply, a change in color can indicate a change in either the amount or composition of the blood flowing through the vessels.

PALE MUCOUS MEMBRANES

Pale mucous membranes may be caused by a decrease in the number of red blood cells in the blood (anemia) or by a constriction of the blood vessels with a corresponding reduction in blood volume. Anemia may be the result of:

- bleeding (trauma, ingestion of rat poisons)
- destruction of red blood cells (immune-mediated hemolytic anemia)
- decreased production of red blood cells (bone marrow disease, kidney disease, many generalized illnesses)

Constriction of the blood vessels may be caused by shock (from severe trauma or illness) or heart disease.

Yellow Mucous Membranes

In **jaundice,** a yellow pigment discolors the body tissues, including the mucous membranes. This pigment, known as **bilirubin,** is not limited to the blood within the blood vessels but actually penetrates the mucous membranes and skin. When sufficiently severe, jaundice will discolor all the body tissues.

Bilirubin is produced from hemoglobin which originates in red blood cells. Normally, as red cells age and are broken down for reprocessing, the pigment is excreted by the liver into the feces and urine. In liver disease or in diseases that accelerate the rate of red cell breakdown, bilirubin accumulates in the blood and eventually finds its way into the body tissues.

Skin and Haircoat Changes

The skin is essential for the maintenance of good health. The skin is the first body organ to contact many toxins and infectious organisms and possesses excellent defense mechanisms to protect the body from disease. The skin and haircoat also serve as useful indicators of disease in other body systems. (*See* Chapter 22, "The Skin and Disorders.")

Itchy Skin

Itchiness (**pruritus**) is an unpleasant sensation that provokes the desire to scratch or chew. It develops into a problem when the chewing or scratching becomes repeated and persistent. Pain can also evoke chewing or scratching at the painful area. The itching sensation is caused by the release of substances from bacteria, fungi, or white blood cells. Causes of itchiness include:

- flea allergy
- allergies to inhaled substances
- food allergy
- allergies to substances in contact with the skin

With regard to flea allergy, it is important to note that some severely allergic dogs can be provoked into continuous itching by a flea bite that occurs *only once every few weeks.* Thus an inspection of the dog for the presence of fleas may produce negative results. Other causes of itchiness include skin parasites (*Sarcoptes* and *Demodex*) and skin infections. (*See* Chapter 23, "External Parasites.")

Prolonged licking at a specific area, usually a leg or paw, can result in the development of a raised, red-to-black circular area of irritation and hair loss (**acral lick dermatitis**). The specific cause of this condition is not known, but boredom appears to play a significant role.

Hair Loss

Dogs lose and regrow hair in a regular cycle that is usually associated with the changing seasons. Most owners are aware that hair loss occurs in their pets at certain times of the year, although many dogs shed a great deal throughout the year. The amount of hair shed may be small or large; so long as the hair is quickly replaced with healthy new hair the process is a normal one. Abnormal hair loss is that which results in a loss of haircoat, either in localized areas or generally over the body.

The pattern of hair loss is an important clue to its underlying cause. Loss of hair primarily on the trunk with sparing of the legs is most often a hormonal disease. Causes include hypothyroidism, **Cushing's syndrome** (excess adrenal hormone production), or alterations in sex hormone levels. Other patterns of hair loss are indicators of other diseases ranging from skin parasites or fungal infections to various immune-mediated diseases wherein the skin is attacked by the body's own immune system.

Changes in the Skin or Ears

The skin should be smooth, dry to the touch, and free from any breaks in its surface. The interior surface of the ear is also skin and is subject to the same diseases as are other areas of skin. Areas of redness, swellings, masses, breaks in the skin, crusts, scaliness, discharges, or changes in skin pigmentation are abnormal. Hormonal disturbances or chronic irritation can produce a marked increase in local skin pigmentation. Masses may represent cancer or noncancerous accumulations of fat or other cells. Breaks in the skin can be caused by trauma, infections, drug reactions, or immune-mediated disease. Certain types of bleeding disorders may first be noted as small, red dots in the skin resembling measles, or as larger bruised areas.

Disease of the skin of the ears is a common problem, often characterized by excessive discharge and a disagreeable odor. If the ear is painful, the dog may hold it to one side and exhibit pain when the ear is touched. Foreign objects such as plant material may fall into the ear and cause irritation. Ear mites are parasites that live in the ear canal and can cause irritation and excessive discharge. (*See* Chapter 20, "The Ear and Disorders.")

Changes in Abdominal Size or Shape

Abdominal size is governed by:

- the size of the internal abdominal organs
- the amount of fluid in the abdomen
- the amount of fat in the abdomen
- the strength of the muscles supporting the abdomen
- the amount of fat under the skin

Changes in abdominal size or shape can be due to pregnancy or body fat gain. Abnormal conditions causing an enlarged abdomen include:

- accumulation of gas and fluid within the stomach or intestines
- accumulation of an abnormal amount of free fluid in the abdominal cavity (as opposed to fluid confined within one of the abdominal organs)
- enlargement of the liver (**hepatomegaly**) or spleen (**splenomegaly**)
- abdominal masses

Abnormal Gait

The normal gait is smoothly coordinated so that the dog moves with ease and strength. A normal gait requires that the bones, joints and muscles of the legs, neck and back function optimally and without pain, and that the brain, spinal cord and associated nerves send and receive messages in a normal fashion.

Lameness

Lameness can be caused by pain alone or by a loss of stability in a bone or joint secondary to broken bones, torn ligaments or tendons, or infection or inflammation of these structures.

Weakness, Paralysis

Weakness is a loss of normal strength. It may be difficult to differentiate from pain and reluctance to walk. Weakness is caused by a malfunction in the nervous and/or muscular system. Nervous system disease may occur in the brain, spinal cord, or peripheral nerves. The nervous system receives input related to the position of the body in space and transmits messages instructing the muscles to contract or relax. The muscles must be able to contract or relax according to these instructions. Weakness can progress to paralysis, a total inability to move. Pressure from an intervertebral disk, blood clot, mass, or broken bones, or localized disease of the nerves or muscles serving a particular limb can cause either weakness or paralysis.

Loss of Coordination or Balance

An incoordinated gait is usually manifested by a tendency to circle or fall while walking, or a high-stepping gait without appreciable loss of strength. A pronounced head-tilt may be present, along with a tendency to fall to one side, or even a complete inability to walk. The dog retains normal strength, but cannot coordinate its movements to stand or walk. An incoordinated gait results from disease within the brain or in the balance mechanism in the ear. It may be caused by masses, blood clots, immune-mediated disease, parasites, or infection.

Seizures and Episodes of Collapse

Seizures (fits) are caused by abnormal brain function that results in the loss of consciousness. The loss of consciousness is usually accompanied by generalized muscle activity such as running movements of the legs and contraction of the neck and head muscles. Episodes of collapse (fainting, or **syncope**) with a loss of consciousness can be caused by a sudden decrease in blood or glucose supply to the brain. It is not always possible to determine whether the seizure or loss of consciousness is due to primary disease within the brain or is secondary to disease external to the brain. Causes of seizures in dogs include epilepsy, distemper, rabies, parasites, tetanus, toxins such as lead or strychnine, heart disease, and brain tumors. Metabolic disorders that affect blood levels of glucose or calcium, or that allow the accumulation of waste products affecting the brain (i.e., kidney or liver failure), can also produce seizure activity.

Prolonged Bleeding

Trauma can damage blood vessels and cause bleeding. This type of bleeding is usually controlled by the formation of a blood clot. Failure to form the clot, however, can result in prolonged bleeding. This is a bleeding or blood-clotting disorder and is due to a malfunction of the blood-clotting system. Prolonged bleeding is significant because it reflects a problem with the blood-clotting mechanism and also because it can result in life-threatening blood loss. (*See* CHAPTER 43, "PROCEDURES FOR LIFE-THREATENING EMERGENCIES.")

Prolonged bleeding may be obvious, as with blood loss from a body opening, or it may be hidden within the body (internal blood loss). Certain types of bleeding disorders result in pinpoint accumulations of blood in the skin that resemble measles. In other types there may be a large accumulation of blood under the skin that resembles a bruise. Internal bleeding can occur in any part of the body; clinical signs will be related to the body part involved. Causes of prolonged bleeding include:

- ingestion of rat poison
- immune-mediated diseases
- bone marrow malfunction
- ulcers
- cancer
- inherited bleeding disorders, such as von Willebrand's disease or hemophilia
- certain drugs, such as aspirin

Abnormalities of the Eyes, Ears, Nose, and Mouth

EYES

The eyes of a dog should be clear and shiny and free of discharge. Red, watery eyes or discharge from the eyes can be caused by allergies, foreign objects such as plant material, infections, or decreased tear production. A painful eye may cause a dog to keep the eyelids partially closed and to avoid light. The pain may be due to:

- ulcers of the **cornea** (the transparent outer coat of the eye)
- inflammation or increased pressure within the eye
- eyelashes growing in toward the surface of the eye
- inflammation of the tissues surrounding the eye

Loss of vision is often noticed only when the dog moves to an unfamiliar environment; for example, the dog may bump into unseen objects or be reluctant to walk in the new area. Vision loss due to **cataracts** (opacity of the lens of the eye) is usually very gradual, while sudden vision loss may be caused by bleeding within the eye or diseases of the vision system within the brain. Many breeds suffer from inherited disorders that interfere with vision. (*See* CHAPTER 19, "THE EYE AND DISORDERS.")

EARS

Ear disease may involve skin disease of the external ear or problems with balance or hearing. Balance and hearing are controlled from the inner ear and the brain. Diseases affecting these areas include infections, foreign bodies penetrating from the external ear canal, cancer, bleeding and inflammation. (*See* CHAPTER 20, "THE EAR AND DISORDERS.")

Nose

The nose should be smooth and shiny without discharge. A sudden onset of sneezing that is persistent is often due to inhalation of plant material into the nasal passages. Nasal discharges may contain blood or secretions and may be caused by allergies, fungal infections or cancer. (*See* Chapter 29, "The Respiratory System and Disorders.")

Mouth

Diseases of the mouth include dental disease of the teeth and gums, ulcers of the tongue or membranes lining the mouth, foreign objects embedded in the mouth, or oral cancer. Dental disease is usually first noticed because of an objectionable mouth odor (**halitosis**). A dog may also exhibit pain by reluctance to chew hard objects or by allowing food to drop out of the mouth. Ulcers of the mouth often are caused by a systemic illness, especially kidney failure. Foreign objects can include a bone lodged in the mouth, spines from various plants, porcupine quills, or small pieces of plant material lodged in the tonsils. (*See* Chapter 21, "Canine Dentistry" and Chapter 27, "The Urinary System and Disorders.")

Owner's Examination

The following guide may help to confirm a dog owner's suspicion that something is wrong so that medical care can be sought. Any marked change in appearance or behavior, whether or not it is included in the following list, should be evaluated by a veterinarian. Redness, heat, swelling, pain, breaks in the skin, masses or growths, bloody or foul-smelling discharge are signs of disease wherever they occur and are not listed repeatedly in this table.

Table 1
Abnormalities That May Be Noted During an Owner's Examination of a Pet

General appearance
depression; lethargy; unresponsiveness; loss of balance; loss of consciousness; altered behavior

Eyes
excessive tears; yellow or thick, ropy discharge; holding eyes closed; cloudy, dark or irregular appearance to surface of eye; red or yellow color of white of eye; unusual eye movements; pupils of different sizes; vision problems

Ears
ears held in abnormal position; scratching at ears especially if pain is evident; foul odor from the ears

Nose
cloudy, yellow or bloody discharge; dryness or cracking of skin; ulceration

Mouth
foul odor from mouth; gums bleeding or pale, yellow or blue; cracked, broken or malaligned teeth; ulcers of tongue or gums; inability to fully open or close mouth; abnormal tongue movements or inability to move tongue; excessive salivation; difficulty eating, drinking; weak or hoarse voice

Heart and lungs
difficult, labored or irregular breathing; pale or blue color of gums; persistent panting when not warm, excited or exercising; frequent coughing, gagging, choking; fainting; decreased tolerance to exercise

Abdomen
vomiting; diarrhea; loose, black or bloody stool; swelling or enlargement of abdomen which does not appear to be due to fat gain; painful or tucked-up abdomen; marked change in appetite or water drinking

Urinary and genital
foul smelling or discolored urine; discharge from vulva in females (unless in heat or shortly after whelping); mammary masses; bloody or foul smelling discharge from nipples; blood dripping from penis; markedly unequal size of testicles; straining to urinate; leaving puddles of urine where resting/sleeping; marked increase or decrease in amount or frequency of urination

Muscles and skeleton
lame, weak or staggering gait; inability to walk in a straight line or up/down stairs as usual; sore neck; persistent circling; loss of muscle size (atrophy); obesity; emaciation; marked loss or gain of body weight

Skin
persistent scratching or licking; crusts or scabs; hair loss; yellow color (jaundice); red spots, streaks or bruises

CHAPTER 40

Surgery and Postoperative Care

by Clare R. Gregory

The surgical technique of **ovariohysterectomy,** or spay operation (removal of ovaries and uterus), for dogs was first described as early as the 16th century, but in those distant days it was only rarely employed. Much later, in the 1930s and 1940s, the development of safe and effective anesthetic agents, antiseptics, and antibiotics, together with an understanding of surgically induced infection and shock, set the stage for the practice of modern canine surgery. As in human medicine the types of procedures now available, as well as their sophistication, is truly remarkable, ranging from the removal of brain tumors to organ transplantation and total joint replacement.

Surgery itself represents only one of several clinical sciences that together combine to provide the canine patient with optimal care, both before and after surgery. Anesthesia is, of course, fundamental to the performance of surgery. The anesthesiologist does not simply render the patient unconscious and insensible of pain, but also monitors the depth of anesthesia, blood pressure, air flow through the lungs, and heart and kidney function. The patient's requirements for oxygen, fluid replacement, anesthetic agents and drugs needed to maintain life vary constantly throughout any surgical procedure. The anesthesiologist thus supports all the vital organ functions of the unconscious dog, and it is precisely this quality of care that makes modern surgical procedures possible. In addition, both surgeon and anesthesiologist provide **analgesics** (pain-killing medication) following surgery to make the patient's recovery as comfortable as possible.

The imaging sciences include radiology (X-ray and gamma-ray sciences), **ultrasonography** (noninvasive technique for visualizing the internal structures of the body by means of sound [echo] reflections; *diagnostic ultrasound*), **computerized axial tomography** (a highly specialized X-ray technique that produces cross-sectional images of the inside of the body; **CAT scan**), **radionuclide scans** (use of injected radioactive elements to identify collections of tumor cells in the body), and **nuclear magnetic resonance imaging** (highly specialized technique for visualizing internal structures of the body using an external magnetic field; **NMR** or

MRI) (*see* CHAPTER 38, "CANCER" and APPENDIX C, "DIAGNOSTIC TESTS"). Such techniques allow the surgeon to view the interior of the body without making a single incision. Using these tools many surgical procedures can be made more effective, or rendered completely unnecessary if it can be determined that the surgical outcome would not be beneficial. For example, if a 12-year-old dog develops a bone tumor of the leg (such as an **osteosarcoma**), X rays of the chest cavity can often determine if the cancer has spread to the lungs, while diagnostic ultrasound may ascertain whether it has invaded the liver, spleen or abdominal lymph nodes. If the cancer has spread from its primary site in the leg to other organ systems, the benefits of removing the tumor from the leg become problematic unless therapy (surgical, chemotherapy, radiation therapy) is directed at these distant sites as well.

Critical-care management is now a vital component of a total surgical program. Intensive-care units provide 24-hour care for canine patients. In a role analogous to that of the anesthesiologist, the critical-care veterinarian supports the vital organ function of the recovering patient until the disease state or injury has resolved. Many surgical procedures are performed on dogs whose physical condition has greatly deteriorated owing to their underlying disease. Often, critical care is required prior to surgery. Heart, lung, kidney, liver and intestinal problems may need to be stabilized prior to induction of anesthesia. Dogs may receive intravenous and intestinal feedings to provide nutrition, blood products or fluid support in order to minimize the impending stresses of anesthesia and surgery.

A successful surgical outcome requires the support of all the clinical sciences. A coordinated approach allows for correct diagnosis, proper preoperative and postoperative care, and the most effective surgical therapy possible.

Types of Surgical Procedures

Surgical procedures can be divided into two major categories, *elective* and *required.* Elective surgeries include spaying, **castration** (sterilization by complete removal of the testicles), **vasec-** **tomy** (sterilization by severing of the testicular tubules), tail amputation (tail docking), dewclaw removal and ear cropping. Required surgeries are those performed after traumatic or disease-induced injury, examples including repair of a fractured thigh bone or removal of a tumor. With either classification, the decision to perform a surgical procedure must be based on a thorough understanding of the risks, possible complications, and consequences of the procedure. *Any anesthetic/surgical procedure can potentially result in the death of the patient.* The chance of death is often very low; however, the perceived benefits of the surgical procedure must always outweigh this inherent risk. When discussing possible surgery, pet owners should as accurately as possible convey their expectations to the veterinarian and have all their questions concerning the contemplated procedure answered to their satisfaction before leaving the examination room.

ELECTIVE SURGERY

Elective surgery is usually performed on healthy dogs. Preoperative management includes bathing the animal and fasting it for 6 to 12 hours prior to surgery. Drinking water should be withheld for the final 2 to 4 hours before induction of anesthesia. Before surgery, the veterinarian will perform a physical examination of the patient and will often submit blood and urine samples to the laboratory for selected tests. The purpose of these tests is to verify that the major organ systems are functioning well and that the dog is a good candidate for anesthesia. Following surgery, the dog will be placed under observation by the veterinarian until all the effects of the anesthetic agents have dissipated. The dog will be discharged to the care of the owner when able to eat, drink and care for itself.

Instructions for home care following elective surgery will vary depending on the surgical procedure performed, and whether bandages or splints were applied. Most animals recovering from surgery will need to have their exercise restricted for 5 to 10 days, or until the incision has healed. For such a purpose, leash walks represent an excellent opportunity for both pet and pet owner to enjoy a moderate form of exercise. (*See* CHAPTER 41, "CONVALESCENCE AND HOME CARE.")

Surgical incisions should be observed by the owner several times daily until the skin **sutures** (stitches) have been removed by the veterinarian. A commonly encountered problem is the premature removal of the sutures by the dog's licking and chewing at the incision site. Discipline alone will seldom prevent a dog from removing sutures. The veterinarian may need to apply a restraining device known as an **Elizabethan collar** (a wide collar that restricts contact between the head and body) to prevent the dog from reaching the incision area. Some surgeons employ an absorbable suture material and "bury" the sutures in the skin so they are not visible.

Incisions should be observed for signs of swelling, heat, redness, and the oozing of **serum** (clear liquid component of blood) or **pus** (fluid produced by an inflammatory process, containing many white blood cells). If any of these signs appear, the veterinarian should be contacted to determine if a serious problem exists. If any internal tissue is observed protruding through the incision line of a spay, a clean towel should be wrapped around the abdomen and the dog taken to a veterinarian immediately.

Ovariohysterectomy

Spaying is the surgical removal of the ovaries and uterus and is most commonly performed for sterilization of bitches. A spay operation may also be performed to treat or control several disease processes, including pyometra. **Pyometra** (accumulation of pus in the uterus) usually results from a severe bacterial infection. This occurs most commonly in older dogs 1 to 2 months following a heat period. If pus is trapped inside the uterus the dog can become gravely ill. Surgical removal of the uterus is often curative. Another disease, **uterine torsion** (twisting of the uterus), usually occurs late in pregnancy when the uterus is very enlarged. The uterus can also rupture owing to external trauma or trauma associated with the birth process. **Uterine prolapse** (bulging or protrusion of the uterus into the vagina) is uncommon in the bitch, but can

occur following **parturition** (the act of giving birth). Removal of the uterus may be necessary when chronic bacterial infections of the uterine wall (**metritis**) cannot be medically controlled. Ovariohysterectomy may also be performed to prevent the recurrence of **vaginal hyperplasia**, which occurs during the normal heat cycle when the wall of the vaginal tract enlarges and protrudes through the opening of the vulva. Once exposed, the sensitive lining of the vaginal tract becomes swollen and may ulcerate (slough its surface layer of cells). Cancer of the uterus is rare in dogs. Fortunately, most uterine tumors are benign. (*See* CHAPTER 14, "REPRODUCTIVE DISORDERS.")

Disease can also affect the ovaries. **Cysts** (fluid-filled cavities) on the ovaries can become very large and may produce hormones that result in fertility problems. The ovaries can also be affected by different types of cancer. If reproductive ability is not of concern, the uterus and both ovaries can be removed at the time surgery is performed to remove a diseased ovary. Normal reproductive cycles can have an effect on other disease problems as well. For example, diabetic bitches and bitches with epilepsy are often easier to manage medically if they have been spayed.

Ovariohysterectomy can be performed at any age depending on the general physical condition of the bitch. Conventionally, most dogs are spayed between 4 and 6 months of age. If spayed prior to the first heat cycle, the adult dog will have a greatly reduced risk of developing cancer of the mammary glands (breast cancer). After the first several heat cycles, this benefit is lost. (*See* CHAPTER 38, "CANCER."). Spaying a mature, adult dog that has developed breast cancer will not reduce the chance of recurrence, but may prevent the development of other disease problems such as pyometra.

There is no evidence that ovariohysterectomy performed prior to puberty is harmful to the dog. Puppies as young as 6 to 8 weeks of age are now being sterilized. Adoption rates at animal shelters are much higher for pups and adults that have been spayed. While further studies are warranted, there is at present no evidence that bitches spayed before puberty suffer any long-term ill effects. (*See* Chapter 15, "Birth Control."). It remains to be seen if such dogs will have a higher incidence of estrogen-dependent urinary incontinence (loss of voluntary control over urination that is correlated with a fall in sex hormone levels) in the last one-third of life. (*See* "Urinary Incontinence" in Chapter 27, "The Urinary System and Disorders.")

The primary benefit of canine ovariohysterectomy for society as a whole is control of the pet animal population. Every year, thousands of unwanted puppies and adult dogs are put to sleep or starve to death. Spaying does not alter the personality of the dog and rarely changes behavioral characteristics unrelated to reproduction. The dog will continue to guard the home and play ball. (*See* Chapter 6, "Canine Behavior," and Chapter 15, "Birth Control.")

The spay operation or loss of the reproductive tract also will not produce obesity per se in most bitches. Often the spay operation is performed late in puppyhood, during a period of rapid growth. As the dog reaches normal adult size, many people continue to feed the same amount of food, or more, as the actual need for food or calories decreases. Thus the cause of obesity, in the vast majority of adult dogs, is overfeeding. There is evidence, however, that some spayed bitches may experience a slight (5–10%) gain in body weight, as a result of the loss of hormonal secretions from the ovaries. (*See* "Behavioral Effects of Spaying and Neutering" in Chapter 6, "Canine Behavior.")

Castration

Castration is performed to sterilize the male dog, to treat certain disease conditions, or to alter some behavioral characteristics. The testicles may be removed to control extensive infection or following severe testicular injury. Testicular cancer, which can develop particularly in older dogs, is another indication for castration. (Fortunately, most testicular tumors in dogs are benign.) Types of cancer include **Sertoli cell** tumors (derived from cells within the testicular tubules that are important for nurture and development of sperm), which can produce **estrogen** (a female sex hormone) and result in a syndrome of male **feminization**

(development of female sex characteristics, such as mammary gland enlargement). Castration is also performed to prevent the recurrence of **perianal adenoma** (benign tumor of glands surrounding the anus). (*See* Chapter 14, "Reproductive Disorders," and Chapter 38, "Cancer.") There is no evidence, however, that castration will prevent the recurrence of **perineal hernia,** a syndrome wherein the wall of the rectum protrudes through the pelvic musculature and becomes impacted with feces.

Cryptorchidism is a congenital (present at birth) testicular defect wherein one or both testicles fail to descend into the **scrotum,** the dependent pouch of skin that normally houses the testicles. They may remain undescended within the abdomen, enter the **inguinal canal** (a passageway deep within the groin area), or be located in the subcutaneous tissues adjacent to the **prepuce** (fold of skin enclosing the penis). Although it may be as long as 6 months after birth before the testicles descend into the scrotum, most cryptorchid dogs are identified during their first examination by a veterinarian at 6 to 8 weeks of age. Cryptorchid testicles retained in the abdomen are more prone to torsion (twisting) and to the development of certain cancers. (*See* Chapter 14, "Reproductive Disorders," and Chapter 17, "Congenital and Inherited Disorders.")

Locating a cryptorchid testicle can be a difficult task, because undescended testicles are often smaller and softer than normal, descended testicles. Testicles retained within the abdomen can only be *palpated* (felt with the hands or fingers) when they become enlarged. Therefore, removal of cryptorchid testicles often requires exploratory surgery. Surgical therapy to place the retained testicle into the scrotum rarely results in a functional gland, and moreover is considered an unethical practice because cryptorchidism is an inherited trait.

Castration is usually performed when a dog is 6 to 9 months of age. This allows the male dog to develop desired secondary sex characteristics (i.e., deep chest, wide broad head, etc.). Castration can be performed at any age, however, depending on the general health and well-being of the dog. Castration performed at 6 to 8 weeks of age is a very simple and rapid procedure and does not result in any long-term physical problems. The adult dog will not develop a "male look," however, and the prepuce and penis will remain small. (*See* Chapter 15, "Birth Control.")

Castration will alter some of the behavioral characteristics of the dog. Some of the roaming and aggressive behavior will be eliminated. As in female dogs, obesity following sterilization is associated with overfeeding rather than the sterilization procedure itself.

Castration is an essential means of canine population control and should be performed on any dog not used for breeding purposes. For dog owners completely opposed to castration, male dogs can be sterilized by performing a vasectomy. In this procedure, the **vas deferens** (testicular tubules) that transport sperm to the penis are cut and tied, the testicles remaining intact. Although vasectomy renders the dog sterile, the roaming and fighting behavior associated with locating a bitch in estrus will continue. (*See* Chapter 15, "Birth Control.")

Cosmetic Surgeries

Cosmetic surgeries of the dog include amputation of the tail, digit (dewclaw) removal, and ear cropping. There has been an ethical debate over these procedures for years; in several countries and communities in the United States such procedures are illegal. However, in most areas of the United States these surgeries continue to be performed, with dog owners seeking out either veterinarians or lay persons to perform them. If cosmetic surgery is performed on a dog, it must be done by a qualified veterinary surgeon under proper aseptic conditions. Surgeries performed by lay persons often produce complications resulting in a poor cosmetic outcome and the need for additional surgery. Moreover, lay persons cannot legally administer anesthetics or certain analgesics to prevent or treat pain in animals.

Amputation of the tail (tail docking) is usually performed for cosmetic reasons, but may be indicated medically following injury, paralysis, cancer, or recurring **perianal fistulas** (chronic draining tracts in the tissues around the anus, most common in German Shepherd Dogs).

Bulldogs can develop a skin infection around the tail ("screw tail") that often requires removal of malpositioned bones in the tail. Some dogs are chronic "tail beaters" and repeatedly injure their tails by swatting them against walls and other hard objects. The best treatment for tail beaters is complete amputation of the tail, as such dogs will continue to injure the tail even if it is surgically shortened. Cosmetic tail docking usually is performed on puppies 3 to 5 days of age. The final length of the docked tail varies according to breed and breeder standards.

Dewclaws are the first toes attached to the carpals (canine equivalent of the wrist) of the forepaws, and on many dogs, especially those of the large breeds, are also the first toes attached to the tarsi (canine equivalent of the ankle) of the hind paws. They represent rudimentary, functionless appendages. The hind dewclaws often lack an internal bone structure so that the nail moves freely. The front dewclaws commonly have a complete internal bone structure and are more difficult to remove. Dewclaws are removed usually for cosmetic reasons, for the prevention of injury, and to prevent ingrowth of the nail. In active dogs, dewclaws often become hooked on objects and torn. In newborn puppies, dewclaws are removed at 3 to 5 days of age. In older dogs, dewclaw removal is often performed at the time of spaying or castration. Following dewclaw removal, the incision lines on the legs of older dogs often are protected by bandages that entirely encircle the leg. The bandages should always be kept clean and dry. When taking the dog outside onto wet grass, the bandages can be temporarily covered with a plastic bag. If a bandage becomes excessively soiled, moist, or begins to exude a foul odor, the veterinarian should be contacted. The toes of the foot should be examined at least twice daily for evidence of swelling—a sign that the bandage may be too tight. The opposite foot, if not bandaged, can be used for a size comparison. If the foot appears swollen, the dog should be taken to a veterinarian to have the bandage changed or removed.

Cosmetic otoplasty (ear cropping) in young dogs is performed strictly for cosmetic purposes, although the **pinna** (external flap) of the ear may need to be partially or completely removed due to injury, infection, or cancer. Ear cropping changes the shape of the pinna from a folded or hanging ear to a prick ear (one that stands erect). Historically, breeds selected for otoplasty include Schnauzers, Boxers, Doberman Pinschers, Great Danes and Boston Terriers. The procedure is usually performed between 8 to 10 weeks of age in most breeds (an exception being Boston Terriers, on whom it is performed at 4 to 6 months of age).

There is no single method of ear cropping that has been found suitable for all dogs. Proper technique and professional judgment must be based on a good deal of surgical experience and postoperative management. Ear cropping must be performed under general anesthesia and postoperative analgesics should be administered. It is very important that careful postoperative management under the guidance of a veterinarian be followed. Ear splints, carriages, and cones to support the ears postoperatively all require special bandaging techniques and must be changed periodically. If the bandages are displaced, become excessively soiled, or begin to exude a foul aroma, the veterinarian should be contacted immediately.

Occasionally dogs are born with deformed ear flaps that are visually displeasing or fail to "stand." This is often a problem in German Shepherd Dogs. Conservative treatment should be initiated as soon as possible with splints and bandages that can form or "train" the **cartilage** (a specialized type of connective tissue) of the ear to hold the desired position. Ears that are not treated early on are very difficult to correct later. Surgical procedures that cut and move segments of cartilage in the ear may provide some general overall improvement.

REQUIRED SURGERY
Required surgeries fall into two major classifications, emergency and nonemergency.

Emergency Surgery
Emergency surgery is performed for conditions that, unless they are corrected swiftly, will result in death of the patient. Examples include intestinal blockage or perforation, gastric dilatation, **dystocia** (difficult birth), and uncontrollable hemorrhage or organ rupture following injury. Surgical procedures to correct each of these conditions must of course be coordinated with excellent anesthetic and critical-care management.

Intestinal blockage in the dog often follows ingestion of bones or large foreign objects such as corncobs or walnuts. Other common obstructing objects include rubber balls, nylon stockings or panty hose, and plastic food wrappers. Dogs with obstruction of the intestine often lose their appetite, vomit, and appear depressed. They may or may not exhibit a painful abdomen. Long-term obstruction of a segment of the intestine can cause it to weaken and rupture. Rupture results in the release of intestinal contents into the abdominal cavity, producing life-threatening contamination and infection. During surgery, the intestine is opened and the obstructing object is removed. Any weakened areas of the intestine are excised.

The intestine can also be perforated by external trauma, particularly by sharp objects such as arrows, or by bite wounds that penetrate through the body wall. With any penetrating wound, surgical exploration of the abdomen should be performed in order to examine the integrity of the intestinal wall.

All dogs, but particularly large breeds (e.g., Great Danes), are subject to **gastric dilatation and torsion** (also called gastric dilatation-volvulus, or bloat). In this condition the stomach twists around until it cannot empty, and then begins to fill with fluid and gas. The twisting and bloating of the stomach inhibit blood flow to the stomach wall, which then begins to die. Death of the stomach wall then leads to complications that eventually kill the patient. The cause of gastric dilatation and torsion is not known. Episodes have been associated with heavy exercise following the consumption of a large meal. The surgeon corrects the problem by untwisting the stomach and attaching it to the abdominal wall so that it lies in a normal position and cannot twist again. However, success rates can be as low as 30–60%. (*See* CHAPTER 30, "THE DIGESTIVE SYSTEM AND DISORDERS.")

All dogs may be susceptible to dystocia, but

the **brachycephalic** (flat-faced) breeds (e.g., Bulldogs) are most commonly affected. Surgery is performed when medical therapy or manual manipulation fail to deliver all the puppies. The fetuses are physically removed from the uterus through an abdominal incision on the midline, a procedure known as a **caesarean section.** If desired by the owner, the bitch may be spayed after the puppies are delivered, since milk will be produced as long as the puppies continue to nurse. The bitch and puppies are returned home as soon as possible after the surgery so that the bitch will initiate normal maternal behavior.

Many emergency surgical procedures result from trauma caused by automobile accidents and dog fights. Exploratory surgery of the abdomen is performed to control bleeding from tears in the liver, spleen or kidney, and to repair ruptured urinary bladders. Open wounds of the chest cavity interfere with the dog's ability to breathe. Free air and fluid must be evacuated from the chest; the lungs and surrounding tissues are then examined for any injuries and the wound is closed.

Nonemergency Surgery

Nonemergency, required surgical procedures are usually classified as either **orthopedic** (involving bone) or *soft-tissue.* Orthopedic disease is classified as either congenital or acquired. Orthopedic surgery corrects problems involving bones, ligaments and joints. Bone fractures are a common problem in dogs. The femur, pelvic bones, tibia, radius and ulna all may fall victim to different types of trauma. The surgeon has several options for the repair of fractured bones; no one procedure is correct for all bones under all circumstances. Fractures can be repaired using metal plates and screws, long pins that fill the bone marrow cavity, wires, or a combination of devices. Pins may also be placed across the fractured segments of bone and fixed to braces outside the skin. If the fractured pieces can be realigned without opening the skin, a splint or cast may be all that is needed to hold the leg in position until the bone heals.

No matter which appliance or device is used to stabilize the fractured bone, there is always a race between the time required for bone healing and failure of the appliance. Most fractures require 6 to 8 weeks to heal. If the plate or cast is stressed beyond its breaking point it will fail before the bone heals. Enforced rest and controlled exercise, therefore, are vital components of home care following surgical correction of a broken bone. Stabilization of the fracture will stop the pain associated with the break, and the dog will try to use the leg normally. A short chase of a squirrel across the park, however, can result in failure of the appliance, refracture of the bone, and a second surgical procedure.

Joint injuries are common in dogs. Dogs often suffer rupture of the **cranial cruciate ligament** of the knee, as do human athletes. In medium- to large-sized dogs, the knee is surgically opened, the injured tissue is removed, and the joint is stabilized using a combination of the dog's own tissues and sutures.

Two common congenital joint problems in the dog are **osteochondritis dissecans (OCD)** of the shoulder and medial patellar luxation of the knee. OCD occurs most often in large, rapidly growing dogs such as Labrador Retrievers. The underlying lesion is a fracture and defect in the cartilage of the shoulder that results in pain and limping. Affected dogs may have the lesion in both shoulders. Treatment involves surgical removal of the defective cartilage as well as any cartilage fragments found free in the shoulder joint, thereby promoting the growth of new cartilage. Medial patellar luxation occurs mostly in small and miniature breeds. The **patella** (kneecap) deviates to the inside of the leg so that the muscles of the leg responsible for straightening the knee are no longer in alignment. The problem can result in little or no lameness or can cause complete nonuse of the leg. At surgery, the patella is moved back into its normal position and fixed firmly in place. (*See* CHAPTER 26, "THE SKELETON AND DISORDERS.")

Postoperative care following joint surgery requires a judicious balance between rest and healing on the one hand, and encouragement of some motion in the joint on the other. The joint tissues and the fluid bathing the joint require motion and weight-bearing to remain healthy. Nonuse of a joint will result in deterioration of the joint cartilage (i.e., "use it or lose it"). Too much rest following surgery may speed healing of the surgical site, but can also result in loss of joint function. Leash walking in a slow, straight line is an excellent exercise for both owner and pet following joint surgery. By walking, the recovering dog is forced to use all four legs—in contrast to trotting, wherein the dog can "cheat" by skipping on the affected limb and thus inadequately exercising the repaired joint.

Once the skin incision has healed, swimming can provide an excellent and safe way to exercise a healing joint. Swimming provides motion without excessive weight-bearing, and dogs cannot swim without using all four legs. *It is very important to remember that swimming is hard exercise.* It is best to begin by having the dog swim for only short amounts of time over relatively short distances—i.e., the dog should not be expected to swim ten Olympian laps, especially after surgery!

Joint injuries may require several weeks of controlled exercise before the dog is allowed to return to its normal level of activity. Owners should not be impatient and attempt to rush the recovery, otherwise healing may be delayed even longer. If use of the limb is not constantly improving, or if a deterioration in function is seen, the veterinarian should be contacted.

Many older dogs are affected by **arthritis** (joint inflammation) of the elbows and hips. Weight-bearing on these joints often results in moderate to severe pain. One of the easiest ways to reduce the pain and increase use of the limb, both in arthritic joints and in joints following surgery, is by controlling the dog's weight. If the dog is obese the joints will have to bear added weight, and weight equals pain. Weight loss often results in improved joint function and/or a more rapid recovery.

Nonemergency, required soft-tissue surgical procedures are numerous and varied. Aftercare depends on the precise organ system and disease entity involved. Many soft-tissue procedures are performed for the removal of tumors from some part of the body. Aftercare may be relatively simple, such as when a small benign tumor is removed from the skin, or may be highly complex if postsurgical chemotherapy and/or radiation therapy is required.

Owners are often asked to assist in the nutritional management of their pets at home. Following surgery of the **esophagus** (the muscular tube extending from the back of the throat to the stomach) for various intestinal ailments, or to provide maximal nutritional support prior to surgery, soft plastic tubes may be surgically implanted in the stomach or intestine. Several times a day a special liquid diet, formulated by a veterinarian, is placed through the tube and into the digestive tract. Following this "feeding," the tube is flushed with water and capped. (An abdominal wrap or Elizabethan collar can be used to prevent the dog from removing and/or eating the tube.) Dogs can be fed for months through such a tube and not only maintain their weight but actually gain some weight. Although they are not able to taste the food, the dogs normally look forward to the feedings once they recognize the routine.

Management of large, open skin wounds may also be performed at home. These are wounds resulting from burns, animal fights, or automobile injuries and are too large or too dirty or contaminated to close with sutures. The veterinarian can instruct the owner on the techniques necessary to clean the wound and change the dressing. The dressings may need to be changed several times a day as the wound begins to heal. Many large skin wounds of the dog are able to heal on their own. Other, larger wounds may need to be covered using grafts or flaps of skin transplanted from another part of the body.

New Directions in Surgery

New directions in surgery include improved management of traumatic injuries and cancer using reconstructive surgical techniques; organ transplantation; total joint replacement; and improved wound healing using growth-promoting substances. Cancer treatment now incorporates the skills of the surgeon, the **radiotherapist** (radiation therapist) or *photodynamic therapist* (a specialist trained in **photodynamic therapy,** involving the use of photosensitizing compounds and light to kill tumor cells), and the medical **oncologist** (cancer specialist). (*See* CHAPTER 38, "CANCER.") Large tissue defects or loss of limb function can sometimes be corrected surgically. Proper use of nonsurgical therapy can reduce the amount of tissue that needs to be surgically removed.

Kidney transplantation is now a recognized treatment for kidney failure in cats. Canine kidneys are far more difficult to transplant, however, owing to the fact that the dog's immune system will rapidly destroy a kidney transplanted from a dog that is not an identical sibling. At present, only very complex immunosuppressive drug therapies can slow rejection of a transplanted canine kidney. Many new and highly potent immunosuppressive medications are now in development for use in human beings; it is hoped that one or more of these may eventually prove effective in dogs as well.

Arthritis of the hips and elbows of dogs is a painful and debilitating disease. Total hip replacement has been successfully performed in dogs for the past 10 years and offers an excellent alternative for the correct surgical candidate. A total elbow replacement is now being tested in canine patients and may be clinically available soon.

Wound healing is a special problem in dogs that are immunosuppressed, diabetic, or afflicted with certain hormonal diseases. Surgery for such dogs poses an exceptional risk, since delayed healing or breakdown of the surgical incision can be a devastating complication. Currently, several growth factors have been identified that can speed the cellular processes involved in wound healing. These substances are now being tested in clinical patients and show great promise for the future.

In summary, successful management of the canine surgical patient requires the cooperative efforts of the veterinarian, the veterinary support staff, and the pet owner. Thorough communication and cooperation, both before and after surgery, will always ensure the best possible treatment outcome.

CHAPTER 41

Convalescence and Home Care

by Janet Aldrich

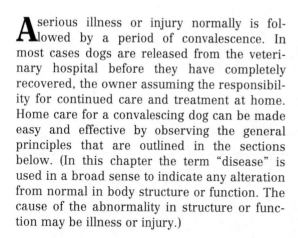

A serious illness or injury normally is followed by a period of convalescence. In most cases dogs are released from the veterinary hospital before they have completely recovered, the owner assuming the responsibility for continued care and treatment at home. Home care for a convalescing dog can be made easy and effective by observing the general principles that are outlined in the sections below. (In this chapter the term "disease" is used in a broad sense to indicate any alteration from normal in body structure or function. The cause of the abnormality in structure or function may be illness or injury.)

Nutritional Support

The importance of nutritional support in promoting recovery from disease cannot be overemphasized. The body's building blocks for the repair of diseased or damaged tissue must come from the diet. Although some dogs will recover normally despite inadequate nutrition during the period of disease, it has been demonstrated repeatedly that proper nutritional support will promote better healing and a faster and more complete recovery.

In healthy dogs, the body's metabolic functions are controlled primarily by the hormones **insulin** and glucagon. Under the influence of these two hormones, the response to malnutrition (i.e., starvation) is to consume the body's fat reserves as the principal source of energy. The healthy dog that is not being fed thus can "live off its fat" for a defined period of time and will only begin to consume its protein reserves as a last resort. However, in sick patients other hormones (**cortisol, catecholamines**) influence the body's metabolic processes and cause a shift toward the consumption of protein for energy. Thus, a sick dog will use up its reserves of muscle protein and spare its fat reserves. In prolonged disease states a loss of muscle mass will occur, even though the patient may still have adequate fat reserves.

The hazards of malnutrition thus include the effects of protein loss. Because most of the protein in the body is in muscle tissue, malnutrition will result in a loss of strength and endurance as well as weight loss. Cardiac and respiratory muscles will eventually lose function. The loss of protein also promotes poor intestinal function, delays wound healing, and eventually will lead to **edema** (tissue swelling) or **ascites** (accumulation of fluid within the abdominal cavity). Moreover, a sick dog also has greater metabolic requirements owing to the disease processes themselves, as there is an increased need for immune function, wound healing and tissue repair.

The problem of malnutrition should be addressed early in the course of any illness. Body weight should be monitored regularly. Dogs that have had a decreased intake of food for more than 5 days, have a body weight less than 85% of the ideal for their age and breed, or weight loss greater than 10% of usual body weight, are candidates for nutritional support. Nutritional support may be as simple as encouraging voluntary intake by hand-feeding, or may require feeding via a **nasogastric tube** (a feeding tube inserted through the nostril and extending through the pharynx and esophagus into the stomach) or **gastric** tube (a tube inserted through the abdominal wall and into the stomach). Dogs with either feeding tube in place may be managed quite well at home by the owner. If the patient's digestive tract is not functioning properly nutritional support may need to be delivered intravenously, but this is usually appropriate only for hospitalized patients.

FOOD

Home care of a dog with a poor appetite should be combined with a plan to thoroughly investigate and treat the disease causing inappetence. Dogs that are convalescing may be reluctant to eat enough food to supply their daily requirements. A variety of techniques may be helpful in encouraging the reluctant eater, including:

- moistening the food
- warming foods to just below normal body temperature
- topping foods with gravy or broth
- offering small amounts of food by hand-feeding

All feeding attempts should be performed gently, in an encouraging but not forceful manner. Force-feeding by placing a small amount of canned food in the mouth or squirting liquid food into the mouth may be successful, provided the dog is tolerant of the procedure. (If the dog resists strongly, this procedure may create an aversion such that the dog will vigorously avoid that particular food in the future.) Drooling or repeated swallowing when food is offered may indicate a feeling of nausea, in which case the food should be removed and several hours allowed to pass before it is offered again.

Dogs may accept new foods more readily than their usual diet. Cooked chicken or liver, all-meat baby food, cottage cheese, and a variety of special diets made specifically for convalescing dogs may be accepted. Liquid diets made especially for dogs and some liquid diets prepared for human use may be of help. (All such diets should be evaluated by a veterinarian on an individual basis, before feeding them to a convalescing pet.) Most liquid diets that are thin enough in consistency to administer with a syringe will contain about 1 calorie per milliliter. A 10-pound dog might require 300 calories per day, meaning that about 1 1/4 cups of the liquid diet would need to be fed per day. The consulting veterinarian can advise owners on the appropriate amount to feed an individual dog. (*See* CHAPTER 8, "CANINE NUTRITIONAL REQUIREMENTS," and CHAPTER 9, "FEEDING DOGS.")

If feeding is followed by vomiting of the food, feeding should be discontinued and the advice of the veterinarian sought. Vomiting carries certain risks, not only of food and fluid loss but also of aspiration of vomited material into the airways, with resulting pneumonia.

WATER

Water intake must be sufficient to meet both the ordinary daily losses in urine, feces and respiration, as well as extraordinary losses such as vomiting, diarrhea or increased urine production. The ordinary daily requirements are estimated based on the dog's body weight and are listed in table 1. (These amounts do not include allowance for extraordinary losses in vomiting, diarrhea or excess urination, which must be added to the listed amounts.) The total daily water intake includes water from all sources, including food (for example, canned dog food contains approximately 80% water).

It is important to note that tables such as these are *only estimates* and that individual patient needs will vary. Such estimates must always be tailored to individual needs. Dogs that are willing to drink more should be allowed to do so unless the veterinarian specifically instructs otherwise.

Water should be clean and fresh and available at all times. If the dog exhibits any difficulty or reluctance in rising or walking to the water bowl, then the bowl should be placed within easy reach. Forcing the patient to drink by squirting or dripping water into the mouth is rarely successful in providing enough water to meet the patient's needs. Dogs that refuse to drink or that persistently vomit cannot be effectively managed at home.

Medication

One of the most important ways to help a convalescing dog is to administer medication exactly as directed by the veterinarian. Studies in human medicine have shown that as many as half of all patients do not completely follow doctor's instructions in taking their prescribed medication. Most commonly, they discontinue taking the medication after they begin to feel better (instead of using up the entire prescription as indicated), or they remember to take it only some of the time. Unfortunately, similar errors may be made when dog owners are asked to administer medication to their pets at home.

The length of time between doses of medica-

tion is determined by studies of the absorption, distribution and metabolism of the drug in the body. For many medications, it is necessary that they be given every 8 hours in order to achieve satisfactory levels in the bloodstream for an entire 24-hour period. For some medications even more frequent dosing may be required (fortunately, these are not as common). Frequent dosing often is an inconvenience; however, if an owner is committed to providing the best home care a schedule can usually be worked out. The veterinarian should be made aware of every medication of any type that an owner is presently giving to a pet, so that potential drug interactions or other adverse effects can be avoided. It is particularly important to recognize that a dog is not just a miniature human being. Dogs' metabolic and drug-handling systems differ from those of people, and seemingly innocuous medications that an owner is accustomed to taking may in some cases represent a danger to a dog's health.

Proper planning is the key to giving medications successfully. Owners should look at things from a dog's point of view and use their knowledge of their pet to make the giving of medication a pleasant experience by adding some particularly favored activity or treat. It is usually unwise to call the dog to the medication-giving area if the experience is going to be unpleasant. By planning ahead one can often administer the medication quickly and follow up with a treat or activity that will leave a good impression in the dog's mind. If the dog slinks away or hides at medication time, it is apparent that this goal has not been accomplished and some rethinking of the procedure is definitely in order.

Table 1
Average Total Daily Water Requirements for Dogs

Body Weight (pounds)	Water (ounces)	Requirement cups
2	4	1/2
4	7	1
6	10	1 1/4
8	12	1 1/2
10	14	1 3/4
15	20	2 1/2
20	24	3
30	33	4
40	41	5
50	48	6
60	55	7
70	62	7 3/4
80	69	8 1/2
90	75	9 1/2

Medication may be given in the form of pills or liquid, or, in a few cases, in injectable form.

PILLS

Pills may be offered inside a small piece of cheese, meat, or canned dog food, provided that the medication can be given with food. This method is easy and avoids struggling, but one must observe the dog closely to be sure that the pill is actually swallowed. Pills may also be placed on the tongue as far back in the mouth as possible. This method is easy to learn, provided that the dog is accustomed to having its mouth handled. (When training a puppy or a newly acquired adult dog, it is often beneficial to spend some time each day gently working around the dog's mouth and lips so as to teach the dog to tolerate this.) One technique is to squeeze the lips gently inward against the teeth with one hand placed over the muzzle. As the dog opens its mouth the lips are pushed in against the teeth, which helps prevent the dog from biting down. The pill is held in the fingers of the other hand and is quickly inserted as far back on the tongue as possible. (It is much safer to insert one's entire hand into the dog's mouth when giving a pill rather than making tentative attempts with a single finger.) The mouth is then closed and the muzzle held until the dog swallows. Swallowing can be encouraged by gently blowing on the dog's nose.

At the time the medication is dispensed, owners should obtain the veterinarian's advice on the method of administration most appropriate for their particular pet. No matter which technique is used, however, some dogs will learn to avoid swallowing the pill. The dog's mouth should be opened and closely inspected after supposed swallowing to be sure that the pill is not stuck to the side of the mouth or on the hairs next to the lips. If such is the case, one must keep trying until the pill is swallowed. Skill at this technique can be gained with a little practice and patience.

LIQUID MEDICATION

Oral Medication

Oral medication in liquid form has an advantage in that the dog's mouth need not be opened to administer it. However, it is also easier for the dog to spit out at least a portion of the dose. When administering the medication, the dog's lower lip on one side at its junction with the upper lip can be pulled out gently to form a small "pouch" between the lip and gum, near the back of the mouth. The liquid is gently squirted into this lip pouch, from where it will flow over the tongue and so be swallowed. When giving the medication the dog's head should be elevated only slightly; too great an elevation will make it difficult for the dog to swallow and can lead to aspiration of the liquid into the airways. If the dog coughs or chokes, administration of the medication should be discontinued immediately so that the dog can relax and recover. If coughing or choking occurs repeatedly, the veterinarian should be consulted on the possibility of switching to a pill formulation. Liquids (even water) should never be squirted directly toward the back of the dog's mouth, as this can easily lead to aspiration of the fluid into the airways.

Eye Medication

Eye medication is given in the space between the eyelid and eyeball, and not directly onto the eyeball. The eyelid should be gently pulled away from the eyeball and the medication dropped into the space. The medication container (tube or bottle) should never be allowed to touch the eye, as injury to the eye or contamination of the medication may result.

Ear Medication

Ear medication should be dropped into the opening of the outer ear canal while the dog's head is steadied by a firm grip on the muzzle. (Prior to giving medication owners should visually locate the opening, since dogs have many folds of cartilage in the external ear that can be mistaken for the entrance to the ear canal.) The sensation of liquid running into the ear will usually cause the dog to shake its head vigorously. The dog should be restrained from doing this, however, until the medication has had an opportunity to flow down into the ear canal. This can be facilitated by gently massaging the ear cartilage just below the opening of the ear for a minute or so after administering the medication.

Injectable Medication

Injectable medications should be administered exactly as instructed by the veterinarian. Owners should ask for a demonstration of the technique and then practice under supervision until they are confident they can administer the injections properly.

Adverse Reactions

Adverse reactions to any medication may occur unexpectedly. Some of the more common reactions include vomiting, fever, diarrhea, and an outbreak of red or moist skin lesions. It is often quite difficult, however, to determine whether such signs are due to the medication or to the disease being treated. When a dog receiving medication exhibits a suspected reaction to that medication, the owner should contact the consulting veterinarian immediately.

Owners should be sure they understand the purpose of each medication they are administering and exactly how often and for how long they are to administer it. They should ask the veterinarian how soon an improvement in their pet's condition should be expected, and devise a contingency plan with the veterinarian in case the expected improvement does not take place. They should also have a clear understanding how long after resolution of the clinical signs the medication should continue to be given. Although most medications are prescribed for a few days to a few weeks, with some illnesses it is absolutely essential that the medication be continued for a much longer period after the disease signs have apparently resolved.

Treatments

In addition to medications, treatments may be prescribed ranging from wound care to physical therapy. Owners should be certain they understand clearly how to perform such treatments before beginning on their own. All the necessary equipment—such as bandages, soaking solutions, scissors, tape, etc.—should be assembled before the dog is brought in. Many treatments are a two-person job and most go better when adequate assistance is provided.

Bandages and casts must not be allowed to get wet. A plastic bag can be temporarily slipped over a cast for the needed trips outside, but should not be left on since the dog may eat it. Healing incisions should be clean, dry and intact, and should be inspected daily. Redness, swelling, heat, apparent pain, or discharge at the incision site are all signs of inflammation and possible infection and should be brought to the veterinarian's attention promptly.

The dog must not be allowed to lick a healing wound or incision. The dog's mouth contains many bacteria that are essentially harmless when in their normal habitat, but may cause a problem if implanted in a wound or incision site. Any cleaning of the affected area should be performed with materials and medications recommended by the veterinarian. An Elizabethan collar may need to be placed on the dog to prevent the dog's licking the wound or incision. This collar is essentially a wide circle of lightweight plastic that fits around the dog's neck and prevents contact between the head (i.e., the mouth and tongue) and the rest of the body. The veterinarian can provide an Elizabethan collar if required. While the dog is wearing the collar, the owner must see to it that food and water dishes are located so that the dog can easily reach them with the collar in place.

Monitoring

Monitoring a dog's convalescence requires more than just casual observation. It is often helpful to keep a daily log so that each important area of monitoring is evaluated and the sequence of changes accurately recorded. Certain areas of monitoring may be of greater or lesser concern, depending on the underlying disease. Appetite is usually recorded as the total amount of food eaten per day. Urination and defecation should be observed as much as possible. The consistency and color of the stool, any discoloration of the urine, and the frequency of urination should be noted. If vomiting is occurring, the **vomitus** (vomited material) should be inspected for color and the presence of food or blood. It should also be noted how long after feeding the vomiting is occurring.

Temperature

Body temperature is controlled by balancing heat produced by metabolism and muscular activity with heat lost by evaporation from the mouth by panting. An increase in body temperature can be caused by the inability to lose heat as fast as it is gained, as occurs with high environmental temperatures or excessive muscular activity. This phenomenon is known as **hyperthermia.** Affected dogs will be seen making efforts to eliminate the excess heat by vigorous panting and seeking a cool environment. **Fever,** on the other hand, is an increase in body temperature caused by disease. With fever the *thermoregulatory* (temperature-regulating) set-point in the brain is temporarily altered so that body temperature becomes reset at a higher level than normal. Consequently, the body will strive to bring its temperature up to this new (abnormally elevated) value. Dogs with fever often can be observed making efforts to conserve heat by seeking a warm environment or sleeping in a curled-up position. Most of us have experienced this need to maintain body temperature at a higher level as the alternating "chills" and "sweats" characteristic of fever.

In general, fever is thought to represent a beneficial mechanism for enhancing the disease-fighting ability of the body. However, when body temperature reaches a level high enough to alter protein structure it becomes dangerous and must be controlled. Normal body temperature for dogs ranges from 100°F to 102.5°F and does not begin to reach dangerous levels until it surpasses 106°F. Because it is fairly uncommon for a fever to exceed 106°F, it is not often necessary to cool a febrile dog. If cooling is necessary it should be performed with lukewarm water applied to the abdomen, chest and legs. (Soaking the entire dog with water should be avoided, because this often results in a sudden drop in body temperature to *below* normal.) If the fever remains below 106°F, the dog should be maintained in a comfortable but not overheated environment with good air circulation. The temperature can be monitored periodically by using a small thermometer well-lubricated with K-Y jelly or vaseline and inserted into the rectum for approximately one minute. (*See* CHAPTER 39, "CLINICAL SIGNS OF DISEASE.")

BREATHING RATE
Breathing rate and effort are important indicators of the functioning of the respiratory system. Home monitoring of the breathing rate involves counting the number of breaths per minute. Each time the chest rises for inhalation and then relaxes for exhalation is counted as a single breath. The normal breathing rate for a dog at rest may be as low as 12 breaths per minute but more commonly is about 20 breaths per minute. An increase in breathing rate can be caused by pain, fever, fear or excitement, as well as by respiratory disease. Dogs with difficulty breathing may refuse to lie down and will often exhibit an anxious expression. The significance of a change in the normal breathing pattern should be evaluated promptly by the veterinarian. (*See* CHAPTER 39, "CLINICAL SIGNS OF DISEASE.")

MUCOUS MEMBRANE COLOR
Mucous membranes are the lubricating membranes lining the internal surfaces of body cavities such as the mouth. Blood vessels running very close to the surface of these membranes impart a normal pink color to them. The mucous membranes in some places can be pigmented and so may obscure the underlying vessels. Many dogs have areas of dark pigmentation in the gums of the mouth, so that one must search for nonpigmented areas to observe the pink color. A few breeds such as the Chow Chow have uniformly pigmented gums and tongue, so that gum color cannot be observed at all.

Normal gum color ranges from pink in the resting dog to red in the exercising dog. It is most useful to compare observations of gum color from day to day, so that one can get a feeling for any changes that might be occurring. In healthy dogs, gum color should never be white or blue. White or very pale pink gums may be caused by shock or blood loss, while bluish gums are usually caused by failure of respiration. These conditions are medical emergencies and should be treated by a veterinarian immediately. (*See* CHAPTER 39, "CLINICAL SIGNS OF DISEASE," and CHAPTER 43, "PROCEDURES FOR LIFE-THREATENING EMERGENCIES.")

Housing

The indoor dog that is convalescing should be provided with its usual comfortable sleeping space. If vomiting, diarrhea, or increased frequency of urination are expected, the dog may need to be confined to an easily cleaned part of the house. In this case, the owner should see to it that the dog has a comfortable place to sleep and receives plenty of assurance that the confinement is not punishment for a supposed misdeed.

Outdoor dogs often are not monitored as closely as are indoor dogs. This should be taken into consideration when deciding whether home care for an individual outdoor dog will be possible. If the dog is kept outside, extra efforts will need to be expended to assure clean, dry sleeping quarters, protection from the elements, and access to potable, nonfrozen water.

Dogs that are unable to rise present special challenges. They must be protected from the formation of decubital ulcers (skin ulcers resulting from prolonged pressure over bony prominences, caused by lengthy recumbency; *bedsores*). The ulcerated areas usually become moist and infected and can present a serious risk to the patient's overall health. Often dogs with a heavy coat will develop extensive ulcer formation before it is noticed because the overlying hair masks the ulcerated skin. Moisture in constant contact with the skin, such as urine or feces, will almost guarantee the formation of decubital ulcers. Urine in contact with the skin can also cause urine scald, a condition similar to diaper rash in babies.

The best prevention for decubital ulcers and urine scald is a soft, padded bed in which the patient is kept clean and dry and turned from side to side every four hours. Nursing a dog that cannot rise requires a substantial commitment of time and effort and constant attention to the fine details of nursing care. It is not an easy job and should not be undertaken without adequate training and preparation.

Exercise

Although the convalescing dog should not be forced to exercise, gentle voluntary exercise may be beneficial to recovery. The duration and activity level of the exercise chosen should be regulated based on the veterinarian's recommendations. No matter what the original plan, exercise should always be halted if the dog exhibits signs of fatigue, such as lying down or excessive panting.

If the dog is recovering from an injury such as a bone fracture or spinal cord trauma, the veterinarian may give instructions for "strict cage rest" (i.e., confinement in a small space with absolutely no exercise for the duration). *Owners should fully understand what is meant by this and closely follow the veterinarian's instructions.* An excellent surgical repair of a fracture can be ruined by allowing a dog to be overly active too soon. Often, however, it may be difficult to adhere closely to cage-rest instructions owing to the fact that the patient feels good and is naturally bored and resents confinement. Concerns in this regard should be discussed at length with the veterinarian so that there is a good understanding of why such strict instructions are necessary, and, of course, ultimately beneficial to the patient.

"TLC"

Tender Loving Care cannot be overemphasized as a contributor to recovery from illness or injury, whether in dogs or human beings. Often, the treatments that must be given involve some discomfort or necessary restraint, which should always be balanced by providing generous measures of love and reassurance.

CHAPTER 42

Home Emergency Care

by Steve C. Haskins

Emergency Prevention

The most important first-aid measure that you can provide as a pet owner is to take steps to prevent emergencies from happening in the first place. Dog owners should be aware of the common ways dogs can unknowingly get themselves into trouble, as well as the ways human beings can inadvertently place their pets in danger.

Puppies should be examined by a veterinarian early in life in order to identify any **congenital** (present at birth) defects that may be pre-

sent. They should also receive appropriate vaccinations or medications for infectious diseases that may be prevalent in the area. (*See* APPENDIX B: "VACCINATIONS.") Young animals are curious and playful, but these endearing qualities commonly predispose them to injury. Pups should not be allowed to play in areas where they will have access to electrical cords (electrocution hazards if chewed upon), children's toys (airway obstructions if they are accidentally inhaled or intestinal obstruction if swallowed), string (foreign-body obstruction if swallowed), or garbage (vomiting, diarrhea, intestinal obstruction). Bones, in general, should not be fed to dogs, particularly bones that splinter or flat bones or vertebrae that can cause obstruction.

Many medications used by human beings are not well tolerated by animals and may even be lethal, even if given at a normal human dosage. Wide species variations exist with regard to tolerance to such medications. *As a general rule dogs should not be medicated without prior veterinary consultation.* A common drug such as aspirin can cause gastrointestinal irritation, vomiting, diarrhea, intestinal bleeding, ulceration and **peritonitis** (inflammation of the lining of the abdominal cavity) in dogs. Acetaminophen (Tylenol) given in high doses to dogs can result in liver failure and blood abnormalities. (Dogs are not, however, as sensitive to the toxic effects of these two drugs as cats are. *See The Cornell Book of Cats.*) All medications should be kept in a safe place where animals (and, of course, small children) will not have access to them. If a dog should ingest a large amount of any medication, a veterinarian should be consulted immediately.

Animals living or traveling in heavily trafficked areas should be leashed or fenced in so that absolute control over their whereabouts can be maintained at all times. Vehicular trauma still comprises a large proportion of the emergencies seen by veterinarians. Animal-induced trauma is another common emergency that, for the most part, is prevented with stringent animal control. Leashing should be done with care so that the animal cannot accidentally hang or strangle itself. Driveway injuries associated with backing over an animal lying underneath the automobile are easily avoided by prior inspection of the undercarriage of the vehicle.

Animals must not be allowed to ride freely in an open vehicle because they may leap or fall out and sustain considerable injury if the vehicle is traveling at speed. An even greater danger is to tie a dog to a lengthy leash in the back of an open vehicle. In such a situation the dog can still jump or fall out, but then would be dragged by the vehicle rather than be allowed to roll and tumble to a stop. If a dog must for some reason be transported in the bed of a truck, it should be tied with a length of leash sufficient to allow it some mobility, but short enough so that the dog cannot make it over the side of the truck.

It is recommended that owners purchase a rectal thermometer, and learn from their veterinarian the proper way to take a dog's temperature. In cold parts of the country one must always consider the dangers of **hypothermia** (abnormally low body temperature), frostbite, and frozen water supplies, while in warm, humid climates, heatstroke hazards prevail. Heatstroke is a concern any time an animal is maintained in a closed environment, such as a car or undersized kennel. The outside environment need not be excessively warm or humid to pose a heatstroke risk to an animal in a confined space (*see* Chapter 43, "Procedures for Life-Threatening Emergencies").

Children should not be allowed to play with unknown dogs, or with any animal in an unsupervised manner. Children may inadvertently abuse an animal, who may then injure the child in self-defense. Dogs with aggressive personalities should be controlled in a manner sufficient to guarantee prevention of injury to other animals or people. In general, dogs with such personality traits probably should not be kept as pets.

Cardiovascular Problems

Normal heart rates vary quite widely, from about 60 to 140 beats per minute in alert dogs. The heart rate can be determined by **palpating** (feeling with the hands and fingers) the lower chest wall behind the shoulder (*see* Figure 1), or by feeling the pulse in the **femoral artery**, which is located high on the inside of each thigh (*see* Figure 2). (Owners should become familiar with these sites prior to a time of crisis. The veterinarian can provide instruction in locating them.) Interested owners might even consider the purchase of a stethoscope so that they can actually listen to their pet's heartbeat. This is an excellent way to determine the heart rate and to listen for rhythm irregularities and abnormal

Figure 1. The heart is located in the lower third of the chest cavity, just behind the foreleg. (Courtesy of Dr. Steve C. Haskins.)

heart sounds. (*See* CHAPTER 24, "THE CIRCULATORY SYSTEM AND DISORDERS.")

An abnormally slow heart rate (**bradycardia**) may be associated with intrinsic electrical con-

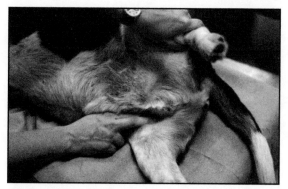

Figure 2. The pulse may be felt in the femoral artery, which is located high on the inside of each hind limb. (Courtesy of Dr. Steve C. Haskins.)

duction disturbances and should be evaluated by a veterinarian. If the heart rate slows too much, even transiently, the dog may faint or lose consciousness. An abnormally rapid heart rate (**tachycardia**) can be caused by excitement, but is also a common compensatory mechanism in many disease processes. The rhythm of the heart or pulse should be regular or regularly irregular (i.e., speeds up and slows down at regular intervals). Irregular irregularities may indicate an underlying heart problem and should be promptly evaluated by a veterinarian.

The pulse quality should be sharp and strong, full and robust. Because pulse quality is a subjective assessment, you should establish a "normal" for your own dog so that any abnormality, if it occurs, can be recognized. A weak or "thready" pulse is indicative of reduced circulatory output from the heart and may or may not be important.

The color of the mucous membranes of the gums and inside of the lips should be assessed. Normally these membranes are a light pink color. If the color is pale pink, gray, or bluish, a veterinarian should be consulted. Pale or white mucous membranes could be a sign of severe **anemia** (low red blood cell count) or shock; gray or bluish discoloration (**cyanosis**) is indicative of

hypoxemia (abnormally low blood oxygen levels) or **methemoglobinemia** (a blood abnormality resulting in reduced ability of the red blood cells to carry oxygen). (*See* CHAPTER 39, "CLINICAL SIGNS OF DISEASE.")

Dehydration (loss of body water) is most often determined by evaluating the pliability of the skin. With the dog lying on its side or resting on its **sternum** (breastbone), lift the skin on the side of the chest up into a fold. When released, the skin should snap back to its normal resting position immediately. If it returns only slowly or remains in a folded or pinched conformation after being released, the dog is moderately or severely dehydrated, respectively, and should be transported to a veterinary hospital for fluid therapy. If a dehydrated dog is still conscious and has not been vomiting, it may swallow water if offered in small amounts or if spooned into the mouth. If the dog does not voluntarily swallow, or gags, coughs or vomits, further water should not be offered.

Respiratory Problems

Animals experiencing respiratory difficulties generally exert a greater effort to breathe than normal animals do. Some nonrespiratory disorders also can cause exaggerated breathing efforts, such as **hyperthermia** (abnormally elevated body temperature) and severe metabolic disorders (kidney failure, shock, decompensated diabetes mellitus). Affected dogs may stand or sit with the head and neck extended but they do not rest. They may develop a "barrel-chested" appearance and make audible noises when they breath, such as snoring, squeaking, or wheezing. The mucous membrane color should be checked. If the membranes are ashen gray or have a bluish discoloration, blood oxygen is likely very low and the dog should be transported immediately to a veterinary hospital. Oxygen, if available, should be administered by face mask. All attempts should be made to calm the dog by offering whatever reassurance seems to help. (*See* CHAPTER 29, "THE RESPIRATORY SYSTEM AND DISORDERS.")

Central Nervous System Problems

Disease of the **central nervous system (CNS)** is broadly divided into diseases of the brain and diseases of the spinal cord. Spinal cord disease is usually manifested by weakness or paralysis of one or more limbs. Diseases of the brain may be characterized by depressed mental activity (behavioral changes, stupor, coma), unilateral (one-sided) weakness or paralysis, a head-tilt, circling, or differences in pupil size in the two eyes. Intracranial disease may be caused by tumors, inflammation, hemorrhage, or systemic diseases such as shock or organ failure. Depressed mental activity caused by systemic disease commonly occurs in proportion to the magnitude of the severity of the underlying disease. Table 1 illustrates the different stages of mental awareness observed with increasing degrees of CNS injury.

Coma (unconsciousness from which the animal cannot be aroused), irregular breathing patterns, **decerebrate rigidity** (all four limbs rigidly extended with the head thrown back), dilated pupils that do not constrict when a bright light is shined on the retina—all these are characteristic of **decerebration** (severe brain damage). Decerebrate rigidity usually indicates that severe and irreversible damage to the brain has occurred.

Table 1
Stages of Mental awareness seen with increasing degrees of CNS injury

Mental State	Clinical Appearance
Demented	Abnormal mental processes, but alert and arousable
Obtunded	Decreased alertness, blunted responses
Stupor	Severely depressed but arousable
Semicomatose	Unconscious, but arousable by deep noxious stimuli
Comatose	Unconscious, nonarousable

Trauma: First Aid and Transport to the Veterinary Hospital

If a dog is found unconscious, the following actions should be taken:

- determine first if the dog is breathing
- determine if the heart is beating
- check the other signs of respiratory and cardiovascular function, as outlined above
- transport the dog to a veterinary hospital

A traumatized dog is often in pain and frightened and can be very dangerous to handle. Regardless of its disposition when healthy, great care must be exercised when handling such an animal in order to avoid personal injury. It is generally a good idea to place a gauze muzzle on an injured dog prior to picking it up or moving it (*see* FIGURE 3). (Dogs with facial injuries or those that exhibit breathing difficulties should not be muzzled, however.) If a muzzled dog acts as though it is going to vomit, the muzzle should be removed immediately.

Dogs that have been struck by a vehicle may have long-bone or spinal fractures. Do not encourage a recumbent dog to get up and move around. Rather, slide a flat board or blanket under the dog and carefully transport it to the veterinary hospital. Unconscious traumatized dogs that are unable to walk should always be transported to the hospital on a board or other flat surface in order to avoid destabilizing any possible fractures. Conscious animals may need to be taped to the board so they will not inadvertently roll off during transport. Conscious animals may also need to be lovingly reassured and cajoled in order to ease their anxiety, fear and confusion.

Exposed wounds, including internal organs that may be exposed, should be covered or wrapped with clean wet towels. Obvious bleeding should be controlled by finger pressure. Injured dogs should be taken to the hospital as quickly and as safely as possible. There are many complications associated with blunt trauma to the abdomen and chest that may not manifest themselves clinically for hours to days. At the hospital, the dog will be observed care-

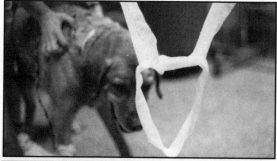

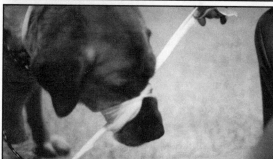

Figure 3. Injured dogs should be muzzled prior to handling to prevent accidental bite wounds to the handler. (First, make a loop in a long length of roll gauze, then pass the loop over the dog's muzzle and cinch it down tight, then tie another half-hitch underneath the dog's muzzle, and finally, secure by tying the gauze behind the dog's head. (Courtesy of Dr. Steve C. Haskins.)

fully during this period of time for changes indicative of such complications. (*See* CHAPTER 26, "THE SKELETON AND DISORDERS.")

Ingestion of Poisonous Substances

Many household cleansers, detergents, insecticides and rodenticides are toxic to animals and must be stored in a safe place to prevent accidental contact or consumption. If a dog is thought to have contacted or ingested a poisonous substance, the animal, the substance container (if available), and a sample of any **vomitus** (vomited material) should be taken to a veterinarian. If you are unable to reach your veterinarian, check the label of the container for instructions "In case of accidental ingestion" and telephone the nearest poison control center for advice and antidotes. The phone number is listed in the "Emergency crisis hotlines" section of your local telephone book. (Ideally, you should record the number in advance, along with other emergency numbers such as fire and police, and keep it in a readily accessible location near the telephone.)

If consumption of a poisonous substance has occurred within the last hour or two, the patient is not seizuring, unconscious, or exhibiting respiratory difficulty—and after consulting your veterinarian by telephone—it may be advisable to induce vomiting. Induced vomiting is *not* appropriate, however, for the following corrosive agents:

> Acids with a pH below 2.0 (antirust compounds, toilet cleaners, gun-cleaning solutions, batteries, swimming-pool cleaners such as muriatic acid and chlorine)
> Alkalis with a pH above 12.5 (drain cleaners, liquid cleansers, lye products, dishwashing detergents)
> Phenol-based disinfectants (check the label)

Vomiting may be induced using syrup of ipecac, hydrogen peroxide, or dry mustard (*see* TABLE 2 FOR DOSAGES). The vomitus should be saved for examination by the veterinarian. A dog with severely depressed mental activity should not be made to vomit owing to the danger of accidentally inhaling the vomitus into the lungs. The dog should be taken to a veterinary hospital as soon as possible because more effective **emetics** (drugs that induce vomiting) are available there and the veterinarian will also be able to pass a stomach tube to wash out the stomach contents.

If the poison is an external toxin, the dog may be bathed with a mild detergent to remove residues from the body surface.

Adsorbents may also be administered to bind the poison and diminish its absorption from the gastrointestinal tract. Activated charcoal, often available in capsule form from local nutrition stores, has been shown to adsorb a large variety of toxins and is quite useful in this regard (dosage: 0.45 to 1.8 grams per pound of body weight, given orally in 50 to 200 ml [2 to 7 ounces] of water). The veterinarian may recommend the administration of a **cathartic** (a drug that induces bowel evacuation) such as Glauber's salt (sodium sulfate), **Epsom salt** (magnesium sulfate), **milk of magnesia** (magnesium hydroxide), or magnesium citrate. A laxative containing **psyllium** (Metamucil) may help reduce absorption and facilitate passage of bowel contents. Ingested acids may be counteracted with baking soda or milk of magnesia, while ingested alkali may be treated with vinegar or lemon juice (*see* TABLE 2).

Rodent poisons, which act by inhibiting blood coagulation, as well as a rat or mouse that has died of such a poison, are often ingested by curious dogs. Some of these rodenticides produce very long-lasting effects and are difficult to treat. Automobile antifreeze (**ethylene glycol**) is very toxic to animals as well and is often ingested by dogs because of its appealing taste. Owners who suspect their dogs have ingested Waferin or ethylene glycol should bring the animal to a veterinarian as this represents a true medical emergency. (*See* CHAPTER 43, "PROCEDURES FOR LIFE-THREATENING EMERGENCIES.")

Surface Burns

Surface burns may result from contact with hot liquids or fire. Local surface burns may be caused by hot-water bottles or electric heating blankets if they are placed in contact with the

---

Table 2
Emergency Treatments for Various Ingested Toxins

To induce vomiting:

Syrup of ipecac (1/4 to 1 teaspoon)

OR

3% Hydrogen peroxide (1–2 teaspoons of a 1:1 peroxide:water mix)

OR

Dry mustard (1–2 teaspoons or 1 tablespoon in 1 cup of water)

For ingested acids:

Baking soda (1–2 teaspoons of a saturated solution)

OR

Milk of magnesia (1 teaspoon per 5 pounds of body weight)

For ingested alkalis:

Vinegar (1–5 teaspoons)

OR

Lemon juice (1–5 teaspoons)

---

skin surface, particularly if the animal is cold or in shock. Water bottles should not exceed 108°F (42°C) in temperature if they are to be placed in direct contact with the skin. It is preferable simply to place hot-water bottles and electric heating blankets *around* the patient and not in direct contact, draping them so as to build a warmed environment ("heat tent") for the patient.

If you are present at the time of the accident, the scalded area should be packed in ice to keep it cool and to minimize the degree of cellular damage. There is a short window of time during which this maneuver will be effective. The patient should then be taken immediately to a veterinary hospital. Time will be required for the wound to heal. Loss of blood plasma at the site of injury and secondary infection are common complications of burn wounds. Large areas of damage may need to be repaired using skin grafting techniques. Burns from chewed electrical cords usually occur on the lips and in the mouth. In such cases, greater problems may result from damage to the lungs and heart caused by the electrical discharge.

Frostbite

If freezing of a limb or toe is suspected because of its cold temperature and white, dry appearance, it should immediately be warmed with warm water. The affected area may become dry and discolored, and some of the tissue may eventually die and slough. Surgical amputation of the affected area may be necessary. Frostbite-affected tissue can be very painful for the patient. The veterinarian should be consulted regarding medications to control the pain arising from such an injury.

Hypothermia

A dog may become hypothermic if it is exposed to excessively low environmental temperatures. Hypothermic animals exhibit depressed mental activity (up to and including unconsciousness) and generally are cold to the touch. The normal rectal temperature for a dog ranges from about 100.5°F (38°C) to 102°F (39°C). Mild degrees of hypothermia (down to about 96°F [36°C]) are not harmful per se and aggressive rewarming techniques are not necessary; it is usually sufficient to cover the dog with blankets and allow passive rewarming to occur. Passive rewarming minimizes further heat loss and allows the patient to warm itself metabolically.

There are a number of ways to rewarm a moderately to severely cold animal (temperature below 95°F [35°C]). Unfortunately, surface warming causes dilation of peripheral blood vessels at a time when the heart is still debilitated by cold, and this may lead to a drop in blood pressure. The rewarming rate should be limited to less than 1°C per hour. Hot-water bottles and electric heating blankets are dangerous because they can burn the skin. As indicated above, they should not be put in direct contact with the skin, but instead should be placed around the patient and draped to build a "heat tent." Infrared heat lamps may also cause overheating of the skin if they are placed too near; however, they are relatively ineffective if placed too far away. The optimal distance is 75 cm (about 30 inches). Hair driers

---

Table 3
Tasks that the dog owner should be able to perform in an emergency situation

Apply a gauze muzzle

Slide an injured dog onto a flat board

Pick up a dog in a manner that is safe and stable for the dog and also safe for the owner

Take a rectal temperature

Palpate a heartbeat

Palpate a femoral arterial pulse (*see* GLOSSARY: FEMORAL PULSE)

A first-aid kit for dogs and dog owners

Roll gauze (3- or 4-inch, depending upon the size of the dog)

Gauze sponges (3- or 4-inch, depending upon the size of the dog)

Oxygen (if possible)

Pen light

Stethoscope

Plastic bag for ice pack (for superficial burns)

60-milliliter syringe

Activated charcoal

Betadine antiseptic solution and ointment

Rectal thermometer

Warm blanket and linen towels

Syrup of ipecac

3% Hydrogen peroxide

Dry mustard

Baking soda

Milk of magnesia

Vinegar

Lemon juice

---

are a good way to warm a smaller dog. The dog may be covered in towels that have been warmed in an oven or warm water, or it may be placed in a warm-water bath (taking care to ensure that open wounds as well as the mouth and nose are not submerged). All warm-water warming techniques (bottles, blankets, baths) should be monitored carefully. Keep in mind that when the temperature of the water drops below that of the patient, the water will then begin to extract heat from the body.

Lacerations

If time allows, lacerations (tears in the skin) and other open wounds should be washed with copious amounts of fresh water and covered with an antibiotic/antifungal ointment. The patient should then be taken to the veterinarian so that the wound may be thoroughly cleansed and **sutured** (stitched together).

Proptosis of the Eyeball

Trauma of sufficient magnitude to "pop" the eyeball out of its socket is very likely to cause severe problems within the eye. The eye should be covered with a wet sponge and manually held in place or bandaged for the trip to the veterinary hospital. The eyeball will require surgical repair followed by postsurgical treatment several times a day. Vision and performance of the ocular muscles will not be assessable until several weeks after surgery. (*See* CHAPTER 19, "THE EYE AND DISORDERS.")

Procedures for Life-Threatening Emergencies

by Steve C. Haskins

Seizures (Fits, Convulsions)
Coma (Unconsciousness)
Apnea (Cessation of Breathing)
Cardiac Arrest (Cessation of the Heartbeat)
Complete Upper-Airway Obstruction
Snoring or Squeaking Respiration
Wheezing Respiration
Penetrating Chest Wounds
Smoke Inhalation and Burns
Drowning
Gastric Torsion
Antifreeze (Ethylene Glycol) Ingestion
Heat Exhaustion/Heatstroke

Most life-threatening situations involve deterioration of the cardiovascular, respiratory or central nervous systems. In the previous chapter, characteristic changes associated with common life-threatening emergencies were described. If you have a question as to whether or not a particular situation is life-threatening, you should speak with your veterinarian either by telephone or by taking your dog in for an examination.

The best course of action is first to recognize that a life-threatening situation might exist, and then to transport the dog to a veterinary hospital for direct evaluation.

Seizures (Fits, Convulsions)

Seizures are very dramatic and frightening. They can be caused by diseases in the brain, metabolic disorders, and numerous toxins and poisons. Seizuring dogs do not "swallow their tongues" and will not suffer an airway obstruction from this cause. Under no circumstance should you insert your fingers into the mouth of an animal that is seizuring—the chances of being bitten are very high. During a seizure episode the animal should be wrapped in a blanket to protect it against self-inflicted trauma. The dog should then be observed closely. If it regurgitates, its head and neck should be tilted downward. If the mucous-membrane color becomes ashen gray or blue (indicating impaired oxygen supply to the tissues), oxygen or mouth-to-nose breathing (see "APNEA," BELOW) should be given.

Characteristics of the seizure should be noted so they can be described to the veterinarian:

1. Was there a sudden collapse, with no muscle movement and a rapid, alert recovery? (*Note*: This may not be a seizure; but may represent a heart problem.)

2. Did all of the muscles become stiff at the same time, or was there thrashing or paddling of the limbs?

3. Was there a loss of consciousness? Did the dog fail to recognize the owner's voice?

4. Was there a change in behavior just prior to the episode?

5. Did the seizure commence with muscle-twitching (facial, a leg, or one side of the body) and remain localized, or did it spread to the entire body?

6. How long did the episode last?

7. The mental condition of the dog immediately following the seizure episode should also be noted, e.g., did the dog act confused, or was it mentally alert when coming out of the seizure?

Coma (Unconsciousness)

If you find your dog unconscious, take the following steps:

1. Check first to see if it is breathing (if it is not, *see* "Apnea," below).

2. Check to see if the heart is beating (if it is not, *see* "Cardiac Arrest," below).

3. Check the other signs of respiratory and cardiovascular function as outlined in chapter 42, "Home Emergency Care."

4. Inspect the immediate vicinity to see if you can identify any obvious cause of the problem.

5. Call your veterinarian.

Because a comatose dog cannot, in general, protect itself from inhaling vomited material into air passages, care must be taken to protect the airway. Make sure the airway is not obstructed (*see* "Complete Upper-Airway Obstruction," below). If the dog regurgitates, tilt the head and neck downward so that the material will flow away from the airway. *Under no circumstance should a comatose dog be given anything by mouth.* Transport the dog to your veterinarian for a complete examination and medical treatment.

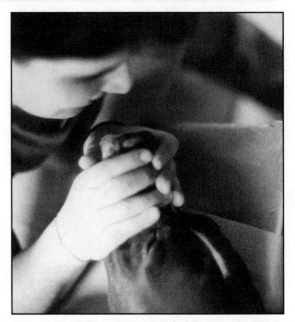

Figure 1. Artificial breathing can be applied to a dog with respiratory arrest. Clasp both hands around the dog's muzzle in order to create an airtight seal of the lips. Then establish an airtight seal around the nose with your lips and blow. Make sure that air does not leak out and that the chest rises up and down. It is possible to blow air into the stomach by this technique, a situation that may cause regurgitation. Make sure that the abdomen does not become progressively distended. Do not attempt to release the air by pressing on the abdomen because of the danger of regurgitation. (Courtesy of Dr. Steve C. Haskins.)

Apnea (Cessation of Breathing)

If the dog is making no attempt to breathe, **ventilatory support** (artificial respiration) is required. The *mouth-to-nose technique* is the simplest way to accomplish this. Clasp both hands around the muzzle so as to make an airtight seal of the lips. Extend the dog's head (stretch the head and neck forward from the body) and blow into the nostrils, making an airtight seal with your lips around the animal's nose (*see* Figure 1).The chest should be observed to expand with each successful breath. If this does not happen:

- the head and neck may not be properly extended
- you may not be blowing forcefully enough

- the air may be leaking somewhere
- there may be an airway obstruction (*see* "COMPLETE UPPER-AIRWAY OBSTRUCTION," BELOW)

If you have been trained in **endotracheal intubation** (passage of a breathing tube into the trachea) and have the proper equipment, you should insert a tube into the trachea rather than try the mouth-to-nose technique outlined above. This also allows examination of the throat region and the bypass of any upper-airway obstructions. Once the breathing tube is in place, the animal can be easily respirated by blowing air into the tube.

Cardiac Arrest (Cessation of the Heartbeat)

The hallmarks of cardiac arrest are:

- unconsciousness
- cessation of breathing
- absence of the heartbeat and of a pulse in the femoral artery on the inside of the thigh (*see* CHAPTER 42, "HOME EMERGENCY CARE")
- ashen discoloration to the mucous membranes
- wide dilation of the pupils

Very little can be done at home if the heart is not beating. A sharp thump over the chest area with the fist may, *in very rare instances,* stimulate an arrested heart to begin beating again. If this maneuver is not successful after two or three attempts, the effort should be abandoned. External compression of the chest over the heart area, in an attempt to produce circulation of the blood, is not a very successful procedure, even when performed by professionals in a hospital situation. It is even less likely to be successful at home. If you feel compelled to try, a recommended procedure follows:

Place the dog on its side on a flat, hard surface that will not bend when the chest is compressed. Apply pressure with the flat of the hand directly over the heart area with a force that is appropriate for the size of the patient, at a rate of about 120 times per minute (*see* FIGURE 2). Apply common sense. A small, fragile dog cannot sustain the same pressure as a large, heavy-boned dog without being injured. The heart is located just behind the front legs, in the lower half of the chest. The compression must be completely released for a brief period of time to allow blood to flow back into the chest and heart between compressions. It is helpful to lay a heavy object such as a sandbag or a book across the dog's abdomen to provide counter-pressure. There should be some improvement in mucous-membrane color if the technique is producing forward blood flow. If you are experienced in feeling for a pulse, you should also be able to detect a femoral arterial pulse (*see* GLOSSARY: FEMORAL PULSE) each time the chest is compressed. In addition to chest compression some artificial breathing must be instituted, as outlined above under "Apnea." This ideally would be performed by a second person after each three chest compressions.

There is no strict rule as to how long one should continue this effort. If the heart has not begun to beat after 5 or 10 minutes, it is probably not helpful to persist. In hospital settings, **cardiopulmonary resuscitation (CPR)** is rarely continued beyond 30 minutes.

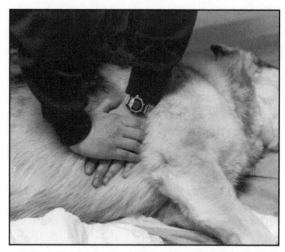

Figure 2. External chest compression may be attempted if a dog suffers a cardiac arrest. With the dog lying on either side, compress briskly over the heart area (just behind the foreleg). The force of compression should be appropriate for the size of the dog, i.e., enough to cause about a 50% compression of the chest wall. (Courtesy of Dr. Steve C. Haskins.)

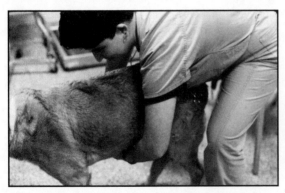

Figure 3. A foreign body may be dislodged from the pharynx by applying a brisk abdominal compression. Position yourself over or behind the dog and wrap your hands or arms (depending on the size of the dog) around the abdomen, behind the rib cage. Briskly compress the chest. The process may be repeated several times if at first it does not succeed. (Courtesy of Dr. Steve C. Haskins.)

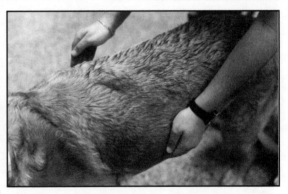

Figure 4. A foreign body may be dislodged from the pharynx by briskly thumping the chest simultaneously on both sides with cupped hands. The process may be repeated several times. (Courtesy of Dr. Steve C. Haskins.)

Complete Upper-Airway Obstruction

Complete upper-airway obstruction is indicated by an acute onset of vigorous breathing efforts that are not associated with air movement. During normal breathing, air is inhaled and the abdomen and chest expand at the same time. With upper-airway obstruction, however, air is inhaled but the chest wall is retracted inward as the abdomen moves outward. This occurs because the **diaphragm** (the large muscle used for breathing which separates the abdominal and chest cavities) is much stronger than the chest muscles. Mucous-membrane color deteriorates very rapidly (in only 60 to 90 seconds) and the dog loses consciousness.

If you think your dog has inhaled a foreign object, you may aid in dislodging the object (prior to the dog's loss of consciousness) by the application of a modified *Heimlich maneuver.* Position yourself behind the dog and wrap your arms or hands (depending on the size of the dog) around the abdomen, beneath or behind the rib cage, and apply a brisk compression (*see* Figure 3).

Try this several times. If this technique is not successful, thump the dog's chest several times, on both sides, with cupped hands (*see* Figure 4). Do *not* insert your fingers into the mouth or

throat while the dog is still conscious; it will be very stressful to the animal, you are unlikely to be successful, and you will most likely receive a severe bite wound.

Once the animal has lost consciousness, you may have 30 to 60 seconds to examine the back of the mouth and throat before the heart stops beating. Extend the head and neck forward from the body, open the mouth widely, and pull out the tongue (*see* Figure 5). This is best accomplished by a second person. Use the lights of the room or a penlight to examine the throat area for foreign objects. Explore the area with your fingers and remove any foreign object you find. You should be aware of the normal structures of the canine larynx, which should not be mistaken for a foreign body (*see* Figure 6).

Snoring or Squeaking Respiration

Animals with partial large-airway obstructions generally make audible snoring or squeaking sounds when they breathe and may exhibit chest-wall retraction during inhalation. This condition should not be confused with a **reverse sneeze,** an inspiratory snoring sound that an animal makes when it is trying to clear the back of its nasal passages. These episodes are quite dramatic but intermittent and are interspersed with long periods of normal breathing.

If the obstruction is rapid and thought to be

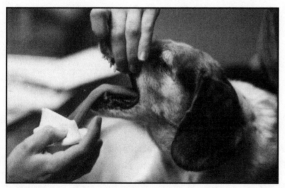

Figure 5. In an unconscious dog, the back of the mouth and pharynx can be examined visually or explored with the fingers by extending the dog's head and neck forward from the body, opening the mouth widely, and pulling out the tongue. Room lights or a pen light may be used to visualize the back of the throat and the larynx. Feel the pharynx with your fingers and remove any foreign objects that you find. (Courtesy of Dr. Steve C. Haskins.)

caused by a foreign body, it may be helpful to apply a modified Heimlich maneuver or chest thump as outlined above for complete airway obstruction. The dog should not be stressed further by abrupt or aggressive handling. It should be kept cool, oxygen should be provided if available, and veterinary care should be sought as soon as possible.

Wheezing Respiration

Wheezing sounds (the sounds typical of a human being with severe asthma) are usually attributed to **bronchoconstriction** (narrowing of the larger airways). Bronchoconstriction is often allergic in nature and may be caused by an insect sting, or it may occur for unknown reasons. Whether you suspect an allergic reaction or do not know the cause, the dog should be taken to the veterinarian for administration of a **bronchodilator** (medication producing expansion of the airways) immediately. Oxygen, if available, will be helpful. One or two doses from an aerosol inhaler containing metaproterenol, albuterol, or terbutaline may be administered orally after consulting with the veterinarian. The medication will be absorbed across the mucous membranes of the mouth and so will reach the target area.

Penetrating Chest Wounds

Penetrating chest-wall trauma may create an opening in the chest wall. As air leaks into the chest cavity, the lungs will collapse and the affected dog will not be able to breath. The wound should be closed with your fingers by pinching the tissues together so as to make an airtight seal. If the respiratory distress is severe and **cyanosis** (bluish discoloration of the mucous membranes, indicative of reduced blood oxygen levels) is present, it may be necessary to place a small tube into the chest cavity prior to pinching the tissue closed. The air should then be removed through the tube using a syringe, turkey baster, or even by mouth. The dog should be transported to the veterinary hospital as quickly as possible.

Smoke Inhalation and Burns

Animals caught in a fire may suffer four consequences:

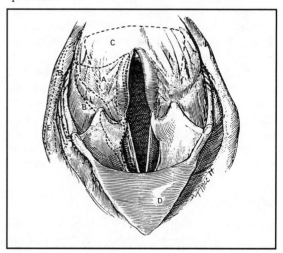

Figure 6. Be aware of the normal structures of the larynx, some of which may be mistaken for a foreign body. (A) arytenoid cartilage; (B) thyroid cartilage; (C) cricoid cartilage; (D) epiglottis; (E) hyoid apparatus. (Reprinted from Grandage, J., and K. Richardson, "Functional Anatomy," in D.H. Slatter, ed., *Textbook of Small Animal Surgery* (W.B. Saunders Co., Philadelphia: 1985, 909.)

1. Thermal burns to the skin surface
2. Upper-airway thermal burns
3. Carbon monoxide poisoning
4. Smoke-induced cellular damage and diffuse lung disease

Extensive surface burns may be life-threatening because they cause the release of activators of the systemic inflammatory response and can be associated with extensive fluid and electrolyte losses, as well as infection at the burn site. Upper-airway burns may be severe enough to cause an airway obstruction. Carbon monoxide produced from combustion will interfere with the ability of red blood cells to carry oxygen. Oxygen therapy is key in removing the carbon monoxide from the red cells. It may take several days for the full magnitude of smoke-induced lung damage to become apparent. Affected dogs will require oxygen therapy and vigorous management of airway secretions and, in some cases, full breathing support. Any dog caught in a fire should be brought to a veterinarian immediately for evaluation and treatment.

Superficial thermal burns to the skin surface should be initially treated with ice packs or by immersing the affected area in cold water. Following this, the area should be dried and then protected with a thin film of *non*-oil-based ointment, such as an eye ointment. A clean fresh dressing should be gently applied and held in place with bandages. The animal should then be taken to the veterinarian for examination of the wound. Deeper burns require immediate veterinary attention. Until you are able to reach the veterinary hospital, keep the wound covered with towels or dressings soaked in cold water.

Drowning

When large amounts of water are aspirated into the lower airways, the resultant collapse of the small airways and **alveoli** (microscopic air sacs in the lungs wherein gas exchange occurs) impairs the lung's ability to infuse oxygen into the blood. Drowning victims should first be evaluated to determine if they are breathing (*see* "APNEA," ABOVE). If breathing, is the breathing adequate? Check the mucous membrane color.

If it is blue or ashen gray the dog is not taking in enough oxygen. If the dog is not breathing, tip the dog head-down and thump the chest with cupped hands to drain any water from the airways (*see* FIGURE 4). In most instances you will be unlikely to obtain much water. The water that is causing most of the problems is lodged deep in the airway. Institute artificial respiration as discussed above in "Apnea." Check to see if the heart is beating and if not, you may elect to try external chest compression (*see* "CARDIAC ARREST," ABOVE).

The duration and effects of the drowning depend somewhat upon the nature of the water. Freshwater is less salty (**hypotonic**) than the blood plasma and tends to be absorbed rapidly—the duration of the lung disturbance thus is shorter and the systemic water intoxication greater. Salt water is **hypertonic** compared to blood plasma, so that the lung disturbances tend to persist and depletion of blood volume may be a problem. In either case veterinary attention must be sought immediately.

Gastric Torsion

An acute, rapidly progressive abdominal enlargement caused by distention and/or twisting of the stomach occurs primarily in large-breed dogs (small breeds on occasion), usually after a large meal (but not always), and can result in death in a short period of time. (*See* CHAPTER 30, "THE DIGESTIVE SYSTEM AND DISORDERS," and CHAPTER 40, "SURGERY AND POSTOPERATIVE CARE.") The enlarged stomach interferes with the return of blood to the heart, breathing, and blood flow to the stomach wall and spleen (which can lead to severe tissue damage). Gastric torsion is a serious life-threatening emergency requiring immediate veterinary care. The attending veterinarian will pass a tube to remove gas from the stomach and then determine whether or not the stomach has twisted along its long axis. Twisting of the stomach requires surgical intervention. The patient may be required to remain in the hospital for follow-up observation because residual organ damage may not become evident for several days.

Antifreeze (Ethylene Glycol) Ingestion

Dogs love to drink **ethylene glycol** (antifreeze), apparently because of its appealing taste. Very small amounts of ethylene glycol cause very serious kidney damage and often irreversible kidney failure. Once a dog has ingested antifreeze there is a 2- to 4-hour window of therapeutic opportunity at most. The consequences of untreated ethylene glycol poisoning are lethal; thus, veterinary attention should be sought immediately if there is even the faintest chance that a dog has consumed a quantity of antifreeze. Antifreeze should *always* be stored in an area inaccessible to pets.

Heat Exhaustion/Heatstroke

Hyperthermia (abnormally elevated body temperature) results when heat production exceeds heat loss. The normal rectal temperature for a dog ranges from 100.5°F (38°C) to 102°F (39°C). The most common causes of hyperthermia include fever in response to an infection; exercise; or confinement in a hot or humid environment. (*See* CHAPTER 39, "CLINICAL SIGNS OF DISEASE.")

Mild degrees of hyperthermia (below 104°F [40°C]) are not harmful per se to the patient and may represent an appropriate response to an underlying disease (e.g., fever of infection). Such "appropriate" fevers should not be treated; effective management of the underlying infection will allow the fever to subside. Aspirin and acetaminophen (Tylenol) can reduce a fever of infection by inhibiting the synthesis of com-

pounds called **prostaglandins** in the brain. These drugs are *not* effective in other forms of hyperthermia or heat exhaustion/heat stroke, however, and should not be administered without consulting a veterinarian.

Heat exhaustion occurs with exercise, particularly on hot or humid days, and may not be associated with much of an elevation in body temperature. Animals with heat exhaustion exhibit acute collapse, normal mental activity, malaise, vomiting, muscle cramps, **tetany** (seizure-like tremors), **tachycardia** (abnormally rapid heart rate), **tachypnea** (abnormally rapid breathing), muscular weakness, and occasionally **syncope** (fainting spell).

Heatstroke, by contrast, is associated with a marked elevation in body temperature. Actually, control of body temperature regulation is essentially lost. Cell damage begins to occur at body temperatures above 108°F (42°C). Severe hyperthermia results in kidney and liver failure, blood-clotting disorders, metabolic abnormalities, gastrointestinal failure, **hypoxemia** (depressed blood oxygen levels), destruction of skeletal muscle cells, brain dysfunction and heart failure.

Effective cooling when the rectal temperature is below 108°F can be achieved by wetting the surface of the dog with cool (but not iced) water and allowing the water to evaporate. Use a fan to keep air moving over the body surface. Ice water should be used only if the rectal temperature is greater than 108°F. As in any other emergency, the heatstroke victim should receive veterinary attention as quickly as possible.

PART VIII

Appendices

An actor is never so great as when
he reminds you of an animal—falling
like a cat, lying like a dog, moving like
a fox.—

—FRANCOIS TRUFFAUT
producer, *New Yorker,* Feb. 20, 1960

Zoonotic Diseases: From Dogs to People

by Bruno B. Chomel

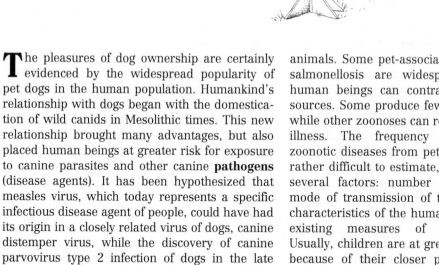

The pleasures of dog ownership are certainly evidenced by the widespread popularity of pet dogs in the human population. Humankind's relationship with dogs began with the domestication of wild canids in Mesolithic times. This new relationship brought many advantages, but also placed human beings at greater risk for exposure to canine parasites and other canine **pathogens** (disease agents). It has been hypothesized that measles virus, which today represents a specific infectious disease agent of people, could have had its origin in a closely related virus of dogs, canine distemper virus, while the discovery of canine parvovirus type 2 infection of dogs in the late 1970s raised some initial concern about the role of dogs in the possible transmission of that agent to human beings (to date it has not been shown to cause disease in human beings, however).

Several parasitic, fungal, or other infectious agents can definitely infect both human beings and dogs, and the diseases they cause are referred to as **zoonoses**—diseases that can be spread between vertebrate animals and human beings. There are more than 150 recognized zoonoses, but only a few are associated with pet

animals. Some pet-associated zoonoses such as salmonellosis are widespread in nature, so human beings can contract them from many sources. Some produce few if any clinical signs, while other zoonoses can result in severe to fatal illness. The frequency of transmission of zoonotic diseases from pets to human beings is rather difficult to estimate, and is dependent on several factors: number of infected animals, mode of transmission of the agent, behavioral characteristics of the human beings at risk, and existing measures of disease prevention. Usually, children are at greater risk than adults, because of their closer physical contact with household pets and their own behavior, which includes exploration of the environment by putting objects in their mouths.

Viral Zoonoses

Among the large variety of viral diseases affecting dogs, rabies is the only one that is recognizably dangerous for human beings. To date no epidemiologic data have supported the purely hypothetical role of canine gastrointestinal viruses (coronavirus, rotavirus, parvovirus) in human cases of diarrhea.

RABIES

The dog is certainly a major animal species associated with rabies and the transmission of rabies virus to human beings. In the developing nations, domestic dogs remain the primary reservoir hosts for rabies and the principal source of human exposure to the virus. Fortunately, rabies remains a rare disease of people in the United States. Since canine rabies was controlled through the mass immunization of dogs, the incidence of human rabies, excluding cases acquired abroad, has fallen from 43 cases per year (0.03 cases per 100,000 people) in 1945 to fewer than 1 per year (< 0.001 cases per 100,000 people) in the 1980s.

Although rabies in the United States is mainly a wildlife disease affecting raccoons, skunks, foxes and bats, human beings are probably still at greater risk of acquiring the disease from a rabid dog, since dogs account for a large majority of bite incidents reported across the country. In 1988 a review of canine rabies cases in the United States found that most cases occurred in young dogs (57% were 1 year or younger) considered as pets (84%) and residing in predominantly rural environments (85%). More importantly, virtually all dogs reported as rabid had either never been vaccinated for rabies, or their vaccination status was unknown.

When introduced into the victim's wound by a bite, the rabies virus multiplies locally at the wound site, and then invades the peripheral nerve(s) supplying that area. The virus migrates up the nerves and reaches the central nervous system, then spreads to various organs, including the salivary glands. The virus is shed in the saliva and can be transmitted to a new victim through a bite. The incubation period of rabies varies from a few days to several months or longer. The virus can be shed in the saliva as much as 1 or 2 weeks *before* the appearance of any clinical signs. This is the rationale for the 10-day quarantine of a dog that has bitten a human being. If the dog remains healthy 10 days after the bite incident, one can assume that the dog was not shedding rabies virus at the time of the bite, and consequently, that the bite victim does not need rabies postexposure treatment with human diploid cell rabies vaccine. (*See* CHAPTER 34, "VIRAL DISEASES.").

Canine rabies is characterized primarily by neurologic and behavioral disorders. During the initial phase (the "prodrome"), an affected dog may appear anxious, nervous and suffer changes in personality. After 2 or 3 days, either the excitatory ("furious") or paralytic ("dumb") form of the disease will become evident. In the excitatory form, lasting from 1 to 7 days, the dog exhibits irritability, aggression, hypersensitivity, disorientation, and sometimes convulsive seizures. In the paralytic form, which may last from 1 to 10 days, the paralysis appears initially in the muscles of the head and neck, the most characteristic sign being difficulty in swallowing. Paralysis then progresses to affect the entire nervous system. The paralytic form always represents the terminal stage of the disease; however, some animals die during convulsive seizures while in the excitatory stage without ever progressing to the final, paralytic stage. Some animals exhibit few if any signs of excitement or "madness," the clinical picture reflecting instead the effects of paralysis. Death occurs inevitably within 10 days of the onset of illness.

Prevention of canine rabies is based on mass immunization of susceptible dogs, confinement of pets, quarantine of biting dogs and removal of strays. Recommendations for state and local rabies vaccination and control measures are published each year by the National Association of State Public Health Veterinarians, Inc. (NASPHV). All states require rabies vaccination of dogs. Interstate movement of dogs usually requires a health certificate and proof of rabies vaccination. Sixteen rabies vaccines are currently marketed for dogs in the United States and should be administered according to the manufacturer's instructions. Puppies should be vaccinated at 3 months of age and revaccinated 1 year later at 15 months of age, after which they should receive boosters every 3 years (or according to individual vaccine specifications). If a dog with a current rabies immunization is exposed to a known rabid animal, it should be revaccinated immediately and confined for observation for 90 days. Exposed, unvaccinated animals are either euthanatized or placed in strict isolation for 6 months and vaccinated 1 month before release. (*See* CHAPTER 34, "VIRAL DISEASES," and APPENDIX B, "VACCINATIONS.")

Bacterial Zoonoses

ANIMAL BITES
An estimated 1 to 2 million animal bites occur in the United States every year, with dogs accounting for 75–90% of all bite wounds requiring medical attention. Children are more likely to be bitten than are adults, and males are twice as likely to be bitten as are females. But only 3–5% of dog bites are likely to become secondarily infected.

Although most bacteriologic studies of dog bite wounds have focused on *Pasteurella multocida,* a wide range of disease-causing bacteria may be present in these wounds, including staphylococci, streptococci, *Moraxella, Bacillus, Neisseria,* and CDC alphanumeric aerobic Gram-negative rods (group IIj, Group EF-4, and *Capnocytophaga canimorsus* [formerly called DF-2]).

Pasteurellosis
Pasteurellosis of human beings is commonly associated with dog bites and even more frequently with cat bites. Pasteurellae are **commensal** (coexisting harmlessly) bacteria commonly found in the mouths of dogs and cats. Carrier rates of *Pasteurella* in dogs range from 22–81% of dogs tested; a recent study indicates that pathogenic strains can be found in 28% of dogs tested, versus 77% of cats. Swelling, inflammation and intense pain at the bite site a few hours after being bitten are the typical presenting symptoms. Penicillin is the antibiotic of choice for treatment. Untreated infections can lead to severe complications, including **septic arthritis** (joint inflammation caused by bacteria) and **osteomyelitis** (infection and inflammation of bone).

Capnocytophaga Canimorsus (DF-2) and Other Dysgonic Fermenter Bacteria
These organisms are common bacteria of the oral cavity of carnivores. They are usually of low virulence, but can cause **septicemia** (bacterial invasion of the bloodstream, accompanied by related clinical signs of illness) in immunocompromised patients.

Miscellaneous Diseases
Certain other disease-causing bacteria can accidentally be transmitted by dog bites, including *Brucella suis* and leptospires. (*See* "BRUCELLOSIS" AND "LEPTOSPIROSIS" BELOW AND IN CHAPTER 35, "BACTERIAL DISEASES.")

GASTROINTESTINAL ZOONOSES

Enteric Campylobacteriosis
Campylobacter jejuni is a leading cause of human **enteritis** (inflammation of the small intestine). Fever, headache, abdominal pain, and severe, watery to bloody diarrhea usually lasting less than a week are the primary symptoms. Food animals, especially poultry, are the major reservoirs of the organism, with human infection usually occurring after consumption of contaminated, untreated surface water, unpasteurized milk, or undercooked meat. However, evidence indicates that contact with infected dogs, especially diarrheic dogs, can increase the risk of acquiring *Campylobacter* infection. The prevalence of infection varies from a few percent in healthy dogs, to 50–75% in diarrheic dogs and puppies. Puppies are more likely to acquire the infection and to exhibit clinical signs (watery diarrhea lasting for 3 to 7 days). Infection can also occur after contact with healthy dogs that are intermittently shedding the organism. It has been estimated that approximately 6% of cases of human enteric campylobacteriosis are acquired from pet animals. Control and prevention of zoonotic infection depend on interrupting contact with contaminated materials. Infected animals should be isolated from other animals and from children. Hands should be washed after handling the pet. The pet's toys, feeding utensils and premises should be thoroughly disinfected with bleach or other strong disinfectants. (*See* "ENTERIC CAMPYLOBACTERIOSIS" IN CHAPTER 35, "BACTERIAL DISEASES.")

Salmonellosis
Salmonellosis is another important gastrointestinal pathogen that can be transmitted to people

from infected dogs. Most human cases of salmonellosis are food-borne; however, as many as 3% of human cases may be pet-associated. Young children are at risk of developing salmonellosis from close contact with pets and failure to wash hands properly after handling the animals.

In human beings and in dogs, salmonellosis presents as a gastroenteritis, characterized by fever, nausea, vomiting, abdominal pain, and a watery diarrhea. After infection, dogs may shed the organism for as long as 3 to 6 weeks. Strict hygienic measures should be instituted. (*See* "Salmonellosis" in chapter 35, "Bacterial Diseases.")

Other gastrointestinal bacterial pathogens that may accidentally be transmitted to people by dogs include *Yersinia enterocolitica* and *Yersinia pseudotuberculosis*.

Vector-borne Zoonoses

Lyme Borreliosis (Lyme Disease)
Lyme borreliosis is an important tick-borne zoonosis in the United States, especially in the eastern part of the country. Several thousand human cases are reported every year to the Centers for Disease Control. The illness is a complex, multisystem disorder that commonly leads to chronic neurologic problems and arthritis.

Lyme borreliosis is caused by *Borrelia burgdorferi*, a tick-transmitted **spirochete** (a filamentous, spiral-shaped bacterium). The first extensive human outbreak described in this country occurred in the town of Old Lyme, Connecticut in the 1970s. The ticks most important in transmission of the disease to people are the deer tick (*Ixodes scapularis*, formally referred to as *Ixodes dammini*) on the East Coast, and the western black-legged tick (*Ixodes pacificus*) on the West Coast. Deer ticks are commonly (25–50%) infected with the Lyme spirochete, while black-legged ticks have a much lower rate of infection (1–5%).

In dogs, infection with the Lyme spirochete is often **asymptomatic** (without clinical signs). When clinical signs are evident, they can include intermittent and painful lameness, inappetence, lymph node enlargement and fever. In people, the first sign of Lyme borreliosis is an expanding, circular red skin rash (**erythema chronicum migrans [ECM]**) that develops at the bite wound where the tick vector had engorged. The appearance of ECM is usually associated with varying degrees of fever, chills, malaise, fatigue, vomiting, headache, lymph node enlargement and neck stiffness. The ECM usually undergoes expansion for several weeks, clears in the center, and then fades. Weeks to months later, a small proportion of infected individuals develops signs of chronic Lyme borreliosis, which can include neurologic, cardiac and joint abnormalities.

Tetracycline is the antibiotic of choice for treatment of Lyme borreliosis in human beings and dogs. Although dogs do not play a direct role in the transmission of the disease to people, they may carry infected ticks on their bodies and bring them into the household. Recently, a Lyme borreliosis vaccine has been marketed for immunization of healthy dogs but it is still difficult to evaluate the efficacy of such a vaccine. It is given by intramuscular injection in two doses spaced several weeks apart. The vaccine reportedly protects for a period of at least 6 months. Currently the vaccine is available in areas of the country where the incidence of Lyme borreliosis is high. (*See* "Lyme Borreliosis [Lyme Disease]" in Chapter 35, "Bacterial Diseases," and Appendix B, "Vaccinations.")

Rocky Mountain Spotted Fever and Boutonneuse Fever
Rocky Mountain spotted fever (RMSF) is caused by a **rickettsia** (specialized bacterium that multiplies only within host cells) called *Rickettsia rickettsii*, which can be transmitted by tick bites to animals (especially dogs) and human beings. Contamination of skin with crushed tissues or feces of the tick may also cause infection. The disease is relatively common in the midwestern plains states and in the mid-Atlantic region, where the major reservoirs and **vectors** (transmitters) are the wood tick (*Dermacentor andersoni*) and the American dog tick (*Dermacentor variabilis*). Infected ticks remain infective for life, commonly as long as 18 months. Dogs can act as transient hosts for the tick vectors, bringing infected ticks into a household of human beings.

Two or 3 days after infection, dogs can develop fever, depression, joint pain and a decreased appetite. Neurologic disorders (partial paralysis, hearing loss, seizures) and ocular disease may be observed in dogs some weeks after the acute illness. Treatment requires supportive care and the use of tetracycline antibiotics for 2 to 3 weeks. In people, RMSF is characterized by a flu-like syndrome, with fever, chills, muscle aches, nausea, vomiting and photosensitivity (sensitivity to light). A skin rash may develop by the 3rd to 5th day of illness, involving the hands, wrists, ankles and feet, and can spread to the rest of the body. When untreated, death occurs in 15–20% of the cases. (*See* "Rocky Mountain Spotted Fever" in Chapter 35, "Bacterial Diseases.")

Boutonneuse fever (Mediterranean spotted fever), caused by *Rickettsia conorii,* is a tick-borne zoonosis occurring in southern Europe, Africa and India. People and dogs can become infected through the bite of the brown dog tick, *Rhipicephalus sanguineus.* The infection is usually asymptomatic in dogs. Although direct transmission from dogs to humans does not occur, dogs can serve as transport hosts to bring infected ticks into a human household. In people, the most common symptoms include fever, a black spot ("tache noir"), and a skin rash. Early treatment with tetracyclines usually leads to a rapid improvement in clinical symptoms.

Ehrlichiosis

Human ehrlichiosis was first described in the United States in 1986. Since then more than 200 cases have been reported, mostly from the southeastern and south central states. Human ehrlichiosis is an acute, febrile illness. The symptoms are nonspecific and can resemble those of Rocky Mountain spotted fever, except that skin rashes are rare. Cases occur during active tick seasons and most of the patients report being exposed to ticks. Once considered as an *Ehrlichia canis*-like organism, the causative agent has been determined by genetic analysis to be a new species, *Ehrlichia chaffeensis.* A recent European epidemiologic study indicated that human beings bitten by brown dog ticks (*Rhipicephalus sanguineus,* the vector for *E. canis*) in areas endemic for *E. canis* did not develop specific antibodies to *E. canis.* No case of human ehrlichiosis has ever been related to an infected dog.

Plague

Bubonic plague caused by the flea-transmitted bacterium *Yersinia pestis* is an endemic disease of rodents in the western United States. In human beings, bubonic plague results from an infected flea bite, usually from a rodent flea, but sometimes from a cat or dog flea. In dogs, plague is a rare and usually mild disease, characterized by a moderate fever and enlarged lymph nodes. In endemic areas, plague antibody prevalence in pet dogs is very low (less than 1%). Increasing cases of plague have been observed in cats in recent years, however. (*See* "Plague" in chapter 30, "Bacterial Diseases," in *The Cornell Book of Cats.*)

OTHER BACTERIAL ZOONOSES

Tuberculosis

Canine tuberculosis is a rare disease, caused mainly by *Mycobacterium tuberculosis,* the primary agent of human tuberculosis. Dogs seem to acquire the infection through contact with tuberculous people who are actively shedding the organism in respiratory secretions. Once infected, dogs can shed the organism themselves and thereby infect other animals and human beings. The recent increase in cases of human tuberculosis in the United States is a major public health concern, and there exists some potential for infection of pet dogs and further spread of the disease.

Canine tuberculosis is characterized clinically by signs of respiratory tract disease, including coughing, retching, and **dyspnea** (respiratory difficulty). Fever, inappetence, weight loss and lymph node enlargement may also be observed. Diagnosis of the disease is not an easy task, however, since skin testing (**tuberculin testing**) as performed in people is not a reliable procedure in dogs. Both diagnosis and therapy of tuberculosis are prolonged, and dogs undergoing treatment represent a potential disease threat to people and animals with whom they are in contact. For this reason, treatment of dogs with tuberculosis is *not* recommended. (*See* "Tuberculosis" in chapter 35, "Bacterial Diseases.")

Brucellosis

Dogs can be infected by various species of the bacterium *Brucella* (including *B. melitensis, B.*

abortus, and *B. suis*) and transmit the infection accidentally to human beings. Dogs may also be infected with a specific *Brucella* biogroup, *B. canis.* Since the first case of human infection with *B. canis* was reported to the CDC, more than 20 cases have been reported in the United States. Human beings are less susceptible to *B. canis* than they are to the other brucellae. Symptoms of human brucellosis caused by *B. canis* include chills, fever, sweating and joint pain. Treatment involves specific antibiotic therapy. (*See* "CANINE BRUCELLOSIS" IN CHAPTER 35, "BACTERIAL DISEASES.")

Leptospirosis

Human cases of leptospirosis are relatively rare in the United States (fewer than 100 cases per year in the last 10 years). Leptospirosis is primarily a water-borne disease, with rodents acting as major reservoirs of infection with the causative **leptospires** (spiral-shaped bacteria belonging to the spirochete group). Human beings are accidental hosts who become infected usually through occupational or recreational exposure. Dogs are the natural carrier host for *Leptospira canicola;* infected dogs shedding the leptospire in urine are a potential source of infection for their human companions. Human infections with leptospires can be severe and may persist for a lengthy period of time. (*See* "LEPTOSPIROSIS" IN CHAPTER 35, "BACTERIAL DISEASES.")

Fungal Zoonoses

RINGWORM

Dermatophytosis, commonly known as *ringworm,* is a common, transmissible, superficial fungal infection of animals (including dogs) and human beings. It affects primarily the hair, skin and nails. The fungi most frequently causing dermatophytosis in dogs are *Microsporum canis* and *Trichophyton mentagrophytes.*

Ringworm is transmitted to people by direct contact with infected animals and indirectly by spores in the hair or scales shed from such animals. In dogs, the lesions are often discrete and localized. **Alopecia** (loss of hair) can be observed with moderately **pruritic** (causing itching) lesions. In human beings, ringworm can affect the scalp or the body. On the scalp it begins as a small **papule** (minute, firm, well-demarcated elevation of the skin). The surrounding hair becomes brittle as the infection spreads in an expanding circle, leaving scaly bald patches. Similar lesions can be found on the body, where they have a tendency to form rings (hence the name "ringworm") with reddish borders. Treatment is based on oral admistration of griseofulvin for at least 4 weeks, and/or a topical antifungal solution. (*See* "RINGWORM" IN CHAPTER 22, "THE SKIN AND DISORDERS.")

Parasitic Zoonoses

ECTOPARASITES

Canine Scabies

Canine scabies is a nonseasonal, intensely itchy, transmissible infestation of the skin caused by the mite *Sarcoptes scabei* var. *canis.* The intense itching results from mechanical irritation caused by the burrowing mites and their production of toxic and **allergenic** (inducing allergy) materials. The primary lesions are erythematous (reddened, due to capillary congestion) papules, with secondary scaling, crusting and **excoriations** (scratches, abrasions). In human beings the "classical" lesion of scabies is the burrow, which consists of a linear scaling lesion that is often **vesicular** (fluid-filled, like a blister). Affected people, especially children, become infested after prolonged contact with an infested pet. Canine scabies can be cured with weekly applications of scabicidal dips (especially lindane). (*See* CHAPTER 23, "EXTERNAL PARASITES.")

Cheyletiellosis

Cheyletiellosis (also called Cheyletiella dermatitis) is a nonseasonal, variably itchy, transmissible infestation of the skin of dogs caused by the mite *Cheyletiella yasguri.* Cheyletiellosis is most often a problem in puppies. Clinical signs usually include some degree of scaling, crusting and **dermatitis** (inflammation of the skin). In people, lesions begin as single or grouped reddened **macules** (discolored areas of skin that are not elevated above the surface), which rapidly evolve into very itchy papules. The complete life cycle of the mite does not occur on humans, so that human infestations are essentially self-limiting. Cheyletiellosis is easily cured in dogs with the weekly application of insecticides (pyrethrins or carbamates). (*See* CHAPTER 23, "EXTERNAL PARASITES.")

ENDOPARASITES: HELMINTHOSES

Four parasitic worm infestations (**helminthoses**) of the dog can be transmitted to human beings. Three are rather common, usually mild infestations: **visceral larva migrans** (caused by roundworm larvae), **cutaneous larva migrans** (caused by hookworm larvae), and **dipylidiasis** (caused by tapeworms). The fourth, **hydatid disease** (or *echinococcosis*), is seldom seen in the United States but is of importance because of its potentially fatal outcome. (*See* CHAPTER 37, "INTERNAL PARASITES.")

Visceral Larva Migrans (Toxocariasis)

Toxocariasis is a common parasitic disease of dogs. Immature eggs of the dog roundworm (*Toxocara canis*) reach the soil in the feces of infested dogs. After a few days, mature embryonated eggs become infective for both dogs and human beings. They can remain infective in the soil for prolonged periods. In people the risk of infection is particularly high in young children, who may ingest embryonated eggs while eating soil ("mud pies") or playing in feces-soiled areas. Once ingested by a child, the embryonated eggs hatch in the intestine and the **larvae** (immature forms of the worm) migrate through various internal organs (liver, lung, muscle, eye, or sometimes central nervous system). Depending on the intensity of the infestation and the localization of the migrating larvae, symptoms develop that can range from **pneumonitis** (inflammation of the lungs), abdominal pain and skin nodules to visual deficiencies or convulsive seizures. Prevention is based on reducing access of children to areas likely to be heavily contaminated with animal feces. Pet access to sandboxes should be forbidden, and the boxes should be covered when not in use. Regular worming of dogs, especially puppies, will also contribute to the control of visceral larva migrans.

Cutaneous Larva Migrans

The **cutaneous** (pertaining to the skin) localization of canine hookworm larvae (*Ancylostoma* spp.) can result in an itchy, creeping skin eruption in people. These common intestinal worms normally are shed as eggs in an infested dog's feces. In warm, moist soils, the eggs hatch and produce infective larvae, which can penetrate the skin of human beings in contact with contaminated soil. An individual larva produces a papule at the site of entry, and the larval tract can be seen in the skin. The lesion may be accompanied by **vesicles** (blisters) that are very itchy. Regular worming of dogs, and banning of dogs from playgrounds (especially from sandboxes), are both useful measures for controlling this zoonotic infestation in humans.

Dipylidiasis

Dipylidium caninum is a common tapeworm that infests both dogs and cats. Adult worms reside in the host's intestinal tract and **gravid proglottids** (tapeworm body segments) are excreted in the feces. The parasite's life cycle requires larval development in fleas or lice. The life cycle is completed when dogs or cats ingest these intermediate insect hosts. Dipylidiasis affects primarily infants and young children, who may accidentally ingest an infected flea. Symptoms are characterized by digestive disorders and irritability. The drug praziquantel is effective in killing the adult tapeworms. Flea control of pets is an important measure to prevent accidental infestation of human beings. (*See* CHAPTER 23, "EXTERNAL PARASITES," and CHAPTER 37, "INTERNAL PARASITES.")

Hydatid Disease (Echinococcosis)

Hydatid disease of human beings is only rarely diagnosed in the United States, but is of importance because of its potentially fatal outcome. The causative tapeworm, *Echinococcus granulosus,* is present in the western United States, Alaska and Mexico. Dogs can carry the adult tapeworm within the intestinal tract, from which eggs are shed into the feces. If ingested by an intermediate host, especially sheep—or, accidentally, a human being—the eggs hatch, releasing larvae that penetrate the bloodstream. The larvae migrate through the body, particularly to the liver and lungs, where they produce exceedingly large, cystic (fluid-filled) structures (hydatid cysts) in which the parasite undergoes a further process of maturation.

Dogs become infested by ingesting hydatid cysts from infested intermediate hosts (sheep viscera and offal). Human beings usually are infected by direct contact with an infested dog. Children are particularly vulnerable, since they may not clean their hands well after petting or playing with an infested dog. Indirect infestation can occur from contaminated water or raw vegetables. Control of hydatid disease is based on worming of infested dogs, preventing dogs from scavenging or eating infected offal, hygienic control of slaughtering, and disposal of infected viscera.

Echinococcus multilocularis, a related tapeworm of wild canids, particularly foxes, can also infest dogs. It has been reported mainly in Alaska, but has spread in recent years to central North America. Infected dogs have not yet been found in the contiguous United States; however, infected dogs are considered to be the main source of human infection in Alaska. In infested areas, pet owners should wash their hands after handling pets and prevent dogs from scavenging.

Endoparasites: Protozooses

Chagas' Disease (American Trypanosomiasis)
Infection with the protozoan parasite Trypanosoma cruzi occurs from the southern United States south to Argentina and Chile. In the southern United States, despite the presence of infected vectors (winged, bloodsucking insects, known commonly as "cone-nose," "kissing," or "assassin" bugs) and wildlife reservoirs, only very few human cases have been reported. Chagas' disease is usually transmitted to humans directly by vectors, especially Triatoma infestans. In poor rural and urban areas of Central and South America, where the incidence of Chagas' disease is much higher, dogs and cats play an important role as reservoirs of T. cruzi infection in the epidemiologic cycle; however, transmission to people is still accomplished by triatomine insects. Dogs can develop a disease similar to human Chagas' disease, with both an acute phase (fever, cardiac disorders, pale mucous membranes, **edema** [swelling] of the eyelids, neurologic

alterations) and a chronic phase (intermittent bouts of fever and cardiac abnormalities). (See Chapter 37, "Internal Parasites.")

Leishmaniasis
Visceral leishmaniasis, or kala-azar (Hindi for "black fever"), caused by the protozoan parasite Leishmania donovani infantum, is a common infection in some areas of the world, especially in Mediterranean countries and the Middle East. Infection of dogs and human beings occurs through the bite of an infected sand fly vector. In endemic areas, dogs are frequently infected and represent a suitable reservoir because they offer the insect vectors direct access to parasitized blood cells present in the characteristic skin lesions. Most cases observed in dogs and people in the United States have been acquired abroad; however, some canine cases of Leishmania donovani infantum infection acquired within the United States have been reported in California, Texas and Oklahoma. Infants and young children are at greatest risk in endemic areas, where sand flies can transfer the parasite from infected dogs to people. In dogs, the skin lesions (hairless areas, small ulcerations) may be found on the nose, ears and back. There is no effective treatment for the canine disease at present, and the prognosis is poor. (See "Leishmaniasis" in Chapter 37, "Internal Parasites.")

Disease transmission from dogs to people is rather uncommon if pet owners follow the tenets of basic hygiene. For the most part, people are more likely to contract transmissible illnesses from one another than they are from their pet dogs or cats. Special attention must be paid to young children, however, who may find themselves in much closer contact with diseased pets and their environment. Responsible dog owners can participate in controlling zoonotic diseases by vaccinating their animals for rabies and instituting routine deworming measures; restricting excessive contact of infants and small children with pets; and maintaining rigorous standards of hygiene in the household environment.

Vaccinations

by Jeffrey E. Barlough and Niels C. Pedersen

Since the days of antiquity, certain learned physicians have advocated the protection of healthy people against illness by treating them with fluids or tissues derived from diseased individuals. This seeming paradox had its very logical basis in the observation that patients who recovered from a particular sickness often developed resistance to it as a consequence (i.e., they had become "immune"). Many successes, but also many failures, were numbered among the results of these earliest and crudest of medical experiments in *active immunization,* which was referred to more commonly as "inoculation." The general citizenry was not always impressed. In relatively recent times, it is sad to relate, public outcry against the "ludicrous" and "dangerous" practice of inoculation even threatened abandonment of some lines of medical inquiry. From our presumably enlightened viewpoint in the twilight of the 20th century, we can only marvel at the courage and insight of some of these pioneers in medical and veterinary research. The early Chinese and Turks, Edward Jenner, Robert Koch, Louis Pasteur, and others— it is on the shoulders of such as these that our society's unprecedented high level of health and relative freedom from infectious disease rest.

In veterinary medicine, as in human medicine, "inoculation" with antiviral and antibacterial vaccines represents the single most important preventive health measure available today. The excellent vaccines against canine distemper, infectious canine hepatitis, rabies and canine parvovirus are only a few of the successes achieved in this area over the past several decades. However, no vaccine is 100% effective; for whatever reason there will always be a small percentage of vaccinated animals (or people, for that matter) in whom full and complete protection is not achieved with a given vaccine.

Types of Vaccines

Two major types of vaccines are currently available to veterinarians for administration to their canine patients: *modified-live* vaccines and *inactivated* ("killed") vaccines.

MODIFIED-LIVE VACCINES

Modified-live vaccines contain an *attenuated* (weakened) strain of the particular **pathogen** (disease agent) of concern. Attenuation usually is accomplished by chemical means. Attenuated strains of disease agents have the advantage that they **replicate** (reproduce) within the host, thus increasing the **antigenic** mass (amount of the agent available for the immune system to react against) without producing serious clinical illness, yet still are able to stimulate protective host defenses—defenses that will now be primed to react should the vaccinated animal subsequently encounter the real pathogen. Modified-live vaccines often require only a single dose to provide an immunity that is both solid and long-lasting (a series of initial vaccinations—"puppy shots"—is usually recommended for pups, however, as a safeguard against possible interference with active immunization by residual maternal antibody; *see* "EFFECTS OF MATERNAL IMMUNITY," BELOW). The immunity delivered by modified-live vaccines develops relatively swiftly, and both humoral and cellular immune responses are stimulated (*see* CHAPTER 33, "THE IMMUNE SYSTEM AND DISORDERS"). Modified-live vaccines closely mimic infection with the virulent disease agent and thus provide the best immune stimulation. Currently, modified-live vaccines available for use in dogs include vaccines for canine distemper, infectious canine hepatitis, kennel cough agents (*Bordetella bronchiseptica,* canine parainfluenza virus), and canine parvovirus (*see* TABLE 1).

INACTIVATED ("KILLED") VACCINES

Inactivated vaccines have certain advantages as well. Because they contain inactivated disease agents they are much more stable than are modified-live vaccines (i.e., the infectivity of the agent need not be preserved, just its antigenic mass) and thus have a longer shelf life. Inactivated vaccines never spread from the vaccinated host to other animals, and there is no possibility that they will revert to a virulent form. They are also safe for use in pregnant animals (the developing fetus may be susceptible to damage by some of the disease agents—even though attenuated—present in modified-live vaccines). Although more than a single dose of vaccine is always required and the duration of immunity is generally shorter, inactivated vaccines are regaining importance in this age of retrovirus and her-

pesvirus infections and concern about the safety of genetically customized microorganisms. Inactivated vaccines available for use in dogs include vaccines for rabies, canine parvovirus, canine coronavirus, leptospirosis, *Borrelia burgdorferi* (the Lyme disease agent), and *Bordetella bronchiseptica* (*see* TABLE 1).

Adjuvants (Enhancing the Immune Response)

Devising a successful inactivated vaccine product requires that the agent in the vaccine be completely inert and thus not replicate in the host. Over the years it has become evident that artificial means must be adopted in order to heighten the immune response of the host to such inert inoculated material. The basic mechanics for eliciting this improved immune response were worked out earlier in this century, using certain specialized mixtures to which the vaccine material was then added. These mixtures are called *adjuvants,* from the Latin *adjuvans* ("aiding"). An adjuvant can thus be defined as a substance that nonspecifically enhances the immune response to a given vaccine.

The secret of success of many commercial inactivated vaccines lies in the composition of their adjuvants. A good adjuvant should be safe and produce an earlier, better and more enduring immune response to the inactivated vaccine than can be elicited by the vaccine alone. Unfortunately, the adjuvant component of inactivated vaccines often is responsible for some of the side effects observed following inoculation (e.g., fever, muscle soreness, malaise, vomiting). A really good adjuvant must minimize such side effects while maximizing its immune boost.

Many different substances can serve as vaccine adjuvants. Those such as **aluminum salts** (aluminum hydroxide, aluminum phosphate) and water-in-oil emulsions act apparently by means of vaccine **sequestration**. By slowing release of the vaccine material into the circulation, they provide a lengthened life span for the vaccine in the body and hence greater exposure to reactive immune system cells—the so-called "depot" effect. Sequestration of vaccine at the inoculation site also promotes an influx of immunocompetent cells secondary to inflammation. Despite some minor side effects, aluminum

Table 1
Canine Vaccine Recommendations (primary immunizations)

Disease	Type of Vaccine	Age at First and Second Vaccinations (weeks)	Age at Third Vaccination (weeks)	Revaccination	Route of Administration
Canine distemper	(1) Modified-live CDV	6–8 and 10-12	14–16	Annual	SC or IM
	(2) Modified-live CDV and modified-live MV	6–8[a]	None	None	None
Infectious canine hepatitis	(1) Modified-live CAV-2	6–8 and 10-12	14–16	Annual	SC or IM
Rabies	(1) Inactivated	12 and 64[b]	None	Triennial	IM
Canine parvovirus	(1) Modified-live CPV-2	6–8 and 10-12	14–16[c]	Annual	SC or IM
	(2) Inactivated CPV-2	6–8 and 10-12	14–16[c]	Annual	SC or IM
Kennel cough	(1) Modified-live CPIV	6–8 and 10-12	14–16	Annual	SC or IM
	(2) Inactivated *Bordetella bronchiseptica*	6–8 and 10–12[b]	None	Annual	SC or IM
	(3) Modified-live CPIV and modified-live *Bordetella bronchiseptica*	2 (minimum)	None	Annual, and/or 1 week prior to possible exposure	IN
Leptospirosis[d]	(1) Inactivated	6–8 and 10-12	14–16	Annual	SC or IM
Canine coronavirus[d]	(1) Inactivated	6–8 and 10–12[b]	None	Annual	SC or IM
Lyme borreliosis[d]	(1) Inactivated	6–8 and 10–12[b]	None	Annual	IM

SC = subcutaneous
IM = intramuscular
IN = intranasal
CDV = canine distemper virus
MV = measles virus
CAV-2 = canine adenovirus type 2
CPV-2 = canine parvovirus type 2
CPIV = canine parainfluenza virus
[a]Only a single dose is normally given
[b]Only two doses required for primary immunization
[c]Optional fourth dose at 18–20 weeks to overcome residual maternal immunity
[d]Vaccination against this disease is considered optional

salt-based adjuvants remain among the most popular adjuvants employed in veterinary vaccines. Some newer adjuvants, many of them still in the exploratory stages, act by enhancing the production of **cytokines,** messenger molecules by which cells of the immune system signal one another and direct each other's activities. Cytokines are essential for the development of proper immune responses to a variety of infectious disease agents that may be encountered by the body.

Route of Vaccine Administration

The route by which a vaccine is delivered to the immune system can be an important determinant of successful immunization. "**Immunization**" and "vaccination" are *not* synonymous terms: a dog can be vaccinated—i.e., inoculated with a vaccine—but if the vaccine is unsuccessful at producing an immune response, the dog has not been immunized. Most vaccines for use in dogs, whether attenuated or inactivated, are given either by injection into a muscle (intramuscular route, IM) or under the skin (subcutaneous route, SC) as instructed by the manufacturer. Most rabies vaccines are given by the IM route, while most canine distemper and infectious canine hepatitis vaccines are given by the SC route. Some vaccines for kennel cough agents (*Bordetella bronchiseptica,* canine parainfluenza virus) are given by instillation into the nasal passages (**intranasal** route, IN) in order to stimulate local, secretory IgA immunity (*see* CHAPTER 33, "THE IMMUNE SYSTEM AND DISORDERS"). Vaccines should always be administered according to the manufacturer's directions in order to assure proper immunization.

Effects of Maternal Immunity

Infectious diseases are most common and most serious in young dogs, so this is the obvious group to immunize. Unfortunately, **maternal immunity** (passive systemic immunity) interferes with vaccination for the first four to six weeks of life. Between 6 and 16 weeks of age this inhibitory effect disappears. The exact age of disappearance will vary greatly, however, from one dog to another. Over 95% of pups will have lost their inhibiting maternal immunity by the time they are 14 to 16 weeks of age.

Maternal immunity is the principal reason why young puppies receive a series of vaccinations. Vaccinations are given at intervals throughout the period when maternal immunity is waning. The final vaccination in the series is given when most pups are sure to respond to it (i.e., at 14 to 16 weeks of age). By giving such a series of vaccinations, the period during which the puppies are most susceptible to natural infection is made as brief as possible. For instance, if a pup loses all of its maternal immunity at 7 weeks of age (owing to a low level of antibody transferred from the bitch) and is not

vaccinated until 14 weeks of age, it will be unprotected for a period of 7 weeks—*almost 2 months!* If the puppy had been vaccinated at 8 weeks of age, then this period of relative susceptibility would have lasted only a few weeks.

Maternal immunity against virulent infections disappears earlier than does immunity against vaccine infection; that is, the level of maternal antibody may be low enough such that the pup is susceptible to infection with the actual disease agent should it be encountered, yet still high enough to interfere with immunization by the modified or killed agent in the vaccine (the so-called "window of opportunity"). This finding has important implications for vaccination programs in kennels and other group-housing situations. If there is a high probability of exposure in a particular environment, then many infections can occur during the window of opportunity before the young pups reach a vaccine-responsive age.

AGE AT VACCINATION
Vaccinations are not usually administered before pups are 6 weeks of age. Most younger pups will still have inhibitory levels of maternal immunity and, moreover, their immune systems are still relatively immature. An exception is the use of intranasal *Bordetella bronchiseptica* vaccine, which can be given at 2 weeks of age. *Bordetella* is one of the agents of kennel cough, an infection usually involving the superficial mucous membranes of the upper respiratory tract. Systemic immunity does not influence such membrane infections; immunity instead is mainly of the local IgA type derived from the secretory immune system (*see* CHAPTER 33, "THE IMMUNE SYSTEM AND DISORDERS"). Intranasal vaccines are particularly effective at evoking a localized secretory type of immunity in the respiratory tract.

The length of the interval between vaccinations in the "puppy shot" series after the primary immunization is decided essentially by two major factors: the biology of the immune response and the cost of the vaccine. A secondary, boosting immune response is not nearly as efficient if evoked sooner than 2 to 3 weeks after initial exposure. Cost also dictates as few vaccinations as possible. This usually translates into two or three immunizations, at intervals of 3 to 4 weeks. Any dose of vaccine given subsequent to the primary immunization, or subsequent to natural exposure, is called a **booster**.

The Vaccines

CANINE DISTEMPER VACCINES

Canine distemper is the most important viral infectious disease of dogs. Most infections with canine distemper virus (CDV) appear to be asymptomatic or very mild in nature. In general, clinical signs of distemper are usually observed in younger dogs. Distemper is characterized initially by acute upper respiratory disease signs and fever, and later by more severe respiratory disease signs, vomiting, diarrhea, and neurologic dysfunction. Because distemper is a highly preventable disease, one cannot overemphasize the value of proper immunization.

All available distemper vaccines are prepared with modified-live virus; inactivated CDV is ineffective. The first inoculation is usually given at 6 weeks of age, and then at intervals of 3 to 4 weeks until pups are 16 weeks old. Annual boosters are also recommended.

Distemper-Measles Vaccine

As an alternative to CDV vaccine the combined CDV-measles virus vaccine may be given as the initial dose in the puppy series at 6 to 8 weeks of age. The measles virus fraction of the vaccine can provide limited immunity against clinical distemper in the presence of residual low levels of maternal immunity that would be sufficient to interfere with modified-live canine distemper vaccine virus. Distemper-measles vaccine is designed to provide temporary protection only and is not indicated for immunization of adult dogs.

INFECTIOUS CANINE HEPATITIS VACCINES

Infectious canine hepatitis, caused by canine adenovirus type 1 (CAV-1), has long been confused clinically with distemper. A closely related virus, canine adenovirus type 2 (CAV-2), is a respiratory pathogen and is involved in the kennel cough complex; vaccination of dogs with modified-live CAV-2 provides cross-protection against CAV-1 without producing the unwanted side effect of CAV-1 known as "blue eye." The vaccine usually is given in concert with distemper vaccine, and so the vaccine schedule reflects the schedule for immunization against CDV. Annual booster vaccinations are recommended.

RABIES VACCINES

Rabies is a disease primarily of bats and carnivores, the latter including the domestic dog and cat. In most of the developing nations, domestic dogs remain the primary reservoir hosts for rabies and the principal source of human exposure to the virus. Rabid animals excrete large quantities of rabies virus in their saliva, which accounts for the primary mechanism by which the virus is transmitted—i.e., by the bite of an infected animal. For both animals and people, rabies is an inevitably fatal illness once clinical signs have appeared.

Mass immunization programs for dogs have been employed for many years to control rabies virus spread by creating an "immunological barrier" between wildlife reservoirs of the disease and human beings (dogs frequently acquiring the infection from wildlife hosts and then subsequently transmitting it to human contacts). In the United States and elsewhere, highly effective, inactivated rabies virus vaccines are available for use in domestic animal species. Immunization of dogs and cats remains the best deterrent to the spread of rabies to human populations. All dogs and cats should be vaccinated for rabies at 3 months, again 1 year from the initial inoculation, and then every 3 years or according to individual vaccine specifications. In comprehensive rabies control programs, only vaccines with a 3-year duration of immunity should be used.

CANINE PARVOVIRUS VACCINES

A worldwide outbreak of a severe and sometimes fatal hemorrhagic gastrointestinal disease of domestic dogs was recognized in 1978, and shown to be caused by a wholly new canine disease agent, canine parvovirus type 2 (CPV-2). The virus is now widespread in canine populations throughout the world. Although infected animals may carry and shed the virus for short periods, the general hardiness of the virus and its astonishing ability to persist in the environment for long periods are believed to be of greater importance in perpetuating the disease.

Most severe cases of CPV-2 infection have been recorded in kennels, pet stores, animal shelters, and the so-called "puppy mills." The disease is less frequently seen in the general canine population. Canine parvovirus infection may be difficult to differentiate from a severe coronavirus infection; dual infections with both viruses may occur in up to 20% of cases (of the two disease agents, CPV-2 is by far the more significant).

Dogs that have recovered from CPV-2 infection acquire a solid and long-lasting immunity. Apart from such natural infection, vaccination using one of several commercially produced vaccines is the most practical and efficient means for preventing parvovirus disease. Residual maternal immunity (antibody derived from the bitch's colostrum and milk) can have a profound interfering effect on vaccination against CPV-2 in puppies; thus, in addition to the three standard doses of vaccine usually administered between 6 and 16 weeks of age, an optional fourth inoculation at approximately 18 to 20 weeks of age is often given (a time when maternal immunity will almost certainly have waned sufficiently to permit active immunization). Annual booster inoculations are generally recommended.

Kennel Cough (Tracheobronchitis) Vaccines

Kennel cough (canine acute tracheobronchitis) has been recognized in dogs for many years. It is a highly contagious respiratory disease that occurs worldwide wherever dogs are allowed to congregate. Clinical illness often follows boarding, showing, or sometimes field trials. A dry, harsh "honking" cough (probably due to laryngitis and swelling of the vocal folds) is a characteristic sign and may persist for weeks in untreated or particularly severe cases.

Kennel cough is a disease of multifactorial origin; that is, a virtually identical clinical syndrome of respiratory disease can be produced by several different infectious disease agents, either alone or in combination. The most important agents involved in producing kennel cough include canine parainfluenza virus (CPIV), canine adenovirus type 2 (CAV-2), and the bacterium *Bordetella bronchiseptica*. Many different vaccines incorporating one or more of these three agents are currently available. Some of the products are for parenteral use (injection), while others are designed for intranasal administration. The parenteral and intranasal vaccines can be given in combination without ill effect. But no vaccine should be given to a dog showing clinical signs of illness.

Intranasal vaccines are aimed at stimulating local IgA immunity in the upper respiratory tract, which is believed to be the most effective route of immunization. Owners should be cautioned that in a small percentage of cases, vaccination with an intranasal kennel cough vaccine may produce transient side effects that include sneezing, coughing or nasal discharge. Vaccinated dogs should receive booster intranasal immunizations against kennel cough approximately 1 week before potential exposure (e.g., boarding, showing, etc.) whether they received a primary intranasal inoculation or not. It may boost immunity derived from natural exposure.

With all kennel cough vaccine products, annual booster inoculations are recommended.

Canine Coronavirus Vaccine

Canine coronavirus is the cause of some cases of diarrheal disease in dogs. Infections range in severity from inapparent to fatal, the latter being extremely uncommon. Younger dogs are more severely affected. In most uncomplicated cases recovery without treatment usually occurs within 7 to 10 days. Mixed infections with other agents (particularly canine parvovirus type 2) may also occur. An inactivated coronavirus vaccine is now available. Vaccination against canine coronavirus is considered optional at the present time. Research suggests that vaccination is best reserved for large kennel operations, particularly those having experienced chronic problems with diarrheal disease in pups. An annual booster inoculation is recommended by the manufacturer.

LEPTOSPIROSIS VACCINES

Leptospirosis is a bacterial disease of dogs and other species characterized often by **jaundice** (yellow discoloration of the skin and mucous membranes) secondary to liver disease, impairment of kidney function, and blood clotting abnormalities. The bacterial agents of leptospirosis are perpetuated in nature by a number of wildlife reservoir hosts, including rodents. Transmission occurs by direct contact with infected urine, by biting, and by ingestion of infected tissue. Like rabies, leptospirosis is a **zoonotic disease** (i.e., it can be transmitted from animals to human beings). Leptospirosis vaccines can be effective at preventing severe disease, but they do not prevent infection. Vaccinated dogs thus may still serve as carriers of the causative bacteria, excreting organisms through the urine for many weeks to months. Moreover, the protection against disease that is conferred by vaccination generally lasts for only 3 to 6 months. Improved vaccines against this particular disease are needed.

Leptospirosis **bacterin** (killed bacterial vaccine) is often included in combination products also containing vaccines against distemper, infectious canine hepatitis, and some others.

LYME BORRELIOSIS VACCINE

Lyme borreliosis (Lyme disease) is caused by a spirochete bacterium, *Borrelia burgdorferi,* that can produce illness in both animals and human beings. Both acute and chronic forms of the disease have been reported in dogs, with lameness being a very common presenting clinical sign. The Lyme borreliosis agent is transmitted among hosts by **ixodid** (hard-bodied) **ticks;** direct transmission from one infected individual or animal to another does not occur.

An inactivated vaccine has recently become available. Use is suggested for those dogs living in areas of the country where Lyme borreliosis among their human companions is prevalent.

Diagnostic Tests

by Linda L. Werner

The veterinarian may recommend that diagnostic tests be performed when the cause of an unusually severe or prolonged illness is unexplained by the patient's history and a physical examination. Routine diagnostic tests, such as **radiographs** (X rays), **urinalysis** (physicochemical analysis of a urine sample), examinations for parasites, and simple blood tests can be performed on site at most private veterinary hospitals. Larger group practices, especially those that offer specialist services, frequently can provide other, more advanced diagnostic capabilities. Most practices, however, rely to some extent on veterinary diagnostic laboratory centers, much like those performing human medical diagnostic services. These larger-volume services employ highly trained medical technologists and veterinary clinical pathologists to perform diagnostic tests, to ensure the accuracy (quality control) of testing methods, and to provide an interpretation of test results. Although human medical diagnostic laboratories offer some tests that are appropriate for animals, veterinary laboratories offer the advantage of a frequently lower cost for the same services, as well as special expertise in animal testing. A consultation service for practicing veterinarians usually is provided in addition to the diagnostic test-

ing service. This is especially important because of the unique differences among the many veterinary species with regard to normal laboratory values and their significance.

Veterinary laboratory testing centers use technically sophisticated equipment (**autoanalyzers**) that becomes economical only when there is a high daily volume of test sample submissions. A practical feature of autoanalyzers is their ability to perform many different tests rapidly on individual blood samples. This series of tests, referred to as a **screening test panel,** can provide a tremendous amount of information about patient health in a much more timely, cost-efficient manner than is possible when ordering many individual tests separately.

When diagnostic testing is elected, it is customary to begin with certain routine screening tests. These typically include a **hemogram** (also known as a **complete blood count,** or **CBC**), a chemistry panel, urinalysis, and possibly X rays. Test results are interpreted, always taking into account the patient's history and physical examination findings. Often this can lead to a specific diagnosis. Even if no specific diagnosis of the clinical problem is forthcoming, valuable clues may still be gleaned from the routine test results. Such clues allow the veterinarian to narrow the list of possible causes (**differential diagnoses**) to those that are the most likely in an individual case. Based upon this list of possible diagnoses, certain other less routine tests may then be selected that will be able to furnish more specific information about the particular problem at hand. Such tests might include, for example, a **biopsy** (procedure to obtain a small sample of tissue for microscopic examination or culture), specialized X-ray procedures, or more sophisticated blood tests.

Hemogram (Complete Blood Count)

The hemogram, or CBC, is an essential component of the initial diagnostic evaluation for almost any type of illness. It is also used as a general health screen for identifying any unusual risks to patients prior to the administration of anesthetics or certain other drugs, and/or before performing certain medical procedures.

Approximately one milliliter (ml) of blood is drawn into a tube containing an **anticoagulant** (chemical that prevents blood from clotting). A number of parameters involving both cellular and fluid components of the blood can be analyzed.

RED BLOOD CELL PARAMETERS
Red blood cells (RBCs), also known as **erythrocytes,** are small disk-shaped cells containing an iron-linked, pigmented protein called **hemoglobin.** It is hemoglobin that carries the oxygen required for all normal body functions. The total number of RBCs, their hemoglobin content, and the percentage of total blood volume (**packed cell volume,** or **PCV;** also called the **hematocrit**) they occupy are included in the CBC report. Any abnormalities in size, shape, color or appearance of the cells are also noted. The RBC parameters are most useful for the detection and diagnosis of many types of **anemia** (low RBC count, reduced PCV, or reduced hemoglobin levels).

WHITE BLOOD CELL PARAMETERS
White blood cells (WBCs), also known as **leukocytes,** are larger than RBC's and are responsible for fighting infection. WBC's thus represent an essential component of the immune system. There are several different types of WBCs that are enumerated in the CBC by total cell counts and by the percentages of the different cells present (**differential WBC count**). Alterations in WBCs frequently accompany many different types of infection or inflammation in fairly predictable patterns. Occasionally, evidence of hormonal imbalance, parasitism, defective immunity, or malignancy involving blood cells (*leukemia*) may be detected. (*See* CHAPTER 33 "THE IMMUNE SYSTEM AND DISORDERS.")

PLATELETS
Platelets are the smallest cells in the blood. They respond very rapidly to injuries that cause bleeding, by adhering to ruptured blood vessel walls and forming a seal or clot with the aid of certain noncellular blood constituents called **clotting factors.** Abnormally low or high platelet counts are found in a number of clinical disorders and can be the cause of abnormal bleeding or excessive clotting, respectively.

NONCELLULAR ELEMENTS
The noncellular elements measured in the hemogram include proteins and other substances within the fluid portion (**plasma**) of an unclotted blood sample. Decreased amounts of *plasma proteins* can be found in blood loss or in liver, kidney, or gastrointestinal disorders, while increased quantities may be produced in certain types of cancer, chronic inflammation, or infection.

The hemogram in and of itself can on occasion provide a specific diagnosis, such as iron deficiency anemia or a blood parasite infection. More commonly, abnormalities on a hemogram point to a more general diagnosis such as chronic inflammation or anemia of unknown cause. These clues afford a rational basis for further testing, in order to determine the exact cause of the clinical and laboratory abnormalities.

In addition to the routine hemogram, certain laboratories also offer blood-typing and cross-matching for blood transfusion purposes; tests for blood-clotting function; and evaluation of bone marrow samples (*see* "CYTOLOGIC EVALUATION [CYTOLOGY] AND FLUID ANALYSIS," BELOW).

Chemistry Panel

The chemistry panel is often included along with the hemogram as an initial screening procedure for any unexplained or lingering illness. It consists of a large number of assays for different substances in the fluid portion of blood. These substances can be found in normal levels in health and in abnormal levels in various disease states.

A chemistry panel provides a large amount of information pertaining to different organ functions. A dozen or more substances are measured using the fluid portion of a blood sample that has been allowed to clot, so that the blood cells and clotting factors are discarded; the fluid that remains is known as **serum** (as opposed to plasma, which is blood fluid with clotting factor proteins intact). Abnormal quantities of the substances measured can point to damage or dysfunction involving the kidneys, liver, muscles, glandular or digestive functions, and various other aspects of body metabolism. Blood sugar (**glucose**), **blood urea nitrogen** (**BUN,** most important in kidney function), cholesterol, and various liver enzymes are among the more common parameters reported on the chemistry panel. Key serum proteins such as **globulins** (which are rich in protective antibodies) are also measured as a group in panel testing. Sustained, highly abnormal serum chemistry values often are an indication to perform more specific tests to determine, if possible, the exact cause or extent of the organ dysfunction involved, and to predict the clinical outcome (the **prognosis**) for the patient.

Biochemical tests can also be performed to evaluate blood levels of hormones, such as thyroid hormone and insulin, minerals such as iron, and many types of toxins.

Urinalysis

Urinalysis is an important screening test for kidney abnormalities and for other problems within the urinary tract. Common clinical signs include increased thirst, increases in frequency of urination or in urine volume, pain, reluctance to urinate, straining upon urination, and abnormal odor or color of voided urine. For routine urinalysis a test strip or "dipstick" is inserted into the test urine. The dipstick can detect certain biochemical abnormalities including the presence of sugar, protein or blood in the urine by producing color changes in specific areas of the strip. The dipstick, together with a small, handheld device

called a **refractometer,** can be used to estimate how concentrated or dilute a urine sample is (a measurement referred to as urine **specific gravity**). Since the kidneys must function properly to produce highly concentrated urine when fluid intake is low (for water conservation) and, conversely, must also allow for the elimination of surplus fluid by making the urine very dilute, measurement of urine specific gravity can provide a rough evaluation of kidney function.

An important part of the routine urinalysis is the microscopic examination of urine sediment. The sediment is obtained by **centrifuging** (spinning at high speed) a urine sample in a tube and collecting the material that is pelleted out at the bottom of the tube. The sediment examination is useful for visualizing bacteria, WBCs, or other evidence of urinary tract infection. Occasionally, microscopic evidence of kidney disease or cancer of the urinary tract can be discovered on a sediment exam.

In selected instances the veterinarian may choose to submit a urine sample for bacterial culture. The accuracy of the results can be affected by the method used to obtain the urine sample. When a cup or other container is used to collect urine as the dog urinates (**free-catch** method), the results may be inconclusive for determining whether a bacterial infection is present. The veterinarian may request that the urine specimen be obtained by inserting a sterile *urinary catheter* (flexible tube for insertion) through the **urethra** (the passage connecting the bladder with the exterior of the body) and into the bladder, or by inserting a small-gauge needle through the lower abdominal wall directly into the bladder (a procedure known as **cystocentesis**) and withdrawing the urine into a syringe. Both of these procedures are well tolerated by most dogs without sedation. They offer the advantage of obtaining a fresh urine specimen quickly and easily without the contamination by bacteria or debris that commonly occurs using the free-catch method of collection.

Parasitology

The common internal parasites of dogs include a variety of intestinal parasites such as roundworms, tapeworms and hookworms, as well as a mosquito-borne parasite that lodges within the heart and pulmonary arteries, the heartworm.

(*See* CHAPTER 37, "INTERNAL PARASITES," and CHAPTER 24, "THE CIRCULATORY SYSTEM AND DISORDERS.") The routine tests for internal parasites include a special preparation of fresh feces called a **fecal flotation.** With the exception of tapeworm segments, the adult parasites living in the intestinal tract are seldom shed or seen in the stool. Instead, the parasites produce eggs or **larvae** (immature forms or stages) that are shed in the feces but are too small to be seen without a microscope. The liquid test mixture for the fecal flotation allows the parasite eggs to float upward toward the surface and onto a microscope slide placed over the specimen vial, while the sediment and debris settle to the bottom. The slide is then placed under a microscope for identification of any eggs or larvae that may be present. Although a quick screening test for intestinal parasites is often performed by examining a direct smear of a very small amount of unprocessed stool, such an examination is not thorough. If a direct smear is negative, a flotation test using a larger volume of feces should then be performed.

Routine heartworm testing is now an integral part of canine health care and disease prevention programs in many areas of the United States and abroad. This test is required not only for diagnosis and treatment of heartworm disease, but also to ensure the absence of heartworm infestation prior to placing a dog on long-term preventive medication. The common blood tests for heartworm are the **Knott's** and **Difil** tests. Both represent methods of processing the blood to concentrate any heartworm prelarval forms (known as **microfilariae**) so that they are more readily visible under the microscope. Occasionally microfilariae are so abundant in the circulation that they can be observed by direct microscopic examination of a drop of unprocessed blood (a negative result with this test method should always be followed up with the Knott's or Difil test, however). Some highly mosquito-infested regions have such a high prevalence of heartworm transmission that two negative tests are recommended to ensure absence of microfiliariae. There are occasional instances of adult heartworm infestation wherein the microfilariae cannot be found in the blood, either because they are not being produced or because they are continually being destroyed by the host's immune response. If the veterinarian suspects that the clinical signs in a dog are due to heartworm disease, but two routine heartworm tests are both negative for microfilariae, radiographs of the chest may be taken to identify abnormalities considered quite typical for heartworm disease. In addition, a serum sample can be tested by newer methods for evidence of heartworm infestation (*see* "VIROLOGY, IMMUNOLOGY AND SEROLOGY," BELOW).

Common external parasites of dogs include fleas, ticks and two types of mites that are not visible without the aid of a microscope. (*See* CHAPTER 23, "EXTERNAL PARASITES.") Tests to detect the presence of skin mites are routinely performed by scraping several areas of skin with a spatula or surgical blade. The dead skin cells, along with any mites or debris, are smeared on a microscopic slide with a drop of oil or salt solution. Both superficial and slightly deeper scrapings that may ooze a very small amount of blood are required, because skin mites that burrow deeply into the skin may be difficult to find. It is not unusual for several office visits and multiple scrapings of the skin to be required in order to arrive at a diagnosis. Skin scrapings and plucked hairs placed in a special clearing solution can also be examined microscopically for the presence of skin fungi (**dermatophytes**) causing a variety of skin lesions, of which **ringworm** is a common example. (*See* CHAPTER 22, "THE SKIN AND DISORDERS.")

Microbiology

The field of microbiology involves the study of microscopic organisms and infectious disease agents, including bacteria, fungi, viruses and protozoa. Diagnostic microbiology is aimed at identifying disease-producing infectious agents in patients exhibiting clinical signs of infection.

Blood, other body fluids, and tissue samples are all appropriate specimens for microbiologic testing. These specimens must be collected into sterilized containers, syringes or tubes that are not contaminated with organisms found normally in or on the body or on environmental surfaces. Routine tests include microscopic examination of specimen smears stained in a variety of ways to enhance the appearance and distinguishing characteristics of different types of organisms. For bacteria, the **Gram stain** is the routine initial identification step. When a more specific identification of bacteria or fungi is required in order to determine the most appropriate therapy, laboratory cultures of the specimen are made. These entail mixing or inoculating the specimen onto a solid (**agar**) or liquid (**broth**) medium, which contains special ingredients either to enhance or inhibit the growth of certain types of organisms. The growth characteristics of the organisms found after a day or two of incubation then allow for more exact identification.

In addition to culture for the purpose of identification, **antibiotic sensitivity testing** can be performed to determine the effect of different antibiotics on the growth of the bacterium involved. If it is found that the organism is resistant to the antibiotic chosen for treatment, a more appropriate selection can be made based on the results of the sensitivity testing. When a more precisely quantitative assessment of the efficacy of antibiotics on a bacterium is performed, the veterinarian can select the lowest effective dose (**minimal inhibitory concentration,** or **MIC**) of the most economical antibiotic choice, minimizing as well any possible side effects of the medication. This type of specialized testing is generally reserved for recurrent infections or infections that do not respond well to routine antibiotic therapy.

Virology, Immunology, and Serology

Viruses are much too small to be visible with ordinary microscopes, and the laboratory conditions required to culture and identify them are much too involved and impractical for routine use in private veterinary hospitals. Other types of infectious disease agents, such as the protozoan *Toxoplasma* and certain fungi, cannot always be found using microscopy or culture. Therefore, alternative testing methods involving the use of antibodies have become standard in the diagnosis of illness caused by these types of **pathogens** (disease-causing agents).

The application of serum **antibodies** (also referred to more generally as **immune serum**) to detect viruses or other infectious disease agents is known as **serologic testing,** or **serology.** In serologic testing, antibodies known to bind only to a particular disease agent can be used, sometimes along with enzymes or dyes, in a test system that will show a positive color reaction if antibody binding has occurred. This is referred to as an antigen-antibody reaction, the **antigen** (commonly a unique protein) being that part of the disease agent to which the antibody attaches. (*See* Chapter 33, "The Immune System and Disorders.") Such tests can be designed to detect either the disease agent itself, or, alternatively, high **titers** (levels) of antibody to the agent, indicating that the patient has mounted a specific immune response.

Whole blood, serum, other body fluids, and processed tissue specimens all may be suitable samples to submit for testing, depending upon the body location of the suspected infection. Smears made on glass slides can also be stained with antibody-containing solutions (**immunostaining**) and examined under a microscope for a color change. An example of this technique has been used in the diagnosis of distemper, looking for large accumulations of distemper virus proteins in cells swabbed from the inner surface of the eyelids.

Liquid samples can be added to small wells in plastic plates coated with either antibody or antigen, in a type of enzyme test called an **enzyme-linked immunosorbent assay** (**ELISA**). Common examples of ELISA tests in canine medicine include tests for canine parvovirus type 2 infection and heartworm disease.

A group of immunologic disorders called *autoimmune diseases* are caused by a failure of the immune system to remain nonreactive (**tolerant**) to the body's own cells. In an autoimmune disease, the patient develops destructive immune responses targeted to one or more body tissues. Frequently this involves the production of autoantibodies and can result in damage to the patient's RBCs, skin, kidneys, and/or joints. There are a variety of immunologic tests available for diagnosing such autoimmune disorders as rheumatoid arthritis and systemic lupus erythematosus (SLE) (*see* Chapter 33, "The Immune System and Disorders"). The **rheumatoid factor (RF)** test and the **antinuclear antibody (ANA) test,** respectively, are screening tests that can aid in making the diagnosis of these two diseases. However, neither diagnosis can be made based solely upon the results of such tests, because they are not as highly specific as many other types of assays. Tests for autoantibodies to RBCs (**Coombs' test**) or to blood platelets are commonly performed to diagnose certain types of anemias and platelet deficiencies.

Many other diagnostic tests are available to evaluate those rare patients suspected of having abnormal or insufficient protective immunity. Immune function tests are not widely available for animal diagnostics, but university veterinary colleges often can provide excellent nonroutine diagnostic services, as well as referral services for private veterinary hospitals.

Cytologic Evaluation (Cytology) and Fluid Analysis

Cytologic evaluation (**cytology**) refers to the microscopic examination of tissue or body fluid specimens fixed onto glass microscope slides and stained to enhance cellular detail. Most often the material for examination is *aspirated* from the tissue in question, frequently a lump or swelling, by drawing it through a fine-gauge needle attached to a syringe (**fine-needle aspirate**, or **aspiration smear**). This procedure offers fairly rapid results and is often the preferred routine screening test to identify inflammatory or infected lesions, benign cysts, and various types of cancer.

The population of cells present on cytologic examination can vary tremendously: various WBCs representing inflammation or infection; different types of microorganisms, such as bacteria or fungi; RBCs, indicating recent hemorrhage; and immature or neoplastic cells representing cancer. Cytologic examination may provide a specific diagnosis, such as bacterial abscess or mammary gland carcinoma, or it may yield a more general diagnosis such as inflammation or cancer of unknown type.

Routine cytologic examination offers the advantage of rapid return of results to the veterinarian, usually within 24 hours or less. Fine-needle aspiration represents a relatively noninvasive, low-risk, nonpainful procedure that can be performed in most cases on an outpatient basis. Sedation of the patient is seldom required. Depending upon the results of the cytology report, further tests such as culture or biopsy may then be recommended. Sometimes a biopsy may be recommended to confirm or classify suspected cancerous lesions more accurately (*see* "HISTOPATHOLOGY," BELOW).

Cytologic evaluation may also be carried out on bone marrow samples from patients exhibiting unresolved or unexplained deficiencies in any of the cellular elements of the blood (i.e., RBCs, WBCs or platelets). These cells are all produced by the active proliferation of precursor or "parent" cells in the bone marrow as part of a normal ongoing process known as **hematopoiesis.** Many types of diseases are the result of defects in hematopoiesis. When hematopoiesis proceeds unchecked by the usual control mechanisms for cell growth, leukemias can develop (*see* CHAPTER 33, "THE IMMUNE SYSTEM AND DISORDERS"). A bone marrow examination thus is essential for the diagnosis and prognosis of leukemia.

Fluid analysis is performed on various body fluids present in certain locations such as the spinal canal or skull cavity (**cerebrospinal fluid [CSF]**) or joint spaces (*joint,* or **synovial, fluid**). Various disease conditions such as trauma, hemorrhage and infection can cause neurologic or joint diseases. Fluid alterations involving excessive fluid quantity, abnormal fluid consistency or color, or changes in certain chemical components of the fluid such as protein or glucose are routinely reported as a part of the fluid analysis result. In addition, routine cytologic examination is performed on the fluid to search for the cause of any reported abnormalities. Abnormal accumulations of fluid in body cavities, such as the chest or abdomen, are also analyzed in this way.

Histopathology

Histopathology refers to the microscopic examination of thin sections cut from tissues or organs at biopsy or during a postmortem examination (**necropsy**). The sections are fixed onto glass microscope slides and stained to enhance detail. Histopathologic evaluation has the advantage of providing information about the organization of cells within the tissue and their relationship to each other and to the overall tissue architecture. Thus, the degree or pattern of spread of an infection or tumor within a particular tissue can be more readily examined by histopathology than by cytologic examination alone. In addition, the degree of tissue damage and/or healing can also be assessed. Many biopsy specimens can be obtained with the patient fully awake, using a local anesthetic similar to novocaine and a specialized small-bore biopsy needle to obtain a **core biopsy.** When more tissue is required or a surgical procedure is necessary to obtain the biopsy, a general anesthetic must be used. Generally, several days to a week will be required for the biopsy report to be issued from the diagnostic pathologist to the attending veterinarian.

Radiology, Special Diagnostic Imaging, and Electrodiagnostics

Radiographs (X rays) are detailed black-and-white film pictures that can reveal anatomic changes such as increased or decreased organ size or irregular organ structure; bone abnormalities; displaced organs; growing masses; or abnormal fluid or air accumulations. Most private veterinary hospitals are equipped to take and evaluate radiographs on site. Occasionally the films may be sent to a specialist, a veterinary radiologist, for review or a consultation. Some specialized radiographic procedures (for example, contrast studies using barium to improve detail within the gastrointestinal tract) are also routinely performed in most veterinary practices. Animals may be referred to a veterinary radiologist or a university veterinary teaching hospital for other, nonroutine radiologic studies, such as dye injection into blood vessels (**angiography**) or the spinal canal (**myelography**), or, less commonly, for special diagnostic imaging. This latter category includes **computerized axial tomography (CAT** or **CT scan)** and **nuclear magnetic resonance imaging (NMR** or **MRI)**. Special imaging techniques offer the advantage of supplying much greater detail so that lesions too small to appear on normal radiographs may be identified. Application of newer technologies such as the CAT scan and NMR remains limited in veterinary medicine at present, however, mainly because of expense.

Another special imaging technique offered by increasing numbers of veterinary practitioners and specialists is **ultrasonography (ultrasound examination)**. This procedure uses sound waves to produce both stationary and moving images of internal organs, such as the heart (**echocardiography**). Ultrasound examination is commonly used to identify internal irregularities and to guide a biopsy instrument to the appropriate site within the body (**ultrasound-guided biopsy**). This can improve both the safety and accuracy of internal biopsy procedures. Functional abnormalities of certain organs can also be identified, such as heart failure or foreign-body obstruction of the gastrointestinal tract.

Endoscopy is a method of enhancing visualization of internal body structures through the use of specialized lighting and magnification devices housed within rigid or flexible tubes, which can be inserted and guided into such areas as the nasal cavity (**rhinoscopy**), trachea (**bronchoscopy**), or accessible regions of the gastrointestinal tract such as the stomach or colon (**gastroscopy, colonoscopy**). Such services are routine usually only in specialist hospitals or at university veterinary teaching hospitals. They are particularly useful for locating lesions and obtaining samples for culture, cytology or biopsy.

A common example of an electrodiagnostic procedure is the **electrocardiogram (ECG)**, which detects the electrical impulses generated by the beating heart and translates them into a recorded tracing on moving paper or a screen monitor. An ECG can provide information about the size of the heart and irregularities of the heartbeat. Along with radiographs, the ECG is considered a routine diagnostic tool for diagnosing heart disease. ECG services are offered by many general practitioners as well as by specialist veterinary hospitals. ECGs are also used to monitor high-risk patients undergoing general anesthesia, and critically ill or injured patients in intensive care. (*See* CHAPTER 24, "THE CIRCULATORY SYSTEM AND DISORDERS.")

Less routinely available electrodiagnostic procedures include **electroencephalography (EEG)** and **electromyography (EMG)** for evaluation of the electrical activity of the brain, nerves and muscles in animals exhibiting signs of neuromuscular disease. As with the special imaging techniques and the ECG described above, performance and interpretation of the results of these procedures require a level of advanced training. EEG and EMG evaluations usually are offered only by certified veterinary neurologists or internists. Likewise the **electroretinogram (ERG)**, an electrical examination of the **retina** (the light-sensitive layers of cells at the back of the eye), is available only through certified veterinary ophthalmologists.

Glossary

Compiled by Jeffrey E. Barlough

abdominal palpation. Applying light pressure to the surface of the abdomen, using the hand and fingers, in order to detect abnormalities within the abdominal cavity.

abiotrophy. Progressive loss of tissue or organ function.

abnormal host. A host infected with a parasite normally found in another host species.

abscess. A walled-off lesion filled with pus.

acanthosis nigricans of Dachshunds. Rare disease of Dachshunds, characterized by hair loss, hyperpigmentation and lichenification.

acariasis. General term for a mite infestation.

accomodation. Ability of the lens to change its shape in order to focus vision effectively on objects at different distances from the eye.

acetylcholine (ACh). Messenger molecule released from axon terminals by a nerve impulse; responsible for transmission of the nerve impulse across the synaptic cleft to the muscle fiber supplied by the nerve.

acetylcholinesterase. Enzyme capable of breaking down acetylcholine.

achondroplasia. A condition of dwarfism characterized by shortening of the limbs.

acquired pattern alopecia. Relatively common skin disease of Dachshunds and certain other breeds, characterized by a gradual, somewhat symmetrical loss of hair on the ears and elsewhere; also called pattern baldness.

acral lick dermatitis. Skin condition caused by prolonged licking at a specific area, usually a leg or paw; also called lick granuloma.

acrodermatitis. Inherited, inevitably fatal disorder characterized by progressively worsening skin inflammation, diminished mental capabilities, inflamed ears and diarrhea.

acromegaly. Chronic disease caused by persistent, excessive secretion of growth hormone in adult dogs; characterized by overgrowth of connective tissue, bone and viscera.

actin. A vital protein component of muscle, one of the proteins responsible for muscle contraction.

actinic keratoses. Single or multiple, firm, elevated, plaque- or papule-like skin lesions that result from excessive exposure to sunlight; considered to be pre-cancerous lesions.

actinomycosis. Pus-producing diseases caused by bacteria of the genus *Actinomyces*.

active immunization. Vaccination.

acute. Of short duration and relatively severe; having a rapid onset.

acute hemorrhagic enterocolitis and gastroenteritis. Disease of smaller breeds of dogs characterized by acute onset of bloody diarrhea.

ad libitum. Free-choice; at will.

Addison's disease. Hypoadrenocorticism; insufficient secretory activity by the adrenal cortex.

adenocarcinoma. Any malignant tumor originating in glandular tissue.

adenoma. Any benign tumor originating in glandular tissue.

adenosine triphosphate (ATP). The major form of energy used by cells in the body.

adhesion. A fusion or sticking together of surfaces.

adipsia. The absence of thirst; avoidance of drinking.

adjuvants. Substances that nonspecifically stimulate immune responses; used in inactivated vaccines to prolong the immune response to vaccine components.

adjuvant chemotherapy. Use of anticancer drugs following surgical or radiation treatments in an effort to destroy residual (microscopic) tumor cells that may have been left behind.

adrenal cortex. The outer layer of the adrenal glands.

adrenal glands. Glands located adjacent to the kidneys, involved in the secretion of several important hormones including cortisol, corticosterone, aldosterone, and epinephrine (adrenaline).

adrenaline (epinephrine). A hormone secreted by the adrenal glands; it acts to increase blood sugar levels and blood pressure and to accelerate the heart rate.

adrenocorticotropic hormone (ACTH). A hormone produced by the pituitary gland in the brain; it exerts a controlling function over the cortex (external portion) of the adrenal glands.

adsorb. To bind to a surface.

adulticide. Medication to kill adult worms.

aerobic. Requiring the presence of oxygen to grow.

aerosol exposure. Exposure to an infectious agent by means of contaminated moisture droplets drifting in the air.

aerosol therapy. Treatment in which drug therapy (antibiotic or other compound) is delivered by misting or spraying the drug into the airways, usually by means of a funnel or cone placed over the nose; useful in treating pneumonia and certain other respiratory ailments. Also called *nebulization.*

alanine aminotransferase (ALT, SGPT). A liver-cell enzyme; increased levels in the bloodstream are indicative of liver-cell injury.

albumin. A major protein component of the blood plasma, important in maintaining osmotic pressure within the blood vasculature and as a transport protein for many substances.

aldosterone. A hormone secreted by the adrenal cortex; important in the regulation of sodium and potassium levels and, in turn, in retaining water within the body.

algae (singular: alga). Single-celled organisms that include seaweed, many freshwater plants, and certain opportunistic pathogens such as *Prototheca.*

allantoin. A highly soluble end product of nucleic acid metabolism, normally excreted in the urine.

allele. An alternative form of a given gene. For each gene there are two alleles, one on each chromosome of a chromosome pair. One allele is inherited from the mother, the other from the father.

allergen. Any substance that can induce an allergic reaction.

allergenic. Inducing allergy.

allergic bronchitis. Allergic inflammation of the bronchi.

allergic colitis. Allergic inflammation of the colon, associated with the ingestion of dietary allergens.

allergic contact dermatitis. An uncommon skin disease caused by a hypersensitivity reaction, as occurs in hikers and backpackers following contact with poison ivy or poison oak.

allergic enteritis. Allergic inflammation of the small intestine, associated with the ingestion of dietary allergens.

allergic gastritis. Allergic inflammation of the stomach, associated with ingestion of dietary allergens.

allergic pneumonitis. Subacute or chronic allergic inflammation of the small bronchioles and alveoli in the lungs, associated with a profound eosinophilia (increased numbers of eosinophils in the blood); most probably associated with inhalant allergens or with heartworm infestation. Also known as pulmonary infiltrates with eosinophilia (PIE) syndrome.

allergic rhinitis. Allergic inflammation of the nasal passages; seasonal in occurrence, associated with the inhalation of allergens.

allergy. A hypersensitive state of the immune response, wherein exposure to a particular substance (an allergen) results in a noxious and sometimes physically harmful immunologic response.

allograft. Tissue graft obtained from an individual of the same species as the recipient.

allopurinol. A medication that acts to decrease the amount of uric acid in urine.

alopecia. Absence or loss of hair.

alveolar crestal bone. The "collar" of bone encircling the neck of each tooth.

alveoli. Small air sacs comprising the innermost structure of the lungs. It is through the delicate walls of the alveoli that gas exchange occurs between the blood (flowing through the pulmonary capillaries) and the inhaled or exhaled air.

amalgam. A restorative for filling cavities in teeth; it is an alloy of mercury, copper, silver, zinc, tin and other metals.

amastigote. Tissue form of trypanosome parasites such as *Trypanosoma cruzi,* the cause of Chagas' disease.

American trypanosomiasis. Alternative term for Chagas' disease, caused by the protozoan parasite *Trypanosoma cruzi.*

amino acids. Nitrogen-containing molecules that form the structural backbone of proteins. All amino acids contain both an amino group (NH_2) and a carboxyl group (COOH).

ammonia. A waste product of protein metabolism; normally excreted through the kidneys.

amylase. Enzyme produced by the salivary glands and pancreas that breaks down carbohydrates.

amyloid. An insoluble protein substance that causes disease (amyloidosis) when deposited in large quantities in tissues.

amyloidosis. Disease process characterized by deposition of amyloid in various tissues of the body, including the kidneys.

anabolism. The body's conversion of simple substances to more complex compounds.

anaerobic. Able to grow in the absence of oxygen.

anagen. The phase of hair follicle activity during which hair is actively being produced.

analgesics. Pain-killing medications.

anamnestic response. Immunologic memory; the ability of the immune system to "remember" a foreign substance to which it has been exposed, and to produce an even more effective response to it upon subsequent reexposure.

anaphylactic reaction (anaphylaxis). A rapidly-developing, exaggerated (and sometimes life-threatening) allergic reaction.

anatomy. The study of body structure.

androgens. Male sex hormones; the primary one, testosterone.

anemia. Low red blood cell count, reduced hemoglobin levels, or reduced volume of packed red cells.

anemic dwarfism. A syndrome of short-limbed dwarfism and mild anemia occurring in Alaskan Malamutes.

anestrus. The sexually inactive period between two estrus cycles.

angioedema. Recurrent wheals or welts in the skin, caused by dilation and/or increased permeability of capillaries.

angiography. The radiographic visualization of blood vessels, accomplished by the intravenous injection of a contrast medium that allows the shape and course of the vessels to be delineated on X-ray examination.

ankyloblepharon. Failure of one or both eyelids of the newborn to open at the appropriate time.

ankylosis. The immobility and consolidation of a joint, secondary to trauma, infection or surgery.

annelids. Segmented worms, such as earthworms.

anorectic. Having no appetite.

anorexia. Loss of appetite; inappetence.

antemortem. Before death.

anterior chamber. The fluid-filled space at the front of the eye, situated between the cornea and the iris.

anterior uvea. The iris and ciliary body of the eye.

anterior uveitis. Inflammation of the iris and ciliary body of the eye.

anthelmintic. Any deworming medication.

anthropomorphism. The tendency to infuse a human persona into an animal, or to interpret an animal's behavior in human terms.

antibiotic. A chemical substance produced by microorganisms that is capable of inhibiting or killing other microorganisms; many antibiotics are used medically for the treatment of serious bacterial infections. Examples of antibiotics include penicillin, tetracycline, and gentamicin.

antibiotic sensitivity testing. Laboratory test procedure for identifying the sensitivity or resistance of a bacterial isolate to several antibiotics.

antibodies (immunoglobulins). Specialized proteins produced by cells of the immune system in response to the presence of foreign material (bacteria, viruses, toxins, etc.); antibodies are capable of binding to the foreign material and thus alerting other immune cells to its presence.

anticoagulant. Chemical that prevents blood from clotting.

antidiuretic hormone (ADH). Pituitary gland hormone that controls water resorption by the kidneys, urine production and concentration, and water balance; also called *vasopressin.*

antiemetics. Medications for controlling vomiting.

antifungal. A chemical substance produced by microorganisms or by other means, useful in the treatment of fungal infections.

antigen. A substance capable of inducing a specific immune response in the body, by binding to a specific antibody; can be a property of bacteria, viruses, other foreign proteins, or even host tissue cells.

antigenic. Having the properties of an antigen.

antimicrobial. Killing or suppressing the growth of microorganisms; also, any antibiotic or antifungal medication.

antinuclear antibody (ANA) test. Test that detects autoantibodies against the DNA of cell nuclei; used as an aid in the diagnosis of systemic lupus erythematosus (SLE, lupus).

antioxidants. Substances, such as vitamin E and selenium, that protect cells against damage caused by byproducts of normal metabolic processes.

antiserum. Serum that contains high levels of antibodies specific for a particular antigen of interest.

antispasmodics. Medications to prevent spasms of the gastrointestinal tract.

antitussives. Cough suppressants.

anuria. Complete cessation of urine production.

aorta. The great vessel arising from the left ventricle of the heart, which feeds blood through the arterial system into the body.

aortic stenosis. Constriction (abnormal narrowing) of the connection between the left ventricle and the aorta.

aortic valve. The semilunar valve on the left side of the heart.

aplasia. Imperfect development or absence of a tissue or organ.

apnea. Cessation of breathing.

apocrine cyst. Cyst caused by obstruction of a sweat gland.

apocrine sweat glands. Sweat glands that empty their contents into an associated hair follicle; they are found throughout the body and produce a scented, fluid secretion that may play a role as a sexual attractant.

appendicular skeleton. That portion of the skeleton composed of the bones forming the limbs and pelvis.

aqueous humor. The fluid occupying the anterior and posterior chambers of the eye.

arachidonic acid. An essential fatty acid found in animal fats; a precursor in the biosynthesis of compounds such as the prostaglandins.

arborize. To branch.

area centralis. Specialized area of the retina, near the optic disk, that possesses an abundance of cone photoreceptors and is largely responsible for the most precise and accurate vision.

argasid ticks. Soft-bodied ticks; distinguished from **ixodid** (hard-bodied) **ticks.**

arrector pili. Muscles in the skin that cause the hair to stand erect.

arrhythmia. Any alteration of the normal heartbeat.

arteries. Thick, muscular vessels that drive oxygenated blood from the heart toward the tissues.

arterioles. Small arteries.

arteritis. Inflammation of an artery.

arthritis. Joint inflammation.

arthropathy. Any joint disease.

arthropod. An invertebrate organism with a hard outer skeleton (exoskeleton) and a segmented body; examples include insects, spiders and crustaceans.

arthrospores. Infective units of the filamentous mold form of the fungal pathogen *Coccidioides immitis,* the cause of coccidioidomycosis ("valley fever").

articular cartilage. Cartilage found within joint structures.

ascariasis. Any ascarid infestation.

ascarid. Type of roundworm commonly infecting dogs, e.g., *Toxocara canis.*

ascites. The accumulation of fluid within the abdominal cavity.

ascorbic acid. Vitamin C.

aspartate aminotransferase (AST, SGOT). A liver-cell enzyme that is also found in muscle cells and red blood cells.

aspermogenesis. Failure to produce sperm.

aspirate. The removal of fluid from a tissue or cavity by means of a syringe and needle.

aspiration pneumonia. Pneumonia caused by accidental inhalation of food or other material into the lungs.

aspiration smear. Diagnostic procedure in which fluid, containing cells, is withdrawn from a tissue or body cavity and then smeared onto a glass microscope slide for examination.

asteroid hyalosis. Common degenerative disorder of the vitreous body (of the eye), characterized by the formation within it of many small, opaque, spherical, refractile bodies composed of calcium and fat.

asthma. A severe, usually allergic reaction resulting in bronchial airway obstruction and life-threatening respiratory distress; common in human beings, but not known to occur in dogs.

asymptomatic. Not exhibiting clinical signs.

ataxia. Incoordination.

atopic dermatitis. A common, heritable hypersensitivity to pollens or other environmental allergens, which results clinically in immunologic and inflammatory reactions in the skin.

atopy. An inherited predisposition toward the development of allergy.

atresia. Congenital absence or occlusion of an orifice or tubular organ.

atrial septal defect (ASD). Rare congenital defect characterized by the presence of a hole in the wall, or **septum,** separating the left and right atria of the heart.

atrioventricular (AV) node. The heart region electrically connecting the atria and ventricles; it slows the conduction of the depolarization wave so that a short period of time is interposed between atrial and ventricular contractions.

atrioventricular (AV) valves. The heart valves that separate each atrium from its corresponding ventricle. The A V valve on the right side of the heart is known as the **tricuspid valve,** and the corresponding valve on the left side is called the **mitral valve.**

atrium (plural: **atria**). One of the two upper chambers of the heart.

atrophia bulbi. Shrinkage or wasting of the eyeball following an attack of ocular inflammation.

atrophy. Shrinking or wasting of a tissue or organ.

atropine. An alkaloid drug that relaxes smooth muscle, increases the heart rate, and in the eye causes dilation of the pupil.

auditory ossicles. Tiny bones in the middle ear that are responsible for transmitting the vibrations of the eardrum to the inner ear.

auscult (auscultate). To listen to the inner sounds of the chest or abdomen with the aid of a stethoscope.

autoanalyzers. Automated equipment for performing serum chemistry panels.

autoantibody. An antibody directed against "self," i.e., against the body.

autoimmune hemolytic anemia (AIHA). Immune-mediated disease wherein broadly cross-reactive autoantibodies called **hemagglutinins** attach to red blood cells, resulting in their immunologic destruction and subsequent anemia.

autoimmune neutropenia. An immune-mediated disease characterized by high fever, depression and decreased levels of circulating neutrophils.

autoimmune response. An inappropriate immune response, directed against the body's own tissues.

autoimmune thrombocytopenia. An immune-mediated disease characterized by hemorrhages caused by decreased numbers of blood platelets (clotting cells) in the circulation.

autonomic nervous system. That part of the nervous system involved in the regulation of the heartbeat, glandular secretions, and smooth muscle contraction and relaxation, and generally not subject to conscious control.

autonomously. Uncontrollably.

autosomal. Referring to any of the chromosomes, excluding the sex chromosomes.

avidin. A constituent protein of egg whites that can impair absorption of the vitamin biotin.

awn hairs. Intermediate-sized hairs forming part of the primary coat.

axial skeleton. That portion of the skeleton composed of the skull, vertebrae, ribs and **sternum** (breastbone).

axilla. Armpit.

axillary. Pertaining to the armpit.

axon. The fingerlike extension of a nerve cell, along which the nerve impulse travels.

axon terminals. Branchings of a nerve axon within muscle, forming neuromuscular junctions with the myofibers supplied by the nerve.

B lymphocytes (B cells). Lymphocytes that upon proper stimulation by an antigen transform into plasma cells, which produce antibody to the antigen.

babesiosis. Any of several diseases caused by protozoa of the genus *Babesia.*

Bacillus Calmette-Guerin (BCG). A live, avirulent bacterial cell preparation of the bovine tuberculosis organism, *Mycobacterium bovis;* useful for immunizing people against tuberculosis and for nonspecifically stimulating the immune system.

bacteremia. Presence of bacteria in the bloodstream.

bacteria (singular: **bacterium**). Minute, single-celled organisms ubiquitous in the environment; they contain a cell wall and a nucleus lacking a delimiting membrane, and divide by **binary fission** (the parental cell dividing into two approximately equal daughter cells).

bacterial endocarditis. Inflammation of the lining of the heart, caused by bacterial infection of one or more heart valves.

bacterial folliculitis. Inflammation of hair follicles, caused by bacteria.

bacterin. Any killed bacterial vaccine, such as leptospirosis bacterin or borreliosis bacterin.

bacteriology. The study of bacteria.

baculum. Penile bone, or os penis; bone present in the penis of male dogs.

balloon valvuloplasty. Therapeutic procedure wherein a catheter with a large, stiff balloon attached is inserted into the heart through a peripheral blood vessel and placed across a narrowing (**stenosis**). The balloon is then inflated in order to widen the stenosis.

barium. Metallic element commonly used as a contrast medium in radiology, particularly useful for examining disorders of the gastrointestinal tract. The barium is first swallowed by the patient and X-ray films are then taken. The general structure and movements of the gastrointestinal tract become visible owing to the inability of the X-ray beam to penetrate the contrast medium.

basal cell layer. The bottom cell layer of the **epidermis** (the outermost layer of the skin).

basal cell tumor. Benign tumor of basal cells, present in the basal cell layer of the epidermis.

base-narrow. Condition wherein the lower jaw is too narrow and/or the lower canine teeth lack the proper lean to the outside in order to fit into the space between the appropriate upper teeth.

basophil. A specialized white blood cell containing histamine and serotonin.

basophilic. Staining dark blue.

Bence-Jones proteins. Immunoglobulins or immunoglobulin fragments detected in blood and sometimes urine in patients with multiple myeloma.

benign. Not malignant; a tumor that is not cancerous (i.e., will not spread).

benign mixed mammary tumor. Benign tumor of the canine mammary glands, often composed of more than a single cell type.

beta blockers. Drugs that block beta-adrenergic nerve impulses; important in treating **tachycardias** (abnormally rapid heart rates).

beta cells. Cells within the islets of Langerhans in the endocrine pancreas; they are the source of the hormone insulin.

bilateral. Occurring on both sides.

bilateral mastectomy. Surgical removal of both chains of mammary glands.

bilaterally symmetrical. Occurring simultaneously in approximately the same place on each side of the body.

bile. Fluid produced by the liver and deposited in the small intestine through the bile ducts, for the purpose of aiding the digestion of nutrients.

bile acids. Steroid acids made from cholesterol, they are components of bile.

bile duct. Duct that discharges digestive fluids (**bile**) from the liver into the small intestine.

bilirubin. A yellow bile pigment, a breakdown product of recycled hemoglobin from red blood cells; the pigment causing jaundice.

binary fission. Method of bacterial and protozoal multiplication wherein the parental cell divides into two approximately equal daughter cells.

binocular fixation. The ability, particularly well-developed in primates, to focus both eyes on a single object.

biological response modifiers. Substances, such as the interferons and the interleukins, that modify immune responses.

biological vector. A vector wherein a developmental stage of a particular parasite necessarily occurs.

biopsy. The procedure by which a small sample of tissue is obtained for microscopic examination or culture, for the purpose of making a medical diagnosis.

Blalock-Taussig shunt. Surgical formation of an artificial patent ductus arteriosus (PDA) in order to increase blood flow through the lungs; a means of treatment for tetralogy of Fallot, a congenital heart condition.

blastocyst. An early stage of the developing embryo.

blepharitis. Inflammatory disease of the eyelids.

blepharospasm. Spasm of the eyelid musculature, causing squinting.

blind spot. That portion of the visual field, behind the line of sight, that cannot be seen without changing eye and head position.

bloat. Gastric dilation-volvulus; distension of the stomach.

blood. The fluid and its component cells that circulate through the blood vessels and carry oxygen and other nutrients to body cells.

blood plasma. The liquid fraction of the blood (as opposed to blood cells).

blood smear. A thin layer of blood smeared on a glass slide, stained and viewed under a microscope; used to identify the maturity and type of blood cells present and to detect any abnormalities of those cells.

blood-typing. Laboratory procedure by which the red blood cells in a blood sample are identified as belonging to one of several blood groups.

blood urea nitrogen (BUN). A measure of the nitrogenous waste products circulating in the blood; elevated levels are usually indicative of kidney malfunction.

blood vessels. Arteries, arterioles, veins, venules, capillaries: the conduits for the transport of blood throughout the body.

blue Doberman syndrome. Older name for color-dilution **alopecia**.

blue dog disease. Alternative name for color-dilution **alopecia**.

blue eye. A transient, immune-mediated clouding of the cornea that often follows infection with canine adenovirus type 1 (CAV-1), caused by virus-antibody interactions in small blood vessels in the eye; vaccine-induced blue eye can be avoided by using vaccines containing canine adenovirus type 2 (CAV-2), which cross-protects against CAV-1 but does not induce blue eye.

boil. A deep-seated bacterial infection of a hair follicle, producing a painful skin nodule containing pus; also called a furuncle.

bone marrow. The soft inner tissue within the bones, containing the blood-forming elements (precursor cells of the red and white blood cells and blood platelets).

bone plating. Method of fracture repair wherein the bone fragments are replaced in their original location and held in place with a perforated metal plate (*bone plate*), which is attached to the fragments with small screws.

bony orbit. The bones of the skull that house and protect the eyeball.

booster. Any dose of vaccine given subsequent to the initial dose, or subsequent to natural exposure, and designed to maintain the immune state or improve it.

borborygmus. Gurgling noises caused by the rapid movement of gas through the intestines.

botulinal toxin. The neurotoxin produced in botulism.

botulism. A rare disease caused by a neurotoxin (botulinal toxin) produced by the bacterium Clostridium botulinum; it targets the neuromuscular nerve endings, producing a flaccid paralysis.

boutonneuse fever. Tick-borne zoonosis occurring in southern Europe, Africa and India; usually asymptomatic in dogs, in people it is characterized clinically by fever and skin lesions. Also called Mediterranean spotted fever.

brachycephalic. Flat-faced, short-nosed; having a short, wide head; said of certain breeds, such as the Pug and English Bulldog.

brachygnathism. Condition wherein the lower jaw is shorter than the upper jaw, placing the lower incisor teeth farther behind the upper incisor teeth.

brachytherapy. Radiation therapy technique wherein a radioactive device is inserted into a tumor and left in place for a period of time, during which the radiation slowly kills the tumor cells.

bradycardia. Abnormally slow heart rate.

bradyzoites. Dormant, encysted forms of the parasite *Toxoplasma gondii.*

brain stem. Portion of the brain containing nerve centers that control the heart rate, respiratory rate and pattern, and level of consciousness.

breath hydrogen test. Test for detecting bacterial overgrowth within the digestive tract.

breech presentation. Birth in which the fetus is delivered rear-end first.

bronchi. The larger air passages leading from the trachea and branching within the lungs.

bronchioles. Smaller branches of air passages leading from the bronchi to the alveoli (the small air sacs within the lungs, through the walls of which gas exchange between the blood and air occurs).

bronchoconstriction. Narrowing of the larger airways.

bronchodilators. Drugs that cause expansion of vital airways in the lungs, allowing for improved respiration.

bronchopneumonia. Lung inflammation that is initiated within the bronchioles.

bronchoscopy. Endoscopic examination of the trachea and bronchi.

budding. Form of asexual reproduction in certain protozoa wherein a dividing cell divides into two unequal parts, the larger part being considered the parent and the smaller one the bud.

bulbus glandis. Penile swelling at one end of the penile bone; during an erection it markedly enlarges, effectively "locking" the male inside the female during intercourse.

bulla. A large vesicle.

bulla osteotomy. Surgical opening and drainage of the middle ear to relieve infection.

bullous pemphigoid. A very rare autoimmune skin disease characterized by the production of autoantibodies and the development of vesicles and bullae beneath the epidermis.

buphthalmos. Gross enlargement of the eyeball.

cachexia. Seriously poor health; malnutrition and wasting.

caesarean section. Delivery of a fetus by surgically removing it from the uterus.

calcification centers. Areas of bone deposit and change within bone tissue.

calcinosis cutis. Disease sign characterized by calcium deposits in the skin, producing nodular irregularities.

calcitonin. A calcium-regulating hormone produced by the thyroid gland.

calcium channel blockers. Drugs useful in treating **tachycardias** (abnormally rapid heart rates).

calculus (plural: calculi). Dental tartar, the mineralized concretions of salivary calcium and phosphorus salts and tooth-surface plaque; also, a urinary stone.

calculogenic. Stone-forming.

calculolytic. Stone-dissolving.

calorie. Unit defined as the amount of energy needed to raise the temperature of 1 gram of water 1 degree Celsius (centigrade). However, the larger **kilocalorie** is usually referred to as a "Calorie" in the nonscientific community.

cancellous bone. Bone tissue having a spongy or lattice-like internal structure; an example is the bone marrow.

cancer. The general term for any malignant tumor.

candidiasis. A relatively uncommon infection of skin and mucous membranes of the oral cavity, respiratory tract and genital area of dogs, caused by yeast of the genus *Candida.*

Canidae. Taxonomic family name for dogs.

canids. Members of the family (*Canidae*) to which dogs belong.

canine acne. Common skin disease of young dogs, characterized by the formation of blackheads or pimples (*comedones*) on the chin and lips.

canine brucellosis. Chronic disease caused by the bacterium *Brucella canis*, and characterized by prolonged bacteremia and disorders of the genital tract, including infertility and abortion.

canine distemper. The most important viral infectious disease of dogs, caused by canine distemper virus (a paramyxovirus); characterized initially by acute upper respiratory disease signs and fever, and later by more severe respiratory disease (**pneumonia**), vomiting, diarrhea and neurologic signs.

canine ehrlichiosis. Alternative name for **tropical canine pancytopenia.**

canine familial dermatomyositis. Inherited inflammatory disease of muscle and skin; seen in Shetland Sheepdogs, Collies, and related crossbreeds.

canine follicular dysplasia. Uncommon disease characterized by hair loss and alterations in coat quality.

canine granulocytopathy syndrome. Rare disease of Irish setters wherein neutrophil counts are actually elevated, but the neutrophils themselves are apparently poorly functional or completely nonfunctioning.

canine viral papillomatosis. A syndrome of multiple infectious **papillomas** (warts) seen most often in young dogs, usually in the mouth and on the cornea, conjunctiva, eyelids, or skin; caused by one or more papillomaviruses of the family Papovaviridae (double-stranded DNA viruses).

canines. Fang teeth, also called cuspids, lying between the incisors and premolars; in the dog there are two upper and two lower canines.

cannula. A tube inserted into a duct or body cavity, for the purpose either of infusing or removing fluid.

capillaries. The smallest blood vessels. They permeate the tissues, serving as microscopic extensions of arterioles and venules; through their semipermeable walls, fluids, nutrients and waste gases are exchanged between the blood and the tissues.

carbuncle. A deep-seated skin infection containing many pockets of pus.

carcinogen. Any cancer-causing substance, such as asbestos, nickel, alcohol or tobacco.

carcinoma. A cancer (malignant tumor) of epithelial cells.

cardiac. Pertaining to the heart.

cardiac arrest. Cessation of the heartbeat.

cardiac catheterization. The passing of a catheter through a peripheral blood vessel and inside the heart, either for diagnostic or therapeutic purposes.

cardiac muscle. Specialized type of muscle found only in the heart.

cardiac tamponade. Acute compression of the heart, caused by filling of the pericardial sac with fluid or blood.

cardiac ultrasound. Examination of the heart by means of ultrasonic sound waves, for the purpose of disease diagnosis; also known as echocardiography.

cardiogenic shock. Shock caused by a diseased heart that has become so dysfunctional that it can no longer pump sufficient blood to the body.

cardiomyopathy. Enlargement of the heart, caused either by thickening of heart muscle (hypertrophic cardiomyopathy) or by its thinning and stretching (congestive cardiomyopathy).

cardiopulmonary bypass. Open-heart surgery wherein a heart-lung machine oxygenates and pumps blood while the heart is stopped.

cardiopulmonary resuscitation (CPR). First-aid technique to revive a patient lacking heartbeat and respiration.

cardiovascular system. The heart and blood vessels of the body.

carious lesions. Tooth cavities, the result of acid demineralization of the tooth surface by oral bacteria, particularly certain streptococci; also called **dental caries.**

carnassial teeth. The upper fourth premolar tooth and the lower first molar tooth on each side of the mouth, which interact in a special shearing overlap when the mouth is closed.

carnitine. Amino acid required for energy production; of therapeutic benefit in certain cases of canine dilated cardiomyopathy (carnitine cardiomyopathy) in Boxers and some large-breed dogs.

carnivores. Meat-eaters.

cartilage. Specialized connective tissue especially important in bone growth and the formation of joints.

castration. Surgical removal of the testes; sterilization of the male.

casts. Solid, tubular deposits in the urine, usually cast off from the walls of kidney tubules.

catabolism. The body's breakdown of complex molecules, such as protein and fat, to simpler compounds.

cataract. Lens opacity in the eye, affecting vision.

catecholamines. Compounds secreted by the adrenal medulla, the most notable of which is **epinephrine** (adrenaline).

cathartics. Drugs to induce evacuation of the bowel.

catheter. A flexible tubular instrument for insertion into a blood vessel or body cavity.

caudal. To the rear of; toward the tail.

cell. The most basic functioning unit of living organisms, composed of a nucleus, cytoplasm, organelles, and other constituents. Cells are the fundamental building blocks of tissues, and in their nuclei contain all the genetic information necessary for the growth and differentiation of a complete organism.

cellular differentiation. The process by which cells mature into specialized, fully functioning units.

cellular (cell-mediated) immune response. The mounting of a **cytotoxic T cell/macrophage/natural killer (NK)** cell immune response to an antigen.

cellulitis. Diffuse inflammation resulting from (usually bacterial) infection of deep connective tissue, sometimes forming an abscess.

cementoenamel junction. The anatomical junction of the crown and root of a tooth.

cementum. Specialized type of connective tissue that covers the tooth roots.

central nervous system (CNS). The brain and spinal cord.

centrifuge. To spin in order to separate the light and heavier particulates in a fluid sample; a machine for performing this procedure.

cercaria. Tadpole-like larval form of flukes that arises from the **redia** stage.

cerebellar abiotrophy. Autosomal recessive disorder characterized by incoordination, lack of balance equilibrium, and head tremors; also called **progressive neuronal abiotrophy (PNA).**

cerebellar hypoplasia. Underdevelopment of the cerebellum, manifested clinically by incoordination.

cerebellum. Portion of the brain concerned with motor function, balance and the coordination of movement.

cerebrospinal fluid (CSF). Fluid bathing the surfaces of the brain and spinal cord.

cerebrum. Portion of the brain concerned with conscious thought, perceptions and learned skills.

ceruminous glands. Glands that produce the waxy coating of the ear canal.

cervical. Pertaining to the neck.

cervical spondylosis. Degenerative and proliferative disease of the neck vertebrae.

cervix. Oval-shaped mass in the female reproductive tract, whose opening connects the uterus with the vagina.

cestocidal. Able to kill tapeworms.

cestodes. Tapeworms; internal parasites having a head unit (**scolex**) and numerous body segments (**proglottids**).

Chagas' disease. Disease caused by the protozoan parasite *Trypanosoma cruzi,* characterized by recurrent fevers, swellings, and gradual enlargement and dysfunction of internal organs (heart, intestines); also known as American trypanosomiasis; transmitted to people and dogs by winged, bloodsucking insects.

chalazion. Chronic inflammatory lesion along an eyelid margin, caused by chronic staphylococcal infection.

cheek teeth. General term for the premolar and molar teeth.

chemosis. Excessive swelling of the **conjunctiva** (membranes covering the inner surface of the eyelids).

cheyletiellosis. Nonseasonal, variably pruritic, transmissible infestation of the skin of dogs (particularly puppies) by the mite *Cheyletiella yasguri.*

choline. A B vitamin important for proper function of the nervous system and for preventing fat deposition in the liver.

chondrosarcoma. A malignant tumor of cartilage.

chorioretinitis. Inflammation of the retina and choroid of the eye.

choroid. Thin, pigmented middle layer of the eye containing nerves and blood vessels; it supplies blood to the retina.

chromosomes. The very large and complex molecules of DNA that occur in the nucleus of every cell and that carry the genetic information needed to make every protein in the body.

chronic. Long-term; of lengthy duration; persisting over a long period.

chronic carrier state. Situation in which an animal or human being maintains (carries) an infectious disease agent for a prolonged period of time.

chronic interstitial nephritis. Chronic, progressive destruction of the kidneys, marked by a reduction in kidney size and scarring of kidney tissue.

chronic superficial keratitis (CSK). Nonulcerative, noninfectious inflammatory condition of the canine cornea that is highly progressive and potentially blinding; also called **pannus.**

cicatrization. Scar-tissue formation.

cilia (singular: **cilium**). Minute, hairlike cellular processes lining much of the respiratory tract; their rhythmic beating movements, in concert with an overlying layer of mucus, effect removal of debris and other foreign material from the airways.

ciliary body. The circular muscle located directly behind the iris of the eye.

circulatory system. The heart, blood vessels, and cellular and fluid components of the blood.

cirrhosis. Liver disease characterized by replacement of functioning liver cells by scar tissue.

clitoris. Small mound of erectile tissue in the female reproductive tract; the female analog of the male penis.

coagulation. Blood clotting.

cobalamin. Cobalt-containing component of vitamin B_{12}.

coccidioidomycosis. The most severe and life-threatening of the systemic fungal infections, caused by *Coccidioides immitis;* also known as "valley fever."

coccidiosis. Disease (usually intestinal) caused by protozoa known as *coccidia.*

cochlea. Curled bone in the inner ear which contains the **organ of Corti,** the actual organ of hearing.

codominant alleles. Genes wherein both members of an allelic pair are fully expressed.

coitus. Sexual intercourse.

cold agglutinins. Autoantibodies that occur only rarely in canine autoimmune hemolytic anemia; they are usually of the IgM class and attach themselves to red blood cells more vigorously at lower temperatures than at body temperature.

colic. Acute abdominal pain.

colitis. Inflammation of the large bowel (colon); contrasts with enteritis (inflammation of the small intestine).

collagen. Protein constituent of connective tissue.

Collie eye anomaly. Inherited ocular disorder of Collies characterized by abnormalities of all three layers of the posterior part of the eyeball.

coloboma. A defect of any tissue of the eye.

colon. The portion of the large intestine connecting the cecum (lowermost portion of the small intestine) with the rectum.

colonoscopy. Endoscopic examination of the colon.

color-dilution alopecia. Uncommon hereditary skin disease seen in color-diluted dogs and characterized by hair loss and poor coat quality; also called **blue dog disease.**

color flow Doppler echocardiography. Technique using sound waves to examine the direction and velocity of blood flow within the heart and great vessels, allowing the cardiologist to observe directly the regions of abnormal blood flow that develop in association with most common cardiac abnormalities.

colostrum ("first milk"). Milk produced by the bitch during the first day or two after the birth of her puppies; it is high in protein and protective antibodies (**maternal immunity**).

coma. Unconsciousness from which one cannot be aroused.

comatose. Unconscious and unable to be aroused.

comedo (plural: **comedones**). A blackhead or pimple.

complement system. A specialized series of blood proteins whose major role is to disrupt the surface structure of microbes and altered body cells, resulting in their destruction.

complete blood count (CBC). Blood analysis containing an enumeration of the number of red and white blood cells per unit of blood volume, the proportions of the different white blood cell types, and the amount of hemoglobin present.

compound follicle. Hair follicle in which more than a single hair is produced.

compound fracture. Fracture that breaks through the skin; open fracture.

computerized axial tomography (CAT scan). Highly specialized diagnostic X-ray technique that produces cross-sectional images of the inside of the body.

conceptus. Embryo or fetus plus the accompanying extraembryonic membranes.

concussion. A violent blow to the head, usually resulting in the loss of consciousness.

conduction deafness. Deafness caused by loss of the bone and tissue structures of the ear that conduct sound.

cones. Photoreceptor cells in the retina of the eye that are responsible for color vision and visual acuity.

congenital hypotrichosis. Hairlessness.

congenital malformations. Birth defects.

congenital testicular hypoplasia. Underdevelopment of the testicles.

congestive heart failure. Syndrome caused by the inadequate pumping of blood by the heart.

conjunctiva. Mucous membrane lining the eyelids and covering the white surface (**sclera**) of the eyeball.

conjunctivitis. Inflammation of the conjunctiva.

connective tissue. A general term encompassing the different types of supportive tissues that hold together many body structures.

constitutional signs. Generalized clinical signs, such as inappetence, lethargy, or weight loss.

continuous heart murmur. A murmur that is present during both contraction and relaxation of heart muscle.

contralateral. On the opposite side.

contusion. A bruise.

convulsions. Seizures.

Coombs' test. An immunologic procedure for the detection of autoantibodies attached to red blood cells; also called an antiglobulin test; important in disease diagnosis as well as in cross-matching blood samples for transfusion purposes.

copepods. Minute aquatic crustaceans.

coracidium. Free-swimming larval form of pseudophyllidean tapeworms.

core biopsy. Biopsy obtained from an awake patient using local anesthesia and a specialized small-bore biopsy needle.

cornea. The transparent outer coat of the eye.

corneal degeneration. Noninherited condition wherein white-to-silver crystalline opacities develop in the cornea, usually in only one eye.

corneal dystrophy. Inherited condition wherein gray-white or silver crystalline opacities develop in the central (or around the central) area of the cornea, usually in both eyes.

corneal melanosis. Black or brown pigmentation of the cornea.

cornified. Converted into hardened tissue; keratinized.

corpus luteum (plural: **corpora lutea**). Ovarian follicle after discharge of the ovum (egg); it secretes the hormone progesterone.

cortex. Outer layer of an organ (kidney, adrenal gland, brain) or hair shaft; contrasted with medulla.

corticosteroids. Steroid hormones (cortisol, corticosterone, etc.) produced by the cortex of the adrenal gland; corticosteroids elevate blood sugar, increase fat and protein breakdown, and exert an anti-inflammatory effect on conditions such as arthritis and dermatitis.

corticosterone. A corticosteroid hormone.

cortisol. A corticosteroid hormone.

cortisone. A corticosteroid hormone (a precursor of cortisol) found in small quantities in the adrenal cortex.

cosmetic otoplasty. Ear-cropping operation.

cranial. Toward the head.

cranial nerves. Nerves originating largely in the brain stem that control the facial muscles and certain specialized activities of the head (sight, smell, hearing).

craniomandibular osteopathy. Formation of excessive dense bone in the jaw; an autosomal recessive disorder of Scottish Terriers and West Highland White Terriers.

creatine kinase (CK). A muscle-specific enzyme found in serum; determination of CK levels represents a useful tool for the diagnosis of muscle disorders.

creatinine. Nitrogen-containing compound generated from the breakdown of ingested proteins.

crepitus. Sensation or sound of grating or scraping, caused when dry joint surfaces or fragments of a fractured bone rub together.

cretinism. Congenital form of hypothyroidism, resulting in arrested physical and mental development.

cricopharyngeal dysphagia. Uncommon neurologic disease resulting in failure of the pharyngoesophageal sphincter to open and close properly, resulting in dysphagia and regurgitation; also called cricopharyngeal achalasia.

cross-bite. Condition wherein the normal tooth-crown overlap is reversed. Anterior cross-bite means that one or more of the lower incisor teeth occlude in front of the upper incisor teeth. Posterior cross-bite is a rare phenomenon in which the carnassial teeth's overlap is reversed so that the lower first molar lies outside the upper fourth premolar when the jaws are closed.

cross-match. Procedure by which blood samples from donor and recipient are tested before blood transfusion, in order to determine compatibility.

crown. The portion of a tooth that lies above the gum line.

crusting, crusts. Residue of dried serum, blood, pus and epidermal, keratinous and bacterial debris on the skin.

cryogen. Any substance, such as liquid nitrogen, used to produce extreme cold during cryosurgery.

cryosurgery. A procedure by which local application of intense cold (freezing) is used to destroy unwanted tissue.

cryptorchidism. Developmental defect wherein one or both of the testicles has not descended into the scrotum.

Cushing's disease (Cushing's syndrome). Hyperactivity of the adrenal cortex; hyperadrenocorticism.

cusps. The sharp points of the tooth crown.

cutaneous. Pertaining to the skin.

cutaneous asthenia. Term used to group multiple rare, heritable, congenital defects of connective tissue, characterized by hyperextensibility and decreased tensile strength of the skin; also known as **Ehlers-Danlos syndrome.**

cutaneous horns. Projections of hardened skin.

cutaneous hyperesthesia. Hypersensitivity to touch.

cutaneous larva migrans. Disease of human beings caused by canine hookworm larvae; disease symptoms are caused by migration of the parasitic larvae through the skin, resulting in an itchy, creeping eruption.

cuticle. The outermost layer of a hair shaft; also, the thick, noncellular covering on the surface of a roundworm (**nematode**) parasite.

cyanocobalamin. Vitamin B_{12}.

cyanosis. A bluish discoloration of the skin and mucous membranes, resulting ultimately from a deficiency of oxygen in the blood.

cyclic hematopoiesis of gray Collies. An inherited condition in gray Collies in which the bone marrow's blood cell-forming machinery shuts down at periodic intervals, creating cyclic deficiencies of white blood cells.

cyclosporin A. An immunosuppressive drug important in organ transplantation; obtained from a soil fungus, it assists in preventing rejection of transplanted tissue.

cyst. Simple, saclike cavity that develops within the skin and usually contains fluid or a semisolid, cheesy or doughy material.

cystadenoma. A benign tumor of cystic and glandular structures.

cystic endometrial hyperplasia. Exuberant overgrowth of the uterine lining, with the formation of cystic structures.

cystitis. Inflammation of the urinary bladder, usually caused by a bacterial infection and sometimes accompanied by the formation of bladder stones.

cystocentesis. Procedure for obtaining a sterile sample of urine by inserting a small-gauge needle through the lower abdominal wall directly into the bladder, and withdrawing the urine into a syringe.

cystolith. A bladder stone, or **calculus** (as found in the urinary bladder or gallbladder).

cytodifferentiation. The production of specialized cells and structures within the developing embryo.

cytokines. "Messenger molecules" by which cells of the immune system signal and instruct one another; the interferons and the interleukins are examples.

cytologic examination (cytology). The microscopic examination of cells obtained by scraping, aspiration or biopsy, for the purpose of disease diagnosis.

cytoplasm. Cell protoplasm; the fluid and particulates within a cell, exclusive of the cell nucleus.

cytotoxic. Harmful to cells.

cytotoxic T cells. T lymphocytes that are responsible for tracking down and eliminating altered or infected body cells.

decerebrate rigidity. Severe brain damage resulting in rigid extension of all four limbs and a throwing back of the head.

decerebration. Severe brain damage.

deciduous teeth. "Baby teeth" or "milk teeth," the temporary teeth that are lost to make way for the permanent teeth.

deep bacterial folliculitis. Form of pyoderma characterized by bacterial infection and inflammation deep within hair follicles.

definitive host. Host in or on which a parasite reaches sexual maturity or undergoes sexual reproduction.

degranulation. Release of granules from a cell.

dehydration. Loss of body water, occurring when the intake of water is insufficient to cover water losses.

dematiaceous fungi. Dark, pigmented fungi represented by the genera *Drechslera, Alternaria,* and others; responsible for causing phaeohyphomycosis and certain **eumycotic mycetomas.**

dementia. Mental deterioration.

demodicosis. Infestation with *Demodex* mites.

dendrites. Short, threadlike extensions of a nerve cell; they act to receive nerve impulses from adjacent nerve cells.

dental caries. Tooth cavities.

dentifrice. Toothpaste.

dentin. The tooth layer lying between the inner **pulp** (containing the tooth's blood and nerve supply) and the overlying **enamel.**

deoxygenated. Having a low oxygen content; said of venous blood.

deoxyribonucleic acid (DNA). The genetic material of living cellular organisms and of certain viruses.

depigmentation. Localized loss of normal color in skin or hair.

depolarization. A change from a negative to a positive charge, generating an electrical wave (as in the production of the heartbeat).

dermal papilla. Structure at the base of each hair follicle that, with the associated **hair matrix cells,** is responsible for the production of hair.

dermatitis. Any inflammatory skin disease.

dermatomycosis. Any fungal skin infection.

dermatophytes. Fungi causing ringworm.

dermatophytosis. Ringworm.

dermatosis. Any skin disease, particularly one without an inflammatory component.

dermis. The middle and thickest major layer of the skin; composed of connective tissue fibers and a ground substance, it lies just beneath the **epidermis,** the outermost layer of the skin.

dermoid cyst. Rare developmental abnormality resembling a follicular cyst; often seen along the back.

dermoids. Congenital problem wherein single or multiple abnormal patches of skin and hair are present on one or more eyelids, in either a pigmented or nonpigmented form.

detoxification. Reduction in toxic properties of compounds.

detrusor. Smooth muscle layer of the bladder wall; contraction of the detrusor results in voiding of urine.

dewclaws. The first toes of the front and hind paws.

dextrose. Glucose; blood sugar.

diabetes insipidus. Disease involving defective synthesis or secretion of **antidiuretic hormone (ADH)** by the pituitary gland.

diabetes mellitus. Diabetes, a chronic disease caused by either insufficient production of insulin by the islets of Langerhans in the pancreas, or by resistance of target tissues to the effects of insulin. Diabetes results in an inability of cells to utilize glucose (blood sugar), with widespread adverse effects owing to impaired utilization of carbohydrates, fats and proteins by the body. Not to be confused with **diabetes insipidus.**

diabetic ketoacidosis. Serious, life-threatening complication of untreated or poorly treated diabetes mellitus, characterized by the buildup of ketone bodies in the circulation and a fall in blood pH, i.e., increasing acidity of the blood.

diaphragm. The large muscle used for breathing which separates the abdominal and chest cavities.

diaphragmatic hernia. Rupture of the diaphragm, with movement of some of the abdominal contents into the chest cavity.

diaphysis. The central shaft of a long bone.

diarrhea. An increase in the fluid content, volume or frequency of bowel movements.

diastole. The relaxation phase of the heartbeat, following **systole.**

diastolic blood pressure. The pressure that occurs when the heart is not pumping blood into the arterial system (i.e., during the relaxation period between contractions).

diastolic heart murmur. Murmur that is present only during *diastole* (the relaxation phase of the heartbeat).

diestrus. Interestrus; the quiescent period between one estrus period and the next.

dietary anion gap. The balance of negatively and positively charged particles in the diet.

diethylcarbamazine. Medication useful in preventing infestation by *Dirofilaria immitis,* the heartworm.

differential white blood cell count. Total white blood cell (WBC) counts and percentages of different WBC types present; component part of a complete blood count (**CBC**).

differentiation. The development of cellular specialization as cells mature.

Difil test. A common blood test for the detection of immature heartworm forms (*microfilariae*).

digestible carbohydrates. Sugars and starches.

digital pressure. Pressure applied by the fingers.

digoxin. Medication that increases the strength of the heartbeat while decreasing the heart rate; used most often for the treatment of congestive heart failure.

dilated. Enlarged or widened.

dilated cardiomyopathy. Disease of the heart muscle characterized by progressive enlargement of the heart that eventually results in heart failure.

dilated fixed pupil. Pupil that does not contract.

dipylidiasis. Human disease characterized by digestive disorders and irritability (primarily in infants and young children); caused by infestation with the common tapeworm (*Dipylidium caninum*) of dogs and cats.

direct life cycle. With regard to parasites, a life cycle that can be completed without the participation of an intermediate host.

discoid lupus erythematosus. Relatively uncommon autoimmune skin disease, possibly caused by an immune reaction against skin cells that have been altered by chronic exposure to sunlight; lesions are restricted usually to the facial skin.

discospondylitis. Inflammation of an intervertebral disk.

dispensable amino acids. Amino acids that can be synthesized by the body so long as a source of nitrogen is present in the diet.

disseminated intravascular coagulation (DIC). A bleeding disorder characterized by the excessive utilization of blood-clotting factors, due to widespread clotting within blood vessels; the resultant hemorrhaging often represents a terminal event in a number of diseases.

distal. Farther, more distant.

distichiasis. Condition wherein eyelashes grow from an abnormal location along the eyelid margin, causing ocular irritation.

disuse atrophy. Loss of muscle mass because of muscle disuse.

diuretic. Any drug that promotes urination.

DNA. Deoxyribonucleic acid, the genetic material of living cellular organisms and of certain viruses.

dolichocephalic. Long-nosed; said of certain breeds, such as the Collie and Shetland Sheepdog.

dominant gene. A gene capable of expressing its trait even when carried by only one member of a chromosome pair.

Doppler echocardiography. Technique using sound waves to examine the direction and velocity of blood flow within the heart and great vessels.

dorsal. Pertaining to the back; toward the back.

duct. Small tube or passageway.

ductus arteriosus. Blood vessel normally present during fetal life that allows blood to bypass the lungs, which of course are nonfunctional at this time; the ductus normally closes shortly after birth.

duodenum. The first part of the small intestine, connecting the stomach with the jejunum.

dysphagia. Difficult or painful swallowing.

dysplasia. Any abnormality in the size, shape or development of cells.

dyspnea. Difficulty breathing; labored breathing.

dystocia. Difficult birth.

dystrophin. A cell protein associated with the inner surface of muscle-fiber membranes; deficiency or lack of dystrophin causes X-linked muscular dystrophy in dogs.

dysuria. Painful or difficult urination.

eardrum. Translucent membrane between the outer and middle ear which vibrates in response to sound vibrations transmitted down the ear canal; also called *tympanic membrane.*

eccrine sweat glands. Sweat glands that empty their contents directly onto the skin surface; found in the footpads and nasal pad.

echinococcosis. Alternative name for **hydatid disease.**

echocardiography. Examination of the heart by means of ultrasonic sound waves, for the purpose of disease diagnosis; also known as **cardiac ultrasound.**

eclampsia. Calcium deficiency in a lactating bitch.

ectoparasite. External parasite; examples include fleas, ticks and mites.

ectopic. In or at an abnormal site; not in the normal position.

ectropion. Eversion (turning outward away from the eyeball) of the margin of an eyelid.

edema. The accumulation of abnormally large quantities of fluid in the intercellular tissue spaces (spaces between cells); **pulmonary edema** refers specifically to fluid buildup in the lungs.

edematous. Swollen with fluid.

effusion. Fluid escaping into a body cavity or tissue.

Ehlers-Danlos syndrome. See CUTANEOUS ASTHENIA.

ehrlichiosis. Acute, febrile, tick-borne illness of people, caused by the rickettsia *Ehrlichia chaffeensis.*

elastin. Protein found in elastic connective tissue fibers that imparts flexibility to the tissue.

electrocardiogram (ECG). Examination of the electrical activity of the heart, for the purpose of disease diagnosis. The ECG records the size and direction of the waves of depolarization that spread across the heart during muscle contraction and relaxation.

electroencephalography (EEG). Examination of the electrical activity of the brain, for the purpose of disease diagnosis.

electrolyte. A molecule that dissociates into ions (atoms having either positive or negative charge due to the addition or loss of an electron) in solution, and thus is able to conduct electricity; examples include sodium and potassium.

electromyography (EMG). Examination of the electrical activity within a muscle at rest or during voluntary or evoked muscular contractions, for the purpose of disease diagnosis.

electrophoresis. Separation of components of a mixture by their differing migration in an applied electric field.

electroretinogram (ERG). Examination of the electrical activity of the **retina** (light-sensitive layer of cells at the back of the eye), for the purpose of disease diagnosis.

electrosurgery. Surgical techniques (such as electrocautery) wherein electrical methods are used to remove tissue and/or seal broken blood vessels to alleviate hemorrhage.

ELISA. *E*nzyme-*l*inked *i*mmunosorbent *a*ssay; any of the many highly sensitive, color-based test methods for detecting either antibody or antigen in blood, serum or plasma.

Elizabethan collar. Wide collar that restricts contact between the head and body.

embolism. Sudden blockage of an artery by a blood clot. (*See* THROMBOSIS.)

emetics. Drugs used to induce vomiting.

enamel. The thin, calcium-rich outer surface of the teeth, overlying the harder dentin layer; it functions to resist wear.

enamel hypoplasia. Underdevelopment or incomplete development of the enamel layer of a tooth.

endocarditis. Inflammation of the innermost lining of the heart (**endocardium**), usually caused by bacterial infection of one or more heart valves.

endocardium. A thin serous membrane, the innermost lining of the chambers of the heart.

endocrine. Pertaining to a gland that delivers its secretions directly into the blood or lymph.

endocrinology. The study of hormones and hormone-producing glands.

endocrinopathy. Hormonal imbalance leading to disease.

endodyogeny. Form of asexual reproduction in certain parasites, wherein two similar daughter cells are formed within a parent cell.

endogenous. Originating within the body.

endometritis. Inflammation of the innermost lining of the uterus.

endophthalmitis. Uncontrolled inflammation of all the internal structures of the eye.

endoscopy. Procedure wherein a small tube (an endoscope) is inserted into an orifice or body cavity, for the purpose of examining the internal portions of that cavity or a hollow organ.

endospore. The type of spore produced during the spherule stage of the life cycle of the fungus *Coccidioides immitis,* the cause of coccidioidomycosis ("**valley fever**").

endotracheal tube. A plastic tube for breathing, commonly inserted into the trachea during general anesthesia.

energy density. The amount of energy contained in a quantity of food.

enophthalmos. Recession of the eye deep within the orbit.

enteric. Referring to the small intestine.

enteric campylobacteriosis. A diarrheal disease caused by bacteria of the genus *Campylobacter.*

enteritis. Inflammation of the small intestine; contrasts with colitis (inflammation of the colon, or large intestine).

enteropathic arthritis. Arthritic condition associated with concomitant inflammatory intestinal disease.

entropion. Inversion (turning inward toward the eyeball) of the margin of an eyelid.

enucleation. Surgical removal of the eyeball.

enzootic. Widespread in a population and always present, but producing disease in only relatively few animals; said of infectious disease agents.

enzyme. Any of a myriad number of different proteins produced by cells, capable of accelerating biochemical reactions occurring within the cells.

eosinophil. A white blood cell that contains granules readily stained with eosin (a red stain used in the laboratory to dye this particular white blood cell); functions in the allergic reaction to parasitic infections.

epicardium. The outermost membrane of the surface of the heart.

epidermal appendages. Collectively the hair follicles, sweat glands and sebaceous glands.

epidermal cell renewal time. The amount of time (approximately 20 to 25 days) required for **keratinocytes** in the skin to progress upward from the **basal cell layer** of the epidermis to the **horny layer.**

epidermis. The outermost layer of the skin.

epidermoid cyst. See FOLLICULAR CYST.

epididymis. In the male, the duct connecting the testis to the vas deferens; used for the storage, maturation and movement of sperm.

epilation. Plucking of hair by the roots.

epilepsy. Brain disorder resulting in seizures.

epinephrine (adrenaline). A hormone secreted by the adrenal glands; it acts to increase blood sugar levels and blood pressure and to accelerate the heart rate.

epiphora. An overflow of tears.

epiphysis. Either end of a long bone.

epistasis. The masking of one gene's activity by another gene.

epistaxis. Bleeding from the nostril; nosebleed.

epithelium. Cellular covering of the internal and external surfaces of the body.

epizootic. Attacking many animals over a short period of time, with resulting high morbidity (high percentage of animals becoming ill); said of infectious disease agents. Also, an acute disease outbreak.

epulis (plural: epulides). The most common benign oral tumor of dogs, it arises from the periodontal ligament.

erectile tissue. Tissue capable of erection, i.e., stiffening following engorgement of blood; found in the penis of the male and the clitoris of the female.

erosion. A superficial denudation of the skin involving only the epidermis.

eructation. Forceful, retrograde expulsion of air from the stomach; "burping" or "belching."

erysipeloid. A deep skin infection of people caused by a bacterium, *Erysipelothrix rhusiopathiae;* it is an occupational illness, often acquired during the handling of infected fish or poultry.

erythema. Reddening of the skin, due to congestion of the underlying capillaries.

erythema chronicum migrans (ECM). A skin reaction seen in human beings with **Lyme borreliosis.**

erythema multiforme. An uncommon skin reaction with a proposed immunologic basis and usually associated with a drug hypersensitivity.

erythrocyte. Red blood cell, the carrier of oxygen in the blood.

erythropoietin. A hormone produced by the kidneys that stimulates red blood cell production in the bone marrow.

esophagitis. Inflammation of the esophagus.

esophagus. The muscular tube extending from the pharynx (back of the mouth) to the stomach.

essential amino acids. Amino acids that cannot be synthesized in sufficient quantities by the body and therefore must be provided in the diet.

essential fatty acids. Fatty acids that have structural functions in cell membranes and serve as precursors for **prostaglandins** and leukotrienes.

estrogens. General term for female sex hormones.

estrus. "Heat"; a recurrent period of varying length, during which the bitch produces a watery secretion from the genital tract, becomes sexually receptive to the male, and ovulates (releases eggs from the ovary).

ethylene glycol. Antifreeze, a potent poison.

etiology. The cause of a disease.

eumycotic mycetoma. A swollen, progressing, tumorlike lesion caused by certain species of fungi.

euthanasia. Humane killing; putting to sleep.

excise. To cut out; remove surgically.

excision arthroplasty. Surgical removal of the head of the **femur** (thighbone); a treatment for **hip dysplasia.**

excisional biopsy. Biopsy sample representing an entire (small) lesion, removed surgically both as diagnosis and treatment.

excoriations. Erosions and ulcerations produced by self-trauma.

excreta (singular: **excretum**). Waste material excreted by the body; feces or urine.

exfoliation. Peeling of the skin.

exfoliative dermatitis. Skin disease characterized by inflammation and peeling, as in sunburn.

exocrine. Pertaining to a gland that delivers its secretions through a duct.

exogenous. Originating outside the body.

exophthalmos (exophthalmia). Protrusion of the eyeball.

exostosis. A benign growth protruding from the surface of a bone.

expectorants. Medications that promote the coughing up (ejection) of mucus or phlegm from the lungs.

expectorate. To cough up or spit.

expiration. The act of breathing air out; exhalation.

external anal sphincter. Anal sphincter or "valve" that discharges fecal waste from the body.

external fixation. Setting of a fracture by means of an external connecting bar, which is attached to pins that have been placed in the broken fragments, thus holding the fragments in place until healing occurs.

external urethral sphincter. Band of muscle that opens and closes the juncture between the bladder and urethra.

extraocular. Exterior to the eyeball.

exudate. A high-protein fluid derived from blood and deposited in tissues or on tissue surfaces, usually as a result of inflammation.

fabella (plural: **fabellae**). Small sesamoid bone occasionally found in the area of the knee.

facultative parasite. A parasite whose life cycle can be completed without a parasitic phase, but which may optionally include a parasitic phase under certain circumstances.

fallopian tubes. *See* UTERINE TUBES

familial. Running in a family line; occurring in a family line with greater frequency than by chance alone.

fasciae (singular: **fascia**). Sheets of fibrous tissue that ensheath the muscles and define their shape.

fat-soluble vitamins. Vitamins A, D, E and K.

febrile. Having a fever.

fecal casts. Minute black, comma-shaped granules of waste from adult fleas, the end product of ingested blood; "flea dirt."

fecal flotation. Laboratory procedure for identification of parasite eggs in a fecal specimen.

feminization. Development of certain female sex characteristics in a male.

femoral pulse. The pulse as measured by pressing on the femoral artery, which lies beneath the inner surface of the hind limbs, in the groin region.

femur. Thighbone.

fetal resorption. Disintegration of the fetus while in the uterus.

fever. A rise in body temperature caused by a change in the thermoregulatory set-point in the brain; usually caused by disease.

fibrin. An insoluble protein that forms the nucleus of a blood clot.

fibrinogen. Clotting factor in the blood, which is converted into its active form (**fibrin**) by the enzyme thrombin.

fibroblast. Immature fibrocyte.

fibrocyte. Common type of cell found in connective tissue.

fibroplasia. Formation of fibrous tissue.

fibrosarcoma. A malignant tumor of connective tissue cells.

fibrosis. Formation of fibrous tissue.

fibrous tissue. Tough connective tissue.

fibrous tunic. The outer layer of the eyeball.

filamentous. Threadlike.

fissures. Cracks in the skin secondary to loss of normal skin tone; associated with inflammatory process.

flatus. Air or gas within the intestinal tract.

flora. The population of microorganisms (bacteria,

viruses, fungi, protozoa) normally resident within an individual host, or within a certain portion of the host (e.g., the intestinal tract).

fluorescein. A chemical compound (fluorane dye us)ed for, among other things, identifying ulcers on the cornea.

follicle-stimulating hormone (FSH). Hormone, produced by the pituitary gland, that stimulates the development of ovarian follicles in the female and sperm production in the male.

follicular cyst. Cyst originating within a hair follicle; also called **epidermoid cyst.**

follicular sheath. Long tubelike structure through which a hair passes through the **dermis** (middle layer of the skin) and exits to the skin surface.

folliculitis. Inflammation of one or more hair follicles.

food allergy. Skin disease believed to result from an allergic reaction to an ingested substance.

fossa. A channel.

foxtail. Grass awn that represents the most common penetrating foreign body affecting dogs in North America; cheetgrass.

free-catch. Method for obtaining a (nonsterile) urine sample by holding a cup or other container under the urine stream as a dog urinates.

free-living stage. A stage in the life cycle of a parasite wherein the parasite exists freely in the general environment and not in or on a host animal.

frozen-section biopsy. Biopsy sample frozen and cut for immediate examination and diagnosis, as during exploratory surgery.

fulminant. Sudden and intense.

fundus. General term for the back of the eye.

fungal tumor. Eumycotic mycetoma.

fungi (singular: **fungus**). A large group of organisms characterized by the presence of a rigid cell wall and the absence of chlorophyll, and whose primary purpose is the decomposition of organic material; examples include the yeasts and molds, mushrooms, smuts and rusts.

furuncle. A deep-seated bacterial infection and rupture of a hair follicle, producing a painful skin nodule containing pus; also called a **boil.**

furunculosis. Disease condition involving the development of multiple furuncles (**boils**).

gametes. Reproductive cells, each containing a single set of chromosomes; **ova** (eggs) in the female and **spermatozoa** (sperm) in the male.

gametogamy. Sexual reproduction involving the formation of male and female reproductive cells which fuse to form a zygote; also called **syngamy.**

gangrene. Death and decay of tissue, usually owing to the loss of blood supply and subsequent invasion by bacteria.

gastric. Pertaining to the stomach.

gastritis. Inflammation of the stomach.

gastroesophageal sphincter. Sphincter located between the esophagus and the stomach.

gastroscopy. Endoscopic examination of the stomach.

gastrula. An early stage of the developing embryo that follows the blastula stage during which the blastocyst is formed.

gene linkage. Phenomenon wherein genes located on the same chromosome tend to be inherited together more often than they are split apart.

genera. Plural form of **genus.**

genes. The individual units of inheritance, composed of stretches of **DNA** found along the **chromosomes** within the nucleus of every cell.

genome. The total genetic information of an individual cell or virus.

genotype. The genetic makeup of a given physical trait; also, the total genetic makeup of an individual organism.

genus (plural: **genera**). One of the major classifying categories of taxonomy, further divided into species or subgenera.

geriatrics. Branch of medical science concerned with the diseases, disabilities and care of aged patients.

gestation. The full period of pregnancy, from fertilization of the egg by a spermatozoon until birth. Gestation in the dog lasts between 58 and 70 days, with an average of 63 days.

gingiva. The gums of the mouth.

gingival hyperplasia. Gum enlargement caused by an increase in the number of cells; a common clinical observation in older dogs, particularly in Collies, Boxers and other large breeds.

gingival sulcus. The area formed by the junction of the tooth and gums.

gingivitis. Inflammation of the gums.

gland. Collection of cells that produces secretions or excretions of a specialized character.

gland of the third eyelid. Lacrimal gland of the third eyelid, that secretes up to 3% of the eye's tears.

glans penis. The cap-shaped termination of the penile shaft.

glaucoma. Group of diseases caused by increased pressure within the eyeball, which damages the optic nerve and can result in blindness.

globe. The eyeball.

globoid-cell leukodystrophy. Inherited, inevitably lethal disorder of Cairn Terriers and West Highland White Terriers characterized by incoordination and hind-limb stiffness, followed by gradual destruction of white matter in the brain.

glomerular filtration rate (GFR). Rate at which the kidney glomeruli filter the blood passing through them.

glomerulonephritis. An inflammatory disease involving the capillaries (small blood vessels) of the kidney glomeruli.

glomerulus (plural: **glomeruli**). Any one of the many tiny clusters of blood vessels within the kidney; they filter waste products from the blood and excrete them in the form of urine, which is transported to the bladder for elimination.

glucocorticoids. Steroid hormones such as cortisol that are produced by the cortex of the adrenal gland; they elevate blood sugar levels, increase fat and protein breakdown and the secretion of stomach acid, and exert an anti-inflammatory effect on conditions such as arthritis and dermatitis.

glucose. Blood sugar, the body's most important fuel molecule.

glucosuria. Spillage of glucose into the urine, as in **diabetes mellitus.**

glutathione peroxidase. An enzyme important for protecting cells against damage caused by by-products of normal metabolic processes.

glycogen. Animal starch; a complex carbohydrate stored primarily in the liver and muscles, and broken down into its component glucose (sugar) molecules whenever they are needed by the body.

GM$_2$ gangliosidosis. Inherited disorder of German Shorthaired Pointers, characterized by increasing nervous behavior, clumsiness, partial blindness, and deafness; caused by a defective enzyme that allows **lipids** (fats) to accumulate in the brain.

goiter. An enlarged thyroid gland.

gonadal hypoplasia. Underdevelopment of the **gonads** (testes or ovaries).

gonads. Ovar*ies* (in the female) and testes (in the male); the reproductive glands that produce **ova** (eggs) in the female and **spermatozoa** (sperm) in the male, as well as the sex hormones **progesterone** and **estrogen** (ovaries), and **testosterone** (testes).

Gram stain. A routine stain used for the laboratory identification of bacteria.

granular cell layer. A layer of cells within the **epidermis**, the outermost layer of the skin; it lies above the prickle cell layer and below the horny layer.

granule. A tiny grain or particle.

granulocytes. White blood cells that contain stainable granules; examples include **neutrophils, eosinophils,** and **basophils.**

granulocytic leukemia. Cancer of granulocytes.

granuloma. Lesion indicative of a chronic inflammatory response, characterized by the accumulation of white blood cells around an offending agent for the purpose of walling off the agent from the rest of the body.

granulosa cell. The cell type that surrounds the developing ovarian follicle.

greenstick fracture. A partial fracture of a bone.

griseofulvin. An antibiotic and antifungal agent, useful for the treatment of ringworm.

gross appearance. Appearance as viewed by the unaided (naked) eye; as opposed to microscopic appearance.

gross energy (GE). Amount of energy produced by the complete combustion (burning) of a food.

growth hormone (GH). Hormone produced by the pituitary gland; it controls the rate of body growth.

growth hormone/castration-responsive dermatosis. Poorly defined, uncommon canine skin disorder associated with a deficiency of circulating growth hormone.

guard hairs. Coarse, thick, straight hairs that taper to a fine tip; also called **primary hairs.**

gum recession. Gradual exposure of the tooth-root surface by a shift in the position of the gingiva and the alveolar crestal bone toward the root; gum atrophy or shrinkage.

gynecomastia. Overdevelopment of the male mammary glands.

habituate. To become gradually accustomed to a particular external stimulus; to become desensitized.

hair bulb. The deepest portion of the hair follicle; its cells are referred to as **hair matrix cells.**

hair follicle. The structural unit of hair production within the skin, containing two major components, the **follicular sheath** and the **hair bulb;** two major types exist, **simple** follicles and **compound follicles**.

hair matrix cells. Cells at the base of the hair follicles that together with the **dermal papilla** are responsible for the production of hair.

hair matrixoma. Benign skin tumor arising from cells at the base of hair follicles (hair matrix cells).

hair root. The lower, anchoring structure of a hair.

hair shaft. The upper, free portion of a hair; as distinguished from the **hair root.**

halitosis. "Bad breath."

hard palate. Bone and tissue composing the roof of the mouth, separating the nasal cavity from the oral cavity.

haw. Third eyelid, located at the inner corner of the eye.

heart base tumor. Tumor that grows around the great vessels of the heart; it grows rather slowly and generally does not spread.

heart murmur. An abnormal heart sound produced when blood flows too rapidly or too chaotically through a portion of the heart; a common sign of heart disease.

heart rate. The heart's rate of contraction (**systole**) and relaxation (**diastole**).

heartworm disease. Infestation of the pulmonary arteries by the parasitic worm *Dirofilaria immitis.*

helminthic. Caused by or related to parasitic worms.

helminthosis. Any parasitic worm infestation.

helminths. Parasitic worms.

helper T cells. T lymphocytes that have a major role in assisting other lymphocytes, known as B cells, to produce antibody against an antigen.

hemagglutinins. Autoantibodies directed against the body's own red blood cells.

hemangioma. Benign tumor of newly formed blood vessels.

hemangiopericytoma. Skin tumor found on the extremities and believed to arise from supporting structures of blood vessels; frequent recurrence following attempted surgical removal is common; also called **spindle cell tumor.**

hemangiosarcoma. Malignant tumor of blood vessels and associated tissue.

hemarthrosis. Bleeding into a joint.

hematocrit. The percentage of red blood cells in a specified volume of whole blood; measurement of the hematocrit is performed to check for anemia; also called **packed cell volume (PCV).**

hematologic. Referring to the blood and/or blood cells.

hematoma. Localized pocket of (usually clotted) blood, most commonly caused by breakage of a blood vessel.

hematopoiesis. The production of new red blood cells.

hematopoietic. Referring to the production of new red blood cells.

hematuria. Presence of blood in the urine.

hemeralopia. "Day blindness," a disorder of the retina characterized by blindness during the day but partial return of vision in dim light.

hemodialysis. Use of an artificial kidney machine to filter the blood.

hemoglobin. An iron-containing pigment found in red blood cells; it serves as the carrier of oxygen to the tissues.

hemoglobinuria. Presence of hemoglobin in the urine; "red water."

hemogram. Results of blood examination including red blood cell count; packed cell volume (PCV), or **hematocrit;** and total and differential white blood cell counts.

hemolymphatic system. The circulatory system and the lymphatic system together.

hemolysis. Red blood cell destruction.

hemolytic. Characterized by red blood cell destruction.

hemolytic disease of the newborn. *See* NEONATAL ISOERYTHROLYSIS.

hemophilia A. Recessive, X-linked bleeding disorder characterized by a deficiency of clotting factor VIII.

hemophilic arthropathy. A metabolic joint disease in which animals with an inherited blood-clotting disorder bleed into the joint capsules.

hemoptysis. Coughing up blood.

hemorrhage. Bleeding.

hemorrhagic diathesis. Disease condition in which an abnormal bleeding tendency exists, as in **disseminated intravascular coagulation (DIC).**

hemorrhagic enteritis. Inflammation of the intestine accompanied by bleeding in the intestinal tract.

hemorrhagic shock. Shock caused by severe bleeding (usually from trauma) resulting in depletion of blood from the circulatory system, so that less oxygen is transported from the lungs to the tissues.

hemothorax. Pooling of blood in the chest cavity.

heparin. An anticoagulant; it prevents blood clotting by indirectly inhibiting the formation of **fibrin** (the chief protein component of blood clots).

hepatic. Pertaining to the liver.

hepatic encephalopathy. Syndrome of neurologic dysfunction secondary to liver failure.

hepatic lipidosis. Abnormal accumulation of fat in liver cells.

hepatic necrosis. Liver-cell death.

hepatomegaly. Enlargement of the liver.

hepatopathic arthritis. Arthritic condition associated with concomitant inflammatory liver disease.

hepatopathy. Any disease of the liver, particularly one characterized by degenerative changes.

hepatosplenomegaly. Enlargement of the liver and spleen.

hermaphroditism. Presence of male and female sex organs in the same individual.

hernia. Protrusion of an organ or tissue through an abnormal fissure; rupture.

heterochromia iridis. Difference of color in different areas of the same iris, or between the two irides.

heterozygous. Having inherited a different allele from each parent, at a given locus on a chromosome; contrasted with homozygous, in which the same allele for a given trait is inherited from both parents.

hip dysplasia. An hereditary developmental disease that is seen in almost all the canine breeds, particularly the larger ones; in essence, it is a failure of proper development of the hip joint.

histamine. Powerful molecule produced by mast cells and basophils that is responsible for many of the unpleasant effects of allergy; it causes contraction of smooth muscle and dilation of capillaries and increases the heart rate, among other effects.

histiocyte. A tissue macrophage.

histiocytoma. Benign skin tumor composed of **histiocytes** (tissue macrophages).

histology. The microscopic examination of normal tissue.

histopathology. The microscopic examination of diseased tissue.

holocrine secretion. Type of secretion in a gland wherein each entire gland cell disintegrates, with the cell contents becoming the secretion.

Holter monitor. A 24-hour recording of an electrocardiogram.

homogeneous. Uniform.

homozygous. Having inherited the same allele for a particular trait from both parents.

hordeolum. Localized inflammatory lesion along an eyelid margin, caused by a staphylococcal infection; also known as a **stye.**

hormone. Any molecule produced by an organ or tissue, usually in extremely small quantities, that has a specific regulatory effect on the activity of another organ or tissue.

horny layer. A cell layer of the **epidermis,** the outermost layer of the skin; it is composed entirely of tightly adherent, dead **keratinocytes** containing abundant quantities of **keratin.**

host. The living organism in or on which a parasite resides.

hot spots. *See* PYOTRAUMATIC DERMATITIS.

human chorionic gonadotrophin (HCG). Hormone produced by the placenta that can stimulate ovulation in an estrous bitch.

humoral immune response. The mounting of an antibody response to an antigen by the immune system.

hydatid disease. Disease caused by the tapeworms *Echinococcus granulosus* and *Echinococcus multilocularis;* characterized by the production in the tissues of large, fluid-filled structures (hydatid cysts), in which the parasite undergoes a further process of maturation.

hydrocephalus. Cerebrospinal fluid accumulation within the brain.

hydrometra. Accumulation of watery fluid within the uterus.

hydrophilic. Having the property of attracting or absorbing water molecules.

hydrophobia. Aversion to water; common in human beings with rabies, much less so in dogs with rabies.

hymen. Membranous tissue that, in virgin bitches, partially or completely covers the external opening of the vagina.

hyper-. A prefix meaning above or beyond; excessive.

hyperadrenocorticism (HAC). Cushing's syndrome (Cushing's disease); hyperactivity of the adrenal cortex.

hyperammonemia. Abnormally elevated ammonia levels in the blood.

hyperandrogenism. Excessive production of male sex hormones.

hypercalcemia. Abnormally elevated levels of calcium in the blood.

hyperchloremia. Abnormally elevated levels of chloride in the blood.

hyperemia. Reddening caused by increased blood flow.

hyperestrogenism. Excessive production of the female sex hormone estrogen.

hyperglycemia. Abnormally elevated levels of **glucose** (blood sugar) in the blood.

hyperhidrosis. Excessive sweating.

hyperkalemia. Abnormally elevated levels of potassium in the blood.

hyperkeratosis. Abnormal overgrowth of the horny layer of the epidermis.

hyperlipidemia. Abnormally elevated levels of fat in the blood.

hypernatremia. Abnormally elevated levels of sodium in the blood.

hyperparathyroidism. Hyperactivity of one or more parathyroid glands.

hyperphosphatemia. Abnormally elevated levels of phosphorus in the bloodstream.

hyperpigmentation. Localized, abnormal darkening of the normal skin color.

hyperplasia. Overgrowth due to an abnormal increase in the number of cells in a given tissue; contrasted with **hypertrophy.**

hyperplastic dermatosis of the West Highland White Terrier (Westie seborrhea). Uncommon, severe, chronic skin disease of West Highland White Terriers, with clinical features similar to primary seborrhea and seborrheic dermatitis.

hyperprogestinism. Excessive production of the hormone **progesterone.**

hypertension. Abnormally elevated blood pressure.

hyperthermia. Abnormally elevated body temperature; also, a method of heating tumors to lethal temperatures in an attempt to kill tumor cells.

hyperthyroidism. Excessive activity of the thyroid gland, with abnormally elevated secretion of thyroid hormones.

hypertrophy. Overgrowth due to an abnormal increase in the size of cells in a given tissue; contrasted with **hyperplasia.**

hyperviscosity syndrome. Abnormal thickening of the blood occurring in certain disease states, such as multiple myeloma.

hyphema. Ocular hemorrhage.

hypo-. A prefix meaning below or under; deficient.

hypoadrenocorticism. Addison's disease; insufficient secretion of steroid hormones from the adrenal cortex.

hypoalbuminemia. Abnormally low levels of the protein **albumin** in the blood, often reflecting abnormally low body stores of protein.

hypoallergenic. Minimizing allergic reactions.

hypocalcemia. Abnormally low levels of calcium in the blood.

hypochloremia. Abnormally low levels of chloride in the blood.

hypodermis. *See* SUBCUTIS.

hypoglycemia. Abnormally low levels of glucose (blood sugar) in the blood.

hypokalemia. Abnormally low levels of potassium in the blood.

hypoluteoidism. Sterility in the female caused by insufficient secretion of the hormone **progesterone.**

hyponatremia. Abnormally low levels of sodium in the blood.

hypoparathyroidism. Insufficient secretion of parathyroid hormone (PTH) from the parathyroid glands.

hypoperfusion. Reduced blood flow.

hypophosphatemia. Abnormally low levels of phosphorus in the blood.

hypoplasia. Underdevelopment or incomplete development of a given tissue.

hypoproteinemia. Abnormally low level of plasma proteins in the blood.

hypopyon. Accumulation of white blood cells (**pus**) in the anterior chamber of the eye.

hyposensitization. Regimen of injections intended to reduce an allergic individual's sensitivity to one or more allergens; "allergy shots."

hypostatic gene. A gene whose expression is masked by another gene.

hypothalamus. The part of the brain concerned with operation of much of the autonomic (unconscious) nervous system; production of specific hormones that are subsequently stored in and released by the pituitary gland; and regulation of body temperature, sleep cycles, and food and water intake.

hypothermia. Abnormally low body temperature; cooling of the body to slow metabolism.

hypothyroidism. Decreased thyroid function, with diminished secretion of thyroid hormone; the most common hormonal disorder affecting dogs.

hypotony. Decreased pressure within the eyeball.

hypotrichosis. Condition characterized by a sparse hair coat.

hypovolemia. Abnormally decreased volume of circulating blood; can lead to shock.

hypoxemia. Abnormally low blood oxygen levels.

hypoxia. Oxygen deprivation.

iatrogenic. Arising as a complication of medical treatment.

idiopathic. Having no known cause.

idiopathic polyarthritis. A polyarthritis (inflammation occurring simultaneously in several joints) of unknown cause, observed most often among sporting breeds of dogs.

idiopathic vestibular disease (vestibular syndrome). Disease of older dogs characterized by a sudden loss of balance, head-tilt, nystagmus, and an inability to walk normally (sometimes an inability to walk at all); usually resolves spontaneously without therapy.

ileus. Loss of normal intestinal motility.

immune complex. Antibody attached to (complexed with) an antigen.

immune-mediated (immunologically mediated). Refers to any condition wherein deleterious effects are caused wholly or in part by components of the immune system.

immunization. The administration of a vaccine to an individual in order to produce protective immunity against the infectious disease agent(s) present in the vaccine.

immunofluorescence assay (IFA). Assay technique for

the detection of antigen or antibody using antibodies labeled with a fluorescent dye.

immunoglobulins (antibodies). Specialized proteins produced by plasma cells (end-stage *B lymphocytes*) in response to the presence of foreign material (bacteria, viruses, toxins, etc.). Antibodies are capable of binding to the foreign material and thus alerting other immune cells to its presence. Often abbreviated Ig, there are five major classes: IgG, IgM, IgA, IgE, and IgD.

immunopotentiator. Any substance with either specific or nonspecific immune-boosting capabilities.

immunotherapy. The use of medications that boost the immune response, to assist in the treatment of a disease.

impetigo. Form of pyoderma characterized by development of superficial pustules not associated with hair follicles.

in utero. Within the uterus.

inactivated ("killed") vaccine. A vaccine in which the infectious agent has been modified in some manner (most often chemically) so that it no longer can infect and replicate within the host, but nevertheless is still capable of stimulating an immune response.

inappetence. Lack of appetite; also called **anorexia.**

inappropriate urination. Voluntary urination by a pet in places of which an owner disapproves.

incisional biopsy. Biopsy sample representing a portion of a larger lesion.

incisors. The front teeth; in the dog there are a total of six upper and six lower incisors.

incontinence. Loss of voluntary control over urination or defecation.

incubation period. The time between exposure to an infectious disease agent and the onset of clinical signs of disease.

indirect life cycle. With regard to parasites, a life cycle that can only be completed with the participation of an intermediate host.

infarct. Localized tissue death resulting from obstruction of the blood supply to the affected site.

infectious canine hepatitis. Disease of dogs and foxes caused by canine adenovirus type 1 (CAV-1); characterized by disease signs involving the liver, kidneys, eyes ("blue eye"), and **vascular endothelium** (cells lining the inner surface of blood vessels).

infectious cyclic thrombocytopenia. Periodic, cyclic decrease in the circulating blood platelet levels, caused by infection with a rickettsia, *Ehrlichia platys.*

infective stage. The specific stage in the life cycle of a parasite that is able to initiate an infection in a definitive or intermediate host.

infertility. Diminished ability to produce offspring.

inflammation. Protective response, often localized, involving white blood cells and other components of the body, wherein a disease agent or other irritant factor is sequestered and attempts are made to destroy it or neutralize its effects.

ingesta. Ingested food.

inguinal. Pertaining to the groin area.

inguinal canal. An opening deep within the groin area for passage of the spermatic cord or the round ligament of the uterus; inguinal ring.

inhalation pneumonia. Pneumonia caused by inhalation of noxious fumes, as during a house or forest fire.

innervation. The distribution of nerves to a particular tissue or body part.

insoluble fibers. Dietary fibers such as cellulose and wheat bran; they are good bulk-forming agents and are only poorly fermented (digested) by bacteria in the large intestine.

inspiration. The act of breathing air in; inhalation.

insulin. Critically important hormone produced by the beta cells of the endocrine pancreas; responsible for regulating the blood concentration of glucose, the body's most important fuel molecule.

insulin-dependent diabetes mellitus. Diabetes mellitus characterized by an inability to utilize blood glucose because of inadequate amounts of circulating insulin.

insulin-like growth factors. *See* SOMATOMEDINS.

insulinoma. Insulin-producing tumor of the endocrine portion of the pancreas; also called beta-cell tumor.

integument. The skin.

interdental spaces. Spaces between the teeth.

interestrus. Diestrus; the quiescent period between one heat period and the next.

interferons. A specialized group of protein molecules capable of inhibiting virus replication and the growth of tumor cells, and of modulating the activities of certain components of the immune system.

intermediate host. A host that (usually) is essential to the life cycle of a parasite and in which the parasite undergoes development to juvenile but not mature stages.

intersexuality. Having characteristics of both sexes intermingling in the same individual.

intertrigo. Superficial skin-fold dermatitis.

intervertebral disks. Cartilaginous, cushioning structures positioned between the vertebrae of the spinal column.

intoxication. Poisoning.

intracranial. Within the skull.

intramedullary pinning. Method of fracture repair wherein a stainless-steel rod (intramedullary pin) is placed down the central, marrow cavity of the fractured bone in order to realign and hold in place the broken pieces.

intramuscularly (IM). A route of injection (into the muscle).

intranasal (IN). Within the nasal passage; a route of administration of a vaccine by instilling it within the nasal passages.

intraocular pressure. The pressure within the eye.

intravenous pyelogram (IVP). Radiograph of the urinary tract after injecting dye for visualization of the various component structures.

intromission. Insertion of one part into another, as of the penis of the male into the vagina of the female during intercourse.

intubation. Insertion of a breathing tube into the trachea during anesthesia.

intussusception. Prolapse ("telescoping") of one section of bowel into an adjoining section.

involution. Period of repair in which there is a return to normal size and composition, as of the uterus following birth and expulsion of the placenta.

ionize. To separate into ions (charged atoms).

ionizing radiation. Radiation capable of ionizing matter;

examples include X rays and radioactive isotopes of elements such as radon, cesium and strontium.

iridocorneal filtration angle. The angle created by the cornea and the iris of the eye, through which the aqueous fluid exits the eyeball.

iridocyclitis. Inflammation of the iris and ciliary body of the eye.

iris (plural: irides). The circular, pigmented structure located behind the cornea; by expanding or contracting its central opening, or **pupil,** it regulates the amount of light penetrating the inner reaches of the eye.

iris cysts. Freely moving, floating brown spheres or "balloons" within the aqueous humor of the eye; in some cases they remain attached to the iris near the pupil margin, poking out from behind the iris into the pupillary space.

irritant contact dermatitis. Uncommon inflammatory skin disease caused by direct contact with an irritating concentration of an offending substance.

islets of Langerhans. The endocrine cells of the pancreas; the beta cells within the islets of Langerhans are the source of the critically important hormone **insulin.**

I.V. Intravenous.

ivermectin. Common medication used for killing the microfilarial forms of *Dirofilaria immitis,* the canine heartworm; also useful as a preventive medication for dogs living in heartworm-infested regions.

ixodid ticks. Hard-bodied ticks; distinguished from **argasid** (soft-bodied) **ticks.**

jaundice. Yellow discoloration of the skin and mucous membranes, caused by the deposition of bile pigment; most commonly a result of liver and/or bile-duct disease.

jejunum. The middle (and longest) portion of the small intestine, situated between the duodenum and the ileum.

jerk nystagmus. Nystagmus that alternates between a slow drift and a quick, jerklike movement.

joint capsule. Thin, saclike structure that envelopes a joint and contains within it all the elements of the joint, such as the the **articular cartilage,** synovial membrane, **synovial fluid,** etc.

junctionopathy. General term for any disorder of the neuromuscular junction.

karyotype. A magnified photographic array of the **chromosomes** derived from an individual cell.

kennel cough. A highly contagious, acute **tracheobronchitis** (inflammation of the trachea, larynx and bronchi) of dogs characterized by a peculiar, high-pitched "honking" cough; caused by the interaction of two or more infectious disease agents capable of infecting the upper respiratory tract.

keratectomy. Surgical removal of a portion of the cornea.

keratin. An insoluble, sulfur-rich protein that represents the principal component of skin, hair and nails.

keratinization. The process whereby keratinocytes in the epidermis mature to form the outer, horny layer of the skin.

keratinocytes. Skin cells that produce **keratin;** they are the major cell type of the **epidermis,** the outermost layer of the skin.

keratitis. Inflammation of the cornea.

keratoacanthoma. Benign skin tumor superficially resembling squamous cell carcinoma.

keratoconjunctivitis sicca (KCS). A serious condition of the eye caused by impaired tear secretion; also called "dry eye."

keratolytic. Capable of causing softening and peeling of the outer (horny) layer of the skin.

ketone bodies (ketones). Organic compounds produced by fatty acid and carbohydrate metabolism in the liver; elevated (toxic) levels are often produced in individuals with diabetes mellitus.

ketonuria. Spillage of ketone bodies (ketones) into the urine in **diabetic ketoacidosis.**

kidney. Either of the two bean-shaped organs in the lower abdmoninal cavity that are responsible for filtering toxic waste products from the blood, producing the important hormone **erythropietin,** and maintaining the body's water and electrolyte balance.

kilocalorie (kcal). Unit defined as the amount of energy required to raise the temperature of 1 kilogram of water 1 degree Celsius (centigrade); the "large" calorie; commonly called simply Calorie.

kilogram. One thousand grams (2.2 pounds).

Klinefelter's syndrome. Chromosomal abnormality in male human beings characterized by an extra X chromosome; in dogs, it is known as 79, XXY testicular hypoplasia and aspermogenesis.

Knott's test. Technique for detecting immature forms (microfilariae) of the canine heartworm (*Dirofilaria immitis*) in a blood sample.

labia. The external lips or folds of the vulva of the female.

labile. Chemically unstable; easily destroyed.

lacrimal gland. Tear gland.

lactase. Intestinal enzyme that breaks down lactose (milk sugar).

lactated Ringer's solution. A sterile salt solution for (usually intravenous, but sometimes subcutaneous) administration containing sodium lactate, sodium chloride, potassium chloride, and calcium chloride; given to restore fluid and electrolyte balance.

lactation. Production of milk by the female.

lactose. Milk sugar.

lagophthalmos. An inability to close the eyelids completely.

Langerhans cells. Cells found in the **epidermis,** the outermost layer of the skin, that are important in generating immune responses in the skin.

laparoscopy. Visual inspection of the interior of the abdominal cavity with a specialized instrument (a laparoscope), inserted through the body wall.

larvae (singular: larva). Immature forms or stages in the life cycle of certain small animals, such as insects or parasites.

laryngitis. Inflammation of the larynx.

laryngoscopy. Visual examination of the larynx.

larynx. Muscular, cartilage-containing structure comprising the upper part of the respiratory tract between the pharynx and trachea, and containing the vocal chords; the "voice-box."

laser therapy. Use of lasers in tumor removal, in an effort to minimize local contamination of the surgical site and to decrease the potential for spreading tumor cells.

latent infection. Dormant stage of certain infections during which the infectious agent is known to be present but is not actively replicating and cannot be detected by usual means.

lecithin. Fatty acid-rich constituent of the outer surface of cell membranes; also called phosphatidylcholine.

leiomyoma. Benign tumor of smooth muscle cells.

leiomyosarcoma. Malignant tumor of smooth muscle cells.

leishmaniasis. Disease caused by protozoa of the genus *Leishmania.*

lens. Transparent refractive structure that finely focuses images onto the retina for clear and sharp vision.

leptospires. Spiral-shaped bacteria belonging to the **spirochete** group.

leptospirosis. Bacterial disease caused by leptospires, characterized by kidney disease, liver disease, or hemorrhages.

lesion. Any disease-induced abnormality of tissue structure or tissue function.

lethargy. An abnormal state of drowsiness or dullness.

leukocoria. A whitening of the pupil of the eye.

leukocytes. White blood cells.

leukocytosis. Increase in the number of circulating white blood cells.

leukopenia. Reduction in the number of circulating white blood cells.

leukotrichia. Whitening of the hair, often localized.

leukotrienes. Compounds that act as modulators of allergic and inflammatory reactions.

level bite. Mild type of **prognathism,** wherein the incisor teeth meet cusp-tip to cusp-tip, rather than having the uppers overlap the lowers.

lichenification. Leathery thickening of the outer layer of the skin, usually caused by excessive scratching or rubbing.

lick granuloma. Skin condition caused by prolonged licking at a specific area, usually a leg or paw; also called **acral lick dermatitis.**

life cycle. The life story of a parasite's development.

ligament. Strengthening band of fibrous tissue, for supporting and stabilizing a joint structure.

ligate. To bind or tie off.

limbus. The line of demarcation between the cornea and sclera of the eye.

linoleic acid. An essential fatty acid acquired from vegetable sources; important in the biosynthesis of cell membranes.

lipase. An enzyme that breaks down fat.

lipid(s). Fat(s).

lipid film. A layering of fat.

lipidosis. Abnormal accumulation of fat within cells.

lipoma. Benign tumor of fat cells.

liposarcoma. Malignant tumor of fat cells.

lobulated. Divided into small lobes, or lobules.

lochia. Vaginal discharge that continues for several days after giving birth.

lockjaw. *See* TRISMUS.

locus (plural: **loci**). The site on a chromosome where a specific gene is located.

lordosis. Downward curvature of the lumbar spine; "swayback."

lumbosacral. Pertaining to the lower back region.

lumen. The interior of a blood vessel or tubular organ, such as the intestine.

lumpectomy. Surgical removal of a mass; used with special reference to masses in the mammary gland.

lupus. Systemic lupus erythematosus (SLE), a multisystemic autoimmune disorder.

luteal phase. In the reproductive cycle, the period during which the ovarian follicle converts to a **corpus luteum** and secretes the hormone progesterone.

luteinization. Conversion of the ovarian follicle to a corpus luteum.

luteinizing hormone (LH). Hormone produced by the pituitary gland; together with follicle-stimulating hormone (FSH) it assists in causing ovulation and inducing production of the hormone **estrogen.**

luteinizing hormone-releasing hormone (LH-RH). Hormone released from the hypothalamus of the brain, that triggers the release of luteinizing hormone (LH) and follicle-stimulating hormone (FSH) from the pituitary gland; also called gonadotropin-releasing hormone.

luxation. Dislocation of a joint; also, total displacement of the lens of the eye from its normal position.

Lyme borreliosis (Lyme disease). An infectious arthritis caused by a spirochete bacterium, *Borrelia burgdorferi.*

lymph. Generally clear fluid drained from tissues, that circulates within the lymphatic vessels and contains fats, proteins and specialized cells (lymphocytes).

lymph node. Any of the body's many nodular accumulations of lymphoid cells; they are interconnected by means of lymphatic vessels.

lymph-node aspirate. Sample of fluid and cells from deep within a lymph node, obtained using a needle and syringe.

lymphadenitis. Inflammation of one or more lymph nodes.

lymphadenopathy. Enlargement of one or more lymph nodes, as from inflammation, infection or cancer.

lymphangiectasia. Disease resulting from dilation of lymphatic vessels of the intestinal tract.

lymphocyte. A type of white blood cell capable of responding to the presence of foreign material in the body; lymphocytes play a central role in directing and coordinating immune responses.

lymphocytic thyroiditis. Immune-mediated inflammation of the thyroid gland; a cause of hypothyroidism.

lymphocytosis. Abnormal increase in the number of circulating lymphocytes.

lymphoma (lymphosarcoma). Both terms indicate malignant tumor of lymphocytes; however, some types of lymphocytic tumors are categorized only as lymphomas.

maceration. Softening or dissolution of skin cell layers, resulting from overexposure to moisture or topical medications.

macroblepharon. Excessively long eyelids.

macropalpebral fissure. An enlarged eyelid opening.

macrophage. A specialized white blood cell of central importance to the body; it ingests cellular debris and foreign material, destroys ingested microorganisms, processes ingested antigens as an initial step in the induction of a specific immune response, and synthesizes a number of important enzymes, coagulation factors and messenger molecules; also referred to as a mononuclear **phagocyte.**

macule. A discolored area of skin that is not elevated above the skin surface.

maintenance energy requirement (MER). The amount of energy used by a moderately active adult dog in a thermoneutral environment, i.e., at optimal ambient temperature.

malabsorption. Faulty absorption of nutrients by the intestinal mucosa.

malassimilation. Defective transport of one or more nutrients from the intestinal contents across the intestinal wall.

maldigestion. Faulty digestion.

malignant. Capable of spreading and invading other tissues; said of tumors.

malocclusion. Abnormal "bite" or fitting together of the teeth when the jaws are closed.

mammary gland. Breast.

mammectomy. Surgical removal of a mammary gland; also called **mastectomy.**

mandible. The lower jaw.

mast cell. A specialized, granule-containing cell found in the skin and lining of the inner body surfaces; it plays a central role in the development of allergy.

mastectomy. Surgical removal of one or more mammary glands; also called **mammectomy.**

mastication. The action of chewing.

masticatory muscle myositis. An inflammatory muscle disease of unknown cause that is limited to the muscles of **mastication** (chewing).

mastitis. Inflammation of one or more mammary glands.

maternal immunity. A form of temporary immunity that is passed from mother to offspring *in utero* (in the uterus) and/or after birth in the colostrum and milk; primarily antibody, maternal immunity serves to protect the neonate until its own immune defenses become fully operative.

maxilla. The upper jaw.

mechanical vector. A vector that merely serves physically to transport a parasite from one host to another.

meconium. The contents of the first bowel movement of a newborn pup.

medial canthus. The inner corner of the eye.

Mediterranean spotted fever. Alternative name for **boutonneuse fever,** a tick-borne zoonosis occurring in southern Europe, Africa and India.

medulla. The innermost part of an organ (kidney, adrenal gland, brain) or hair shaft; contrasted with **cortex.**

megaesophagus. Enlargement of the esophagus, caused by paralysis of the esophageal musculature and resulting in regurgitation.

megakaryocyte. A giant cell found in the bone marrow; it is the precursor of the blood platelets.

megalophthalmos. Congenital defect characterized by an oversized eyeball.

meibomian glands. Sebaceous glands of the eyelids.

meiosis. Process involved in the formation of **gametes** (reproductive cells), wherein cell division produces new cells (**spermatozoa** and **ova**) containing only one set of chromosomes.

melanin. Dark pigment of skin and hair.

melanoblasts. Immature melanin-forming cells that originate early in fetal life.

melanocytes. Cells of the **epidermis,** the outermost layer of the skin, that produce the skin pigment **melanin.**

melanoma. A (usually) malignant tumor of pigmented skin cells.

melanotrichia. Abnormal darkening of the hair color.

melena. Dark, pitchy stool caused by bleeding into the digestive tract.

meninges. The three protective membranes surrounding the brain and spinal cord; specifically, the *d*ura mater, pia mater, and arachnoid.

meningitis. Inflammation of the meninges.

meront. *See* SCHIZONT.

merozoites. The daughter cells resulting from either **schizogony** or **endodyogeny** (asexual forms of reproduction in certain protozoa).

mesenteric. Pertaining to the mesentery, the membrane that lines the abdominal organs and attaches them to the body wall.

mesothelioma. Rare, highly malignant tumor of the lining surfaces of the lungs, heart, chest or abdominal cavity; possibly associated with exposure to asbestos.

mesovarium. Fold of tissue that holds the ovaries in place.

metabolic energy (ME). The caloric content of a diet; can be roughly estimated from the proximate analysis.

metabolic water. Water the body obtains from solid food and the breakdown of ingested fat, carbohydrate and protein.

metabolism. All the life-sustaining biochemical processes in the body; the conversion of nutrients into energy.

metabolites. By-products of metabolism.

metabolizable energy (ME). The difference between the gross energy of a food and the energy that is lost in urine and feces.

metacercaria. Infective larval form of flukes that arises from the cercaria stage.

metastasis. Spread of tumor cells from the primary tumor site to distant body sites; a characteristic of malignant tumors (cancers).

metestrus. In the estrus cycle, the period of subsidence of follicular activity that follows **estrus** ("heat").

methemoglobinemia. Blood abnormality resulting in reduced ability of the red blood cells to carry oxygen.

metritis. Inflammation of the uterus.

microbe. Any minute living organism, particularly one capable of causing disease; viruses, because they are not living organisms, technically are not considered "microbes," but are more correctly referred to by a term such as "infectious agent."

microfilaremia. Presence of microfilariae in the bloodstream.

microfilaria (plural: **microfilariae**). Minute prelarval stage of the heartworm parasite, *Dirofilaria immitis.*

microfilaricide. Medication to kill microfilariae.

microphthalmos. Developmental abnormality resulting in an undersized eyeball.

microscopic agglutination test (MAT). Standard serologic assay for detection of antibodies to leptospires.

microvasculature. The smallest blood vessels (**capillaries**).

miliary dermatitis. Miliary eczema; disease characterized by many small, reddened, crusty skin lesions.

mineralocorticoids. Corticosteroids whose primary function is regulation of water and electrolyte balance; they act by retaining sodium and excreting potassium within the kidney tubules.

minimal inhibitory concentration (MIC). Laboratory test procedure for determining the sensitivity or resistance of a bacterial isolate to several antibiotics.

miotic. Any ophthalmic medication that causes the pupil to contract.

miracidium. Free-living larval form in the life cycle of flukes.

miticide. Medication that kills mites.

mitochondria (singular: **mitochondrion**). Specialized structures within body cells that are responsible for producing energy.

mitosis. Process wherein a body cell divides into two exact copies of itself, each new cell receiving two complete sets of chromosomes.

mitotic. Actively undergoing cell division.

mitral regurgitation. Partial backflow of blood through a dysfunctioning mitral valve.

mitral valve. The **atrioventricular valve** on the left side of the heart.

Mittendorf's dot. Opaque dot on the back of the lens, representing a persistent remnant of the fetal hyaloid artery that supplies the eye with blood in utero.

modified-live virus (MLV). Attenuated (weakened) virus that no longer produces clinical disease in the host but retains the ability to induce a protective immune response; can be used as a vaccine; technically a misnomer, since viruses are not living organisms.

molars. The grinding teeth lying behind the premolars; in the dog, there are a total of four upper and six lower molars.

monocyte. Nondescript (but hardly mild-mannered) white blood cell found in the circulation, which converts into an active **macrophage** upon entry into tissue.

morphogenesis. The progressive development of form and shape of an organism, or of an individual organ or tissue within the organism.

morphology. The shape and structure of an organ or of an entire organism.

motile. Capable of movement.

motility. Ability to move.

motoneuron. A nerve cell that supplies myofibers in skeletal muscle.

motor nerve conduction velocities. Electrodiagnostic test that provides information about the integrity of nerve fibers, principally the fastest-conducting motor nerve fibers, for the purposes of disease diagnosis.

motor unit. The basic functional and anatomical organization of nerves and muscle fibers within skeletal muscle.

mucociliary escalator. A coordinated and forceful wavelike movement of the *cilia* lining the air passageways from the trachea to the bronchioles; essential for the normal removal of mucus and inhaled particulate matter and bacteria.

mucocutaneous junctions. Areas where mucous membranes and skin adjoin, such as the lip margins.

mucoid. Resembling mucus.

mucometra. Presence of mucus in the uterus.

mucosal-associated lymphoid tissue (MALT). Lymphoid tissue associated with the linings of the digestive, respiratory and urogenital tracts.

mucous membranes. Lubricating membranes lining the internal surfaces of body cavities, such as the mouth, digestive tract, respiratory tract and urinary tract.

mucus. Slimy substance secreted by certain membranes (mucous membranes); contains a variety of secretions, salts and cells.

multiple myeloma. An uncommon malignant tumor of plasma cells arising from the bone marrow.

murmur. An abnormal heart sound produced when blood flows too rapidly or too chaotically through a portion of the heart; a common sign of heart disease.

muscle action potential. The wavelike electrical impulse that spreads throughout a muscle and triggers the events leading to muscle contraction.

mutation. A permanent genetic change, sometimes resulting in altered structure or function.

myasthenia gravis (MG). A disorder of the neuromuscular junction caused by a deficiency of acetylcholine receptors on the myofiber membrane; characterized primarily by muscular weakness.

mycetoma. General term for a swollen, progressing, tumorlike skin lesion caused either by fungi or certain bacteria.

mycology. The study of fungi.

mycoplasmas. Microscopic organisms closely related to bacteria that are ubiquitous inhabitants of the respiratory and genital tracts; they appear to contribute to some extent to the total disease syndrome in **kennel cough.**

mycosis fungoides. Unique skin tumor involving lymphoid cells.

mydriatic. Any ophthalmic medication that dilates the pupil.

myelin. Fatty substance forming the outer tunic (myelin sheath) around many nerve axons; facilitates the conduction of nerve impulses along the axons.

myelogenous. Originating within the bone marrow.

myelography. Radiologic study of the spinal canal; myelogram.

myelopathy. General term for any degenerative disorder affecting the spinal cord.

myiasis. Infestation of body tissue by fly maggots.

myocarditis. Inflammatory heart-muscle disease.

myocardium. The muscular layer of the heart; heart muscle.

myoclonus. Involuntary rapid, jerky twitching or contraction of muscles; a common complication of canine distemper.

myofibers. Muscle fibers.

myofibrils. Slender threadlike structures, bundles of which make up each muscle fiber.

myofilaments. Smaller threadlike elements making up

the myofibrils of muscles.

myonecrosis. Muscle-cell death.

myopathy. General term for any muscle disorder.

myosin. One of the proteins responsible for muscle contraction.

myositis. Muscle inflammation.

myxedema. Swelling or puffiness of the skin caused by hypothyroidism.

myxoma. Benign skin tumor derived from primitive connective tissue cells; often found as a component of benign mixed mammary tumors.

myxosarcoma. Malignant skin tumor derived from primitive connective tissue cells.

nanogram. One billionth of a gram.

nares. The two halves of the nasal passages; also, the external and internal openings of the nasal passages.

nasal septum. Vertical dividing wall that separates the two nasal passages.

nasopharynx. The rear portion of the pharynx, above the soft palate.

natural killer (NK) cells. Specialized lymphocytes that are important in detecting and eliminating tumor cells and virus-infected cells.

nebulization. Conversion of a liquid into a spray or mist; employed in aerosol therapy, wherein a drug (antibiotic or other compound) is delivered by misting or spraying it into the airways, usually by means of a funnel or cone placed over the nose; useful in treating pneumonia and certain other respiratory ailments.

necrolysis. Separation or peeling of tissue caused by cell death.

necropsy. Examination of an animal after death; postmortem; autopsy on an animal.

necrosis. Cell death.

necrotic. Composed of dead cells.

necrotizing. Causing cell death.

Negri bodies. Intracellular inclusion bodies sometimes found in brain cells of animals or humans with rabies.

nematode. General term for a roundworm.

neonatal. Newborn.

neonatal isoerythrolysis. Acute hemolytic anemia of the newborn caused by ingestion of antibodies in the dam's colostrum and milk that are directed against the neonate's red blood cells; also called **hemolytic disease of the newborn.**

neoplasia. Uncontrolled, progressive proliferation of cells under conditions that normally should be restrictive of cell growth; formation of a tumor.

neoplasm. Tumor.

neovascularization. Growth of new blood vessels into an abnormal site, such as a tumor.

nephritis. Kidney inflammation.

nephrolith. Kidney stone.

nephrosclerosis. Scarring of kidney tissue; a principal cause of the normal, progressive deterioration of kidney function that accompanies aging.

nephrotic syndrome. Abnormal fluid retention as edema or ascites, resulting from glomerular disease of the kidneys.

nervous tunic. *See* RETINA.

neural deafness. Congenital deafness caused by failure of the sound-receptor cells in the ear to form.

neuritis. Inflammation of a nerve.

neurofibroma. Benign tumor of the nervous system arising from Schwann cells.

neuromuscular junctions. The intimate connections between muscle cells and adjacent nerve cells, representing a specialized extension of the *sarcolemma.*

neuromyopathy. General term for any disorder affecting both neurons and muscle fibers.

neuron. An individual nerve cell.

neuronal ceroid-lipofuscinosis. Inherited, inevitably fatal disease characterized by signs of impaired vision and mental degeneration; caused by deposition of fat granules in nerve cells.

neuropathy. Any disorder of the peripheral nervous system.

neurotoxin. Any toxin targeting the nervous system.

neutropenia. An abnormal decrease in the number of circulating neutrophils.

neutrophil. A type of white blood cell capable of engulfing and destroying bacteria and other disease agents, immune complexes, and cell debris.

neutrophilia. An abnormal increase in the number of circulating neutrophils.

nevus (plural: nevi). Any stable, well-defined lesion of congenital origin affecting any cellular component of the skin; birthmark.

nit. Louse egg.

nocardiosis. Bacterial infection with similarities to actinomycosis; caused by members of the genus *Nocardia.*

nocturia. Excessive urination at night.

nodule. A large papule; small lump.

nodulectomy. Surgical removal of a nodule; used with special reference to nodules or masses in the mammary glands.

nuclear magnetic resonance imaging (NMR, MRI). Highly specialized diagnostic technique for visualizing internal structures of the body using an external magnetic field.

nuclear sclerosis. Common disorder wherein the central region of the lens of the eye becomes dense and hard compared to the peripheral region; a consequence of the aging process.

nucleic acids. General term for **deoxyribonucleic acid (DNA)** and **ribonucleic acid (RNA)**, DNA serving as the genetic material of all living organisms and some viruses.

nucleotide. An individual unit of DNA.

nulliparous. Having never given birth.

nutritional secondary hyperparathyroidism. Disease caused by a calcium deficiency, a marked imbalance in the ratio of calcium to phosphorus in the diet, or a combination of both; the end result is the withdrawal of calcium from the bones.

nystagmus. Rapid, involuntary, rhythmic eye movements, often indicative of central nevous system dysfunction.

obligatory parasite. A parasite whose life cycle cannot be completed without a parasitic phase at some stage.

occlude. To close off or obstruct.

occlusion. A blockage or closure; also, the fit or "bite" of the upper and lower teeth together when in contact following closure of the mouth.

ocular. Pertaining to the eyes.

ocular larva migrans. Disease of human beings caused usually by the canine ascarid *Toxocara canis,* and very rarely by the feline ascarid *Toxocara cati;* disease symptoms result from migration of the parasitic ascarid larvae through the eyes.

odontoblasts. Cells lining the pulp chamber of the tooth; they manufacture dentin.

old dog vestibular syndrome. Disorder of elderly dogs characterized by very sudden onset of severe vestibular signs (loss of balance, circling, abnormal position or movements of the eyes).

olfactory. Pertaining to smell.

oliguria. Reduction in the amount of urine excreted.

omnivore. Any organism that can subsist on either plant or animal tissue.

omphalophlebitis. Infection (usually bacterial) of the veins of the umbilical cord in the newborn; "navel ill."

oncogenesis. The process of tumor development.

oncologist. Cancer specialist.

oocyte. Developing egg cell (**ovum**) in the ovary.

oocyst. An encapsulated ovum (egg) of a sporozoan parasite such as *Toxoplasma gondii,* usually excreted in the feces.

oömycosis. Uncommon disease caused by organisms of the genus *Pythium,* and thus also called **pythiosis;** characterized by swellings, skin ulcerations, lymph node enlargement and draining tracts, with or without involvement of internal organs; also known by the more general term **phycomycosis.**

opacification. Loss of transparency.

opacity. An opaque area or spot, as in the lens or cornea of the eye.

open bite. Severe form of wry bite wherein the upper and lower incisor teeth are unable to come together when the jaws are closed.

open reduction. Any procedure to repair a fracture wherein the broken bone is exposed surgically.

ophthalmoscope. Instrument for viewing the interior of the eye.

opportunistic pathogen. Any organism that is able to induce disease only if the host's immune or other defenses are compromised.

optic disk. That portion of the optic nerve visible at the surface of the retina; also called optic nerve head.

optic nerve. An extension of the brain, which reaches to the back of the eye (**retina**) and transmits signals derived from light energy that are translated into a visual image by the brain.

optic neuritis. Inflammation of the optic nerve.

orchitis. Inflammatory disease of the testicle.

organ of Corti. The spiral-shaped organ of hearing within the inner ear, containing specialized sensory receptors.

oropharynx. The back of the throat; tonsillar area, between the soft palate and epiglottis.

os penis. Penile bone, or **baculum;** bone present in the penis of male dogs.

ossicles. Small bones.

osteoblast. A bone-forming cell.

osteochondrosis dissecans (OCD). A genetic disease seen in young, fast-growing, active dogs of medium and large breeds; characterized by degeneration of bone underlying the articular cartilage of joint surfaces, often accompanied by a rupture or break in the cartilage itself; also called osteochondritis dissecans.

osteomalacia. Vitamin D and calcium deficiency disease in adult dogs, characterized by bone softening.

osteomyelitis. Infection of bone with pus formation, usually caused by bacteria.

osteopenia. Loss of bone calcium.

osteoporosis. Thinning and weakening of bone.

osteosarcoma (osteogenic sarcoma). A malignant tumor of bone.

osteotomy. Surgical cutting of bone.

otitis externa. Inflammation of the outer ear.

otitis interna. Inflammation of the inner ear; also called labyrinthitis.

otitis media. Inflammation of the middle ear; also called **tympanitis.**

otoplasty. *See* COSMETIC OTOPLASTY.

otoscope. Medical instrument equipped with a light for inspecting the ear canal.

ova. See *ovum.*

ovarian follicle. An **ovum** (egg) and its surrounding cells.

ovariectomy. Surgical removal of one or both ovaries.

ovaries. Paired organs of the female responsible for the production of ova (eggs).

ovariohysterectomy (OVH). Surgical removal of the uterus and ovaries; spay operation.

oviducts. *See* UTERINE TUBES.

ovotestes. Abnormal gonads containing both testicular and ovarian tissue.

ovulation. Release of an egg from an ovary.

ovum (plural: ova). Egg.

oxidation. The cellular "burning" of glucose, amino acids and fatty acids to produce energy in the form of **adenosine triphosphate (ATP),** the major form of energy used by cells.

oxygenated. Filled with oxygen; said of arterial blood.

oxytocin. A hormone formed in the hypothalamic region of the brain and stored in the pituitary gland; it stimulates contraction of the uterus and milk ejection, and is of therapeutic value in certain cases of **dystocia** (difficult birth).

pacemaker. Nerve tissue that controls the heart's rate of contraction and relaxation; also known as the **sinoatrial node.** An artificial pacemaker is an electrical device implanted surgically to treat abnormally slow heart rhythms (**bradycardias**).

packed cell volume (PCV). A measurement of the volume of red blood cells in relation to the volume of blood fluid, expressed as a percentage; also called the **hematocrit.**

palliation. Alleviation of clinical signs in the absence of specific treatment of the underlying disorder.

palpable. Detectable by touch or feeling.

palpate. To examine by feeling with the hands and fingers.

palpebral. Pertaining to an eyelid.

palsy. Paralysis.

pancreatic exocrine insufficiency. Digestive disorder caused by loss of function of the exocrine portion of the pancreas; characterized by a ravenous appetite, voluminous stool, and failure to gain weight.

pancytopenia. Condition in which red blood cell, white blood cell and platelet cell numbers are all decreased in the circulation.

panniculitis. Inflammation of subcutaneous fat.

pannus. Nonulcerative, noninfectious inflammatory condition of the canine cornea that is highly progressive and potentially blinding; also called chronic superficial keratitis and German Shepherd pannus.

papilledema. Swelling of the optic nerve.

papillomas. Warts.

papule. A minute, firm, well-demarcated elevation of the skin.

papulocrustous. Characterized by minute, firm, crusty elevations of the skin.

papulopustular dermatitis. Inflammatory skin disorder characterized by the presence of both papules and pustules (pus-filled nodules).

paralysis. Total absence of voluntary movement in a muscle or set of muscles.

paransal sinuses. Passages within the upper respiratory tract that are actually holes in the skull that empty directly into the nasal cavity; in the dog, there are three paranasal sinuses, the frontal, maxillary and sphenoid sinuses.

parasite. Any organism that is dependent in some manner for its continued existence on another organism (its host), most often to the detriment of the host.

parasitemia. Presence of a parasite in the blood circulation.

parasitism. Any parasite infection or infestation.

parasitology. The study of parasites.

paratenic host. An "optional" host in a parasite's life cycle in which juvenile stages may persist but do not develop.

parathyroid glands. Twin, small pairs of endocrine glands located adjacent to the thyroid gland; they secrete parathyroid hormone (PTH), which is essential for the regulation of calcium and phosphorus balance in the body.

parathyroid hormone (PTH). Hormone secreted by the parathyroid glands that regulates the metabolism of calcium and phosphorus in the body.

parenteral. By injection (i.e., not by the oral route); injectable.

paresis. Diminished ability to move a muscle or a body part voluntarily.

parietal pleura. Thin, transparent membrane that forms the inner lining of the chest cavity.

paronychia. Pus-forming (usually bacterial) infection of a nail bed.

paroxysm. A sudden bout.

parthenogenesis. Mode of reproduction wherein the female produces offspring without the need for fertilization by a male.

parturition. The act of giving birth.

pasteurellosis. In people, a major complication of dog (and cat) bites, caused by the bacterium *Pasteurella multocida;* manifested clinically by swelling, inflammation and intense pain at the site of the bite.

patch. A large macule.

patella. Kneecap, a small triangular sesamoid bone located in front of the the knee and within the tendon of the quadriceps extensor femoris muscle.

patellar luxation. Displacement of the kneecap.

patent. Unobstructed, open.

patent ductus arteriosus (PDA). Abnormal persistence after birth of the embryonic blood vessel connecting the pulmonary artery to the aorta; requires surgical intervention to prevent the recirculation of arterial blood through the lungs.

patent infection. With regard to parasites, an infection in a definitive host that results in the appearance of products of the parasite's reproduction (eggs, larvae, etc.).

pathogen. Any microbial agent capable of causing disease.

pathogenesis. The cellular, biochemical and pathological mechanism(s) underlying the development of a disease.

pathogenic. Able to cause disease.

pathogenicity. The relative ability of an organism to cause disease.

pattern baldness. *See* ACQUIRED PATTERN ALOPECIA.

pectinate ligaments. Lattice-like layers of fine strands that bridge the angle created by the cornea and iris of the eye.

pedicle. A small stalk or stem.

pedunculated. On a stalk.

pelvic rotation. A surgical treatment for **hip dysplasia,** wherein the hip socket is moved outward to provide more coverage of the head of the **femur** (thighbone).

pelvic symphysis. The joint formed by the union of the two halves of the pubic bone of the pelvis.

pelvis. Hip.

pemphigus foliaceus. An uncommon autoimmune disease characterized by autoantibody production and the subsequent development of vesicles and pustules in the superficial layers of the skin.

pemphigus vulgaris. A very rare autoimmune disease characterized by the development of vesicles in the skin.

pendular nystagmus. Nystagmus characterized by smooth and equal movement of the eyes in both directions.

penicillins. A large group of antibiotics derived primarily from fungi of the genus *Penicillium;* of pivotal importance in the treatment of diseases caused by certain bacteria such as the streptococci, clostridia, and spirochetes, penicillins interfere with the vital synthesis of bacterial cell walls.

penile bone. Bone found in the penis of certain species, including dogs; **os penis,** or **baculum.**

peptide. A short chain of amino acids; peptides form the building blocks of proteins.

peracute. Of extremely rapid onset.

percutaneous needle biopsy. Technique by which a sample of organ tissue is obtained for examination by maneuvering a biopsy needle through the skin and into the organ of interest (often the kidney or liver).

perianal. In the region of the anus.

perianal adenoma. Perianal gland tumor.

perianal fistulas. Chronic draining tracts in the tissues around the anus, most common in German Shepherd dogs.

perianal gland. Modified sebaceous glands found in the vicinity of the anus in dogs.

perianal gland tumor. Common (usually benign) tumor of the perianal gland in older male dogs; perianal adenoma.

pericardial effusion. Abnormal accumulation of fluid in the pericardial sac.

pericardial sac (pericardium). The layered, membranous sac that surrounds the heart and is attached at its base to the diaphragm.

perinatal period. The period shortly before and after birth.

perineal hernia. Syndrome wherein the wall of the rectum protrudes through the pelvic musculature and becomes impacted with feces.

perineum. Region between the thighs encompassing the anus and genitalia.

periodontal disease. Progressive, bacteria-induced disease of the tooth-holding structures, the end-result being tooth mobility and tooth loss; the most common cause of tooth loss in dogs, cats and people.

periodontal ligament. Structure composed of tiny fibers that serves to attach the tooth root to the bone of the jaw.

periodontal pocket. A gingival sulcus that has become diseased as the result of chronic gingivitis/periodontitis (periodontal disease).

periodontitis. Inflammation of the gum tissue surrounding the basal portion of a tooth, characterized by loss of the microscopic gum-tooth attachment and alveolar bone destruction.

periorbit. Eye socket.

periosteum. The highly sensitive connective tissue sheathing the bones; it contains a rich blood supply and provides for the nutrition, growth, repair, and protection of the underlying bone.

peripheral nervous system (PNS). The cranial, spinal and peripheral nerves and their connections to muscle or to sensory receptors.

peristalsis. Muscular movements of the intestinal tract that function to propel contents longitudinally through the tract.

peritoneal dialysis. Procedure to compensate for failing kidney function by using the lining of the peritoneal cavity as a filter to remove waste products from the blood.

permeability. Leakiness; ability to be penetrated.

persistent hyperplastic primary vitreous. Congenital ocular abnormality caused by failure of the fetal hyaloid artery (part of the developing eye's internal vascular system) to regress, accompanied by the formation of fibrous tissue, leading to development of a plaque of fibrous, vascular tissue on the back of the lens.

persistent primary vitreous. Condition wherein the fetal hyaloid artery (part of the developing eye's internal vascular system) persists as a posterior remnant, seen as a red or white "tail" in front of the optic disk.

persistent pupillary membranes. (PPMs). Tiny strands in the eyes of some juvenile and adult dogs, representing remnants of the fetal iris vessels and tissues.

pH. A measure of the hydrogen ion concentration of a solution, reflective of acidity (pH below 7) or alkalinity (pH above 7), with a pH value of 7 representing neutrality.

phacoemulsification. Technique for removing the lens of the eye, involving fragmentation of the lens by ultrasonic vibrations.

phaeohyphomycosis. An uncommon chronic infection of the subcutaneous tissues caused by dark, pigmented fungi (*dematiaceous* fungi).

phagocyte. Any cell type (such as a neutrophil or macrophage) able to engulf and digest minute particulate matter.

pharyngeal. Pertaining to the pharynx.

pharyngoesophageal sphincter. Sphincter located between the pharynx and esophagus.

pharynx. Area extending from the rear of the mouth and nasal passages to the larynx and esophagus.

phenotype. The visible, physical expression of a genetic trait, e.g., blue eyes or red hair.

pheochromocytoma. Catecholamine-producing tumor of the adrenal medulla.

pheromones. Chemical secretions that elicit a specific behavioral response (often attraction) in another individual of the same species.

phlebotomy. Therapeutic bloodletting.

phlegm. Viscous secretion produced by the respiratory tract.

phosphofructokinase deficiency. Syndrome of hemolytic anemia in English Springer Spaniels caused by a deficiency of a red blood cell enzyme, phosphofructokinase.

phospholipids. Fats containing phosphorus.

photodynamic therapy. Use of a photosensitizing compound and light to kill tumor cells.

photon. The energy unit of visible light, having characteristics both of a wave as well as a discrete particle.

photoperiod. The length of time per day that an animal is exposed to natural or artificial light.

photophobia. Visual hypersensitivity to light.

photoreceptors. Specialized light receptors (**rods** and **cones**) present in the retina of the eye.

photosensitizing. Sensitizing to the effect of light.

phthisis bulbi. Shrinking or wasting of the eyeball, with such internal scarring that no recognizable structures remain.

phycomycosis. General term for diseases caused by a number of fungi, including *Mucor, Rhizopus, Absidia* and *Pythium,* and characterized by inflammation and blockage of small blood vessels.

physiology. The study of body function and metabolism.

physis (plural: physes). A growth plate of a bone; an area where new bone growth originates.

phytates. Form of inositol (a sugarlike compound) found in plants; excessive amounts in the diet can interfere with the absorption of zinc from the digestive tract.

picogram. One trillionth of a gram.

piloerection. Reflex by which the muscles at the base of the hair shafts cause the hair to "stand on end."

pinna. The external portion, or flap, of the ear.

pituitary dwarfism. Developmental defect in German Shepherd dogs caused by an insufficiency of growth hormone from the pituitary gland.

pituitary gland. Endocrine gland located at the base of the brain, and connected to it by a narrow stalk; it stores and/or secretes many hormones of pivotal importance to body function, including growth hormone (GH), thyroid- stimulating hormone (TSH), follicle-stimulating hormone (FSH), luteinizing hormone (LH), oxytocin, antidiuretic hormone (ADH, vasopressin) and adrenocorticotropic hormone (ACTH).

plague. Severe, life-threatening illness caused by the bacterium *Yersinia pestis* and transmitted by fleas.

planum nasale. The (usually black) tip of a dog's nose, characterized by a "cobblestone" architecture.

plaque. The mixture of oral bacteria, bacterial sugars, salivary proteins, and food and cellular debris that accumulates on the teeth; also, a flat area in the skin.

plasma. The fluid portion of the blood (excluding the blood cells).

plasma cells. End-stage B lymphocytes (B cells), whose function is to produce antibodies.

plasmacytic-lymphocytic synovitis. Inflammation of the lining membranes of joints, with infiltration by plasma cells and lymphocytes; has a particular predilection for the stifle (knee) joints.

platelets. Cell fragments released from megakaryocytes, that play an important role in blood clotting.

plerocercoid. Minute larval form of pseudophyllidean tapeworms that develops inside a freshwater fish.

pleura. Thin, transparent membrane covering the lungs and lining the chest cavity.

pleural cavity. The potential space between the visceral pleura and parietal pleura.

pneumonia. An inflammatory condition of the lungs; characterized by the filling of air spaces with fluid, resulting in impaired gas exchange.

pneumothorax. Accumulation of air within the pleural cavity, inside the chest but outside the lungs, impeding the ability of the lungs to expand normally; collapsed lung.

pododermatitis. Inflammation of the footpads.

pollakiuria. Increased frequency of urination.

polyclonal gammopathy. Increase in serum gamma globulins (blood proteins that include most of the antibody classes) that tends to be spread over a wide range of protein types.

polycythemia. An excessive number of red blood cells.

polydipsia. Excessive thirst.

polygenic traits. Traits that are the result of the action of more than a single gene.

polymorphism. Genetic variation.

polymorphonuclear leukocyte. Any white blood cell having a lobular nucleus, such as a neutrophil.

polymyositis. Term referring to a varied collection of generalized inflammatory muscle diseases that can be caused by several different infectious disease agents, as well as by ill-defined immunologic mechanisms.

polyneuritis. Inflammation occurring simultaneously in more than one nerve.

polyp. A small fleshy mass projecting from the surface of a mucous membrane.

polypeptide. Any peptide containing two or more amino acids; often referred to simply as a peptide.

polyphagia. Excessive eating.

polyuria. Excessive urination.

portacaval (portasystemic) shunt. Abnormal persistence of an embryonic blood vessel within the liver.

post-clipping alopecia. Relatively common syndrome of hair loss seen after hair clipping and attributed to an arrest of the normal hair-growth cycle; primarily observed in sled-dog breeds.

posterior chamber. That portion of the eye between the iris and the lens.

posterior paresis. Partial paralysis of either or both hind limbs.

postpartum. Occurring after birth.

postprandial. Occurring after a meal.

predilection. Preference.

premature ventricular contractions (PVCs). Abnormal contractions of the ventricle that are caused by diseased heart muscle rather than by normal heart pacemaker (**sinoatrial node**) stimulation.

premolars. The teeth lying between the canines and molars; in the dog there are a total of eight upper and eight lower premolars.

premunition. Maintenance of immunity to a parasite by the persistent presence of small numbers of the parasite, usually in the gastrointestinal tract; premunition immunity wanes if the parasite is completely eliminated from the body.

prepatent period. The time elapsing between the initiation of a parasite's infection of a definitive host and the appearance of the products of parasite reproduction, e.g., eggs, larvae, etc.

prepubertal. Pertaining to the period before sexual maturity.

prepuce. Fold of skin enclosing the penis in dogs.

prickle cell layer. A layer of cells within the **epidermis,** the outermost layer of the skin; also known as the **squamous cell layer,** it lies above the basal cell layer and below the granular cell layer.

primary hairs. Coarse, thick, straight hairs that taper to a fine tip; also called **guard hairs.**

primary hyperparathyroidism (PHP). Hyperparathyroidism resulting from excessive, relatively uncontrolled secretion of parathyroid hormone (PTH) by one or more abnormal parathyroid glands.

primary hypoparathyroidism. Hypoparathyroidism resulting from an absolute or relative deficiency of secretion of parathyroid hormone (PTH).

primary immunization. Initial immunization series given to puppies.

primary lymphoid organs. Organs in which the production and maturation of lymphocytes takes place; in dogs, they include the bone marrow, the mucosal-associated lymphoid tissue (**MALT**) and the **thymus.**

primary seborrhea. A narrowed definition of seborrhea, referring exclusively to inherited disorders of **keratinization** occurring in specific breeds of dogs.

procercoid. Larval form of pseudophyllidean tapeworms that develops inside a **copepod** (minute aquatic crustacean).

proestrus. In the estrus cycle, the period just before estrus.

progesterone. Hormone secreted by the corpus luteum, adrenal cortex and placenta, whose primary function is to prepare the uterus for pregnancy; also called progestin.

progestogen. Any compound with progesterone-like activity.

proglottid. One of the chain of segments comprising the **strobila,** or body, of a tapeworm parasite.

prognathism. Condition characterized by an elongated lower jaw, as seen "normally" in the **brachycephalic** (flat-faced) breeds.

prognosis. The outlook for recovery from a disease.

progressive neuronal abiotrophy. (PNA) Autosomal recessive disorder of Kerry Blue Terriers characterized by incoordination, lack of balance equilibrium, and head tremors; also called **cerebellar abiotrophy.**

progressive retinal atrophy (PRA). Inherited, progressive degeneration of the retina, occurring in either a central or generalized form.

prolactin. Hormone secreted by the pituitary gland that simulates and sustains lactation; also called lactogenic hormone.

prolapse. A bulging through or protrusion of a tissue or organ.

prophylaxis. Disease prevention.

proptosis. Bulging or protrusion of the eyeball from the eye socket; also called **exophthalmos.**

prostaglandins. A group of fatty acid-derived compounds that are important as regulators of a number of physiological processes involving allergic reactions, contraction of smooth muscle, dilation of blood vessels, blood clotting and others.

prostate gland. Gland in male mammals that surrounds the neck of the bladder and is important in the production of seminal fluid.

prostatitis. Inflammation of the prostate gland.

prosthesis. An artificial limb, or other substitute for a missing body part.

proteins. Molecules, composed of amino acids, that make up many of the structural components of the body and that are needed to maintain all normal body functions.

proteinuria. Excessive loss of protein into the urine.

proteolytic. Capable of breaking down protein.

prothrombin time. A measure of the clotting ability of the blood.

protozoa. Simple organisms that are usually composed of a single cell; most are free-living but some are capable of producing disease in animals or humans.

proximate analysis. A measure of the nutrient content of a diet, including the maximum moisture, maximum fiber, minimum crude protein, and minimum crude fat content.

pruritus. Itchiness.

pseudopregnancy. A condition wherein the bitch exhibits signs of pregnancy following a nonfertile mating; false pregnancy.

ptyalism. Excessive drooling; hypersalivation.

puerperal tetany. Eclampsia; milk fever in a lactating bitch.

pulmonary. Pertaining to the lungs.

pulmonary edema. Noninflammatory buildup of fluid in the tissues and air spaces within the lungs.

pulmonary embolism. A detached clot from elsewhere in the body occluding a blood vessel within the lungs.

pulmonary infiltrates with eosinophilia (PIE) syndrome. *See* ALLERGIC PNEUMONITIS.

pulmonic stenosis. A common congenital heart defect, characterized by a narrowing **(stenosis)** of the connection between the right ventricle and the pulmonary artery.

pulmonic valve. The semilunar valve on the right side of the heart.

pulp. The blood vessels, nerves, lymphatic channels and cells that line the pulp chamber, or root canal, of each tooth.

pulp chamber. The chamber within each tooth that contains nerves, blood vessels and lymphatic channels; also known as the **root canal.**

pulpectomy. Removal of damaged pulp from a tooth.

pulpitis. Inflammation of dental pulp.

pulse. The regular, rhythmic pulsation of an artery, which is taken as a measure of the heartbeat and the strength of heart muscle contraction.

pulse pressure. The difference between systolic and diastolic pressure; the pressure one is actually detecting when feeling the pulse.

Punnett square. Checkerboard diagram for delineating possible outcomes of mating two individuals of defined genotype.

pupil. The central opening of the iris, through which light penetrates into the inner reaches of the eye.

purulent. Pus-forming.

pus. Fluid produced by an inflammatory process, containing many white blood cells.

pustule. A skin vesicle containing pus.

putrefactive. Pertaining to the normal decomposition of organic matter by microorganisms.

pyelonephritis. Any infection of the kidney involving the renal pelvis.

pyloric sphincter. Sphincter located between the stomach and duodenum.

pylorus. The terminal portion of the stomach, connecting it with the **duodenum** (first part of the small intestine).

pyoderma. General term for any skin disease in which pus is formed.

pyometra. Accumulation of pus within the uterus, resulting usually from a severe bacterial infection.

pyometritis. Purulent inflammation of the uterus.

pyothorax. Accumulation of pus within the chest; also called thoracic empyema.

pyotraumatic dermatitis. Self-induced, traumatic skin disease; also called hot spots.

pyruvate kinase deficiency. Sydrome of hemolytic anemia in Basenjis caused by a deficiency of an essential red blood cell enzyme, pyruvate kinase.

pythiosis. *See* OÖMYCOSIS.

quaternary ammonium compounds. Important class of chemicals useful as disinfectants for surfaces.

radiograph. An X-ray film.

radiography. The use of X rays or gamma rays to view the internal structures of the body.

radioisotopes. Radioactive elements.

radionuclide scan. Use of injected radioactive elements to identify collections of tumor cells in the body.

radiotherapy. Radiation therapy.

recessive gene. A gene that can be expressed only when both members of a chromosome pair contain the same

allele for a given characteristic (i.e., the same allele must be inherited from both parents).

recombination. Genetic exchange among chromosomes, producing new combinations of genes.

rectum. Lowermost portion of the large intestine, immediately adjacent to the anus.

redia. Larval stage of flukes arising from the **sporocyst** stage.

reduction. The setting of a bone fracture.

reflex. In general, muscle movement orchestrated by the nervous system in response to a stimulus and without conscious (voluntary) control; an example is the knee-jerk reflex.

reflux. Backflow.

refractive. Light-bending.

refractometer. Small, handheld device that can be used for determining how concentrated or dilute a urine sample is (a measurement referred to as urine **specific gravity**).

regional mastectomy. Surgical removal of a series of mammary glands.

regurgitation. Involuntary return of undigested food to the mouth after swallowing; differs from vomiting in that it is a passive process (i.e., unaccompanied by the reflex action, propulsive movements characteristic of vomiting) or the backward flow of blood in the heart.

renal. Pertaining to the kidneys.

renal pelvis. "Collecting funnel" deep within each kidney into which the kidney tubules drain filtrate.

reservoir host. An animal from which infection may be passed to domesticated stock or to human beings.

resorption. Biochemical dissolution or loss of tissue.

respiration. Breathing.

retching. Abdominal contractions in preparation for vomiting.

retina. The light-sensitive layer of cells at the back of the eye.

retinal dysplasia. Congenital disorder characterized by abnormal development of the retina.

retinitis. Inflammation of the retina.

reverse sneeze. Inspiratory snoring sound made when an animal is trying to clear the back of its nasal passages.

rhabdomyoma. A benign tumor of striated muscle cells.

rhabdomyosarcoma. A malignant tumor of striated muscle cells.

rheumatoid arthritis. A chronic, progressive, immune-mediated arthritis that resembles idiopathic (of unknown cause) polyarthritis in its earlier stages, but deviates significantly in that, in rhematoid arthritis, virtually complete destruction of the affected joints occurs; seen primarily in toy breeds of dogs.

rheumatoid factor (RF). An autoantibody found in rhematoid arthritis and some other autoimmune diseases, and believed to play a prominent role in disease development.

rhinitis. Inflammation of the nasal passages, unaccompanied by fever; "head cold."

rhinoscopy. Visual examination of the nasal passages, using an endoscope, otoscope, or other instrument.

rhinosporidiosis. An uncommon fungal disease caused by *Rhinosporidium seeberi* and characterized by the formation of **polyps** (small, fleshy growths) within the nasal passages.

rhythmic segmentation. Rhythmic muscular movements of the intestinal tract that serve to delay the passage of intestinal contents until digestion and absorption have been completed.

ribonucleic acid (RNA). A nucleic acid occurring in all cells and involved in cell division, gene expression and protein synthesis; also serves as the genetic material for some viruses.

rickets. Vitamin D deficiency in young dogs, characterized by joint enlargement, bone fractures, bowed legs, and abnormal jaw formation and tooth eruption.

rickettsia. A group of specialized bacteria that multiply only within host cells and that are transmitted to animals and human beings by lice, ticks, fleas or mites; examples include *Rickettsia rickettsii,* the cause of **Rocky Mountain spotted fever,** and *Ehrlichia canis,* the cause of **tropical canine pancytopenia** (*canine ehrlichiosis*).

ringworm. A common skin infection caused by ringworm fungi (**dermatophytes**), that invade the outer, superficial layers of the skin, hair and nails; also called **dermatophytosis**.

RNA. *See* RIBONUCLEIC ACID.

Rocky Mountain spotted fever. A tick-borne infection caused by a rickettsia, *Rickettsia rickettsii,* and characterized in dogs by fever, depression, vomiting, diarrhea, enlarged lymph nodes, ocular and nasal discharge, muscle or joint pain, decreased blood platelet counts, and multiple small hemorrhages on the oral or genital mucous membranes.

rods. Photoreceptor cells in the retina of the eye that are responsible for night vision and detection of motion.

root. The portion of a tooth that lies below the gum line.

root canal. The chamber within each tooth that contains nerves, blood vessels and lymphatic channels; also known as the **pulp chamber.**

root-canal therapy. A common salvage procedure for treating crown fractures or deep cavities that result in irreversible damage to the tooth pulp; during the procedure the pulpal contents are taken out, the root canal is cleaned and reshaped, and the empty pulp chamber is then sealed with a biocompatible material.

root planing. Peridontal therapy that involves scaling the tooth-root surface of plaque, calculus and dead cementum. Closed root planing is performed without gum surgery, while open root planing necessitates surgical intervention.

saline. A physiologically balanced salt solution; physiological sodium chloride solution.

salmon disease ("salmon poisoning"). An acute, rapidly progressive and frequently fatal gastrointestinal disease of dogs that occurs shortly after feeding on raw salmon or trout infected with one or both causative rickettsiae, *Neorickettsia helminthoeca* and the *Elokomin fluke fever agent.*

salmonellosis. A primarily diarrheal disease caused by members of the bacterial genus *Salmonella.*

San Joaquin valley fever. Coccidioidomycosis ("**valley fever**").

sarcolemma. The outer membrane surrounding every skeletal muscle fiber.

sarcoma. General term for malignant tumors of connective-tissue cells (those cells within an organ or structure that bind it together and support it).

satiety. Appeasement of the appetite; a feeling of sufficiency or satisfaction with regard to food intake.

scabies. Skin infestation by the itch mite, *Sarcoptes scabiei*

scale, scales. Accumulated fragments of the horny layer of the epidermis.

scaling. Teeth cleaning with the use of dental instruments.

scapula. Shoulder blade.

schizogony. A form of asexual reproduction seen in certain protozoa, in which the nucleus of the organism divides several times before the remainder of the cell divides; also called multiple fission.

schizont. A developmental stage of certain protozoa, specifically, a dividing cell undergoing **schizogony;** also called a **meront.**

Schnauzer comedo syndrome. Relatively common, usually asymptomatic skin disease seen exclusively in Miniature Schnauzers and related crossbreeds; may be caused by abnormalities in hair follicle development.

Schwann cells. Large cells that are wrapped around certain nerve axons to form a myelin sheath, which serves to facilitate the conduction of nerve impulses along the axon.

sclera. The white outer covering of the eyeball, continuous with the **cornea.**

sclerotic. Hardened.

scolex. The "head" of a tapeworm parasite, armed with hooks or suckers and used for attachment and locomotion.

scotoma. A localized, disease-caused "blind spot" in the retina.

scrotum. Dependent pouch of skin containing the testicles.

sebaceous adenitis. Sebaceous gland inflammation.

sebaceous duct cyst. Uncommon cyst involving the ducts leading from sebaceous glands to their associated hair follicles.

sebaceous glands. Minute skin glands, many of which are attached to hair follicles; they secrete **sebum,** an oily secretion that lubricates and protects the skin.

seborrhea. General term used to describe clinical signs of excessive scaling, crusting and greasiness of the skin.

seborrhea oleosa. Seborrhea in which oiliness or greasiness predominates.

seborrhea sicca. Dry, waxy, scaly dermatitis; dandruff.

seborrheic dermatitis. Disorder characterized by severely inflamed lesions of primary seborrhea.

sebum. The oily secretion of the sebaceous glands, containing fats, bacteria and dead skin cells; it lubricates and protects the skin surface.

secondary hairs. Fine hairs making up the undercoat; also called underhairs.

secondary lymphoid organs. Organs wherein antigens are trapped and destroyed by immune system cells; they include the lymph nodes, spleen, and portions of the bone marrow and the mucosal-associated lymphoid tissue (MALT).

seizures. Relatively brief episodes of neurologic derangement caused by abnormal bursts of electrical activity within the brain; also called **convulsions** or fits.

selective IgA deficiency. An uncommon disease characterized by an inability to produce sufficient quantities of IgA.

self-limiting. Said of disease, with reference to any illness that will run its (usually benign) course without the need for treatment.

semen. Seminal fluid from the male, containing also the male reproductive cells, or **spermatozoa** (sperm).

semicircular canals. Structures in the inner ear that are concerned with the sensation of balance.

semilunar valves. The heart valves that separate each ventricle from the great artery with which it is connected (either aorta or pulmonary artery). The semilunar valve on the right side of the heart is known as the pulmonic valve, and the corresponding valve on the left side is called the aortic valve.

seminiferous tubules. Small channels within the testes wherein the spermatozoa (sperm) develop.

septic arthritis. Inflammation of the joints caused by an infectious agent.

septicemia. The presence of bacteria in the blood circulation, accompanied by related clinical signs of disease.

septic shock. Shock caused by invasion of the body by bacteria that produce substances injurious to cells, such that the cells can no longer utilize oxygen.

septum (plural: septa). A dividing wall, such as that dividing the right and left sides of the heart or the right and left nasal cavities.

sequestrum (plural: sequestra). A fragment of dead bone that has broken off from the underlying normal bone tissue.

serology. The use of specialized diagnostic tests for the detection of antigens and antibodies in serum.

serovar. Variant or subspecies of leptospire.

Sertoli cells. Cells within the testicular tubules that are important for nurture and development of **spermatozoa** (sperm).

serum. Blood plasma minus the clotting factor **fibrinogen;** the clear liquid that remains after the blood clots, containing many important blood proteins including antibodies (**immunoglobulins**).

serum alkaline phosphatase (SAP). An enzyme present in the blood that is produced in many body tissues and is of greatest diagnostic significance in diseases of the bone and liver.

sesamoid bone. Any small, nodular bone (such as the kneecap) that is located within the tendon of a muscle or the capsule of a joint.

sex-linked diseases. Genetic diseases of males caused by defective genes located on the X chromosome; also called X-linked diseases.

sexual dimorphism. Size differences between the sexes, as seen with certain parasites.

shock. Failure of the blood vascular system to provide adequate circulation to the vital organs; circulatory collapse; a life-threatening emergency condition requiring immediate veterinary medical attention.

sick sinus syndrome. Degeneration of the **sinoatrial node** (the heart's natural pacemaker), resulting in **bradycardia** (an abnormally slow heart rate).

sign. A characteristic of a disease; "signs" are seen by observation, while "symptoms" are characteristics reported by the patient; thus, animals exhibit signs of disease, while human beings report symptoms.

silent heat. A heat period that goes unnoticed simply because there may be little vulvar swelling, bleeding, attraction of males, or behavior change.

simple follicle. A hair follicle in which only a single hair is produced.

sinoatrial (SA) node. A collection of specialized cardiac muscle fibers found at the junction of the right atrium and the vena cava; it is the heart's natural pacemaker, generating the electrical discharges that stimulate the beating and pumping of the heart.

sinus arrhythmia. A normal heart rhythm wherein the heart rate accelerates during inhalation and slows during exhalation.

sinusitis. Inflammation of a sinus.

sinus tachycardia. An accelerated heart rhythm that can be caused by fever.

skeletal muscle. The type of muscle making up most of the muscles of movement attached to the skeleton; also known as **striated muscle.**

smooth muscle. The type of muscle found in the walls of blood vessels and the major internal organs.

snuffling. Abnormal breathing sounds.

soft palate. At the rear of the mouth, the soft, fleshy posterior partition separating the nasal and oral cavities.

soft-tissue orbit. The nonbony structures (muscles, nerves, blood vessels) that lie within the bony orbit.

solar dermatitis. Inflammatory skin disease induced by sunlight; also called actinic dermatitis.

soluble fibers. Dietary fibers as found in fruits, oat bran, and psyllium (the chief component of commercial stool softeners such as Metamucil); they attract water and form a gel, are highly fermentable (able to be digested by bacteria) in the large intestine, and have been shown in people to slow emptying of the stomach and to inhibit the absorption of cholesterol.

somatomedins. Small proteins produced mainly in the liver that exert an anabolic effect on the body, resulting in proliferation of bone, cartilage and soft tissues, and enlargement of body organs; also known as **insulin-like growth factors.**

spay operation. Surgical removal of the ovaries and uterus; also known as an **ovariohysterectomy (OVH).**

species. One of the major classifying categories of taxonomy, representing divisions of a genus, and sometimes further classified into subspecies.

specific gravity. A measurement of the concentration of urine in a urine sample; determined by using a small handheld device called a refractometer.

sperm. *See* SPERMATAZOA.

spermatic cord. Combined structure extending from the groin area to the testes, through which run the **vas deferens** and a number of vessels and nerves.

spermatozoa (sperm). The mature reproductive cells of the male; produced by the testes, their role is to fertilize the female egg (**ovum**).

spherule. The parasitic, noninfectious stage of the fungus *Coccidioides immitis,* formed during the organism's growth phase in host tissue.

sphincter. Circular band or ring of muscle that serves to open or close a tube or orifice; analogous to a valve.

spina bifida. General term encompassing all developmental anomalies related to failure of the vertebrae to encircle the spinal cord.

spinal nerves. Nerves arising from the spinal cord that form nerves of the **peripheral nervous system (PNS).**

spindle cell tumor. *See* HEMANGIOPERICYTOMA.

spirochetes. Filamentous, spiral-shaped bacteria, such as the leptospires and *Borrelia.*

spleen. Large abdominal organ that removes senescent (aged) red blood cells and foreign material from the bloodstream; an important component of the immune system.

splenectomy. Surgical removal of the spleen.

splinting. Tightening of the muscles in an area in order to avoid pain associated with muscle movement.

split heat. An incomplete heat period, with each apparent proestrus failing to be followed by ovulation; frequently seen as a female behavior problem.

spore. Highly resistant, thick-walled "resting stage" formed by certain bacteria to ensure their survival during periods of unfavorable environmental conditions; it germinates quickly once favorable conditions have been restored to produce a new generation of bacteria. Also, a general term referring to the reproductive cells of certain microorganisms, particularly fungi and protozoa.

sporocyst. Larval stage of flukes that arises from the free-swimming miracidium stage.

sporotrichosis. An uncommon chronic, pus-forming infection caused by the dimorphic fungus *Sporothrix schenckii.*

sporozoites. In certain protozoa, the daughter cells resulting from division of a fertilized cell (**zygote**).

sprain. Joint injury involving damage to one or more ligaments, but without actual ligament rupture.

squamous cell carcinoma. A malignant skin tumor of cells within the squamous cell layer of the epidermis.

squamous cell layer. A layer of cells within the **epidermis,** the outermost layer of the skin; also known as the **prickle cell layer,** it lies above the basal cell layer and below the granular cell layer.

standing heat. Behavioral estrus; the full behavioral signs of estrus.

status epilepticus. An emergency medical condition of rapidly repeated seizure episodes.

stenosis. A constriction or narrowing of a vessel or duct.

stereopsis. Depth perception.

sternum. Breastbone.

steroid. Common term for corticosteroid.

stifle joint. Knee joint.

stomatitis. Inflammation of the lining of the mouth.

strabismus. The condition of being cross-eyed; squint.

strangulation. Constriction resulting in impairment of the blood supply.

striated muscle. Skeletal muscle.

stricture. Narrowing of the diameter of a hollow tube, usually the result of contraction caused by local tissue damage.

stridor. Loud, strained, high-pitched noise on inhalation.

strobila. The body of a tapeworm parasite, comprised of

a chain of segments called **proglottids.**

struvite. Magnesium-ammonium-phosphate crystals that form in the urinary tract during infection with certain bacteria; also called triple phosphate crystals.

stye. Localized inflammatory lesion along an eyelid margin, caused by a staphylococcal bacterial infection; also known as a **hordeolum.**

subalbinism. Partial but not total absence of iris pigmentation.

subcutaneous (SC). Beneath the skin; a route of injection.

subcutaneous edema. Accumulation of fluid beneath the skin.

subcutaneous emphysema. Formation of air pockets under the skin, usually caused by an injury to the chest.

subcutis. The skin layer lying beneath the **dermis,** and composed of fat cells and strands of collagenous connective tissue; also called hypodermis.

subfertility. A state of being less than normally fertile, but not infertile.

subgingival. Below the gum line.

subinvolution. Partial **involution** (return to normal size) of an organ, as of the uterus following delivery of the fetus.

subluxation. Partial dislocation of a joint; also, a slight alteration in the position of the lens of the eye.

submandibular. Beneath the lower jaw.

sucrose. Table sugar.

sulfur granules. Yellowish clumps of bacteria mixed with dead and dying cells, commonly observed in the pus draining from lesions of actinomycosis.

superfecundation. Fertilization of an **ovum** (egg) by separate matings during a single ovulatory cycle; it is thus possible for a litter of puppies to have more than one father.

superfetation. Fertilization of another **ovum** (egg) occuring when a fetus is already developing in the uterus.

superficial bacterial folliculitis. Form of pyoderma characterized by development of superficial pustules in association with hair follicles; also called **superficial pyoderma.**

superficial pyoderma. Superficial bacterial folliculitis.

superficial spreading pyoderma. Form of pyoderma characterized by reddened macules that frequently expand and coalesce.

suppurative. Producing pus (said of bacterial infections).

surfactant. A soaplike substance produced by specialized cells lining the alveoli of the lungs; responsible for decreasing the pressure (surface tension) within the alveoli and preventing them from collapsing during normal respiratory movements.

suspensory ligament. Ligament made of numerous fine strands (zonules) that holds the lens of the eye in place.

suture. A surgical stitch.

symptomatic therapy. Therapy aimed at alleviating the signs or symptoms of a disease rather than treating its underlying cause.

synaptic cleft. The space between an axon terminal and the myofiber it supplies, and across which the nerve impulse is transmitted by means of "messenger molecules" such as **acetylcholine.**

syncope. Fainting spell.

syngamy. *See* GAMETOGAMY.

synovial fluid. Joint fluid, the material that lubricates the joint surfaces.

synovial sarcoma. A malignant tumor of the lining membrane of a joint.

systemic. Throughout the body; pertaining to the body as a whole.

systemic lupus erythematosus (SLE, lupus). A rare, chronic, multisystemic autoimmune disorder, characterized by the production of autoantibodies to DNA and normal cellular constituents.

systole. The contraction phase of the heartbeat.

systolic blood pressure. The pressure that occurs when the heart contracts and pushes blood into the arterial system.

systolic heart murmur. Murmur that is present only during systole.

T lymphocytes (T cells). Specialized lymphocytes that mature within the thymus; two important types are **cytotoxic T cells** and **helper T cells**.

tachycardia. Abnormally fast heart rate.

tachypnea. Abnormally rapid breathing.

tachyzoites. Actively dividing form of the parasite *Toxoplasma gondii* found in the tissues of an infected animal.

tail head. Site where the tail joins the body.

tapetum lucidum. The highly reflective and colorful upper portion of the interior of the canine eyeball, lying directly beneath the retina; aids in night vision.

tapetum nigrum. The lower half of the interior of the canine eyeball, consisting of a broad area of heavy pigmentation that guards the sensitive retina from overhead glare during the daylight hours.

taxonomy. The classification of organisms into different categories on the basis of their individual physical, genetic and biochemical relationships to each other.

teletherapy. Radiation therapy using a concentrated beam of radiation directed at a tumor target.

telogen. The phase of hair follicle activity during which the follicle is resting and not producing new hair.

temporal region. Area of the head in front of the ears and lateral to the forehead.

tendon. Fibrous tissue that attaches muscle to bone.

Tensilon test. Intravenous injection of a short-acting cholinesterase inhibitor known as edrophonium ("Tensilon"); used to provide a preliminary diagnosis of myasthenia gravis; a positive test results in marked, transient improvement in clinical weakness and exercise intolerance.

teratogen. Any compound or agent that disrupts normal development *in utero,* producing defects in the developing embryo.

teratology. The study of abnormal development and congenital malformations.

test cross. A mating between a homozygous recessive and an animal with the phenotype of the dominant allele.

testes (testicles). Paired reproductive organs of the male wherein the **spermatozoa** (sperm) are produced.

testosterone. The principal male sex hormone, produced

in the testes.

tetanospasmin. The neurotoxin produced in tetanus.

tetanus. Acute, often fatal disease caused by a toxin from the bacterium *Clostridium tetani;* characterized by violent muscle spasms and contractions, hyperreflexive responses, and "lockjaw" (**trismus.**)

tetany. Seizure-like tremors caused most often by a decrease in circulating calcium levels.

Tetralogy of Fallot. Congenital heart defect characterized by the presence of a ventricular septal defect (VSD) and severe pulmonic stenosis together with an abnormally placed aorta.

tetraplegia. Paralysis of all four limbs.

thalamus. Portion of the brain that serves as a relay center for sensory information coming from the rest of the body, and for nerve impulses concerned with balance and coordination arising from the cerebellum.

thelaziasis. Conjunctivitis caused by a worm parasite, *Thelazia californiensis.*

theriogenology. Study of the physiology and pathology of animal reproduction.

thiacetarsamide. Arsenical compound used to kill adult forms of the canine heartworm, *Dirofilaria immitis.*

thiaminase. An enzyme that destroys thiamine (vitamin B_1).

third degree AV block. Degeneration of the atrioventricular node within the heart, resulting in **bradycardia** (abnormally slow heart rate).

thoracic. Pertaining to the chest.

thoracocentesis. Procedure in which a sterile hypodermic needle is inserted into the chest cavity in order to remove accumulated air or fluid, or to obtain a sample of fluid or lung tissue for examination.

thromboembolism. Obstruction of a blood vessel by a clot originating at another site.

thromboplastin. A protein essential for blood clotting.

thrombosis. Formation of a blood clot (**thrombus**) that results in obstruction of a blood vessel at the site of clot formation; contrasts with **embolism,** which is a blood-borne clot that lodges at a site distant from its site of formation.

thrombus. A blood clot causing obstruction of a blood vessel at the site of clot formation.

thymus. Lymphoid organ located in the chest that produces hormones (thymopoietin, thymosin) and that regulates the maturation process of specialized lymphocytes known as **T cells.**

thyroid gland. Endocrine gland located on either side of the trachea that produces hormones (**thyroxine (T_4), triiodothyronine (T_3)**) important in regulating the body's metabolic rate.

thyroid hormone. Collective name for the two major hormones produced by the thyroid gland, **thyroxine (T_4)** and **triiodothyronine (T_3).**

thyroidectomy. Removal of all or part of the thyroid gland.

thyroid-stimulating hormone (TSH). Hormone elaborated by the pituitary gland that stimulates the thyroid gland to produce the hormones **thyroxine (T_4)** and **triiodothyronine (T_3).**

thyroxine (T_4). One of two important iodine-containing hormones secreted by the thyroid gland that assist in regulating the cellular metabolic rate of the body.

tick paralysis. A reversible paralysis of motor function associated with an infestation of ticks; caused by a toxin in tick saliva.

tinea. Ringworm.

titer. A quantitative measure of the concentration of an antibody or antigen in blood serum; determined in principle by making serial dilutions of serum and identifying the highest dilution at which the antibody or antigen can still be detected.

tocopherols. General term for vitamin E.

tolerance. The normal state whereby the immune system remains nonreactive or "tolerant" to the body's own cells.

tonsils. Masses of lymphoid tissue at the rear of the mouth.

total ablation of the ear. Surgical removal of the entire ear canal.

toxemia. Presence of toxins in the blood, accompanied by related signs of disease.

toxic epidermal necrolysis. Rare, severe, ulcerative disorder of the mouth and skin with an apparent immunologic basis; usually associated with a drug hypersensitivity.

toxoplasmosis. A protozoan disease caused by *Toxoplasma gondii.*

trabecular network. Lattice-like layers of fine strands that bridge the angle created by the cornea and iris of the eye.

trace elements. Minerals that are required in the diet only in very minute amounts; e.g., zinc, iron, copper, manganese, cobalt and iodine.

trachea. Cartilage-lined tubular airway that descends from the larynx into the chest and branches at its lower end into two bronchi that enter the lungs; it conducts air between the upper nasal passages and the lungs; colloquially known as the windpipe.

tracheal collapse. Syndrome most commonly recognized in aging small- and toy-breed dogs, such as Poodles and terriers, in which the normally rigid structure of the trachea is weakened, making the trachea easily collapsible by external or internal pressures.

tracheitis. Inflammation of the trachea.

tracheobronchitis. Inflammation of the trachea, larynx and bronchi.

tracheostomy. Surgically created opening through the skin into the trachea, to allow for insertion of a tube for breathing and to clear airway obstructions.

transmammary. Through the milk or **colostrum.**

transmissible venereal tumor. Sexually transmitted tumor affecting the genital region.

transplacental(ly). By way of the placenta; across the placenta.

transport host. An animal in which part of the immature phase of a parasite's life cycle is spent, but no development occurs.

transtracheal wash. Flushing of material from the trachea and bronchi for diagnostic purposes, by needle puncture and aspiration through the skin and tracheal wall.

trematodes. Parasites generally ingested in insufficiently cooked fish and vegetables; flukes.

trichiasis. Condition wherein facial hair or eyelashes arising from normal sites are misdirected and contact the cornea or conjunctiva.

trichoepithelioma. Benign skin tumor composed of multiple cysts and originating in hair follicles.

tricuspid valve. The **atrioventricular valve** on the right side of the heart.

triglycerides. A component of fat, consisting of fatty acids linked to glycerol.

triiodothyronine (T3). An important iodine-containing hormone secreted by the thyroid gland that assists in regulating the cellular metabolic rate of the body; much more powerful than its companion hormone **thyroxine (T4)**, it is considered to be the active form of thyroid hormone in tissue.

trismus. "Lockjaw," caused by spasm of the chewing muscles.

trophozoites. Motile feeding forms of the parasite *Giardia;* they multiply in the small intestine by means of binary fission.

tropical canine pancytopenia. A tick-borne disease of dogs caused by a rickettsia, *Ehrlichia canis,* and characterized by fever, lethargy, bloody nasal discharge and blood-clotting abnormalities; also called **canine ehrlichiosis.**

trypsinogen-like-immunoreactivity test. Test for diagnosing pancreatic exocrine insufficiency.

tubal ligation. Sterilization procedure in the female wherein the oviducts are clamped off, preventing eggs from reaching the uterus.

tuberculin testing. Procedure testing for exposure to the bacteria causing tuberculosis.

tuberculosis. Chronic disease of human beings and some animals, primarily affecting the respiratory tract and caused by bacteria of the genus *Mycobacterium;* the name is derived from the many small inflammatory nodules ("tubercles") that are characteristic of the disease in some species.

tumor. A large nodule, or obvious cancerous mass.

turbinates. Delicate, scroll-like, rolled bony structures within the nasal cavity that filter, warm and humidify inhaled air; also referred to as the nasal turbinates.

Turner's syndrome. Chromosomal abnormality in women characterized by a missing X chromosome; also called female gonadal dysgenesis; in dogs, it is known as 77,X gonadal dysgenesis.

tympanic membrane. Eardrum.

tyrosinase. Key enzyme produced by **melanocytes** in the skin; it converts the amino acid tyrosine to the skin pigment **melanin.**

Tyzzer's disease. An extremely rare and highly fatal liver disease caused by a spore-forming bacterium, *Bacillus piliformis.*

ulcer, ulceration. A severe sloughing of the surface of an organ or tissue as a result of a toxic or inflammatory response at the site.

ulcerative colitis. Chronic inflammatory condition of unknown cause, producing ulceration of the surface of the colon (large intestine) with recurrent bouts of abdominal pain and bloody stool.

ulcerative keratitis. Inflammation of the cornea accompanied by corneal ulceration.

ultrasonography. Noninvasive diagnostic technique for visualizing the internal structures of the body by means of sound (echo) reflections; ultrasound.

ultrasound. Ultrasonography.

ultraviolet radiation. High-energy radiation existing beyond the violet region of the electromagnetic spectrum; ultraviolet rays emitted by the sun are responsible for a number of effects on the skin, including tanning, burning and activation of vitamin D.

underhairs. Fine hairs making up the undercoat; also called **secondary hairs.**

undifferentiated sarcoma. Malignant tumor derived from primitive connective tissue cells.

unicellular. Single-celled.

unilateral. Occurring on only one side.

unilateral mastectomy. Surgical removal of one entire chain of mammary glands.

unthrifty. Unkempt in appearance and failing to thrive.

urate calculi. Uric acid (urate) bladder stones.

urea. Nitrogen-containing compound generated by the breakdown of ingested proteins.

uremia. Abnormally elevated levels of urea and other nitrogenous waste products in the blood.

ureter. Membranous tube that transports urine from the kidney to the urinary bladder.

ureterolith. Urinary stone lodged in the ureter.

urethra. Membranous tube that transports urine from the urinary bladder to the exterior of the body.

urethritis. Inflammation of the urethra.

urinalysis (UA). Panel of physicochemical tests carried out on urine, as an aid in the diagnosis of urinary-tract disorders.

urinary calculus (plural: calculi). General term for a stone lodged anywhere within the urinary tract; also known as a **urolith.**

urine. The fluid filtrate of the kidneys.

urine sediment. Urine solids obtained by centrifuging a urine sample.

urolith. General term for a urinary stone.

urolithiasis. The process of formation of urinary stones; disease associated with the presence of urinary stones and (usually) bacterial infection of the urinary tract, particularly the bladder.

urticaria ("hives"). Acute, usually localized skin swelling caused by an increased permeability of capillaries, producing a net outflow of fluid into the tissue spaces; often a manifestation of an allergic process.

uterine horns. Paired branchings of the uterus leading from the body of the uterus to the uterine tubes.

uterine inversion. Protrusion of a portion of the uterus through the cervix; uterine prolapse.

uterine prolapse. Uterine inversion.

uterine torsion. Twisting of the uterus, which may occur late in pregnancy when the uterus is very enlarged.

uterine tubes. Paired **fallopian tubes** of the uterus, wherein fertilization of the eggs with sperm occurs; also called **oviducts.**

uterus. Organ in the female wherein the fertilized egg implants and develops through embryonic and fetal stages until birth; womb.

uvea. Cellular layer of the eye that contains blood vessels, the iris, ciliary body and choroid.

uveitis. Inflammation of the uvea of the eye.

vacuolar hepatopathy. Liver disease characterized by the presence of vacuoles in liver cells.

vacuole. Small, round to oval space or cavity within a cell.

vagina. The genital canal of the female, extending from the cervix of the uterus outward to the vulva.

vaginal exfoliative cytology. Procedure wherein the microscopic appearance of cells shed from the vagina is assessed, in order to monitor the estrus cycle; used as an aid in determining when a bitch should be bred.

vaginitis. Inflammation of the vagina.

vaginoscopy. Visual inspection of the vagina, using a speculum.

valley fever. Coccidioidomycosis.

valvular degeneration. Heart disease, particularly of smaller breeds, wherein the leaflets or cusps comprising a heart valve curl back on themselves, allowing the valve to leak.

vas deferens. Ducts that serve as the transport conduit for sperm from the testes to the urethra; also called ductus deferens.

vascular. Pertaining to blood vessels.

vascular endothelium. Cells lining the inner surface of blood vessels.

vascularization. The formation of blood vessels at a tissue site.

vascularized. Supplied with blood vessels.

vascular ring defect. Abnormal retention of embryonic blood vessels in the region of the aorta.

vasculature. The blood vessels—**arteries, arterioles, capillaries, venules** and **veins**—that traverse the body.

vasculitis. Inflammation of a blood vessel or vessels; also called angiitis.

vasectomy. Sterilization of the male by severing the testicular tubules (**vas deferens**) without removing the testes.

vasodilation. Dilation (expansion in diameter) of a blood vessel.

vasopressin. *See* ANTIDIURETIC HORMONE (ADH).

vector. A term usually applied to insects, ticks and mites that carry disease-causing microorganisms from an infected animal to a noninfected animal.

veins. Large, thin-walled vessels that direct deoxygenated blood from the tissues back to the heart.

venipuncture. Taking a blood sample (from a vein, usually in either a foreleg or the neck).

venous. Pertaining to veins or venules.

ventilatory support. Artificial respiration.

ventral. In a direction toward the belly surface.

ventricles. The two muscular, lower chambers of the heart that are primarily responsible for pumping blood out of the heart; also, cavities in the brain within which is produced the cerebrospinal fluid.

ventricular fibrillation. Rapid, repeated firing of ventricular muscle fibers without coordinated contraction of the muscle itself; can result in cardiac arrest and death.

ventricular septal defect (VSD). Uncommon congenital abnormality wherein a defect, or hole, exists in the wall, or **septum,** separating the left and right ventricles of the heart.

ventricular tachycardia. Abnormal condition wherein damaged or diseased heart muscle within a ventricle begins contracting on its own, which it normally does not do.

venules. Small veins.

verminous pneumonia. Pneumonia caused by parasitic worms.

vertebrae. Blocklike bones that make up the spinal column and through which the spinal cord runs.

vesicle. A circumscribed elevation of the epidermis, filled with serum; blister.

vesicular. Fluid-filled; causing blisters.

vestibular. Pertaining to the balance mechanism in the inner ear and brain.

vestibular syndrome. Term for **idiopathic vestibular disease.**

vestibule. Outer portion of the vagina into which the **urethra** (the connecting tube from the urinary bladder) empties.

villi (singular: villus). Tiny hairlike projections lining the interior of the small intestine, which serve to increase greatly the surface area available for the absorption of nutrients.

viremia. Presence of virus in the bloodstream.

virilizing. Producing male characteristics.

virology. The study of viruses.

virulence. Measure of the disease-causing capacity of an infectious disease agent.

virulence factor. Any factor that enhances the ability of an infectious disease agent to infect the host and damage tissue.

viruses. Minute, nonliving infectious disease agents composed primarily of protein and nucleic acid (either RNA or DNA), and characterized by absence of metabolism and an inability to replicate outside susceptible host cells.

virus isolation. Procedure of propagating a virus artificially in the laboratory; more specifically, the process of recovering a virus from a tissue or fluid sample of an infected animal or human being.

viscera (singular: viscus). The large interior organs of the body.

visceral larva migrans. Disease of human beings usually caused by the canine ascarid *Toxocara canis,* and very rarely by the feline ascarid *Toxocara cati;* disease symptoms result from migration of the parasitic ascarid larvae through internal organs; also called toxocariasis.

visceral pleura. Membrane covering the surface of the organs in the chest cavity.

vital pulpotomy. Dental procedure in which the damaged portion of the tooth pulp is removed, leaving behind some living pulp tissue; contrasted with **root-canal therapy,** in which the entire pulp is removed, resulting in a dead tooth.

vitamin. General term for a number of substances required in very small quantities for the normal functioning of the body's metabolic processes.

vitiligo. Uncommon, acquired disorder of pigmentation characterized by progressive, usually well-circumscribed, areas of pigment loss in the skin.

vitrectomy. Surgical removal of the vitreous body of the eye.

vitreous body. Viscous fluid filling the posterior portion of the eyeball (behind the lens); also called simply *vitreous.*

vitreous chamber. The deepest chamber of the eye, behind the lens.

vitreous syneresis. Degenerative process characterized by liquefaction of the vitreous body, predisposing the eye to retinal tears and detachments.

vocal folds. The vocal chords of the dog.

vomiting. The forceful ejection of contents of the stomach and upper small intestine through the mouth.

vomiting center. Portion of the brain that initiates vomiting.

vomitus. Vomited material.

von Willebrand's disease. Autosomal dominant bleeding disorder characterized by a deficiency of clotting factor VIII.

vulva. The external genitalia of the female, representing the entrance to the vagina; composed of the external lips or folds (**labia**) and the **clitoris.**

warm agglutinins. Autoantibodies that are by far the most common type found in canine autoimmune hemolytic anemia; they are usually of the IgG class and attach to red blood cells more avidly at body temperature than at lower temperatures.

wheal. A discrete, well-circumscribed, reddened skin swelling with a flat top and steep-walled margins, produced by *edema* in the dermis; often associated with allergic reactions, i.e., **urticaria;** also called a "hive."

whelp. To give birth; said of female dogs.

whole-body hyperthermia. Cancer therapy involving elevation of the core body temperature as an aid in killing tumor cells.

wry bite. Condition resulting from asymmetric growth of the skull or jaw, resulting in a midline malalignment; a form of unilateral brachygnathism or **prognathism.**

X-linked diseases. Genetic diseases of males caused by defective genes located on the X chromosome; also called **sex-linked diseases.**

X-linked muscular dystrophy. A rare X-linked muscle disease of dogs characterized by a deficiency of **dystrophin,** a cell protein associated with the inner surface of muscle-fiber membranes; similar to the well-known Duchenne muscular dystrophy of young male children.

XX sex reversal. Autosomal recessive disorder which, when homozygous, causes an XX (female) animal to develop either partially or completely into a male.

Zepp-LaCroix resection. Surgical removal of the vertical portion of the ear canal.

zona pellucida. Thick, transparent outer envelope or casing that surrounds an **ovum** (egg).

zonules. Numerous strands making up the **suspensory ligament,** which holds the lens of the eye in position.

zoonotic disease (zoonosis). Any disease that can be spread between animals and human beings; examples include plague, rabies, salmonellosis and ringworm.

zygomycosis. Uncommon diseases caused by several different fungi (*Rhizopus, Absidia, Mucor*) and characterized by locally spreading inflammation and the blockage of small blood vessels; also known by the more general term **phycomycosis.**

zygote. Fertilized **ovum** (egg).

Index

Italicized page numbers indicate figures;
page numbers followed by *t* indicate tables.

Esophagus, 177, 295
  enlargement of, 297
  inflammation of,
    297–298
  motility problems in,
    297
  obstruction of, 298
  surgery on, 442
Essential fatty acids,
  89–90, 108
Estrogens, 118
  excess of, 225
  for mismating, 137–138
  Sertoli cell tumors and,
    438
Estrus, 10–11, 69, 115,
  119, 119–120
  behavior during, 72,
    125
  cancer and, 416
  clinical signs of, 120
  duration of, 120
  hormonal changes in,
    119
  prevention of, 151–153
Eumycotic mycetoma,
  385
Euthanasia, 9, 49–50, 65,
  412
Excoriation, 217
Exercise
  during convalescence,
    450
  motivation for, 49
  for older dogs, 60
  pregnancy and, 134
  for puppies, 56
Exfoliative cytology,
  121–123, *123*
Exfoliative dermatitis,
  217, 222, 240
Exophthalmia, 193, 260
Expectorants, 328
Eye(s), 178–181, *179*
  anatomy of, *179,*
    179–181
  disorders of, 181–193,
    433, 434t
    Collies and, 170–171,
      190–191
    congenital, 167–168
    distemper and, 345
    older dogs and,
      61–62
  dry, 184
  evaluation of, 11
  medication for, 447
  movements of, 181
  parasites in, 391
  trauma to, 458
Eyelid(s)
  disorders of, 181–182
  inability to close, 62
  inflammation of,
    183–184

third, 179
  eversion of, 186
  prolapse of, 185
  protrusion of,
    185–186
  tumors of, 62, 184,
    186

Factor VIII deficiency,
  168–169
Fangs, 201
Fat
  dietary, 89–90
  subcutaneous, 106
Fecal flotation test, 487
Feeding, 70–71, 94–104.
  See also Diet;
    Nutrition
  excessive, 103, 109
  guidelines for, 99–103,
    100t, 101t
  management of,
    103–104
Feline immunodeficiency
  virus, 336, 351
Feminization, 146, 225,
  438
Femur, 263
Fertilization, 130–131.
  See also
    Reproduction
Fever, 71, 425, 449
Fiber, dietary, 89
Fibrocytes, 214
Fibroma, 415t
Fibroplasia, 189
Fibrosarcoma, 265, 415,
  415t
Filarial nematods, 396
Finnish Spitz, 35, 38,
  40–41
First aid, 454–458. *See
  also* Emergency
    care
  kit for, 457t
Fits. *See* Seizures
Fleas, 235–237, *236*
  allergies to, 197
  dermatitis from,
    237–238
Fluke parasites, 401–402
Fluorosis, 212
Folacin, 93
Follicle-stimulating hor-
  mone, 119
Follicular cysts, 233
Follicular dysplasia, 231
Follicular sheath, 215
Folliculitis, 218, 227
Food, 95–97
  additives to, 104, 445
  allergies to, 111,
    220–221
  aversions to, 70, 111,
    300

caloric content of, 99t
  preservatives in, 104
  selection of, 97–99, 98t,
    99t
  storage of, 99
Foxhounds, 20
Foxtails, 229, 286, 288,
  367
Fractures, 266–268
Frostbite first aid, 457
Fungal diseases,
  378–386, 474
  rhinitis from, 288
  skin, 219–220
Furunculosis, 218

Gait, abnormal, 432
Gallbladder, 177
Gangliosidosis, 167
Gastric dilatation, 85,
  111, 299–300, 440
Gastric torsion, 464
Gastritis, 298–299, 329
Gastroenteritis, 301
Gastrointestinal tract
  anatomy of, 295–296
  bleeding in, 300, 301
  diseases of, 296–304,
    471–472
  flukes in, 401–402
  lymphosarcoma of, 335
Genes, 154
  coat color, 161–162,
    163t
  defective, 166–171
  dominant, 156–158
  linkage of, 159
  recessive, 156–158
Genetics, 154–162, 163t
Geriatric dogs, 58–65
  cancer in, 409–410
  dental disease in, 61
  diet for, 59–60,
    102–103
  distemper and, 344
  encephalitis in, 344
  health evaluation of, 59
  hookworms and, 393
  housing for, 60
  incontinence in, 428
  kidney disease in, 63
  misbehavior in, 60–61
  obesity in, 59–60
  tracheal collapse in,
    292
  urinary disorders in, 63
  vestibular syndrome in,
    283
German Shepherd Dogs,
  38, *42–43,* 163t
  bloating in, 299–300
  characteristics of, 15
  demodicosis in, 240t
  dermoids in, 182
  dwarfism in, 266

maldigestion in, 301
  neuropathy in, 284
  pancytopenia in, 325,
    374
  pannus of, 187
  perianal fistulas in, 439
Gestation, length of,
  131–132
GH. *See* Growth hormone
  (GH)
Giardiasis, *392,* 405
Gingival disorders,
  205–207
Glaucoma, 62, 180
Globoid-cell leukodystro-
  phy, 167
Glomerular filtration rate,
  270
Glomeruli, 269
Glomerulonephritis,
  272–273, 333, 374
Glucocorticoids, 317,
  334–335
Glucose, 86
Glucosuria, 316
Glutathione peroxidase,
  91
Goiter, 314
Gonadal dysgenesis, 166
Gram stain, 487
Granular cell layer, 213
Granulocytopathy syn-
  drome, 337
Granuloma, lick, 232
Grass awns, 229, 286,
  288, 367
Great Danes, 24, *30–31,*
  161, 163t
  bloating in, 299–300
  demodicosis in, 240t
  ear cropping for, 440
  hypothyroidism in, 313t
Great Pyrenees, 24,
  30–31
Greyhounds, 20, 24, 29,
  36–37
Griffon
  Brussels, 29, *36–37*
  Wirehaired Pointing,
    17, *22–23*
Grooming, 56
Growth factors, 169
Growth hormone (GH),
  226, 312
Gum disease, 205–207
Gynecomastia, 146, 226

Hair
  abscence of. *See*
    Alopecia
  changes in, 431–432
  depigmentation of, 108
  evaluation of, 11
  facial, abnormal, 183
  follicles, 215